SPINOZA

Baruch Spinoza (1632–77) was one of the most important philosophers of all time; he was also, arguably, the most radical and controversial. Born into a Portuguese Jewish merchant family living in Amsterdam, Spinoza was banished from the Sephardic community as a young man, apparently for his heretical views. He devoted the rest of his life to the search for truth, freedom, and moral well-being. He also pursued his vision of "true religion" and of the secular, tolerant state.

This is the first complete biography of Spinoza in any language and is based on detailed archival research. More than simply recounting the story of Spinoza's life, the book takes the reader into the heart of Jewish Amsterdam in the seventeenth century and, with Spinoza's exile from Judaism, also into the midst of the tumultuous political, social, intellectual, and religious world of the young Dutch Republic.

Although the book will be an invaluable resource for philosophers, historians, and scholars of Jewish thought, it has been written for any member of the general reading public who has a serious interest in philosophy, Jewish history, seventeenth-century European history, or the culture of the Dutch Golden Age.

Steven Nadler is Professor of Philosophy and a member of the faculty of the Center for Jewish Studies at the University of Wisconsin at Madison.

Spinoza
A Life

Steven Nadler

CAMBRIDGE
UNIVERSITY PRESS

SANTIAGO CANYON COLLEGE
LIBRARY

PUBLISHED BY THE PRESS SYNDICATE OF THE UNIVERSITY OF CAMBRIDGE
The Pitt Building, Trumpington Street, Cambridge, United Kingdom

CAMBRIDGE UNIVERSITY PRESS
The Edinburgh Building, Cambridge CB2 2RU, UK   http://www.cup.cam.ac.uk
40 West 20th Street, New York, NY 10011-4211, USA   http://www.cup.org
10 Stamford Road, Oakleigh, Melbourne 3166, Australia

First published 1999

Printed in the United States of America

Typeface Ehrhardt 10/12 pt.   *System* QuarkXPress™ 4.0 [AG]

*A catalog record for this book is available from
the British Library.*

Library of Congress Cataloging-in-Publication Data
Nadler, Steven M. (date)
Spinoza : a life / Steven Nadler.
p.   cm.
Includes bibliographical references and index.
ISBN 0-521-55210-9 (hardcover)
1. Spinoza, Benedictus de, 1632–1677.   2. Philosophers –
Netherlands – Biography.   I. Title.
B3997.N33   1999
199′.492 – dc21
[B]   98-36034

ISBN 0 521 55210 9 hardback

for my family

Contents

Acknowledgments   *page* ix

Preface   xi

1   Settlement   1

2   Abraham and Michael   27

3   Bento/Baruch   42

4   Talmud Torah   61

5   A Merchant of Amsterdam   80

6   *Cherem*   116

7   Benedictus   155

8   A Philosopher in Rijnsburg   182

9   "The Jew of Voorburg"   203

10 *Homo Politicus*   245

11 Calm and Turmoil in The Hague   288

12 "A free man thinks least of all of death"   320

A Note on Sources   353

Notes   355

Bibliography   389

Index   401

Acknowledgments

No project such as this can be accomplished without a great deal of help. I have asked for a lot of favors over the past few years, and at this point all I can do is express my thanks to various individuals and institutions for their services, generosity, support, and friendship. Maybe I'll also give them a free copy of the book.

First of all, I am enormously grateful to Jonathan Israel, David Katz, Marc Kornblatt, Donald Rutherford, Red Watson and especially Pierre-François Moreau, Wim Klever, Piet Steenbakkers, and William Klein for reading through the entire manuscript and providing copious comments on matters of both substance and style. Their suggestions, corrections, and criticisms were essential in moving this book from its early drafts to a publishable form.

I also thank a number of people who read individual chapters, steered me to the right sources, responded to my queries, lent me material that they owned, looked things up, ran local and international errands, or just provided much-needed encouragement: Fokke Akkerman, Amy Bernstein, Tom Broman, Ed Curley, Yosef Kaplan, Nancy Leduc, Tim Osswald, Richard Popkin, Eric Schliesser, and Theo Verbeek. I would especially like to give my thanks to the director of the Bibliotheca Rosenthaliana of the University of Amsterdam, Adri Offenberg, who was most kind in resolving a number of my perplexities about the Amsterdam Portuguese-Jewish community in the seventeenth century. Finally, Henriette Reerink was a perfect friend – and an indispensable assistant – in Amsterdam. Besides finding me a bicycle to use, she hunted down some important records at the Municipal Archives and helped me navigate my way, under glorious Dutch skies, to the cemetery at Ouderkerke. She also knows where to find the best *poffertjes* in town.

Work on this book was supported by a summer stipend from the National Endowment for the Humanities, by a research fellowship from the

Romnes Foundation, and by a number of summer research grants from the Graduate School of the University of Wisconsin–Madison. I also benefited from a year's sabbatical from the University of Wisconsin, for which I am enormously grateful.

Some of the material from Chapter 6 on the reasons behind Spinoza's excommunication was presented to audiences at University College, London; the University of Chicago; and the History of Science Department and the Logos Society of the University of Wisconsin–Madison. I am grateful for the invitations to speak, and especially to Martin Stone in London, and for the comments and suggestions that I received on those occasions.

And then there are those to whom this book is dedicated, whose love and support kept me going: my wife, Jane, and my children, Rose and Benjamin; my parents, Arch and Nancy; my brother, David, and my sisters, Lauren and Linden. I owe you more than words could ever express.

Preface

Baruch de Spinoza (1632–77) was the son of a prominent merchant in Amsterdam's Portuguese-Jewish community. He was also among the more gifted students in its school. But something happened around his twenty-third year – whether it was sudden or gradual, we do not know – that led to the harshest excommunication ever proclaimed by the leaders of the Amsterdam Sephardim. The result was Spinoza's departure from the community – indeed, from Judaism entirely. He would go on to become one of the most important and famous philosophers of all time, and certainly the most radical and controversial of his own.

The young man's transformation (if that's what it was) from ordinary Jewish boy – living, to all appearances, a perfectly normal orthodox life and remarkable perhaps only for his intelligence – to iconoclastic philosopher is, unfortunately, hidden from us, possibly forever. We have only the *cherem* document, full of oaths and maledictions, that was composed by the community's governors. There is so little surviving material, so little that is known for certain about the details of Spinoza's life, particularly before 1661 (when his extant correspondence begins), that we can only speculate on his emotional and intellectual development and on the more mundane matters that fill out a person's existence. But what a rich field for speculation it is, particularly given the fascination of its subject.

Metaphysical and moral philosopher, political and religious thinker, biblical exegete, social critic, grinder of lenses, failed merchant, Dutch intellectual, Jewish heretic. What makes Spinoza's life so interesting are the various, and at times opposing, contexts to which it belongs: the community of Portuguese and Spanish immigrants, many of them former "marranos," who found refuge and economic opportunity in the newly independent Dutch Republic; the turbulent politics and magnificent culture of that young nation which, in the middle of the seventeenth century, was experiencing its so-called Golden Age; and, not the least, the history of philosophy itself.

As a Jew, even an apostate one, Spinoza was always, to a certain extent, an outsider in the Calvinist land in which he was born and from which, as far as we know, he never traveled. But after his excommunication from the Talmud Torah congregation and his voluntary exile from the city of his birth, Spinoza no longer identified himself as a Jew. He preferred to see himself as just another citizen of the Dutch Republic – and perhaps, as well, of the transnational Republic of Letters. He nourished himself not only on the Jewish traditions to which he had been introduced in the synagogue's school, but also on the philosophical, theological, and political debates that so often disturbed the peace of his homeland's first hundred years. His legacy, of course, was as great as his appropriation. In many respects, the Dutch Republic was still groping for its identity during Spinoza's lifetime. And as much as Spinoza's Dutch contemporaries reviled and attacked him, there can be no denying the significance of the contribution that he made to the development of Dutch intellectual culture. It is, perhaps, as great a contribution as that which he made to the development of the character of modern Judaism.

This is the first full-length and complete biography of Spinoza ever to appear in English. It is also the first to be written in any language in quite a long time. There have, of course, been short studies of one aspect or another of Spinoza's life, and practically every book on Spinoza's philosophy begins with a brief biographical sketch. But the last substantial attempt to put together a complete "life" of Spinoza was Jacob Freudenthal's *Spinoza: Sein Leben und Sein Lehre* at the beginning of this century.[1] A great deal of research into the history of Amsterdam's Portuguese Jews and on Spinoza himself has been done since Freudenthal published his valuable study, however. As a result of the enormously important work of scholars such as A. M. Vaz Dias, W. G. Van der Tak, I. S. Revah, Wim Klever, Yosef Kaplan, Herman Prins Salomon, Jonathan Israel, Richard Popkin, and a host of others, enough material has come to light over the last sixty years about Spinoza's life and times, and about the Amsterdam Jewish community in particular, that any earlier biography is, essentially, obsolete. And I should make it clear for the record that, without the labors of those individuals, this book could never have been written. I can only hope that I have made good use of their work.

Let the scholarly reader beware: it was not my intention to track down and present the various sources of Spinoza's thought, all the possible thinkers and traditions that may have influenced him. That would be an infinite task, one that no individual could accomplish in a lifetime. This is, in other words, most definitely not an "intellectual" biography. At certain points it was important – indeed, essential – for me to look closely at what seemed to be Spinoza's intellectual development. But I make no claims for exhaustiveness in my research on his philosophical origins. Nor is this a study of Spinoza's philosophy. Books and articles on his metaphysical and other doctrines are a dime a dozen, and I had no desire to add to the growing bibliography of literature for specialists. Rather, I have tried to provide the general reader with an accessible overview of Spinoza's ideas. If I appear to some Spinoza scholars to be guilty at times of simplification or distortion, then I plead nolo contendere: I do not want to pick any academic fights on the finer details of Spinozism. Let that be for a different time and place. What I am interested in – and what I hope my reader is interested in – is the life and times and thoughts of an important and immensely relevant thinker.

The question that lies at the heart of this biography is how did the various aspects of Spinoza's life – his ethnic and social background, his place in exile between two such different cultures as the Amsterdam Portuguese-Jewish community and Dutch society, his intellectual development, and his social and political relationships – come together to produce one of history's most radical thinkers? But there is another, more general question that interests me as well: what did it mean to be a philosopher and a Jew in the Dutch Golden Age? The quest for answers to these questions must begin almost two hundred years earlier, in another part of Europe.

Settlement

O N MARCH 30, 1492, Spain committed one of those acts of great self-destructive folly to which superpowers are prone: it expelled its Jews. For centuries, the Jews had been a rich and thriving presence in Iberia. Not incidentally, they were also a great economic benefit to their Moslem and, later, Catholic hosts. To be sure, the land they knew as *Sepharad* was no utopia for the children of Israel. They suffered harassment, slander, and, on occasion, physical attack. And the Catholic Church took a particularly keen interest when Jews were accused of encouraging *conversos* – onetime Jews who had converted to Christianity – to return to Judaism. Moreover, Jewish political and legal rights had always been severely circumscribed. But the Jews of Spain nonetheless enjoyed favor at a high level. Though some of the monarchs who protected them may have been moved by humanitarian feelings, most were thinking mainly of their own political and material self-interest. The king of Aragon, for one, recognized the practical benefits of having an economically active Jewish community within his realm. They were skilled merchants, and they controlled a far-flung commercial network. Up to the end of the fourteenth century, the Jews were able to carry on in their communities with a tolerable amount of peace and security. Some of the scholars among them even occupied posts at the royal courts.

All of this changed in 1391. Beginning in Castile, the largest kingdom in medieval Spain, unruly crowds – usually from the lower classes and incited by demagogic preachers – began burning synagogues or converting them into churches. Jews were either killed outright, forced to convert to Christianity, or sold to Moslems as slaves. Anti-Jewish riots soon spread to Catalonia and Valencia. In the face of such popular and widespread reaction, the Spanish rulers could do nothing but look on helplessly. Eventually, some semblance of order was restored and a few Jewish communities were partially rebuilt. But those who had been forcibly converted in mass baptisms were held to their new religion. Any attempt to return openly to Judaism or to continue Jewish practices in secret was considered heresy.

During the early decades of the fifteenth century, there was renewed anti-Jewish activity, now more systematically inspired by the yearning to compel the Jews to admit the truth of the Christian faith. In 1414, there was a particularly large number of mass conversions. Once an individual converted, he fell within the domain of Christian ecclesiastical authority. Conversos were under the constant scrutiny of the church, whose officers were always concerned with the spiritual condition of the members of their flock (regardless of the circumstances under which those members joined up). The lack of organized Jewish resistance only incited further violence, as one community after another fell to the onslaught. This time the kings, who were desperately seeking to save the backbone of their economies, tried to intervene and put an end to the persecutions. But the damage had been done. By the middle of the century, Spain's Jewish population was decimated, its remnants demoralized. The vibrant life and culture – not to mention the productivity – of the Jewish community was gone; its "Golden Age" was over.

The Jews called the conversos *anusim* ("forced ones") or *meshummadim* ("converted ones"). A more derogatory term, used primarily by Christians to refer to those whom they suspected of being secret Judaizers, was *marranos*, or "swine." Many conversos undoubtedly became true and sincere Christians. Some, on the other hand, probably did continue to observe some form of Judaism in secret.[1] These Judaizing "New Christians" grew adept at hiding their practices, and it became difficult for observers (or spies) to grasp the reality behind the appearance of conversion. Consequently, "Old Christians" always suspected conversos of insincerity in the faith. Conversos were constantly being harassed by the general populace; soon, they would also find themselves cruelly persecuted by the Inquisition.

The situation for Jews and conversos continued to deteriorate after the marriage of Isabella of Castile and Ferdinand of Aragon in 1469 and the union of their two kingdoms in 1479. The royal couple passionately pursued religious unity and orthodoxy in Spain, and thus kept a watchful eye on their converso population. Hoping to isolate conversos from the pernicious influence of Jews who might attempt to persuade them to return to Judaism, they adopted a policy of segregating Jews from Christian communities. In 1478, Pope Sixtus IV granted Ferdinand and Isabella the power to appoint Inquisitors in Castile. Over the next twelve years, the Spanish Inquisition claimed to have discovered – invariably through violent and irresistible means – over 13,000 Judaizing conversos. (Naturally, the Inquisition tended to leave professed Jews alone, as its concern extended only to heretics and not to infidels.)

In 1492, after the elimination of Moslem control in Granada, the Christian reconquest of Spanish soil was complete. With the "Moslem problem" well in hand, the monarchs and their ecclesiastic allies were free to turn all their attention to the Jews. This would be the final stage in their project of national religious uniformity. On March 31, 1492, Ferdinand and Isabella signed an expulsion order covering all the territories under the crowns of Castile and Aragon, "to prevent Jews from influencing conversos and to purify the Christian faith."

We have been informed that within our kingdom there are evil Christians who have converted to Judaism and who have thereby betrayed our holy Catholic faith. This most unfortunate development has been brought about as a result of the contact between Jews and Christians. . . . We have decided that no further opportunities should be given for additional damage to our holy faith. . . . Thus, we hereby order the expulsion of all Jews, both male and female, and of all ages, who live in our kingdom and in all the areas in our possession, whether such Jews have been born here or not. . . . These Jews are to depart from our kingdoms and from all the areas in our possession by the end of July, together with their Jewish sons and daughters, their Jewish servants and their Jewish relatives. . . . Nor shall Jews be permitted to pass through our kingdoms and through all the areas in our possession en route to any destination. Jews shall not be permitted in any manner whatsoever to be present in any of our kingdoms and in any of the areas in our possession.

The Jews were, in fact, given a choice: conversion or exile. Within months there were, officially, no more Jews in Spain.

The majority of the exiles (about 120,000) went to Portugal. Others left for North Africa, Italy, and Turkey. The Jews who remained behind in Spain converted to Christianity, as the law required. But their life as conversos was no easier than their life as Jews. They continued to suffer at the hands of their incredulous Old Christian neighbors, and were now harassed by the Inquisition as well. Many must have regretted not having joined the exodus.

For those who did choose exile, Portugal proved to be a safe haven of brief duration. On December 5, 1496, Manuel, the ruler of Portugal, issued a

royal decree banishing Jews and Moslems from his realm. His motive ostensibly was to expedite his marriage to Isabella, the daughter of the Spanish monarchs. But Manuel was less short-sighted than his future in-laws.
He recognized that whatever immediate gain would result from expulsion
(including the confiscation of Jewish wealth) would be offset by a greater
long-term loss. Thus, to make sure that the financiers and traders remained
a part of his economy, he decided that forced conversion was to be the only
option offered the Jews. On March 4, 1497, he ordered all Jewish children
to be presented for baptism. There was as yet no Inquisition in Portugal,
and many of these new conversos – their numbers increasing due to continued converso flight from the Spanish Inquisition – were able to Judaize
in secret with minimal difficulty. For a while, the marranos of Portugal enjoyed a degree of toleration (although they were officially forbidden to leave
the country), and this fostered a rather strong crypto-Jewish tradition.

The reprieve did not last long. In 1547, a "free and unimpeded Inquisition" was fully established in Portugal by papal order. By the 1550s, persecution of conversos suspected of Judaizing – and what converso escaped
such suspicion? – was in full force, paralleling the situation in Spain. The
Portuguese Inquisition, in fact, proved to be even harsher than its Spanish counterpart, particularly after the union of the two nations under one
crown in 1580. Many conversos started emigrating back to Spain, where
they hoped to blend in with some anonymity and, perhaps, recapture their
former prosperity. Conversos returning from Portugal, however, were under an especially strong suspicion of being Judaizers, and this inspired the
Spanish Inquisition to pursue its task with even greater zeal.

Throughout the second half of the sixteenth century, as the Inquisitions
in Portugal and then Spain grew increasingly more ruthless, there was a
marked increase in converso flight from the Iberian peninsula altogether.
A good number of refugees went to northern Europe. Some directly departed from Portugal, while others went north only after a temporary sojourn in Spain. Still other emigrants came from those families which had
never left Spain in the first place. Among these sixteenth-century exiles
there must have been many Judaizers, remnants or descendants of those
who were so committed to the Jewish faith that they chose exile over conversion in 1492 and then surreptitiously continued to practice their religion in Portugal. They now trekked to the outer reaches of the Spanish
Empire in the hope that there the power and influence of the Inquisition
would be weaker. Having refused to become sincere and inwardly con-

forming Christians in either Portugal or Spain, they sought a more tolerant environment where, even if they could not live openly as Jews, they could nonetheless practice their religion in secret without the constant harassment they faced in Iberia.[2]

Portuguese conversos started settling in the Low Countries as early as 1512, when they were all still under Hapsburg control. Most of them went to Antwerp, a bustling commercial center that afforded the New Christians great economic opportunities and whose citizens perceived the financial advantage of admitting these well-connected merchants. In 1537, the Holy Roman emperor Charles V (also Charles I of Spain and ruler of the Netherlands) officially gave his permission for this immigration to continue as long as the New Christians did not revert openly to Judaism or even Judaize in secret. Although he was later forced to issue an edict banning New Christians from settling in his northern domains, it was never strongly enforced. By the 1570s, Antwerp had a converso community numbering around five hundred. Most of the Portuguese in Antwerp were probably not Judaizers, but many undoubtedly were.

᠀

There is not much reliable information on the founding and earliest development of a truly Jewish community in Amsterdam.[3] The dates usually given by historians for the initial settlement of Amsterdam's Jews range between 1593 and 1610. What makes this question especially difficult to resolve with any certainty is the number of myths that surround the arrival of the first Portuguese New Christian immigrants in Holland.

Two stories in particular stand out. According to one account, whose events are variously dated between 1593 and 1597, the English, who were then at war with Spain, intercepted a ship carrying a number of New Christian refugees fleeing Portugal. Among the passengers was the "strikingly beautiful Maria Nuñes" and some of her relatives. The ship and its cargo were seized and brought back to England. The duke who was commanding the British fleet immediately fell in love with Maria. After they reached port, he asked for her hand in marriage, but she refused. Queen Elizabeth heard about the affair and ordered the young woman to be brought into her presence. She, too, was struck by Maria's beauty and grace, and promenaded her about London high society. Despite generous promises and amorous entreaties, all designed to entice her to stay in England, the brave and steadfast Maria insisted on continuing her journey to the Low

Countries, where she intended to convert back to Judaism. The queen finally relented and gave her and her companions safe passage to Holland. In 1598, after the arrival from Portugal of her mother, her sister, Justa, and two older brothers, Maria married her cousin, Manuel Lopes, in Amsterdam. Thus the establishment of the first converso (and possibly Jewish) household in Amsterdam.[4]

A second tale more explicitly involves the introduction of Jewish observance into Amsterdam. Around 1602, the story runs, two ships arrived in Emden in East Friesland bearing a number of Portuguese marranos and their possessions. The refugees disembarked and, after walking through the town, came upon a house with a Hebrew motto (which they could not read) written above the door: *'emet veshalom yesod ha'olam* ("Truth and peace are the foundation of the world"). After some inquiring, they learned that this was the home of a Jew, Moses Uri Halevi. They went back to Halevi's house and tried to communicate with him in Spanish, which he did not understand. Halevi called in his son Aaron, who knew the language. The visitors told him that they were recently arrived from Portugal and wished to be circumcised because "they were children of Israel." Aaron responded that he could not perform the ceremony in a Lutheran city such as Emden. He directed them to go to Amsterdam, where they were to rent a particular house in the Jonkerstraat. He said that he and his father would soon follow them there. Several weeks later, Moses and Aaron Halevi found the group in Amsterdam, circumcised the men, and led them in regular Jewish services.

It did not take the Amsterdam authorities long, however, to become suspicious of this secret, unfamiliar activity taking place in their Protestant city. One Friday evening, neighbors reported the sounds of a strange language emanating from the house in which the Jews were praying during a Shabbat service. The sheriff's deputies, Calvinists one and all, and convinced that the unfamiliar sounds must be Latin, burst into the house expecting to find a mass surreptitiously being celebrated. The gathering was broken up, and Moses and Aaron Halevi were arrested. They were soon released, however, when the matter was cleared up by a fellow Portuguese resident, Jacob Tirado (alias Jaimes Lopes da Costa). Tirado explained that they were in fact Jews, not Catholics, and that the strange sounds were Hebrew, not Latin. Tirado also pointed out to the authorities the economic benefits to Amsterdam of having a Jewish community established there. The appeal succeeded, and Tirado was granted permission to set up a congregation, with Moses Halevi as its rabbi.[5]

Each of these stories has a kernel of historical truth. All the main characters were real people living in Amsterdam in the first decade of the seventeenth century. There is a record of Maria Nuñes's marriage in 1598, for example, as well as the report of a Dutch envoy in London to the States General of the Netherlands in April of 1597 regarding a ship captured with Portuguese merchants and a girl dressed as a man on board. Jacob Tirado was in Amsterdam from 1598 to 1612, along with his wife, Rachel, and their children, and he is identified in notary documents as a "merchant of the Portuguese Nation of Amsterdam." Between 1598 and 1608, ships from Emden regularly sailed between Iberia and Amsterdam, often with Portuguese New Christians on board. Finally, there was a man named Moses Halevi working as a kosher butcher in Amsterdam as early as 1603.[6]

But the truth behind the establishment of the Portuguese Jewish community in Amsterdam is, for the most part, more mundane than these inspirational stories suggest. In the final years of the sixteenth century, there were a number of Portuguese individuals residing in Amsterdam, most of them apparently New Christians. The first official text pertaining to these immigrants as a group is a decision taken on September 14, 1598, by a board of burgemeesters regarding citizenship for "Portuguese merchants." It was decreed that they were allowed to take the *poorterseed* ("citizen's oath"), but the board added a warning that public worship outside of the officially recognized churches was forbidden.[7] In the minds of Amsterdam's municipal governors, this was clearly not a question of allowing Jews (or even crypto-Jews) to settle in the city, for they explicitly note in their resolution that the Portuguese "are Christians and will live an honest life as good burghers." From where did these earliest New Christian residents emigrate? Most of them journeyed to the banks of the Amstel directly from Portugal and Spain, especially before 1600, but a substantial number also came up from Antwerp.

Antwerp was the hub of trade for Portuguese and Spanish firms dealing in East India spices and Brazilian sugar. The local agents for these firms were, almost exclusively, Portuguese New Christians living there. From Antwerp, the colonial goods would be distributed to Hamburg, Amsterdam, London, Emden, and Rouen. This arrangement operated relatively smoothly for a while. But the economic health of Antwerp began to take a turn for the worse after the signing of the rebellious Union of Utrecht in 1579. When the seven "United Provinces" of the northern Low Countries (Holland, Zeeland, Utrecht, Gelderland, Overijssel, Friesland, and Groningen) officially declared their independence from Spanish dominion – Philip II of Spain had inherited the Netherlands from his father, Charles V,

in 1555 – they initiated a new stage in their already decade-old armed revolt. Various military strategies by the northern provinces in the 1580s and
1590s undermined the control that Antwerp (which was part of the still
loyal southern Low Countries) exercised over the distribution of northern
European trade and helped foster the rapid economic growth of Amsterdam. But it was the imposition in 1595 of a full-scale maritime blockade of
the south – effectively cutting off Flemish seaports from Dutch and neutral shipping and not lifted until 1608 – that ultimately forced the Lisbon
dealers to send their Antwerp agents to alternative northern distribution
points. Initially the middlemen went to Cologne and other northern German cities, as well as to Bordeaux, Rouen, and London. But many eventually ended up in Amsterdam.

The Thus, a good number of the Portuguese who were in Amsterdam at the
close of the sixteenth century were New Christian merchants who had come
north from Antwerp for economic reasons. These immigrants, regardless
of their ancestral (Jewish) or present (ostensibly Catholic) religious persuasions, were usually welcomed by Dutch cities, which were always on
the lookout for their material advantage.[8] Many of Amsterdam's Portuguese settlers were also, no doubt, motivated by fear of the Inquisition.
This would be particularly true of those conversos who arrived directly
from Portugal or Spain, or who came from Antwerp just after that city fell
to the duke of Parma in 1585. Some may even have been seeking the opportunity to return to Judaism. They would have been attracted by the
promise of religious toleration offered explicitly in article 13 of the Union
of Utrecht: "Every individual should remain free in his religion, and no
man should be molested or questioned on the subject of divine worship."
With this proclamation, extraordinary for its time, the signatories to the
treaty stipulated that no one could be persecuted for his religious beliefs,
although the public practice of any religion outside of the Reformed
Church was forbidden.

There is no evidence that there was any organized Jewish observance
among the "Portuguese" – and this term is used generally to describe even
those with a Spanish background – who were of Jewish descent living in
Amsterdam in the last years of the sixteenth century.[9] There were, however, a number of individuals who, just a few years later, played an important role in initiating an active, if still rather private, Jewish community. Of
particular interest in this regard are Emanuel Rodriquez Vega and Jacob
Tirado, who were employed as agents for exporters in Portugal.

Rodriguez Vega came to Amsterdam from Antwerp around 1590. He is identified in notarial records in 1595 as a "merchant of Amsterdam," and two years later he was able to buy his citizenship. He was, by the early 1600s, a major figure in the Portuguese Jewish community's economic life, trading in sugar, wood, cloth, grain, salt, spices, metals, and fruit, with business in Brazil, England, Portugal, Morocco, and various cities and principalities in the German lands. He even had some business dealings with the Spinoza family. In 1596, he authorized Emanuel Rodriguez de Spinoza (alias Abraham de Spinoza, the great-uncle of Baruch), then living in Nantes, France, to reclaim a cargo of textile goods that had been seized by Spanish soldiers.[10] It was the wealth and international connections of men like Rodriguez Vega that made possible the establishment and rapid growth of the Portuguese community.

Tirado, on the other hand, is often credited with being one of the prime movers of Jewish worship in Amsterdam (where he lived until 1612, when he emigrated to Palestine). There is no reason to believe that any of the marranos in the United Provinces showed their true Jewish colors until around 1603, and then they did so slowly and cautiously. That is the year Halevi and his son are supposed to have arrived in Amsterdam to perform circumcisions and, according to records, to serve as *schochetim*, or ritual slaughterers. Tirado seems to have been in contact with Halevi, and not just for business purposes. He may, around this time, have been organizing Jewish services in his house and actively (but quietly) encouraging others to join in.[11]

Two cities in the United Provinces were, in fact, explicitly willing to admit Jews and allow them to practice their religion openly: Alkmaar, in 1604, and Haarlem, in 1605 (although the burgemeesters of Haarlem put so many conditions on their offer that it effectively prevented any Jewish community from developing there).[12] Portuguese petitioners came to Haarlem from Amsterdam, apparently hoping to bargain for a greater degree of religious liberty than they had in Amsterdam. This suggests that by 1605 at the latest Jewish services were being held in Amsterdam with some regularity – in private, to be sure, but probably known and tolerated by the authorities.[13] Portuguese Jews were organized and open enough about their Judaism to make a request for burial grounds within the municipal boundaries in 1606 and again in 1608, a request the city of Amsterdam denied.[14]

The first organized congregation in Amsterdam was called "Beth Jacob",[15] in honor of Jacob Tirado. In 1609, Joseph Pardo arrived from Venice

with his son David to become their rabbi. In 1608, a second congregation
was formed, Neve Shalom ("Dwelling of Peace").[16] Their first rabbi was
Judah Vega, from Constantinople. Thus, by 1614, the year the Portuguese
Jewish community was finally able to purchase some land close to Amsterdam – in Ouderkerk – to serve as a burial ground, there were two well-
attended congregations. Beth Jacob continued to meet in Tirado's home
until around 1614, when they began renting an old warehouse (called
"The Antwerpen") on the Houtgracht. Neve Shalom met for a time at the
house of Samuel Palache, Morocco's Jewish ambassador to the Netherlands. The members of Neve Shalom tried to build a synagogue in 1612
(also on the Houtgracht), and to this end hired a local Dutch builder, Han
Gerritsz, with the stipulation that no construction work should take place
between sundown Friday and sundown Saturday. The city authorities,
however, at the insistence of Calvinist preachers (who were growing increasingly nervous at the presence of a burgeoning Jewish community in
their midst), forbade the Jews to furnish and use the building. From 1616
onward, Neve Shalom had to make do with a house rented from a prominent Dutch burgher. When he died in 1638, his wife sold the house to the
congregation.[17]

ॐ

The rapport between the Jews and the Dutch in the first quarter of the
seventeenth century was uneasy: each side recognized the economic and
political value of their relationship, but also regarded the other with a certain degree of suspicion. It is not surprising that it took a long time for the
Portuguese community to lose the feeling of insecurity that one would naturally expect to find among a group of persecuted refugees dependent on
the goodwill of their hosts for protection. Indeed, the city of Amsterdam
was slow in granting formal recognition to the Jews as a religious community with the right to practice their religion openly and to live according
to their laws, although it clearly tolerated the existence of "secret" (that is,
discreet) worship. In 1615, when the States General – the central legislative organ of the United Provinces as a whole, made up of representatives
from each province – authorized resident Jews to practice their religion,
Amsterdam was still forbidding public worship. In the same year, the States
of Holland – the governing body of that province, composed of delegations
from eighteen towns, along with a delegation representing the nobility –
set up a commission to advise them on the problem of the legal status of

the Jews. The commission consisted of Adriaan Pauw and the great jurist Hugo Grotius, the pensionaries or chief legal advisers of Amsterdam and Rotterdam, respectively. While Grotius and Pauw deliberated, the municipal authorities of Amsterdam issued, in 1616, a warning to the "Jewish nation." Among other things, the Jews were ordered to refrain from criticizing the Christian religion, not to attempt to convert Christians to Judaism, and not to have sexual relations with Christians. Behind the ordinance lay the machinations of the local Calvinist consistory, which was clearly unhappy about seeing yet another religious "sect" take up residence in the land. The clergy redoubled their efforts when they learned of various amorous affairs (some of them adulterous) between Jewish men and Christian women and of a number of conversions from Christianity to Judaism.[18] Still, relations between the Jews and the citizens of the city of Amsterdam were tranquil enough for Rabbi Uziel to write, also in 1616, that "at present people live peaceably in Amsterdam. The inhabitants of this city, mindful of the increase in population, make laws and ordinances whereby the freedom of religions may be upheld." He adds that "each may follow his own belief, but may not openly show that he is a different faith from the inhabitants of the city."[19]

In 1619, after having studied drafts of ordinances submitted by the ad hoc commission, the States of Holland rejected the restrictions on Jewish–Dutch relations recommended by Grotius[20] and concluded that each town should decide for itself whether and under what conditions to admit Jews. They added that if a town did decide to accept Jews, though it could assign them a special residential quarter, it could not compel them to wear any special marks or clothing. Even Grotius, despite his misgivings and his concerns to safeguard the interests of the Reformed Church, conceded that for theological and moral (not to mention practical) reasons Holland should give the Jews the refuge they sought and the hospitality they deserved: "Plainly, God desires them to live somewhere. Why then not here rather than elsewhere? . . . Besides, the scholars among them may be of some service to us by teaching us the Hebrew language." That same year, the Amsterdam city council followed suit and officially granted the Jews of Amsterdam the right to practice their religion, with some restrictions on their economic and political rights and various rules against intermarriage and certain social activities with Christians.[21] The council also demanded that the Jews keep to a strict observance of their orthodoxy, adhering scrupulously to the Law of Moses and never tolerating deviations from the

belief that there is "an omnipotent God the creator . . . [and] that Moses
and the prophets revealed the truth under divine inspiration, and that
there is another life after death in which good people will receive their rec-
ompense and wicked people their punishment." It was not until 1657 –
nine years after Spain, with the signing of the Treaty of Münster, conceded
official recognition to the sovereignty of the Dutch Republic – that the
States General actually proclaimed that Dutch Jews were citizens of the
republic and thus entitled to its protection in their travels abroad and business dealings with foreign firms or governments. Prior to this, they were
still a "foreign group."[22]

Some of the difficulties in the relationship between the Jews and the
Dutch, particularly the opposition among the Calvinist clergy to formally
granting the Jews the right to practice their religion, have their source in
the religious controversy that raged within the Dutch Reformed Church
during the second and third decades of the seventeenth century.[23] It is
likely that at least part of the reason for Amsterdam's resistance to recog-
nizing the Jews were the strong conservative theological tendencies in the
city at that time and the power exercised there by the Calvinist *predikanten* and their allies.

In 1610, a group of forty-four ministers, all followers of Jacobus Arminius, a liberal theology professor at the University of Leiden, issued a "Remonstrance" in which they set forth their unorthodox views on certain
sensitive theological questions. Anticipating the impending reaction, they
also asked the States of Holland for protection. The Arminians, or "Remonstrants," explicitly rejected the strict Calvinist doctrines of grace and
predestination. They believed that a person had the capacity to contribute,
through his actions, to his own salvation. They also favored a separation
between matters of conscience and matters of political power, and dis-
trusted the political ambitions of their orthodox opponents. Like many religious reformers, the Arminians saw their crusade in moral terms. In their
eyes, the true spirit of the Reformation had been lost by the increasingly
dogmatic, hierarchical, and intolerant leaders of the Reformed Church.[24]
The Remonstrants had on their side Johan Oldenbarneveldt, the Advocate
or political adviser (later called the "Grand Pensionary") of the States of
Holland, the most important and powerful office in the republic after the
Stadholder, whose own domain extended to several provinces. (The stadholder was also the commander-in-chief of all Dutch military forces and,
by tradition, a symbol of Dutch unity; the post was traditionally given to

a member of the House of Orange/Nassau.) With the Advocate's intervention, what was initially a doctrinal dispute within the Calvinist Church and the university faculties quickly took on political overtones. The States of Holland, urged on by Oldenbarneveldt, granted the Remonstrants their demands, which in effect served only to solidify opposition to the Remonstrant cause. The Counter-Remonstrant theologians accused the Arminians of papism – an accusation that the Remonstrants threw right back at them[25] – while Oldenbarneveldt's political enemies, of which there were many, saw in his support for the liberals an opportunity to label him a traitor who was working on behalf of Spain, their Catholic enemy. Over time, the Remonstrant/Counter-Remonstrant battle over theology became intertwined with opposing views on domestic affairs (such as whether civil authorities had the right to legislate over the church and to control what it taught) and foreign policy (especially how to conduct the war with Spain and how to respond to the recent Protestant uprisings in Catholic France). For a while, Amsterdam was a stronghold of Counter-Remonstrant activity, the town's regents choosing to side with the local orthodox ministers, mainly out of political expediency. There was frequent, and sometimes quite violent, persecution of Remonstrants. Many of them were stripped of their offices and perquisites. By 1617, the Stadholder himself, Prince Maurits of Nassau, entered the fray on the Counter-Remonstrant side. This was a purely political move by the prince, part of his opposition to Oldenbarneveldt's policies of seeking peace with Spain and staying out of French affairs.

The Synod of Dort, a meeting of Dutch Reformed ministers from all the provinces, was convened from November of 1618 to May of 1619 to consider the Remonstrant issue. The synod ultimately resolved to expel the Remonstrants from the Calvinist Church. The representatives to the synod reiterated their commitment to freedom of conscience but nonetheless insisted that public worship and office holding be restricted to orthodox Calvinists. There was a purge of the church at all levels. Meanwhile, Oldenbarneveldt was convicted of treason and beheaded. The harassment of Remonstrants continued for a number of years, although by the mid-1620s things had quieted down somewhat. Amsterdam itself eventually gained a reputation as a city favorable to Remonstrants.[26]

The consequences of this crisis within Calvinism for the Jews of the Dutch Republic were both material and psychological. Certainly, any backlash against those who were not strict Calvinists would hit not just Reformed

dissenters but Jews as well. In fact, one of the resolutions taken by the
Synod of Dort was "that there be found a way to stop the blasphemy practiced by the Jews who live among us." To be sure, in the minds of the Reformed leaders the Jews represented less of a threat than any dissidents
from within the church. Moreover, even the Counter-Remonstrants, with
their interest in the sacred texts of Hebrew Scripture, thought that the
Jews, as the remnants of the ancient Israelites, the people of the "Old Testament," could be a useful asset to their culture. Still, the whole affair
strengthened the hand, for the time being, of the less tolerant elements
within the Calvinist Church. Any kind of departure from Calvinist orthodoxy became more suspect than usual. Jews, Catholics, and deviant Protestant sects all felt the heat generated by the Counter-Remonstrant forces.[27]
When the Amsterdam city council issued its order in 1616 warning Jews
not to make attacks, written or verbal, on Christianity, and to regulate their
conduct; and when it granted them official recognition in 1619 on the condition that they keep to a strict observance of Jewish law, these were, in part,
efforts to ensure that the Jews stayed out of the fray and kept to themselves.[28]

The Portuguese Jews, recently resettled in a society divided by religious
strife, clearly felt a certain degree of insecurity. They worried – and not without good reason – that the fury of the Calvinists could turn on them at any
moment and on any pretext, and that the protection they found in Holland was but a fragile one. This insecurity found expression in various internal regulations enacted by the leaders of the Jewish community – for
example, the order threatening to punish anyone who tried to convert a
Christian to Judaism.[29] Through such measures, the Jews hoped to reassure their hosts both that they could keep their own house clean and that
they had no intention of meddling in Calvinist affairs.

In spite of the various legal restrictions imposed upon them, once the
members of the Amsterdam Portuguese-Jewish community won the right
to live openly and practice their religion in a public manner, they enjoyed
a good deal of autonomy. The Sephardim were allowed to run their affairs
according to their own devices. Naturally, they did have to exercise some
caution. The lay leaders of the community, who represented it before the
Amsterdam magistrates, were responsible for ensuring that their fellow
congregants observed the regulations regarding Jews issued by the city.
And the Dutch claimed jurisdiction in criminal matters and on most legal
issues that went beyond the management of social mores. Although the
rabbis, for example, were free to perform weddings, all non-Reformed mar-

riages had to be legalized before the municipal authorities.[30] But with respect to religious and social legislation, and the punishment of transgressions thereof, the leaders of the community looked not to Dutch law but to both Jewish law and (just as important) their own eclectic traditions.

ن‌

Because most of the founding members of the Portuguese Jewish community in Amsterdam were either conversos returning to Judaism or Judaizing New Christians who now, for the first time, practiced openly, the Judaism inherited by the community had a special, rather unorthodox character. It had been formed over the centuries during which Iberian Jewish practice intermingled with, and later was forced to submerge itself within, Catholic society. The converso communities in Spain and Portugal were effectively cut off from the mainstream Jewish world. Their grasp of the rules and practices of normative Judaism was, particularly among later generations, somewhat distorted and incomplete. Many laws and customs existed only in memory, as it had not been possible to observe them with any consistency. One historian notes that by the end of the sixteenth century marranos had given up not only circumcision, kosher ritual butchery, and many funerary customs – public acts that would be difficult to maintain under the watchful eyes of their neighbors – but also the use of tefillin or phylacteries, ordinary Jewish prayers (their prayers consisted mostly in the recitation of specific psalms), and the celebration of certain holidays, such as Rosh Hashonah (the Jewish New Year).[31] Nor were conversos able to turn to rabbinical authorities or consult many of the central texts of their ancestral religion. They had no access to the Torah, Talmud, Midrash, or any of the other books of rabbinic literature, the study of which is so central to an informed Jewish life. Thus, particular laws, or even just aspects of laws, were promoted while others, no less important, fell into neglect.

In addition to this inevitable process of attrition there were the natural effects of cultural assimilation. Converso crypto-Judaism, and even Iberian Judaism before the Expulsion, was strongly influenced by many of the rites, symbols, and beliefs of local Catholicism. There was, for example, a concern with eternal salvation, albeit by way of the Law of Moses and not Jesus Christ. There were also various cults around Jewish "saints." "Saint Esther," the heroine whose bravery is commemorated on the Purim holiday, had a particular significance for these Jews, for she herself was a kind of marrano, having been compelled to hide her Jewishness from her husband, the Persian king Ahasuarus. She finally revealed herself in order to save her people from the evil plot of the king's minister, Haman.[32]

For these reasons, the earliest Jews of Amsterdam required outside guidance for their reintegration into the Judaism from which they and their ancestors had been removed for so long. The story of how the Ashkenazim from Emden, Moses and Aaron Halevi, helped the first group of Portuguese merchants return to Jewish practice is only the most legendary instance of this. Most of the leading rabbis of the Amsterdam Portuguese Jews in the first half of the seventeenth century came from outside the community. Joseph Pardo had been born in Salonika but was living in Venice when he left to serve as rabbi for Beth Jacob. He did much to re-educate that congregation's members in Sephardic rites; whatever Halevi might have taught them would have been Ashkenazic in character. Neveh Shalom imported, first, Judah Vega, from Constantinople, followed in 1616 by Isaac Uziel from Fez, Morocco. Uziel, in turn, trained Menasseh ben Israel and Isaac Aboab da Fonseca, both of marrano background (from Madeira and Portugal, respectively). The most important rabbi of the community in the period, Saul Levi Mortera, was not even Sephardic. Born into an Ashkenazic family in Venice, he arrived in Amsterdam in 1616 and became head rabbi of Beth Jacob two years later. These rabbis, or *chachamim* ("wise men") of non–converso background corrected or abolished altogether various practices that they deemed inconsistent with Jewish tradition, and they supervised the conformity of the community's activities with halachic (legal) requirements. Pardo, for example, prohibited the members of Beth Jacob from gathering in the synagogue on the three Saturdays preceding the ninth of Ab to mourn the destruction of the Temple, as they were wont to do, because (he argued) this violated the holiness of the Sabbath day.[33]

Venice played an important normative role in this process of organizing and rectifying the Amsterdam *kehillah*. The Venetian Sephardic community – one of the largest and most prosperous of its day and the most important for marrano refugees seeking to return to Judaism – not only supplied rabbis for their northern coreligionists, but also served as a model for the internal order of the newer community. Right from the start, Beth Jacob and Neve Shalom adopted the Venetian structure of authority, whereby real power in the congregation was vested not in the rabbis but in the lay governors. The governing board regulated political, business, judicial, and even religious affairs – everything from the butchering and sale of kosher meat to excommunicating people for moral or religious offenses. The power of the rabbi was, at least de jure, rather narrowly defined. He was technically a salaried official working for the governing board and was to serve mainly as a spiritual leader and teacher.

This arrangement did not always run smoothly. In 1618–19, a conflict over the division of power split apart one of the congregations. The exact origin of the dispute is not entirely clear. It involved various charges made against one David Farar, a physician, one of the leaders of the Beth Jacob congregation and a man with a reputation for being a liberal, even (at least according to his opponents) a freethinker. On one observer's account of the schism, Farar was accused of having appointed as *schochet* a man whom the rabbis subsequently concluded was unqualified for the job; Farar reportedly refused to remove him.[34] According to another witness, what was at issue were various heterodox opinions – about the interpretation of biblical texts and the practical efficacy of kabbalah – that Farar was alleged to have been propounding. (The affair over the *schochet,* on this second view, concerned not Farar himself but his father-in-law, Abraham Farar).[35] Farar was denounced (or perhaps even put under a ban, or *cherem*) by Joseph Pardo, the rabbi of Beth Jacob, who apparently was supported by Isaac Uziel, the strict, conservative rabbi of Neve Shalom. Farar countered by reasserting his views and rejecting the rabbis' right in this matter. He may also have questioned their authority to issue a ban on an individual, claiming that this was the prerogative of the governing board (the *parnassim*) of the congregation, of which he was a member. What is certain is that, as a result of the dispute, Beth Jacob divided into two camps: one group backed the *parnas* Farar, the other group stood behind Rabbi Pardo. The Pardo camp decided to secede from Beth Jacob and form a new congregation, called Ets Chaim ("Tree of Life") and, later, Beth Israel. Their first act was to blockade and seize control of the house Beth Jacob had been using as a synagogue and thus initiate a fight over the congregation's property. Meanwhile, with Pardo's departure, Saul Levi Mortera took over as chief rabbi of Beth Jacob. He was joined in the pro-Farar faction by, among others, Abraham de Spinoza, recently arrived from Nantes.

The Beth Jacob affair was finally settled in 1619 after a Dutch court appointed arbiters.[36] The Farar group, which continued using the name 'Beth Jacob', was awarded title to the synagogue. But both groups also requested a ruling from the leaders of the Venetian community and sent representatives to Venice to press their claims. Venice refused to blame either Pardo or Farar and tried to resolve both the issues surrounding Farar's alleged heterodoxy and the practical and administrative questions over property in a spirit of reconciliation and compromise.[37] In addition to demonstrating how the lay governors and the rabbis were sometimes at odds over questions of power within the early community, this episode – and it was not the only time that an appeal was made to Venice – reveals the role that the Sephardim of the Italian republic played as a source of legal and religious authority for the Amsterdam Jews.

Each of the three congregations that existed after 1619 had its own governing board and its own set of rabbis. There were five officials on each governing board: three *parnassim* and two assessors, all eventually called *parnassim*. (When the three congregations later merged into one, the boards consolidated into a single *ma'amad*, composed of six *parnassim* and a *gabbai*, or treasurer.) The chief rabbi for Beth Jacob after 1618 was Mortera. He was seconded by Moses Halevi (until 1622, when Halevi returned to Emden). Among the *chachamim* for the Neve Shalom congregation in the period after Isaac Uziel's death in 1622 were Menasseh ben Israel and Samuel Cohen. David Pardo took over as head rabbi of Beth Israel in 1619 after his father's death; he was joined from 1626 until 1629 by Joseph Delmedigo, from Crete. Isaac Aboab da Fonseca, soon to be a prominent figure in the community, was also named *chacham* of that congregation in 1626, at the young age of twenty-one.

Despite their administrative independence from one another, Beth Jacob, Neve Shalom, and Beth Israel managed to cooperate a good deal, particularly on projects that were of special importance to the Portuguese Jewish community as a whole. In the beginning, Beth Jacob and Neve Shalom each had its own Talmud Torah association for education. But by 1616 they banded them together into a single educational brotherhood. There was a joint *Bikur Cholim* association to look after the sick and help transport the dead for burial; the *Honen Dolim*, established in 1625, for loans; and (modeled on a similar association in Venice) a charitable society for supplying dowries to orphan girls and poor brides, the Santa Companhia de dotar orfans e donzelas pobres ("Dotar," for short), founded in 1615.[38] Dotar was not just for residents of Amsterdam, or even of the Netherlands. Any poor girls who were "members of the Portuguese or Spanish nation, Hebrew Girls," whether they lived in France, Flanders, England, or Germany, were eligible to apply for assistance. The only condition was that they marry a circumcised Jew under a bridal canopy (*chuppah*) in a Jewish ceremony.

By 1622, a joint board of representatives, the Senhores Deputados, was set up to oversee issues of concern to the community at large. The board consisted of two *parnassim* from each congregation, although on questions of particular importance all fifteen *parnassim* – the Senhores Quinze – would meet. The *deputados* were authorized to regulate, among other things, internal taxation (especially the *imposta*, a tax levied upon import and export transactions and an extremely important source of funds for the community treasury); the appointment of *shochetim* and the provision of kosher meat; burial, through the Beth Chaim society; and immigration.

Immigration was an issue of great importance to the community in the 1620s. In 1609, the Sephardic Jewish population of Amsterdam was about two hundred individuals (out of a total municipal population of 70,000); by 1630 it was up to one thousand (as the city's population climbed to 115,000). And it was an increasingly heterogeneous population. The majority still consisted of those of Portuguese or Spanish descent, Jews of Iberian marrano heritage. Their everyday language in the street and in the home was Portuguese, with some Hebrew, Spanish, and even Dutch words thrown in. (Spanish was considered the language of high literature and Hebrew was reserved for the liturgy. Because almost all the adult members of the community up to around 1630 had been born and raised in Christian environments and educated in Christian schools, very few actually knew much Hebrew.) But a visitor to the neighborhood would also be likely to hear French, Italian, and perhaps even a little Ladino as well, as Jews from France, Italy, North Africa, and the Near East, many also of converso heritage, arrived in Amsterdam, attracted by its renowned freedom and wealth. To the great consternation of the Portuguese, not all of these Sephardim had achieved the level of cultivation and prosperity of the original merchant families. One way of regulating the community's population (and, indirectly, its character) was by encouraging many of these new, often indigent, immigrants to settle elsewhere. The *imposta*, in fact, was instituted in part to help raise money to send the Jewish poor to places where the cost of living was lower than in Amsterdam.[39]

It was even more difficult to assimilate the Ashkenazic Jews who started arriving from Germany and Poland in the second decade of the seventeenth century.[40] Most of these Yiddish-speaking easterners initially came from ghettos and in small numbers. But as the Thirty Years' War made life

more difficult for Jews in the German lands, and as pogroms became
harsher and more frequent, the Ashkenazic population of Amsterdam grew
significantly. By the end of the century, the German, Polish, and Lithuanian Jews would outnumber the Sephardim by almost two to one.

The differences between Amsterdam's Sephardim and Ashkenazim in
these first decades were striking. Whereas the Portuguese were relatively
well-off and highly organized, the *tudescos* were, for the most part, poor
and lacking any communal organization of their own. With very few exceptions (Rabbi Mortera being one), educated Ashkenazim tended not to
emigrate to Amsterdam. The settlers were mostly tradespeople, such as
peddlars and butchers. They quickly became dependent upon the Portuguese community, both economically and spiritually. The Sephardim gave
them employment (as slaughterers, meat sellers, printers, even as domestic servants), let them pray in the congregations' synagogues, and (until
1642) allowed them to bury their dead at Ouderkerk. Slowly, the Ashkenazim managed to organize themselves socially and religiously independently of the Portuguese community, and in 1635 they established their first
congregation.

Even if they were not particularly learned, the Ashkenazim who settled
in Amsterdam had not been cut off as a group from normative Judaism
and forced to assimilate into local gentile society, as the marranos from
Portugal and Spain had been. Rather, for centuries they and their ancestors had been living the traditional life of the Jew, isolated from the surrounding culture. They knew the language of the Torah and the demands
of *halacha*. For this reason, some Ashkenazim were able to achieve promi-
nence as teachers in the Portuguese community. On the whole, however,
the Sephardim were rather contemptuous of the German and Polish Jews
in their midst. They resented their shabby clothes and their archaic and
"uncultivated" habits and practices. The Ashkenazim of seventeenth-
century Amsterdam were never able to acquire the prestige or status of the
Portuguese. The differences between the two groups were immediately
apparent to anyone walking down the main thoroughfares of the Jewish
quarter. Etchings of the period (some by well-known Dutch artists) show
that the dress of the Sephardim was stylish, well-tailored, and in many respects indistinguishable from that of the Dutch. From their hairstyles,
hats, and capes to their stockings and boots, the Portuguese affected the
manners of the Amsterdam mercantile class, with whom they had regular
business and social contacts. The Ashkenazim, on the other hand, clearly

stood out, in their long dark coats, untrimmed beards, and unfashionable caps.

Despite the cultural and social disparities between the two groups – Ashkenazic/Sephardic marriages were strongly discouraged – as well as the apparent embarrassment the Ashkenazim caused the Sephardim before the Dutch, the Portuguese were financially generous toward the impoverished central and eastern Europeans. This was especially the case after 1628, when the *deputados* decided to earmark a certain amount of money from the *imposta* for distribution to the Ashkenazic poor. This sympathy and generosity would not last long, however. The Portuguese soon became impatient with their indigent neighbors. In 1632, the year of Spinoza's birth, a bylaw was passed setting up two charity boxes to collect alms for the Ashkenazim, "to prevent the nuisance and uproar caused by the Ashkenazim who put their hands out to beg at the gates." In 1664, private individual charity to German, Polish, or Lithuanian Jews was punishable by a ban. Some institutional support continued – most notably through the Avodat Chesed society – but significant amounts of the community's revenues were specifically allocated "for sending our poor brethren" back to their countries of origin.[41]

It is difficult to determine just how well-off the Sephardim of Amsterdam were. Some individual families were quite wealthy, although not as rich as the wealthiest of the Dutch. According to the tax rolls of 1631, Bento Osorio had a pretax income of 50,000 guilders, while Cristoffel Mendes took in 40,000.[42] The more affluent Dutch entrepreneurs, on the other hand, had incomes well into the six figures. And in 1637, the income of Prince Frederik Hendrik, the Stadholder, was 650,000 guilders. At the Amsterdam Exchange, a historian notes, "there were Jews in different places, but they did not dominate it, as some have assumed. Their capital was insufficient. Among the great bankers there was not a single Jew, and, when we compare their wealth with that of the great merchants and regents, they are insignificant."[43] Moreover, most of the Jewish wealth was concentrated in the hands of less than 10 percent of the families. This still allowed the Sephardic community as a whole to attain, by the third quarter of the century, a higher degree of average wealth than the Amsterdam populace in general.[44] In the 1630s, most of the Portuguese families were, it seems safe to say, modestly comfortable.

The main source of the Amsterdam Portuguese-Jewish community's prosperity – and the domain of their indisputable contribution to the rapid growth of the Dutch economy in the first half of the seventeenth century – was trade. There were physicians, surgeons, printers, scholars, and other professionals among them, depending upon which guilds did not exclude Jews. But by far the greatest number were merchants and brokers. By the 1630s, the Jews controlled a relatively significant portion of Dutch foreign commerce: estimates are as high as 6–8 percent of the total for the Republic, and 15–20 percent for the city of Amsterdam.[45] Jewish trade with Spain and Portugal and their colonies was a fair match for the trade of the Dutch East and West Indies Companies. In 1622, according to the records of the *imposta* – the business tax that was calculated according to the total value of a transaction, including merchandise, transportation costs, duties, insurance, and so on – Jewish merchants, trading on their own account or on behalf of others, did business worth 1.7 million guilders; the next year, it was over 2 million guilders. Between 1630 and 1639, they were averaging a commercial turnover of nearly 3 millions guilders annually.[46] What is even more impressive is that they were able to carve out such a relatively large and profitable share of the economy on the basis of what was, in fact, a rather narrowly confined area of operations. During the first three decades of the century, the most important routes for Jewish traders were those between Holland and Portugal and its colonies (especially Brazil). Their activity centered on a few select products: from the north they exported grain (particularly wheat and rye) to Portugal, as well as various Dutch products to the Republic's New World colonies; from Portugal they brought salt, olive oil, almonds, figs and other fruit, spices (such as ginger), wood, wine, wool, and some tobacco. Of the greatest importance by far in those years was sugar from Brazil, along with other Portuguese colonial products (wood, spices, gems, and metals). The Sephardim controlled well over half of the sugar trade with Brazil, much to the annoyance of the directors of the Dutch West Indies Company. According to a document drawn up by Amsterdam Jewish merchants in 1622 – in an attempt to demonstrate to the Dutch the "profits these provinces enjoy from the navigation and commerce" controlled by the Jews and thus to gain an exemption from the monopoly over trade with Brazil just granted to the Company – the growth in sugar imports over the previous twelve years was such that twenty-one new sugar refineries had to be built in Amsterdam alone.[47] As long as the Twelve Years' Truce between the United Provinces and Spain was in effect (from 1609 to 1621), the colonial products were carried to Lisbon, Oporto, Madeira, and the Azores, and then on to Amsterdam and other northern cities. With the resumption of the war, which kept Dutch ships out of Spanish and Portuguese ports, the goods often went directly from Brazil to Amsterdam.

The Amsterdam Jews worked with Portuguese partners – usually New Christian merchants – and tended to invest their money in their own companies and ships rather than in the powerful Dutch companies. When the Portuguese settling in Amsterdam returned to Judaism, they often took Jewish names for use within the community while retaining their Portuguese New Christian names for business and other purposes (much as Jews today have Hebrew Jewish names in addition to their ordinary family or given names). The man most Dutch merchants knew as Jeronimo Nunes da Costa was called Moseh Curiel by his fellow Jews; Bento Osorio was called David Osorio, and Francisco Nunes Homem was David Abendana. In their dealings with their Portuguese (and, on occasion, Spanish) partners, however, the Sephardim often used Dutch aliases to conceal their Iberian origins from the eyes of curious Inquisitors and their spies. Thus, Abraham Perera became "Gerardo van Naarden," David Henriques Faro became "Reyer Barentsz Lely," and (more literally) Josef de los Rios became "Michel van der Rivieren" and Luis de Mercado became "Louis van der Markt."[48] Their real names would have given them away as Portuguese residents of Amsterdam (and, thus, as probably Jewish), hence endangering their Portuguese partners or even their own relatives still living in Iberia. Any kind of Jewish connection rendered one suspect in the eyes of the Inquisition, which continued to keep a close watch on its converso population. (On occasion, the Inquisition still managed to touch, and even deeply wound, those who had escaped beyond its immediate grasp. The Amsterdam community was horrified when it received word of the public burning of Isaak de Castra-Tartos, one of its own, in 1647. He had left Amsterdam as a young man, traveling to Spain and Portugal to try to convert marranos back to Judaism. It was a foolhardy project. He was caught, of course, and readily confessed to his "crimes." It was reported that, as he stood on top of the pyre, he screamed out the *shema:* "Hear O Israel, the Lord our God, the Lord is one." A funeral service was conducted for him in Amsterdam by Rabbi Mortera.)

When the truce ended in 1621, the Dutch Jews' economic fortunes suffered greatly, as direct trade between Holland and Spain or Portugal was officially prohibited by the Spanish Crown. Under these circumstances, many Jews chose to emigrate to neutral territory (such as Hamburg or Gluckstadt) to continue business as usual. But Dutch Sephardic–Iberian trade, now contraband, continued nonetheless. Through the use of neutral vessels, loopholes in the embargo on Dutch shipping, and, especially, secret contacts in Portugal and Spain via relatives or the converso network, the Jews who remained in Amsterdam managed to carry on, although at a substantially lesser volume. They were even able at this time to expand their trade with Morocco (munitions and silver) and Spain (fruit, wine, silver, and wool), as well as with Italian cities such as Leghorn and Venice (silk and glass).

The overseas trade controlled by the Sephardim did wonders for the Dutch domestic economy by stimulating industries from shipbuilding and related activities to the refining of sugar. The Jews themselves were rather restricted in their local business options. They were excluded from shopkeeping and the retail trades, as well as from most of the traditional crafts governed by guilds (with the exception of physicians, apothecaries, and booksellers). Although Jewish merchants could purchase citizenship, they were not therefore entitled to all burgher rights (and their citizenship was neither hereditary nor even transferable to their children). An Amsterdam ordinance of 1632 expressly stipulates that "Jews be granted citizenship for the sake of trade . . . but not a license to become shopkeepers." And yet they were still able to profit at home from the new opportunities opened up as a result of colonial trade, as these tended to be in areas not covered by the established guilds or run by well-entrenched interests: diamond cutting and polishing, tobacco spinning, and silk weaving, to name but a few. The Dutch Jews even managed to become involved in the refining of sugar, although this was a trade from which they were officially excluded until 1655.[49]

ം

Jewish life in seventeenth-century Amsterdam was, for the most part, concentrated in a fairly well-defined neighborhood. There were never any legal restrictions on where Jews could live in Amsterdam; but because of the lack of space in the old parts of the city, as well as the need for Jews to live in close proximity to one another (and to their synagogue) in order to develop a properly orthodox community, the Jews arriving in the first few decades of the seventeenth century tended to settle together within the new section that resulted from the city's 1593 extension project. There was, first of all, the Vloonburg (or Vlooienburg) quarter, a square island of recently drained land surrounded by canals and the Amstel River and accessible by way of four bridges. (The once-inundated quarter got its name from the Dutch word for flood, *vloed*). Vlooienburg was cut into four main plats by two central streets that crossed in the middle of the island, with two additional plats on the Amstel side. Here, in the district now known as the "Waterlooplein," was the Nieuwe Houtmarkt, the Houtgracht, the Leprozenburgerwal, Lange Houtstraat, Korte Houtstraat, and Binnen Amstel. Before the influx of the Jews, much of this area was given over to the processing and marketing of wood (*hout* in Dutch), which was of great importance for the building of Holland's celebrated mercantile and military fleets. It was, then, in addition to the Jews, a neighborhood of wood dealers and warehouses. The houses in the interior of the island were made mostly of wood, not brick like the wealthier homes along the city's main canals. By the 1630s, the poorer Ashkenazim were settling in these narrow inner streets and alleyways. The better-off among the Sephardim lived on the broad and open boulevards along the outside border (especially on both sides of the Houtgracht).

The other main thoroughfare of the Jewish quarter was the Breestraat (later called the "Jodenbreestraat," or Jews' Broad Street), which ran parallel to the street that was the horizontal axis of the Vlooienburg island. The Breestraat and Vlooienburg were connected by a short city block and a canal bridge. The community built its magnificient new synagogue at the western end of the Breedestraat in 1679; it still stands there today. In 1650, 37 of the 183 houses on the Vlooienburg island (or about 20 percent) were wholly or partly owned by Portuguese Jews. The Portuguese also comprised about 24 percent of the property owners of the Jewish quarter as a whole, although they constituted a much greater percentage of the residents of the district, since many Dutch-owned houses there were rented to Jews. Eighty percent of the Sephardim who registered in the city's marriage records between 1598 and 1635 lived in the Vlooienburg/Breestraat neighborhood.[50]

The Jewish quarter was certainly no ghetto. Many non-Jews also lived and worked in these streets (including, for a time, Rembrandt, as well as a number of other well-known painters and art dealers: Hendrick Uylenburgh, Paulus Potter, Pieter Codde, and Adriaen van Nieulant). The wealthiest Jews, on the other hand, tended to move out of this district and onto

Amsterdam's more upscale canals. Manuel Baron de Belmonte, for example, lived on the Herengracht, and the De Pinto family lived in a mansion on the St. Anthoniesbreestraat. The Sephardic community was not an isolated one, and the Portuguese Jews were in close business, intellectual, and social contact with their Dutch neighbors. There were Christian maids in Jewish households (a situation that naturally gave rise to rumors of sexual scandals, some of them true) and joint business ventures between Jews and the Dutch. Jews were also known to frequent Amsterdam's cafés and taverns, where they presumably drank nonkosher wine and beer.[51]

Contemporary engravings from Spinoza's time show the main thoroughfares of the Jewish quarter to be neat, prosperous-looking, tree-lined streets, with all of the commercial and social activity one would expect in a seventeenth-century Dutch urban quarter. Most of the brick houses are standard fare for Amsterdam, typically tall and narrow, although there are a few rather broad, mansion-like structures – dwellings, no doubt, of more prosperous families. Not all the buildings were residential; there were still timber yards, warehouses, mercantile offices, and other businesses. During the day, the streets were filled with people conducting their affairs, strolling, or shopping – visiting, for example, the *groenmarkt*, or vegetable market, on the Houtgracht – while boats and barges of various sizes were moored along the canal right alongside the street. The trip to the cemetery at Ouderkerk was a straight and fairly short barge trip up the Amstel. To all appearances, the Portuguese Jewish quarter into which Spinoza was born was practically indistinguishable from any other part of the city. The sounds – the words being spoken or sung – and perhaps even the smells emanating from the kitchens were Iberian, the complexions of its inhabitants were darker and more Mediterranean-looking, but the sights were distinctly Dutch. The Sephardim had, in less than three decades, managed to recreate on the banks of the Amstel what they had been forced to leave behind in Spain and Portugal one hundred and forty years earlier: a rich and cosmopolitan but distinctly Jewish culture. It is altogether fitting that Amsterdam should have become celebrated as the "Dutch Jerusalem."

2

Abraham and Michael

O N A TYPICAL day in the 1610s, both sides of the Houtgracht, the canal separating the square island in Vlooienburg from the neighborhood surrounding the Breestraat, would be teeming with activity. Besides the wood trade operating out of warehouses in the district, which sent barges loaded with lumber up the canal and out to the Amstel, as well as the art dealers marketing their paintings, there was the hustle and bustle of the Jews going about their ordinary daily affairs. All three of the community's synagogues fronted the canal. A member of the Portuguese *gemeente*, whether he lived in the interior of the island or in the more upscale Breestraat quarter, would find himself on the Houtgracht several times in a day. He might be on his way to or from synagogue, attending to congregational or communal business, striking a deal with another merchant, or taking his children to the community's school.

Among the Sephardim who could be found working or worshiping along the canal was one Abraham Jesurum de Spinoza, alias Emanuel Rodriguez de Spinoza. He often went by the name Abraham de Spinoza de Nantes, to distinguish himself from another member of the community, Abraham Israel de Spinoza de Villa Lobos (alias Gabriel Gomes Spinosa). The name "de Spinoza" (or "Despinosa," or "d'Espinoza," among other variants) derives from the Portuguese *espinhosa* and means "from a thorny place." The family may originally have been Spanish, escaping, like so many others, to Portugal in the fifteenth century. Abraham was, for all we know, born in Portugal. But the first extant record concerning him places him in Nantes in 1596. He fled to France probably sometime in the early 1590s, most likely along with his sister Sara. There seems also to have been a brother, Isaac, and his family. Perhaps some relative or friend had been denounced as a Judaizer to the local church tribunal. The voracious Inquisition was rarely satisfied with single individuals, and they had ways of loosening tongues and getting more names. Often, as soon as a converso clan suspected that the authorities were taking an interest in even one of its members, no matter how distant, they all departed en masse, and quickly.

In December of 1656, Emanuel Rodriguez Vega, who was in Amsterdam by around 1590, granted power of attorney to Abraham de Spinoza of Nantes to act on his behalf and recover some merchandise that had been seized by the Spanish. These goods – twenty-two pieces of baize, belonging to Rodriguez Vega himself; eight buffalo hides and thirty-two pieces of shot, belonging to Rodriguez Vega and his brother, Gabriel Fernandes, of Antwerp; ten pieces of baize belonging to Luis Fernandes of Antwerp and Manuel de Palachios of Lisbon; twenty-five pieces of baize, belonging to Bartholomeus Sanches of Lisbon; four pieces of baize, belonging to Symon Dandrade of Porto; and a shipment containing some Haarlem cloth, belonging to Bartholomeus Alveres Occorido, "Portuguese merchant" (presumably of Amsterdam) – were on the Dutch ship *De Hope*, captained by Jan Rutten and bound for Viana in Portugal. As Holland and Spain were still at war, the ship and its cargo were impounded by Spanish soldiers and brought to port at Blavet, France. Rodriguez Vega, identified as a "merchant of the Portuguese nation, at present in Amsterdam," authorized "the honorable Emanuel Rodrigues Spinosa, residing in Nantes in Brittany, to prosecute and find . . . the said goods . . . [and] to do in this respect everything the deponent, if he were present himself, could or would be able to do."[1] It is not exactly clear why Rodriguez Vega commissioned Abraham to take on this chore. Were there family connections? Past business relations? Did Abraham have a particularly good reputation for handling assignments of this sort? The affair does show the wide network that the Portuguese Jews (and New Christians) had in place. They were able to rely on each other across international borders. Amsterdam's Sephardim were frequently commissioning Jewish or New Christian agents in various other countries to act on their behalf, particularly when it came to dealing with Spain when no truce was in effect.

Whatever the origins of the relationship between Abraham Spinoza de Nantes and Emanuel Rodriguez Vega, within twenty years both were members of the same congregation in Amsterdam, Beth Jacob. Abraham left Nantes to settle in the Netherlands sometime before 1616. The other family members either accompanied him or followed close behind. Both Abraham and Sara went to Amsterdam, while an Isaac Espinoza "who came from Nantes" ended up in Rotterdam.[2] In 1616, Abraham was living on the Houtgracht with a son, Jacob, and a daughter, Rachel, both of whom were probably born in France. We know that he was in Amsterdam in that year, because on June 18 "Abraham Jeserum despinosa denantes" joined Dotar, the charitable fund for orphaned girls, with a subscription of 20 guilders, "assuming the obligation to fulfill and to adhere to all regulations of this holy society for himself and his heirs." He was identifying himself in public notary deeds as a "Portuguese merchant in the city of Amsterdam" and was now the one authorizing Portuguese agent in France to act on behalf of Amsterdam firms. His business must have consisted, at least in part, in the importing of fruit and nuts from Portugal. In 1625, he agreed (under the name Manuel Rodrigues Spinosa) to trade in almonds with Antonio Martines Viega. He was, to all appearances, moderately successful in his business, although certainly not one of the more prosperous members of the community. His account at the Amsterdam Bank of Exchange was in the black, but in 1631 his payment for the States of Holland's 200th Penny Tax (a one-half-of-one-percent tax on one's fortune if it exceeded one thousand guilders) was only twenty guilders. This means that his wealth in that year was around four thousand guilders. According to A. M. Vaz Dias, one of this century's most important historians of Dutch Jewry, that was "not a great fortune, even in those days and particularly not for a Portuguese merchant."[3]

Abraham played a prominent and important role in the Beth Jacob congregation, as well as in Amsterdam's Jewish community at large, and it is partly because of his efforts that the Spinoza family came to occupy the respectable place it did. From 1622 to 1623 (5383, by the Jewish calendar), Abraham was the representative from the Beth Jacob congregation on the administrative board of the community's cemetery, Beth Chaim, at Ouderkerk. In 1624–5 (5385), and then again continuously from 1627 to 1630 (5388–90) he was one of the *parnassim* on the *ma'amad*, or lay governing board, of Beth Jacob. This meant that he also, during that same time, served on the joint governing board (the Senhores Quinze dos tres Mahamad) of the Portuguese Jewish community. The Senhores Quinze did not meet together except on extraordinary occasions. Most of the affairs that were of general community interest were dealt with on a regular basis by the group of deputies from the three congregations' governors, the Senhores Deputados. Abraham was designated one of Beth Jacob's *deputados* in 1627–8 (5388) and 1628–29 (5389).

There were, of course, other, less fortunate – and, in the eyes of some of his colleagues, less honorable – episodes in Abraham de Spinoza's life in the Amsterdam Sephardic community. On December 3, 1620, Abraham and his maidservant were released from custody by the municipal authorities. The notice read as follows:

Emanuel Rodrigues Spinosa, Portuguese, was released from custody by the judicial board with the solemn promise that whenever the Lord Sheriff summons him on the orders of the judicial board, he will again appear in court, this on the condition that he provides security. Dr. Francisco Lopez Rosa and Francisco Lopez Dias stand surety and promise herewith that they will produce the said Emanuel Rodrigues in court or else to comply with the verdict of the judicial board. Promised thus etc. Done on the 3rd of December, in the presence of the honorable Frederick de Vrij, presiding mayor as sheriff, Jan Petersz. de With and Joris Jorisz., member of the judicial board. Toboda Ockema of Nantes, maid-servant of the said Emanuel Rodrigues, was released as above in all respects.[4]

We do not know why Abraham and his maid were arrested in the first place. Toboda may have originally come with the family to Amsterdam from Nantes or even Portugal, or perhaps Abraham (availing himself once again of the converso network) brought her to Holland later. Were they having an affair? Vaz Dias thinks so, noting that this was something that Amsterdam's Portuguese Jews (including the rabbis) were frequently accused of doing. He suggests that "one must remember . . . that among the Israelites who had come from the south there was a different set of moral values than among the strict Calvinists."[5] Polygamous (and adulterous) relationships between masters and servants were not uncommon in Iberia, and the Jews, long assimilated to Spanish and Portuguese customs, may have added this practice to their other departures from the precepts of the Torah.

In 1619, Abraham was on the other side of the bail bond. In August of that year, Rabbi Saul Levi Mortera, newly appointed as the chief rabbi for the Beth Jacob congregation, was in judicial detention, for reasons that remain unknown. Abraham and Jacob Belmonte, one of the wealthier members of the community, stood surety for Mortera. It could be that Abraham was simply acting on behalf of his congregation, which was trying to get its rabbi out of jail. But Abraham was not yet, at this time, one of the governors of Beth Jacob. A more plausible suggestion is that Abraham and Rabbi Mortera were on rather good terms, perhaps even close friends. In 1625, Mortera acted as a witness to a notarial deed in which Abraham, "ill in bed but in full control of his mind and speech," conferred the power of attorney on Michael d'Espinoza, his nephew and son-in-law, to represent him with the Amsterdam Exchange Bank, "to write off from and add to his account there, to bring cash into the bank and to withdraw it and to do all that is required and to grant a power of attorney if necessary."[6] This shows not only the faith that Abraham had in Michael, but also the close relationship he had with Mortera, who took the time to come to the sick man's house in order to witness this ordinary business transaction. Perhaps their friendship had its roots in the dispute that split apart the Beth Jacob congregation in 1618. Both Abraham and Mortera stayed in Beth Jacob with the more liberal Farar group, rather than following Rabbi Pardo and his supporters, who went on to establish the Ets Chaim/ Beth Israel congregation.[7] Little could Abraham suspect that his friend would be the chief rabbi of the united Talmud Torah congregation when his grandnephew was excommunicated.

&a.

The notary deed in which Abraham conferred power of attorney upon Michael d'Espinoza also indicates that Michael was in Amsterdam no later than 1625. In fact, there is reason to believe that Abraham's nephew and future son-in-law was in Amsterdam as early as 1623. There is a child buried at the Portuguese Jewish cemetery in Ouderkerk who died on December 3 of that year and is identified in the Beth Chaim record books as "a child of Micael Espinosa."[8]

Michael was born in Vidigere, Portugal, in either 1587 or 1588. It is all but certain that the Isaac Espinoza who went from Nantes to Rotterdam was his father. Michael's father was Abraham's brother, and the flight from Portugal to Nantes and then to the Netherlands in the same period by two Jewish men named d'Espinoza, Abraham and Isaac, must be more than mere coincidence. Although Isaac died in Rotterdam (on April 9, 1627), he was buried in the Ouderkerk cemetery, probably because he had immediate family (say, a brother and a son) in one of the Amsterdam congregations. Moreover, Michael named his eldest son – who would die young, in 1649 – Isaac, and it is common Jewish practice to name the firstborn male after the paternal grandfather. There can be little doubt, then, that the Isaac Espinoza living in Rotterdam was both brother to Abraham and father to Michael; that would also make him the philosopher's grandfather.[9]

If Isaac and Abraham left Portugal at around the same time, as seems likely – and it would have been sometime between 1588, when Michael was born, and 1596, when Abraham was doing business in Nantes – then

Michael would have been a young boy when his family took flight.[10] When Michael arrived in Amsterdam in 1623 or a short time before, it was probably from Nantes and possibly also via Rotterdam. Soon after settling in, Michael married Rachel, the daughter of Abraham. There is no surviving record of their marriage, although it probably took place in 1622 or early 1623, the year they lost the child. The infant is not named in the book of records of Beth Chaim, indicating that it may have died before it could be named on the eighth day. A second child, premature and stillborn, died on April 29, 1624.[11] The unfortunate Rachel, young and childless, died on February 21, 1627.

What brought Michael to Amsterdam in the first place? Perhaps it was Abraham's doing, as he sought to arrange a marriage between his daughter and his brother's son. Or it could be that Michael was hoping to get ahead in business. The economic opportunities in Amsterdam, particularly for a Jew (or a marrano seeking to return to Judaism), were far superior to those in either Nantes or Rotterdam. Maybe Uncle Abraham, in addition to providing Michael with a wife, was offering to set him up in business. The two men did have a close personal and financial relationship; for this we have the testimony of the document in which Abraham grants Michael power of attorney over his accounts in the Amsterdam Exchange Bank. And although there is no evidence to suggest that Abraham took Michael in as a partner in his own business, the two did engage in a "partnership in trade" involving goods from the Barbary Coast.

This joint trading venture later became a source of contention between Michael and Abraham's son, Jacob, soon after Abraham died in 1637. Relations between the two cousins were initially cordial, to all appearances. According to the notary records arising out of the dispute, Jacob Espinosa had been living in "Grancairo in Palestine" (probably Cairo, Egypt), where there was an active Jewish community. He probably returned to Amsterdam in 1637 when his father died, although the notary deeds (which identify him as "living" in Cairo and only "sojourning" or "presently" in Amsterdam) indicate that his residence in Holland was temporary. In December of that year, Michael petitioned to allow Jacob to take his father's place as a member of Dotar. Michael himself had joined the society only six months earlier, paying the required twenty guilders and "binding himself to fulfill all duties of this holy society." Dotar's board unanimously agreed to accept Jacob "as the only legal son in the place of his father."[12]

There must have been a disagreement, however, between Michael and

Jacob concerning the profits and goods related to Michael's and Abraham's business relationship. It seems that Jacob, as Abraham's heir, felt that he was owed some money from the Barbary venture. Things appear to have been resolved to Jacob's satisfaction, as on January 14, 1639, in the presence of the notary Jan Volkaertsz. Oli, Jacob discharged Michael of his obligations:

The said deponent [Sr Jacob Espinosa] declared to have received for himself and his heirs, from Michael despinosa, Portuguese merchant here in this city, the sum of 220 carolus guilders, six stuivers and eight pennies as the remainder and final settlement of accounts. These concern the money that was partially recovered for his, the deponent's, deceased father from the partnership in trade that the latter had with the said Michael Despinosa to Salle in Barbary, as well as the goods from this partnership that were delivered by the said Michael Despinosa to him, the deponent, in his afore-mentioned capacity. Therefore he, the deponent, acknowledges to have been paid to his full satisfaction from the last penny to the first by the above-mentioned party for what issued from the said trading-partnership to Salle. . . . Therefore he . . . thanks the said Michael Despinosa for his good payment as above and for his settlement of the accounts and receipts which Michael Despinosa finally rendered to him in the presence of Joseph Cohen and Joseph Bueno.

Jacob goes on to declare that

He fully receipts Michael Despinosa and his heirs and descendants for everything regarding the above matter and promises that neither he, personally, nor others through him, will make any claims, demands on the said Michael Despinosa or his heirs, either now, or later, directly or indirectly, by means of law or otherwise in any way.

But not all was well between the two cousins. Twelve days later the two were back in the presence of the same notary. A new deed mentions the matter of Jacob's inheritance. Perhaps Michael, Abraham's closest male relative in Amsterdam before Jacob's arrival, was the executor of his uncle's/ father-in-law's estate; or maybe this is a continuation of the first dispute over money and goods related to the Barbary business; or it could be a new dispute over other business-related profits or debts. Since "a matter and controversy had arisen between them because of a certain inheritance claimed by the said Jacob Espinosa . . . from the said Michael Despinosa," the two agreed to submit their "differences concerning the mentioned inheritance as well as all other matters, differences and claims with everything that

belongs to this matter" to arbitration, "in order to prevent a lawsuit, trouble and costs." They asked Doctor Jacob Bueno, Matthatias Aboaf, and
Joseph Cohen, all prominent citizens of the Portuguese community, to render judgment on the dispute. They also agreed that if either party failed to
honor the verdict of the arbiters, he had to pay four hundred guilders "for
the benefit of the poor . . . one half of which will be used for the poor of
this city and the other half for the poor of the Jewish nation."[13]

For two months the arbiters listened carefully to the arguments of both
parties, examined all the relevant documents, and considered any additional information that might help them render a fair verdict. On March 21,
the arbiters felt they could state that they had "effected an amicable agreement and compromise between the parties." On the one hand, Michael
had to pay Jacob six hundred and forty guilders, which Jacob received
"to his full satisfaction and contentment and for which he thanks the said
Michael d'Espinosa for his good payment." For his part, Michael and his
heirs had the right, "forever and hereditarily," to any future "remainders,
debts, shares and credit, none excepted, as could be collected from whatever place or whatever person or persons, either issuing from the joint
trading venture he had with the father of the said Jacob d'Espinosa or from
other matters in whatever way of the said Jacob d'Espinosa or from other
matters in whatever way or from whatever matter there might be." Whatever other money or goods might henceforth come in as a result of the
business partnership Michael had with Abraham would belong exclusively
to Michael, "as his free and unencumbered own property, without him
having to pay anything to the said Jacob Espinosa or his relatives." The arbiters and the notary were careful to make it clear that this should be the
end of the matter, and to insure that there would be no further claims from
either side.[14] Michael must have known that there were some further profits to be drawn out of the business; it is hard to believe that he would otherwise have agreed to such a compromise.

Abraham, as the older and more established partner, seems to have
given his son-in-law a good start in business. Michael would eventually
become a moderately prosperous merchant in his own right, importing dried
and citrus fruits (from Spain and Portugal), oil (from Algeria), pipes, and
other goods. We do not know exactly when Michael established his own
firm, but it could have been as early as the mid-1620s. These were tough
years for Amsterdam's Portuguese-Jewish merchants, however, and he
would have had a hard time getting a business under way.

The treaty inaugurating the Twelve Years' Truce in 1609 was a boon for the Dutch economy, for it opened up direct and uninhibited shipping routes to Portugal and Spain and facilitated commerce to both Spanish and Portuguese colonies in the Western hemisphere and around the coast of Europe to North Africa and Italy. The truce was of particular importance for the Portuguese-Jewish merchants in Amsterdam, given the centrality of the Iberian trade for their businesses. The Jews' economic fortunes began to flourish with the end of the Spanish embargoes on these shipping routes and the cessation of the harassment of Dutch ships. Between 1609 and 1620, the number of Sephardic Jewish accounts at the Amsterdam Exchange Bank rose from 24 to at least 114. The rapid increase in sugar imports, a market controlled by the Jews, led to the construction of over twenty new sugar refineries in Amsterdam during this period.[15] As Jonathan Israel, a historian of the economy of the Dutch Jews, has shown, the truce years between 1609 and 1621 were a period of the fastest and most vigorous growth both for Amsterdam as a whole and for the Sephardic community in particular. This was the boom that gave the Dutch Golden Age its impetus.[16]

The party ended when the truce expired in 1621, a year or so before Michael's arrival in Amsterdam. The Dutch economy as a whole hit a slump, and naturally this affected the fortunes of Amsterdam's Jews. Because direct trade between Holland and Spain or Portugal was officially prohibited by the Spanish Crown, Jews who did not emigrate to neutral territory but remained in Amsterdam had to make use of their secret converso or family networks in order to keep things going. These Portuguese contacts (in both Spain and Portugal, as well as in neutral countries such as France) gave them an advantage over non-Jewish Dutch merchants, but it was still a hard time for any trading business operating out of the Netherlands. It was a particularly bad moment to start a business, and it may be that the initial failures of the Dutch West India Company, established in 1621, can be seen as at least partially a result of these general difficulties.

Given the kinds of products in which Abraham and Michael dealt, typical for members of the community, their own business fortunes would have registered the pressures of the times. However, as they had relatively recently lived in Nantes, they may have had family or friends or especially strong business contacts among the converso community in that important port city. Michael and his uncle could have taken advantage of French shipping or of Portuguese (or French) merchants in France to help them circumvent the obstacles to Iberian–Dutch trade and facilitate the importing of their raisins, almonds, and other goods.

Business was certainly good enough for Michael to establish himself, by the early 1630s, as a successful entrepreneur in the Jewish community, and as someone who was reliable and whose word was good. He appears as a witness, for example, in a fair number of notary documents from this period. On July 15, 1631, a notary deed reported that there was a warehouse on the Prinsengracht "in which miscellaneous merchandise was stored, such as sugar, brazil-wood and candied ginger." Michael did not own the warehouse, although the candied ginger stored there may have been one of his imports. Nonetheless, he, along with one Philips Pelt, had a key to the warehouse. According to Vaz Dias, this shows that Michael was regarded as trustworthy by the community.[17]

A business in trade, of course, will have its ups and downs. In 1633, a shipment of fifty small casks of raisins that Michael was expecting from Malaga did not arrive in good order, and he had recourse to the usual legal procedures to try to recoup his loss.[18] And by the early 1640s, Michael's finances – including a debt that he assumed voluntarily by standing surety for another member of the community – began to grow troublesome. But the late 1620s and early 1630s seem to have been generally good years for Michael d'Espinoza as he tried to make a name for himself as a Portuguese merchant of the Jewish nation in the city of Amsterdam.

ð

When Rachel died in 1627, Michael was about thirty-eight years old.[19] It was not long after her death that he decided to try again to build a family. Around 1628, Michael married Hanna Deborah Senior, the daughter of the merchant Henrique Garces, alias Baruch Senior, and his wife, Maria Nunes. She was one of three children; her brothers were named Joshua and Jacob. We do not know where Hanna was born, nor even how old she was when she married Michael. In fact, we know practically nothing about her at all, except the dates on which her children were born and the date of her death. In 1629, Michael and Hanna had a daughter, whom they named Miriam, after Hanna's mother. Sometime between 1630 and early 1632, a son was born, Isaac.[20] In November 1632, Hanna gave birth to a second son, Baruch, named for his maternal grandfather.

As Michael's family grew so did his status in the Portuguese-Jewish community. In the years before 1639, when there were still three congregations, each with its own governing board of five men, becoming a *parnas* (or member of the board) may have been more of a communal obligation to be shared among the congregation's members than the true honor it would later become after the union into one large congregation. As one recent historian has noted, the *kahal kodesh,* or "holy community," had not yet fully developed into the aristocratic structure that would characterize it after 1639;[21] and many of the community's posts were filled by members who were certainly not among its wealthiest or most distinguished citizens. About seventy businessmen served as members of the Senhores Quinze during this period, and it may have been a matter simply of "taking your turn."[22] Even so, serving on the board would have been a position of some power, and becoming one of the *parnassim* an indication that one had achieved a relatively high degree of respect in the community. Being one of the *Senhores Quinze,* a representative among the Senhores Deputados, or even one of the governors of the educational board was still an honor, if only because it was a reflection of the confidence being placed in the person. The members of Beth Jacob, as well as the other congregations, entrusted their *parnassim* not just with running the synagogue and its various agencies, but also (as members of the Senhores Quinze) with the overall governing of the community, including whatever dealings with the municipal authorities were necessary. The *parnassim* were the official representatives of the Jewish community before the Dutch public, and it is hard to believe that just anyone was entrusted with this task. Finally, any honor attached to these leadership posts would also derive from the fact that it would have been considered a *mitzvah,* or deed that fulfills some obligation incumbent upon a Jew, to serve the community in this way. In other words, not everyone got to "take a turn."

In the years before the union in 1639, Michael was quite active in the community's leadership and organizations, more so than he would be in the 1640s. Like all the successful merchants of the community, including his uncle Abraham, he did his philanthropic duty and joined Dotar in 1637, contributing his membership dues (still twenty guilders) to help the poor Sephardic girls of northern Europe. He first served as a member of the Senhores Quinze, and thus as one of the five *parnassim* of Beth Jacob, in 1633, the year after Baruch's birth. At the same time, he began a two-year stint, along with Josef Cohen, as one of Beth Jacob's representatives on the

board of deputies. In 1635–6 (5395), he was one of six *parnassim* on the
governing board of the educational foundation, "Talmud Torah," charged
with running the schools and distributing fellowships. And in 1637–8
(5398), he returned again to Beth Jacob's governing board – along with
Abraham da Costa, brother of the famous heretic Uriel da Costa – and,
thus, to the Senhores Quinze.[23]

During these years, much of the *parnassim*'s time was taken up, as usual,
with issues of ongoing concern both to their individual congregations and
to the community at large. They were worried about the inconvenience
and "scandalous effects" being caused by the German Jews, who were constantly in doorways begging for alms; about the publication of books in
Hebrew and Latin by members of the community without permission
from the *deputados;* and about the upkeep of the burial grounds in Ouderkerk. They drafted one ordinance forbidding people to bring weapons
into the synagogues, and another forbidding members to elevate their seats
in the synagogue, an act that would be taken as an insult by others (it was
probably intended as such). In 1631, at the behest of the municipal authorities, the *deputados* ordered all members of the community to refrain
from trying to convert Christians to Judaism; violators of this rule would
be punished by a ban. In 1632, the Senhores Quinze resolved to designate
three members to speak with the States-General, which was at that time
engaged in peace negotiations with Spain, regarding those points of the
negotiations that would affect Jews and their possessions. On the same day,
they issued some regulations related to what they took to be the extrava-
gance of the recent celebrations of Simchat Torah, the holiday celebrating
the end of the annual Torah reading cycle. They were clearly concerned
about how such public displays were perceived by the Dutch. In 1635, after the Ashkenazim had become organized enough to establish their own
congregation and synagogue, the deputies warned the members of the
"Portuguese nation" that they must not buy meat that had been butchered
by anyone except the three men who had been examined and commissioned to act as *shochetim* by the Sephardic community, namely Aaron
Halevi (Moses' son, himself an Ashkenazic Jew), Isaac Cohen Lobatto, and
Isaac de Leao.

In 1633, Michael's first year as a Beth Jacob *parnas*, the Senhores Quinze
to which he belonged met on the eighth of Elul at the house of Abraham
Farar. They agreed to increase the endowment of the *imposta*, the tax that
was used to help finance the relocation of indigent Ashkenazim. At the

same meeting they issued a very strong warning against using Jewish family names in letters to people in Spain. Anyone who violated this regulation would be put under a ban. During that year, the three *ma'amadot* met together again in order to take up the issue of Neve Shalom's contribution to the *imposta* funds, which that congregation was having trouble paying. The Senhores agreed that from then on Beth Jacob and Beth Israel would each pay three-eighths, while Neve Shalom would only have to pay one-quarter. As a member of the Senhores Quinze once again in 1637–8, Michael would have been involved in the initial discussions about uniting the three congregations into one.[24]

Judging from the notary records of the time, these were busy years for Michael. He seems to have been involved in numerous business ventures, both with fellow Portuguese Jews and with Dutch merchants. These included importing transactions initiated by his own firm, as well as acting as a secondary agent in transactions initiated by others. In June of 1634, he, along with the brothers Pieter and Wijnant Woltrincx, accepted from David Palache, "Portuguese merchant," the transfer of all the merchandise aboard ship *De Coningh David* (*The King David* – was it a Jewish-owned ship?), which was sailing home to Amsterdam from Salé in Barbary. Palache, as the notary deed states, made this move in order to reduce his debts, and one wonders whether Michael accepted the transfer in order to help Palache or because it was a wise business deal. In 1636, he was engaged in negotiations over a parcel of insured goods with Jacob Codde, a member of a prominent and liberal Dutch family in Amsterdam. The goods had been lost in a shipwreck, and in the notary record Michael acknowledges having received from Codde, who may have been responsible for their transport, the insurance.[25]

Michael's name also appears in several notary records in the 1630s because he was standing surety for someone, further testimony to his reputation as a trustworthy and reliable man. This also shows that business was good and that his finances were in order, for no one would accept the surety of a man who was unsuccessful or who could not meet his own expenses. On September 8, 1637, "Migael d'Espinosa" and Abraham da Fonseca, "also a Portuguese merchant," stand surety "of their own free will, with their persons and goods for Abraham de Mercado, doctor of medicine," who had just been released from prison.[26] Michael's willingness to stand surety for others, however, would soon cause him and his heirs, including Baruch, great difficulties.

On June 30, 1638, the Amsterdam notary Jan Volkaertsz. Oli, accompanied by Antonio Francisco de Crasto, "Portuguese merchant within this city," went to the home of the recently deceased Pedro Henriques, "during his life also Portuguese merchant of this same city." De Crasto was a creditor of Henriques, and he and the notary were at the house in order to serve Henriques's widow, Esther Steven, with a bill of exchange requiring payment. Henriques had accepted the bill some time before, and now payment was past due. Oli notes that "the said widow answered that she could not pay," but goes on to state that on the following day "Michael Despinosa . . . declared that he would accept and pay the above bill of exchange in honor of the letter."[27] Michael had performed the same service on behalf of the late Henriques two months earlier, on April 25. By June 8, Michael had been officially appointed, by the municipal authorities of Amsterdam, as one of the trustees of Henriques's bankrupt estate, along with Dr. Joseph Bueno. They were stepping in for Diego Cardozo Nunes, who had initially been appointed but later withdrew. Michael's action on June 30 was apparently in fulfillment of his curatorial duties. It is not clear what Michael's relationship to Henriques was, nor why he would take on such a burden, as it should have been obvious, even before Henriques's death, that his financial condition was precarious. Michael must have known that acting as one of two trustees of a bankrupt estate would be time-consuming and would involve him in complex and protracted legal proceedings. It could also potentially cost him a lot of money, since he was responsible for paying off Henriques's debts. He seems, in fact, to have had some trouble collecting money that was due to Henriques' estate – and that would help him satisfy its creditors – because on January 26, 1639, he and Dr. Bueno authorized a third party, Jan Nunes, to collect several debts owed to the estate. On January 31, Michael granted the power of attorney to Pedro de Faria, a merchant in Nantes – perhaps an old friend or business contact from his days in that city – and directed him "to arrest all goods and properties of Gaspar Lopes Henriques from Hamburg, that may be in Nantes." We do not know if this Gaspar Lopes Henriques was related to the late Pedro of Amsterdam, but he may very well have been; and this action could have represented an attempt on Michael's part to impound some of the Henriques family goods to help pay off the estate's debts.

The affairs of the Henriques estate would trouble Michael d'Espinoza for some time, and may have seriously affected his own finances by the late 1640s or early 1650s. Even as late as 1656, the new curators of the estate of Pedro Henriques were submitting claims on Michael's own estate, no doubt to pay off Henriques's creditors. Michael's estate would have been responsible for covering the debts and obligations that he had assumed in his lifetime. This whole business would be a particular burden for Michael's third child.

3

Bento/Baruch

IN 1677, shortly after Spinoza's death, Jean Maximilian Lucas, a French Protestant refugee living in Holland, began writing his *La Vie et l'esprit de Monsieur Benoit de Spinosa*. Lucas was about the same age as Spinoza and had known him personally. In the opening of his book, he summarizes practically all that we know for certain of Spinoza's earliest years: "Baruch de Spinoza was born in Amsterdam, the most beautiful city of Europe."[1] Johan Köhler (or Colerus, as he has come to be known), a Lutheran minister from Dusseldorf who lived in The Hague at the end of the seventeenth century and who was Spinoza's other early biographer, supplies one or two additional facts: "Spinoza, that philosopher whose name makes so great noise in the world, was originally a Jew. His parents, a little while after his birth, named him 'Baruch'. . . . He was born at Amsterdam on the twenty-fourth of November in the year 1632."[2] Unlike Lucas, who was sympathetic to Spinoza and an admirer of his ideas (referring to him as his "illustrious friend"), Colerus – like most of his contemporaries – was hostile to his subject, although that did not keep him from trying to produce as complete and accurate a biography as possible. Still, he could not compensate for the dearth of extant information on the circumstances and events of Spinoza's boyhood.

If Spinoza was born on November 24, 1632, then, like all Jewish males, he would have received his name at his circumcision ceremony, or *brit milah*, eight days later, on December 1. In most of the documents and records contemporary with Spinoza's years within the Jewish community, his name is given as "Bento." The only exceptions are the membership roll of the Ets Chaim educational society, the book of offerings listing contributions to the congregation, and the *cherem* document in which he is excommunicated, all of which refer to him as 'Baruch', the Hebrew translation of Bento: "blessed."

In the years immediately leading up to Spinoza's birth, the Dutch Republic was enjoying the early stages of its so-called Golden Age, although the prosperous young nation's ability to take advantage of the possibilities open to it was still limited by the bitter struggle against Spain, now in its seventh decade. In 1632, the painter Johannes Vermeer and the scientist Anthonie van Leeuwenhoek, the great developer of the microscope, were both born in Delft. The Grand Pensionary of the States of Holland, Adriaan Pauw, who also served as the chief adviser for the States General of the United Provinces, was that year leading the Dutch delegation at the peace negotiations with Spain and the southern Netherlands. Prince Frederik Hendrik, the son of William I, Prince of Orange (also known as William the Silent, the popular hero of the republic's struggle for independence, who was assassinated in 1584), was in possession of Holland's stadholdership. Rembrandt, since the previous year a regular houseguest on the Breestraat in the Jewish quarter, where he would shortly buy his own house, was – along with the Utrecht Italianist Gerard van Honthorst – one of the stadholder's unofficial court painters. In 1632 he was painting portraits of Amalia van Solms, Frederik Hendrik's wife, and of Charlotte de la Trémoille, as well as his *The Abduction of Europa* and several self-portraits.[3] Meanwhile, just around the corner, Rabbi Saul Levi Mortera was preaching for the Beth Jacob congregation and teaching in the community's school, and getting paid an annual salary of nearly six hundred guilders for his work. He was also, by this time, running his own yeshiva, Roshit Chochma ("Beginning of Wisdom"), founded in 1629.

When Spinoza was born, his father, Michael, was serving his first term on the *ma'amad* of the Beth Jacob congregation. It was also the year of Michael's first stint as one of the Portuguese-Jewish community's *deputados*. He was therefore probably quite busy when his second son was born, performing these duties for the community at the same time that he was trying to run his business and provide for a growing household. Lucas and Colerus disagree about how successful he was at that and how well-off the Spinoza family was at this time. Lucas, for some reason, insists that the family was poor. Spinoza "was of very modest origin [*d'une naissance fort médiocre*]," he tells us. "His father, who was a Portuguese Jew, did not have the means to get him started in commerce, and resolved to have him learn Hebrew literature."[4] Pierre Bayle, another seventeenth-century philosopher and a harsh critic of Spinoza, claims that "there is reason to believe that [Spinoza's family] was poor and of little consequence [*pauvre et très-peu considerable*]." He draws this conclusion from the fact that, after his departure from the Jewish community, Spinoza relied on a friend's generosity in order to maintain himself; and that, according to some accounts, the Jewish community offered him a pension if he would return to the orthodox fold.[5]

Colerus's opinion, however, is probably the more accurate one, and certainly agrees with what the documents testify about Michael's activities in the 1630s: "Although it is commonly written that he [Spinoza] was poor and was of an inconsiderable family, it is, however, certain that his parents were respectable and well-to-do Portuguese Jews."[6] It is likely as well that when Baruch was born the family was living, not on one of the crowded backstreets of the less desirable interior of the Vlooienburg island (as some writers have assumed),[7] where so many of the poor Ashkenazim settled, but right on the Houtgracht itself. If they were in the same house that they occupied in 1650, for which we have the tax records establishing Michael's residence, they were renting from Willem Kiek, a Dutchman who owned some property in this part of town; Michael, as far as we know, never owned his own house.[8] The thoroughfare on which they lived was also sometimes referred to as the Burgwal. It was a stately street, and the Spinoza home – which Colerus calls *een vraay Koopmans huis* ("a nice merchant's house") – was near one of the busiest and most public intersections of the Jewish quarter. There were a vegetable market and a variety of businesses there, along with some very attractive homes.

The house that Michael rented from Kiek fronted the Houtgracht. Looking down and across the "wood canal," the family could see "The Antwerpen," the house that served as a synagogue for the Beth Jacob congregation. Next to the synagogue were two houses that the community was renting and using for classrooms. Thus, when it was time for Baruch to go to school, all he had to do was cross over the Houtgracht by the bridge that was practically in front of his home and walk down the Houtgracht on the other side of the canal. The house being used as a synagogue by the Neve Shalom congregation was one house down from the Spinoza home, whereas the Beth Israel synagogue – which would serve as the sole synagogue for the united congregation after 1639 – was only eight houses, a warehouse, and an alley away. The Spinoza family, then, lived at the heart of the Jewish quarter. Simply by walking out their door they could not help but run into others on their way to one of the synagogues or the community's school.

Behind Spinoza's house, in the same plat but on the diagonally oppo-

site corner and facing the Breestraat, was the home of Hendrik Uylenburgh, a well-known art dealer and Rembrandt's agent. Rembrandt lived
with Uylenburgh off and on for a number of years after he returned, in
1632, from Leiden to the city where he had done his apprenticeship. In
1639, after marrying Uylenburgh's niece Saskia, Rembrandt bought the
house next door to Uylenburgh on the Breestraat, around the corner from
Spinoza, a stone's throw from the house of Menasseh ben Israel, and
across the St. Anthoniesluis from Rabbi Mortera's home.

By the time Baruch was born, Miriam was three years old and Isaac –
if indeed he was Hanna's son – somewhat younger. Michael also had another daughter, Rebecca, but we do not know if she was Hanna's child or
the child of Michael's third wife, Esther. When she and her nephew made
claims on Baruch's estate after his death in 1677, she was identified in the
petition as the sister (and not the half-sister) of "Baruch Espinosa."[9] This
lends support to Colerus's claim that the eldest of Michael's daughters
was Rebecca, and that she was one of Baruch's two sisters.[10] It is also
telling, as Vaz Dias notes, that Esther, in her last will and testament, leaves
all of her property at her death, "nothing excepted," to Michael, "her husband, so that he will possess all and enjoy all, for ever, as he does his own
goods, without contradiction from anyone." There is no mention in this
document of any children that Esther may have had with Michael, which
suggests that Michael's third marriage was a childless one.[11] Finally, and
perhaps of the greatest importance, Rebecca named her daughter Hanna,[12]
presumably after her (and Baruch's) mother. On the other hand, the people
among whom she spent her last days were apparently under the impression that she was Baruch's half-sister, and the daughter of Esther. Sometime between 1679 and 1685, Rebecca, by then a widow of twenty years,
moved with her sons Michael (named, it would seem, after his maternal
grandfather) and Benjamin to Curaçao, then a Dutch possession. There
was a significant Portuguese-Jewish community in the West Indies, many
of whom were refugees from the failed Brazil community, with ties to the
Amsterdam congregation. Rebecca and Michael both died in the yellow
fever epidemic of 1695. In the official history of Curaçao's Jews, the author writes that "our Ribca [Hebrew for Rebecca] was the Philosopher
Spinoza's half-sister, the daughter of Michael Spinoza and his third wife
Ester de Solis."[13]

There was also a third son, Abraham (alias Gabriel), who was probably
younger than Baruch and born sometime between 1634 and 1638. A dating

later in that range seems more likely, as Abraham was almost certainly named after Michael's uncle and the father of his first wife, Abraham de Spinoza de Nantes, who died in either 1637 or 1638.[14]

In the 1630s, then, the Spinoza household was rather full and probably very hectic. There were four, perhaps five children. Michael was busy with his importing activities and congregational duties. Hanna would have tried to stay on top of things, but there is reason to believe that she was never very healthy. She may have suffered, as Baruch was to do, from respiratory problems, probably tuberculosis, and lived only a few years after Baruch's birth. Perhaps by the time Gabriel was born Miriam was able to help out around the house. A notary record from September of 1638 affords a rare momentary glimpse inside their home:

Today, the eighth of September 1638, I &c in the presence &c at the request of Sr. Simon Barkman, went to the house and the sick-beds of Sr. Miguel d'espinoza and his wife and requested acceptance of the bill of exchange I showed there, addressed to the said Miguel despinoza and copied out above, upon which the wife of the said Miguel despinoza, who was lying ill in bed on another bed in the same room, answered, because of the illness that has befallen my husband, the bill of exchange will not be accepted.[15]

On September 8, 1638, Hanna was sick in bed. Less than two months later, she was dead.

The language spoken in the Spinoza home was, of course, Portuguese. The men, at least, knew Spanish, the language of literature. And they prayed in Hebrew. All the boys in the community were required to study the "holy tongue" in school, while the older generation, raised in Catholic environments, may have had only a phonetic familiarity with the language. Most of the members of the family probably also learned how to read and speak some Dutch, as this was necessary for getting around in the markets and for communications and documents related to business, although at least one of the notaries whom the Jewish merchants often employed had an assistant who understood Portuguese. (Michael, however, seems not to have understood spoken Dutch very well. In a notary document of August 1652 it is stated that when the notary came to the Spinoza household to read to Michael a protest being lodged against him by the skipper of a ship – the seaman was complaining about how badly he had been treated by Michael's agents in Rouen and Le Havre, France – Michael's daughter had to translate for him.)[16] But if Michael d'Espinoza and his children needed to be multilingual in their mundane and sacred affairs, still, like most of the families of the community, the language they used in the street and in running their household was Portuguese. Even when he was older, Spinoza, although perfectly fluent in Latin and knowledgeable in Hebrew, was always more comfortable in Portuguese than in any other language. In 1665, writing to Willem van Blijenburgh in Dutch, Spinoza closes by saying, "I would have preferred to write in the language in which I was brought up [*de taal, waar mee ik op gebrocht ben*]; I might perhaps express my thoughts better"; he then asks Blyenburgh to correct the mistakes in the Dutch himself. It is clear that the *taal* he is referring to here is Portuguese, and not, as some scholars have assumed, Latin.[17]

The 1630s, like the previous decade, were a difficult time for the United Provinces. It was a period of economic stagnation, even recession, as the war with Spain dragged on, draining financial and material resources and continuously generating obstacles to trade. It was also a time of political and religious conflict. There were irrational upheavals in the markets and serious outbreaks of the plague. And, through it all, Amsterdam's Jews, ever conscious of their status as a group of resident aliens, kept a nervous eye on developments both within and outside their community.

In the summer of 1632, Spain suffered a number of significant setbacks in its military pursuit to maintain a strong presence in the Netherlands. Frederik Hendrik, leading the army of the northern Netherlands, did not succeed in stimulating a revolt in the southern Low Countries against the Spanish crown, despite his promise that the Catholic clergy in any towns that came over to the side of the States General would be allowed to stay and continue serving Catholics in their churches. But the Stadholder's siege of Maastricht did bring about that city's capitulation, following the earlier surrenders of Venlo and various other small towns. The southern provinces were demoralized and not a little alarmed, and they forced Isabella – daughter of Philip II and the local governor for the reigning Spanish monarch, Philip IV – to convene the States General of the south. The representatives to that body, concerned about the future of their union as a Catholic land, voted to open peace negotiations with the north. Talks in The Hague began that fall.

Philip IV was not the only one who was unhappy about these pacific developments. The Dutch themselves were divided. Some felt that, as the republic was really no longer in any grave danger and the war was now just a matter of limiting (or even rolling back) Hapsburg power in the southern Netherlands, it was time to stop fighting. Peace, they argued, could only be a good thing. It would certainly ease the strains on the economy and reopen trade routes. Besides, France was becoming a major power in its own right and would help counterbalance the Hapsburgs. Adriaan Pauw, a strong advocate for peace and someone who was deemed acceptable to both Arminians and Counter-Remonstrants – now no longer just theological adversaries but also identified, respectively, as the tolerant liberal and the narrow conservative political camps – led the Dutch delegation to the talks. He was initially supported by Frederik Hendrik himself, as well as by the two major cities of the province of Holland, Amsterdam and Rotterdam, whose mercantile economies stood to benefit the most from peace. On the other side stood many Counter-Remonstrant towns, which were in favor of continuing the war and mobilizing for the final defeat of the Catholic forces.

As the peace conference became less productive – hindered both by the north's insistence that members of the Reformed Church be allowed to practice openly in the south and by the south's demand that the Dutch relinquish their possessions in Brazil – the division in the Dutch camp grew. Pauw and the Arminians favored the end of hostilities above all else and were willing to modify the Dutch conditions for peace. The Counter-Remonstrants argued against making any concessions to the south, particularly in the matter of religion and territory, and they insisted that the negotiations be broken off immediately. Frederik Hendrik gradually moved over to the "war camp," especially when he saw that an alliance with France against Spain, which would increase his power, was possible. By late 1633, the Stadholder (backed by the Counter-Remonstrants) and the Grand Pensionary (allied with the Arminians) were locked in a battle for control of the States of Holland and thus, given the power of the States of Holland in the United Provinces as a whole, for political domination of the republic. In essence, it was not only a fight over whether or not to pursue peace with Spain, or even over foreign policy as a whole: what was at issue was the political identity of the union of the northern provinces. Pauw and his allies basically stood for the preeminence of the States, and thus for a republican form of government. Frederik Hendrik and his Counter-Remonstrant supporters, though generally not monarchists and certainly not committed simply to jettisoning the apparatus of a republic, stood for the preeminence of the office of Stadholder, primarily the Prince of Orange, over any representative body. Pauw was, to be sure, no Oldenbarneveldt; and Frederik Hendrik lacked the ruthlessness of Prince Maurits. But, as was the case in the 1610s, confrontation between the Stadholder and the liberal wing of the States of Holland, led by its Grand Pensionary, became the dominant theme of Dutch politics in the 1630s. Even though the Counter-Remonstrants remained somewhat suspicious of the Stadholder, given Frederik Hendrik's tendency of toleration toward Remonstrants and even Catholics, they tied their cause – including their hope for renewed repression of Remonstrants within the republic – to his fortunes.

They soon had the upper hand. By 1635, the Netherlands had allied itself with France, which declared war on Spain in May. The campaign was back in full strength as the Dutch invaded the Spanish Netherlands from the north while France attacked from the south. In 1636, the Stadholder secured Pauw's departure from the post of Grand Pensionary of the States of Holland and his replacement by Jacob Cats, the celebrated Dutch poet who was viewed as a man of moderate and practical political opinions (and, thus, as someone more liable to go along with the Stadholder's policies).[18] For the time being, at least until 1650, it was the Stadholder and the strict Calvinists who called the shots. The States party was never fully marginalized, however, and the tension between the two groups would be an important factor in Dutch politics for the rest of the century. The pendulum would soon enough swing once again toward the more liberal and republican camp.

These struggles in the military, political, and religious domains in the 1630s were matched by various social and economic disturbances. In 1635 and 1636 there was a particularly severe outbreak of the plague. It had been ten years since the last epidemic, in 1624–5, which took over eighteen thousand lives in Amsterdam alone. The latest episode was even more fatal. Over twenty-five thousand people died in two years in Amsterdam (20 percent of the city's population), accompanied by eighteen thousand deaths in Leiden (almost 30 percent of that city).[19] The plague virus does not discriminate among religions, and there is no doubt that Amsterdam's Jews – mingling with the rest of the city's population as they did – were as hard-hit as any other group. It may be that the Ashkenazim, living in close and crowded quarters on the Vlooienburg island, suffered a particularly high rate of infection.

Of the tempests experienced by the Dutch during this period, however, perhaps the most famous – and certainly the most colorful – was the tulip mania that struck in the middle of the decade.

The tulip is not native to the Netherlands. It was a sixteenth-century transplant from the Near East – Turkey, to be exact – which happened to flourish particularly well in the Dutch soil and climate, particularly around Haarlem. It quickly became *the* fashionable flower of northern Europe and an object of great aesthetic and scientific admiration. It did not take the Dutch long to become adept at growing and cultivating the tulip, and they developed an incredible number of varieties by modifying the flower's color, size, and shape. Interest in the tulip soon spread beyond the circle of horticultural specialists and professional gardeners to the middle and lower classes, which saw in the flower not just an attractive way to spruce up a small garden or decorate a house, but also a commodity in which to invest. Unlike rarer or more expensive goods, the trade in tulips – particularly the less extraordinary varieties – was something into which the nonwealthy could buy, although on a much smaller scale than rich investers. Buying and selling tulip bulbs, sometimes by the basket or even by the individual bulb, became a popular way of making a couple of guilders.

In the mid-1630s, however, when the market in bulbs started to become less a straightforward exchange of money for merchandise and more a matter of speculation, many were drawn into what was, increasingly, an exercise in high-risk gambling. People were buying bulbs and making deals out of season, several months in advance of the proposed delivery date. The buyer often never saw the actual bulbs, or even a sample of the variety being promised. Between the signing of the deal and the delivery of the bulbs, many buyers would sell their interest in those bulbs to a third party at a higher price. This market in tulip futures rapidly expanded, with more and more people deciding to play the game. The number of transactions surrounding a single delivery deal, and thus the number of interested parties, would multiply dangerously as the secondary buyers turned around and offered their interest to others. Because the transfers were usually made on promissary notes, only rarely did any actual money change hands. It was simply a matter of time before this activity around the paper became a market in its own right. By 1637, the interests themselves, rather than any tulip bulbs, were the real object of speculation. All of this, of course, sent tulip bulb prices skyrocketing. And the value of the paper interests rose dramatically as the date of delivery approached. People went to all extremes to get in on a deal that looked particularly good. Jacob Cats, in his

Sinne-en Minnebeelden, a book of pictorial emblems with moral significance, tells us that one person, probably a farmer, paid two thousand five
hundred guilders for a single bulb, in the form of two bundles of wheat,
four of rye, four fat oxen, eight pigs, twelve sheep, two oxheads of wine,
four tons of butter, a thousand pounds of cheese, a bed, some clothing, and
a silver beaker.[20] When the crash came – and come it surely would – a lot
of people were going to be hurt.

It was, in the end, like the children's game of "hot potato": one did not
want to be caught holding the paper when the delivery date arrived. Rather
than making a profit, the final buyer would be stuck with a bunch of tulip
bulbs. The High Court of Holland could not stand by any longer watching the republic's usually sober-minded citizens ruin themselves in the
midst of this hysteria. When rumors that the authorities were about to intervene began circulating, prices fell precipitously as people tried quickly
to unload their interests. In April 1637, the court nullified all deals made
after the planting of 1636; any disputed contracts would have to be taken
up with the local magistrates. A great many families and fortunes were
ruined in the ensuing crash. It took the tulip growers some time to recover
both their financial losses and their damaged reputations, as many blamed
them for fueling the mania in the first place.[21]

We do not know to what degree the Jews were swept up by the enthusiasm. They certainly felt the indirect effects of this brief but powerful crisis in the Dutch economy, and it would be somewhat surprising if they
themselves, with their commercial instincts, were not tempted to enter the
fray. Because the growing of tulips was a relatively new enterprise, it was
not covered by any established guild. It was therefore an area where Jews
were free to try their hand, as Francisco Gomez da Costa did on a relatively large scale outside Vianen.

≈

The 1630s were trying years for Amsterdam's Portuguese-Jewish community as well. It was a time both of division and of union. Perhaps the most
significant crisis within the *naçion* involved what was initially a theological
debate between two of the community's leading rabbis from the congregations Beth Jacob and Neve Shalom. The complexity of the issues, however,
made it more than a mere disagreement on a technical matter of dogma and
addressed some very deep and pressing concerns for the members of the
Portuguese *kehillah*. The rift, in fact, may have led to the departure of one

of the rabbis from Amsterdam. It probably also contributed to the decision to unite the three congregations in 1639.

Sometime around 1636, Rabbi Isaac Aboab da Fonseca, of the Beth Israel
congregation, composed a treatise entitled *Nishmat Chaim* ("The Breath
of Life"). This document was at the center of the dispute and reflected his
disagreement both with the views of Saul Levi Mortera and with the judgment of the rabbis in Venice. Rabbi Aboab had been born a New Christian
in Portugal in 1605. After a brief sojourn in France, his family moved to
Amsterdam – presumably to return to Judaism – in 1612, while Isaac was
still a young boy. In Amsterdam, he studied with Rabbi Isaac Uziel, the
conservative rabbi of Neve Shalom. Aboab must have been a precocious
student, because by 1626, when he was only twenty-one, he was already a
chacham for Beth Israel. He had a rather mystical bent, more so than the
other rabbis in the community, and a deep interest in *kabbalah*. In this respect, he could not have been more unlike his opponent in the dispute,
Rabbi Mortera of Beth Jacob, who was inclined toward a rationalistic and
philosophical approach to religion. Moreover, unlike Aboab, Mortera was
an Ashkenazic Jew, and thus had never gone through the marrano experience. Although he lived out his life among the former conversos of Amsterdam and preached to them in fluent Portuguese, it is easy to imagine
his lack of empathy with what the members of his congregation (or their
ancestors) had endured, and perhaps his impatience with their loose and
unorthodox approach to some Jewish beliefs and practices. This difference
in their backgrounds helps to explain Mortera's confrontation with
Aboab.

An important question for Amsterdam's Jews was the theological and
escatalogical status of their brethren who remained in Spain and Portugal
and who, although of Jewish descent, were living Christian and not Jewish lives. Were they still, technically, Jews? And if so, what did their continuing apostasy mean for the fate of their souls after they died? The
Mishnah, in *Sanhedrin,11*:1, declares that "All Israelites have a portion in
the world-to-come [*olam ha-ba*]." Does it follow that whoever belongs to
the nation of Israel, no matter how grave his sins and no matter how long
he remains a sinner, is promised an eventual place in the world-to-come,
the ultimate reward? Will a Jew never suffer eternal punishment for his
sins? Mortera did not think so. According to him, "Israelite" refers to a
righteous person. And someone who has failed to follow the laws of the
Torah, and who has openly denied the principles of the faith, is no right-

eous person and will be eternally punished for his transgressions. There is no guarantee that just because a person has a Jewish soul he can avoid eternal punishment in hell for his sins.

Apparently, a significant number of young members of the Amsterdam community believed otherwise and argued loudly for the unconditional salvation of all Jewish souls. This would be an attractive thesis for former marranos (who may still have had marrano relatives in Iberia), as it meant that even those Jews who once practiced, or were still practicing, Catholicism in the old country – perhaps as grave an offense as can be imagined – would be guaranteed a place in *olam ha-ba*. According to various documents, including Mortera's own report on the controversy, sometime in early 1635 Mortera's sermons were being disrupted by "some young men" who took offense at his claim that "the wicked who commit grave sins and die without repentance do incur eternal punishment."[22] These "young rebels," or "immature disciples" – corrupted, Mortera argued, by kabbalists (which may be his way of referring to Aboab and others) – asked the leaders of the community to issue an injunction forbidding Mortera to preach the doctrine of eternal punishment. Such a doctrine, Mortera's opponents insisted, came dangerously close to Christian beliefs on reward and punishment. They also worried about the consequences of such a strict doctrine for their marrano cousins.

The matter was too big for the relatively young community to handle by itself, especially because it involved a question of orthodoxy, something on which the community's leaders were perhaps still educating themselves. Once again they turned to Venice, and asked the Beth Din of the Jewish community there to rule on the dispute. Mortera and his opponents submitted their respective pleas, with Mortera marshaling a great deal of textual evidence – from the Bible and the Talmud, as well as from Jewish philosophers such as Maimonides – to argue for the doctrine of eternal punishment for unrepentant sinners, even if they were Jews. To the Venetian rabbis it seemed a very delicate matter. They hesitated to bring it up before the Beth Din, in part because they did not want to justify the dispute by making it seem as though this was indeed a difficult question to answer and for which there were good reasons on both sides. Their initial recommendation was that the lay leaders of the Amsterdam community try to find a way to settle it among themselves, mainly by persuading Aboab to set an example for his younger protégés – if indeed they were simply following his directions – by publicly renouncing his opinion. It appears that this approach did not work, and so the Venetians wrote to Aboab himself, in early 1636: "We were hoping for the day that would bring the message of peace . . . but our expectation has been frustrated. For we were again informed that the conflict persists and that the spokesman of those denying the belief in the eternality of punishment is none other than you, Sir, and that you preach thus openly and publicly."[23] They appealed to Aboab, in gentle and flattering but firm terms, to be reasonable and abandon an opinion explicitly denied by the sages of the Talmud and other rabbinical authorities.

The letter did not have its desired effect, and in response Aboab wrote his *Nishmat Chaim*. In the treatise, he directly addresses the questions "Is there eternal punishment of souls or not? And what did our rabbis, of blessed memory, intend by saying 'The following have no share in the world-to-come'?" He insisted that the true answers to these questions were to be found in kabbalah, not in philosophy or the Talmud (as Mortera had argued); and that the kabbalistic texts show authoritatively (if not unambiguously) that *all* Jewish souls ultimately receive salvation. Many of these souls, as a result of their sins, would have to go through a painful process of purification by way of longer or shorter periods of transmigration. But they still belonged to Israel: "All Israelites are a single body and their soul is hewn from the place of Unity."[24]

Given the background of the overwhelming majority of the Jews in the Portuguese community, there is no question that many members were sympathetic to Aboab's views. On the other hand, Venice's rabbis, whom they regarded with great respect, had made their own opinion on this matter quite clear: Mortera was right, Aboab was wrong. Although there is no indication that Aboab ever retracted his views, it would seem that – at least as a practical matter – Mortera prevailed, as in less than three years he was made head rabbi of the united congregation, with Aboab occupying the lowest rank (behind David Pardo and Menasseh ben Israel). In 1642, Aboab left for Brazil to minister to the Amsterdam Jews who had settled in Recife. His departure from Amsterdam may have been the result of lingering tensions with Mortera, who was then running things.

It is also possible that it was this dispute that made it clear to the lay leaders of the Amsterdam Sephardim that having three rabbis of such different temperaments and persuasions leading three congregations was much too troublesome a situation and served only to increase the potential for further dispute – and, perhaps, even schism. They were no doubt aware of the problems that resulted from the fragmentation of the Sephardic Jews of Salonika (where Rabbi Pardo of Beth Israel had been born), which had five Spanish and three Portuguese congregations. It was also likely becoming much too difficult to manage the increasingly complex affairs of the community, which now contained well over a thousand individuals. The members of the board of *deputados*, or even the Senhores Quinze, representing both the community at large as well as their respective congregations, may have been unable to handle the job. A more centralized and efficiently structured organization of the Sephardic community was required.

After some consultations and negotiations between the governing boards of the three congregations, probably with the advice of the Venetian community, the Senhores Quinze met in September of 1638 (28 Elul 5398) to conclude their agreement on the merging of the three congregations – Beth Jacob, Neve Shalom, and Beth Israel – into one, to be called "Talmud Torah" (after the Sephardic congregation of Venice). Within a month, the members of each congregation approved the merger agreement, and it was signed in the spring of 1639.[25] Any Jew of "the Portuguese and Spanish nation" residing in Amsterdam in 1638 or who settled in the city after that year automatically became a member of the united congregation; non-Sephardic Jews could not become members and could attend services only with special permission. The house on the Houtgracht that had been serving as the synagogue for the Beth Israel congregation – the largest house of the three, and eight houses down from the Spinoza home – would henceforth serve as the synagogue for Talmud Torah. A contemporary Dutch visitor described the "house of prayer":

The Portuguese have a fairly large place for which they have put together two houses; below, you enter a hall or large bare vestibule containing a water-butt that can be turned on with a tap. Upon it you will find a towel, for the Jews wash their hands before they enter the church; on either side there are stairways by which you reach their church; the women, who are separated from the men and cannot be seen by them, are seated high up in a gallery. At one end of the church there is a large wooden cupboard with two doors; it contains many precious things, among them the Books of Moses wrapped in rare embroidered cloths. Their teachers stand on a raised platform some three feet higher than the other congregants; the men don white shawls over their hats which hang down over their shoulders and trunk and each holds a book in his hand, all of which are in Hebrew.[26]

The three congregations' rabbis all became the *chachamim* of Talmud Torah, although they were decidedly ranked. Rabbi Mortera, from Beth Jacob, was now head rabbi of the entire community and principal of the school. He was required to preach three times a month and to give Talmud lessons to advanced students. He was paid six hundred guilders per year, along with one hundred baskets of turf for his heating needs. Rabbi David Pardo (the son of Joseph Pardo), from Beth Israel, was the second rabbi. His duties included serving as the administrator of *Beth Chaim,* the congregation's cemetery at Ouderkerke, and he was paid five hundred guilders. Third in rank came Rabbi Menasseh ben Israel, formerly the rabbi for Neve Shalom. He was to preach on one Shabbat each month and was paid one hundred and fifty guilders. And Rabbi Isaac Aboab da Fonseca would be responsible for teaching elementary school and giving evening sermons to students, at a salary of four hundred and fifty guilders a year. (This unexplained discrepancy between the salaries of Menasseh and Aboab was a source of tension between the two and a sore point in Menasseh's relationship with the congregation.) The four rabbis would all sit together, in order of rank, during services on an appointed bench while the *chazzan* – in 1639, Abraham Baruch (for an annual salary of three hundred and ninety guilders) – led the congregation in prayers and read from the Torah. They were also jointly responsible for deciding, by majority vote, all matters of *halacha,* or religious law, that arose within the community.

The rabbis were not, however, the chief executives of the community. It was not their role to run the congregation's day-to-day affairs, nor were they responsible for adjudicating in secular matters, or even for directing the community's religious life. All executive and legislative and non-halachic judicial powers – including the right to excommunicate members – were invested in a board of laymen. With the merger, the fifteen *parnassim* of the three congregations were reduced to a single *ma'amad* composed of seven individuals: six *parnassim* and a *gabbai,* or treasurer. This new governing board served, in effect, as a constitutional committee and drew up an additional fifty-six regulations for the new congregation to supplement the original *ascamot* of the three congregations. And the first of their new regulations laid it down in no uncertain terms that "the *ma'amad* has an absolute and incontestable authority; no one may avoid its resolutions, [disobedience will be] under punishment of *cherem.*"[27]

Membership on the governing board, a position of honor, was a matter of cooptation: one was elected by the seven members sitting on the board,

and a majority was required. There was no outside consultation or oversight over the *ma'amad*'s election of its members. The only limitations
were that one had to have been a Jew for at least three years and that three
years had expired since one's last term on the board. Moreover, close relatives (by blood or marriage) could not serve on the board at the same time:
"a father cannot be elected to the *ma'amad* with a son, a brother with a
brother, a grandfather with a grandson, an uncle with a nephew, a brother-
in-law with a brother-in-law, or a parent of these." Finally, no one elected
to the board could refuse to serve. The *ma'amad* met on Sundays, and all
of its deliberations were secret.

The executive board was the highest authority in the community. There
was no appealing its decisions. Among their multifarious duties, the members of the *ma'amad* imposed the community's taxes, regulated the appointment of community officers and employees, ran the schools, broke ties when
a vote of the *chachamim* was evenly divided, resolved business disputes between Portuguese Jews, distributed charity, licensed the carrying of arms
among members of the congregation, oversaw ritual slaughtering and the
training of *shochetim*, authorized the publication of books, granted per-
missions for circumcision of Portuguese men returning to Judaism, authorized divorce proceedings, nominated the *chatan torah* ("bridegroom
of the Torah") for the holiday of Simchat Torah, and basically controlled
the celebration of the holidays ("There shall be no games or riddles in the
synagogue during *Simchat Torah* nor on any other occasion"; "On Purim,
all members of the congregation shall disburse *maot Purim* [Purim money]
for the purpose of *sedaca* [*tzedakah*, charity]"). The *parnassim* were even
responsible for assigning seats in the synagogue – to men only; women had
to fend for themselves and grab the first vacant seat they could find in their
gallery – and for setting the time for services. They also had the power to
punish anyone caught violating any of the regulations, either by fines or –
in more serious cases – by *cherem*, excommunication.

Although much of the inspiration for the internal political organization
of the community undoubtedly came from Venice, the power structure,
particularly in its social dimensions, closely resembled that of Calvinist
Amsterdam itself. The members of the *ma'amad* came from prominent
and well-to-do – although not necessarily the wealthiest – families. They
were usually drawn from the pool of successful merchants of the community, as well as from its professional class (particularly its medical doctors).
When it came time to elect new members, the sitting board knew just where

to turn to ensure continuity. It was simply a matter of wealth and/or status. The community was, in effect, governed by a self-perpetuating economic elite, an aristocracy – or, better, oligarchy – that both selected its own successors and made all appointments to other offices and boards.[28] In this sense, it was a microcosm of Amsterdam politics. For the city, too, was no democracy. The municipal government was not composed of delegates elected by the general populace, representing the interests of the many social and economic strata of Amsterdam and occupying offices open to all. Political power in Amsterdam in the seventeenth century – and this was true of most Dutch cities and towns of the time – was vested in a relatively small and well-defined number of families, known as "regents." The regents were basically the members of some of the wealthiest families of the city that constituted its oligarchic class. The regent families came from professional as well as merchant and manufacturing backgrounds. As in the Jewish context, they were not necessarily the wealthiest families in the city. Although wealth was indeed a necessary condition for membership in the regent class, money alone was not sufficient. There were many rich families that never gained admittance to the clique. It was also a matter of social status, political and family connections, and historical contingency. The regents, according to one historian, were not a separate social or economic class but "a politically privileged section of the upper-bourgeoisie."[29] They were not nobles but financially successful families who simply had a monopoly on political power. It included both those families whose members were actually sitting on the *vroedschap*, or town council, at a given time, and those families whose members had sat on the council in the past and would no doubt do so again in the future. It was generally a closed system, although during the periods of political upheaval and reversal – the so-called *wetsverzettingen* – there occurred significant changes in the membership of the regent class. One could also marry into a regent family and thus improve the connections of one's own blood relations.

Members of regent families filled all the important and powerful offices in Amsterdam. The *schout*, or chief police official and prosecutor, was usually from a local regent family, as were the *burgemeesters*. These were the officials responsible for the day-to-day administration of the town, and were usually chosen from the *vroedschap*. Amsterdam, like most towns, had four *burgemeesters*, each holding office for only a year or two. The *vroedschap*, the real core of the regent system, was more preoccupied with general policy than with daily administration. It usually consisted of thirty-six members, who were concerned both with matters of importance to the province as a whole, particularly as these affected Amsterdam – they were charged with giving voting instructions to the city's delegates to the States of Holland – and with the internal economic and political life of the town. Unlike those of the Jewish community's *ma'amad*, which it resembled in its legislative and executive functions and in the scope of its authority, members of the *vroedschap* served for life. When a place did open up on the *vroedschap*, a replacement was elected by the council's sitting members, as in the *ma'amad*. Moreover, their deliberations (like the deliberations of the *parnassim*) were kept secret. There was even a regulation against "consanguinity" resembling that of the Portuguese Jews: fathers and sons, brothers, and other blood relatives (but not relatives by marriage) could not serve on the council at the same time.[30] The names differed, of course – Bicker, Six, Van Beuningen, and De Graeff, as opposed to Curiel, Farar, Da Costa, and Cohen – as did the language of deliberation. But the nature of the concentration of political power was remarkably similar among the Dutch and the Portuguese Jews in their midst.

଼

In the fall of 1639, the year the merger went into effect, Baruch de Spinoza turned seven. This meant that he was at the age when most boys in the community began their compulsory education in the congregation's elementary school. His mother had died a year earlier, on November 5, 1638, and it was probably not a happy time in the Spinoza household. Michael was once again a widower, but this time he had five children to care for.

The young Baruch, we can be sure, excelled in his studies as he moved up through the grades of the school's curriculum, and he must have made his father quite proud. Lucas relates that Spinoza's father "had not the means to help him on in business and therefore decided to let him take up the study of Hebrew letters."[31] In another early biographical account it is suggested that Michael greatly resented his son's preference for literature over business.[32] This seems most unlikely. There can be no doubt that Michael wanted to insure that his sons – born, unlike him, as Jews in a thriving religious community – receive a proper Jewish upbringing. He clearly cared a great deal about education, as he served twice (in 1635–6 and 1642–3) as a *parnas* on the board of governors overseeing the community's educational institutions. He also made sure to inscribe himself

and his three sons in the membership roll of the Ets Chaim society, the
educational brotherhood, as soon as it was founded in 1637; the foundation was, among other things, responsible for providing scholarships for
gifted students. He both paid the admission fee of eighteen guilders and
made a donation of fifty-two guilders.[33] These facts make it hard to believe that the education of one of the seventeenth century's most important philosophers was merely a reluctant concession of a disappointed
father.

4

Talmud Torah

A ROUND 1640, Rabbi Sabatti Scheftel Hurwitz of Frankfurt, on a journey to Poland, went out of his way to make a detour through Amsterdam. Among the Jews there, he tells us, he encountered "many reputable and learned people." He went to observe the Portuguese community's schools and was impressed enough by what he saw to lament the fact that "nothing of such a sort was found in our land."[1] Another visitor to Amsterdam, Shabbethai Bass, a Polish scholar, related that

[In the schools] of the Sephardim . . . I saw "giants [in scholarship]: tender children as small as grasshoppers," "kids who have become he-goats." In my eyes they were like prodigies because of their unusual familiarity with the entire Bible and with the science of grammar. They possessed the ability to compose verses and poems in meter and to speak a pure Hebrew. Happy the eye that has seen all these things.[2]

Bass goes on – obviously taking much delight in what he saw – to describe the structure of the school day and the levels of teaching. He remarks on the great number of students in the classrooms ("and may they keep on increasing!") and notes the progress the pupils made in their studies as they advanced from one grade to the next.

The foundations for the educational system that so impressed Jewish (and Gentile) visitors to Amsterdam's Jewish quarter were established early, in 1616, when Beth Jacob and Neve Shalom instituted the Talmud Torah Society. This was an educational brotherhood initially devoted to providing instruction for the sons of families who could not afford to hire private tutors. The society set up a school, which, after 1620, met in a house it was able to rent next door to the Beth Jacob synagogue on the Houtgracht. In 1639, when the congregations merged, the united Talmud Torah community was given as a gift that house and the one next to it for their school, also called Talmud Torah.[3] Tuition was free for elementary education, and both rich and poor families sent their sons to be taught the essentials of Judaism. It was this school, a relatively short walk from his house across the canal and down the other side, which Spinoza started attending around 1639.

In 1637, a second educational society was founded, Ets Chaim. At first this was intended to be primarily a scholarship organization. It was devoted to raising enough capital to generate the interest that, supplemented by donations, could provide stipends for the more gifted students and allow them to continue their education at the higher levels. However, Ets Chaim soon began to function as a Talmudic college for older boys, and it was responsible for the formal training of rabbis.

Instruction in the Portuguese community's school was divided into six classes. The four lower classes, generally for boys aged seven to fourteen and attended by all pupils, covered the basic religious, cultural, and literary material that any educated Jew was expected to know. In 1639, when Spinoza probably began, Mordechai de Castro was teaching the first class. Like the other elementary-school teachers, Castro went under the title "Rubi." He earned one hundred and fifty guilders a year for giving instruction in the Hebrew alphabet and spelling. Shabbethai Bass tells how "in the first class the younger children study until they are able to read the prayer book; then they are promoted to the second class." Once promoted to the second grade – and a student's time in any one grade was dependent only upon the progress he made and usually lasted much more than a year – the students first gained some basic skills in reading the Torah in Hebrew from Joseph de Faro. They then spent the rest of the year learning each week's Torah portion ("with the accents") from Jacob Gomes. According to Bass, Gomes (who earned a yearly salary of two hundred and fifty guilders), or whoever was teaching this level at the time of his visit, would lead the boys through the Pentateuch "until they are well versed in the Five Books of Moses down to the last verse," with the emphasis placed on chanting the Hebrew text. They also began working on translating parts of the Torah.

By the time the students finished the third grade, they were translating the week's Torah portion, or *parshah*, into Spanish under the direction of Abraham Baruch. Because Baruch was the same man who served as *chazzan*, he no doubt emphasized, as well, the melodic dimension to the reading of the Torah. Third-grade students also studied Rashi's commentary on the *parshah*. In the fourth grade, Salom ben Joseph taught the prophets and Rashi. Bass relates that in this class (which Salom may no longer have been teaching by the time of his visit) "one of the boys recites the verse at the top of his voice in Hebrew and then explains it in Spanish while the others listen. Then a second one takes his turn, and so on."[4]

Instruction in the elementary school was conducted mainly in Spanish, as it was in practically all Sephardic communities around the world. Spanish was the language of learning and literature (including sacred literature), even for Jews whose vernacular was Portuguese. The translation of the Bible that all of the students in Talmud Torah were expected to know by heart was Ferrara's Spanish version from 1553. As Cecil Roth, a historian of the marranos, puts it, "Portuguese was spoken; but Spanish, the semi-sacred language, was learned."[5] Many of the congregation's teachers, in fact, came from Ladino- (or Judeo-Spanish-) speaking parts of the Jewish world.[6] Besides, at this early stage in the Amsterdam community's existence, it would have been the rare student indeed who understood Hebrew as a language of conversation.

Classes began at eight in the morning. The teachers and their students worked for three hours, until the bell rang at eleven. They presumably went home for lunch (and perhaps some recreation), and returned to the school at two. In the evening they were dismissed at five (except in the winter, when classes began "as appropriate" and they stayed only until it was time for the evening service at the synagogue).[7] Many households may have supplemented this public education with private lessons in the home. Bass notes that "during those hours when the boys are home, their father engages a tutor, who teaches writing in Hebrew and other languages, poetry, reviews with the student what he has learned, directs his education, and teaches him that which may be of particular interest to him."[8] All students under the age of sixteen were also expected to be present every day in the synagogue for evening prayers and to sing psalms.

The end of the fourth grade – when a student was around fourteen years old – represented the end of elementary school education. The next two grades were devoted, among other things, to studying Talmud, both Mishnah and Gemara, and other classical texts. Many fewer students attended these higher classes than were graduated from the elementary levels. The course of study that now lay ahead would take at least six years and essentially constituted a rabbinical training. The article in the congregation's *ascamot* dealing with the duties of the *chachamim* states that "Chacham

Isaac Aboab will teach Hebrew grammar and give primary instruction in
Gemara." Bass described this fifth grade as follows:

> The boys are trained to study the Mishnaic law by themselves until they acquire
> understanding and intelligence and reach the category of *bocher* [Talmud student].
> In that class they speak in no other tongue but Hebrew except to explain the law
> in Spanish. They also study the science of grammar thoroughly. Every day they
> also learn one Mishnaic law with its Gemara comment.

(As Bass was writing some time after the years in which Spinoza attended
the school and Aboab taught Gemara, it is hard to gauge how much of what
he describes is an accurate picture of what was going on in the classrooms
when Spinoza was a student. It is not clear, in particular, whether in the
1640s the students, or even Aboab himself – once a marrano – had a sufficient verbal command of Hebrew to "speak in no other tongue" and a
good enough reading knowledge of Hebrew and Aramaic to study the Talmud in its original languages. It could be that the main passages of these
texts were translated into Spanish).[9]

The fifth level – which was taught for a time by Menasseh ben Israel,
after Aboab left for Brazil in 1642 – is also where the students, now young
men, learned the halachic requirements for the Jewish holidays:

> When a holiday or festival draws near all the students then study the relevant chap-
> ters in the *Shulchan Aruch* [the sixteenth-century codification of Jewish law by Rabbi
> Joseph Caro]; the laws of Passover for the Passover, and the laws of Sukkot for
> Sukkot. This is kept up until all the boys are familiar with the holiday regulations.

The sixth, or highest, grade was taught by the congregation's chief rabbi,
Saul Levi Mortera. He was responsible for educating the most advanced
students in the Talmud and, basically, for training them as rabbis, although
not all of the students would go on to become *chachamim* themselves. Under
Mortera's watchful gaze, they spent a number of years studying Gemara,
Rashi, and the Tosafot, along with Maimonides' commentaries and other
rabbinical and philosophical texts.

There is no doubt that Spinoza attended the Talmud Torah school up
through the fourth grade, until he was about fourteen. It used to be nearly
universally assumed that he also trained for the rabbinate and thus attended the upper levels of the school. Indeed, it was widely believed, perhaps romantically, that he was one of Mortera's prize students. Lucas, for
one, insists that "Mortera, a celebrity among the Jews and the least igno-

rant of all the Rabbis of his time, admired the conduct and the genius of his disciple. . . . Mortera's approval enhanced the good opinion that people had of his disciple."[10] There are, however, good reasons for doubting that Spinoza's Jewish education went past the fourth (or, at most, the fifth) grade, and thus that he ever studied to be a rabbi.

Spinoza must have excelled in his studies, acquiring both a command of the Hebrew language – sufficient to allow him later to write his own Hebrew grammar – and a deep knowledge of the Bible and of important rabbinical sources. He was an extraordinarily intelligent young man, one who would have easily stood out from his fellow students. According to Colerus, "Spinoza was endowed by nature with a clever mind and a quick perceptive faculty."[11] Just how clever and perceptive he was is revealed by an anecdote that Lucas tells. The story is perhaps a little too convenient and clearly drawn to be credible (although, given Lucas's personal acquaintance with Spinoza, the story may have been told to him by the philosopher himself). Nonetheless, it gives us a glimpse of the young and precocious Spinoza in the early 1640s. Michael, a "good man who had taught his son not to confuse superstition with genuine piety," one day decided to test Bento, who was then only ten years old.

He instructed him to go and collect some money that a certain old woman in Amsterdam owed him. When he entered her house and found her reading the Bible, she motioned to him to wait until she finished her prayer; when she had finished it, the child told her his errand, and this good old woman, after counting her money out to him, said, as she pointed to it on the table, "Here is what I owe your father. May you some day be as upright a man as he is; he has never departed from the Law of Moses, and Heaven will only bless you in the measure in which you will imitate him."

If Michael was indeed trying his son's ability to size up character, he was not disappointed:

As she was concluding these remarks she picked up the money in order to put it into the child's bag, but, having observed that this woman had all the marks of false piety against which his father had warned him, he wanted to count it after her in spite of all her resistance. He found that he had to ask for two more ducats, which the pious widow had dropped into a drawer through a slit specially made on the top of the table, and so he was confirmed in his thought.[12]

❧

The 1640s did not have an auspicious beginning for the Jews around the Breestraat. There was great excitement and hope over their growing strength as a united community and their increasing numbers. More and more Sephardim from various parts of Europe and around the Mediterranean – not to mention numerous Ashkenazim from eastern Europe – were migrating to Amsterdam, *Eleutheropolis*, "city of freedom." But the decade began for the congregation under a dark shadow of heterodoxy and tragedy.

In 1640, Uriel (or Gabriel) da Costa, a member of a prominent and respectable family in the community, shot himself in the head. The Da Costas were merchants and former marranos from Portugal. With the exception of the unstable Uriel – who seems, in fact, to have been partly responsible for the family's original return to Judaism – they settled comfortably into an orthodox Jewish life in their new homeland and quickly established themselves as upstanding members of their congregation. Uriel's brother, Abraham, sat on the *ma'amad* of Beth Jacob with Michael d'Espinoza in 1637–8, and would also sit on the Talmud Torah educational board with him in 1642–3. Perhaps there was a close relationship between the two families, although we cannot be sure. There seems, at least, to have been some connection between Uriel da Costa's family and the family of Spinoza's mother, Hanna, that went back to their days in northern Portugal.[13] Either way, there is no doubt that Spinoza himself, like any member of the community at the time, was familiar with Da Costa's heretical ideas; he probably meditated long and hard over them.

Uriel da Costa was born in 1585 to an aristocratic family in Porto. His father, Bento da Costa, was, according to Uriel himself, an "authentic Christian,"[14] but his mother, Branca, seems to have been a Judaizer. Uriel underwent an ordinary Christian education, eventually studying canon law at the University of Coimbra and later serving as a church treasurer. His life was, to all appearances, a perfectly pious one: he feared eternal damnation and confessed his sins regularly. But there were doubts. As he wrote in his autobiography:

The more I thought about these things, the greater the troubles that arose in me. In the end, I fell into an inextricable state of perplexity, restlessness, and trouble. Sadness and pain devoured me. I found it impossible both to confess my sins according to Roman rites in order to obtain valid absolution and to accomplish all that was demanded of me. I also began to despair over my salvation. . . . Since I found it difficult to abandon a religion to which I had been accustomed ever since the cradle and which, thanks to faith, had established deep roots in me, I uttered these doubts (when I was around twenty-two years old): Could what is said about another life be a fiction? Does the faith given to such sayings agree with reason? For reason directly repeats for me a number of things and ceaselessly whispers things altogether contrary [to faith].[15]

Having articulated, at least to himself, these doubts about the compatibility of Christian faith with human reason, Uriel found rest, he claims, and continued with his ecclesiastical life. But he soon started reading the Torah and the prophets, to see what Judaism had to offer. He became convinced, he says, that the Law of Moses was truly revealed by God and decided thenceforth to follow it. Of course, living openly (or even secretly) as a Jew was not permitted in Portugal. He resigned his benefice, abandoned the house his father had built in the well-to-do quarter of the city, and left Portugal with his mother and two brothers. They traveled north and settled in Amsterdam, "where we found Jews living, without fear, as Jews," in 1612. Uriel and his brothers were circumcised and began to familiarize themselves with the rituals and observances of regular Jewish life.

Disappointment quickly followed. Uriel claims to have been seeking the religion of the Bible, a pure devotion to the Law of Moses, and not some rabbinically altered religion of meaningless and superfluous rules. "Hardly had several days passed when I realized from my experience that there was a great disagreement between the customs and dispositions of the Jews, on the one hand, and the laws prescribed by Moses, on the other hand." The time frame here may be a bit foreshortened, but the nature of the discrepancy he perceived survives the demands of narrative tension: there was what he calls "the absolute law," and then there were the "inventions" of the so-called Jewish sages, "additions totally foreign to the law." Perhaps Da Costa was, in his description of this revelation, being a bit disingenuous. It is not likely, as one scholar has noted, that Uriel was so naive as to think that somewhere he could find, in seventeenth-century Europe, a communal life of pure biblical Judaism; and he could not have been totally surprised at the way in which contemporary Jewish life was shaped by rabbinical Judaism.[16] The Judaism that Da Costa would have been familiar with on a practical level, from his Judaizing mother and others, was in fact the peculiar Judaism of the marranos, with its small but unmistakable traces of the postbiblical, rabbinic religion.[17]

Whatever his actual expectations, Uriel was dismayed by the Judaism he found in Amsterdam. In his eyes it was nothing but a sect led by latter-day

Pharisees. He moved to Hamburg and in 1616 published his *Propostar contra a Tradicao*, a set of ten theses attacking, among other things, the validity of the Oral Law (that is, the Talmud) and demonstrating "the vanity and invalidity of the traditions and ordinances of the Pharisees."

It is by itself enough to cause the destruction of the foundation of the Torah if one says we should interpret the ordinances of the Torah according to oral reports and that we must believe in these reports as we believe in the Torah of Moses itself. By holding them to be true, we thereby create changes in the Torah and, in fact, create a new Torah opposing the real one. [But] it is impossible that a verbal Torah exists. . . . It would make the word of man equal to that of God to say that we are obliged to keep all the laws of the Talmud just as we are to keep the Torah of Moses.[18]

He was also, it seems, still plagued by his doubts about the immortality of the soul and an eternal life in the hereafter, doctrines that he would go on to attack at length in his later writing.

Venice responded to the publication of Da Costa's book with a *cherem* pronounced against him on August 14, 1618, by Rabbi Leon Modena. Modena condemned those "who contradict the words of our sages and who, notwithstanding the gaze of Israel, destroy above all the fences around the Torah, claiming that all the words of our sages are a chaos and calling stupid all those who believe in these words."[19] Modena's judgment would have great force in Hamburg and Amsterdam, given the mentoring relationship that existed between those communities and the Venetian congregation. Rabbi Modena also took it upon himself to refute Da Costa's views and defend the Oral Law in a book, *The Shield and the Buckle* ("Strive, O Lord, with those who contend against me: fight with those who oppose me. Take hold of shield and buckle, and rise up for my help" [Psalm 35, line 2]) "for the defense of our sages against a stray and stupid man, wise in his own eyes, whose name is insane."[20]

Da Costa was also put under a ban in Hamburg. He returned to Amsterdam a short time afterward, where he continued to propound his views. According to Samuel da Silva, a medical doctor in Hamburg who was asked by the rabbis of the Amsterdam community to refute Da Costa's opinions, Da Costa was claiming that

the Oral Law is lies and falsehoods, that the written law does not need any such explication, and that he and others like him can provide it. He affirms that the laws by which Israel was governed and still governs itself were entirely the invention of ambitious and evil men. . . . He claims that all of Israel practices a strange cult that he intends to destroy.[21]

Da Costa, added Da Silva, rejected the rite of circumcision and mocked the usage of various articles of Jewish ritual, including *tefillin* (phylacteries), *tallitot* (prayer shawls), and *mezuzot*.

The most important matter in Da Silva's eyes, however, was Da Costa's denial of the immortality of the soul. Da Costa was arguing that the human soul is mortal and does not survive the death of the body. A soul, he claimed , is naturally engendered by one's parents. It is not created by God separately and then placed in the body. It comes into being along with the body itself, as it really is just a part of the body, namely, the vital spirit residing in the blood. In this respect the human soul is no different from the souls of animals. The only distinguishing feature of the human soul is that it is rational. Thus, it is necessarily as mortal and perishable as the human (or any) body. It follows that there is no afterlife, and no eternal reward or punishment. "Once he is dead, nothing remains of a man, nor does he ever return to life."[22] Preserving *this* life is the reason for obeying God and his commandments, and the fruit one reaps will simply be the rewards of one's works here. The Law, Da Costa insisted, does not say that the soul is immortal, nor that there is some life after death, a life of reward or punishment. On the contrary, the Torah tells us that the human being, and not just the human body, is "dust, and to dust shall return." He concluded, as well, that there are a great number of errors, evils, and superstitious behaviors – grounded in our most irrational fears and hopes – that have their source solely in the belief in the soul's immortality.

On May 15, 1623, the ban under which Da Costa had been placed by Hamburg and Venice was – not surprisingly – endorsed by the Amsterdam community.

The sirs, Deputies of the Nation, make it known that they have learned of the arrival in this city of a man named Uriel Abadot. He brings with him numerous erroneous, false, and heretical opinions directed against our very holy law. Moreover, he was already declared a heretic and excommunicated in Venice and Hamburg. Desiring to lead him back to the truth, they have on several occasions, with all gentleness and grace, taken the necessary steps through the mediation of the *chachamim* and the elders of the nation in the presence of the said Deputies. Learning that, through sheer arrogance and obstinacy, he persists in his wickedness and in his false opinions, they declare, with the *ma'amadot* of the communities and the said *chachamim*, the following ordinance: that he be ostracized as a sick man, cursed by the Law of God; that no one, no matter what their rank, speak with him, whether they be man, woman, parent, or stranger; that no one enter into the house he is occupying nor show him any favor, under the penalty of being included under the same *cherem* and being separated off from our community. Out of respect for the convenience of his brothers, we grant them a delay of eight days before they must separate from him. Amsterdam the thirtieth day of Omer 5383 [1623]. Samuel Abarbanel, Binhamin Israel, Abraham Curiel, Joseph Abeniacar, Raphael Jesurun, Jacob Franco.[23]

Da Costa's response was defiant. "The situation having come to such a point," he wrote, "I resolved to compose a book in which I demonstrate the just character of my cause and in which, basing my argument on the Law itself, I show explicitly the vanity of the traditions and observances of the Pharisees, as well as the discrepancy between their traditions and institutions and the Mosaic Law."[24] Da Costa's *Examination of the Pharisaic Traditions*, published in 1624 by the same Dutch publisher who published Da Silva's attack, the *Treatise on Immortality*, is an elaboration of his earlier refutation of the immortality of the soul and assault on the oral tradition. For his heretical opinions – as much an affront to Christians as to Jews – he was arrested by the city of Amsterdam; he spent ten days in jail and was fined fifteen hundred guilders. The book was burned, and all that has come down to us is a single copy.[25]

His mother stood by him, however, and this caused a delicate problem for Amsterdam's Jewish leaders. Sarah (née Branca) da Costa was the mother not only of the heretic Uriel, but also of two well-respected and influential members of the community. Uriel's brothers abided by the terms of the *cherem*. They condemned their brother and broke off all ties with him. But their elderly mother continued to live in the same house with Uriel, hold his hand, eat meat that he himself had butchered, and even (we are told) follow his doctrines. By the regulations of the community, she, like anyone who defied the governors and died without making amends, should have been denied a burial place in the Jewish cemetery. What ought they to do if she died in such a state of rebellion? The Amsterdam rabbis wrote to Jacob Halevi in Venice for his opinion on this matter. Halevi mercifully responded that, "from the point of view of Jewish law, one cannot refuse a place in an Israelite cemetery to an honest woman."[26]

Meanwhile, Da Costa's ideas were becoming ever more extreme: "I came to the conclusion that the Law did not come from Moses, but is only a human invention, just like many other such inventions in the world. It contradicts the law of nature in many respects, and God, the author of the law of nature, could not contradict himself, which he must have done if he ordered man to fulfill commandments which are contrary to a nature of which we know the author."[27] At this point, however, Da Costa decided that there was no sense in trying to maintain a solitary life, particularly from a financial perspective. He resolved to swallow his pride and try to reconcile with the Jewish community, "to reunite myself with them and fall into step, acting according to their wishes, apeing the apes, as they say."[28] (He may also have been motivated by a desire to marry, as the second *cherem* that he would shortly receive forced him to break off an engagement into which he had recently entered.) He publicly retracted his opinions and tried to live by orthodox standards. This effort to conform must have been quite a burden for him, and the act did not last for long. His nephew reported to the authorities that Uriel was violating the dietary laws, giving rise to the suspicion "that I was not a Jew." More seriously, he was caught trying to dissuade two Christians, one from Spain and one from Italy, from converting to Judaism and joining the community – "they did not know the yoke they were about to put around their necks" – and was hauled before the rabbis and the lay leaders. In 1633, a new *cherem*, reportedly more severe than any previous one, was pronounced against him.[29] He was offered an opportunity to atone by submitting to flagellation, but he refused to go through with it. Seven years later, however, poor and alone, he changed his mind.

I entered the synagogue; it was filled with men and women gathered for the show. The moment came to climb the wooden platform that, situated in the middle of the synagogue, served for public reading and other functions [the *bima*]. I read out in a clear voice the text of my confession, composed by them: that my deeds made me worthy to die a thousand times, I had violated the Sabbath, I had not kept the faith, and I had even gone so far as to dissuade others from becoming Jewish. For their satisfaction, I consented to obey the order they imposed on me and to fulfill the obligations they presented to me. In the end, I promised not to fall back into such turpitude and crime. I finished my reading, descended from the platform, and the chief rabbi approached me and told me, in a low voice, to retire to a certain corner of the synagogue. I went, and the keeper told me to undress. Naked down to my waist, my head veiled, barefooted, I had my arms around a column. My guard approached and tied my hands around the column. Once these preparations were finished, the cantor approached, took the whip and inflicted thirty-nine lashes upon my side, as required by tradition. . . . A psalm was sung during the flagellation. When it was finished, I sat down on the ground, and a cantor or a *chacham* approached and released me from all excommunication. . . . I then put on my clothes and went to the threshold of the synagogue. There I laid myself out while my keeper supported my head. And all who came down to exit the synagogue passed over me, stepping with one foot over the lower parts of my body. Everyone, young and old, took part in this ceremony. Not even monkeys could exhibit to the eyes of the world such shocking actions or more ridiculous behavior. When the ceremony was over, with no one left, I got up. Those who were beside me washed the dirt off of me . . . and I went home.[30]

It was more than Uriel could take. A few days later, after writing his autobiography, the *Exemplar humanae vitae* (A model of human life), which he concludes by accusing the Amsterdam magistrates of not protecting him from the injustices perpetrated against him by "the Pharisees," he killed himself.

Scholars have questioned the authenticity of Da Costa's memoir, especially this account of his final punishment, perhaps the first major act of the congregation that had united so triumphantly the year before.[31] It has been suggested that some of it sounds like the work of someone with an anti-Semitic agenda, a Christian who may have doctored Uriel's original text – or even written much of it himself – to make the Jewish community look bad.[32] And there is no question that Da Costa's work was used to portray the Amsterdam congregation in a poor light.[33] But it is not as if there were no precedent in the community for this kind of punitive action. In 1639, just before Da Costa's final attempt at a reconciliation with the congregation, Abraham Mendez sought the removal of the excommunication that had been pronounced on him for violating one of the congregation's regulations regarding marriage. When he asked for forgiveness, he was told that he would have to "go up to the pulpit and read the declaration the members of the *ma'amad* give to him. Then he will publicly be lashed in front of the congregation. And he will place himself at the foot of the stairs so that the members of the congregation can pass over him."[34]

Spinoza, only eight years old at the time of Da Costa's suicide, was as yet nowhere near the kinds of doubts and heretical thoughts that plagued Uriel. Nonetheless, Da Costa's views on the immortality of the soul, the status of the Torah – whether it had been written by Moses communicating the word of God or was simply an "invention" by a number of people at some later time – and the superstitious nature of organized religion were widely discussed and long remembered within the community, and without question had an impact on Spinoza's intellectual development. On the other hand, any suggestion that Spinoza formed his opinions while sitting on Da Costa's knees, as is depicted in one overwrought painting from the nineteenth century, is pure fantasy.

≥≈

In 1640, the Spinoza family had more immediate things to think about than the suicide of a heretic. Hanna had been dead over two years, and Michael was probably concerned about finding a new wife to keep house and care for his children; the eldest, Miriam, was still only eleven or twelve, and the youngest may have been only three. On April 28 of the following year, the fifty-two-year-old Michael married Esther (Hester) Fernand, alias Giomar de Soliz. Esther was around forty years old at the time. She had arrived in Amsterdam from Lisbon just that year and was living in the city with her younger sister, Margrieta; both of their parents were dead. Perhaps Michael, with the help of Margrieta, whom he may have known through the congregation, was responsible for bringing her sister to Amsterdam for the purpose of marrying her. On the same day that Michael and Esther registered their intention to wed with the Amsterdam authorities, Margrieta declared her own forthcoming nuptials with Emanuel de Tovar from Faro, "with parents living in Brazil, himself living on Uylenburg."[35]

We thus know slightly more about Esther than we do about Michael's first two wives, but the information is still very sparse. She may have been related to Abraham Farar, a prominent member of an important family in the community. She probably never learned Dutch, because her last will and testament – a legal document that had to be drafted before a Dutch notary (in this case, Jan Volkaertsz. Oli, a notary frequently used by Michael, probably because of his Portuguese-speaking assistant) and hence would ordinarily be in Dutch – is in Portuguese.[36] We do not, however, have a clue about the nature of Spinoza's relationship with his stepmother, or what he thought of her. This is unfortunate, as she basically raised him from the age of eight on and thus surely had a strong influence on the boy. If Rebecca was indeed Hanna's child, then Esther never had any children of her own.

≥≈

After the Da Costa affair, the spirits of the Talmud Torah congregation were probably in need of a lift. They must have been somewhat revived in 1642 by the Stadholder Frederik Hendrik's decision to pay a visit to the Houtgracht and grace the Portuguese community's synagogue with his presence.

The office of Stadholder was a remnant from the days when the Low Countries were a part of the lands of the Duke of Burgundy, who always appointed a governor to keep an eye on his northern subjects. When the Hapsburgs inherited the territory, the Spanish Crown made it a practice to nominate a member of the higher nobility to act as the sovereign's representative. The Dutch kept the office and used it, ironically, to their own advantage against the Spanish. The most popular and important (and legendary) Stadholder ever was William I, who in the 1570s and 1580s led the United Provinces in their revolt against Spain. After the beginning of the war and throughout the seventeenth century, the Stadholder was a provincial appointment made by the local states, although someone from the House of Orange generally held the stadholdership in a number of provinces at the same time, with two members of the family dividing the seven stadholderships. There was always a dominant Stadholder, however (with the exception of the stadholderless period from 1650 to 1672), namely, the one who occupied the post for the provinces of Holland, Zeeland, Utrecht, Overijssel, and Gelderland. This served, in effect, as a national office, not unlike a monarchy, particularly as a symbol – indeed, *the* symbol – of Dutch unity. The Stadholder was ex officio president of the Court of Holland, and was responsible for maintaining public order and justice in the province. He was also charged with defending the "true religion," the Reformed Church. Perhaps most important, from a practical perspective, he was the commander-in-chief of the army and navy of the Dutch Republic. From 1625 to 1647, the Stadholder of Holland and certain other provinces was Frederik Hendrik, son of William I.

Frederik's decision to visit the Talmud Torah synagogue was a remarkable one. The Jews were still officially considered "resident aliens" in the republic; it was not until 1657 that they were declared to be "truly subjects and residents of the United Netherlands."[37] They were also considered *unwelcome* resident aliens in many quarters of the Reformed Church. By visiting the Jews' house of worship, the Stadholder was essentially demonstrating his refusal to be governed by the intolerance of certain Calvinists. He was giving his seal of approval to a community that he must have recognized as an important factor in Dutch economic growth and of-fering them, at least tacitly, his protection.

The occasion for the Stadholder's visit to the synagogue – the first ever by a member of the House of Orange – was the arrival in the Netherlands of Queen Henrietta Maria, wife of Charles I of England. The English queen was bringing her daughter, the ten-year-old Mary, to wed Frederik Hendrik's son, William. Henrietta Maria wanted to see the Jews at prayer, something she could not do in her own country, which had expelled its res-ident Jews in 1290 and would not officially readmit them for many more years. But there was a more materially pressing motive for the visit. The queen had brought her crown jewels along with her from England and was hoping to get the Jewish merchants to lend her money on them, money her beleaguered husband desperately needed. The Amsterdam Jews re-portedly said that they would make the loan only if the Stadholder stood surety. Thus, partly in the cause of international politics and familial rela-tions (and the two were rarely unconnected in the seventeenth century), Frederik Hendrick accompanied her on the visit to the synagogue, along with Prince William II and his bride-to-be, Princess Mary. On May 22, the royal visitors were warmly greeted by the Portuguese community and wel-comed into the Talmud Torah's *beit hamidrash*. A delegation from the Jew-ish community thanked the Stadholder for the protection he had given them over the years, and Jonas Abrabanel read a poem he had composed for the occasion. But it was Rabbi Menasseh ben Israel who was given the honor of presenting the official welcoming address:

We no longer look upon Castille and Portugal, but upon Holland as our Father-land. We no longer wait upon the Spanish or Portuguese King, but upon Their Excellencies the States General and upon Your Highness as our Masters, by whose blessed arms we are protected, and by whose swords we are defended. Hence, no one need wonder that we say daily prayers for Their Excellencies the States Gen-eral and for Your Highness, and also for the noble governors of this world-renowned city.[38]

Frederik Hendrik was no doubt gratified by the sentiments expressed by his Portuguese merchants, and probably even happier that they were will-ing to help out financially. And when Menasseh traveled to England thir-teen years later, he hoped to use the general economic argument to good effect in convincing Charles I's replacement, Oliver Cromwell, to allow Jews once again to settle in that country.

Dutch visitors to the Jewish synagogue in fact became fairly common
around this time, even during hours of worship. On October 29, 1648, a
number of burgemeesters and magistrates of the city together made a visit
to the Houtgracht building. Among them were Andries Bicker, a rich and
powerful merchant and a member of one of the foremost regent families
in Amsterdam, and Captain Frans Banning Cocq. It was Cocq's company
of civic guardsmen (from Precinct 2 on the Nieuwe Zijde) whom Rembrandt had immortalized six years earlier in the painting commonly known
as *The Nightwatch*.

Rembrandt himself was a less transient presence in the Breestraat
neighborhood during the 1640s. He was now living in an expensive
home – perhaps too expensive in light of his later financial troubles – on
the boulevard. Since shortly after his arrival in Amsterdam, he had been
drawing, etching, and painting his Jewish neighbors, both for his own
artistic purposes and for the Jews themselves. There is, for example, a
1636 etched portrait that appears to be of Menasseh ben Israel, who lived
across the street from him. He also produced a likeness of Dr. Ephraim
Bueno, a friend of Menasseh's and a learned scholar in his own right.
(These two seem to have been popular sitters for Dutch artists: Bueno's
portrait was also made by Rembrandt's onetime partner, Jan Lievens;
Menasseh's was painted in 1636 by Rembrandt's former pupil Govert
Flinck). There is, in addition, an etching from 1648 showing a number of
elderly Polish Jews ostensibly gathered outside their synagogue, as well as
some rough drawings of Jews in the street. Unlike Romeyn de Hooghe,
however, who depicted the Jews and their environs in the 1670s, Rembrandt's intention in drawing the Sephardim and Ashkenazim was not
simply to record them (and their architecture) in their daily lives but to
compile preliminary works for his biblical and history paintings. The faces
and bodies that we see in his sketches of Jewish men, young and old, reap-
pear in his paintings of Old Testament scenes and figures, paintings that
the Sephardim themselves were keen on buying.

The Portuguese Jews, like the Dutch, were enthusiastic collectors of art.
The Pinto home, for example, contained "precious paintings to the total
value of one ton of gold."[39] Alphonso Lopez, who acted as the Amsterdam
agent for Louis XIII of France and his prime minister, Cardinal Richilieu,
bought – and may even have commissioned – Rembrandt's *The Prophet
Balaam* in 1626. Then there is the less successful transaction involving
Diego d'Andrade. D'Andrade had commissioned Rembrandt to make an

image of a certain young girl and paid a deposit for it. When d'Andrade saw the painting, however, he insisted that the portrait "bore not even the least resemblance to the person or face of the girl." He asked Rembrandt either to change it or to make another one. Rembrandt refused to do either, and d'Andrade refused to accept the painting. When d'Andrade asked for his money back, Rembrandt said that he would change the painting, but only if d'Andrade paid the whole amount up front. He would then leave it up to the judgment of the governors of the Guild of St. Luke – the painters' guild – whether or not it was a good likeness.[40]

There has been a great deal of debate over just how much contact, beyond the merely observational, Rembrandt had with the Jews living in the houses around him – literally, as Daniel Pinto, a tobacco merchant, lived to one side of his house and the family of Salvator Rodrigues the other side. There were business deals over works of art and his use of anonymous Jewish models, as well as the occasions on which individuals sat for their portraits. There is, moreover, no denying that Rembrandt had a fairly close working relationship with Rabbi Menasseh. In 1635, he must have consulted with Menasseh on a point of biblical exegesis (and perhaps for help with his Hebrew script) for the painting *Belshazzar's Feast*, in which the king of Babylon receives a divine warning (in Aramaic) in a form conformable to Menasseh's own theory of the event.[41] Rembrandt also collaborated on Menasseh's *Piedra gloriosa de la estatua de Nebuchadnesar*, by providing four engravings to illustrate Menasseh's text, which he published in 1655. There were also the kinds of disputes into which neighbors unfortunately but naturally fall. In May 1654, Rembrandt and Pinto argued over some work done on their houses for which Rembrandt never paid his share, and over the amount of noise that Rembrandt was causing in the basement.[42]

It would seem reasonable, then, to speak of Rembrandt's "rapport with the Jews of Amsterdam"[43] and to portray him as engaged in close mutual relations with them.[44] One Rembrandt scholar, however, calling this a "sentimental conjecture," insists that "Rembrandt did not penetrate deeply into the Jewish community" and that his contacts were limited to the few individuals "who ventured furthest into the Christian world."[45] There is admittedly not much documentary evidence one way or the other, besides the portraits of Menasseh and Bueno and the joint projects with Menasseh. But with Rembrandt's undeniable curiosity for things Jewish, on the one hand, and, on the other, the cosmopolitan nature of the Sephardic community, it is hard to accept the more restrictive view. Why would Rembrandt have to limit his contacts to those Jews who "ventured furthest into the Christian world" when he himself lived in the midst of Amsterdam's Jewish world? Rembrandt must have had more than casual contact with the many intellectual and artistically minded Portuguese Jews living in his neighborhood.

The most fascinating question, however, is whether Spinoza himself was acquainted with Rembrandt. It is tantalizing to assume that these two great figures of seventeenth-century Dutch culture knew each other. There could have been many opportunities to meet beyond the chance encounter in the street, although there is no reason why Rembrandt would have been at all interested in making Spinoza's acquaintance at this point. Some scholars have conjectured that Menasseh served as an intermediary.[46] Perhaps Rembrandt visited the synagogue or the school in the company of Menasseh (or possibly even Mortera, whose portrait he may have painted) and was introduced by the rabbi to the young Spinoza, one of the school's outstanding pupils. Or they could have met at Menasseh's home. Unfortunately, these speculations are entirely groundless. Although it is common to call Menasseh ben Israel "Spinoza's teacher," it seems likely that Spinoza was never formally Menasseh's pupil at the Talmud Torah school. Menasseh took over the fifth grade in 1642, when Rabbi Aboab went to Brazil and Spinoza would have been in only the second grade, at the most, at that point. Menasseh was still teaching the fifth grade by the time Spinoza was of the age to enter the upper classes, but he would soon be replaced by Judah Jacob Leao.[47] There is simply not enough evidence that Spinoza and Menasseh ever had a close relationship, and thus no good reason for believing that Menasseh would have thought, especially in the 1640s, of bringing Rembrandt and Spinoza together.

It is also conceivable that Spinoza met Rembrandt sometime in the 1650s, although this too is pure speculation. One of the students in Rembrandt's workshop, Leendert van Beyeren, reportedly lodged in the home of Franciscus van den Enden, Spinoza's Latin tutor, until Van Beyeren's death in 1649. Van Beyeren made copies of Rembrandt's paintings and served as a bidder for Rembrandt at art sales. Van den Enden had an abiding interest in art – he was an art dealer when he first moved to Amsterdam – and may have cultivated an acquaintance with his lodger's famous master. If he continued that relationship after Van Beyeren's death, he could have introduced the artist to his new star pupil when Spinoza arrived sometime in the mid-1650s.[48] But that goes well beyond any evidence at hand. In the end, there is no arguing with the judgment of a Rembrandt scholar who wrote that "the fond wish of many to link Rembrandt to Spinoza has no historical basis."[49]

&.

Between Michael's marriage to Esther in 1641 and the death of his son Isaac in 1649, we have no significant information about Spinoza and his family, aside from the fact that in 1642–3 Michael served a second term (although it was his first for the united congregation) as a *parnas* on the community's educational board (now called Talmud Torah e Tezoureiro de Es Haim). There is the occasional business deal, such as the trading agreement Michael made in 1644 with Abraham Farar and Antonio Fernandes Carvejal, "merchant in London" (who was there despite England's official ban on Jewish residents, and who would go on to become one of the founders of the first synagogue in London).[50] But nothing is known about Bento's activities during these years, aside from whatever ordinary assumptions one can legitimately make about the life of a young man in an orthodox Jewish community in Amsterdam. After years of intensive study and training, Bento would have celebrated his bar mitzvah in 1645, when he turned thirteen. But we do not know what Michael had in mind for his son's educational future. Did he intend him to join the family firm after he finished his elementary schooling, or did he want his son to continue his studies through the higher grades and, perhaps, become a rabbi? Unforeseen events soon rendered that issue moot.

5

A Merchant
of Amsterdam

WHEN MICHAEL'S ELDEST SON, ISAAC, died in September of 1649, Spinoza was about to turn seventeen. This means that, if all was going well, he would have been entering the first level of the upper classes at Talmud Torah, the fifth grade. At this time it was being taught by Rabbi Menasseh, although he would soon be relieved of these duties by Judah Jacob Leao (also known by the nickname 'Templo', because of his almost fanatical devotion to building a scale model of Solomon's Temple). Until early in the twentieth century, it was assumed that Spinoza went on to complete his schooling through the upper grades and, thus, trained to be a rabbi. This may be just what his father had in mind for his second son. In light of his service to the community's educational boards, we know that Michael cared a good deal about education; and Bento must have been a naturally gifted student. What greater source of honor and pride for a former marrano than to have his son become a *chacham?* What greater achievement for a young Jewish man of Spinoza's intelligence?

If Spinoza did indeed have rabbinical aspirations, it would add much drama to the story of his eventual fall from grace. On the basis of documents that he discovered in the Amsterdam Jewish archives in the 1930s, however, Vaz Dias has shown that Spinoza was not, in fact, attending the highest class, or *medras* – that taught by Rabbi Mortera and including advanced lessons in Gemara and readings in rabbinic and philosophical literature – when he should have been, in the early 1650s. There was a register kept by the Ets Chaim brotherhood to record the grants that the society made to students attending the higher *medrassim* (as well as the fines for nonattendance). In the register for 1651, when the eighteen-year-old Spinoza would have been in Mortera's class, probably for the first time, his name does not appear.[1] Nor is he listed in the registers for the preceding or subsequent years. This does not mean that Spinoza never studied Talmud or Jewish philosophy with Saul Levi Mortera, but it does mean that

his official education in the curriculum ordained by the Ets Chaim seminary was cut short. Spinoza did not train to be a rabbi.

An obvious explanation for Spinoza's absence from the school's records
for the uppermost level is that, after Isaac's death, Michael needed Bento
in the family business. Thus, Spinoza, who by 1654 is referred to in notarial documents as a "Portuguese merchant in Amsterdam," probably
abandoned his formal studies and joined his father's importing and ex-
porting firm in late 1649 or soon thereafter. He may have stopped attending classes even earlier than that, just after finishing the elementary grades
(around 1646 or so), and gone right to work when he was about fourteen.
As his name appears nowhere in the registers for the *talmudim* at Ets
Chaim for the years 1647–50 (5407–5411), there is no evidence that he attended even the fifth grade.[2] Perhaps Michael pulled young Bento out of
school before he could start the advanced course of study. If so, then his
father never intended for him to enter the rabbinate in the first place. Like
himself, his son would become a merchant (although being a rabbi did not
preclude one from also engaging in mercantile activities – Mortera, Menasseh, and Samuel de Casseres, all rabbis in the community, traded in a
substantial way).

Michael was elected to the *ma'amad* of the Talmud Torah congregation
in 1649, an indication that he was still held in high esteem by his colleagues.
Things must have been going fairly well. Despite some debts – particularly his ongoing responsibilities for the troublesome Henriques estate –
he had good money in the bank.[3] Moreover, the business that he ran, now
with Bento at his side, would have been picking up over the last several
years, particularly because of important political developments affecting
Dutch (and especially Dutch-Jewish) trade.

In December of 1640, Portugal seceded from its political union with
Spain and went its own diplomatic and economic way. This opened the
door for the Sephardim of Amsterdam to begin reestablishing their mercantile links with Portugal and its colonies. These were the routes, curtailed
since the truce with Spain expired in 1621, that had been so crucial to the
community's initial economic development. If Dutch shipping could move
freely once again in this arena, it would allow the Jews to regain their mo-
mentum. Such an opportunity would be especially good news for Michael,
who dealt in nuts and fruits from the Algarve, in southern Portugal. The
Sephardim took an active role in the alliance negotiations between Portugal and the Netherlands (against Spain), working hard to ensure free trade

between Holland, Portugal, and Brazil. They also lobbied for protection for the Jewish residents in that part of Brazil occupied by the Dutch. By 1644, there were over fourteen hundred Jews in Brazil, centered mainly in Recife. These Dutch-Jewish emigrés facilitated direct mercantile traffic between Brazil and the Netherlands, which was particularly important when the war made it impossible to go through Portugal or Spain.[4] Ultimately, however, the peace between the Dutch Republic and Portugal did not last very long. In 1645, Portuguese Catholic planters in Dutch Brazil revolted. Portugal came to their aid and within months had reconquered almost all of the territory occupied by the Dutch. This paralyzed the sugar trade,[5] which the Jews dominated, and sent the Dutch residents (including Recife's Jews) scattering: to the islands of the Caribbean, to New Amsterdam, and back to Holland itself.

Peace with Spain, on the other hand, was finally secured in 1648 with the signing of the Treaty of Münster. After eighty years of hostility, interrupted only by the Twelve Years' Truce, the Republic of the Netherlands, the southern Low Countries, and the Hapsburgs were able to agree on terms for ending the war. This had been Frederik Hendrik's project when he died in March 1647, although he was opposed by his son, William II, and his Calvinist advisers, who wanted to go on the offensive and "liberate" the provinces of the south. Even though William II immediately took over as the dominant Stadholder, the States of Holland – led by their Grand Pensionary, Adriaan Pauw, and Andries Bicker, a burgemeester of Amsterdam – were firmly in control of the States General and, thus, of the political direction of the republic. In the spring of 1648, they secured the ratification of the seventy-nine articles of the Treaty of Münster and, in the process, established their temporary dominance over the House of Orange. The new Stadholder opposed the peace, but there was simply nothing he could do about it.

With the signing of various agreements between the States General and the Spanish Crown, the Jews were more than able to make up for the loss of Portuguese trade after 1645 through renewed trade with Spain and Spanish colonies (especially in the Caribbean). Historians generally agree that the end of the war in 1648 inaugurated "the Golden Age of Dutch Sephardi Jewry."[6] From now on, Spanish ports would be open to Dutch shipping; and (according to Philip IV's decree) Jews who were Dutch subjects would be permitted to trade with Spain, but only through Catholic or Protestant agents. The Jews soon controlled a substantial amount –

upward of 20 percent – of the traffic with Spain, carrying timber and grain from northern Europe in exchange for wine, raisins, olive oil, syrup, almonds, and citrus fruits.[7] This would have been a big boost for Michael's business after the sluggish period during the war. In the years Spinoza began to take a larger role in the firm, it should have been expanding in volume and increasing its profits due to the ease with which the cargo in which they dealt was now able to move.

꿙

Peace with Spain did not mean that all was well inside the republic. On the contrary, the debates over peace leading up to the treaty only exacerbated political and religious tensions among the various Dutch factions. For years, Amsterdam and other towns had been arguing strongly for reductions in military spending and for concluding some kind of treaty with the enemy, if only for the sake of economic well-being. When the peace was concluded, the divisions between the generally liberal regents who controlled the States of Holland (and who were pro-peace) and the orthodox Calvinists (with the Stadholder on their side) were so strong that the fundamental political principles of the republic were put into question.

Although he was on the losing side over the issue of peace with Spain, William II was not one to give in, and he quickly took advantage of the discord between Holland and the other provinces to drive a wedge between them. There were many issues at stake during the political crisis of 1649–50. How tolerant should the republic be to its resident Catholics and Arminians? Now that the war was over, was it really necessary to maintain such a large army? William, along with several provinces, favored keeping the army at its present level (around thirty-five thousand men). He also backed a measure – opposed by Holland – that would exclude Catholics from all posts in lands controlled at-large by the States General (the so-called Generality Lands), thereby hoping to shore up his support among orthodox Calvinists. These, in turn, saw in the friendly Stadholder an opportunity to resume their campaign against the Remonstrants. A general economic slump, the failure of the Dutch West Indies Company (which many blamed on Holland's refusal to come to its rescue), bad weather, high bread prices, and poor harvests only contributed to the general malaise. But the real question that lay behind all of these particular issues concerned the political nature of the republic. The so-called States party-faction – centered on six towns in Holland: Amsterdam, Dordrecht, Delft, Haarlem, Hoorn,

and Medemblik – argued that the Dutch Republic was a league of sovereign provinces. Their opponents, the Stadholder's faction (or "Orangists")
insisted that it was a united federation with power vested in a central authority, and that the provinces had given up a degree of their sovereignty
to the States General when they joined the union. The States party questioned the need for a quasi-monarchical figure like the Stadholder in a republic; the Orangists pointed to the important political and military role
played by an "eminent head," a unifying figure who could defend the public church and serve as captain-general of the republic's relatively large
standing army.[8]

William hoped eventually to gain control of the States of Holland and
make it more pliable to his wishes. To do this, he would have to weaken the
opposition. He accordingly plotted to arrest those regents leading the States
party-faction (especially Pauw and the Bicker brothers). He also wanted
to replace the "Arminian" pro-regent preachers in Amsterdam with more
loyal, and less tolerant, Orangist preachers. In May 1650, the crisis came
to a head when Holland gave the Stadholder the excuse for which he was
looking. When the province moved unilaterally to disband a number of
army units, William, with the backing of the States General, staged a coup.
The States General (with Holland and Gelderland dissenting) authorized
him to enter any town in Holland that had voted for disbandment. In July,
after entering Amsterdam and being treated rudely by its burgemeesters,
William arrested the leading regents of the opposition while States General troops marched on the city. The Bicker brothers and their allies were
purged from the *vroedschap*, and Amsterdam, now surrounded by 12,000
soldiers, yielded to the Stadholder's demands on military numbers.

The victory for the Orangist camp was brief. On November 6, 1650, to
the great dismay of his supporters, William II died of smallpox. The political changes brought about by the Stadholder in Amsterdam and in the
States of Holland never had a chance to take root. Amsterdam immediately reverted to its previous political balance, with the liberal "Arminians"
firmly in control of the city. After the crisis of 1650, real power in the republic once again devolved to the local regents of the cities and towns. The
province of Holland, for its part, went back to running its own affairs, now
under the pensionaryship of Jacob Cats, and continued to assert its sovereignty in the face of any federalist claims. The States of Holland again dominated the States General and took over many of the political and military
functions of the Stadholder. Despite the fact that William's son, William

III, was born just after the Stadholder's death in 1650, there would be no Stadholder outside the provinces of Friesland and Groningen until 1672.

Many questions still remained after these tumultuous events, some of them of direct interest to the Jews. Among the problems discussed at the Great Assembly that convened in The Hague in early 1651 to address the political situation in the republic was the issue of religious toleration. The orthodox Calvinists still hoped for a theologically regimented state, if not a confessionally homogeneous one. They were concerned about the rise of Catholicism and the increase in the number of non-Reformed or dissenting-Reformed Protestant congregations (especially Lutherans, Mennonites, and Remonstrants).[9] But they saved their particular ire for the Jews. These "blasphemers against Christ," it was argued, should not be allowed to practice their religion publicly anywhere in the republic.[10] While Holland did allow some concessions to the synods of the Reformed Church, and agreed that unorthodox Reformed or non-Reformed congregations "in future will not be permitted in any other places than where they are already practiced," the Jews were left in peace.

ॐ

The early 1650s were an emotionally and materially unsteady time in the Spinoza household. Michael no longer held a position on the *ma'amad*, although he was appointed administrator of *Bikur Cholim*, the community's loan society, in 1650. In June 1650, Spinoza's sister Miriam wed Samuel de Casseres, a rabbinical student in the Talmud Torah school. Michael, for some reason, could not be present when the couple registered their intention to marry with the city. Esther accompanied them, however, and it is noted that "Michael de Spinose, the father, gave his consent to the marriage."[11] De Casseres, "with no parents alive and living in the Batavierstraet," was twenty-two years old at the time. He was still studying in the highest *medras* with Rabbi Mortera, with another two years to go. Unlike Spinoza, he finished his studies and became a rabbi. Samuel was, in fact, one of Mortera's protégés, and would give the funeral oration for his teacher in 1660, shortly before his own death. He never became one of the rabbis of the Talmud Torah congregation, but he did serve as a *sofer*, or scribe, in the community. He was also a merchant, and he and Michael engaged in some business together in 1652.

Miriam and Samuel had a son, Daniel, sometime between March and September 1651. On September 6, 1651 – little over a year after her marriage –

Miriam died, perhaps from giving birth to Daniel. Samuel, conscious of the need for a mother for his young son, married Miriam's sister (or half-sister), Rebecca.[12] When Samuel himself died in 1660, Rebecca took on full responsibility for raising her nephew/stepson, along with the three children she and Samuel had had together (Hana, Michael, and Benjamin). Daniel married Judith de David Moreno in Amsterdam in 1678, but the marriage ended in divorce. Soon after that, Rebecca and her two sons moved to Curaçao.

Two years after Miriam's death, Michael became a widower for the third time. On October 24, 1653, Esther died. She may have been ill for quite a while, for a year earlier she thought to compose her last will and testament, a document that she was too sick at the time to confirm ("The testatrix, not being able to sign because of weakness, requested us [the notary] to confirm for her").[13] Spinoza's father himself was probably not well when his wife was buried, for five months later Michael d'Espinoza died.

This must have been a depressing period for Bento. He lost his father, his stepmother, and his sister all in the space of three years. By 1654, at the age of twenty-one, Spinoza was without parents, both of whom had probably been sick for a while anyway ("in his formative years," as Vaz Dias puts it, "he would not have had a great deal of fatherly guidance").[14] The family may also have been having financial difficulties, as the estate that Spinoza inherited was heavily in debt.[15] And, whether he wanted to or not, he was now running a business, one that had probably just been through some tough years and that was plagued by creditors.

In Michael's final years, whatever gains his firm may have seen as a result of renewed Spanish trade would have been offset by the adverse effects of British interference with Dutch shipping in the very areas and routes of his commerce. For no sooner had relations with Spain been normalized then the English Parliament passed the Navigation Act of 1651, which prohibited all Dutch ships from carrying southern European products to English ports and outlawed Dutch commerce with English colonies in the Caribbean. Such inflammatory measures, along with the usual English harassment of Dutch shipping on the high seas, could lead only to a military response by the Dutch. The first Anglo–Dutch War broke out in 1652. This was greeted with great excitement by the Orangist party, who saw in the confrontation an opportunity to help restore Charles II to the British throne and to place William III in his father's shoes as Stadholder, but with great dejection by anyone engaged in trade, as the regents and Sephardim of Amsterdam were.

By the time Bento took over from his father, the war with England was over (soon to be replaced by an Anglo-Spanish war, which was good for Dutch business), but the firm's debts remained. Spinoza did have a business partner, however: his younger brother Gabriel (Abraham). The firm of Bento y Gabriel de Spinoza was, most likely, simply a continuation of Michael's trading business, in which Bento at least (and probably Gabriel as well) had had several years' experience.

The extant documents concerning the activities of the firm in these early years, while Spinoza was still involved, usually name Bento as the primary agent, acting "for himself as well as for Gabriel de Espinosa, his brother and partner."[16] After Spinoza's expulsion from the Jewish community in 1656, however, all members of the congregation – indeed, anyone belonging to the "people of Israel" – were forbidden to communicate with him, either orally or in writing. Naturally, this would have made running a business from within that community, and benefiting from all the networks to which it was connected, impossible. If Gabriel wanted to keep the company going, and do so without being excommunicated himself, he would have to run it without his anathematized brother. This is just what he did – still identifying himself as a representative of the firm Bento y Gabriel Espinoza[17] – until 1664 or 1665, when he left Amsterdam for the British West Indies. There was a sizable population of Sephardic Jews in Barbados and Jamaica by the middle of the seventeenth century. They traded with the Amsterdam Jews and acted as agents in the Caribbean for Dutch-Jewish firms, much to the consternation of the English Crown, which was again at war with the Dutch in the 1660s. After just a few years in the islands, Gabriel must have had a good sense as to which way the political winds were blowing. In 1671, after moving from Barbados to Jamaica, he successfully applied to become a naturalized English subject. He never returned to Holland.[18]

Some notary records from April and May 1655, related to Spinoza's activities on behalf of the firm, provide an interesting glimpse into his character and acumen as a businessman. There were in Amsterdam three Portuguese Jewish brothers, Anthony, Gabriel, and Isaac Alvares, who had emigrated from Paris and were now living on Uylenburg in a house called De Vergulde Valck ("The Gilded Falcon"). They were jewel dealers, and apparently rather shady characters. Spinoza possessed a bill of exchange – basically, a debt or I.O.U. – for the amount of five hundred guilders to be paid by Anthony Alvares. This bill went back to November 1654 and was originally owed to Manuel Duarte, a member of a prominent Jewish family. Duarte signed the bill over to Spinoza, and it was now his to collect. (Duarte was also a jewel dealer, and perhaps this transaction between Spinoza and Duarte indicates that Spinoza had expanded the family business to include trading in jewels.[19] The "rich" trades were doing particularly well at this time, and it would have been a wise move.) Alvares procrastinated about paying the bill for some time, always "saying he would pay within two or three days or a week." When Spinoza finally pressed the issue, Anthony offered to satisfy some of the account by giving Spinoza a bill of exchange for two hundred guilders on his brother Gabriel Alvares, with a promise that he would pay the remaining balance soon. Spinoza, for some reason, accepted this offer. Not surprisingly, Gabriel Alvares refused to cooperate and would not pay the bill that his brother had drawn on his name. So Spinoza went back to Anthony, returned the bill on Gabriel to him, and demanded full payment of the five hundred guilders. Alvares, despite "daily promises to pay," still delayed payment. Spinoza, who began to lose patience, insisted on either being paid the money or given jewelry as surety, but Alvares was not forthcoming on this offer until it was too late. Alvares did have one more trick up his sleeve, however. He claimed that the original bill on him was payable only in Antwerp, where it would be covered by one Pedro de Palma Carillo. Spinoza basically told Alvares that enough was enough, and that he had begun court proceedings against him.

Tired of the game – and this had been going on for several months now – Spinoza finally had Anthony Alvares arrested in May 1655. Alvares was taken to the inn De Vier Hollanders ("The Four Dutchmen") and held until he paid the full amount Spinoza was owed. The notary document itself best tells the tale of the subsequent events: "Anthonij Alveres then asked the requisitionist [Spinoza] to come to the inn to reach an agreement with him. . . . When [Spinoza] arrived there, the said Anthonij Alveres hit the requisitionist on the head with his fist without there having been spoken a word in return and without the requisitionist doing anything." Spinoza and Alvares did come to some kind of agreement, however, although it apparently included Spinoza paying the costs of the arrest. Spinoza went out to get some money to pay for it, and when he returned to the inn, Anthony's brother Gabriel was waiting for him: "Upon his [Spinoza's] return to the said inn, Gabriel Alveres, also a brother of the said Anthonij Alveres, was standing in front of the inn and hit the plaintiff on the head with his fist without any cause, so that his hat fell off; and the said Gabriel Alveres took the requisitionist's [Spinoza's] hat and threw it in the gutter and stepped on it." Notwithstanding this somewhat rough treatment, Spinoza was still willing to negotiate with Anthony, and on that same day, with the innkeeper and everyone else who saw the assault as witnesses, they came to an agreement. Anthony would provide surety – we are not told what, but it may have been jewels – for the five hundred guilders he owed Spinoza. Spinoza, for his part, was now no longer willing to pay for the expenses of the arrest, but – astoundingly – he did agree to loan Alvares the money to pay those charges. Isaac Alvares promised to pay this money back, along with "the damages and interests suffered by [Spinoza] as a result of the default of the payment and his not having the said money back." He also promised to reimburse Spinoza for the hat.

We do not know if Spinoza ever saw a cent of the money the Alvares brothers owed him.[20]

ॐ

Just because Spinoza was now a businessman did not mean that his studies had come to an end. He may not have attended the upper *medrassim* of the Talmud Torah school, but there were many avenues for advanced education in the Sephardic Jewish community. The most important and organized of these was the yeshiva. The *jesibot* were religious and literary study groups for adults. They were led by the community's *chachamim*, usually met once a week, and were sometimes financed by wealthy Jews in a philanthropic spirit, individuals who wanted to help fellow Sephardim fulfill the *mitzvah* of continuing to study Torah and other religious texts throughout their lives. In 1629, Rabbi Mortera set up his first yeshiva, Roshit Chochma, "Beginning of Wisdom." By 1643, he was leading the group Keter Torah ("Crown of the Law"). Ephraim Bueno, the same doctor who had his portrait painted by Rembrandt, and Abraham Israel Pereira, a rich merchant, established Tora Or ("The Law Is Light") in 1656 for Rabbi Aboab to run. This study group probably had a rather mystical bent, and Aboab may have led them in the reading of kabbalistic texts, along with the Spanish literature and poetry that Bueno favored.

Tora Or was not the Pereira family's first or last foray into running a yeshiva. Abraham and his brother, Isaac – both of whom were raised as crypto-Jews in Spain and were reunited in Holland after fleeing the Inquisition – had founded an academy in Amsterdam soon after their arrival in the city and their reconversion to Judaism in 1643. Menasseh ben Israel was the leader of that group, and he was provided with a staff and a generous endowment with which to work.[21] And in 1659 Abraham set up a foundation for establishing a yeshiva in Hebron, Palestine, for the training of rabbis. Abraham Pereira was, moreover, a learned and serious thinker in his own right. He published a number of moralistic works in Spanish (including *La Certeza del Camino* in 1666) and was one of the few individuals within the Portuguese Jewish community to attack Spinoza's views after they were published in 1670.

Given Spinoza's intellectual gifts and what must have been a great urge for learning, it is all but certain that he was attending one of the community's yeshivot in the early 1650s, at the same time that he was active as a merchant. Vaz Dias believes that, in fact, the yeshiva Spinoza attended was Rabbi Mortera's Keter Torah. Daniel Levi (alias Miguel) de Barrios was the Amsterdam Sephardic community's resident poet-historian, and in his *Triumpho del govierno popular y de la antiguedad Holandesa* he provides an account of Mortera's "academy."

The Crown of the Law [Corona de la ley, i.e., Keter Torah], ever since the year of its joyous foundation, never ceased burning in the academic bush, thanks to the doctrinal leaves written by the most wise [*Sappientisimo*] Saul Levi Mortera, lending his intellect to the counsel of Wisdom and his pen to the hand of Speculation, in the defense of religion and against atheism. *Thorns* [*Espinos*] are they that, in the *Fields* [*Prados*] of impiety, aim to shine with the fire that consumes them, and the zeal of Mortera is a flame that burns in the bush of Religion, never to be extinguished [emphases in the original Spanish version].[22]

The references (italicized by De Barrios himself) to Spinoza and Juan de Prado, another heretic in the community excommunicated not long after Spinoza, suggest, according to Vaz Dias, that they were both connected with the Keter Torah yeshiva and, thus, that Mortera directed their studies. What makes it even more reasonable to assume that Spinoza attended Keter Torah is that there were old connections between Mortera and the Spinoza family going back to the days in Beth Jacob; both Abraham and Michael had a fairly close relationship with their rabbi. If, as seems highly plausible, Spinoza was looking for somewhere to study, then why not choose the yeshiva run by an old family friend? It was also the yeshiva that his brother-in-law, Samuel de Casseres, was attending.[23] It is likely, then, that Spinoza *was* Mortera's "student" or "disciple," although not in the Talmud Torah school. That would explain why Mortera himself was imagined, by Lucas and others, to have felt so much personal disappointment and resentment when he learned of Spinoza's apostasy.

Saul Levi Mortera, unlike the community's other rabbis, Menasseh and Aboab, was not of marrano background. In fact, he was not even a Sephardic Jew: he had been born, in 1596, to an Ashkenazic family in Venice.[24] He studied with Leon Modena – the same Venetian rabbi who was consulted on the Da Costa case – and completed a solid and traditional rabbinical training at a very early age. Mortera left Venice in 1612 for Paris with Elias Rodrigues Montalto, a physician whom Modena had reconverted to Judaism and who was on his way to take up his duties as official court doctor for Marie de' Medici. In addition to serving as Montalto's secretary, Mortera tutored Montalto and his children in the Hebrew language and Jewish law, while Montalto, in turn, taught Mortera Portuguese. When Montalto died in 1616, Mortera brought his body to Amsterdam for burial. He decided to stay on in that city, marrying Ester Soares (recently arrived from Lisbon via Nantes) and taking over as *chacham* of Beth Jacob when that congregation split in 1618 and Rabbi Joseph Pardo and his followers left to form Beth Israel.

From the beginning of his service to the Amsterdam community, Mortera was recognized by his colleagues as a learned Talmudist and an outstanding scholar of Jewish thought. Already in 1621, when he was only twenty-five years old, he was giving two three-hour Talmud classes per day (except Friday and Saturday) in the school. On Friday afternoons, after lessons in Hebrew grammar, he spent two hours with his students translating the week's Torah portion, and on Saturday he was responsible for giving the sermon at services. Mortera's sermons, models of erudition, usually consisted of an introductory Hebrew text from the week's portion, translated into Portuguese so that most of his audience would understand it, followed by some passages from the Talmud or other rabbinical work. He would draw a connection between these writings, provide an interpretation, and finally bring out a practical or moral lesson, supported by other biblical or rabbinical citations.[25] Much of his time was also taken up with responding to questions from Jews elsewhere in the Netherlands on points of Jewish law, as he was basically *the* authority in the republic on matters of *halacha*. In the mid-1630s, Antonio Gomes Alcobaca (alias Abraham Jessurun) asked Mortera whether the ownership of paintings and the hanging of them in a Jewish home violated the commandment against making graven images. The rabbi replied that it did not, as long as the pictures

themselves were not objects of worship by non-Jews or did not portray beings or objects that were worshiped by non-Jews. By the 1640s, he enjoyed
a great international reputation, and, like his teacher in Venice, was consulted by foreign rabbis on moral and juridical issues.

Mortera was a strict but very popular teacher. He was devoted to his
students – more so than the resentful Menasseh ben Israel, who looked
upon teaching as a necessity that took up valuable time and was somewhat
beneath him – and they seemed to have had a genuine affection for him.[26]
He was not, however, above punishing a student with a temporary ban for
violating his rules regarding classroom decorum (for example, for introducing the Trinity into a discussion during one of his lessons, as one student apparently did). He also took a very hard line on doctrinal matters.
In response to a query from a Spanish priest in Rouen, he harshly warned
that "Jews who are not circumcised and who do not observe the law in lands
where they are not permitted to do so" risk eternal punishment. If they
continue to confess the Christian faith (even "against their wishes"), worship images, attend mass, and deny that they are Jews "when, in their hearts,
they really are," then they are "guilty before God." He was no liberal when
it came to the proper understanding of Jewish law. His approach to *halacha*, to morality, and to religion in general was rigorous, sober, and highly
intellectual (as opposed to the mystically spiritual Rabbi Aboab or the more
messianistic Menasseh). His commitment to religious orthodoxy, however, did not keep him from being interested in the leading philosophical
and scientific ideas of his time. Mortera was not the unenlightened and
uncultured obscurantist that his critics – presumably to explain his hostility to Spinoza – have made him out to be. Although the Venetian community in which he grew up was confined to a ghetto, its members could
not help absorbing much of the cosmopolitan culture that surrounded
them. Well-traveled (he spent four years in Paris) and widely read, Mortera
was learned in more than just the texts of Jewish tradition. In his writings
there are references to Patristic writers, ancient and medieval philosophers
(Jewish and non-Jewish), and Italian humanists, as well as to rabbinical
authorities. He was also in favor of theological dialogue and intellectual
exchange with Christians. His *Treatise on the Truth of the Law of Moses*
(1659–60), for example, is an oddly ecumenical work directed toward certain anti-Trinitarians among the Baptists. These "Socinians," he believed,
were actually fairly close to the true Noachite religion (based upon the
seven laws revealed to Noah). Were they to purify their doctrines and bring
them into conformity with the religion of the Hebrew Bible, they could –

though there was no question of their converting to Judaism – at least worship "the God of Israel" and serve as a bridge between the Jews and Protestants. To this end, Mortera undertook to demonstrate in his treatise that the Law of Moses is of divine origin and thoroughly self-sufficient, and does not need to be completed by the "New Testament."

Mortera's Keter Torah group was devoted primarily to studying "The Law" (presumably written *and* oral), although he, as the rabbi with the most solid knowledge of Jewish religious literature in the community, would certainly have supplemented these lessons in Torah and Talmud with discussions of other rabbinical texts. He may also have provided his more enterprising and capable students – among whom, no doubt, he counted Spinoza – with readings in medieval Jewish Bible commentary (particularly Rashi and Ibn Ezra) and classical Jewish philosophy. Given his preference for a rationalistic approach to religion – where the key to understanding the law is reason, not some mystical or nonrational intuition – Mortera would have introduced his students to the works of Maimonides, Saadya Gaon, and Gersonides, among others.

In this yeshiva, then, Spinoza could have received at least some of the religious and philosophical instruction from Mortera that he would have received had he stayed in school through the highest class. Spinoza was extremely well versed in Scripture and in the major commentaries on it (his own copy of the Bible, in Hebrew, included Rashi's commentary).[27] He also closely studied the great Jewish philosophers, and we can almost certainly date the beginning of his familiarity with them to this period of his life. Lucas's claim, however, that "after the examination of the Bible, [Spinoza] read and re-read the Talmud with the same closeness," is highly doubtful.[28] Attending a study group once a week will not make one a serious Talmudist; and it is not likely that, with his business activities, he had much time to devote to independent study of Mishnah and Gemara, much less to learning Aramaic.[29] Spinoza cites the Talmud only rarely in his writings – just six times, in the *Theological-Political Treatise* – and even then his citations are careless and secondhand.[30] His familiarity with Talmud was, in spite of Mortera's weekly meetings (if indeed Spinoza attended Keter Torah), superficial at best.

᠅

It is usually claimed that, in addition to being Mortera's disciple, Spinoza was greatly influenced by Menasseh ben Israel, perhaps the most worldly –

and, especially among Christians, widely known – rabbi of the seventeenth century and third in rank among the Amsterdam *chachamim*.

Born Manoel Diaz Soeiro in Madeira (a Portuguese colony off the coast of Africa, not far from the Canary Islands) in 1604, Menasseh moved with his family first to La Rochelle, in southwestern France, and then, sometime around 1610, to Amsterdam. They were fleeing not any abstract and general threat by the Inquisition against New Christians, but very concrete persecution against particular family members. His father, when he was living in Spain, had been seriously injured by his Inquisitors' methods, and there was reason to believe that he would soon be arrested once again. When they reached Holland, Senior Diaz and his sons were circumcised and the family took the name ben Israel. They joined the Beth Jacob congregation, and Manoel, now Menasseh, was taught in the community's school by Mortera and Rabbi Uziel. He was a precocious student, and particularly well-spoken in both Portuguese and Hebrew. "In my youth," he wrote, "I was so given to rhetoric and was so eloquent in the Portuguese language that, when I was fifteen years of age, my speeches were very acceptable, applauded, and well-received."[31] When Uziel died in 1622, Menasseh, already teaching in the elementary school, was selected to replace him as *chacham* of the Neve Shalom congregation. Menasseh was well-respected for his preaching (many non-Jews used to come to the synagogue to hear his sermons) and his knowledge of Scripture, but it seems that some had their doubts about his skills as a Talmudist. He was never really held in great esteem by the other rabbis, and he took it as a great insult when, in 1639 with the union of the three congregations, he was given the third rank behind Mortera and Aboab. His relations with the congregation's leaders were somewhat rocky, and he chafed under what he felt were the undignified limitations put on him.

In 1640, his rapport with the community reached one of its low points when Menasseh was put under a ban by the *ma'amad*. Someone had been posting placards on the gates of the synagogue and around the community in which the business practices of some leading members of the congregation were castigated. The posters continued to appear, along with other writings, even after a ban was pronounced on their anonymous author(s). It was later discovered that they had been written by Jonas Abrabanel, Menasseh's brother-in-law, and Moses Belmonte. The offenders humbly begged forgiveness, paid a fine, and the ban was rescinded. Menasseh, however, passionately objected to the way in which his relative had been treated. He made his case in front of the assembled congregation in the synagogue after services one day (noting, among other indignities, that his brother-in-law had been referred to in the public proclamation detailing the affair without the title *senhor*) and apparently made quite a nuisance of himself. Despite the fact that two members of the *ma'amad* approached him and told him to hold his peace, threatening to put him under a ban, he continued with his harangue. Faced with this challege to their authority, the *ma'amad* felt that they had no alternative but to issue a ban against the irate rabbi, who in turn reportedly replied: "I under the Ban? It is I who can proclaim the Ban upon you!"[32] The *cherem* – which prohibited Menasseh from attending services in the synagogue and others from communicating with him – lasted only a day, but it was enough to add to Menasseh's sense of humiliation. For good measure, he was also relieved of his official rabbinical duties for a year. Throughout his career in Amsterdam, it seemed to Menasseh that, compared to the effort that the members of the community made to show their appreciation for Rabbi Mortera, they went out of their way to show their lack of respect for him.

There was no love lost between the two rabbis. They differed not only in their intellectual accomplishments – Menasseh would never be the Talmudist Mortera was – but also in their approaches to religion. Menasseh, unlike the more reserved Mortera, had a particular fascination for messianic themes. It was also rumored that Menasseh, with his many Christian contacts, may have been less than fastidious when it came to Jewish observance. He certainly could be careless: once, while in the company of a Gentile, he took up a pen in his hand and only then realized that it was the Sabbath.[33] Menasseh and Mortera reportedly attacked each other in their sermons, and at one point the leaders of the community – perhaps fearing another schism – had to step in. On this occasion, both rabbis were punished (they were forbidden from preaching for a period of time) while the leaders tried to reconcile their differences and put an end to the constant antagonism.[34]

Given the narrow scope of his rabbinical duties, as well as the meager compensation he received for them (one hundred and fifty guilders, compared to Mortera's six hundred), it is not surprising that Menasseh directed his considerable energies toward many other projects. He must have done fairly well by running and teaching in the Pereiras' yeshiva, although his work there probably took more time than he would have liked. His days at this point were rather full. To a correspondent he wrote:

So that you can see that I am not exaggerating, this is how I allocate my time. Each day I devote two hours to the temple, six to the school, one and a half to the Pereiras' Academy, both the public classes and individual work, of which I am president, and two to the correction of my typographical proofs, as I am alone in this work. From eleven o'clock until noon I receive all those who come to me for advice. This is all indispensable. Your Grace may be the judge of the amount of time I have to deal with my domestic cares, and to answer four to six letters a week.[35]

Menasseh also, like the other rabbis, engaged in some mercantile business – in his case in Brazil with his brother and brother-in-law. But he felt that having to supplement his salary as a rabbi in this way was insulting. "At present, in complete disregard of my personal dignity, I am engaged in trade. . . . What else is there for me to do?"[36]

Menasseh's real love was his printing press. He became, in short time, an internationally known bookseller and printer, publishing several Hebrew Bibles, Pentateuchs, and prayer books (and Spanish translations of these), an edition of the Mishnah, and numerous treatises in Spanish, Portuguese, Hebrew, and Latin. He also acquired a great reputation among Christians for his own writings, some of which were addressed directly to them. He was, without question, the most famous Jewish apologist of his time and, perhaps more than anyone else, took on the responsibility for explaining the doctrines and beliefs of Judaism to the Gentile world. Pierre Daniel Huet, bishop of Avranches and no friend to the Jews, praised him as "a Jew of the first order . . . I have had long and frequent conversations with him on religious subjects. He is an excellent man – conciliatory, moderate, sensible to reason, free from numerous Jewish superstitions and the empty dreams of the kabbalah."[37]

One of Menasseh's most widely read works was the *Conciliador*. In this book, which took almost twenty years to write and which he did not complete until 1651, he tried to reconcile the apparent inconsistencies in Scripture with the help of ancient and modern commentaries. He wrote the *Conciliador* in Spanish (although it was quickly translated into Latin) so that marranos, above all, could see that the central text of Judaism is not full of contradictions. The *Hope of Israel* (1650), on the other hand, was published immediately in both Spanish and Latin so that it would reach a wide audience. The book caused quite a stir among both Jewish messianists and Christian millenarians. Menasseh composed it as a response to recent rumors that some of the lost tribes of Israel had been discovered in the New World. Antonio Montezinos (alias Aaron Levi) was a Portuguese

New Christian who arrived in Amsterdam in 1644 after a voyage to South America. He claimed to have found a group of Indians consisting of descendants of the tribe of Reuben in "New Granada" (now Colombia). In his report, he says that these Indians recited the *shema* to him and proclaimed that "our fathers are Abraham, Isaac, Jacob and Israel, and they signified these four by the three fingers lifted up; then they joined Reuben, adding another finger to the former three."[38] Menasseh had a chance to interview Montezinos during his stay in Amsterdam. Although he did not believe the general theory, popular among some of his contemporaries, that the American Indians were the Ten Lost Tribes of Israel, he was inclined to accept Montezinos's claim that the Indians *he* came across were indeed part of one of the lost tribes. And for Menasseh – as for many of his readers – the fact that there were Jews in the New World had messianic implications.

For Jews, it is a matter of common belief that the coming of the Messiah, a descendant of the House of David, will mean the reestablishment of the Jews in the Holy Land and the beginning of an era of universal peace. There is a great deal of disagreement among Jewish authorities and thinkers, however, as to in what exactly the messianic period will consist. Maimonides, for example, discouraged people from hoping for an otherworldly paradise; he insisted, rather, that the Messiah will be a mortal human being who will restore the Kingdom of David, rebuild the sanctuary, and gather all the dispersed of Israel under his dominion. Quoting the Talmud, he claimed that "the only difference between the present and the messianic days is a deliverance from servitude to foreign powers."[39] Menasseh's conception of what the Messiah will bring is more robust. "Those who hope for a temporal Messiah err just as much as the Moors who hope for a sensuous paradise."[40] The coming of the Messiah will involve not just the political restoration of the Jewish homeland but will mean spiritual redemption as well, and will be accompanied by true happiness for those who have led a virtuous life.

Menasseh could not say for sure when redemption was to arrive – 1648 was a date bandied about by certain kabbalists – but he believed it to be close at hand, "for we see many prophecies fulfilled."[41] Because the arrival of the Messiah must be preceded by the thorough dispersion of the tribes of Israel, whom he will then lead back to Jerusalem, locating at least some of those lost tribes in faraway lands was considered of crucial importance. And not just for Jews: the Second Coming of Christ, according to Christian millenarians (so-called because that coming will inaugurate a reign of a thousand years), will not occur until after the Ten Tribes of Israel are reunited and restored to their kingdom.

Menasseh's messianist persuasions were behind what he had hoped would be the crowning achievement of his life: arranging for the readmission of the Jews to England, from which they had been banned since 1290 (although there were, at least unofficially, a fair number of Jews in London by the 1650s).[42] The dispersal of the Jews, according to tradition, would not be complete until they were residing in all nations and living among all peoples ("And the Lord shall scatter you among all people, from one end of the earth to the other" [Deuteronomy 28:64]). Christian millenarians in England had their own reasons for working with Menasseh on his readmission project, for the Second Coming also required the conversion of the Jews. If the Jews were allowed back into England, not only would their dispersal be extended, these millenarians believed, but their conversion would be facilitated and the millennium brought one step closer.

Menasseh, then, received a good deal of encouragement from English friends and others to apply for the readmission of the Jews. Although he was preparing to cross the channel to begin negotiations as early as 1653, he was delayed by the Anglo-Dutch War. When he was finally able to go over in 1655, accompanied by his son Samuel, he made his presentation to Oliver Cromwell. Menasseh appealed to him through both theological and (perhaps more important) economic arguments. He was particularly mindful to bring to the Lord Protector's attention the financial benefits that have usually attended the presence of a thriving Jewish community in a country. After noting that "merchandising is, as it were, the proper profession of the nation of the Jews," Menasseh went on to remind Cromwell that "there riseth an infallible Profit, commodity and gain to all those Princes in whose Lands they dwell above all other strange Nations whatsoever."[43] Cromwell was quite taken by the Dutch rabbi and gave him a sympathetic hearing. Public opinion, however, was by no means so well disposed toward readmission. Some argued that strong and humiliating conditions should be imposed upon the Jews (for example, they were not to be admitted to any judicial function, employ Christian servants, or be granted many of the other privileges or rights they had been enjoying for decades in Holland). After several sessions, the conference convened by Cromwell to consider the issue was deadlocked; it adjourned before anything was resolved.[44] Menasseh was greatly disappointed by the lack of tangible results, particularly as he had devoted several years of his life (two of them in England) to this project. When Samuel died in England in September 1657, the blow was too much for him. Menasseh himself died two months later, after bringing his son's body back to Holland.

It is possible that this enterprising, cosmopolitan, and well-connected rabbi with messianic interests was, at some point, Spinoza's teacher. Their paths would have crossed in the Talmud Torah school only if Spinoza was present in the fifth grade while Menasseh was still teaching in Rabbi Aboab's place. There is only a small window of opportunity here, however, as Spinoza would likely have begun attending that first level of the higher *medrassim* – if indeed he did so – in 1648 at the earliest, and Menasseh was replaced by Leao in 1649.[45] Spinoza may have attended a yeshiva directed by Menasseh, but there is no evidence that he did. Perhaps Michael, with an eye to his son's continuing education after he pulled him out of school to help with the family business, hired Menasseh – always on the lookout to supplement his income – to tutor Baruch privately. Or Menasseh could very well have served as a kind of informal intellectual mentor to the young man in the early 1650s, particularly if Spinoza – already out in the world and mixing with Christian merchants at the Exchange – was at this time interested in learning more about the kinds of things to which the more conservative Mortera would not likely have been willing (or able) to introduce him: kabbalah or Jewish mysticism, heterodox currents in Jewish and Christian thinking, or non-Jewish philosophy. Menasseh was familiar with the writings of Isaac La Peyrere, a French Calvinist who held that Moses was not the author of the Pentateuch, that there were many people in existence before Adam and Eve (they are not mentioned in the Bible because the Bible is the history only of the Jews, not of all humankind), and that the arrival of the Messiah expected by the Jews was imminent. Menasseh, who wrote a refutation of the "pre-Adamite" theory in 1656, may have been responsible for introducing the "young rebels" in the Jewish community to La Peyrere's ideas.[46] Spinoza could certainly have been among his circle. He owned a copy of the *Prae-Adamitae* and used material from it in his own Bible criticism, and his familiarity with La Peyrere's theses may stem from the time when he was still in the Jewish community. Spinoza also owned a copy of Rabbi Joseph Salomon Delmedigo's kabbalistic work, the *Sefer Elim,* which Menasseh edited in 1628. Delmedigo, originally from Crete, studied in Padua with Galileo and served briefly as a rabbi in the Amsterdam community in the 1620s. He was a good friend of Menasseh's in the Neve Shalom congregation, and perhaps it was Menasseh who initially encouraged Spinoza to look into this material. Moreover, Spinoza was familiar with Menasseh's own writings: he owned the Spanish edition of the *Hope of Israel* (which was dedicated to the Talmud Torah congregation's *ma'amad,* on which Michael d'Espinoza sat in the year the book was published), and certainly read *El Conciliador* closely. All of this, along with the less tangible elements of temperament and interest, suggests – but by no means establishes – that Menasseh played some kind of formative role in the broadening of Spinoza's intellectual horizons.[47] With his contacts among Christians, Menasseh would have been the perfect conduit to the larger theological and philosophial world in which Spinoza the merchant must have been developing an interest.[48]

᪣

Of course, if one was bold enough, one could go outside the Jewish community to that world itself and seek its learning there. Nothing prohibited Jews from studying with Gentile scholars – nothing, that is, except rabbinical opprobrium. While many Dutch scholars were eager to learn from the Jews, and even sought them out in order to be taught Hebrew and the principal texts of the Jewish religion, the Jewish leaders, for their part, no doubt frowned upon members of the congregation turning to the non-Jewish world to further their education (unless it was for purposes of professional training, such as in medicine or the law). It was one thing to read secular Spanish poetry and literary classics, as these were a part of their own heritage. But one probably risked censure by stepping too far into the contemporary domain of Gentile letters and sciences.

Lucas remarks that, with respect to his studies so far, all within the community and all perfectly conventional, Spinoza "found nothing difficult, but also nothing satisfying."[49] It was around the age of fifteen, according to the only extensive biographical account written by someone who actually knew and talked with Spinoza, that he began encountering problems "which the most learned among the Jews found it hard to solve." Baruch kept his suspicions to himself, however, lest his doubts embarrass – or, worse, irritate – his teachers, and "pretended to be very satisfied with his answers." Although he continued to follow his lessons – or, if he was already no longer attending school, the discussions in the yeshiva – with all due attentiveness, he nonetheless had come to the conclusion that "henceforth he would work on his own and spare no efforts to discover the truth himself." Within just a few years, Spinoza must have been feeling a sufficient lack of contentment with the education he had acquired, and having some rather serious doubts about Judaism, both its dogma and its practices, was ready to seek enlightenment elsewhere. By the time Baruch was twenty-two, he may in fact have been undergoing a kind of spiritual and intellectual crisis similar to that experienced by Uriel da Costa over thirty-five years earlier. Perhaps the rules and expectations of a properly Jewish life, now that his father was dead, were of diminishing importance and interest to him; and the ancient learning to which he had devoted so much time too narrow to satisfy his natural curiosity for ideas. His contacts in the Dutch world, particularly the friendships that would have developed out of the business relationships he cultivated at the *bourse,* or mercantile exchange, could only have encouraged him to widen his intellectual pursuits. Circulating among the merchants he met there – many of whom were members of dissenting Protestant sects, such as the Mennonites, and thus broader in their reading and much more open in their thinking than orthodox Calvinists – Spinoza would have been exposed to a variety of liberal theological opinions and come across much talk of new developments in philosophy and science, such as Descartes's recent innovations in physics and mathematics. Spinoza may even, at this time, have begun attending meetings of one or another of the groups of freethinkers that proliferated in seventeenth-century Amsterdam and participating in their discussions of religion, philosophy, and politics.

It was not, however, only lack of satisfaction with his education and the religious life in the Jewish community and a vague intellectual curiosity that awakened in Spinoza a desire to search, through philosophy and the sciences, for a broader knowledge of the world. He also began to experience what historically must be one of the prime motivations behind anyone's choice of a philosophical vocation: a deep sense of the *vanitas* of ordinary pursuits, particularly the materialistic pursuits of an Amsterdam merchant, and a desire for "truth" – not just empirical truths about nature but, more important, an understanding of the "proper goods" of a human life (to borrow a phrase from Socrates). It was probably to this period in his life that Spinoza was referring when he wrote, in his *Treatise on the Emendation of the Intellect,* that

after experience had taught me that all the things which regularly occur in ordinary life are empty and futile, and I saw that all the things which were the cause or object of my fear had nothing of good or bad in themselves, except insofar as [my] mind was moved by them, I resolved at last to try to find out whether there was anything which would be the true good, capable of communicating itself, and which alone would affect the mind, all others being rejected – whether there was something which, once found and acquired, would continuously give me the greatest joy, to eternity.

He was not unaware of the risks involved in his this new enterprise:

I say that "I resolved at last" – for a first glance it seemed ill-advised to be willing to lose something certain for something then uncertain. I saw, of course, the advantages that honor and wealth bring, and that I would be forced to abstain from seeking them, if I wished to devote myself seriously to something new and different; and if by chance the greatest happiness lay in them, I saw that I should have to do without it. But if it did not lie in them, and I devoted my energies only to acquiring them, then I would equally go without it.[50]

By this point, Spinoza had more than a suspicion that "the greatest happiness" did not lie in the life of a businessman leading an observant Jewish life.

There can be no question, then, that by 1654 or early 1655, Spinoza's education was taking a decidedly secular – and, in the eyes of the rabbis, troubling – turn. And what he would have learned, first of all, is that in order to pursue his studies any further he would need Latin, the language in which practically every important work of science, philosophy, and theology had been written since late antiquity. There is no particular reason why he should have had to go outside the Jewish community just to learn Latin. Rabbis Mortera and Menasseh ben Israel both knew Latin well, as did the many members of the Sephardic community who had been raised as Christians and attended universities in Portugal and Spain, where Latin was the language of instruction. But as his interest was not in learning Latin per se, but also in gaining some secular pedagogical direction, he needed outside help. Besides, around the time he decided to learn Latin, and almost all of his early biographers date this before the excommunication, Spinoza may not have been having much to do with the Jewish community beyond what was required for his commercial activities and what was minimally expected of a member-in-good-standing of the congregation. It is likely that he was no longer attending Mortera's *Keter Torah* by this point. Lucas relates that he had so little intercourse with the Jews for some time that he was obliged to associate with Christians, and he formed ties of friendship with intellectual people who told him that it was a pity that he knew neither Greek nor Latin, although he was well-versed in Hebrew. . . . He himself fully realized how necessary these learned languages were for him; but the problem was in finding a way of learning them, as he had neither the money, the birth, nor the friends to help him out.[51]

Spinoza's first Latin tutor, according to Colerus, was "a German student";[52] another writer reports that it was "a learned virgin."[53] Whatever the true story behind Spinoza's earliest foray into Latin, however, the experience was nothing in comparison to what he would learn from the man who was certainly more than just a language teacher to him.

In a house on the Singel, one of the grand concentric canals that radiate outward from the center of Amsterdam, there was a Latin master who had set up in his home a kind of preparatory school. Prominent families, reluctant to send their sons to the public Latin school run by the strict Calvinists, would employ him to give their boys (and, on occasion, girls) the language skills and humanistic background that they would need for their studies at a university. This was not Franciscus van den Enden's first attempt at earning a living in Amsterdam. When he and his family first moved to the city, sometime in the mid-1640s, he tried running an art gallery and bookshop – called *In de Konstwinkel* ("In the Artshop") – out of a house in the quarter of town called The Nes. That did not last long, and in 1652 Van den Enden was a fifty-year-old man with a large family and a failed business who quickly needed to find a steady source of income. So he started teaching Latin.

Apparently he was a very fine Latin teacher indeed and attracted many students from distinguished homes. Van den Enden himself had been trained in Latin, first by the Augustinians and then by the Jesuits, in Antwerp, where he was born in 1602.[54] He formally entered the Jesuit order at the age of seventeen but was kicked out two years later, for unknown reasons. In a contemporary account of his life, we are told that the young Van den Enden "had a great penchant for women" and that the reason for his dismissal was that he had been caught in a compromising position with the wife of a distinguished military officer.[55] He must have soon been reconciled with the order, however, for he then spent a number of years studying philosophy and ancient classics at a Jesuit college in Louvain, after which he went home to Antwerp to teach Latin, Greek, and belles-lettres, as well as to obtain a degree in grammar. After giving lessons in grammar, poetry, and eloquence in a number of Flemish towns, he returned in 1629 to Louvain to study theology and become a Jesuit priest. Once again, however, he was dismissed by the Jesuits ("because of his errors"), whereupon he finally gave up any plans for the religious life. Somewhere along the way, before his marriage in 1642 to Clara Maria Vermeeren (from Danzig) in Antwerp, Van den Enden acquired the title *medicinae doctor,* but there is no record of where or when he actually studied medicine. Soon after the birth in 1643 of their first daughter, also called Clara Maria, the family moved to Amsterdam, where the twins Anna and Adriana Clementina were born in 1648, followed by Jacobus in 1650 and Marianna in 1651 (Anna and Jacobus died at a very young age). It was a highly intellectual, artistic, and musical household, and Van den Enden made sure that his daughters were well-educated and capable of holding their own with his male students. The girls were reportedly able to give their father a hand in conducting Latin lessons.

The Van den Enden's was not, however, a religious household, at least if we are to believe the account provided by one of his former lodgers. According to Du Cause de Nazelle, a young French officer who lived with them after he had moved his Latin school to Paris in the 1670s, Van den Enden was a man of no religion, except perhaps a kind of harmless, non-dogmatic deism. Colerus, looking for the root of Spinoza's evil, is a bit harsher, blaming Van den Enden for "sowing the first seeds and foundations of atheism in his young students."[56]

Van den Enden taught in Amsterdam until 1671. He was fond of his adopted country and saw it as a fine, if flawed, example of republicanism. His own preference, however, was for true democracy. In two political works probably written in the early 1660s, the *Free Political Propositions and Considerations of State* and *A Short Narrative of the New Netherlands' Situation, Virtues, Natural Privileges, and Special Aptitude for Population,*[57] he argues – much as Spinoza would in his own political works – for a radically democratic state, one that respects the boundary between political authority and theological belief and in which religious leaders play no role in the government. Only such a liberal state would be truly stable and strong enough to fulfill securely its role in the lives of its citizens. The *Short Narrative* contains a proposal for a constitution for Dutch colonials in North America, and Van den Enden takes the opportunity to present a picture of his ideal polity. He insists on strict civil, political, and legal equality between all members of the state, absolute freedom of speech, religion, and opinion; and freedom of "philosophizing." He also goes so far as to propose that preachers, "who always rouse and congeal everybody's private opinion" and thus introduce a "ruinous pestilence of all peace and concord," be banned from the colony. No one is to dominate over anyone else, and the state's leaders are to be elected to limited terms by its well-educated citizenry (men *and* women). On particularly important issues, the citizens are to resolve their disagreements for themselves by majority vote.

Van den Enden certainly did not think that the Republic of the Netherlands measured up to his ideal. For one thing, the leaders of the Reformed Church played too great a role in running the political affairs of the provinces. Moreover, he found the oligarchical way in which the regent families controlled the cities and towns – the real loci of political power in Holland – insufficiently democratic and egalitarian. During his sedition trial in France, he is reported to have said that "there are three kinds of republic, namely, that of Plato, that of de Groot [i.e., the Dutch Republic], and that of More, which is called utopian." He claimed to have constructed a fourth kind, one in which "virtue is always rewarded."[58] He even discussed with others "the means of establishing a free republic in Holland" and transforming the country into a democracy. In spite of these disappointments with the Dutch political situation, Van den Enden tried to take an active part in the defense of the country when it was threatened by its enemies, monarchies one and all. In 1662, during a brief interruption in the wars with England, he wrote to Johan de Witt, the Grand Pensionary of the States of Holland, with some ideas about improving the offensive capabilities of Dutch ships. When the republic was invaded by the army of Louis XIV in 1672, he allegedly adopted even stronger measures, joining a plot to overthrow the king.

Van den Enden's affection for the Dutch Republic, however, was not reciprocated. His extreme democratic ideas received a hostile response from Calvinist leaders. In 1670, he moved to Paris, possibly to take up an appointment as a counselor and physician to Louis XIV,[59] and established there another fashionable Latin school, called the Hôtel des Muses. He married again in 1672, and he and his new wife, the fifty-three-year-old widow Catharina Medaens, turned their home into an intellectual salon. For a time, he succeeded in attracting members of Paris's philosophical and scientific elite to his gatherings (the German philosopher Leibniz is reported to have frequented Van den Enden's house during his years in the French capital). But even in his old age – he was now seventy-two – he was not

content to live the contemplative life. It seems that his political enthusi-
asms spurred him to action, and the consequences were, in the end, tragic.

In 1674, Van den Enden was implicated in a plot against the French
Crown. According to De Nazelle, who claimed to have overheard the conspirators laying out their scheme when they met in Van den Enden's house,
the plan was to remove Louis XIV and establish a republican form of government in France. The leaders of the conspiracy were Chevalier Louis de
Rohan, a former high master of the hunt for France, and Gilles du Hamel
de Latréaumont, a retired officer from Normandy and a former pupil of
Van den Enden's in Amsterdam. They were unhappy with the latest round
of wars, particularly the French invasion of the Netherlands in 1672, and
blamed recent domestic problems on Louis's expansionist ambitions; Rohan was also enticed by the promise of sovereignty over Bretagne should
the plan succeed. Van den Enden was, for the most part, moved by his concern for the security of what he considered his home country, the Netherlands, and by his hatred of the ministers who were behind the French ag-
gression against the republic. He argued that such an unjust war violated
the rights of men, and would never have been waged by a democratic form
of government, which is not subject to the whims of any one individual. It
was rumored that the Dutch (and perhaps even the Spanish) supported
the conspiracy and had promised the plotters material support; in fact,
Dutch ships were lying just off the coast of France at the time the plot was
discovered, although Holland's leaders denied any knowledge of the intrigue against the king. The scheme was foiled when De Nazelle revealed
what he knew to Louis's war minister. The conspirators were seized, and
Rohan was beheaded (Latréaumont had been shot while resisting arrest).
Because he was a foreigner and a spy – and, perhaps more important, not
a noble – Van den Enden was hanged.

One of the great uncertainties in Spinoza's biography concerns when
he began studying with Van den Enden. It could have been as late as 1657.
But given what can reasonably be surmised about his increasing dissatisfaction with his Jewish religious studies and his growing desire to learn
more about philosophy and science (particularly contemporary developments in those fields), processes that almost certainly peaked while he was
still a merchant and thus in his early twenties, it is plausible that Spinoza
turned to the ex-Jesuit for instruction in Latin sometime around 1654 or
1655 – that is, *before* his excommunication from the Jewish community.[60]
He may have been directed to Van den Enden by his mercantile acquain-

tances, the same people who, in the late 1650s, would be among his most intimate friends and the members of a close circle devoted to encouraging Spinoza to expand on his ideas and to discussing his and other philosophical opinions. Van den Enden was undoubtedly on familiar terms with these individuals – among them Pieter Balling, Jarig Jellesz, Simon Joosten de Vries (who, like Van den Enden, also lived on the Singel), and Jan Rieuwertsz (who may have printed Van den Enden's *Short Narrative* in 1665, two years after publishing Spinoza's own study of Descartes's *Principles of Philosophy* and five years before he published the explosive *Theological-Political Treatise*). Given the similarities between Van den Enden's political and religious views and the liberal opinions of these theological dissidents and freethinkers, it would not be surprising if during this period Van den Enden – and perhaps even Spinoza – was, on occasion, present at the Collegiant meetings (attended by disaffected Mennonites, Remonstrants, Quakers, and others). Like the Collegiants (and, later, Spinoza), Van den Enden insisted that religious belief was a personal matter, not to be dictated by any organization or authority. True piety consisted only in the love of God and of one's neighbors; that – in a phrase remarkably similar to how Spinoza puts it in the *Theologico-Political Treatise* – is "the whole sum of the Law and the Prophets."[61] The outward expression of that love, the form it takes in public religious practice, is irrelevant and often borders on superstitious behavior.

Spinoza's matriculation at Van den Enden's school – where, after his expulsion from the congregation and the end of his life as a businessman, he probably also lodged and helped with the teaching[62] – was of crucial importance to his intellectual and personal development. It is true that Spinoza was already well along in his ideas by the time he took up the study of Latin. He must, by that point, have been articulating, at least in his own mind and perhaps also to others (which may have led to his excommunication), his dismissive views of religion. He may also have begun formulating, if only in a rudimentary form, the radical political, ethical, and metaphysical principles to which he would eventually give written systematic expression. Thus, Van den Enden's role in the formation of Spinoza's thought should not be exaggerated.[63] It can hardly be doubted that Spinoza was an original and independent thinker at a relatively early age. Still, at this point in his life he had much to learn, and at Van den Enden's he would have been exposed to an impressive range of important texts, ideas, and personalities.

There is no documentation of what exactly Van den Enden was teaching his pupils in the mid-1650s. But if it was like any other "college" or preparatory school, then the lessons in Latin grammar would have been supplemented with a general introduction to the arts and sciences. This is confirmed by the testimony of one of Van den Enden's former students. Dirk Kerckrinck was at the school at around the same time as Spinoza, overlapping perhaps for a year or two. He had been born in Hamburg in 1639 to a well-to-do family and was studying with Van den Enden in order to learn Latin and other propadeutical material so that he could begin his medical studies at the University of Leiden, which he entered in 1659. In a work on anatomy that he would publish some years later, he praises Van den Enden and credits his former teacher with inculcating in him a passion for learning and with "introducing me to the liberal arts and philosophy."[64]

Kerckrinck never did complete his studies for a medical degree, but he went on to practice medicine in Amsterdam and became famous for his work in anatomy and chemistry. (At one point, he took upon himself the investigation of Amsterdam's drinking water as the cause of various illnesses that had been breaking out in the city.) He and Spinoza kept up their acquaintance even after Spinoza left Amsterdam. In his microscope he used lenses ground by Spinoza, whereas Spinoza had some of Kerckrinck's books in his library. According to Colerus, however, this professional friendship initially began as a rivalry for the affections of Van den Enden's daughter, Clara Maria.

Van den Enden had an only daughter [*sic*], who understood the Latin tongue, as well as music, so perfectly that she was able to teach her father's students. Spinoza often said that he fell in love with her and that he wanted to marry her. Although she was rather feeble and misshapen in body, nonetheless he was taken by her sharp mind and excellent learning. However, his fellow student Kerkring, born in Hamburg, noticed this and became jealous.[65]

Kerckrinck was not about to allow himself to be bested in love. He redoubled his efforts and, with the help of a pearl necklace, won the girl's heart.

This is the only report of any romantic interest in Spinoza's life. And, unfortunately, the story seems apocryphal. Kerckrinck joined Van den Enden's school in 1657, when Clara Maria would have been only thirteen years old – a bit young, perhaps, for the attentions of a twenty-five-year-old like Spinoza, even in those days. Not too young for the eighteen-year-old Kerckrinck, however. He and Van den Enden's daughter must have developed some kind of mutual affection – one capable of surviving the stresses of time and separation – for in February 1671, twelve years after Kerckrinck's departure from Van den Enden's school (and, we are told, after Kerckrinck's conversion from Lutheranism to Catholicism), they wed.[66]

What Kerckrinck meant by "the liberal arts and philosophy" was just the kind of humanistic education that was expected by the urban, upper-bourgeois families who sent their children to the school, and that was used generally by Latin masters of the time to improve their students' fluency in grammar, syntax, and, above all, style. Van den Enden would have had his students read the ancient classics of poetry, drama, and philosophy – the literary legacy of Greece and Rome – as well as neoclassical works of the Renaissance. They were introduced, at least in a broad manner, to Platonic, Aristotelian, and Stoic philosophy; to Seneca, Cicero, and Ovid; and perhaps even to the principles of ancient skepticism. They would also have read the great epics, tragedies, comedies, and histories of antiquity. Spinoza's writings abound with references to classical Latin authors, and he had in his relatively small library works by Horace, Caesar, Virgil, Tacitus, Epictetus, Livy, Pliny, Ovid, Homer, Cicero, Martial, Petrarch, Petronius, Sallust, and others – testimony to a passion that was probably aroused during his time with Van den Enden.

Van den Enden was particularly fond of the dramatic arts and encouraged in his students a taste for theater. He frequently had them rehearse dramatic speeches as a way of developing their eloquence in Greek and Latin. This was not an uncommon practice in Dutch schools in the seventeenth century. It was believed that by having students act out passages from Latin plays they would better acquire the skills in pronunciation, phrasing, and "gesture" (bodily and vocal) so essential to rhetorical success. They were often assigned monologues to compose or memorize and then perform, not just recite.[67] Occasionally, these dramatic exercises culminated in the public production of some play. In Leiden in 1595, for example, the students in the city's Latin school – the same school Rembrandt later attended – put on Beza's *Abraham Sacrifiant*.[68] The budding young thespians under Van den Enden's direction performed at the wedding celebration of an Amsterdam burgemeester's daughter in 1654. On January 16 and 17, 1657, at the Amsterdam Municipal Theater, they put on Terence's *Andrea*, which they had been rehearsing for some time. That same month they acted in two performances of Van den Enden's own *Philedonius*, also at the Municipal Theater. This must have been the high point of Van den Enden's pedagogical career. The production of his neoclassical allegorical work was a great success – the two burgemeesters whose sons had roles in the play were particularly pleased – and the play was later published. The following year, the school put on Terence's *Eunuchus,* along with "a Greek farce."[69] (Not everyone was enthusiastic about the productions. Calvinist preachers, scandalized by the fact that the roles of women were played not by boys *en travestie* but by Van den Enden's female students, tried to halt the productions of 1657.)[70]

It is fairly certain that Spinoza participated in the Terence productions. As several scholars have shown, Spinoza's writings reveal an intimate knowledge of Terence's works. Latin phrases and sentences are sometimes taken directly from the Roman playwright, particularly from the two comedies that Van den Enden had his students perform in 1657 and 1658.[71] Spinoza must have known his parts well, and thus retained and adapted what he needed for his own writings and correspondence. This fondness for the theater that Spinoza acquired from his teacher can also provide the context for an alarming incident that allegedly took place before his excommunication. Pierre Bayle, in a famous article on Spinoza in his seventeenth-century *Dictionnaire historique et critique,* relates that around the time that Spinoza was feeling alienated from his Jewish upbringing and education he started to "distance himself little by little from the synagogue." Nonetheless, he continues, Spinoza would have been perfectly willing to maintain contact with the congregation, at least for a little while longer, "had he not been treacherously attacked by a Jew who struck him with a knife when he was leaving the theater. The wound was minor but he believed that the assassin's intention was to kill him."[72]

It is hard to know how much credibility to give this story. Perhaps there was, as one scholar suggests, a climate of deep hostility in the Jewish community regarding apostasy, of which Spinoza was around this time showing early but unmistakable signs. Frustrated by recent conversions to Christianity from within the community, the Portuguese Jews may have been "pushed to adopt a passionate and murderous attitude" toward members of its congregation who defected or seemed likely to do so.[73] These conversions were said to have been encouraged by Calvinist pastors, who often promised various rewards for any Jews who made the leap: Moses ben Israel was given a military commission after his baptism; Samuel Aboab, before converting, asked for help in seizing his uncle's inheritance.[74] In any

case, when the assault reportedly took place, Spinoza may have been acting in or attending one of the productions of Van den Enden's school.

In addition to the education they received in classical literature and philosophy, Van den Enden's students were almost certainly introduced to
more modern material, including recent developments in natural science.
It seems likely that Spinoza's familiarity with sixteenth- and seventeenth-
century thinkers began under Van den Enden's tutelage. His teacher could
have given him lessons in the "new science" and had him read Bacon,
Galileo, and the Italian Renaissance philosopher Giordano Bruno. He may
also have directed him to humanists such as Erasmus and Montaigne, and
to the sixteenth-century Dutch spiritualist Dirk Coornhert. And Spinoza's
interest in political and theologico-political questions no doubt sprouted
when Van den Enden, a radical knowledgeable in the history of political
thought, told him to read Machiavelli, Hobbes, Grotius, Calvin, and
Thomas More.

The most interesting question about Spinoza's intellectual apprenticeship, however, concerns when and how he started reading Descartes, the
most important philosopher of the seventeenth century and, without a
doubt, the dominant influence on Spinoza's philosophical growth. When
Lucas says that Spinoza, after taking up with Van den Enden, "thought only
of making progress in the human sciences,"[75] he is referring above all to
Descartes's investigations into nature. Descartes was, as Colerus puts it,
Spinoza's "master teacher [*Leermeester*]," whose writings would guide
him in his search for knowledge.[76]

Although he was born in France in 1596, René Descartes lived in Holland for most of his adult life. He decided to settle there (in late 1628 or
early 1629), he claimed, because of the richness and variety of the country's commerce, the innocence of its inhabitants, and the moderation of its
climate. "Where else on earth could you find, as easily as you do here, all
the conveniences of life and all the curiosities you could hope to see? In what
other country could you find such complete freedom, or sleep with less
anxiety, or find armies at the ready to protect you, or find fewer poison-
ings, or acts of treason or slander?" Most important, he was able to find in
the Netherlands the peace and solitude that he desired in order to pursue
his work uninterrupted, something he could not find in Paris. "In this large
town where I live [Amsterdam, ca. 1631], everyone but myself is engaged
in trade, and hence is so attentive to his own profit that I could live here
all my life without ever being noticed by a soul."[77] Descartes published

his philosophical works in Amsterdam, and the Dutch Republic contained his most devoted followers, as well as his harshest critics.

If around 1654–5 Spinoza's desire for learning in philosophy and the sciences was truly as intense as we are led to believe – and all the indications are that it was – then there can be no doubt that his curiosity would have turned immediately to the writings of Descartes and his Dutch disciples. Descartes's work in physics, physiology, geometry, meteorology, cosmology, and, of course, metaphysics was widely discussed and debated in the universities and urban intellectual circles. It was also violently condemned by the more conservative Calvinist leaders. From the mid-1640s onward, disputes over Cartesianism became intertwined with the basic ideological divisions that ran through Dutch society and basically split the members of its political and theological worlds into warring camps. Whether they were for or against him, Descartes's name was – even after his death in 1650 – on the lips of practically all educated citizens in the republic.

There are a number of ways in which Spinoza's interest in Cartesian philosophy could initially have been piqued. Most of his friends at the Amsterdam Exchange – Jellesz, Balling, and the others – were devotees of Cartesian thought.[78] Spinoza would have heard mention of the "new philosophy" from them either at the *bourse* or, if he was attending them, at their Collegiant meetings, which often functioned as philosophical discussion groups. On the other hand, he would have had a ready tutor in Cartesianism in Van den Enden. Van den Enden, in fact, had a reputation for being, as well as an atheist, a Cartesian.[79] Thus, among the "sciences" into which he was initiating some of his better students, at least privately and discreetly, would certainly have been those of a Cartesian character. He probably had them read Descartes's *Discourse on Method* along with the mathematical and scientific essays that accompanied it; the *Meditations on First Philosophy;* the treatises on human physiology and the human passions; and, above all, the *Principles of Philosophy*, Descartes's attempt to compose a full-length textbook of philosophy based on Cartesian rather than Aristotelian-Scholastic principles, starting with the most general elements of metaphysics and culminating in the mechanistic explanations of particular natural phenomena (such as magnetism and human sensory perception).

This does not prove beyond a doubt that Spinoza's familiarity with Descartes's philosophy stems from this period and thus predates by a year or so his excommunication from the Jewish community. And his deep investigation and critical analysis of that system would really only take place in the late 1650s, when he regularly participated in the discussions of the Amsterdam Collegiant circles and may also have studied under Cartesian professors at the University of Leiden. But if, as his early biographers claim, his search for philosophical and scientific enlightenment began around the early 1650s, then it is hard to believe that he would have waited very long before turning to those works which at the time were causing such a stir in the Netherlands. And if he was indeed meeting, however occasionally, with his Mennonite merchant friends and studying with Van den Enden before the *cherem* in 1656, then he would have had every opportunity to hear about and even read Descartes.

An even more tantalizing hypothesis is that, in addition to a familiarity with Latin language and literature and modern philosophy and science, Spinoza gained at Van den Enden's home a political education, not just in the sense that Van den Enden gave him the classic works of political thought to read (including Aristotle's *Politics*, Machiavelli's *The Prince* and the *Discourses*, Hobbes's *De Cive*, and Grotius's republican writings), but also that Spinoza's commitment to a secular, tolerant, and democratic state was influenced both by his tutor's own opinions and by those whom he might have met in the house on the Singel. Spinoza's liberal persuasions were probably fairly well set, at least in a general way, by the time he began his lessons with Van den Enden. But there is much about his mature political views (in the *Theologico-Political Treatise* and the *Political Treatise*) that resembles what is found in Van den Enden's *Free Political Propositions* and in his constitutional proposals for the New Netherlands. Moreover, it is conceivable that Van den Enden, during the years Spinoza was his student, was visited by many of the freethinkers in Amsterdam who shared his politics. Contrary to what some historians have claimed, Spinoza would not have met the radical Adriaan Koerbagh at Van den Enden's at this time, because from 1653 onward Koerbagh and his brother, Jan, were away from Amsterdam, studying first at the University of Utrecht and then, after 1656, at the University of Leiden. The Koerbagh brothers would go on to become infamous and inflammatory writers; and Adriaan did indeed have close relations with Spinoza and Van den Enden in the early 1660s. But there were other liberal and radical republicans in town with whom Van den Enden might have crossed paths and to whom he might have introduced his star pupil, an intellectually mature young man who seemed to share many of his political views. It has sometimes been assumed, for example, that Spinoza knew the well-known political writer and advocate of toleration Pierre de la Court (Pieter van den Hove), and their acquaintance could have been initially mediated by Van den Enden.[80]

Influence, of course, can always be a two-way street. Spinoza was no child when he started with Van den Enden. He would have been substantially older than the other students at the school, whom he apparently helped to teach.[81] And he probably gave Van den Enden himself lessons in Hebrew and Spanish. When he set up shop in Paris, Van den Enden taught, in addition to his usual subjects, those two languages, and Spinoza could easily have been *his* tutor in those and perhaps other areas (such as biblical exegesis and Jewish philosophy). Spinoza was no intellectual novice at the time he took up the study of Latin. Moreover, even if he was with Van den Enden as early as 1654, there were additional avenues by which he could have made the progress in his education that he was seeking, both within the Portuguese Jewish community (with the help of Menasseh ben Israel and the more heterodox individuals with whom we find him spending time around the mid-1650s) and without (his Mennonite friends). Nonetheless, though Van den Enden was probably not the "hidden agent behind Spinoza's genius," and although it is an exaggeration to say that he played the role of Socrates to Spinoza's Plato,[82] Spinoza no doubt benefited greatly from his lessons with the ex-Jesuit. In addition to a knowledge of Latin, at Van den Enden's he picked up a sound humanistic training, and probably also an increased sophistication in his political and religious opinions.

ন্ম

Although Spinoza never did pursue, in a formal manner, a higher education in the Talmud or rabbinical training, when he began to drift away from the Jewish community he had a solid familiarity with the Jewish philosophical, literary, and theological tradition. This is something that no other major philosopher of the period possessed. And, to all appearances, Spinoza remained interested in that tradition – albeit for his own philosophical purposes – throughout his life. When he died, he had in his library, among other Judaica, works by Joseph Delmedigo, Moses Kimchi, Menachem Recanati, and a Talmudic lexicon, as well as a Passover Haggadah.[83] He also seems to have continued to relish the Spanish literature which the community regarded as its cultural heritage. Works by Cervantes, Quevedo, and Perez de Montalvan stood next to the Hebrew Bibles and Latin comedies.

From 1654 (and perhaps even earlier) onward, Spinoza was supplementing the education of his Jewish and expatriate Iberian upbringing with a grounding in the ancient classics and in the philosophy and science of his day. Spinoza the merchant was no doubt aware of what the choice of the philosophical life would mean for him in material terms. But he had perhaps decided already that "the advantages that honor and wealth bring" are of no account when compared to the rewards of knowledge and understanding and of leading (to quote Socrates again) "a life worth living for a human being." Just as important, he must also have been aware of what the consequences of his pursuit of knowledge beyond the confines of the Houtgracht and the Breestraat would be for his relations with the Jewish community. Van den Enden's reputation for atheism, and thus for corrupting the city's youth, probably does not extend as far back as 1654–5, when he was still a relative newcomer to Amsterdam's intellectual and political scene. But the fact that Spinoza was, when not engaged in business, off studying Latin and philosophy – perhaps even the works of the infamous Descartes! – with a former Jesuit priest must have been worrisome to the rabbis. By early 1656, they had even stronger reasons for concern.

6

Cherem

THE YEARS 1654–6 were generally prosperous ones for Holland's Portuguese Jews. The economic growth that had begun after the end of the war with Spain and was now fueled by a temporary truce with England continued, and they took great advantage of the opportunities that peacetime offered. Still, there were new pressures on the community. The end of Dutch colonial rule in Brazil in 1654, when the Portuguese recaptured all of their most important (and lucrative) New World possessions, was a devastating blow to Amsterdam's Jews. Not only did it mean the final collapse of the sugar trade and, with the deterioration of the Dutch–Portuguese rapprochement, the suspension of mercantile relations with Portugal, but the Talmud Torah congregation had also placed great hopes in the growing Jewish community in Pernambuco, or Recife (where their own Rabbi Aboab was serving). There, beyond the reach of the Inquisition, was an opportunity for emigrating New Christians to return to Judaism. In 1644, there were slightly more than fourteen hundred Jews in Netherlands Brazil; by 1654, there were five thousand in Recife alone, living in conditions of extraordinary freedom, privilege, and protection.[1] Many of them owned plantations in outlying areas, and there were a number of Sephardic congregations in small villages within the Dutch zone. By 1654, however, Recife was the last surviving outpost of Brazilian Jewry. When it fell to the Portuguese early that year there was an exhaustive migration. Those Jews who did not stay in the New World and go to the Caribbean or New Amsterdam went back to Europe.

The Sephardim of Amsterdam found themselves overwhelmed by a large number of returnees from the Brazilian enterprise. This was in addition to the continuing influx of New Christians who had been fleeing Spain in greater numbers since the revival of an aggressive Inquisition there after 1645. Many of the refugees did not remain in Amsterdam for very long, either moving on to Italy or (unofficially) to London or turning around and heading back to the Caribbean. Of those who stayed in the Netherlands, a good number settled not in Amsterdam but in Rotterdam and Middelburg.[2] The Amsterdam Jews nonetheless had to find room for those who did remain in their city, although they probably welcomed the increase in their numbers, not to mention the boost this skilled and productive influx gave to their economy.

The Ashkenazic Jews who were arriving in increasing numbers in the early 1650s were a bigger problem. These more indigent groups were fleeing new waves of attacks upon Jews in the German lands and Poland. A number of cities in the Holy Roman Empire (such as Augsburg, Lübeck, and Lauingen) also formally expelled their Jews. Amsterdam's Sephardim were less prepared – and less willing – to accommodate the increased immigration from the east, and the city's own Ashkenazic community simply did not have the resources to deal with them. Some Dutch towns, such as Amersfoort and Maarssen, were opening up to Jews at around this time, and this eased the pressure on Amsterdam somewhat. But the members of the Talmud Torah congregation still had a significant resettlement problem on their hands.

The plague was particularly severe in the years 1655 and 1656. After a respite of almost twenty years since the last outbreak, Amsterdam suffered over seventeen thousand deaths, while Leiden saw close to twelve thousand perish.[3] At this time, the Sephardic population of the city was nearly two thousand individuals, a little over 1 percent of the city's total population. There is no record of how many Jews were carried away by the epidemic, but it is reasonable to assume, once again, some proportionate contagion among them, particularly among those who were still living in the poorer center of Vlooienburg.

な

In the first and seventh months of every Jewish year – that is, in Tishri (September or October) and in Nisan (March or April) – the Talmud Torah congregation assessed the taxes and collected the pledges that its members owed. In addition to the *imposta,* the business tax that was calculated according to the total value of an individual's trade for the period, there were the *finta,* a contribution to the community that was expected of every member (a kind of dues payment) and was calculated according to one's wealth, and the *promesa,* a voluntary offering or *tzedakah* that went into the general charity fund. The *promesa* was pledged in the synagogue and added to the *finta* and *imposta* assessments made by the *gabbai*, or communal treasurer.

In the first month of 5414 (September 1654), after the death of his father, Spinoza took over the payments for his family and their business. In the year that followed, Spinoza made significant contributions to the charity fund, promising eleven guilders and eight stuivers in September and forty-three guilders and two stuivers in March (in addition to two *finta* payments of five guilders each, and a one-time contribution of five guilders to a fund for the Jewish poor in Brazil).[4] These high sums may represent memorial offerings for his father. They indicate, as well, that Spinoza was still, in mid-1655, an at least nominally active – if not necessarily enthusiastic – member of the congregation, keeping up appearances and willing to do his part in satisfying the basic obligations that were expected of every *yehudi*. During that year Spinoza may also have been attending synagogue on a fairly regular basis, at the very least to say *kaddish* for his father, which requires a *minyan* or quorum of ten Jewish males.[5] On Rosh Hashonah (the New Year) of the following year, 5415 (September, 1655), he pledged a noticeably smaller sum, four guilders and fourteen stuivers (again accompanied by a five-guilder *finta* payment). Three months later, on the Shabbat of Hannukah, he offered six small pieces of gold.[6] In Nisan of that year (March 1656), he pledged a *promesa* of only twelve stuivers, a sum that was never paid.

It is tempting to read these figures as a reflection of a rebellious Spinoza's flagging commitment to the Talmud Torah congregation, indeed to Judaism, and of his strained relations with the leaders of the community.[7] While Spinoza's faith must indeed have suffered a serious decline by the end of 1655, the explanation for the rapid and significant decrease in his payments to the community may, on the other hand, simply be a financial one. The fact that during the same period his *imposta* payments also dropped from sixteen guilders to six in half a year, and then to nothing six months later, indicates that business had fallen precipitously, and that either the value or the volume of his trade was way down. The lack of a *finta* payment in March 1656 is perhaps a sign that his personal wealth was too low or his finances too precarious to warrant an assessment.

This economic interpretation of Spinoza's declining payment record[8] is supported by the fact that in March 1656 he took drastic steps to relieve himself of the debts he inherited along with his father's estate. Among those liabilities were the continuing responsibilities for the Henriques estate that

Michael had taken on some eighteen years earlier. Spinoza paid off some of the debts, so that (according to a document submitted to the High Magistrates of the Court of Amsterdam)[9] "afterwards he could more easily (if this could be done with little expense) act as heir of his father." By taking this action, he originally indicated his acceptance of his father's estate and his willingness to satisfy the demands of his father's creditors. But as "the said inheritance is encumbered with many arrears to the extent that the said inheritance would be extremely detrimental to the said Bento de Spinoza," he concluded that the best thing now would be to try to reject the inheritance ("to abstain from it in all respects") and get himself excused from his obligations to the creditors. His primary concern was to secure whatever money was due to him from his mother's estate – reportedly "a considerable sum" – which was initially incorporated into Michael's when she died. Spinoza claimed that he "never received to his contentment anything from the fruits of this [his mother's money] in his father's lifetime." He was, in effect, attempting to clear himself of responsibility for Michael's debts and establish himself as a privileged creditor on his father's estate.[10] He decided to try to take advantage of a Dutch law that protected under-aged children who had lost their parents. Because he was a year and a few months shy of his twenty-fifth birthday, he was still technically a minor. Spinoza was thus able to file a petition that legally declared him to be an orphan. The Orphan Masters for the city of Amsterdam then appointed a guardian for him, Louis Crayer, the same person who later worked to protect the rights of Titus Rembrandt, the painter's son and heir to his estate. Crayer filed his brief with the court on March 23, arguing that

Bento de Spinosa . . . be discharged from any such act as he, in any way, could have committed regarding the inheritance from his said father and from all omissions and failures he could have brought about in any way; the said Bento de Spinosa, with his claim on his mother's goods, will be given preference above all other creditors and in particular above Duarte Rodrigues, Lamego Anthonio, Rodrigues de Morajs and the curators of the estate of Pedro Henriques with regard to the goods of the said Michael de Spinosa.

Spinoza was certainly in a bleak financial situation in early to mid-1656. The quick decline in payments to the Jewish community may be no more than a reflection of this fact. Indeed, for the next ten years, until his departure from Amsterdam for the West Indies, his brother Gabriel – who took over responsibility for the payments when Spinoza left the community and

of whom, as far as we know, there was never any question of heterodoxy –
made only nominal *promesa* contributions and no payments for the *finta* or
imposta.[11]

Still, it is hard to believe that there was no connection whatsoever between the mere twelve stuivers that Spinoza promised on March 29, 1656,
and the events that soon followed.

ða

On July 27, 1656, the following text was read in Hebrew from in front of
the ark of the synagogue on the Houtgracht:

The Lords of the *ma'amad*, having long known of the evil opinions and acts of
Baruch de Spinoza, have endeavored by various means and promises, to turn him
from his evil ways. But having failed to make him mend his wicked ways, and, on
the contrary, daily receiving more and more serious information about the abominable heresies which he practiced and taught and about his monstrous deeds, and
having for this numerous trustworthy witnesses who have deposed and born witness to this effect in the presence of the said Espinoza, they became convinced of
the truth of this matter; and after all of this has been investigated in the presence
of the honorable *chachamim*, they have decided, with their consent, that the said
Espinoza should be excommunicated and expelled from the people of Israel. By
decree of the angels and by the command of the holy men, we excommunicate, expel, curse and damn Baruch de Espinoza, with the consent of God, Blessed be He,
and with the consent of the entire holy congregation, and in front of these holy
scrolls with the 613 precepts which are written therein; cursing him with the excommunication with which Joshua banned Jericho and with the curse which Elisha cursed the boys and with all the castigations that are written in the Book of
the Law. Cursed be he by day and cursed be he by night; cursed be he when he
lies down and cursed be he when he rises up. Cursed be he when he goes out and
cursed be he when he comes in. The Lord will not spare him, but then the anger
of the Lord and his jealousy shall smoke against that man, and all the curses that
are written in this book shall lie upon him, and the Lord shall blot out his name
from under heaven. And the Lord shall separate him unto evil out of all the tribes
of Israel, according to all the curses of the covenant that are written in this book
of the law. But you that cleave unto the Lord your God are alive every one of you
this day.

The document concludes with the warning that "no one should communicate with him, neither in writing, nor accord him any favor nor stay with
him under the same roof nor come within four cubits in his vicinity; nor

shall he read any treatise composed or written by him." A Portuguese version was later entered into the community's record books.[12] Through this proclamation, a *cherem* – a ban or excommunication – was pronounced on Baruch de Spinoza by the *parnassim* sitting on the community's *ma'amad* in 1656. It was never rescinded.

Cherem as a punitive or coercive measure exerted by a Jewish community upon its recalcitrant or rebellious members goes back at least to the Tannaitic period, the time of the development of the Mishnah, in the first and second centuries. Originally, in its biblical use, the term *cherem* designated something or someone that is separated from ordinary things and with which common use or contact is forbidden.[13] It can also mean "destroyed." The reason for the separation may be that the object or person is sacred or holy; or – and this would be the grounds for destruction – it may be that it is polluted or an abomination to God. The Torah, for example, declares that anyone who sacrifices to any god other than the Israelite God is *cherem* (*Exodus* 22:19). He is to be destroyed, and the idols he worshiped burned. *Deuteronomy* (7:1–2) declares that the nations occupying the land that God has promised to the Israelites are *cherem* and thus must be destroyed. On the other hand, something that has been devoted to the Lord (*cherem l'adonai*) is "most holy to the Lord [*kodesh kadashim*]" (*Leviticus* 27:29) and thus cannot be sold or redeemed. There are also in the Bible occasions when a separation or destruction is used to threaten or punish someone who disobeys a command. The people of Israel are commanded to destroy (*tacharemu*) the population of Yavesh-gil'ad because they failed to heed the call to battle against the tribe of Benjamin (*Judges* 21:5–11). In the postexilic period, Ezra declared that anyone who did not obey the proclamation to gather in Jerusalem within three days would "lose [*yacharam*] all of his property and . . . be separated from the congregation of the exiles" (*Ezra* 10:7–8).

Among the sages of the Mishnah, *cherem* (or, more properly, *niddui*) came to function as a form of excommunication. A person who has violated some law or command is punished by being declared *menuddeh*, or "defiled." He or she is therefore to be isolated from the rest of the community and treated with contempt. *Niddui* may also have indicated, more narrowly, some kind of expulsion from the ranks of the Pharisees or scholars.[14] Over time, *cherem* came to be considered a more serious form of punishment than *niddui*. Maimonides discusses the case of a *chacham*, or wise man, who has sinned. At first, a *niddui* is pronounced upon him. If, after thirty days, the learned *menuddeh* has not reformed his ways, he is given another thirty days. During the time that he is under a *niddui*, he is to act and be treated as someone who is in mourning: he cannot cut his hair, he cannot wash his clothes or even his body, and no one may come within four cubits of his vicinity. If he should die while the *niddui* is still in effect, then it is not permitted to accompany his coffin to burial. If, after the sixty days under *niddui*, the sinner is still unrepentant, he is given a *cherem*. It is now forbidden to engage in business with him; he may not sell or purchase anything, nor negotiate or bargain. He is also forbidden to teach others and to be taught by someone else (although he is permitted to teach himself, "lest he forget his learning").[15] There were also less stringent forms of warning and correction. The *nezifah* was only a reprimand and initiated a period of seven days during which the sinner was to contemplate the error of his ways; and the *nardafa* involved corporal punishment, possibly a lashing. There has always been much disagreement among halachic authorities, the arbiters of Jewish law, over terminology, definition, sequence, and degree of punishment. Some argue that a *niddui* is to be pronounced only after the milder forms of punishment have failed to work, and that only when neither the *niddui* nor the *cherem* – both of which hold out hope of a reprieve – has succeeded in producing the desired contrition is the final and most rigorous punishment, the *shammta*, to be employed.[16] On the other hand, Maimonides (unlike Rashi, for example) draws no distinction between a person who is *b'shammta* (under the punishment of *shammta*) and the *menuddeh* (the person under a *niddui*).[17]

Among the offenses for which one would be given a *niddui* were, according to Maimonides, showing disrespect for rabbinical authority, personally insulting a rabbi, using a Gentile court of law to recover money that would not be recoverable under Jewish law, performing work on the afternoon before Passover eve, hindering someone else from performing a commandment, violating any of the laws surrounding the preparation and consumption of kosher meat, intentional masturbation, not taking sufficient precautions when owning dogs or other potentially dangerous things, and mentioning God's name in everyday discourse.[18] Rabbi Joseph Caro, the author of the *Shulchan Arukh*, the sixteenth-century compendium of Jewish law that was of particular importance to Sephardic communities, adds a number of other acts for which one would deserve a *niddui*, including breaking an oath, performing work while a corpse lies unburied in town, demanding the performance of the impossible, and the taking over of a teacher's functions by one of his students.[19]

To be put under a *cherem* was of great consequence for an observant Jew. It affected the life of a person and his family in both the secular and the religious spheres. The person under a *cherem* was cut off, to one degree or another, from participating in the rituals of the community and thus from performing many of the everyday tasks that make life meaningful for a Jew. The harshness and duration of the punishment usually depended upon the seriousness of one's offense. Because of the restrictions on dealing and bargaining, not to mention conversation, the *muchram* was, first of all, isolated from his ordinary business and social contacts. He might also be forbidden from serving as one of the ten men required for a *minyan,* or from being called to the Torah in synagogue, or from serving in a leadership post of the congregation, or from performing any number of *mitzvot*, deeds that fulfill the halachic obligations incumbent upon any Jew. In extreme cases, the punishment extended to the offender's relatives: as long as he was under a *cherem,* his sons were not to be circumcised, his children were off-limits for marriage, and no member of the family could be given a proper Jewish burial. Clearly, a *cherem* carried tremendous emotional impact. As one historian puts it, "the excommunicated individual felt himself losing his place in both this world and the next."[20]

The power to excommunicate an individual was traditionally vested in a community's rabbinical court, the Beth Din. But during the medieval period this became a rather contentious issue, as prominent lay members of various communities took on many of the leadership functions that had earlier been reserved for rabbis. The ceremony of pronouncing a severe *cherem* was usually conducted in the synagogue, where a rabbi or *chazzan* read the ban either in front of the Torah in the open ark or from the pulpit. The *shofar* would be blown while members of the congregation held candles (sometimes described as black) that were extinguished after the *cherem* was proclaimed.[21]

There is no evidence that such a powerful symbolic drama was carried out in the case of Spinoza's *cherem*. Lucas, in fact, claims that Spinoza's excommunication ceremony did not follow this procedure:

When the people have assembled in the synagogue, the ceremony they call *cherem* begins with the lighting of a number of black candles and the opening of the Tabernacle, where the books of the law are stored. Afterwards, the cantor, from a slightly elevated place, intones in a gloomy voice the words of the Excommunication, while another cantor blows a horn, and the wax candles are turned upside down so that they fall drop by drop into a vessel filled with blood. At which point the people, animated by a holy terror and a sacred rage at the sight of this black spectacle, respond Amen in a furious voice, which testifies to the good service which they believe they would be rendering to God if they could tear the excommunicant apart, which they would undoubtedly do if they were to run into him at that moment or when leaving the synagogue. With respect to this, it should be remarked that the blowing of the horn, the inverting of the candles and the vessel filled with blood are rituals which are observed only in cases of blasphemy. Otherwise they are content simply to proclaim the excommunication, as was done in the case of Spinoza, who was not convicted of blasphemy but only of a lack of respect for Moses and for the law.[22]

The text of the excommunication could have been read by Rabbi Mortera, although Colerus says that some "Jews of Amsterdam" told him that "old *chacham* Aboab" – who happened to be presiding over the Beth Din at the time – was responsible for this.[23] But even if the task of making the public pronouncement was given to a rabbi, the authority to issue a *cherem* was, among the Amsterdam Sephardim, firmly in the hands of the community's lay leaders. The regulations of the Talmud Torah congregation leave no question whatsoever on this point: the *ma'amad* has the absolute and sole right to punish members of the community who, in their judgment, have violated certain regulations.[24] They were, of course, permitted and even encouraged to seek the advice of the rabbis before issuing a ban against someone, particularly if the alleged offense involved a matter of *halacha*. But such consultation was not required. The *ma'amad*'s exclusive right to excommunicate members of the community went virtually unchallenged in the seventeenth century. Only Rabbi Menasseh ben Israel, when he was angry over the treatment he and his family had received at the hands of the *ma'amad* in 1640, protested that the right of excommunication properly belongs to the rabbis. For his impertinence – and perhaps to make sure that he got the point – he was excommunicated, albeit only for a day.[25]

There were various degrees of punishment of which the *ma'amad* of Talmud Torah could avail itself. They could, first of all, simply issue a warning. But offenders might also be denied admission to the synagogue on Yom Kippur, the Day of Atonement; or they could be denied admission to all services in the synagogue. They could be forbidden from being called up to read from the week's Torah portion, that is, from performing *aliyah*, a great honor and privilege; they could be denied charity from the community's treasury; or they could be prevented from holding some communal office. The *chazzan*, Abraham Baruch Franco, was at one time under prolonged punishment by a sentence of flogging, which took place before every new moon for two years. The directors of the community thus recognized, at least tacitly, the range of sanctions running from *nezifah* to *nardafa*. But the ultimate punishment was the ban. And in the Amsterdam Sephardic congregation, there seems to have been no distinction between different forms or degrees of excommunication. Some excommunications as a matter of fact (but not as a matter of proclamation) lasted longer than others; there were differences in the wordings of the proclamations (including the addition of curses); and there was some variety in the nature of the extended punishment to which the banned person was subject: sometimes it was sufficient to ask forgiveness and pay a fine; on other occasions the banned person would, after reconciling with the community, be prohibited from performing certain *mitzvot* for a specified period. But whatever the length of separation or the severity of penance, each act of excommunication was referred to simply as a *cherem*. A differentiation among *niddui*, *cherem*, and *shammta* seems not to have operated in the congregation.[26]

Disregarding Maimonides' admonition to use this form of punishment sparingly, Amsterdam's Sephardic leaders employed the *cherem* widely for maintaining discipline and enforcing conformity within the community. In many cases, excommunication was directly attached by the community's regulations to violations of specific laws. In fact, there were certain laws for the breaking of which an excommunication was mandatory: establishing a *minyan* for common prayer outside the congregation; disobeying orders of the *ma'amad;* raising a hand against a fellow Jew with the intention of striking him, either inside the synagogue or in its vicinity; arriving at synagogue with a weapon (although an exception would be considered for people who were in a quarrel with a Christian and felt that they needed to carry a weapon for protection); circumcising non-Jews without the permission of the *ma'amad;* speaking in the name of the Jewish nation without permission of the *ma'amad;* brokering divorce documents without the permission of the *ma'amad;* dealing in contraband coins; and engaging in common prayer with persons who had never been members of the synagogue or who had rebelliously left the synagogue.[27]

An excommunication was attached to the violation of certain rules regarding religious and devotional matters, such as attendance at synagogue, the purchase of kosher meat, and the observance of holidays. One could not, for example, buy meat from an Ashkenazic butcher.[28] Then there were ethical regulations: one could be banned for gambling or for lewd behavior in the streets. Social precepts protected by the ban included a rule against marrying in secret, that is, without parental consent and not in the presence of a rabbi. There were also regulations deriving from the political and financial structure of the community. For example, one could be banned for failing to pay one's taxes, or for showing personal disrespect to a member of the *ma'amad* (as Menasseh quickly learned).

Other bannable activities included making public statements derisive of other members of the community, especially the rabbis; publicly defaming the Portuguese (but not the Spanish!) ambassador (a regulation that was maintained at least before the crisis over Brazil); writing letters to Spain containing any mention of or reference to the Jewish religion, which might jeopardize the recipient – most likely someone of converso descent – by putting him or her under the suspicion of being a secret Judaizer; printing a book without permission from the *ma'amad;* and removing a book from the congregation's library without permission. Women were forbidden, under threat of excommunication, to cut the hair of Gentile women, and Jews were forbidden to engage Gentiles in theological discussions.[29]

It goes without saying that the public expression (orally or in writing) of certain heretical or blasphemous opinions – such as denying the divine origin of the Torah or slighting any precept of God's law or demeaning the reputation of the Jewish people – would also warrant excommunication.

In 1639, Isaac de Peralta was excommunicated for disobeying and insulting a member of the *ma'amad* and then attacking him in the street. Jacob Chamis was excommunicated for a couple of weeks in 1640 when he circumcised a Pole without permission; in his own defense, he claimed that he was not aware that the man was a non-Jew.[30] Joseph Abarbanel was put under a *cherem* in 1677 for buying meat that was kosher, but from an Ashkenazic butcher. Several individuals were given a ban for adultery.[31] In all, between 1622 and 1683, as the historian Yosef Kaplan has discovered, thirty-nine men and one woman were excommunicated by Spinoza's congregation, for periods ranging from one day to eleven years. (The woman, the wife of Jacob Moreno, was excommunicated in 1654 together with her husband when they failed to heed the warning that they were causing a scandal in the community by allowing Daniel Castiel to enter their house when Jacob was not home.) Rarely – as in the case of Spinoza – was the ban never removed. All of this indicates that an excommunication was not intended by the Jewish community of Amsterdam to be, by definition, a permanent end to all religious and personal relations. It might, on occasion, turn out to have that result, as it did for Spinoza. But it seems usually to have been within the power of the individual being punished to determine how long it would be before he fulfilled the conditions set for his reconciliation with the congregation.

The *cherem*, then, was used to enforce the social, religious, and ethical conduct thought appropriate to a proper Jewish community, and to discourage deviancy not just in matters of liturgical practice but also in matters of everyday behavior and the expression of ideas. All of these would be particularly important issues for a community founded by former conversos and their descendants, most of whom had long been cut off from Jewish texts and practices and who had only recently been introduced to orthodoxy and educated in the norms of Judaism. The leaders of Talmud Torah had to work hard to maintain religious cohesion among a community of Jews whose faith and practices were still rather unstable and often tainted by unorthodox beliefs and practices, some of which stemmed from their experiences with Iberian Catholicism. Moreover, such a community might feel insecure about its Judaism, and thus in compensation be particularly inclined to resort frequently to the most rigorous means to keep things "kosher." The Amsterdam Sephardim did use the sanction of excommunication for offenses for which other congregations, such as those of Hamburg and Venice, adopted less extreme measures.[32]

The text of Spinoza's *cherem* exceeds all the others proclaimed on the Houtgracht in its vehemence and fury. There is no other excommunication document of the period issued by that community that attains the wrath directed at Spinoza when he was expelled from the congregation. The matter-of-fact tone of Peralta's *cherem* is more typical:

Taking into consideration that Isaac de Peralta disobeyed that which the aforesaid *ma'amad* had ordered him, and the fact that Peralta responded with negative words concerning this issue; and not content with this, Peralta dared to go out and look for [members of the *ma'amad*] on the street and insult them. The aforesaid *ma'amad*, considering these things and the importance of the case, decided the following: it is agreed upon unanimously that the aforesaid Isaac de Peralta be excommunicated [*posto em cherem*] because of what he has done. Because he has been declared *menudeh*, no one shall talk or deal with him. Only family and other members of his household may talk with him.[33]

After four days, Peralta begged forgiveness and paid a fine of sixty guilders, and the ban was removed. David Curiel was able to remove his *cherem* in 1666 by paying one thousand guilders to the congregation's charity fund, "considering the long time that he was outside the community and the pressing needs of the poor."[34] But there is no mention in Spinoza's *cherem* of any measures that he could take that would serve as a sufficient sign of repentance or of any means by which he could reconcile with the congregation. Even the *cherem* of Juan de Prado, Spinoza's friend and fellow *mucharam* in 1656 (and presumably guilty of similar offenses), though it is just as uncharacteristically long as that of Spinoza and rules out any further reconciliation overtures, is nonetheless relatively reasoned and mild in its tone. Prado will not again be allowed to beg forgiveness and profess the mending of his ways; and the board of governors ask him and his family to move away from Amsterdam, preferably overseas. But there is none of the anger and violence that characterizes their condemnation of Spinoza.[35]

The formula for Spinoza's *cherem* seems to have come from Venice, brought by Rabbi Mortera from his mentor, Rabbi Modena. In 1618, Mortera traveled to Venice, along with other members of the Beth Jacob congregation and representatives of the breakaway group (soon to become Beth Israel) led by Rabbi Pardo. These were the two factions that had split over the Farar affair, and they were attempting, with Venice's help, to effect a reconciliation, or at least gain a judgment from the rabbis and leaders of the Venetian Sephardim. The *parnassim* of the Talmud Torah congregation in Venice counseled the Amsterdam congregants to settle their difference amicably but nonetheless threatened to put under a *cherem* those who "sowed the seeds of schism." The *cherem* text that Mortera carried with him to Amsterdam was adapted – most likely by Modena – from chapter 139 of the *Kol Bo* ("The Voice Within"), a late-thirteenth- or early-fourteenth-century compilation of Jewish lore and customs printed in Naples around 1490.[36] Mortera's Venetian teacher produced a text full of curses and imprecations, one *maldicion* after another; their sheer quantity makes the *cherem* actually used for Spinoza seem mild by comparison. From it was probably also drawn the formula that was used when the Venetian congregation pronounced a *cherem* on Uriel da Costa in 1618. In the Spanish translation from a Hebrew original are found maledictions identical with or similar to those which were later directed at Spinoza: "We excommunicate and expel, separate, destroy, and curse . . ."; "cursing him . . . with the excommunication with which Joshua excommunicated Jericho, with the curse with which Elijah cursed the boys . . . with all the oaths and curses written in the book of the law"; "God will blot out his name from under heaven, and God will separate him unto evil from all the tribes of Israel according to the curses written in the book of the law"; and, echoing (like Spinoza's *cherem*) the famous phrases from Deuteronomy 4:7: "cursed be he when he comes in; cursed be he when he goes out . . . cursed be he when he lies down; cursed be he when he rises up." The words of Deuteronomy 4:4 come toward the end of both texts: "You that did cleave to the Lord your God are alive every one of you this day." The document that Mortera brought back from Venice must have been the model to which the Amsterdam Sephardim turned when the case that called for a ban was a particularly serious one. The same text was used by the congregation again in 1712, when David Mendes Henriques and Aaron and Isaac Dias da Fonseca were excommunicated because they were believed to be "following the sect of the Karaites" and thus denying the validity of the Oral Law.[37]

The obvious question is, why was Spinoza excommunicated with such extreme prejudice? Neither his *cherem* nor any document from the period tells us exactly what his "evil opinions and acts [*más opinioins e obras*]" were supposed to have been, nor what "abominable heresies [*horrendas heregias*]" or "monstrous deeds [*ynormes obras*]" he is alleged to have taught and practiced. He was only twenty-three years old at the time and had not yet published anything. Nor, as far as we know, had he even composed any treatise. Spinoza never referred to this period of his life in his extant letters, and thus did not himself offer his correspondents (or us) any clues about why he was expelled. Turning away from his Jewish studies – and perhaps the Keter Torah yeshiva – to seek a philosophical and scientific education elsewhere might have incited his "teachers" within the Jewish community, particularly Mortera. And the rabbis would surely not have been happy with his attending lessons at Van den Enden's, if indeed he was doing so at this time. Moreover, if after the end of the period of mourning for his father he did begin to drift from regular attendance at synagogue and proper observance of Jewish law (perhaps with regard to respect for the Sabbath or compliance with the dietary laws), then the *parnassim* might have resorted to the threat of a *cherem* to bring him back into the fold. But none of this is sufficient to explain the vehemence of his excommunication.

Spinoza would not have been alone in his lax conformity to orthodox behavior. There must have been numerous individuals in the community

who were somewhat less than zealous in their performance of their religious obligations. When Abraham Mendez was in London, he did not join
a *minyan* there and pray on a regular basis. His punishment, in 1656, was
that he could not be called to the Torah for two years. Another man was
threatened with excommunication for failing to circumcise his sons. As
Kaplan has noted, "acts of that sort were typical of daily life in the community."[38] It thus does not seem likely that the origins of the impassioned
expulsion of Spinoza lie simply in his departure from the behavioral norms
of Judaism. Nor would he have been alone in frequenting gentile establishments or maintaining educational and intellectual connections with
non-Jews. These Portuguese Jewish merchants were in constant commercial and social contact with their Dutch neighbors and business associates.
They were known to visit the city's cafés and eating establishments, where
neither the wine nor the food were likely to be kosher. And Menasseh's extensive intellectual network in the gentile world, while an object of concern and even disdain to the other rabbis, was never itself the occasion for
a threat of punishment. The problem cannot have been Spinoza's pursuit
of secular learning per se. Amsterdam's Portuguese Jews were not obscu-
rantists inhabiting a cultural and intellectual ghetto. The rabbis were all
well-read in the pagan classics of Greece and Rome, as well as in the modern classics of Holland, France, Italy, and Spain. Like many members of
the community, they were interested in contemporary European learning.
Even the kabbalistic Aboab owned works by such down-to-earth thinkers
as Machiavelli, Montaigne, and Hobbes.[39]

The answer, then, must lie rather in Spinoza's "heresies" and "evil opinions."[40] Evidence that this is so is found in a report that an Augustinian
monk, Tomas Solano y Robles, made to the Inquisition in 1659 when he
returned to Madrid after some traveling that had taken him to Amsterdam
in late 1658. The Spanish Inquisitors were no doubt interested in what was
going on among the former marranos in northern Europe who had once
been within its domain and who still had connections with conversos back
home. Tomas told them that in Amsterdam he met Spinoza and Prado,
who were apparently keeping each other company after their respective excommunications. He claimed that both men told him they had been observant of Jewish law but "changed their mind," and that they said that
they were expelled from the synagogue because of their views on God, the
soul, and the law. They had, in the eyes of the congregation, "reached the
point of atheism."[41]

Charges of "atheism" are notoriously ambiguous in early modern Europe and rarely provide a clue as to what exactly the subject of the accusation actually believed or said. But if we take as our guide Spinoza's written works, most of which were not published until after his death, it is not very difficult to imagine the kinds of things he must have been thinking – and probably saying – around late 1655 and early 1656, particularly with the help of Brother Tomas's report, as well as the report made to the Inquisition on the following day by Captain Miguel Perez de Maltranilla, another recent visitor to Amsterdam. For all of Spinoza's writings, both those he completed and those left unfinished (and including the later treatises), contain ideas on whose systematic elaboration he was working continuously from the late 1650s onward.

In both the *Ethics*, Spinoza's philosophical masterpiece begun in the early 1660s, and the *Short Treatise on God, Man and His Well-Being*, a somewhat earlier work (possibly from as early as 1660, only four years after the excommunication!) that contains many of the thoughts of the *Ethics* practically fully expressed or in embryonic form, Spinoza basically denies that the human soul is immortal in the sense of enjoying a life after death. Although he is willing to grant that the mind (or part of it) is eternal and persists in God even after the death of the body, he believes that the personal soul perishes with the body.[42] Thus, there is nothing to hope for or fear in terms of eternal reward or punishment. In fact, he suggests, hope and fear are merely the emotions that religious leaders manipulate in order to keep their flocks in a state of worshipful submission. The notion of God acting as a free judge who dispenses reward and punishment is based on an absurd anthropomorphizing. "They maintained that the Gods direct all things for the use of men in order to bind men to them and be held by men in the highest honor. So it has happened that each of them has thought up from his own temperament different ways of worshipping God."[43] Superstition, ignorance, and prejudice are thus at the basis of organized religion. In truth, he insists, God is simply the infinite substance and, as such, is identical with Nature.[44] Everything else follows from God's nature with an absolute necessity. Spinoza also denies that human beings are free in any significant sense, or that they can do anything "of themselves" that would contribute to their salvation and well-being.[45]

One of the primary lessons of the later *Theological-Political Treatise* is that the Pentateuch, the first five books of the Hebrew Bible, was not in fact written by Moses, nor are its precepts literally of divine origin. Rather, while there is indeed a "divine message" conveyed by its moral teaching, the Bible was the work of a number of later authors and editors, and the text we have is the result of a natural process of historical transmission. Spinoza also maintains that if the Jewish people are "elected" in any meaningful sense, it is only a matter of their having been granted a "temporal physical happiness" and autonomous government. With God's help, they were able to preserve themselves for an extended period of time as a nation, as a social unit under certain laws. The notion of the Jews as a "chosen people" has no metaphysical or moral significance; and such an election is not necessarily something unique to them. The Jews are neither a morally superior nation nor a people surpassing all others in wisdom.

> We conclude, therefore (inasmuch as God is to all men equally gracious, and the Hebrews were only chosen by Him in respect to their social organization and government), that the individual Jew, taken apart from his social organization and government, possessed no gift of God above other men, and that there was no difference between Jew and Gentile. . . . At the present time, therefore, there is absolutely nothing which the Jews can arrogate to themselves beyond other people.[46]

He adds that if the "foundations" of the Jewish religion have not "emasculated the minds [of the Jews]" too much, they may someday "raise up their empire again."[47]

These are not sentiments likely to endear one to the rabbis of a Jewish community in the seventeenth century. And there are persuasive grounds for thinking that some of these opinions, which Spinoza would begin to commit to writing by 1660 at the latest, were already fairly well-developed by 1656. Several sources claim that immediately after his expulsion from the synagogue Spinoza composed an *Apologia*, or "justification," for his "departure" from the Jewish religion.[48] Allegedly written in Spanish (according to Bayle), the legendary manuscript, which was supposed to have borne the title *Apologia para justificarse de su abdicacion de la sinagoga*, was never printed and has never been discovered. If such a composition did exist, it was most likely not something he intended actually to send to the *parnassim* or the rabbis of the congregation; there is no reason to think that Spinoza made or even contemplated any attempt formally to address those who excommunicated him.[49] In this first written expression of his views was reportedly to be found much of the material that later appeared in the *Theological-Political Treatise*, including, presumably, the denial of the divine origin of the Torah and the claims regarding "the election of the Hebrew people." Salomon van Til, a professor of theology at Utrecht, one of Bayle's sources and our witness on this matter, wrote in 1684 that

this enemy of religion [Spinoza] was the first who had the audacity to undermine the authority of the books of the Old and New Testament, and he tried to show to the world how these writings had been transformed and modified many times by the work of men and how they had been elevated to the authority of divine writings. He exposed these ideas in detail in a dissertation against the Old Testament written in Spanish, under the title "Justification for my departure from Judaism." But, on the advice of his friends, he withheld the writing and tried to insert these things more skillfully and more economically in another work that he published in 1670 under the title *Tractatus theologico-politicus*.[50]

In fact, what Van Til, Bayle, and others are referring to could have been an early draft of (or notes for) those parts of the *Theological-Political Treatise* that deal with the Bible. It is possible that Spinoza was working on that treatise in some form or another as early as the late 1650s. This is, in fact, suggested by a letter from the Rotterdam regent Adriaen Paets to Arnold Poelenberg, a professor at the Remonstrant seminary in Amsterdam. Paets was a cultured man with Arminian sympathies and was known to be a supporter of religious toleration. In his letter, dated March 30, 1660, he notes that he has seen a certain booklet (*libellum*),

a theological-political treatise [*tractatum theologico-politicum*], by an author certainly not wholly unknown to you, but whose name for now should be kept quiet. [The treatise] contains an argument of the greatest utility for these times, most of which will not be found anywhere else. Above all, the author subtly and accurately questions the distinction between constitutional and natural laws. I foresee that there will be many individuals, principally theologians, who, swayed by their emotions and obnoxious prejudices . . . will calumniate greatly against a book they do not understand.[51]

If Paets is indeed talking about an early version of Spinoza's *Theological-Political Treatise*, then he was prescient about the eventual public reaction to the work. His description of the content of the manuscript captures some, at least, of the political doctrines of Spinoza's treatise; and there was apparently no other work published in the Netherlands in the seventeenth century bearing a title containing the phrase *theologico-politicus*.[52] As the political ideas in Spinoza's work are so closely related to his theological conclusions, any draft of the *Treatise* would have included, even if only in rudimentary form, the major elements of his Bible criticism and critique of organized religion. Although the absence in Paets's letter of any mention of Spinoza's unmistakably bold pronouncements on the Bible is noteworthy, he and Van Til may still be referring to the same work (or different parts thereof).[53]

Spinoza must have begun forming his views on the origins of the Torah early on, certainly by the end of his studies – formal and informal – within the Jewish community. His having reached those conclusions about the status of the Pentateuch would in fact help to explain his disillusionment with the Jewish religion. His familiarity with the Bible commentary of the medieval Jewish philosopher Ibn Ezra, who argued that Moses could not have written all of the books of the Bible traditionally ascribed to him, probably stems from before his excommunication. Around this time he might also have read Isaac La Peyrère's work on the pre-Adamites, which was published while La Peyrère, a friend of Menasseh's, was in Amsterdam in 1655. La Peyrère argues, among other things, that the Bible we possess is actually a compilation from several sources. All of this points to the plausibility of Spinoza's denying the divine origin and Mosaic authorship of the Torah already around the time of his *cherem*. Indeed, he himself insists, at the heart of his discussion of the Bible in the *Theological-Political Treatise*, that "I set down nothing here which I have not long reflected upon."[54]

There are, in addition to rumors of long-lost treatises, more tangible grounds for believing that the ideas of Spinoza's written works – particularly regarding God, the soul, and the Torah – were in his head (and possibly on his tongue) as early as the mid-1650s. First there is the testimony of an old man who claimed to have known Spinoza personally. When the German traveler Gottlieb Stolle talked with him in 1704, he claimed that the reason Spinoza was excommunicated was because he was claiming that "the Books of Moses were man-made [*ein Menschlich Buch*], and thus not written by Moses."[55] Then there is the story of Spinoza's "interrogation" by fellow students in the community. In Lucas's chronology of the events leading up to the *cherem*, there was much talk in the congregation about Spinoza's opinions; people, especially the rabbis, were curious about what the young man was thinking. As Lucas tells it – and this anecdote is not confirmed by any other source – "among those most eager to associate with him there were two young men who, professing to be his most intimate friends, begged him to tell them his real views. They promised him that whatever his opinions were, he had nothing to fear on their part, for their curiosity had no other end than to clear up their own doubts."[56] They suggested that if one read Moses and the prophets closely, then one would be led to the conclusion that the soul is not immortal and that God is material. "How does it appear to you?" they asked Spinoza. "Does God have a body? Is the soul immortal?" After some hesitation, Spinoza took the bait.

I confess, said [Spinoza], that since nothing is to be found in the Bible about the non-material or incorporeal, there is nothing objectionable in believing that God is a body. All the more so since, as the Prophet says, God is great, and it is impossible to comprehend greatness without extension and, therefore, without body. As for spirits, it is certain that Scripture does not say that these are real and permanent substances, but mere phantoms, called angels because God makes use of them to declare his will; they are of such kind that the angels and all other kinds of spirits are invisible only because their matter is very fine and diaphanous, so that it can only be seen as one sees phantoms in a mirror, in a dream, or in the night.

As for the human soul, "whenever Scripture speaks of it, the word 'soul' is used simply to express life, or anything that is living. It would be useless to search for any passage in support of its immortality. As for the contrary view, it may be seen in a hundred places, and nothing is so easy as to prove it."

Spinoza did not trust the motives behind his "friends' " curiosity – with good reason – and he broke off the conversation as soon as he had the opportunity. At first his interlocuters thought he was just teasing them or trying merely to shock them by expressing scandalous ideas. But when they saw that he was serious, they started talking about Spinoza to others. "They said that the people deceived themselves in believing that this young man might become one of the pillars of the synagogue; that it seemed more likely that he would be its destroyer, as he had nothing but hatred and contempt for the Law of Moses." Lucas relates that when Spinoza was called before his judges, these same individuals bore witness against him, alleging that he "scoffed at the Jews as 'superstitious people born and bred in ignorance, who do not know what God is, and who nevertheless have the audacity to speak of themselves as His People, to the disparagement of other nations."[57]

Finally, there are the more credible reports of Brother Tomas and Captain Maltranilla. According to their testimony before the Inquisition, both Spinoza and Prado were claiming in 1658 that the soul was not immortal, that the Law was "not true [*no hera verdadera*]," and that there was no God except in a "philosophical" sense. In his deposition, Tomas says that he knew both Dr. Prado, a physician, whose first name was Juan but whose Jewish name he did not know, who had studied at Alcala, and a certain de Espinosa, who he thinks was a native of one of the villages of Holland, for he had studied at Leiden and was a good philosopher. These two persons had professed the Law of Moses, and the synagogue had expelled and isolated them because they had reached the point of atheism. And they themselves told the witness that they had been circumcised and that they had observed the law of the Jews, and that they had changed their mind because it seemed to them that the said law was not true and that souls died with their bodies and that there is no God except philosophically. And that is why they were expelled from the synagogue; and, while they regretted the absence of the charity that they used to receive from the synagogue and the communication with other Jews, they were happy to be atheists, since they thought that God exists only philosophically . . . and that souls died with their bodies and that thus they had no need for faith.[58]

If Spinoza was saying these things about God, the soul, and the Law in 1658 – and to strangers, no less! – then the likelihood of his having been saying them two years earlier is quite strong, particularly as that would help to account for the seriousness with which the leaders of the congregation viewed his "heresies" and "evil opinions."

The "truth" of the Torah and the existence of a God who is a free creator, giver of laws, and judge – and not just an "infinite substance" – are two central and (according to Maimonides) indispensable tenets of the Jewish religion. They are found among the thirteen articles of faith that Maimonides insists are required beliefs for any Jew. The first fundamental principle, he insists, is the existence of God the creator; and the fifth principle stipulates that God is separate from all natural processes, and that only he is a totally free agent. The eighth principle states that the Torah came from God.[59] In the *Mishneh Torah* he insists that "he who says that the Torah is not of divine origin" is to be "separated and destroyed."[60] The Amsterdam *chachamim*, and especially Mortera and Menasseh, held Maimonides in the highest regard; and the chief rabbi would certainly have consulted the great twelfth-century *chacham* in matters of *halacha*.[61]

Of equal importance, and perhaps greater practical relevance, is the fact that the immortality of the soul and the divine origin of the Torah were issues of immediate concern to the rabbis of the Talmud Torah congregation. It was certainly his denial of the immortality of the soul and of the validity of the Oral Law, among other things, that led to their harsh reaction against Uriel da Costa. Furthermore, when Mortera was arguing, in his debate with Aboab in the mid-1630s, for the eternal punishment of the souls of unrepentent sinners, he was revealing his deep commitment to a strong doctrine of immortality. For such punishment would, of course, require the eternal existence of the soul after the death of the body. In fact, Mortera had composed a long work defending the immortality of the soul some ten years earlier.[62] And in 1652, Menasseh published his own *Nishmat Chaim*, in which he insists that "the belief in the immortality of the soul" is "the foundation and essential principle" of the Jewish faith.[63]

As for the "truth" of the Law, if Spinoza had been expressing his considered views on this question in 1656, he would have brought down upon himself the full wrath of Mortera, whose magnum opus was a long defense of the divine origin and *verdade* of the Torah. Mortera did not start writing his *Treatise on the Truth of the Law of Moses* until 1659, but there is no question that the issues he addresses in that work (including the "proof" of the divinity of the Mosaic Law) had been occupying his mind for some time. The topic recurs several times in his sermons.[64]

Thus, if in 1655–6 Spinoza was denying the immortality of the soul (along with the related doctrines of eternal reward and punishment) and the divine origin of the Torah – and a good deal of evidence suggests that he was – he could not have picked a more dangerous set of topics. He also could not have been unaware of the risks. With his learning and experience, it is impossible that he did not know what the reaction to his opinions would be among the *chachamim*. Lucas claims, in another unverifiable and unlikely but nonetheless impressive story, that when Mortera heard about the reports from the young men who had questioned Spinoza on his views, he was initially incredulous and encouraged the young men to continue their interrogation, whereupon they would see that they were mistaken. But when he heard that Spinoza had been hauled before the Beth Din, he ran to the synagogue, fearing for "the peril in which his disciple was placed." He quickly discovered that the rumors were indeed true.

He demanded of him whether he was mindful of the good example he had set him? Whether his rebellion was the fruit of the care that he had taken with his education? And whether he feared falling into the hands of the living God? [He said] that the scandal was great, but that there was still time for repentence.[65]

There is some debate over the nature and intimacy of Mortera's relationship with Spinoza and his role in the disciplinary process. It would certainly add a sentimental element to the unfolding drama if there had been

such an emotional response by the head rabbi – a formidable figure even
at the best of times – to the fate of his favorite pupil. One can imagine
Mortera's feelings of sadness at the young man's separation from Judaism
mixed with an angry sense of betrayal over the fact that his efforts to educate and improve him should have been so repudiated. Unfortunately, it
is impossible to say with any certainty how active a role Mortera took in
the excommunication of Spinoza or what his personal feelings about Spinoza's apostasy were. Perhaps it was, after all, at his request that the extraordinarily harsh *cherem* text that he himself had brought back from Venice
almost forty years earlier should be dusted off and used against Spinoza
(but, interestingly, not against Prado, who was banned shortly after Spinoza and, it seems, for practically the same offenses).

೩

There is a game that Spinoza scholars play in which they speculate on the
identity of the individuals responsible for Spinoza's "heretical" ideas on
religion, God, the soul, politics, and Scripture. It has become, in essence,
a search for Spinoza's "corruptors" and, by extension, for the remote causes
of his forced departure from the Jewish community. According to some,
Spinoza's unorthodox thought was molded early by various influences
from outside the Sephardic congregation; others insist that we need look
no further than certain heterodox tendencies within the Amsterdam Jewish community itself. In a sense, the whole quest is misguided, not just because we can never know the answer for sure, but, more important, because
any adequate investigation must take into account *all* of these various contexts, as well as Spinoza's own autodidactic erudition and undeniable originality. By his early twenties, Spinoza was already living within a relatively
complex web of intellectual and spiritual influences, many of them mutually reinforcing. Before turning seriously to the study of gentile philosophers, he was probably reading works such as Maimonides' *Guide for the
Perplexed;* the *Dialogues on Love,* by the sixteenth-century Platonist Judah
Abrabanel (Leone Ebreo), in which one finds many elements that would
later appear in Spinoza's writings;[66] and Joseph Salomon Delmedigo's
Sefir Elim (Book of the gods), a treatise on Galileo's science that was published by Menasseh.[67] And whatever opinions regarding the nature of the
human soul or the status of Scripture or the relationship between God and
creation Spinoza might have acquired from his reading of Jewish philosophical texts and from unorthodox acquaintances in the Jewish commu-

nity could have supported (and, in turn, been supported by) what he would have heard about "true" religion and morality from the various dissenting Christians with whom he was in contact from 1654 onward.

Although Van den Enden certainly played some role in Spinoza's philosophical and political education, Spinoza's developing views on religion and Scripture probably drew greater sustenance from within another setting.[68] Among Spinoza's closest friends during this period, including his mercantile acquaintances from the Amsterdam Exchange, were a number of individuals who regularly attended the Collegiant gatherings that had been meeting in Amsterdam since around 1646. These Collegiants – so called because their biweekly Sunday reunions were named "colleges" – were disaffected Mennonites, Remonstrants, and members of other dissenting Reformed sects who sought a less dogmatic and nonhierarchical form of worship. Like the Quakers, whose "meetings" their gatherings resembled in their egalitarian and nonauthoritarian structure, the Collegiants shunned any official theology and refused to be led by any preachers. Any adult who felt so moved could, at their worship/study sessions, take his turn at elaborating on the meaning of Scripture.

The first Collegiant community appeared in 1619 at Warmond, partly in response to the reactionary resolutions of the Synod of Dort, which had expelled the Remonstrants from the Reformed Church. The group soon moved its primary base of operations to Rijnsburg, just a few miles outside Leiden. By the 1640s, there were "colleges" in several cities around the Netherlands, including Groningen, Rotterdam, and, above all, Amsterdam. The Amsterdam group, trying to be circumspect, usually met in the homes of its members, although they were also known to gather at Jan Rieuwertsz's bookshop, "Book of Martyrs," or (when they were trying to gain some respite from their harassment by Calvinist preachers) in the sacristy of the Anabaptist community. Together they would pray, read and interpret Scripture, and engage in the free discussion of their faith. They believed that both the official Reformed Church and the organized dissenting Reformed churches were no better than the Catholic Church when it came to dogmatic sectarianism. True Christianity, they asserted, was non-confessional. It consisted in an evangelical love for one's fellow human beings and for God and an obedience to the original words of Jesus Christ, unmediated by any theological commentary. Beyond the few simple and general truths contained in Jesus' teachings, each individual had the right to believe what he or she wanted and no right to harass others for what they believed. Salvation was attained not through any superstitious rites or signs, nor by belonging to any organized cult, but only by a heartfelt inner faith. The Collegiants had no use for pastors; anyone who felt inspired to speak at a meeting could do so. They rejected any doctrines of predestination as incompatible with Christian liberty, and (like the Anabaptists, who comprised many of the Collegiants' members) they recommended baptism for freely consenting adults only. Anticlerical to the core, the Collegiants sought to liberate Christianity from the constrictions imposed upon worship and deed by institutionalized religions. Moral action was, for these pacifistic "Christians without a Church" (to use Kolakowski's celebrated phrase), more important than any set of dogmas. True religious feeling and the proper behavior that accompanied it could flourish only where sentiment, thought, and speech were unconstrained by any ecclesiastical power.[69]

Among the founders of the Amsterdam Collegiants was Adam Boreel (1603–65), a learned and committed partisan of liberty and equality for all who wished to express their faith in a sincere and unfettered manner. For Boreel, the only recognized authority in spiritual matters was the direct word of the Bible, open to all to read and interpret (and debate) for themselves. The message of Scripture was simple and neutral with respect to the particular forms that everyday worship might take. Boreel was a close friend of Menasseh ben Israel – who could have introduced him to Spinoza, with whom he would have been able to converse in Portuguese or Spanish[70] – and was ecumenical in his attempts to encourage Jews, Lutherans, and Quakers to join the movement.[71]

It did not take long for the orthodox Calvinists to become suspicious of the Collegiants. They were accused – perhaps, in some cases, correctly – of being antitrinitarian. The Reformed clergy came down hard on them, just as they had on the Remonstrants decades earlier, particularly as they perceived the Collegiant meetings as redoubts of Socinianism, perhaps the most reviled and persecuted of antitrinitarian doctrines. In addition to denying God's tripartite nature as Father, Son, and Holy Ghost, the followers of the sixteenth-century Italian theologian Fausto Sozzini rejected both the divinity of Christ and the doctrine of original sin, all regarded by the leaders of the Reformed Church as the fundamentals of Christianity. In 1653, in the midst of an anti-Socinian campaign, the Calvinist *predikanten* succeeded in persuading the States of Holland and West Friesland to issue an edict – aimed primarily at the Collegiants – forbidding antitrinitarian (and especially Socinian) "conventicles" from meeting.[72] The members of Boreel's group tried to keep a low profile and hoped to benefit from the generally tolerant attitude of the Amsterdam regents. But the persecution of Collegiants continued in some provinces well into the next century.

It is by no means implausible that Spinoza was attending Collegiant gatherings before his expulsion from the Jewish community, perhaps as early as late 1654. At the very least, he was, before the break, well acquainted with a good number of Collegiants, some of whom may have encouraged him to join them for a meeting or two.[73] Many of Spinoza's most intimate and lasting friendships commenced around this time and involved people such as Simon Joosten de Vries, Pieter Balling, and the Mennonites Jarig Jellesz and Jan Rieuwertsz – all of whom were members of Boreel's Amsterdam "college." With his knowledge of Hebrew and the Torah, Spinoza would no doubt have been of great use to these inveterate readers of Scripture; conversely, Spinoza would have found much of interest in the moral and religious opinions of Boreel and his colleagues. Liberal in their politics, tolerant in their religion, nondoctrinaire in their interpretation of Scripture, and generally anticlerical, the Collegiants would have held a great attraction for Spinoza.[74]

Despite his extracurricular interests, Spinoza was, before July 1656, still technically (and, to all appearances, actively) a member of the Talmud Torah congregation. And his ideas, while perhaps nourished by his Collegiant contacts, seem also to have found a sympathetic corner in the Vlooienburg district itself, where unorthodoxy, skepticism, and even outright unbelief were not uncommon. The rabbis of the *kahal kodesh* were doing their best to maintain religious cohesion and doctrinal propriety among a population of Jews whose ranks were still being augmented by converso immigration. Ever mindful of the Da Costa tragedy, they were particularly on their guard against heterodox views on the most fundamental principles of the Jewish faith, such as the nature of the soul and the status of the Law. Given the cosmopolitan nature of their young community and the background of many of its members, however, their task was necessarily a difficult one. Not only were former marranos reluctant to give up beliefs and practices that had been in their families for generations, but (like Da Costa) they often found that the Judaism to which they had "returned" was not exactly what they had thought (or hoped) it would be.

Among the recent returnees to Judaism newly settled in Amsterdam was one Juan de Prado.[75] Prado was born into a Judaizing converso family in Andalusia, Spain, in 1612. He studied medicine at the university in Toledo and earned his doctorate in 1638. Already in 1639 he was encouraging other marranos to observe Jewish law, an activity that naturally attracted the attention of the Inquisition. Prado himself was never arrested by the Holy Office, although his wife and other members of his family were detained at one point. Although that did not keep them from remaining in Spain for a number of years, by the early 1650s Prado had decided that living within the domains of the Inquisition was becoming too dangerous. The decisive event was probably when one of his relatives confessed, under torture, that Prado had persuaded him to return to Judaism. Prado secured an appointment as the personal physician of the archbishop of Seville, Domingo Pimental, who was off to Rome to take up his new duties as a member of the College of Cardinals. This allowed him, along with his wife and mother, to leave Spain for good. He did not stay in Rome long, however, and by 1654 Prado was in Hamburg, where he changed his name to 'Daniel' and became an active member of the Sephardic congregation. His sojourn in that city was even shorter, and sometime in 1655 he arrived in Amsterdam, joined the Talmud Torah congregation, and registered to practice medicine with the city's *collegium medicum*. His medical practice could not have been very successful, for he was never assessed a *finta* by the community and was often supported by the congregation's charities.[76]

Although Prado was, while in Spain, an active proselytizer for Judaism, and later (in Hamburg and initially in Amsterdam) an outwardly observant Jew himself, there is some question about the orthodoxy and even the consistency of his own religious views and practices. He was reportedly expressing deistic opinions to friends around 1643, claiming that all religions were capable of delivering salvation to their adherents and providing them with an awareness of God, and that Judaism was no more privileged in this regard than Christianity or Islam.[77] In Amsterdam, he joined Mortera's yeshiva, Keter Torah, where, the scholar I. S. Revah believes, he first met Spinoza, but it was not long before he began to raise philosophical objections to Jewish principles. According to Isaac Orobio de Castro, a prominent member of the Amsterdam congregation who had known Prado in Spain and who, after Prado's expulsion from the community, developed an interest in the evolution of his religious views and engaged in a polemical correspondence with him, Prado fell into the abyss of unbelief soon after his open return to Judaism.[78] His "evil opinions" were serious enough to earn him an admonition (and possibly an excommunication, or at least the threat thereof) from the *ma'amad,* who ordered him to retract his opinions and make amends. Consequently, in the summer of 1656, around the same time as Spinoza's *cherem,* Daniel de Prado mounted the *theba* in the synagogue and read the following document:

Having had evil opinions and having shown little zeal in the service of God and the Holy Law, I mount this platform at the order of the *Senhores* of the *ma'amad* and, on my own free will, I confess, before blessed God and the Holy Law, before all of this holy community, that I have sinned and erred, in words as well as in action, against blessed God and his Holy Law and causing scandal in this holy community. I strongly repent for this and I humbly beg pardon to God and to the Holy Law, and to all of this community for the scandal I have caused it. I willingly undertake to execute the penance prescribed by the rabbis, and I promise never again to revert to such sinful deeds. I pray you to ask the Lord of the universe to pardon my sins and to have pity upon me. May there be peace upon Israel.[79]

It seems that Prado's retraction was less than sincere, however, and that he continued in his deviant ways. The *ma'amad* commissioned an inquiry into his behavior and that of Daniel Ribera, a friend of Prado's who had been teaching nonreligious material in a special school that the congregation set up for poor students. Several of the school's pupils denounced Prado and Ribera for their "scandalous actions," such as mocking Jews on their way to synagogue and showing disrespect for the *ma'amad.* "It seems," Prado allegedly said, "that these little Jews want to establish an Inquisition in Amsterdam." They also, according to the students' depositions, planned to compose a number of "scandalous and immoral" letters and leave copies at Mortera's house and in his yeshiva. Along with these provocations, Prado and Ribera, who came from an Old Christian family (his original name was José Carreras y Coligo) but had converted to Judaism in 1653, reportedly made various heretical remarks to the students. Among other things, one young man claimed that Prado had told him it was not forbidden to comb hair or carry money on Shabbat. The members of the *ma'amad,* along with Rabbis Mortera and Aboab, were persuaded by the testimony that something had to be done. Ribera seems to have left Amsterdam while the inquiry was in progress (he had expressed to one of the students a wish to join his brother in Brussels, although, as Revah discovered, he actually turned up in England as a member of the Anglican Church[80]), but Prado was still around. On February 4, 1658, a *cherem* – possibly his second – was pronounced upon him.

Since Daniel de Prado has been convicted by various witnesses before the *Senhores* of the *ma'amad* of having reverted very scandalously, of having desired anew to seduce different people with his detestable opinions against our Holy Law, the *Senhores* of the *ma'amad*, with the advice of the rabbis, have decided unanimously that the said Daniel de Prado should be excommunicated and separated from the nation. By the threat of the same excommunication, they order that no member of this Holy Community should communicate with him, neither verbally nor in writing, neither in this city nor outside it, with the exception of the members of his family. May God spare his people from evil, and peace be upon Israel.[81]

Prado was distraught. Unlike Spinoza, he had no desire to leave the community. Also unlike Spinoza, he was a relative newcomer to the Netherlands, had no extensive family and business connections, and probably knew very little Dutch. More important, he was dependent on the congregation's financial support. Brother Tomas, the Augustinian monk who reported to the Inquisition, noted that Prado told him how much he "regretted the loss of the charity that [he] had been receiving from the synagogue."[82] The *ma'amad*, sensitive to the difficulties of his situation and the needs of his family, offered to help them relocate overseas "to some region where Judaism is practiced." Prado declined their offer, instead protesting his innocence and requesting that the excommunication be removed. His son, David, wrote a letter to the community's leaders in defense of his father's orthodox faith and against the unfairness of the proceedings against him. He particularly resented the way Prado had been treated by Rabbi Mortera, who opted to insult and attack rather than teach and reform.[83] Prado himself appealed to the *ma'amad* of the Hamburg Sephardic community to which he had once belonged to intercede on his behalf, but the German congregation refused to do so. Sometime after 1659, Prado left Amsterdam. He eventually settled in Antwerp, outside the United Provinces, where there was a Portuguese Jewish community.

In the course of his defense, Prado admitted that, although he was not accused of any explicit practical transgressions of Jewish law (which is false, as Ribera's students claimed that both men were eating *treyf* food and purchasing meat, cakes, and cheese from gentile merchants, as well as violating the restrictions on various activities during the Sabbath), he may have "unwittingly" propounded heretical opinions.[84] We can get a sense of what those opinions were from the Inquisitional testimony of Brother Tomas and Captain Maltranilla. According to the monk – who describes Prado as "large and thin, with a big nose, brownish complexion, black hair and black eyes" – he (like Spinoza, Tomas alleges in his statement) was denying in 1658 the "truth of the Law of Moses," asserting that God exists "only philosophically" and claiming that the soul, rather than being immortal, died with the body.[85] The information gathered from Ribera's students by the congregation's investigators corroborates that these were just the kinds of things that the two men were professing several years earlier. Prado, they charged, denied both the immortality of the soul and the resurrection of the body, as well as the divine origin of the Torah. Along with Ribera, he insisted that the Mosaic law is no different from the sets of laws observed by other religions, all of which are for children and other individuals who have not reached the proper stage of intellect and understanding. For free and responsible adults, on the other hand, the only authority to be followed is reason itself. From Orobio de Castro's attacks on Prado's views, too, as well as from other documents, it is evident that Prado was denying that either the written or the oral law had its source in a revelation from God and asserting that Scripture, such as it exists, is merely a compilation of human writings. He mocked the pretension of the Jews to be God's "elected people" and derided the Torah as a useless set of anthropomorphisms. Furthermore, Prado allegedly argued that there is no demonstration that the world had a beginning in time, thus rejecting the biblical account of creation (although, in the defense he composed in response to his judges, he denied ever having held such a view). Finally, Orobio's counteroffensive indicates that Prado asserted that God was neither the creator nor the governor nor the judge of the universe – in a word, as Brother Tomas charged, that God existed "only philosophically."[86]

There is, then, a remarkable convergence between the views Prado is said to have propounded around 1655–7 and those which Spinoza almost certainly held at the same time. That there was a close intellectual and even personal relationship between the two apostates – a relationship that had its roots in their mutual connections to Mortera's yeshiva – is suggested by the poet Daniel de Barrios. Writing in 1683, he picturesquely but unmistakably couples Spinoza and Prado:

The Crown of the Law [Mortera's Keter Torah], ever since the year of its joyous foundation, never ceased burning in the academic bush, thanks to the doctrinal leaves written by the most wise Saul Levi Mortera, lending his intellect to the counsel of Wisdom and his pen to the hand of Speculation, in the defense of religion and against atheism. *Thorns* [in Spanish, *Espinos*] are they that, in the *Fields* [*Prados*] of impiety, aim to shine with the fire that consumes them, and the zeal of

Mortera is a flame that burns in the bush of Religion, never to be extinguished. (emphases in original)[87]

Barrios is only echoing the phrases penned by Abraham Peyrera seventeen years before: "What is this world except barren ground, a field full of thistles and thorns [*espinos*], a green meadow [*prado*] full of venomous serpents."[88]

When the testimonies of Brother Tomas and Captain Maltranilla reveal, in less metaphorical terms, that Spinoza and Prado, in their ostracism from the Jewish community, were keeping each other company in Amsterdam – Maltranilla asserted that they and others were meeting regularly at the home of Joseph Guerra, a nobleman from the Canary Islands – any reasonable doubt that Spinoza and Prado were intimately acquainted with each other even before July of 1656, while both were still members of the Talmud Torah congregation, is dispelled. To Orobio de Castro (who did not arrive in Amsterdam until 1662, well after all these events had transpired), Peyrera, Barrios, and other members of the community, there was never any question that the apostasies of Spinoza and Prado were linked. Prado's contrite retraction and apology is entered into the community's record books on the page just before the record of Spinoza's *cherem*, possibly an indication that the two men were excommunicated by the *ma'amad* at the same time (with only Prado asking for forgiveness). One recent historian goes so far as to say that for the Portuguese Jews of Amsterdam in the seventeenth century, in fact, there was never any "Spinoza" affair – only a "Spinoza/Prado" affair.[89]

Spinoza's heretical ideas, then, may very well have found a collegial reception and even encouragement – if not their source – among some former marranos of dubious orthodoxy in Amsterdam's Portuguese Jewish quarter.[90] The Collegiants, whose views on religion and morality had much in common with Spinoza's, did not question the immortality of the soul or assert that God exists "merely philosophically."[91] Nor, as far as we know, did they deny the divine origin of the Torah. Whether the more worldly Dr. Prado, almost twenty years older than Spinoza, was indeed the young man's "corruptor" it is impossible to say for sure.[92] More likely it was the other way around. Spinoza, with his schooling (aborted as it was), could not have had much to learn from Prado (who knew little or no Hebrew) about interpreting Scripture; and his philosophical education (Jewish and otherwise) up to this point would have provided his inquisitive mind with sufficient food for thought on the nature of the soul and of God.

The Netherlands in the seventeenth century

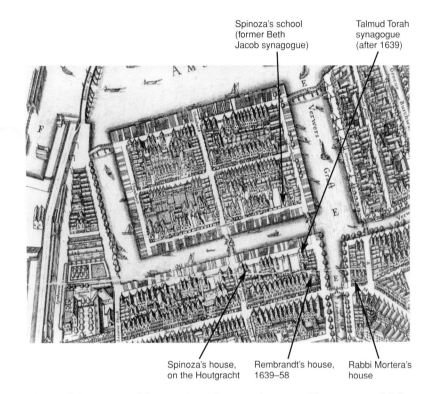

Spinoza's school
(former Beth
Jacob synagogue)

Talmud Torah
synagogue
(after 1639)

Spinoza's house,
on the Houtgracht

Rembrandt's house,
1639–58

Rabbi Mortera's
house

The Jewish quarter of Amsterdam, from a 1625 map (Gemeentearchief Amsterdam)

Rembrandt, *The Jews in the Synagogue* (1648) (Graphic Arts Collection, National Museum of American History, Smithsonian Institution)

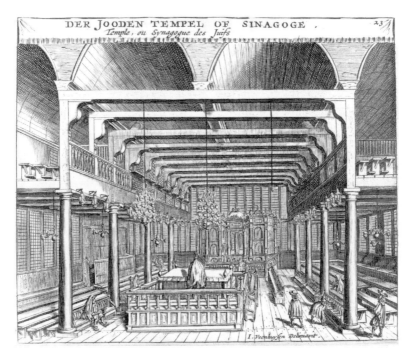

The Amsterdam Portuguese Synagogue (interior), 1639–75 (Library of
the Jewish Theological Seminary of America)

The Amsterdam Portuguese Synagogue (exterior), 1639–75 (Spinoza's synagogue) (Bibliotheca Rosenthaliana, University of Amsterdam)

Rabbi Isaac Aboab (Library of the Jewish Theological Seminary of America)

Rabbi Menasseh ben Israel (Library of the Jewish Theological Seminary of America)

Henry Oldenburg
(The Royal Society)

Christiaan Huygens
(Haags Historisch
Museum, The Hague)

Johann de Witt
(Museum Boijmans
van Beuningen,
Rotterdam)

Gottfried Wilhelm
Leibniz (Niedersach-
sische Landesbiblio-
thek, Hanover)

Politically radical ex-Jesuits, Collegiants with Socinian tendencies, apostate Jews, possibly even Quakers and freethinking libertines – if one must search for the "corruptor" of Spinoza, then, in a sense the real culprit is Amsterdam itself. Heterodox ideas flourished in that comparatively liberal and tolerant city. Writers and publishers, if they were sufficiently circumspect and willing to play by the rules, could disseminate their ideas and products without too much trouble. And religious dissenters of all stripes – even, at certain times, Catholics – if they kept a low profile and did not disturb the peace, could pursue their worship (or nonworship) as they saw fit. The stricter Calvinists were ever vigilant against heretics and nonbelievers, and they frequently attempted to rouse the regents from their nondogmatic slumber. The members of the municipal ruling class, for their part, were reluctant to threaten the relatively peaceful political and social equilibrium (not to mention the cultural vibrancy) that was so crucial to Amsterdam's economic success. Spinoza, venturing far from the Houtgracht in pursuit of business and a knowledge of Latin, clearly took advantage of the intellectual opportunities the city offered him. While there were other Jews in the community who shared his doubts about Jewish law, God's providence, and the immortality of the soul, there is no question that he was also stimulated both by what he read at Van den Enden's school and by what he observed among the Reformed dissenters with whom he was spending time.

&.

There is a broader context for Spinoza's *cherem*, one that takes it beyond being merely a matter of "internal affairs" whereby the Sephardic congregation was punishing one of its members for his doctrinal deviancy and acts of disobedience. Like the other excommunications of the period, Spinoza's ban certainly finds part of its explanation in what Yosef Kaplan has called the "social function" of the *cherem*, its role as a disciplinary tool wielded by the *ma'amad* for maintaining religious orthodoxy and moral conformity within the community. Insofar as Spionza's actions and opinions threatened the *kehillah*'s governors' and rabbis' project of a unified and uniform community, one of whose functions was to educate its members in, and reintegrate new arrivals into, traditional Judaism, then he would suffer their strongest censure. But there is also a political dimension to the case.

There may be a very direct and obvious sense in which this is so. Spinoza's mature, and probably even his early, political views were profoundly

democratic. He was, in his ideas on the state and society, a liberal republican for whom sovereignty lay in the will of the people. He argued strenuously for freedom of thought and speech and for a polity in which the
rights of citizens were protected against any abuses of power. On the other
hand, the leaders of Amsterdam's Portuguese Jews were wealthy merchants
who ran the affairs of the community in an autocratic manner. They had
a substantial economic stake in the Dutch status quo – an oligarchy – and
their own political opinions must have been rather conservative. Some of
them may even have been supporters of the Orangist faction in Dutch politics, the party calling for the return of the quasi-monarchical stadholdership. Spinoza's democratic persuasions, and his contacts with would-be
revolutionaries like Van den Enden and social radicals like the Collegiants
(many of whom were fairly critical of capitalism), would no doubt have
irritated the *parnassim.*[93]

But there is a more interesting and substantial political dimension to
the Spinoza affair. As a population of former refugees – and many of the
congregation's members were only recently arrived from Iberia – the Jews
were conscious of their dependence on the goodwill of their Dutch hosts.
Though life in the Dutch Republic may have superficially resembled the
peaceful landscapes of Ruisdael or the well-ordered social interiors of Vermeer and De Hooch, the Jews were well aware of the political tensions and
theological divisions running barely beneath the surface of Dutch society
in the seventeenth century, and of their potential dangers. Whenever the
less tolerant elements of the Calvinist Church gained the upper hand – as
they did in 1618 and again in the late 1640s – Jews, Catholics, and dissenting Protestants all keenly felt their vulnerability in the face of these
reactionary forces.

When the Jews were officially allowed to settle in Amsterdam in 1619,
the city council expressly ordered them to refrain from making any attacks,
written or verbal, on the Christian religion, and to regulate their conduct
and ensure that the members of the community kept to a strict observance
of Jewish law. This was right after the Synod of Dort, when the strict
Calvinists expelled the Remonstrants and solidified their control over the
Reformed Church. The warning to the Jews was, at least in part, an effort
to make sure that they kept to themselves, at least in religious matters. The
recently resettled Sephardim thus found themselves in a precarious situation. They were refugees living in a society torn by religious division.
They were tolerated and even allowed to practice their religion. But the

city of Amsterdam officially and explicitly told them to keep their house clean, to enforce Jewish orthodoxy, and not to let their affairs stray into the Dutch arena. This must have left the Jews with a deep sense of insecurity and a very strong desire to be careful not to do or permit anything in their community that would attract the attention of the Amsterdam authorities or bring down upon themselves any unfavorable judgments.

Nearly twenty years later, there was still evident among the Sephardim a sensitivity about how they were regarded by the Dutch. In the regulations adopted in 1639 when the three congregations merged, there is a prohibition against public wedding or funeral processions, lest non-Jews be offended by the display and the Jews be blamed for the ensuing disturbance. There is also, in accordance with the city's wishes, a regulation prohibiting Jews from discussing religious matters with Christians and from attempting to convert them to Judaism, for this might "disturb the liberty we enjoy."[94] Even in 1670, over fifty years after being granted the right to live openly as Jews in Amsterdam, they are cautious about maintaining an appearance of rectitude and of being a well-ordered society-within-a-society. On November 16 of that year, Rabbi Aboab submitted to the city of Amsterdam a request from the Portuguese Jews to build a new synagogue – the magnificent one still in use at the end of the Jodenbreestraat. They needed a building that would be large enough to accommodate their expanding population, which at this point had reached over two thousand and five hundred individuals. People, Aboab says in his request, were fighting for seats, and the "unpleasantnesses" were so disturbing services "that we cannot pay attention to praying to our creator."[95] On the very next day, the elders of the community brought another petition to the city magistrates, this time asking them to reauthorize the regulations adopted by the community in 1639. In this second request, they included and explicitly cited the right of the *parnassim* to excommunicate "unruly and rebellious people."[96] This seems a tactful but clear reminder to the Amsterdam regents that the same community which is expanding and wants to build a new synagogue has also vested its leaders with strong disciplinary powers, that they had nothing to worry about with a large and active Jewish community in their midst.

The Jews, then, knew that there were limits to the famed Dutch toleration, and they often looked for ways to reassure their hosts that their community was a controlled and orthodox one. Perhaps their insecurity was a bit exaggerated, their fears slightly out of proportion to any real dangers

to their position. The Amsterdam regents were well aware of the important contribution their Portuguese residents made to the city's economic
life. They were not about to commit, or allow anyone else to commit on
their behalf, the enormous mistake made by the Spanish monarchs in
1492. In the 1650s, in particular, with the inauguration of the period of
"True Freedom" under the new Grand Pensionary, Johan de Witt, the political power of the intolerant elements within the Calvinist Church was
limited. In 1656, the year of Spinoza's *cherem,* the republicans were in firm
control of the city of Amsterdam, much to the consternation of their
Orangist opponents. Still, the Jews were aware that Dutch politics were
subject to sudden and often revolutionary changes, including what the
Dutch call *wetsverzettingen,* the power shifts that occurred under crisis
conditions. They could completely change the makeup of a town's ruling
body and reverse the direction of its policies, as briefly happened in Amsterdam and other towns in 1650. The caution of Amsterdam's Jews – as
well as the lessons of history – would have prevented them from placing
too much confidence in the durability of the current climate of tolerance.
Their use of the ban, in addition to its function in maintaining internal
discipline, was a public act that was meant to communicate to the Dutch
authorities the message that the Jews ran a well-ordered community;[97]
that they – in accordance with the conditions laid down when the city
granted them the right to settle openly – tolerated no breaches in proper
Jewish conduct or doctrine.

Moreover, when the *parnassim* issued their *cherem* against Spinoza, they
were banning someone whose views would be considered heretical not just
by Jews but by any mainstream Christians as well. The immortality of the
soul and a full-bodied conception of divine providence are of as much importance to a Calvinist preacher as to a rabbi. Thus, excommunicating
Spinoza was a way of demonstrating not just that they tolerated no breaches
in Jewish orthodoxy but also that the Jewish community was no haven for
heretics of any stripe. Perhaps the singular animosity of the ban against
Spinoza is a reflection of the *ma'amad*'s concern that the Dutch would
look particularly harshly at a community that harbored deniers, not just
of the principles of the Jewish faith, but also of those of the Christian religion.

The Jewish leaders may also have wanted to make it clear to the Dutch
that the community was no haven for Cartesians either. In the 1640s, open
battles over Descartes's philosophy raged in the Dutch universities. The

conflict eventually spread across intellectual, religious, and political society at large and created schisms not unlike those caused by the Remonstrant controversy.

In 1642, the University of Utrecht, at the instigation of the archconservative theologian (and rector of the university) Gibertus Voetius, condemned the teaching of Descartes's philosophy. The "new science," Voetius argued, threatened to undermine the principles of the Christian religion. He insisted that the Copernican view (which Descartes never explicitly argued for but clearly supported) that the sun, not the earth, is the center of the planetary and stellar orbits was inconsistent with Scripture; that Descartes's methodology led inexorably to radical skepticism and, hence, a loss of faith; that Descartes's metaphysics seemed to be inconsistent with various Christian dogmas; and, above all, that it was incompatible with "the ancient philosophy " that was the standard curriculum in the schools. In 1646, the University of Leiden followed suit, decreeing that only Aristotelian philosophy should be taught to its students. The university's senate forbade its professors in the faculties of philosophy and theology from even mentioning Descartes and his novel ideas in their theses and debates.[98] Other institutions of higher learning soon issued their own prohibitions, culminating in the proclamation of 1656, just before Spinoza's excommunication, by the States of Holland and West Friesland. The provincial council declared that all professors of philosophy, "for the sake of peace and calm," needed to take an oath promising "to cease propounding the philosophical principles drawn from Descartes's philosophy, which today give offense to a number of people."[99]

The attacks on Cartesian thought waxed and waned, depending on time and place. Enforcement of the bans was, at some universities, notoriously lax. Even when they had the support of the university's administration, the prohibitions were of dubious efficacy. Cartesianism slowly infiltrated the university faculties, aided no doubt by the fact that Holland's Grand Pensionary – and the republic's main political leader until 1672 – Johan de Witt, a decent mathematician in his own right, was sympathetic to the principles of the new philosophy. The two universities that initially led the assault on Descartes, Leiden and Utrecht, were known, by the early 1650s, to be well populated with Cartesian professors.

The reason why Cartesianism caused such a reaction and aroused such passions was that, in the eyes of its opponents, it threatened to undermine their entire intellectual and religious edifice. For centuries, philosophy and theology in the schools and university faculties were deeply wedded to the philosophy of Aristotle (at least as this was interpreted by medieval commentators). The new philosophy and science dispensed with many of the concepts and categories of Aristotelian thought. According to the mechanistic philosophy of Galileo and Descartes, the physical world is made up solely of particles of matter in motion. All explanations in science are to refer only to moving material parts (and collections of such parts), whose shape, size, and motions are describable in purely mathematical terms. There are, in bodies, none of the occult powers or spiritual principles or mentalistic tendencies that so populated the scientific worldview of the Aristotelians. There is no room in the material world for the soul-like agents that university professors employed to understand the behavior of ordinary physical objects and that theologians used to explain extraordinary events, such as Eucharistic transubstantiation. This radical division between the realms of matter and mind – called 'dualism' – is the central thesis of Descartes's metaphysics. Some later Cartesians went so far as to suggest that this new world picture, with its strictly mechanistic determinism, required a nonliteral approach to the Bible. Because the miracles described in Scripture were, they argued, incompatible with the universal mathematical laws of nature, passages recounting such events had to be read figuratively. Voetius and his allies also argued that Descartes's "method of doubt," whereby proper philosophizing begins with a doubting suspension and critical examination of all one's previously accepted beliefs, can lead only to skepticism and even atheism. In these ways, the disputes over Descartes grew to be about more than just academic philosophical and theological principles. To rigid Calvinists, his was a dangerous philosophy that would destroy the religion and morals of ordinary people.

In 1656, the campaign against Cartesianism was in one of its periodic peaks. By the late 1650s, Spinoza was well-known (and even admired) among his acquaintances as an expositor of Descartes's ideas. If, as Colerus claims,[100] Spinoza had indeed been reading and talking about the new philosophy just a few years earlier, around the time of his *cherem* – perhaps under the tutelage of Van den Enden or at the recommendation of some of his Mennonite friends, who kept abreast of the latest intellectual developments – then this would definitely have caused some concern among the Jewish community's leaders. The excommunication of an apparent "Cartesian" by the *ma'amad,* who must have had an eye on the anti-Cartesian activity among the Dutch, could have been a signal to the authorities that subversive philosophy was no more tolerated in the Talmud Torah synagogue than it was in the province of Holland at large.

ॐ

It is highly unlikely that the community's rabbis and governors simply cut Spinoza off without making a concerted effort to persuade him to repent and return to the congregation's fold. The *cherem* document, in fact, states that the members of the *ma'amad* "endeavored by various means and promises to turn him from his evil ways." According to Lucas, Mortera himself, after rushing to the synagogue to see if the reports of his disciple's rebellion were true, "urged him in a most formidable tone to decide for repentance or for punishment, and vowed that he would excommunicate him if he did not immediately show signs of contrition." Spinoza's response was calculated to push the rabbi over the edge: "[I] know the gravity of the threat, and in return for the trouble that [you] have taken to teach [me] the Hebrew language, allow [me] to teach [you] how to excommunicate." The rabbi left the synagogue in a fit of rage, "vowing not to come there again except with a thunderbolt in his hand."[101]

If the *ma'amad* had followed the process prescribed by Maimonides, Spinoza would have been given a warning to repent and change his ways, followed by two thirty-day periods for reflection. Only at the end of those sixty days, if he still refused to ask forgiveness, would the final punishment have been implemented.[102] Although there is no documentary evidence that the Talmud Torah congregation formally observed this sequence of stages, various sources do relate that the members of the *ma'amad* went to great lengths to try to get Spinoza to reform, or at the very least to keep up appearances and act like an upstanding member of the congregation. They reportedly even tried to bribe him into attending synagogue and conforming outwardly with their behavioral norms. Thus, claims Bayle, "it is said that the Jews offered to tolerate him, provided he would adapt his exterior behavior to their ceremonial practices, and that they even promised him an annual pension."[103] Spinoza's landlord in The Hague, speaking with Colerus, confirmed this, claiming that Spinoza himself told him that they had offered him one thousand guilders "to appear now and then in the synagogue."[104] Spinoza is said to have replied that "even if they offered him ten thousand guilders" he would not accept such hypocrisy, "for he sought only truth and not appearance."[105]

When the *cherem* was read to the assembled congregation on July 27 (the sixth of Ab), Spinoza was probably not present. He did have the right to appeal to the city's magistrates if he thought he was being punished unjustly or too harshly. The city, when it authorized the community's regulations in 1639, expressly recognized the right of the Jewish community's governors to excommunicate disobedient members, although they were apparently willing to step in and adjudicate if the banned person formally requested their intercession.[106] Spinoza did not do so. Nor, unlike Prado, did he appeal to another congregation to intercede on his behalf. In fact, he did not even ask the Talmud Torah congregation itself to reconsider its judgment. He simply quit the community. Brother Tomas, describing his two Jewish acquaintances in Amsterdam who had been expelled from the congregation two and a half years earlier, told the Inquisition that "they regretted the absence of the charitable funds that they were given by the synagogue and the communication with other Jews."[107] But he is most likely referring here only to Prado and not to Spinoza, for only Prado received any financial support. Spinoza, in contrast, seems to have departed without any regrets. His attitude toward his expulsion is probably best captured in the words attributed to him by Lucas: "All the better; they do not force me to do anything that I would not have done of my own accord if I did not dread scandal. But, since they want it that way, I enter gladly on the path that is opened to me, with the consolation that my departure will be more innocent than was the exodus of the early Hebrews from Egypt."[108]

7

Benedictus

B Y THE END OF 1656, Spinoza was twenty-four years old. From the descriptions provided by Brother Tomas and Captain Maltranilla three years later, he seems to have been a good-looking young man, with an unmistakably Mediterranean appearance. According to the friar, Spinoza was "a small man, with a beautiful face, a pale complexion, black hair and black eyes." The officer adds that he had "a well-formed body, thin, long black hair, a small moustache of the same color, a beautiful face."[1] The German philosopher Gottfried Wilhelm Leibniz, who visited Spinoza in 1676, described him as having "an olive-colored complexion, with something Spanish in his face."[2] Portraits from the period that are purportedly of Spinoza (including one by the famous chronicler of his artistic contemporaries, a kind of Dutch Vasari, Samuel Van Hoogstraten) show a long, thin, beardless face with a coloring that confirms these reports.[3] Spinoza was never in robust health. He suffered from a respiratory ailment for most of his life – perhaps something akin to what was responsible for his mother's early death – and his thinness and pallor (Tomas describes him as *blanco*) were no doubt a reflection of this.

Spinoza was gone from the Vlooienburg district soon after his excommunication; he may even have left the neighborhood well before the *cherem* was pronounced against him. By the terms of the *cherem*, his family and friends were required to break off all relations with him. If he and his brother Gabriel were, while in business together, living under the same roof, that arrangement had to end. We do not know exactly where he went to live at this time. Most likely he moved in with Van den Enden, if he was not lodging there already (as Lucas claims). In this way he could continue his studies and perhaps earn his room and board by doing a little teaching on the side. The evidence from Spinoza's works that he participated in the plays that the Latin school produced in 1657 and 1658 – possibly playing a role in one of Terence's comedies – suggests that he was still with Van den Enden at this point.[4] Spinoza, then, would have been living on the Singel, one of the more upscale of the city's canals and a decent distance from the Houtgracht.[5]

Lucas, in a perhaps prejudiced attempt to depict the Jews as a petty and vindictive lot, insists that it was not enough for Mortera and the community's leaders to have expelled Spinoza from their midst. They wanted him out of the city, he claims, for the apostate's mere presence in Amsterdam, getting on with his life, was a continual provocation to them. "Mortera especially could not abide the fact that his disciple and he lived in the same city, after the affront that he thought he had received from him." They could not bear to see Spinoza "outside their jurisdiction and subsisting without their help."

The Jews [were] much agitated because their thrust had missed and because he whom they wanted to get rid of was beyond their power. . . . But what could [Mortera] do to drive him out of [Amsterdam]? He was not the head of the city, as he was of the synagogue. Meanwhile, malice in the guise of a false zeal is so powerful that the old man attained his goal. He got a rabbi of the same temper and together they went to the magistrates, to whom they argued that if he had excommunicated Spinoza, it was not for ordinary reasons, but for execrable blasphemies against Moses and against God. He exaggerated the falsehood by all the reasons that a holy hatred suggests to an irreconcilable heart and demanded, in conclusion, that the accused should be banished from Amsterdam.[6]

The Amsterdam magistrates, according to Lucas, saw that this was a matter of personal enmity and vengeance rather than piety and justice. They tried to pass the buck by sending the matter on to the Calvinist clergy. The preachers, for their part, could find nothing "impious in the way in which the accused had conducted himself." Still, out of respect for the importance of the office of rabbi (and thinking perhaps of its similarity to their own), they recommended to the magistrates that the accused be condemned to exile from the city of Amsterdam for several months. "In this way," Lucas concludes, "Rabbinism was avenged."

It is a dramatic episode, and Lucas's personal acquaintance with Spinoza lends it some credibility. However, apart from Lucas's report, there is no evidence that any such appeal to the city government or the banishment ever took place. There is no legal record of any forced exile of Spinoza, nor even of any request by the Jewish community to have one of its members punished in this way. Moreover, according to the congregation's regulations, only the *ma'amad* had the authority to communicate with the municipal authorities regarding official community business. It is unlikely that a rabbi would take it upon himself to approach the Amsterdam magistrates directly on a matter of such importance.[7]

Nonetheless, some historians believe that the rabbis did indeed ask the municipal authorities to exile Spinoza.[8] Mortera or Aboab, they argue, could have made a convincing case that, as a heretic, Spinoza would influence others, including Christians. But it seems implausible that the relatively liberal regents who controlled the city at this time would have let themselves be persuaded by the Calvinist clergy, much less by the Jewish clergy, to condemn to exile someone who had not published anything. While it was not unheard of for people to be banished from the city by the magistrates at the insistence of the Calvinist consistory, this was usually for publishing something judged to be dangerous; it helped, moreover, if the work was in Dutch, thus threatening the piety of ordinary citizens. Even when someone's banishment was sought merely because of their allegedly heretical religious beliefs or activities, the accused either had a fairly well-established reputation for his views or appeared to be connected in some way to a movement regarded with suspicion by the authorities (such as Socinianism). In 1657, a number of English Quakers were imprisoned and banished from Amsterdam soon after they had begun regular meetings.[9] But they were probably caught up in the general campaign against the Collegiants and other antitrinitarians, with whom the Quakers, in the minds of the authorities, were often associated. On the whole, the city's leaders were reluctant to banish (or even punish with a milder sanction) people on questions of religious orthodoxy. They did, at the instigation of the Reformed ministers, throw Adriaan Koerbagh, a friend of Spinoza's, in jail in 1668 for his "blasphemous" views; he was to be banished after serving a ten-year term but died in prison within a year of his arrest. Like Spinoza, Koerbagh denied the divine authorship of the Bible. But the year before his arrest Koerbagh had published his opinions in a book in the vernacular. Moreover, the political circumstances were significantly changed by the late 1660s: the sun was setting on De Witt's "True Freedom," and the revived Orangists and their allies among the Calvinist preachers had more leverage. Adriaan's brother Jan, on the other hand, who had been arrested with him, was released by the magistrates with only a warning. The authorities claimed that in the republic even people who held heretical views could not be punished if they did not write books or organize gatherings.[10]

It seems safe to say, then, that Spinoza was never banished from Amsterdam. In fact, he appears to have been in that city throughout most of the period from his excommunication in 1656 to the beginning of his extant correspondence in 1661, often called the "dark period" of his life, as so little is known of his activities and whereabouts during this time. Colerus claims that, after developing his skills as a lens grinder, and with no longer any need to stay in Amsterdam, Spinoza left the city and lodged in the house of a friend on the road to Ouderkerk.[11] The way to this small village about ten miles outside of Amsterdam, where the Sephardic cemetary was located, runs right alongside the Amstel River. It was lined with some well-apportioned "country homes," where the city elite and their families could tend their gardens and enjoy some fresh air and a respite from the crowded urban spaces (and, in the summer, from the stench of the canals). Spinoza may have stayed at the house of Conraad Burgh, an Amsterdam judge and one of the wealthiest men of the city. Burgh was sympathetic to the Collegiants, and the connection with Spinoza could have run through his Mennonite friends. Spinoza was also friendly with Burgh's son, Albert. The two probably met in the late 1650s at Van den Enden's, where Albert studied Latin before going on to the University of Leiden, and acted together in some of the plays the school put on.[12]

There is no evidence to support Colerus's report. And even if there was a sojourn in or near or "on the way to" Ouderkerk, either to live there for a time or simply to pay an extended visit to some friends, Spinoza's main activities and primary residence throughout this period were in Amsterdam. (It would have been only a short trip into the city along the river, particularly if by *op de weg naar Ouwerkerk* Colerus means nothing more than a house on a particular road but still very close to the Amsterdam city limits.) Spinoza's continued contacts, theatrical and otherwise, with Van den Enden and his school, as well as his regular attendance at the home of Joseph Guerra (as witnessed by Captain Maltranilla) all indicate this. That he was still in Amsterdam as late as May 1661, just before his move to Rijnsberg that year, is suggested by an entry for that month in the diary of Olaus Borch, a learned Danish traveler. When he was in Leiden, Borch heard from a friend that "there are some atheists in Amsterdam; many of them are Cartesians, among them a certain impudent atheist Jew."[13] This is, without question, a reference to Spinoza.

William Ames, an Englishman who was leading the Quaker mission in

Amsterdam, may also have been referring to Spinoza when he wrote to Margaret Fell, often called "the mother of the Quakers," in April 1657 that

there is a Jew at amsterdam that by the Jews is Cast out (as he himself and others sayeth) because he owneth no other teacher but the light and he sent for me and I spoke toe him and he was pretty tender and doth owne all that is spoken; and he sayde tow read of moses and the prophets without was nothing tow him except he came toe know it within; and soe the name of Christ it is like he doth owne: I gave order that one of the duch Copyes of thy book should be given toe him and he sent me word he would Come toe oure meeting but in the mean time I was imprisoned.[14]

If Ames is indeed speaking of Spinoza, then this letter reveals not only that Spinoza was still in Amsterdam after his excommunication but that he was in contact with the Quakers not long after – and perhaps even before[15] – the event. His introduction to them could have come through his Collegiant friends. The dissenting Mennonites and Remonstrants in Adam Boreel's "college" had much in common with the English sect. With their stress on the importance of the "inner light" and individual independence in interpreting the word of God, as well as their antiauthoritarian approaches to worship, the two groups held similar opinions on religion, piety, and even morality. The Quakers, moreover, were interested in making contact with Jews. The year 1656 was widely predicted by contemporary millenarians – all anticipating the Second Coming of Christ – as the year in which the Jews would convert to Christianity, a necessary step heralding the imminent arrival of the millennium.[16] In fact, the Quaker mission in Amsterdam was established in part because of the large and open Jewish population there. The missionaries were to meet with Jews in that city and enlighten them as to their historic mission. They attended the synagogue and visited Jews in their homes, arguing with them and trying to win them over. Fell herself had already tried to open communications with Menasseh ben Israel during his stay in England in 1655–7, when he was working for the readmission of the Jews to that country. She hoped that he would distribute her conversionist pamphlet, originally an open letter entitled "For Menasseth-Ben-Israel: The Call of the Jews out of Babylon, Which Is Good Tidings to the Meek, Liberty to the Captives, and of Opening of the Prison Doors," among his Jewish congregants. Though he was, with his own messianistic convictions, in close touch with

a number of philo-semitic millenarians and perfectly willing to discuss with
them the subject of the Messiah's arrival, Menasseh would certainly have
had no interest in fostering Jewish conversion. Anyway, he died soon after
his return to the Netherlands and seems never to have taken any notice of
Fell's plea.

Spinoza would have been perceived by the Quakers as a good candidate
to help them further their cause. Because he left the Jewish community
without any regrets, they probably assumed that he shared none of a rabbi's
qualms about conversionist programs. And with his knowledge of Hebrew
he could have fulfilled Fell's desire to have her writings translated into that
language to facilitate its dissemination among the Jews. The original intermediary between Spinoza and Ames could have been Peter Serrarius
(Pierre Serrurier), one of the foremost millenarians in Amsterdam and a
regular presence at the Collegiant meetings at Boreel's home.[17] Serrarius,
whom Spinoza may have first encountered among the members of the
Amsterdam "college" and with whom he developed a good friendship, was
interested in both the Quakers (for their millenarian views) and the Jews
(for the momentous role they were to play in the "end" of history). Born in
London in 1580 to a Huguenot family, Serrarius moved to Amsterdam just
after his marriage in 1630 and had many close colleagues in the two countries. He was friendly both with Menasseh, with whom he shared a taste for
escatology and who may have first introduced him to Spinoza, and with
Ames. Perhaps Spinoza was even present at Serrarius's house when Boreel
presented a paper to the assembled Collegiants and Quakers on the recent
turmoil generated by an English Quaker claiming to be the Messiah.[18]

After translating Fell's letter to Menasseh from English into Dutch, Ames
gave it to his Jew to translate into Hebrew, sometime in early 1657. Fell appears to have been most gratified by the results, for toward the end of 1657
she asked another Quaker missionary in Amsterdam, William Caton, to have
a second pamphlet of hers translated into Hebrew. Caton wrote back:

> I have been with a Jew and have shewed him they booke, & have asked him what
> Languadge would bee the fittest for them hee told mee portugees or Hebrew, for
> if it were Hebrew they might understand it at Jerusalem or in almost any other
> place of the world; And he hath undertaken to translate it for us, he being expert
> in severall Languadges.[19]

Because the Jew who was to translate the work into Hebrew "could not
translate it out of English," Caton wrote to Fell a few months later, he, like

Ames, first had to have it translated into Dutch. "He hath it now and is translating of it, like he has done the other [i.e., the letter to Menasseh]." He adds that "the Jew that translates it, remaines very friendly in his way."[20]

This second work, *A Loving Salutation, to the Seed of Abraham among the Jews, where ever they are scattered up and down upon the face of the Earth*, is a maternal but forceful plea to the Jews to enter into the "New Covenant," where they will be warmly welcomed. Fell exhorts the Jews to be "cleansed of [their] iniquity" and to "turn to the light within you," away from sin and toward righteousness. There, in the "Covenant of light and love," they will be able to partake of the "everlasting riches and inheritance that never fades away." She speaks often of the Quakers' benevolent desire to see the Jewish people enjoy the rewards of joining the righteous: "So here is the Lords love freely tendered to you, if ye come into the *light*, by which the Lord God *teacheth his People;* that in the pure obedience, of the leading and teaching, and guiding of the *light*, which convinceth of the *Sinne* and *Evil*. Here you will come to have your hearts *Circumcised*, and the fore-skin of your hearts taken away."[21]

Fell has nothing but warm tenderness and concern for the Jews, whose eternal happiness rests in the balance. Threats for continued resistance to conversion are saved for Samuel Fisher's letter to the Jews, which was appended to the translation of Fell's work when it was published. Whereas Fell speaks of God's love, Fisher, a leading polemicist among the Amsterdam Quakers who frequently engaged the Jews in debate, stresses God's anger. In his letter, Fisher warns of what will happen to those whom "He has called and they have not obeyed." The Jews, he insists, "have done evil in His eyes and . . . have chosen that which He did not want for you." Rather than listening to the law, they have despised it. He ends on an ominous note: "Be wise and take counsel, Children of Israel! Remember you are rebellious!"[22]

Caton notes that the Jew enlisted to translate Fell's *Loving Salutation* was the same person as Ames's translator, the "Jew at amsterdam that by the Jews is Cast out." If it was indeed Spinoza, then these pamphlets represent what one scholar has called "Spinoza's earliest publication." Spinoza would have become, for a brief time in 1657 and 1658, a kind of Jewish expert and consultant for the Quakers, translating for them and perhaps giving them advice on how best to approach the Jews of Amsterdam. When George Fox, the Quaker leader, asked Ames about having *his* treatise for the Jews translated into Hebrew, Ames once more took the step of having the work translated first into Dutch. But after talking it over "with one who hath been a Jew" – perhaps, again, Spinoza – he decided that, as most of Amsterdam's Jews did not know Hebrew anyway, it would be best to leave it in Dutch, which they could read and speak.[23] This time the Jewish adviser, after giving some thought to the matter, must have made it clear to Ames that those who *could* read Hebrew would be the least likely to be won over, whereas those who, in the eyes of Ames, might have been open to conversionist pleas would not have been able to get the message through a Hebrew text.

Even in light of Spinoza's broken relationship with Judaism at this point in his life, not to mention his hostile relations with the Amsterdam congregation, it would be surprising to see him – if he is Ames's and Caton's accommodating Jew – providing services to a Christian sect actively working to convert the Jews. Contrary to the reports of some seventeenth-century writers,[24] Spinoza did not become a church-attending Christian after his "departure" from the Jewish religion. And there is absolutely no question of his ever having officially joined the Quakers, a group of enthusiasts with whom he would have had little in common other than an egalitarian view of worship and a tolerant conception of the inner nature of "true" faith. In fact, whatever relationship he may have had with the Quakers was probably over by 1658, when the Amsterdam missionaries were deeply divided over the claim of James Naylor, an English Quaker, to be the Messiah. Collegiants such as Boreel and Serrarius ridiculed the excited messianists among the Quakers and in their attitude toward the sect would have carried Spinoza along with them.[25] Still, his views on religion and Scripture at this time probably harmonized quite well with Quaker beliefs and practices, just as they did with those of the Collegiants; and his initial attraction to the Quakers, if there was one, could have been due to these doctrinal affinities.

Moreover, working with the Quakers could have been a useful and intellectually important experience for Spinoza. If he was in contact with Samuel Fisher, collaborating with him on Fell's second pamphlet, then he would have been exposed to some of the period's most radical ideas on Scripture. Fisher, who knew Hebrew, was a leading figure in the debates over the origins and status of the Bible that, from 1656 onward, occupied many Christian scholars and clerics in England, France, and Holland. Fisher argued that it is highly unlikely that the words of the Bible have been transmitted perfectly intact from their original revelation from God.

The written text almost certainly is, in fact, many times removed from the authentic communication. What we have are simply copies of copies of copies, and so on, all produced by (fallible) human hands. Fisher made a distinction between God's eternal and supernatural Word and the historical, natural processes through which, in time, that Word has been transmitted to us and during which it must have undergone various mutations and additions, including the contingent canonization procedure carried out by the rabbis and scribes who edited it. Nor, he argued, does it seem possible that Moses is the author of all of the Pentateuch. Thus, the "inner light" is a much better guide to the word of God than the written Bible.[26] It is quite possible that many of Spinoza's own radical ideas on the authorship and redaction of Scripture found reinforcement – or even their origin – in discussions he had with Fisher and other Quakers in 1657.[27]

ta.

If the "Jew" referred to in these documents relating to the Quakers' mission in Holland was Spinoza, then they establish that he was in Amsterdam throughout 1657 and 1658.[28] However, it also appears that sometime before early 1659, when (at the latest) he was talking in Amsterdam with Brother Tomas and Captain Maltranilla, he was either staying in or making periodic visits to Leiden to study at the university there. It is Brother Tomas himself who provides this information. In his report to the Inquisition, he relates that Spinoza "studied at Leiden, and was a good philosopher." Spinoza, in fact, probably began studies at Leiden precisely in order to expand his philosophical education. Now that he was no longer a merchant, and thus free to devote more of his energies to philosophy, Spinoza must have felt that it was time to supplement whatever knowledge of Cartesianism he might have acquired from Van den Enden, his Collegiant friends, and his own reading. There is no record of his having formally enrolled as a student at the university, but he could have audited classes without officially matriculating in any faculty. (It may have been his association with university life – where all instruction and learned discourse was in Latin – that first moved Spinoza to use the Latinized version of his first name, Benedictus.) What must have made the University of Leiden, where Descartes himself had studied mathematics in 1630, particularly attractive to Spinoza, and the natural choice for his purposes, was not just the fact that it was the oldest and best university in the republic, but also its reputation for being well-endowed with Cartesian professors.

Despite the decrees against teaching Descartes's philosophy that had been issued by the university senate in 1646 and by the States of Holland as recently as 1656, there were a number of individuals in both the philosophy and theology faculties at Leiden who were openly committed to Cartesian thought and its various applications to physics, medicine, logic, and metaphysics. There was Jacob Golius, a professor of oriental languages and a mathematician, as well as Abraham Heidanus (Abraham van der Heyden), who had been appointed professor of theology in 1648. And Frans van Schooten the younger, who drew the figures for the appendices of Descartes's *Discourse on Method,* taught mathematics at Leiden until his death in 1660. But for Spinoza, it would have been the members of the philosophy faculty – responsible for instruction in logic, physics, metaphysics, psychology, and ethics – whose courses he would have had the most interest in attending. Here Cartesianism practically flourished, as the university tended to let its philosophy teachers go their own way as long as they did not stray into theology. This restriction, at least in theory, was acceptable to the philosophers, who usually stressed the importance of maintaining the distinction between reason (the proper tool for philosophizing) and faith.

Among Leiden's philosophers was Adriaan Heereboord (1614–61), a professor of logic who, by the early 1650s, was well known for his eclectic devotion to Descartes's thought. Heereboord had a tendency to ridicule his Aristotelian colleagues for being slavish followers of the opinions of others rather than true investigators of nature. He was particularly taken by Cartesian philosophical method and the role of the *cogito ergo sum* ("I think, therefore I am") argument as the first truth and foundation of all knowledge. Into his lectures and the disputations he directed among his students, Heereboord introduced many important Cartesian theses on the proper conduct of reason in the search for knowledge, including the role to be played by the "method of doubt." Descartes himself acknowledged that Heereboord "declares himself more openly for me and cites me with more praise than Regius [Henri Le Roy, an overly enthusiastic disciple of Descartes's at the University of Utrecht] has ever done."[29] When the curators of the university, in 1647, again ordered all professors in the faculties of philosophy and theology to refrain from discussing Descartes and his ideas, their warning was directed mainly at Heereboord.[30] He ignored the decree.

Although Heereboord was still around in the late 1650s, his drinking problem had begun to catch up with him and he was eventually relieved of his teaching responsibilities.[31] In any case, his importance as a leading exponent of Cartesian ideas had, by that time, been eclipsed by that of Johannes de Raey (1622–1707). De Raey was a student of Regius at Utrecht before moving to Leiden. He was a professor of philosophy at the university and lectured on natural philosophy and other subjects (as well as medicine after 1658, much to the dismay of the medical faculty). Descartes, always looking to encourage his Dutch disciples, reportedly remarked that De Raey taught his philosophy better than anyone else.[32] In 1648, not long after receiving his degrees in the arts and in medicine at Leiden and when he was still giving private lessons to students, De Raey, too, received a reprimand from the university senate. It was decided that his tutoring, which must have been well laced with Cartesianism, would henceforth be more closely supervised: "Mr. De Raey will be told on behalf of the curators that private courses may be given only after he has deliberated with the rector and with the professors of all the faculties. Moreover, that any teaching of Cartesian philosophy is not allowed."[33] De Raey was ecumenical in his fidelity to Descartes. He was willing to incorporate elements of Aristotle's thought and intent on showing that Descartes's system was not such an iconoclastic break from traditional philosophy. He would later distance himself from Spinoza and others who were perceived as "radical" Cartesians. Around 1658 – perhaps while Spinoza was still around – De Raey was joined at Leiden by Arnold Geulincx (1623–69). Geulincx had been forced to flee the University of Louvain, in the southern Low Countries, most likely because of his Cartesianism. When he arrived in Leiden, newly converted from Catholicism to Calvinism, he immediately fell into the university's Cartesian circle, under the sponsorship of Heidanus. There is much in common between Geulincx's thought and Spinoza's – in fact, after his death Geulincx was accused by a Calvinist minister of having fallen into the "sin" of Spinozism – and it is possible that they were acquainted with each other in Leiden.

Spinoza was probably well-prepared in his reading for the lectures on Cartesian science, method, and metaphysics that he would have audited at the university. Descartes's major philosophical works, including the *Meditations on First Philosophy* (1641) and *Principles of Philosophy* (1644), were all published in Latin. Even the widely read *Discourse on Method* (1637), along with its scientific (but not its mathematical) essays, originally published in French (a language Spinoza seems not to have known very well),[34] were available in Latin after 1644. Spinoza owned a copy of the 1650 edition of Descartes's *Opera Philosophica*, which contains all of these works. After the initial publication of some of Descartes's letters in 1657, Spinoza would, as well, have been able to begin reading in his philosophically rich correspondence. But the unfinished *Rules for the Direction of the Mind*, an early and influential treatise in philosophical method, though it circulated in manuscript among a small circle of devotees, was not published until 1701 (a Dutch version appeared in 1684).[35]

Spinoza also took time to study the important contemporary Cartesians who were continuing to develop Descartes's metaphysical and scientific thought, although not always in ways of which the master himself would have approved. It could have been De Raey, at whose lectures on Descartes's *Discourse on Method* and *Principles of Philosophy* Spinoza must have been present,[36] who first directed Spinoza to the writings of Johannes Clauberg. A German who had been De Raey's student at Leiden in the 1640s, Clauberg had, by the late 1650s, already published a number of important philosophical treatises, including the *Defensio Cartesiana* of 1652 (a copy of which Spinoza owned). In his mathematical education, Spinoza seems to have relied a good deal on the texts of Frans van Schooten the elder, one of Descartes's more faithful disciples, who was also responsible for translating the geometrical essay of the *Discourse* into Latin in 1649.[37]

In the late 1650s, then, Spinoza was steeping himself in the works of Descartes (or, as his good friend Jarig Jellesz put it, the *Scripta Philosophica Nobilissimi & summi Philosophi Renati des Cartes*)[38] and his followers, ruminating on the essential features of the expatriate French philosopher's system. So much of what Descartes said (or, in many cases, left unsaid) must have seemed liberating and, even better, right to Spinoza. The new dualistic metaphysical picture of the world that, with the complete separation of the mental from the material, provided the foundations for a purely mechanistic physics would allow for fruitful, clear, and nonabstruse explanations of the phenomena of nature – a nature whose structures and dynamics could be captured in purely mathematical terms. The unity of the Cartesian scientific enterprise in all of its dimensions would promote the quest for certainty in various disciplines and expand the possibilities for productive experimental work in the particular sciences. There was also Descartes's optimistic picture of the knowing mind, of reason's capacity to penetrate nature's inner workings. For Descartes, the intellect, if guided by the proper method, was able truly (and usefully) to know the world in all its minute detail through its own conceptual tools, its "clear and distinct ideas." More important, at least to Spinoza, the mind could also know its own place in that world.

Unlike the tradition-bound studies of his Jewish education, including the logically rigorous but antiquated exercises of rabbinical commentaries and the cosmological speculations of Judaism's philosophical texts – for even the great Maimonides was committed to an essentially Aristotelian system – here was a progressive philosophical home in which Spinoza felt comfortable. Cartesianism was a relatively young philosophy, and there was still much work to be done. Not that he would bind himself to Descartes in the way others had bound themselves to Plato or Aristotle. If he was ever a naive disiciple, it was only for the briefest of times. Spinoza was too original and independent a thinker, and possessed too analytically acute a mind, to be an uncritical follower.

Perhaps what he saw, above all, was that within a basically Cartesian framework he could begin to pursue his own philosophical agenda, a project whose outline was becoming increasingly well defined around this time and that seemed to arise naturally out of his own experience. What interested Spinoza was the nature of the human being and his place in the world. What is this creature who is a knower both of himself and of the world of which he is a part? What can be concluded from the human being's relationship to the rest of nature about his freedom, his possibilities, and his happiness? What is the nature of his emotional responses to the world and of his actions within it?

Spinoza must have made rapid progress in his philosophical apprenticeship; for by early 1661 he was already well known as someone who "excelled in the Cartesian philosophy."[39] He also had good company in his enterprise, for the *scientia nova* was a frequent topic of conversation among his circle of friends in Amsterdam. They seem to have met on a regular basis to discuss philosophical and religious ideas,[40] with Spinoza – perhaps because of his recent experience in Leiden, but also simply because he was their intellectual superior – acting as a kind of resident, if often critical, expert on Descartes's thought. Lucas reports that "his friends, most of whom were Cartesians, would propose difficulties to him that they insisted could be resolved only by the principles of their master." He adds that Spinoza would "disabuse them of an error into which the learned men had fallen by satisfying them by entirely different arguments [than Descartes's]."[41] Among these individuals were, of course, the Collegiants and their fellow travelers with whom he had been associating for a number of years, but there were also some new acquaintances recently made either in Amsterdam or in Leiden.

Spinoza probably first met Jarig Jellesz (short for Jelleszoon, "Jelle's son"), a close and lifelong friend, at the Amsterdam mercantile exchange in the early 1650s. Born in 1619 or 1620 into an affluent Amsterdam family of Frisian descent, Jellesz became a grocer dealing mainly in spices and dried fruit. He engaged in both wholesale and retail trade and frequently did business with the Portuguese Jews. He may even have been a customer of Spinoza's family firm: in 1655, he was buying raisins from Simon Rodrigues Nunes, and these were one of the commodities imported by Michael Spinoza and his sons. According to a friend who added a biographical note to Jellesz's "Confession of the Universal and Christian Faith," Jellesz gave up his business at a relatively young age when he "realized that the accumulation of money and goods could not satisfy his soul. He thus sold his shop to an honest man and, without ever getting married, withdrew from the turbulence of the world to practice in quietness the knowledge of the truth, looking for the true nature of God and to obtain wisdom."[42] Jellesz, whose family belonged to the Flemish Mennonite community in Amsterdam, was perhaps one of the more pious members of the city's group of Collegiants. He believed deeply that faith is a personal affair, a matter of inner conviction and religious experience, and consequently he rejected external authority, organized confession, and theological dogmatizing. Human happiness, he insisted, consists simply in the knowledge of God, a purely rational communion with the divine understanding.[43]

Jellesz's "Confession" was published in 1684 by Jan Rieuwertsz ("Rieuwert's son"), the radical and intrepid printer and bookseller who published works that other publishers would not touch. Rieuwertsz, who was born in 1616, also came from a Mennonite family. He met Spinoza either through the Collegiants whose works he was producing (perhaps through Jellesz himself), or by way of Van den Enden, with whom he and Spinoza shared many of the same intellectual interests, particularly Cartesian philosophy and radical political theory. In 1657, around the time he would have joined Spinoza and his other friends in their Cartesian meetings, Rieuwertsz began publishing the Dutch translation of Descartes's works, a task that would take him almost thirty years. The translator of those works, another member of the Cartesian "roundtable," was Jan Hendrik Glazemaker, the same man who later translated most of Spinoza's works into Dutch. Glazemaker probably knew Jellesz from childhood, as he too was born around 1620 to a family in the Flemish Mennonite community in Amsterdam, and he could have first met Spinoza through the grocer.[44]

Spinoza may also have met Pieter Balling, soon to become one of his more faithful disciples, through the Collegiant network. Balling was a highly educated Mennonite merchant who, with his knowledge of Spanish, probably also did business with the Portuguese Jews; at one point he served as the representative in Spain for certain Dutch merchants. He was one of Spinoza's greatest admirers and an enthusiastic participant in the Amsterdam philosophical discussions. While he did his best to help disseminate Spinoza's works, he also composed his own Spinozistic treatise, which he published anonymously in 1662. In *The Light upon the Candlestick*, a book that – with its emphasis on "the light" – many people assumed to have been written by the Quaker Ames, Balling argues for a personal, non-confessional and tolerant approach to religious worship. Taking a somewhat more mystical approach than Jellesz, he claims that a natural, intuitive, "inner" experience of the divine is possible for everyone. Any individual can commune with God through his own rational faculties, regardless of his knowledge of Scripture or his confessional background. The "light on the candlestick" is reason, "the clear and distinct knowledge of the truth," which he identifies with the Word, Christ, and the mind of God.[45] The book was, naturally, published by Rieuwertsz.

In his biography, Colerus takes particular note of the love and devotion to Spinoza on the part of Simon Joosten de Vries.[46] His report is confirmed by their letters, which at times show a personal warmth and intimacy rare in Spinoza's extant correspondence. De Vries was born around 1634 into a large upper middle-class merchant family of Mennonite background. He, too, may have come to know Spinoza through Collegiant circumstances. In the 1660s, the philosopher would develop an uncharacteristically close relationship with De Vries' extended clan. Before dying at an early age in 1667, Simon did his best to insure that his friend would be well cared-for financially, a commitment that his sister and brother-in-law honored.

Despite the fact that the group had a reputation for being "atheistic Cartesians,"[47] it is clear that Jellesz, Balling and many of the other members of Spinoza's intellectual circle were committed primarily to religious reform and toleration, to the freedom of the individual to worship God in his own manner – guided only by his own intellectual faculties, unconstrained by any dogma and rites, and unmolested by any authorities, theological or otherwise. They shared with Spinoza an enthusiasm for Cartesian philosophy. They were particularly taken by its rationalism, with the emphasis on the power of independent reason to attain higher truth. Like Spinoza, they were convinced that human happiness – in the strong sense of what the ancient Greeks called *eudaimonia,* or flourishing, and what Christians called "salvation" – lay in the unfettered but disciplined use of the intellect directed toward its proper object. Spinoza, for his part, was no doubt interested in his friends' views on "inner experience," morality, and toleration. But unlike Spinoza, their motivations were deeply religious; and the truth to which reason led them was usually a devout Christian one. One wonders whether the Amsterdam Cartesian discussion group resembled, at times, a meeting of Boreel's "college."

In addition to those friends of Spinoza who came to their philosophical meetings from a Collegiant or Mennonite background, there were several individuals whose acquaintance he may have made while attending lectures at the University of Leiden. The radical political and religious thinker Adriaan Koerbagh, for example, was studying at Leiden from 1656 to 1661. Although he was enrolled in the medical faculty, having done his philosophical training a few years earlier at Utrecht, he may have also attended the same philosophy lectures on Descartes given by De Raey that Spinoza did. Since De Raey was also teaching medicine after 1658, perhaps Koerbagh was curious enough about his medical lecturer's Cartesian proclivities to go and see what he was professing in a purely philosophical context. Although Koerbagh could have met Spinoza through their mutual friend Van den Enden, with whom he shared a taste for democratic politics, a Leiden connection seems more plausible.

Over time, Spinoza and Koerbagh developed a close, mutually influential relationship. They agreed in their political views and in their attitudes toward religion. There is an unmistakable strain of Spinozism running throughout Koerbagh's metaphysical doctrines, while Spinoza's *Theological-Political Treatise* has much in common with Koerbagh's bold ideas on the state and on Scripture (Koerbagh would certainly have seen an early draft of the work, which Spinoza was composing from 1665 onward). Spinoza's decision to publish the *Treatise,* in fact, was at least partly inspired by Koerbagh's death in prison in 1669, after he had been arrested by the city authorities for blasphemy at the instigation of the Calvinist consistory. When Spinoza argued for freedom of thought and speech and for noninterference by ecclesiastical authorities in the social and political arena, there is no question that he had his friend's fate in mind.

Although he seems not to have been a particularly religious man, Koerbagh nonetheless shared with Jellesz, Balling, and the others a rationalist and, in his own case, at least nominally theocentric conception of human happiness. A human being finds his *beatitudo* in the knowledge of God. This apprehension of the divine is not some mystical insight, but reason's intellectual grasp of an eternal, immutable essence. On this basis, Koerbagh argued against irrational theology and superstitious religious rites. True religion, he insisted, is an inner, personal matter. The true teaching of God is simply a love of and obedience to God and a love of one's neighbor. Everything else is accidental or superfluous. There is also an explicit element of Socinianism in Koerbagh's views: he denied the trinity and the divine nature of Jesus.[48] He must have felt right at home among Spinoza's other friends, and may have been strongly influenced by his contact with the Amsterdam Collegiants.

Lodewijk Meyer, on the other hand, did not even pretend to share the piety of Spinoza's other acquaintances. He came from a Lutheran, not a Mennonite family; and while he was friendly with the Collegiants, and may even have attended some of their meetings, his real love was for philosophy and the arts, particularly theater and literature. He became the director of the Amsterdam Municipal Theater from 1665 to 1669, and the founder of the dramatic and literary society Nil Volentibus Arduum ("Nothing Is Difficult to Those Who Are Willing") in 1669. Meyer was a man of broad humanistic culture, and if he spoke on religious matters at all it was to help end the theological quarrels that so disturbed the peace of the republic. His personal and intellectual devotion to Spinoza was grounded not just in their shared philosophical tastes (particularly for Descartes) but also in what Meyer himself took to be a joint dedication to the search for truth. Thus, he more than anyone else was responsible for bringing Spinoza's writings to publication, both while Spinoza lived and after his death with the posthumous publication of his collected works.

Meyer was born in 1629 in Amsterdam. He originally hoped to be a Lutheran pastor, but this enthusiasm did not last long. As a young man he developed a strong interest in language, and in 1654 he reedited a book that explained thousands of foreign terms in use in seventeenth-century Dutch. That same year, he matriculated at the University of Leiden, studying first philosophy and then, after 1658, medicine; he took doctorates in both faculties in 1660. At Leiden, he must have been acquainted with Koerbagh, as they were in the same faculty and would have attended the same lectures. It was probably also at Leiden, and not at Van den Enden's (as most scholars have assumed), that Meyer initially met Spinoza. During the period in which Spinoza was attending Van den Enden's school, 1654 to early 1658, Meyer was not even in Amsterdam; but he *was* at Leiden when Spinoza would have been spending time there.

Meyer's philosophical importance, beyond his being Spinoza's close friend and promoter, lies in his own radically rationalistic theory of Bible interpretation. In order to end the religious sectarianism that threatened the well-being of civil society in the Netherlands, Meyer proposed an exegetical method that, he believed, would reveal the true and unequivocal meaning of Holy Scripture, one that would "affirm and propagate the incorruptible doctrine of heavenly truth and allow our souls to enjoy salvation and happiness." The method found in Meyer's *Philosophia S. Scripturae interpres* (*Philosophy, Interpreter of Holy Scripture*), which he published anonymously in "Eleutheropolis," is Cartesian to the core. It emphasizes the importance of relying only on the clear and distinct ideas of the intellect. That is, *Philosophia*, or reason, and not faith or institutional authority is the proper guide for intepreting Scripture. To get what Meyer calls the "true sense" of the biblical text, the sense or meaning intended by its author, one should rely only on what is clearly and distinctly perceived by natural reason, and not simply on what tradition or the church councils or the pope dictate. This is because the ultimate author of the Bible – although not the immediate author of the written text as we have it – is God. God is omniscient and necessarily veracious, and therefore whatever propositions God intended to convey will be not just the "true sense" of his words, but the *truth* itself. Since reason is the faculty for discovering truth – logical, natural, and spiritual – and since the "true meaning" of Scripture is also the absolute truth, then reason is the proper tool for getting at the meaning of Scripture.[49]

Reason also tells us when the words of Scripture should be read literally and when they should be read figuratively by revealing what can and cannot be properly attributed to God. For example, the Bible speaks of God's feet, his finger, and his anger. But we know, by reason, that to have feet or fingers or emotions requires a body, and that having a body is incompatible with being an infinitely perfect, eternal being such as God. Therefore, passages referring to God in these ways must be read figuratively.[50]

Meyer's work was banned together with Spinoza's *Theological-Political Treatise*. (Some people even thought that Spinoza himself had written the *Philosophia S. Scripturae interpres*.)[51] His outraged critics believed that Meyer abused the Cartesian separation of reason and faith, and actually made theology subordinate to philosophy. Descartes himself was very reluctant to apply his method to theological matters. Meyer's own lack of scruples led him to conclude that the biblical text was full of inconsistencies, confusions, and falsehoods. It was not only orthodox Calvinists with Voetian sympathies who took offense. Even Cartesians like Professor Heidanus at Leiden and generally tolerant types like Serrarius were vocal in their condemnation.[52]

Possessed of a real enthusiasm for philosophy and what seems to have been a good deal of energy, the latecomer[53] Meyer must have been an invigorating presence at the Amsterdam meetings. Accompanied by his "old and faithful friend" Johannes Bouwmeester, a man of equally wide literary, philosophical, and scientific interests[54] – and who also studied philosophy and medicine at Leiden from 1651 to 1658, where he may have known Spinoza independently or through Meyer's introduction – Lodewijk Meyer was undoubtedly responsible, at least in part, for the group's reputation for "freethinking." Whether this ambiguous label was warranted or not, Spinoza's Amsterdam circle toward the end of the 1650s and the first year and a half of the 1660s (when Meyer and Koerbagh, recently finished with their university degrees, would have joined the group) comprised an eclectic mix of passions and personalities: from pious, nonconfessionalist reformers and iconoclastic Bible critics to cultured humanists and radical democrats, all interested, for varied reasons, in discussing Cartesianism and other philosophical and religious matters.

❧

Before the discovery of the Inquisitional testimony of Captain Maltranilla, it was usually assumed that Spinoza, after his expulsion from the Jewish community, no longer had any contacts with Amsterdam's Sephardim. And Colerus insists that Spinoza had once declared that "from that time he neither spoke nor had any intercourse with them." He adds that "some Amsterdam Jews, who knew Spinoza very well, have told me that that is well known."[55] But when the Spanish officer testified in 1659 that, around that time, Spinoza and Prado "regularly frequented the house of Joseph Guerra," along with Dr. Miguel Reinoso and a confectioner and tobacco merchant named Pacheco, he revealed that certain Portuguese Jews were willing to defy the ban and be in the same company as the condemned heretics. It is clear from Maltranilla's report – and we know from independent sources – that Reinoso and Pacheco, both from Seville, were upstanding members of the Talmud Torah congregation: to the captain they confessed themselves to be "Jews who observed their law; and though they had once been offered swine's flesh they refrained from eating it."[56] Don Guerra, on the other hand, was a wealthy non-Jew who hailed from the Canary Islands. He was in Amsterdam hoping to be cured of his leprosy. Holland was often visited by foreigners seeking medical treatment,[57] and Guerra, who surely spoke no Dutch, must have sought out a Spanish-speaking doctor. Reinoso was probably his attending physician, perhaps accompanied in his visits from time to time by an old friend from his marrano days in Spain, Pacheco.

Reinoso's presence in Spinoza's and Prado's company in 1658–9 is particularly interesting. For living the life of a Judaizing converso in Iberia he was denounced to the Inquisition in 1655 by Baltazar Orobio de Castro – the same Orobio de Castro, also from Seville, who, when he too was a doctor in Amsterdam and a member of the Portuguese congregation (going by the name Isaac), fulminated against the excommunicated Prado and Spinoza. Orobio and Reinoso, as well as Prado, had apparently been partners in crypto-Judaism in Seville. When Orobio was imprisoned and tortured by the Inquisition in 1655, he named names, among them Miguel Reinoso and Juan de Prado. This indicates that Guerra's visitors Reinoso and Prado, and probably Pacheco too, had known each other for quite a while and under very different circumstances. Fortunately for them, Reinoso and Prado had already left Spain by the time of Orobio's confession – it was common to denounce only those whom one knew to be dead or gone – and were well beyond the Inquisition's reach.[58] There seem to have been no hard feelings, as Reinoso (going by the Jewish name Abraham) and Orobio later worked together in Amsterdam on various medical cases.[59] One wonders, however, whether Orobio, when he initiated his crusades against the ideas of Prado and, later, Spinoza, was aware that his fellow physician and old Judaizing comrade had defied the congregation and kept company with the two heretics a few years earlier. As Reinoso and Pacheco did not arrive in Amsterdam until just around the time of Spinoza's excommunication, Spinoza was probably introduced by Prado to his fellow former-marranos from Seville sometime after his departure from the community. Reinoso and Pacheco were never punished by the *ma'amad* with a ban for entering within four cubits of Spinoza's vicinity and probably kept their meetings with him to themselves.

≥

Spinoza's earliest philosophical writings date from the final years of his Amsterdam period – about the same time as his visits to the home of Guerra and while he was still present in person (and not just by correspondence) at the meetings of the Cartesian circle. If the Rotterdam regent Adriaen Paets, in his letter to the Remonstrant professor in March 1660, was indeed referring to a short work by Spinoza when he mentioned a *tractatus theologico-politicus* by "an author not wholly unknown to you," then by the late 1650s the philosopher was already committing to paper his views on some of the same issues that elicited his excommunication – biblical authorship and exegesis – along with various matters concerning political and religious authority and natural and civil law.[60] (This suggests, as well, that the *Theological-Political Treatise* that he published in 1670 was not simply a response to the Dutch political crises of the late 1660s or to the personal trauma of Koerbagh's death in prison in 1669, but rather the culmination of a long-term project focused on the state, liberty, toleration, and, of course, religion.) At the same time, Spinoza's mind was clearly turning to broad questions of ethics, knowledge, and metaphysics. In fact, from 1658 to around 1665, despite what may have been his work on the "little book" that Paets had in hand, Spinoza's theological-political interests were of secondary importance while he labored, through various fits and starts, to construct a full-blown philosophical system.

The *Treatise on the Emendation of the Intellect* (*Tractatus de intellectus emendatione*) is an unfinished work on method and knowledge. It has always been considered one of Spinoza's early pieces, but scholars usually dated it to around 1662, later than some other writings (including initial work on his masterpiece, the *Ethics*). There are good reasons, however, for thinking that the *Treatise* is, in fact, the first of Spinoza's extant original philosophical treatises. Its thematic content, its terminology, its specific doctrines of knowledge and of the operations of the human mind, its likely sources, and its function as introductory material to more systematic treatment of various philosophical issues all suggest a dating before the *Short Treatise on God, Man and His Well-Being*, which he probably began sometime in late 1660 or early 1661.[61]

Spinoza conceived the *Treatise on the Emendation of the Intellect* as part – perhaps the first part – of some larger work. The *Treatise* was to address the preliminary question of philosophic method and some basic problems concerning the nature and varieties of knowledge, all in the context of a broad conception of what constitutes "the good" for a human being. These issues would also receive a deeper treatment in the rest of the work, which Spinoza refers to in the *Treatise* itself as "our Philosophy [*nostra Philosophia*]*." Apparently not yet written at the time he was composing the *Treatise,* this "Philosophy" would be an extensive and systematic inquiry into the mind, metaphysics, physics, morality, and other subjects. What seems to have happened is that, for one reason or another, he decided in late 1659 or early 1660 to abandon the *Treatise* and start again, this time working on what would become the *Short Treatise on God, Man and His Well-Being,* whose own methodological chapters overlap with the material in the *Treatise* in various respects.[62]

While clearly intended as an introduction to the proper method to be followed in the search for truth, the *Treatise* is also (like Descartes's *Discourse on Method*) partly an autobiographical sketch of Spinoza's own intellectual itinerary and partly an appeal to the reader – presumably one with at least a passing familiarity with Cartesian philosophy – to follow the same road and convert to the philosophical life.

What is required for such a conversion even to begin to be contemplated is a feeling of dissatisfaction, perhaps not yet fully articulated, with the life one is leading. One must question the values one has adopted and that have guided one's actions and ask after the "true good" for a human being, "the eternal source of the greatest joy." One must, in other words, begin to lead what Socrates called "the examined life." What Spinoza saw was that this search for the good requires a radical change in one's way of living. One must suspend the pursuit of ordinary "goods," such as honor, wealth, and sensual pleasure. These reveal themselves, upon reflection, to be fleeting and unstable – in sum, not at all what is expected of the true good for a human being. Moreover, such perishable things often lead to our downfall and destruction.

There are a great many examples of people who have suffered persecution to the death on account of their wealth, or have exposed themselves to so many dangers to acquire wealth that they have at last paid the penalty for their folly with their life. Nor are there fewer examples of people who, to attain or defend honor, have suffered most miserably. And there are innumerable examples of people who have hastened their death through too much sensual pleasure.[63]

The true good, on the other hand, is the love of something eternal and immutable. And it is never a source of sadness or danger or suffering, but only of joy.

What this true good consists in is having a certain "nature," being in a certain condition that is natural for a human being and that represents the perfection of human nature. Because human beings are essentially knowers – rational animals, to use a common philosophical definition – our good, our perfection, consists in having a kind of knowledge. What that knowledge is, what we should strive for, is the comprehension of our place in Nature. Or, as Spinoza puts it, it is "the knowledge of the union that the mind has with the whole of Nature."[64] The human being does not stand outside of Nature, but is an intimate and inextricable part of it, subject to all of its laws. When one sees the way in which this is so, and strives so that others may see it too, then one has achieved the good for a human being, "the highest human perfection."

In order to be realized, the true good requires a thorough knowledge both of Nature itself and of human nature, a clear and exhaustive understanding of the metaphysics of matter and of mind, the physics of bodies, the logic of our thoughts, and the causes of our passions. But before any of this can be approached – and these are the materials for the more substantive discussion of the subsequent part of the work, "Philosophy" – there is need for a method. This is not a project to be undertaken haphazardly. The intellect must be purified and prepared for the task of inquiring into Nature. Without a method, our hope of ever attaining our goal of "understanding things successfully" – a goal upon which our happiness depends – is doomed to failure.

There are, Spinoza insists, four different ways of "perceiving things." We know some things merely by report or signs. This is a rather indirect, and thus (absolutely speaking) insecure way of apprehension. We know through report or conventional sign what our date of birth was, or who our parents are. These are not things of which we can be directly and immediately certain. We know or perceive other things by means of "random experience," that is, experience not guided or critically reviewed by the intellect or reason. These are our chance encounters with things. Sometimes, when our experience is not contradicted, we can draw general inferences from a number of similar cases. But although the results of such induction may in fact be true, they are (again, absolutely speaking) uncertain and possibly subject to change. Spinoza notes that it is only by random experience that he knows he will die, "for I affirm this because I have seen others like me die, even though they had not all lived the same length of time and did not all die of the same illness." Similarly, I know by random experience that oil feeds a fire and water puts it out, that dogs bark, and "almost all the things that are useful in life."

What is lacking in random experience is a deep knowledge of things. We need also to know not just how things appear, in what order and with what apparent (past) connections with other things; we need to know *what* and *how* they are, and *why* they are as they are. This is what Spinoza calls knowing the "essence" of a thing. It involves knowing a thing's essential properties (those properties without which it would not be *that* thing), as well as the universal causes in Nature and its laws that explain its coming to be. We need, above all, certainty in our knowledge of these matters, something our sense experience alone can never provide.

There are two ways of coming to know the essence of a thing. The first is when we reason to the essence from some other thing. This discursive or inferential "perception" explains how we sometimes know, working back from our experience of some effect, what its cause was; or when we deduce some particular fact from a universal truth or general proposition. If I perceive that the sun is actually larger than it appears to be, but only because I reason from general principles regarding the nature of vision (such as that one and the same thing looks smaller from a great distance than from close up), then my knowledge of the size of the sun, while certain and true, is only inferential. For Spinoza, there is still a kind of inadequacy at the heart of inferential reasoning. It is inferior to perceiving a thing "through its essence alone." This fourth kind of knowledge consists in an immediate, intuitive, noninferential grasp of the essence of a thing. I can know that the soul is united to a body by inferring this from the fact that there are sensations in the soul whenever the body is affected in certain ways; or, I can know immediately that the soul is united to a body simply by understanding the nature of the soul and seeing that it is of the essence of the soul to be united to a body.

Our goal, then, is to know – in this most adequate, intuitive, and perfect sense – our own nature exactly as it is in itself, and as much of the nature of things as is necessary to distinguish them one from another, to know what their actions and receptivities are, and to compare them with the nature and power of the human being.

The purpose of method is to show us how to achieve this kind of knowledge of Nature and of its order and causal connections in a systematic, rule-governed (and not fortuitous) manner. It begins with reflection upon the knowledge that we do have. We must, on that basis, learn how to distinguish "true ideas" – ideas that reveal the essences of things – from fictions, "clear and distinct" perceptions from confused ones. We must strive for precision and clarity in our concepts, such that we are certain they include nothing that does not belong to the essential nature of a thing; and that the properties that do belong essentially to the thing are all distinguished one from another and are seen to follow from the thing's nature. In this way, we can perceive, for example, that the sum of the interior angles of a triangle equals one hundred and eighty degrees, and that the soul cannot have material parts. In other words, in our pursuit of knowledge – and, ultimately, of well-being – we must rely on the intellect, not on the imagination or the senses. If one should inquire as to the reliability of the intellect itself and raise the epistemological question as to how we can be sure that our clear and distinct ideas really are objectively true and not just subjectively certain, then (like Descartes before him) Spinoza appeals directly to the benevolence and veracity of God.[65] Because a supremely perfect God, who gave us our knowing faculties in the first place, cannot be a deceiver, if we use those faculties properly we will arrive at truth.

When the ideas in the mind truly and adequately represent the essences of things and reflect the order of Nature, then we have reached our desired state of perfection. But, Spinoza insists, this will happen only when we connect all the ideas of things in Nature with the idea of the being that is the source of all of Nature.

The aim, then, is to have clear and distinct ideas, i.e., such as have been made from the pure mind, and not from fortuitous motions of the body. And then, so that all ideas may be led back to one, we shall strive to connect and order them so that our mind, as far as possible, reproduces objectively the formal character of nature, both as to the whole and as to the parts. . . . It is required, and reason demands, that we ask, as soon as possible, whether there is a certain being, and at the same time, what sort of being it is, which is the cause of all things, so that its objective essence may be the cause of all our ideas, and then our mind will (as we have said) reproduce Nature as much as possible. For it will have Nature's essence, order, and unity objectively.[66]

To know Nature and our place in it is to perceive that Nature has its origin in a most perfect being. Consequently, we must do all we can to ensure not just that we have a clear idea of this perfect being, but also that all of our other ideas follow in the proper order from the idea of this being. "It is evident that for our mind to reproduce completely the likeness of Nature, it must bring all of its ideas forth from that idea which represents the source and origin of the whole of Nature, so that that idea is also the source of the other ideas."[67] Spinoza never, in the *Treatise*, calls this being "God," but that is clearly what is suggested (and what perhaps might have been made explicit in the subsequent parts of the work). There is a certain "fixed and eternal" aspect to Nature, including its laws and the most general natures of things. All natural beings and events, all series of causes and "singular, changeable things" follow necessarily from these universal and immutable elements. When we see that this is the case, and how things causally flow from "the first cause," "the source and origin of Nature" – what in the *Ethics* is expressly identified as God and his attributes – then we have grasped the highest truth of all.

It is not clear why Spinoza left the *Treatise* unfinished. Much of its content – including the idea of a fixed and inviolable order of nature that has its source in a higher being, as well as the radical ethical notion that nothing is good or bad in itself but only relative to human ends – reappears in his more mature works, so it was certainly not because he felt there was something fundamentally wrong with its main doctrines. Perhaps he sensed an inadequacy in his presentation, or some flaws in his arguments. Or Spinoza may have simply concluded that there was no need to put all of the material on method up front in a distinct treatise; the *Short Treatise on God, Man and His Well-Being*, on which he began to work soon after abandoning the *Treatise*,[68] includes its methodological elements within the main body of the work.

⋅❧

According to the Danish traveler Olaus Borch's diary, Spinoza was still in Amsterdam as late as May 1661, the "impudent Jew" among the "atheistic Cartesians" meeting in that city.[69] The first letter of Spinoza's extant correspondence, however – a brief epistle from Henry Oldenburg in London dated August 26, 1661 – indicates that by that time Spinoza had already been living in Rijnsburg for about a month (Oldenburg begins by fondly recalling his recent visit "to your retreat at Rijnsburg"). Thus, in the summer of 1661 Spinoza moved to that small village a few miles outside Leiden. Perhaps, as his friend Jellesz suggests, he was seeking the peace and quiet of the countryside and some respite from the constant interruptions of his friends so that he could devote himself to the "investigation into truth" and be "less disturbed in his meditations."[70] This may be what, some years later, he told Lucas, who wrote that "[Spinoza] hoped to disengage himself from the madness of a large city, when people started bothering him." It was, he insists, "the love of solitude" that motivated Spinoza to leave Amsterdam for Rijnsburg, "where, far from all the obstacles [to his studies] which he could only overcome by flight, he devoted himself entirely to philosophy."[71] There probably were no longer any reasons of a family nature to remain in the city of his birth. His brother Gabriel was still living in Amsterdam, as was his sister (or half-sister) Rebecca. But by the terms of the *cherem* they were forbidden to communicate with him, although we do not know how scrupulously they adhered to that prohibition. Because Spinoza no longer had a part in the family business, which Gabriel seems to have run by himself until he left for the West Indies, there was no financial incentive to stay in Amsterdam.

Spinoza may have been directed to Rijnsburg by his Collegiant friends. The village had been, some years before, the center of Collegiant activity in Holland. By the early 1660s, though, it had diminished in importance to the movement; the "college" there now met only twice a year.[72] Another German traveler, Gottlieb Stolle's companion, a man named Hallmann, reports in his journal that Rijnsburg enjoyed a strong reputation for tolerance, and that it was a particularly good place for refugees seeking religious freedom.[73] That may have had some influence on Spinoza, although he certainly was no refugee – he was not hounded out of Amsterdam, either by the rabbis or by anyone else. A more likely explanation for his choice of Rijnsburg was its proximity to Leiden. It afforded him easy access to the university, where he probably still had friends from the time he had studied there. Rijnsburg thus combined the virtues of a quiet retreat in the country with the resources of a university town, all the better to pursue his philosophical work.

A Philosopher
in Rijnsburg

B Y THE MIDDLE OF THE SUMMER OF 1661, Spinoza was living in
Rijnsburg. He lodged with Herman Homan, a chemist-surgeon, in a
house on the Katwijklaan, a quiet street removed from the center of the
village. Homan belonged to the local "college," and it was probably through
his Amsterdam Collegiant friends that Spinoza was referred to his new
landlord. The house is still there, its facade graced, since 1667 (after Spinoza's departure), with a stone bearing a Dutch inscription from a play by
Dirk Camphuysen:

> Alas, if all humans were wise
> And had more good will,
> The world would be a paradise.
> Now it is mostly a hell.

In the back of the house was a room where Spinoza set up his lense-
grinding equipment. It was a craft he must have begun working on while
still in Amsterdam, for by the time he settled in Rijnsburg he was fairly
skilled at it and ready to get to work. As early as fall 1661, he was known
for making not just lenses but also telescopes and microscopes.[1] Spinoza
may initially have taken up the production of lenses and instruments to
support himself. When he was forced to break off all relations with the
Jewish community completely, and therefore could not conduct his importing business, he had to seek his living by other means. But the firm
"Bento y Gabriel Despinoza" was not bringing in very much income from
1655 onward anyway, certainly not enough to cover the debts he inherited
from his father, and Spinoza could not have felt his forced retirement from
the business to be much of a pressing loss. Moreover, from the opening
paragraphs of the *Treatise on the Emendation of the Intellect* it is clear that
Spinoza had independent, philosophical reasons for leaving the world of
business, to turn from the pursuit of money and other mutable goods to

the search for the "true good": "I found that, if I devoted myself to this new plan of life, and gave up the old . . . I would be giving up certain evils for a certain good."[2] He made an effort all his life to keep his material needs to a minimum, and his friends provided a good deal of financial help.

The work on lenses, then, more likely arose not primarily from pecuniary need but from scientific interest. Spinoza, with his general enthusiasm for the new mechanistic science, was interested in the latest detailed explanations of the microphenomena of biology and chemistry and the ever-improving observations of the macrophenomena of astronomy, as well as in the principles of optics that made such discoveries possible. He wrote to Oldenburg in 1665, with evident delight, about some new instruments he had heard of from the Dutch scientist and mathematician Christiaan Huygens: "He has told me wonderful things about these microscopes, and also about certain telescopes, made in Italy, with which they could observe eclipses of Jupiter caused by the interposition of its satellites, and also a certain shadow on Saturn, which looked as if it were caused by a ring."[3]

Spinoza himself did not do much significant original work in the physical or mathematical sciences. He did have a solid grasp of optical theory and of the then current physics of light, and was competent enough to engage in sophisticated discussion with correspondents over fine points in the mathematics of refraction. Writing in 1666 to the mathematician Johannes Hudde, who had an interest in the cutting and polishing of lenses, Spinoza offered a geometrical argument for why he believed that convex/plane lenses are more useful than convex/concave lenses.[4] But, despite Lucas's claim that "if death had not prevented it, there is reason to believe that he would have discovered the most beautiful secrets of optics,"[5] Spinoza was not particularly noted among his contemporaries for his theoretical contributions to the science. He did, however, have a well-recognized talent for practical optics, as well as a passion for microscopic and telescopic observation. Over time, he earned praise from some notable experts for his expertise in lense and instrument construction. Huygens, writing to his brother from Paris in 1667 (when Spinoza was living in Voorburg), noted that "the [lenses] that the Jew of Voorburg has in his microscopes have an admirable polish."[6] A month later, still using the somewhat contemptuous epithet – occasionally replaced in his letters by "our Israelite" – he wrote that "the Jew of Voorburg finishes [achevoit] his little lenses by means of the instrument and this renders them very excellent."[7] By the early 1670s,

Spinoza's reputation was sufficiently widespread that the German philosopher Leibniz called him "an outstanding optician, a maker of rather famous peeptubes" and told him directly that "among your other achievements which fame has spread abroad I understand is your remarkable skill in optics . . . I shall not easily find someone who can judge better in this field of studies."[8] Even Dirk Kerckrinck, his old colleague from Van den Enden's school, now an established and skilled physician and married to his former teacher's daughter, lauded Spinoza's handiwork: "I own a first-class microscope made by that Benedictus Spinoza, that noble mathematician and philosopher, which enables me to see the lymphatic vascular bundles. . . . Well, this that I have clearly discovered by means of my marvelous instrument, is itself still more marvelous."[9]

Grinding and polishing lenses, in Spinoza's day, was a quiet, intense, and solitary occupation, demanding discipline and patience – in a word, an occupation perfectly suited to Spinoza's temperament. Unfortunately, it was not as well suited to his physical constitution, and the glass dust produced by the process probably exacerbated his respiratory problems and contributed to his early death.

&

Soon after taking up residence on the Katwijklaan, Spinoza received a visit from Henry Oldenburg, who was on one of his periodic trips to the Continent. Born around 1620 in Bremen, where his father taught philosophy (and where he was originally named Heinrich), Oldenburg began an extended stay in England, perhaps as tutor for some wealthy family, sometime after finishing his theology degree in 1639. By 1648, he was back on the Continent to travel and, eventually, to spend some time in his hometown. In 1653, the Bremen town council, apparently impressed by Oldenburg's contacts in England, asked him to go back to that country to negotiate with Oliver Cromwell over Bremen's neutrality during the first Anglo–Dutch war. He remained in England throughout most of the mid-1650s, studying at Oxford and tutoring aristocratic youth, and there became friendly with such notable intellectuals as the poet John Milton, who was also Cromwell's Latin secretary, and the philosopher Thomas Hobbes.

During his studies, Oldenburg had developed an interest in scientific matters, a passion later strengthened by a visit to the French Académie des Sciences and to the famous group of savants who had been meeting at the house of Henri-Louis Habert de Montmor in Paris. Back in London in mid-1660, he joined the group of individuals meeting at Gresham College to conduct "experimental inquiries into the secrets of nature." Oldenburg became an active member of this club, and when they incorporated in 1662 as the Royal Society he was given the job of secretary. His numerous international contacts in the scientific world, including Huygens, made him the natural choice for the post. He would be responsible for maintaining the society's correspondence with its continental colleagues, and for gathering news and data from various far-flung investigators.

Before taking up his duties with the new society, Oldenburg made a trip to Bremen and to the Netherlands. He intended to pay a visit to Huygens, whom he would bring up to date on scientific developments in England. Before reaching The Hague, however, he passed through Amsterdam and Leiden. In one of those cities – or perhaps both – he heard mention of Spinoza, either from mutual Collegiant or Cartesian acquaintances in Amsterdam such as Peter Serrarius[10] or Jan Rieuwertsz,[11] or from Johannes Coccejus, the liberal professor of theology at the University of Leiden and a good friend.[12] His curiosity piqued, he set out in mid-July from Leiden to Rijnsburg to call on the recently relocated philosopher. The two men got along well; their first exchange of letters after the visit is full of warm regards and wishes for a speedy reunion. Spinoza must have made quite an impression on his visitor, who wrote that "it was so difficult to tear myself away from your side, that now that I am back in England I hasten to unite myself with you, so far as is possible, even if it is only by correspondence." He urges upon Spinoza that they should "bind ourselves to one another in unfeigned friendship, and let us cultivate that friendship assiduously, with every kind of good will and service."[13] Spinoza, for his part, proclaims "how pleasing your friendship is to me," but fears appearing too eager in the eyes of the more worldly and experienced Oldenburg:

I seem to myself rather presumptuous, to dare to enter into friendship with you (particularly when I think that friends must share all things, especially spiritual things). Nevertheless, this step must be ascribed to your courtesy and good will, rather than to me. The former is so great that you have been willing to belittle yourself, the latter so abundant that you have been willing to enrich me, that I might not fear to enter into the close friendship you continue to offer me and deign to ask of me in return. I shall take great care to cultivate it zealously.[14]

In Spinoza's rooms they talked about God and his attributes, the union of the human soul with the body, and the philosophies of Descartes and

Bacon – all topics of immediate concern to Spinoza. For the last several months he had been laboring over a systematic philosophical treatise. In this work, he would examine the metaphysical, ethical, theological, psychological, methodological, physical, and epistemological questions that he had been pondering for some time, and that were only hinted at (as his "Philosophy") in the *Treatise on the Emendation of the Intellect*.

When Spinoza first wrote back to Oldenburg in September 1661, the *Short Treatise on God, Man and His Well-Being* was still very much a work in progress.[15] It was most likely begun while he was still in Amsterdam, at the instigation of his friends. They must have recognized that Spinoza was well beyond merely discussing with them the doctrines of others – especially Descartes – and they may have wanted a concise exposition of his own developing philosophical ideas, preferably something on paper that they could study and discuss. Spinoza obliged them, composing a work in Latin probably sometime between the middle of 1660 and his departure for Rijnsburg. When they asked for a Dutch version, perhaps for those members of the group whose Latin was less than fluent, Spinoza reworked the text, making additions and emendations along the way, sometimes in response to his friends' queries and suggestions.[16] This process of composition and revision continued throughout 1661. Though Spinoza seems to have thought of eventually publishing the treatise,[17] his remarks at the end of the work make it clear that it really was mainly a presentation of his philosophy for his friends:

To bring all this to an end, it remains only for me to say to the friends to whom I write this: do not be surprised at these novelties, for you know very well that it is no obstacle to the truth of a thing that it is not accepted by many. And as you are also aware of the character of the age in which we live, I would ask you urgently to be very careful about communicating these things to others.[18]

Spinoza clearly recognized, not just the extraordinary originality of his ideas, but the certainty of their appearing too radical in the eyes of the Dutch Calvinist authorities.

The *Short Treatise* starts out innocently enough, with several proofs for the existence of God. And, like the *Treatise on the Emendation of the Intellect,* the conclusion of the work is that human happiness and well-being, indeed our "blessedness," consists in a knowledge of God and of how all things in nature depend on him. This is accompanied by an exhortation to love God as our highest and true good. However, the God whose existence is demonstrated is not a God who would have been familiar to the members of the Reformed Church, or indeed of any religion. It is not God the benevolent and free creator of whom Spinoza speaks. His God is not a lawgiver and judge in any traditional sense. He is not a source of comfort or reward or punishment, nor is he a being to whom one would pray. Spinoza explicitly denies that God is omniscient, compassionate, and wise. Rather, God is "a being of whom infinite attributes are predicated." God is what Spinoza calls "substance." Substance is simply real being. It is, by definition and demonstration, infinitely perfect as well as infinite and unique in its kind; that is, it is not limited by any other substance of the same nature. It is also causally independent of anything outside of itself: substance exists necessarily, not contingently.

Thus, the thinking substance, the substance of which thought is an attribute or nature, is infinite and unique; there is only one thinking substance. The same is true of the extended substance, or the substance of which extension (or dimensionality, the essence of matter) is an attribute. In fact, thought and extension are just two attributes or natures of the one infinite and perfect substance. The substance of which thought is an attribute is numerically identical with the substance of which extension is an attribute. All of the attributes that are in nature – and we have knowledge of only two of them – are, despite their apparently substantial diversity, simply different aspects of one single being. Nature is a unity, a whole outside of which there is nothing. But if Nature is just the substance composed of infinite attributes, the underlying productive unity of all things, then Nature is God. All things in nature "exist in and are understood within God." God is not outside of nature. He is not some distant cause. Rather, God is the immanent and sustaining cause of all there is. God is also the free cause of all things, although this does not imply that things could have happened otherwise than as they did happen or that things could have been more or less perfect. Everything flows from God – from Nature – with an eternal necessity. Nothing in nature is contingent or accidental. There are no spontaneous or uncaused events. Nothing could have *not* happened as it did. It is all "predestined" and necessitated by the eternal attributes of God.

Spinoza calls God *Natura naturans*, or "naturing Nature" – the active, eternal, and immutable dimension of nature. "Nature" in this sense is invisible: it consists in the unseen but universal attributes of thought and extension – the two natures that are known to us of all that exists – along with the laws governing each, the laws of thought and the laws of extension (that is, geometry). The world as we know it, the world of matter and motion (including physical bodies) and of intellect (including the ideas or concepts of bodies), is *Natura naturata*, or "natured Nature." This world is no more but the product of the infinite substance that generates and sustains it. Singular things and their properties are what Spinoza calls "modes" of that substance – ways in which the attributes of the substance express themselves. Unlike the underlying substance itself, they come into being and go out of being according to nature's unchanging laws.

This is the metaphysical background for Spinoza's ethics and anthropology. Because everything in nature just *is*, and follows necessarily from God, one consequence of Spinoza's radical determinism is that good and evil are nothing real in themselves. "Good and evil do not exist in nature," he insists, but are only "beings of reason," products of the mind. All good and evil is relative to our conceptions. These moral categories are merely labels that we attach to things when they measure up or fail to measure up to our ideals. A "good" person is simply a person who meets our criteria of a perfect human being, just as a bad hammer is a hammer that fails to correspond to our idea of a perfect hammer.

The human being is a composite of soul and body. But, unlike the dualism in Descartes's metaphysics, the human soul and the human body are not, for Spinoza, two distinct substances. Our soul is just a mode of one of God's substantial attributes, thought. It is, in fact, the mode in thought – it is an idea or knowledge – that corresponds to a particular mode in the extensional attribute of God, which is all that the body is.[19]

Because a human being consists in a mind (a mode of thought) and a body (a mode of extension), he is the subject both of "perceptions" (or ways of knowing) and of passions, with different passions naturally attending different kinds of knowledge. As for our perceptions, Spinoza distinguishes, as he did in the *Treatise on the Emendation of the Intellect,* among opinions acquired through report or random experience, true beliefs acquired through the art of reasoning, and (best of all) an intuitive grasp of the thing itself through a clear and distinct concept. Unlike indirect acquaintance and random experience, rational knowledge, whether it be inferential or immediate, is not subject to error. It is a stable cognitive state and provides an apprehension of the essence of its object. The better the object, the better the knowledge; the better the knowledge, the better the condition of the knower. "The most perfect man," he claims, "is the one who unites with the most perfect being, God, and thus enjoys him."[20]

These different ways of perceiving have their specific affective consequences. Spinoza carefully catalogues, analyzes, and evaluates the different
passions of human beings – love, joy, hate, sadness, envy, shame, desire, grat-
itude, remorse, and so on – and demonstrates which are most conducive
to human happiness and which contribute to our destruction. As long as
we rely on report and random experience, valuing and chasing the fleeting objects of our imagination and senses, we will be governed by the passions of desire, hate, love, sadness, wonder, lust, fear, despair, and hope.
Corruptible things are completely outside our power. We have no control
over them, and both their properties and our possession of them are subject to many accidents. This kind of love and attachment can lead only to
misery. True belief, on the other hand, brings us to a clear understanding
of the order of things and allows us to perceive in an intellectual manner
how the objects outside of us actually all depend on their ultimate cause
and origin. We eventually come to know God himself and "the eternal and
incorruptible things" that depend immediately on God, as well as the ways
in which corruptible things follow from these.

The knowledge of God just is the knowledge of Nature in its broadest
dimension. And this knowledge leads to Love of the highest being on
whom everything else depends. In this way, we can condition ourselves to
act without passions such as hate and envy, all of which are based anyway
on misconceptions and false evaluations of things, as well as on a lack of
insight into their necessity. The proper use of reason will eliminate those
harmful passions from our lives. We will abide in the stable contemplation
of an unchanging being. "If a man comes to love God, who always is and
remains immutable, it is impossible for him to fall into this bog of the passions. And therefore, we maintain it as a fixed and unshakeable rule, that
God is the first and only cause of all our good, and one who frees us from
all our evil."[21]

What one also comes to perceive is that the human being himself is a
part of nature and is indissolubly linked within its causal nexus to the order of things. We, too, are determined in our actions and passions; freedom,
understood as spontaneity, is an illusion. "Because man is a part of the
whole of nature, depends on it, and is governed by it, he can do nothing,
of himself, toward his salvation and well-being."[22] We need to learn that
our body, and through it our mind, is subject to the same laws of nature as
any other thing. "We depend on what is most perfect in such a way that we
are a part of the whole, i.e., of him [God], and so to speak contribute our
share to the accomplishment of as many well-ordered and perfect works

as are dependent on him." This knowledge "frees us from sadness, despair, envy, fright, and other evil passions, which . . . are the real hell itself." Above all, we will no longer fear God, "who is himself the greatest good and through whom all things that have any essence – and we who live in him – are what they are."

This is the road to well-being and happiness. The knowledge and love of God, by diminishing the power that our bodies have over us, will free us from the disturbances of the passions and, at the same time, maximize our "true freedom" (understood as a "firm existence that our intellect acquires through immediate union with God" and a liberation from external causes). Herein lies our "blessedness."[23]

Despite Spinoza's theological language and what look like concessions to orthodox sentiment ("the Love of God is our greatest blessedness"), there is no mistaking his intentions. His goal is nothing less than the complete desacrilization and naturalization of religion and its concepts: "Man, so long as he is a part of Nature, must follow the laws of Nature. That is true religion. So long as he does this, he has his well-being."[24] The existence and nature of God and of his providence (reduced by Spinoza to the natural inertia in beings to preserve themselves), predestination (the causal necessity in the world), salvation, and "God's love of man" are all given a naturalistic interpretation in terms of substance, its attributes and modes, and the laws of nature. Even the immortality of the soul is taken to be nothing more than an "eternal duration." As long as the soul is united only with the body, it is mortal and perishes with the body. When it is united with an immutable thing, however (such as occurs when it knows God or substance), the soul too partakes of immutability. It is not a personal immortality in which one can take much comfort.

The *Short Treatise* is a difficult and complex work. Spinoza devoted a great deal of energy to clarifying and revising its content and presentation. He may have shown some parts of a copy of the latest Latin manuscript to Oldenburg when he stopped in Rijnsburg in the summer of 1661, but he seems to have been cautious about revealing too much detail to his visitor: Oldenburg recalls that "we spoke as if through a lattice."[25] Oldenburg was deeply intrigued by what he heard or read, but also confused, particularly by the metaphysics of the system. Among other things, it was couched in what seemed to be Cartesian terms, yet did not appear to be propounding ordinary Cartesian doctrines. Spinoza was willing to help clarify matters to his new friend, but, despite his claim that "you will easily be able to see what I am aiming at," Oldenburg seems to have had trouble putting it all together.

Spinoza worked on the *Short Treatise* throughout 1661 and into 1662, "transcribing and emending it," as he told Oldenburg.[26] He hesitated to publish it, however, not so much because it was never finished – he seems, in fact, to have regarded it as a complete work by early 1662, even if it needed more polishing – but because he feared that "the theologians of our time may be offended and with their usual hatred attack me, who absolutely dread quarrels."[27] Even in July 1663, he was holding on to the manuscript, waiting to see what the public reaction would be to his soon-to-be-published critical summary of the principles of Descartes's philosophy.[28] He had still not sent even a summary of the *Short Treatise* to Oldenburg, who was anxious to have a copy.[29] The secretary of the Royal Society nonetheless encouraged him, several times, to go forward: "Let it be published, whatever rumblings there may be among the foolish theologians. Your Republic is very free, and gives great freedom for philosophizing."[30] Either Oldenburg's conception of the extent of Dutch toleration was slightly exaggerated or he failed to grasp the deeper theological implications of Spinoza's work.

Along with his queries and promptings, Oldenburg, aware of Spinoza's interest in scientific matters and carrying out his duties as the secretary for the Royal Society, sent to Rijnsburg in the fall of 1661 a copy of the Latin translation of "some physiological essays" by Robert Boyle, the great seventeenth-century English scientist and author of the law on the expansion of gases. Boyle was primarily a chemist and an important proponent of the mechanist paradigm. His main programmatic concern was with demonstrating that chemistry, like the other physical sciences, could be pursued in purely mechanistic terms, without the occult qualities and mysterious powers of the Aristotelian scientists. Chemical reactions, physical alterations, and the qualitative and causal properties of things could all be explained as the result of the motion, rest, connection, and impact of minute particles of matter (or "corpuscles") of varying shapes and sizes. No longer would the coldness of snow be explained by the presence in it of the quality *frigiditas*, or "coldness," or the power of opium to put one to sleep by the "dormitive virtue," as Molière so famously satirized the Aristotelian mode of explanation. From now on, Boyle hoped, scientific explanation could proceed in a clear, perspicuous manner by appealing only to the quantitative features of matter. If a certain compound tasted

salty or bitter, it was only because of the way in which the microscopic particles constituting the elements of the compound interacted with the pores
of the tongue.

Oldenburg saw Boyle and Spinoza as similarly motivated colleagues in
the search for scientific truth. Over the course of his correspondence with
Spinoza, acting as a facilitator and mediator between his two friends, he
tried to smooth over whatever differences they had on the details of particular phenomena and bring their agreement on general principles to the
fore. What seemed most important to him was their mutual commitment
to the new science. He looked forward to the contributions that, together,
they could make to that enterprise according to their particular but com-
plementary talents.

I would . . . encourage you both to unite your abilities in cultivating eagerly a genuine and solid Philosophy. May I advise you [Spinoza] especially to continue to
establish the principles of things by the acuteness of your Mathematical understanding, as I constantly urge my noble friend Boyle to confirm and illustrate this
philosophy by experiments and observations, repeatedly and accurately made.[31]

In the "Essay on Niter," one of the pieces included in the book that Oldenburg sent Spinoza, Boyle argued through reasoning and experiment that
niter, or saltpeter (potassium nitrate), is of a "heterogeneous" or mixed nature, composed of "fixed parts" (potassium carbonate) and "volatile parts"
("spirit of niter," or nitric acid) both of which differ from each other and
from the whole that they constitute. He melted some niter in a crucible,
placed a hot coal in it, and allowed it to kindle. He continued to heat the
mixture until all of the "volatile part" was gone. What remained was the
"fixed part," which he then reconstituted into niter by adding drops of
spirit of niter and then allowing the solution to evaporate and crystallize.
What he hoped to demonstrate was not only that this particular compound
was made up of particles that differ from each other in kind (the particles
of spirit of niter being fundamentally different from the particles of the
fixed niter), but, more generally, that the distinctive properties of niter and
of its constituent parts (such as their taste, smell, etc.) – and indeed of any
substance – can all be explained by differences in the shape, size, relationship, and motion of their particles. According to Oldenburg, Boyle wrote
these essays primarily "to show the usefulness of Chemistry for confirm-
ing the Mechanical principles of Philosophy."[32]

Spinoza shared absolutely Boyle's commitment to the mechanical philosophy, to the corpuscularian explanation of this and other chemical, physical, and sensory phenomena. But he wondered why, if the confirmation of the general principles of mechanism was Boyle's goal, he went to so much experimental trouble. For while experiment may tell us something about the particular nature of niter itself, the fact that niter's nature is a mechanistic one to begin with – and, more importantly, that nature in general operates solely according to the principles of the mechanist philosophy – is not something that can be revealed by experiment but only by the intellect, as Descartes and Bacon showed so well.[33] Besides, Spinoza argued, even Boyle's conclusions about the heterogeneous nature of niter were not warranted by his experiments. He claimed that those experimental results were perfectly consistent with the hypothesis of the homogeneity of niter. In fact, he provided his own experiments to support the hypothesis that niter and spirit of niter are, in fact, the same substance, made up of the same kind of particles. The only difference is that when those particles are at rest it is niter, and when they are in motion it is spirit of niter. The "reconstitution" of niter, he argued, is simply the coming to rest of the particles of spirit of niter. What Boyle called the "fixed niter," the salt that remained when the spirit of niter has been cooked away, is nothing but an impurity in the original niter.[34]

In his correspondence with Oldenburg about Boyle's writings, Spinoza shows himself to be, if not as accomplished a chemist as Boyle, at least skilled in conducting experiments and in his employment of the scientific method of formulating hypotheses and testing them against experimental results. His interest in chemistry, his familiarity with up-to-date chemical theories, and his facility with the ingredients, hardware, and processes of chemical experimentation probably date to his days in Amsterdam. There were a number of well-known chemists and alchemists working in that city, including Paul Felgenhauer and Johannes Glauber. Van den Enden and Serrarius were frequent attendees at the discussions on chemical experiments held at Glauber's laboratory, where much work on niter was being done in the late 1650s.[35] It seems plausible – even, in light of Spinoza's easy familiarity with experimentation on niter in 1661, certain – that Spinoza accompanied his former Latin tutor to those discussions.

ॐ

Over time, and particularly in the minds of his biographers, there arose the myth of Spinoza the recluse, a loner living in seclusion and working in a solitary manner on his philosophy. From what we know about his life in Rijnsburg, however, it appears that nothing could be further from the truth. He had several close and devoted friends whose company he enjoyed and valued, and many acquaintances, with some of whom he kept up a lively and philosophically fruitful correspondence.

The population of Rijnsburg, tolerant and generous though it was, may not itself have been a great source of educated companions and intellectual stimulation. There is no way of knowing how close Spinoza was to the Collegiants in the village, and whether he attended their meetings or even socialized with them. None of his extant letters from Rijnsburg mention the group, whose "college" was fairly dormant by the early 1660s. He would certainly have found among them some with whom he could discuss religion and morality, and he must have been on at least friendly if not intimate terms with the local colleagues of his anticonfessional Amsterdam friends. But he was very engaged at this time with his writing, studies, and lense grinding, and there is no reason to think that he became a regular member of the Rijnsburg Collegiants, as some have suggested.

Spinoza often left sleepy Rijnsburg and the quietude of his "retreat" to visit one city or another to meet with his friends. On at least one occasion, perhaps in late 1662, he was in The Hague and there spoke with Simon de Vries.[36] He also made several trips into Amsterdam, sometimes staying for a couple of weeks, no doubt to spend time with De Vries, Jellesz, Meyer, and the rest of the company. And then there must have been frequent visits to nearby Leiden, perhaps to hear some of the lectures being given by De Raey (now professor of philosophy at the university) or by his fellow Cartesian Arnold Geulincx, and to partake of the town's intellectual life. Spinoza actually had a reputation in Leiden. When Olaus Borch was taking in the tourist sites in the area, a medical doctor told him about a certain "Spinoza who, from being a Jew, became a Christian and was now almost an atheist, and was living in Rijnsburg; that he excelled in the Cartesian philosophy, what is more, that he even superseded Descartes with his distinct and probable ideas."[37]

The traffic between Rijnsburg and the cities of Amsterdam and Leiden was two-way, and Oldenburg was not the only visitor to the corner house on the Katwijklaan. Spinoza appears to have seen much of Pieter Balling, who acted as a kind of courier between Spinoza and the Amsterdam group. Balling traveled to Rijnsburg on several occasions to talk with his friend and to carry letters back and forth between Spinoza and the others. Among

Spinoza's acquaintances in Leiden were a number of students from the
university who, possibly inspired by De Raey's lectures, seem to have made
a habit of going to Rijnsburg to seek enlightenment on the finer principles
of Cartesian philosophy. There was, first, another Dane, Niels Stensen
(Nicolaus Steno, in the university's Latin register), who would go on to
become an accomplished anatomist. Writing in 1671, Steno recalled Spinoza as "a man who was once my good friend" and elsewhere claimed to be
well acquainted with "the many Spinozists in the Netherlands."[38] The
university records also show that Jan Koerbagh, brother of Adriaan, had
returned to Leiden from Amsterdam in 1662 to finish his studies in theology.[39] He would certainly have found time to pay a visit or two to his
brother's friend. Abraham van Berckel, a friend of the Koerbagh brothers,
was studying medicine at the university. He shared Spinoza's and Adriaan
Koerbagh's interest in political philosophy. In 1667, he would perform the
important service of translating Thomas Hobbes's *Leviathan* (1651), one
of the seminal works in the history of political thought, into Dutch. Dirk
Kerckrinck, as well, was still around Leiden, probably finishing his medical studies. He, too, may have gone out, either alone or with others, to see
his old companion from Van den Enden's Latin school.

Then there was a young man named Burchard de Volder. He was born
in Amsterdam in 1643 into a Mennonite family and may have first met
Spinoza while they both were still living in that city; perhaps De Volder,
too, learned his Latin at Van den Enden's, possibly with Spinoza's assistance. He went on to study philosophy and mathematics at the University
of Utrecht, and then medicine at Leiden. He was in Leiden until 1664,
when he took his degree and returned to Amsterdam to set up his medical
practice. With his interest in Cartesian philosophy, De Volder, like the others, would have made the short trip to Rijnsburg during his student days
to talk with that village's resident expert on Descartes. What is certain is
that, by the mid-1660s, De Volder and Spinoza were good friends. In fact,
Dr. Hallman – who, with his traveling companion Stolle, actually talked
to De Volder after the latter had become a professor of philosophy at the
University of Leiden – wrote in his diary that Rieuwertsz's son had described De Volder to them as "Spinoza's special friend."[40] De Volder knew
Spinoza's work well, as his conversation with Stolle reveals, and he may
even have held views similar to those of his Jewish friend.[41] Although his
work as a physician kept him busy, De Volder maintained a steady interest
in mathematical and scientific questions. He published a number of works

in philosophy, including a long defense of Descartes against a vicious condemnation by the French bishop Pierre-Daniel Huet; and he kept up a lively intellectual correspondence with Leibniz, Huygens, and others. In 1697, he was made rector of the University of Leiden, a significant indication of how far Cartesianism had come since its initial condemnation at that university in the 1640s. It is unlikely that those who appointed him to this post were aware of his past long and close relationship with the reviled heretic from Amsterdam.

Spinoza seems to have had a talent for attracting a coterie of like-minded individuals who were eager to hear and discuss what he had to say on various philosophical matters, and it is possible that, during his time in Rijnsburg, a circle developed in Leiden that paralleled the group in Amsterdam. One gets the impression that Spinoza had a fairly charismatic personality, in his own quiet way. Lucas tries to convey just this when he writes that

[Spinoza's] conversation had such an air of geniality and his comparisons were so just that he made everybody fall in unconsciously with his views. He was persuasive although he did not affect polished or elegant diction. He made himself so intelligible, and his discourse was so full of good sense, that none listened to him without deriving satisfaction. These fine talents attracted to him all reasonable people, and whatever time it may have been one always found him in an even and agreeable humor. . . . He had a great and penetrating mind and a very complacent disposition. He had a wit so well seasoned that the most gentle and the most severe found very peculiar charms in it.[42]

One of the Leiden students who regularly visited Spinoza ended up staying for extended lessons. This gave Spinoza a constant but not altogether welcome companion and housemate for a time. Johannes Casear (or Casearius) was born in 1642 in Amsterdam. He may originally have met Spinoza at Van den Enden's in the mid-1650s; perhaps there he received his first lessons from Spinoza, in Latin grammar. He left Amsterdam for Leiden to study theology at around the same time that Spinoza moved to Rijnsburg. Casearius lived briefly in Leiden itself, on the Salomonsteeg in the home of Jacob van der As, but soon left town and moved in with Spinoza. His aim was to obtain a thorough instruction in the Cartesian philosophy. A few years after Spinoza relocated to Voorburg, Casearius, after a short sojourn at the University of Utrecht, returned to the city of his birth, where he began his career as a Reformed preacher. He had a great desire, however, to be posted to an exotic locale. When, at the end of 1667, the Dutch East Indies Company made known their need for pastors in the colonies, Casearius jumped at the chance. He went to Malabar, on the south-west coast of India, where he developed an interest in botany. When not attending to his pastoral duties, he spent many hours in the company of the governor-general, classifying native flora. He died young there in 1677, from dysentery.[43]

In his lessons to Casearius, Spinoza concentrated on Parts Two and Three of Descartes's *Principles of Philosophy*. This book was intended by Descartes to be his *summa philosophiae*, a complete and systematic exposition of his philosophy and science. Basically a textbook in the Cartesian philosophy, the *Principles* is an ambitious attempt to cover all the usual topics in method, metaphysics, and natural philosophy, much like the Scholastic textbooks – Aristotelian to the core – that he dreamed it would someday replace in the university curriculum. All the scientific explanations that Descartes offers for a great variety of phenomena are mechanistic, and the physics as a whole is grounded in his dualistic metaphysics, in the exclusive and exhaustive ontological division between the world of mind and the world of matter. What Descartes actually published in 1644 may have been something less than he had initially hoped for, and he was frustrated in the accomplishment of some important aspects of his project. Still, the *Principles* represents the most extensive and detailed presentation of his mature thought.

In Part One, Descartes first covers the foundational epistemological material that he had already worked through in the *Meditations on First Philosophy*, including the proofs that God exists and is not a deceiver and thus that our rational faculties are, when used properly, a reliable means to the truth. Then, after introducing the fundamental categories of mind–body dualism and of his metaphysics of substance, he moves, in Part Two, to consider the nature of matter and motion and the most general principles of physics, including the laws of nature and the rules governing impact between bodies in motion and at rest. Part Three of the treatise, "The Visible Universe," is devoted to an overview of his celestial physics. Descartes cautiously but nonetheless confidently throws in his lot with Copernicus. Among other things, he offers his famous vortex account of the heavens and uses it to explain how the planets are carried around the sun, describes what sunspots are, and provides a theory of the cause of the motion of comets. In Part Four, he turns to the terrestrial world, and, in the terms of the new science and employing in his hypotheses only particulate matter in motion, explains such phenomena as gravity and magnetism and establishes the foundations for a Cartesian chemistry and material science.

The lessons in Spinoza's house proceeded with the teacher dictating to his student a precise but occasionally critical exposition of Descartes's philosophy, focusing on Part Two and some of Part Three of the *Principles of Philosophy*, which contain the most important elements of Cartesian science. In his lectures, Spinoza reworked the material on matter, motion, and their laws into a more rigorous "geometric style," complete with postulates, definitions, axioms, and demonstrated propositions.[44] He also introduced Casearius to "some of the principal and more difficult questions that are disputed in Metaphysics, and that had not yet been resolved by Descartes."[45] These questions almost certainly included the nature of Being, the distinction between essence and existence, and the being of God. What Spinoza did *not* do, however, was initiate Casearius into the principles of his own developing philosophical system, for which he did not think his student was ready.

When Spinoza's friends in Amsterdam heard that he was giving lessons in Cartesian philosophy, and that the beneficiary of these was even living in the same house as Spinoza, they were envious. Simon de Vries wrote to Spinoza in February 1663 to express his ardent desire to see him soon (although the winter weather still prevented any travel) and to complain about the distance that separated him from his friend. He made no attempt to conceal his envy: "Fortunate, indeed most fortunate, is your companion, Casearius, who lives under the same roof with you, and can talk to you about the most important matters at breakfast, at dinner, and on your walks."[46] From Spinoza's reply the following month, we learn that Casearius was an eager but rather undisciplined pupil. Spinoza found him immature, impatient, and hard to teach. The task of tutoring such a person in a philosophy beyond which he himself had moved – a job that Spinoza may have undertaken for income – was clearly something of a burden. But, recalling perhaps his own youthful intellectual enthusiasm, he regarded these defects as simply the shortcomings of Casearius's age. Spinoza had high hopes for the young man, and saw some real talent in him, even if he was not yet prepared to reveal to him – or allow anyone else to reveal to him – his own metaphysical ideas. He replied to De Vries:

there is no need for you to envy Casearius. No one is more troublesome to me, and there is no one with whom I have to be more on my guard. So I should like to warn you and all our friends not to communicate my views to him until he has reached greater maturity. He is still too childish and unstable, more anxious for novelty than for truth. But I hope that in a few years he will correct these youthful faults. Indeed, as far as I can judge from his native ability, I am almost certain that he will. So his talent induces me to like him.[47]

ॐ

Serving as a tutor in Descartes's philosophy for Casearius must also have been a distraction for Spinoza from more pressing projects, such as working on the presentation of his own philosophical system. In early 1662, he was still revising the material in the *Short Treatise*. His ideas on God, nature, and human well-being were, in essential respects, well formed by then. But he was intent on reworking some important details, such as the nature of the relationship between mind and body, the division between kinds of knowledge, and the cataloging of the passions. What particularly concerned him at this point, however, was the mode of exposition of his ideas. In an "Appendix" that appears at the end of the extant manuscripts of the *Short Treatise*, and probably written sometime after the completion of the main body of the work, are seven axioms about substance and its attributes and causality. Following the axioms are demonstrations of four propositions on the uniqueness, independence, infinitude, and existence of substance – essentially the same material from the first two chapters of Book One of the *Short Treatise* proper, except now reorganized into a "geometrical" format. This appendix may, in fact, have been part of an early draft of the *Ethics*, the philosophical magnum opus in which all of the most important doctrines from the *Short Treatise*, along with a great deal more material, is given a complete geometrical presentation. Spinoza had been thinking about a mathematically formatted exposition of his ideas since the fall of 1661. Referring to three of the propositions that would appear, slightly differently, in the appendix (which was probably not yet composed), Spinoza told Oldenburg in September:

Once I have demonstrated these things, then (provided you attend to the definition of God), you will easily be able to see what I am aiming at, so it is not necessary to speak more openly about these matters. But I can think of no better way of demonstrating these things clearly and briefly than to prove them in the Geometric manner and subject them to your understanding.[48]

Even while continuing to emend the *Short Treatise*, then, Spinoza was conceiving – and perhaps even starting to write – a work on a grander scale, one that would provide a more effective and rigorous presentation of his system.

The model for certain knowledge in the seventeenth century was mathematics. Its propositions were clearly formulated, its arguments (when properly attended to) indubitable, and its methods (when properly employed) foolproof. Euclid's *Elements,* the most popular paradigm for the discipline, begins with twenty-three basic definitions ("A point is that which has no part," "A line is a breadthless point"), five postulates ("That all right angles are equal to one another"), and five "common notions" or axioms ("Things which are equal to the same thing are also equal to one another," "If equals be added to equals, the wholes are equal"). With these simple tools in hand as premises, Euclid proceeded to prove a great number of propositions about plane figures and their properties, some of them extremely complex. (The first proposition of Book One, for example, lays out the method for constructing an equilateral triangle on a finite straight line; the fifth proposition is that in an isosceles triangle the angles at the base are equal to one another. By Book Ten, he is demonstrating how to find two rational straight lines that are commensurable in square only.) The demonstration of each proposition uses – besides the definitions, postulates, and axioms – only propositions that have already been established. No unproven assumptions are introduced into the demonstrations; nothing is presupposed except what is self-evident or demonstrably known. In this way, the results are guaranteed to be absolutely certain.

With this model in mind, Spinoza hoped to expand upon and fulfill Descartes's own dream of maximum certainty in the sciences. Like his mentor, he thought that philosophy (understood broadly to include much that today would more properly fall under the natural, human, and social sciences) could reach a degree of precision and indubitability that approximated if not equaled that achieved by mathematics.[49] In short, Spinoza wanted to do for metaphysics, epistemology, physics, psychology and ethics what Euclid had done for geometry. Only in this way could philosophy, the discipline that must prescribe for human beings the path to happiness and well-being, become truly systematic and its conclusions guaranteed to be valid. The means for accomplishing this goal was literally to put metaphysics and the other fields in the exact same form in which Euclid had organized his material. The clarity and distinctness of their presentation would then reveal their truths in a perspicuous and convincing manner. Here Spinoza went beyond anything that Descartes himself had envisioned.[50] Descartes certainly recognized the need for order and rigor in philosophy. He insisted many times throughout his life that one must proceed systematically from indubitable first principles to what can be derived, by means of a validated method, from them with certainty. And he believed that mathematics provided the proper methodological model for all the sciences:

Those long chains composed of very simple and easy reasonings, which geometers customarily use to arrive at their most difficult demonstrations, had given me occasion to suppose that all the things that can fall under human knowledge are interconnected in the same way. . . . Of all those who have hitherto sought after truth in the sciences, mathematicians alone have been able to find any demonstrations – that is to say, certain and evident reasonings.[51]

He argued that "the method that instructs us to follow the correct order, and to enumerate exactly all the relevant factors, contains everything that gives certainty to the rules of arithmetic," and he believed that this same method could be used to resolve the problems of the other sciences as well. At the end of his *Principles of Philosophy*, Descartes suggests that even his detailed mechanistic explanations of particular natural phenomena are absolutely certain. "Mathematical demonstrations have this kind of certainty . . . and perhaps even these results of mine will be allowed into the class of absolute certainties, if people consider how they have been deduced in an unbroken chain from the first and simplest principles of human knowledge."[52]

For Spinoza, however, Descartes did not go far enough. Descartes did not think that the application of "the geometrical method" to philosophy and the sciences required them literally to take on the pattern of Euclid's writing. That is why he never seriously attempted to present his results in true geometric form. And this is what Spinoza tried, in part, to rectify in his lectures to Casearius. He must have felt the same disappointment with his own *Short Treatise*, and it was around the time of his letter to Oldenburg that the explicitly geometrical presentation of his doctrines on God and substance began to occupy much of his intellectual energy. By the end of 1661, in other words, Spinoza was already working on what would become the early parts of his *Ethics*.

He was not the only one interested in the progress of his work. Soon after Spinoza left Amsterdam, his friends seem to have stopped meeting regularly to discuss philosophy. Spinoza had undoubtedly been the leader of their conferences, and now that he was in town only sporadically, the group lacked its catalyst. But sometime in late 1662 or early 1663 its members reconvened. This time, however, it was more of a Spinozist circle than a Cartesian one. For the stimuli for the renewed meetings were Spinoza's own writings, which he had begun sending to his Amsterdam friends for their questions and comments. "Though our bodies are separated from one another by such a distance," De Vries wrote to Spinoza in February 1663, "nevertheless you have very often been present in my mind, especially when I meditate on your writings and hold them in my hands."[53] What De Vries had a copy of, and shared with his colleagues, was part of an early draft of what would be Part One of the *Ethics*, "On God." Balling had brought the manuscript to De Vries when he returned from one of his trips to Rijnsburg. De Vries and the others read through the material, and such was their admiration for their absent friend that they started gathering together in order to discuss it and come to a deeper understanding of Spinoza's thought. De Vries reported to Spinoza that "not everything is clear enough to the members of our group – which is why we have begun meeting again." At these meetings, each individual present – and they probably included De Vries, Meyer, Jellesz, Rieuwertsz, Bouwmeester, Balling, and possibly even the Koerbagh brothers – took a turn reading through the latest assignment, explained its basic sense "according to his own conception," and then performed, for the benefit of all, the demonstrations, "following the sequence and order of your propositions." More obscure points were then debated and discussed. When all else failed, they turned to the author himself for clarification.

If it happens that one [of us] cannot satisfy the other[s], we have thought it worthwhile to make a note of it and to write to you, so that, if possible, it may be made clearer to us, and under your guidance we may be able to defend the truth against those who are superstitiously religious and Christian, and to stand against the attacks of the whole.[54]

The format of the Amsterdam meetings was not unlike that of a Collegiant gathering, although the text being interrogated was no longer *Holy* Scripture. No philosopher could hope for more eager and devoted disciples.

9

"The Jew
of Voorburg"

IN 1665, the village of Voorburg, just outside The Hague, was in the grip
of a rancorous civil dispute over who would be the next pastor of the local church. In a petition composed by one party to the dispute written for
the municipal government of Delft, within whose bailiwick Voorburg lay,
mention is made of a Daniel Tydeman, in whose house lodged "a certain
A[msterdammer?] Spinosa, born of Jewish parents, who is now (so it is
said) an atheist, that is, a man who mocks all religions and is thus a pernicious element in this republic." The petitioners added that a number of
learned individuals and preachers could attest to these facts.[1]

Tydeman was a master painter as well as a once and future soldier. He
lived with his wife, Margarita Karels, in a house on the Kerkstraat (Church
Street), probably near the center of town. They were members of the Reformed Church, but Tydeman seems to have had Collegiant proclivities.[2]
These appear, in fact, to have been responsible for his being on the losing
side of the 1665 dispute. When Spinoza moved from Rijnsburg to Voorburg in the spring of 1663, it may have been at the recommendation of his
own Collegiant friends that he chose to rent a room in Tydeman's house.

Voorburg was substantially larger than Rijnsburg but still small enough
for the peace and quiet that Spinoza sought.[3] It was no farther from The
Hague than Rijnsburg was from Leiden – a couple of miles – so it too had
the advantage of proximity to a major city and its social and intellectual resources. Colerus tells us that Spinoza had "a great many friends" in The
Hague; and during his years in Voorburg he seems once again to have acquired a circle of admirers. "They were often in his company" – perhaps
making the trip out to Voorburg as often as he traveled in to the city – "and
took a great delight in hearing him discourse." When Spinoza later moved
to The Hague itself, it was most likely at their instigation.[4] The Huygens
family owned a country estate in the vicinity of Voorburg, which Constantijn Huygens – Christiaan's father, Descartes's friend, and, in an earlier

time, secretary to the Stadholder Frederik Hendrik, who held court in The Hague – called "a village that knows no equal."[5] After he and Christiaan Huygens became friends, probably around early 1665, Spinoza must have occasionally spent time at the property *Hofwijk*, a five-minute walk from Spinoza's house, when Huygens was not off on scientific business in London or Paris.

Through Tydeman, Spinoza seems not only to have entered local Voorburg society, and thus become involved in the controversy over the preachers, but also to have learned something of the fine arts. Colerus claimed to have had in his possession a portfolio of drawings made by Spinoza, which he says he acquired from his (and Spinoza's) landlord in The Hague, who was also a painter. The philosopher apparently had a preference for portraits:

He taught himself[6] the art of drawing, and he could sketch someone with ink or charcoal. I have in my hands a whole book of these, his art, in which he has portrayed various considerable persons, who were known to him and who visited him on occasion. Among other [drawings], I found on the fourth sheet a fisherman in a shirt, sketched with a net on his right shoulder, just as the famous Neapolitan rebel Massaniello is generally represented in historical prints. Mr. Hendrik Van der Spyck, his last landlord, told me that this portrait bore a striking resemblance to Spinoza himself and that he certainly had drawn it after his own face.[7]

The collection of drawings has never been found.

Although Voorburg was even farther away from Amsterdam than Rijnsburg was, Spinoza kept in close touch with his friends in that city, both by letter and in person. De Vries, for one, paid him a visit during that first summer, in 1663, and would return several times over the next couple of years. Spinoza, in turn, enjoyed returning to Amsterdam, and did so quite often. In fact, no sooner had he moved his furniture and lense-grinding equipment into Tydeman's house at the end of April, than he was back in Amsterdam for a stay of several weeks. The occasion for his prolonged absence from Voorburg so soon after relocating there was the preparation for publication of the lessons on Descartes that he had given to Casearius. His Amsterdam friends, still envious of Casearius's good fortune, wanted their own copy of Spinoza's elucidation of the principles of Cartesian philosophy. At that point, the work existed only in dictated form, in Casearius's hand. When Spinoza came to town, they asked him to compile for them an expanded version and then urged him to allow them to publish the treatise at Rieuwertsz's press. Writing to Oldenburg at the end of July, he excuses himself for not having responded more promptly to his last letter (from the beginning of April) and explains why he only just received it.

Some of my friends asked me to make them a copy of a treatise containing a precise account of the Second Part of Descartes' *Principles,* demonstrated in the geometric style, and of the main points treated in metaphysics. Previously I had dictated this to a certain young man to whom I did not want to teach my own opinions openly. They asked me to prepare the First Part also by the same method, as soon as I could. Not to disappoint my friends, I immediately undertook to do this and finished it in two weeks. I delivered it to my friends, who in the end asked me to let them publish the whole work. They easily won my agreement, on the condition that one of them, in my presence, would provide it with a more elegant style and add a short preface warning readers that I did not acknowledge all the opinions contained in this treatise as my own, since I had written many things in it which were the very opposite of what I held, and illustrating this by one or two examples. One of my friends, to whose care the publishing of this little book has been entrusted, has promised to do all this and that is why I stayed for a while in Amsterdam. Since I returned to this village where I am now living, I have hardly been my own master because of the friends who have been kind enough to visit me.[8]

The friend who so graciously agreed to help polish Spinoza's Latin style and write the preface to the work was Lodewijk Meyer, who was also the primary moving force behind the publication of the treatise. Meyer had been hoping to "translate" Descartes's doctrines into the geometrical style himself, but other, more pressing matters interfered.[9] He believed that the "method of the mathematicians," with its definitions, axioms, and deduced propositions, was the best way to settle many interminable disputes in philosophy and science and "to build the whole edifice of human knowledge."[10] He was disappointed, moreover, that Descartes, for whom he had great admiration ("that brightest star of our age," he called him) did not fully exploit this method. Thus, he was quite pleased to learn about Spinoza's project and worked hard to see the *René Descartes' Principles of Philosophy, Parts I and II, Demonstrated According to the Geometric Method by Benedict de Spinoza of Amsterdam* through to publication. Meyer took seriously his responsibility for "the whole business of printing and publishing" the work "entrusted to my care," as well as his duties to a friend.[11] He advised Spinoza on various stylistic and even substantive issues throughout the preparation of the manuscript – asking him at one point whether it would be better to delete the statement that "the son of God is the father

himself," lest he give offense to theologians, who were always on the lookout for signs of Socinianism – and Spinoza often deferred to his judgment.
"Do as it seems best to you," Spinoza told him more than once.[12] In writing his preface, Meyer was sensitive to Spinoza's concerns and clearly took
care to accommodate his wishes.

Spinoza agreed to publish the treatise, accompanied by an appendix containing "Metaphysical Thoughts [*Cogitata Metaphysica*] in which are briefly
explained the chief things that commonly occur in the general part of Metaphysics, concerning Being and its Affections," in part because, as he told
Oldenburg, he wanted to see what kind of reception he could hope for for
his own ideas and possibly to win some favor among influential people.

Perhaps it will induce some who hold high positions in my country to want to see
other things I have written, which I acknowledge as my own, so that they would
see to it that I can publish without any danger of inconvenience. If this happens,
I have no doubt that I will publish certain things immediately. If not, I shall be
silent rather than force my opinions on men against the will of my country and
make them hostile to me.[13]

The "other things" to which Spinoza is referring here might be the *Short
Treatise,* but it is more likely the more up-to-date geometrical reworking
of that work's material, the *Philosophia,* that is, the early *Ethics,* which Spinoza may have overoptimistically anticipated as being near completion in
mid-1663.[14]

Spinoza, in fact, had to interrupt briefly his work on the *Ethics* to put
together the *Descartes' Principles of Philosophy.* Ever anxious about public
reaction to the book, he wanted people to know that "I composed it within
two weeks. For with this warning no one will think I have set these things
out so clearly that they could not be explained more clearly, and therefore
they will not be held up by a word or two if here and there they happen to
find something obscure."[15] Even after he was back in Voorburg, however,
it continued to occupy his attention, to one degree or another, through the
end of the summer of 1663, when he conferred by letter with Meyer over
the preface.

Besides serving as a means of testing the waters for his own metaphysical and ethical ideas, which are present in the "Metaphysical Thoughts"
and somewhat more subtly in the *Principles* itself, these two works – the
only writings that Spinoza published under his name during his lifetime –
were intended by him "for the benefit of all men." He wished it to be

known that the motivation behind their appearance was "a desire to spread the truth" and "a good will inviting men to study the true philosophy and . . . aiming at the advantage of all."[16] And the "true" philosophy, the one most beneficial to humanity, was, without question, the modern one. Unencumbered by the stale and unenlightening schemata of Scholasticism, it was progressive in its aims and roughly Cartesian in its inspiration.

But Spinoza in 1663 was by no means an uncritical disciple of Descartes – in fact, if he ever had been, it was well before 1661 – and in *Descartes' Principles of Philosophy* he makes it clear, and wants Meyer to reinforce the point, that he is not therein offering his own views.

For since he had promised to teach his pupil Descartes' philosophy, he considered himself obliged not to depart a hair's breadth from Descartes' opinion, nor to dictate to him anything that either would not correspond to his doctrines or would be contrary to them. So let no one think that he is teaching here either his own opinions, or only those which he approves of.

In his preface, Meyer points out only the most remarkable divergencies between Spinoza's opinions and those of Descartes: Spinoza "does not think that the will is distinct from the intellect, much less endowed with such freedom," nor that the mind is a substance in its own right. There is no knowing to what degree the published work, which is sometimes critical of Descartes and occasionally suggests Spinoza's real doctrines, reflects what he dictated to Casearius. Because he considered Casearius not yet mature enough to hear his own views, one wonders how much of the critique of Descartes was present in his lessons to the young man. Perhaps in most of those lectures he did not, in fact, "depart a hair's breadth" from Descartes's opinions.

What Jan Rieuwertsz published in the fall of 1663, though, was certainly not a mere summary of Descartes's opinions. Although much of the material is right out of Descartes's writings – primarily the *Principles of Philosophy* itself, along with the *Meditations on First Philosophy* and Descartes's responses to objections that he received to the *Meditations* – it is, first of all, rearranged and reordered to fit the demands of the geometrical presentation. And, as Spinoza notes in a letter to Meyer, sometimes he demonstrates things that Descartes only asserted, uses proofs different from those employed by Descartes, and even adds things that Descartes omitted.[17] But Spinoza was not interested only in giving an accurate, if somewhat supplemented, picture in geometric form of what Descartes said and how he argued (or should have argued). He also saw himself as using Cartesian principles to solve some problems with which, he believed, Descartes did not adequately deal. As Meyer notes, many things in the treatise were not explicitly said by Descartes but nonetheless can be "deduced validly from the foundations he left." Spinoza clarifies, interprets, explicates, expands, gives examples, justifies, adds suppressed premises, improves the arguments; in short, he acts at times like a faithful albeit creative Cartesian, doing what many other more or less orthodox Cartesian philosophers did in the seventeenth century. But he also queries, criticizes, suspends judgment ("I do not know whether it is a greater work to create [or preserve] a substance than to create [or preserve] attributes"), corrects, and outright denies things Descartes asserted. Sometimes he gives Descartes the benefit of the doubt ("I think Descartes was too intelligent to have meant that"); elsewhere he takes him to task.

Spinoza's achievement in the *Descartes Principles of Philosophy*, even with respect only to his geometrical exposition of Descartes's ideas, should not be underrated. If the material was originally intended for the benefit of a less-than-stellar student or to assuage persistent friends, still it was no casual and disinterested work undertaken on the side. Spinoza's selection and "translation" of the most important elements of the Cartesian system were of great service to many people interested in a serious and critical study of that system, as well as to enhancing his own philosophical reputation.

He begins with a review of the epistemological issues that Descartes deals with in Part One of the *Principles* and in the *Meditations*. The "method of doubt," for Descartes, is the proper way to begin philosophizing and to "discover the foundations of the sciences." By adopting at the outset a skeptical pose, the inquirer into truth can "lay aside all prejudices," uncover the causes of error, and eventually find the way to a clear and distinct understanding of all things. The first certainty of all, as Descartes so famously demonstrated, is our own existence. Even in the face of the most radical skeptical doubt, I cannot but perceive the absolute indubitability of the proposition "I am, I exist" (or, as he puts it elsewhere, "I think, therefore I am"). But what Descartes presented as a simple, intuitive truth – simply to think "I exist" is to be convinced of its truth – Spinoza demonstrates geometrically.

PROPOSITION 2: I am *must be known through itself*
DEMONSTRATION: If you deny this, then it will not become known except through

something else, the knowledge and certainty of which (by Axiom 1 ["We do not arrive at knowledge and certainty of an unknown thing except by knowledge and certainty of another thing which is prior to it in certainty and knowledge"]) will be prior to us in this proposition, *I am*. But this is absurd (by Proposition 1 ["We cannot be absolutely certain of anything so long as we do not know that we exist"]). Therefore, it must be known through itself.[18]

From the certainty of my own existence, I can also become certain of the existence of a nondeceiving God who created me, and thus of the reliability of the rational faculties with which he has endowed me. As long as I rely only on my clear and distinct conceptions of things, I will arrive at the truth.

With these preliminaries out of the way, Spinoza first considers the metaphysical foundations of Cartesian science as laid out in Parts One and Two of the *Principles*. This includes the ontology of substance, the nature of thought and extension, the distinction and relationship between the mind and the body, and God. What follows, once the relevant metaphysical propositions are established, is the bulk of what constituted Spinoza's lectures to Casearius. This includes the universal features of the world and the most general principles of Cartesian physics: the nature of matter, motion, and force (which Descartes defined in purely scalar terms as the product of a body's mass and speed), the composition and properties of physical bodies, and the laws governing bodies in motion, both solids and fluids. Descartes identified the matter of bodies with extension alone; a body is not distinguished from the space it occupies. And all the properties of a body must therefore be modes of extension, quantifiable aspects such as shape, size, divisibility, and motion or rest. It follows from this, Descartes believed, that a vacuum is impossible: where there is space, there is matter. Descartes thus rejected one particular model of the corpuscular mechanistic world – namely, the atomistic model, according to which indivisible atoms move and impact with each other in empty space – in favor of a plenum. There are no empty spaces, and when matter moves, it takes the place of, and is displaced by, other matter. The only way in which one parcel of matter (a body) moves another parcel of matter is by pushing it.

Although such impact between bodies is the cause for the particular motions that bodies have, the universal, primary, and sustaining cause of motion in the universe is God. God introduced motion into matter and (being immutable) conserves the same quantity of motion therein. This allowed Descartes to deduce from God's nature the most general law of nature, his conservation law, that the total quantity of motion in the universe is constant. From this law, in conjunction with further premises about how God sustains bodies in motion, others follow. Thus, Spinoza, staying close to Descartes's text, demonstrates the Cartesian principle of inertia:

PROPOSITION 14: *Each thing, in so far as it is simple, undivided, and considered in itself alone, always perseveres in the same state as far as it can.* This proposition is like an axiom to many; nevertheless, we shall demonstrate it.

DEMONSTRATION: Since nothing is in any state except by God's concurrence alone (Part I, Proposition 12) and God is supremely constant in his works (IP20, corollary), if we attend to no external, i.e., particular causes, but consider the thing by itself, we shall have to affirm that insofar as it can it always perseveres in the state in which it is, q.e.d.[19]

Part Three of the work begins with a summary of Descartes's remarks on scientific method and a presentation of some general hypotheses about the world that he believed would allow him to explain a great number of phenomena. Thus, the reader is introduced to the vortex theory of the heavens and some details about the universal matter that composes both the terrestrial and the celestial realms. But the treatise ends rather abruptly, after only two propositions about the particles into which that matter is divided. Spinoza probably never went further than this in his lessons to Casearius. Having already spent more than two weeks in Amsterdam expanding the text into Part One for his friends, he must have decided not to take any more time and energy away from his work on the *Ethics* to pursue the *Principles* beyond these fragments from Part Three.

At some point, Spinoza determined that his *Descartes' Principles of Philosophy* should be accompanied by a philosophical appendix containing a discussion of classical metaphysical problems that, he believed, Descartes did not adequately address. Spinoza's purpose with the "Metaphysical Thoughts" – which may have been written even before the geometrization of the *Principles* – was to clarify the major concepts, categories, and distinctions of philosophy that, to his mind, had been neglected or, worse, obscured by earlier thinkers. Most of his criticism is directed at the Scholastics, both medieval thinkers and more recent neo-Aristotelians such as Professor Heereboord of Leiden. At times, his approach is straightforwardly Cartesian; on other occasions, the careful reader catches a glimpse of Spinoza's own metaphysical ideas ("The whole of *natura naturata* is only one being. From this it follows that man is a part of nature"). The nature and varieties of Being, the distinction between essence and existence, and the differences among necessary, possible, and contingent existence all receive extended treatment. God and his attributes – his eternity, simplicity, knowledge, omnipresence, omnipotence, will, and power – are examined particularly to clear up some confusions bequeathed by earlier writers. Spinoza dismisses such "absurdities" as the vegetative soul that the Scholastic philosophy accorded to plants and the duration that some thinkers have attributed to God. There are opinions in the *Principles* and the "Metaphysical Thoughts" that clearly are not Spinoza's – for example, a recommendation that the best way to interpret Scripture's meaning is by evaluating the truth of its purported claims;[20] and, as Meyer notes, he seems to be asserting that the human will is free.

Uninformed or casual readers would have had some trouble distinguishing which claims presented in the two works Spinoza endorsed and which he rejected; one of his correspondents, the Dutch merchant Willem van Blijenbergh, suffered just this confusion. But the book was well suited to its intended task, at least as he had described this to Oldenburg: to bring himself to the attention of the learned and of those in high places and perhaps to stimulate their interest in (and thus gain some protection for) the publication of his own ideas. The treatises seem to have been widely read and discussed, particularly in Leiden, and to have earned Spinoza a reputation for being a talented commentator on the Cartesian philosophy.[21] The book's reception was sufficiently encouraging that Spinoza's friends immediately made plans for a second Latin edition. While that edition never did materialize, a Dutch translation by Pieter Balling, underwritten by Jarig Jellesz (who also financed the publication of the Latin original), did appear the following year. Spinoza had a hand in the production of what was practically another edition.[22] He made revisions and corrections in the text, and probably examined Balling's translation very closely. When the translation came out, Spinoza was able finally to put all of this behind him. Writing to Blijenbergh at the beginning of 1665, he states that "I have not thought about the work on Descartes nor given any further attention to it since it was published in Dutch." The reason for this, he adds, "would take too long to tell."[23]

&

In the summer of 1663, the plague returned to northern Europe. Though it took a while for the disease to reach its maximum potency, it struck with particular virulence and lasted for over six years. Writing to Spinoza in 1666, Oldenburg told him that the disease was so "violent" in London that the meetings of the Royal Society were suspended while its scientists sought refuge in the country. "Our Philosophical Society holds no public meetings in these dangerous times." Some had retired with the king to Oxford, others were scattered around England. Many of the fellows did "not forget that they are such" and continued to work on their private experiments.[24] The intrepid Oldenburg stayed on in London, fulfilling his correspondence duties as the society's secretary. Even during such crises, he never missed an opportunity to urge Spinoza to publish his thoughts – "I shall never stop exhorting you until you grant my request," he wrote in August 1663, just before the outbreak – or at least to allow him to see some of his writings. "If you were willing to share with me some of the main results, how much would I love you! how closely would I judge myself to be bound to you!"[25] Oldenburg was most anxious to receive a copy of *Descartes' Principles of Philosophy*. He asked Spinoza to send one to him by way of Serrarius, with whom both men were in occasional contact and who often acted as the Amsterdam-based postmaster (and even, when he was traveling to England, as the courier) for Spinoza's international correspondence while he lived in the country.

In Amsterdam, where the plague reportedly began, there were almost ten thousand deaths in 1663; the following year the toll climbed to over twenty-four thousand. The English diplomat Sir George Downing reported in July 1664 that "there dyed this last weeke at Amsterdam 739, and the plague is scattered generally over the whole country even in the little dorps and villages, and it is gott to Antwerp and Brussells."[26] In June 1664, Pieter Balling's son, still a young child, died. Spinoza, who had a warm relationship with Balling, was clearly touched by his friend's loss and commiserated with the man who had just finished translating his work on Descartes.

It has caused me no little sadness and anxiety, though that has greatly decreased as I consider the prudence and strength of character with which you are able to scorn the blows of fortune, or rather opinion, when they attack you with their strongest weapons. For all that, my anxiety increases daily, and therefore by our friendship I beseech and implore you to take the trouble to write me at length.

Balling believed he had had some "omens" about his son's impending death – "when your child was still healthy and well," Spinoza recalls, "you heard sighs like those he made when he was ill and shortly afterwards passed away" – and wrote to Spinoza seeking his interpretation of them. In his reply, Spinoza, in addition to offering what he hoped would be some comforting remarks on the sympathetic ties that bind a father's soul to that of his son, related a dream he himself had had a year earlier: "One morning, as the sky was already growing light, I woke from a very deep dream to find that the images that had come to me in my dream remained before my eyes as vividly as if the things had been true – especially [the image] of a certain black, scabby Brazilian whom I had never seen before."[27] There is no telling what significance Spinoza attached to the content of this dream, nor what solace Balling took from his friend's words. This is the last letter we have between Spinoza and Balling, who himself probably died of the plague within the year. Spinoza's grief was no doubt great, although any expressions of it were probably consigned to the flames by his posthumous editors along with much of his other personal correspondence.

During the plague years, those urban residents who were able fled to the Dutch countryside. Voorburg was close enough to The Hague, and big enough in its own right, to be in some danger of contagion. Thus Spinoza, almost certainly prodded by the solicitous Simon, took advantage of his connections with the De Vries family and, in the winter of 1664, left town for several months. He stayed at a country house in the vicinity of Schiedam, a medium-sized village near Rotterdam. The farm, called De Lange Boogert ("The Long Orchard"), was owned by Jacob Simons Gijsen, the father-in-law of Simon de Vries's sister. The Gijsen family was another well-to-do clan of Anabaptist merchants, having made their fortune in herring and salt. Spinoza had probably first made their acquaintance ten years earlier. When Simon's sister Trijntje married Alewijn Gijsen in 1655, Simon could not have failed to invite one of his closest friends to the wedding. Although Alewijn's father owned the farm, the young couple and their children lived there. The Gijsen and De Vries families were, in fact, related by blood, as Jacob Gijsen was the brother of Simon's maternal grandmother, and thus

his great-uncle. After the plague struck, members of both clans retired to
the farm to decrease their chances of infection. Spinoza joined them in
December and stayed until February 1665. It was a beautiful setting, with
a well-apportioned farmhouse and fruit trees overlooking a river. But the
visit could not have been a very happy one. Alewijn's brother had died,
most likely of the plague, earlier in 1664. So did Trijntje's and Simon's
mother, Maria de Wolff, and their brother Frans Joosten de Vries and his
wife, Sijtien Jacobs Uien, all in the month of June.[28] It must have been
gratifying for Simon, however, to be able to spend an extended period of
time with Spinoza, even if the circumstances of their reunion were not
particularly cheerful.

In January 1665, Spinoza's peace at Schiedam was disturbed by a series
of letters from someone who considered himself a fellow "seeker after
truth." Willem van Blijenbergh was a grain merchant and broker from
Dordrecht, a major port for grain from the Baltic on its way to other parts
of Europe and to the New World. While much of his time was taken up
with business, he had always had a penchant for theology and philosophy,
and obviously relished the opportunity to discuss philosophical matters
with a published intellectual such as Spinoza. He himself was the author
of a book published in 1663, *The knowledge of God and Religion, defended
against the Outrages of Atheists, In which it is demonstrated with clear and natural reasons that God has created and revealed a Religion, that God also wishes
to be served in accordance with this religion, and that the Christian Religion
corresponds not only to the Religion revealed by God but also to our innate reason.* Spinoza clearly knew nothing about this work and had no idea about
the convictions of the man with whom he was about to begin – quickly to
his regret – an exchange of long letters.

Blijenbergh had read only *Descartes' Principles of Philosophy* and the
metaphysical appendix and, understandably, had some trouble telling when
Spinoza was offering his own views and when he was merely summarizing those of Descartes. Even when he did manage to make that distinction,
he had a hard time understanding what exactly Spinoza was saying; he was
neither the most penetrating nor the most generous of correspondents.
Still, he raised some very interesting and important questions about Spinoza's exposition of Descartes and about his own doctrines. "As I have
found many things in [your treatise] that were very palatable to me, so also
have I found some I could not easily digest."[29] In his letters, Blijenbergh
pressed Spinoza on the status of good and evil (which, according to Spin-

oza, are not something real in the world) and particularly on God's relationship to sin. If God is the cause and continuous conserver of all things and their affections, then God must also be the cause of all "motions" or volitions in the soul. Now some of those volitions are sinful. "From this assertion it also seems to follow necessarily, either that there is no evil in the soul's motion or will, or else that God himself does that evil immediately." He also wondered how there can be any room for human freedom if, as Spinoza says, everything follows necessarily from the immutable will of God. And he perceptively recognized that, given what at least seem to the reader of Spinoza's work to be his own metaphysical views of the mind and the body, there is some difficulty in understanding how the soul is immortal.

> When I consider this short and fleeting life, in which I see that my death may occur at any moment, if I had to believe that I would have an end, and be cut off from that holy and glorious contemplation, certainly I would be the most miserable of creatures, who have no knowledge that they will end. For before my death, my fear of death would make me wretched, and after my death, I would entirely cease to be, and hence be wretched because I would be separated from that divine contemplation [when I shall exist again]. And this is where your opinions seem to me to lead: that when I come to an end here, then I will come to an end for eternity.[30]

In his first reply, Spinoza carefully tried to explain to Blijenbergh how God is the cause only of what is positive in things, and how evil is merely a privation or falling short of a more perfect state of a thing, relative to our conceptions. He warned his new correspondent against being taken in by the inaccurate and misleading ways of speaking about God common to the vulgar, and not to think that we, by our actions, are capable of "angering" God. But Blijenbergh's further queries show that he was a man of narrow intellectual horizons. His letters are long, prolix, and tedious, and he clearly did not share many of Spinoza's philosophical presuppositions. Already by his second reply, Spinoza's patience was wearing thin as he began to realize the kind of person he was dealing with. "When I read your first letter, I thought our opinions nearly agreed. But from the second . . . I see that I was quite mistaken, and that we disagree not only about the things ultimately to be derived from first principles, but also about the first principles themselves." He suggested, politely but firmly, that they break off their correspondence. "I hardly believe that we can instruct one another with our letters," he wrote, and expressed his opinion not only that

Blijenbergh did not understand his views, but also that he was *incapable* of understanding them.[31] The two men had little in common. They were attached, in Spinoza's eyes, to incommensurable points of view. Blijenbergh deferred to the authority of Scripture on all matters theological *and* philosophical.

I see that no demonstration, however solid it may be according to the laws of demonstration, has weight with you unless it agrees with that explanation which you, or theologians known to you, attribute to sacred Scripture. But if you believe that God speaks more clearly and effectively through sacred Scripture than through the light of the natural intellect, which he has also granted us, and which, with his divine wisdom, he continually preserves, strong and uncorrupted, then you have powerful reasons for bending your intellect to the opinions you attribute to sacred Scripture.

When reason and faith clash, on Blijenbergh's view, it must be reason that is defective. Spinoza's opinion could not have been more different. For him, there was no authority above reason. In a passage that is very revealing of Spinoza's own intellectual and spiritual orientation, he tells Blijenbergh that

for myself, I confess, clearly and without circumlocution, that I do not understand Sacred Scripture, though I have spent several years on it. And I am well aware that, when I have found a solid demonstration, I cannot fall into such thoughts that I can ever doubt it. So I am completely satisfied with what the intellect shows me, and entertain no suspicion that I have been deceived in that or that Sacred Scripture can contradict it. . . . For the truth does not contradict the truth. . . . And if even once I found that the fruits which I have already gathered from the natural intellect were false, they would still make me happy, since I enjoy them and seek to pass my life, not in sorrow and sighing, but in peace, joy and cheerfulness. By so doing, I climb a step higher. Meanwhile, I recognize something that gives me the greatest satisfaction and peace of mind: that all things happen as they do by the power of a supremely perfect Being and by his immutable decree.[32]

It is not that Spinoza does not see Scripture as a source of truth. Rather, in order to be able to see those truths that it does contain and to give it the authority it deserves, one must first free oneself from "prejudice and childish superstitions." Above all, one must cease thinking of God in human terms and anthropomorphizing his ways, which Spinoza sees as part of the reason for Blijenbergh's failure to grasp properly his doctrines. God is not a judge, nor is he subject to the emotions and passions (anger, jealousy, desire, etc.) that theologians – seeking to take advantage of the hopes and fears of ordinary people – absurdly attribute to him.

> Because theology has usually – and that not without reason – represented God as a perfect man, it is appropriate in theology to say that God desires something, that he finds sorrow in the acts of the Godless and takes pleasure in those of the pious. But in philosophy we understand clearly that to ascribe to God those "attributes" that make a man perfect is as bad as if one wanted to ascribe to man those that make an elephant or an ass perfect. Therefore, speaking philosophically, we cannot say that God desires something, nor that something is pleasing or a cause of sorrow to him. For those are all human "attributes," which have no place in God.[33]

Blijenbergh was taken aback by Spinoza's tone, and by the insinuation that he himself was less than truly philosophical. "In view of your request and promise, I expected a friendly and instructive reply. But what in fact I received was a letter that does not sound very friendly."[34] But Blijenbergh was nothing if not persistent and was willing to forgive Spinoza his temporary lapse of etiquette, if only he would answer a few more questions. He was coming to Leiden, he wrote Spinoza in early March, and planned on paying the philosopher a visit. Spinoza, despite what must have been a great reluctance to take any more time away from his own studies for the grain dealer, received him cordially. They talked about freedom, sin, and the nature of the soul. It must have been no small source of annoyance to Spinoza to hear later from Blijenbergh that when he tried to put it all down on paper after he left, he could not remember what they had discussed and what Spinoza's answers to him had been. "I found then that in fact I had retained not even a fourth of what was discussed. So you must excuse me if once again I trouble you by asking about matters where I did not clearly understand your meaning or did not retain it well."[35] That was enough for Spinoza. He wrote back to Blijenbergh telling him in polite but clear and unmistakable terms to leave him alone. "I wanted the opportunity to talk with you in the friendliest way, so that I might ask you to desist from your request [for a further proof of his opinions]."[36]

By this point, even the plodding Blijenberg can have been under no illusions about their differences. Nine years later, after Spinoza published the *Theological-Political Treatise*, expanding his views on Scripture, Blijenbergh responded with a five-hundred-page tome, *The Truth of the Christian Religion and the Authority of Holy Scripture Affirmed against the Arguments of the Impious, or a Refutation of the Blasphemous Book Entitled*

"*Tractatus Theologico-Politicus*," which he published in Leiden in 1674.
His correspondence, however, may in the end have been of some service
to Spinoza. For, as one recent scholar has noted, Blijenbergh's inability to
comprehend, and his prejudiced reaction to, Spinoza's views caused Spinoza to realize that the time might not, in fact, have been ripe for the publication of his own doctrines, particularly the *Ethics*.[37] The exchange with
Blijenbergh could only have increased Spinoza's apprehensions about how
his opinions would be received by the public, and especially by the less
philosophically talented members of the Reformed Church.

 za.

As if the plague had not made life difficult enough in the Dutch Republic
in the mid-1660s, in 1664 war between the United Provinces and England
loomed once again on the horizon. The English navy had been expanding
ever since 1660, when Charles II was restored to the throne and hostilities
with Spain ended. This troubled the Dutch, who had been taking advantage of Britain's military distraction to increase its control over maritime
shipping. While they appreciated the peace that settled over the sea routes
and were generally glad to be rid of Cromwell, whose hostility toward the
Netherlands never waned, Dutch merchants were nervous about England's growing economic and military power. De Witt and the regents,
meanwhile, were anxious about Charles's intentions toward William III.
The young man's mother was Mary Stuart, Charles's sister, and his father
the late Stadholder, William II. The Orangists were putting pressure on
the States of Holland to give William, still an adolescent, his rightful place
as heir to his father's stadholderships. They were hoping that Charles
would come to the aid of his nephew.

In fall 1662, a treaty of friendship, long in the making, was finally signed
by England and the Netherlands. But the relationship between the two
nominal allies was too poisoned for this to be of any significance. There
was, first, an intense competition between the Dutch East Indies Company and its English counterpart for supremacy in the South Pacific. And
the restrictions that Charles had placed upon foreign fishing rights off the
English coast hit the Dutch fishing industry particularly hard. There were,
moreover, tensions over Caribbean, North American, and West African
colonies. By 1664, New Netherlands had been overrun by the English and
was now New York. The Dutch clearly had legitimate complaints against
England, particularly when British ships began harassing and comman-

deering Dutch ships on the high seas. But the English were in no mood for appeals to justice or law. Old jealousies, grievances, and enmities that had been festering just beneath a thin veneer of cordiality between the two great maritime powers began to surface with a vengeance. The English had a clear military superiority, and their confidence in a quick and profitable victory made them bolder by the day. According to Samuel Pepys, the English were "mad for a Dutch war."[38]

In March 1665, war officially broke out. In the beginning, the Dutch were slow to engage. Over a hundred ships with twenty-one thousand men lay in harbor, waiting for the appropriate time to move out. Many citizens of the republic were growing impatient with the admirals, and Spinoza himself wondered if they were being overcautious. "I hear much about English affairs, but nothing certain," he wrote to Bouwmeester in Amsterdam in June 1665.

The people do not cease suspecting all sorts of evils. No one knows any reason why the fleet does not set sail. And indeed, the matter does not yet seem to be safe. I am afraid that our countrymen want to be too wise and cautious. Nevertheless, the event itself will finally show what they have in mind and what they are striving for. May the gods make things turn out well. I would like to hear what people think there, and what they know for certain.[39]

What the event finally showed was disaster. Later that month, the Dutch fleet was routed. And it was only the first of many setbacks. Not until 1666 were the Dutch able, with French and Danish help, to reverse substantially the tide of the war. Charles did not show any willingness to make peace until after his ports had been blockaded, his ships captured in large numbers, and his colonies in the East Indies taken over. Financially drained and suffering low morale, England signed the treaty with the Netherlands at Breda in July 1667. England got to keep New York but had to return several other important and lucrative colonies captured from the Dutch.

Some time had passed since Oldenburg and Spinoza had last written to each other, and now the war made communication between Voorburg and London difficult. Still, in April 1665, Oldenburg, who heard through Serrarius that Spinoza was "alive and well and remembered your Oldenburg," took the initiative to see how he was holding up. As usual, he immediately renewed his plea for publication. "Mr. Boyle and I often talk about you, your erudition and your profound meditations. We would like to see the fruit of your understanding published and entrusted to the embrace of the

learned. We are sure that you will not disappoint us in this."[40] Spinoza was
genuinely pleased to hear from his English friend and to learn that he was
well. Throughout that summer, they exchanged letters on books, scientific
news, mutual acquaintances, and the progress of the war. Oldenburg was
as capable of nationalistic sentiments as the next man. To Boyle, he wrote
as if the responsibility for the war lay in Dutch intransigence: "If they
would come downe from their haughtiness, they would find much generosity and equity in ye English, of granting ym such terms, whereby they
might handsomly continue their trade for a comfortable support of their
country; and they hardly deserve more, in my opinion."[41] In his letter to
Spinoza from the same month (September 1665), however, he seems to be
only fed up with the whole mess.

This terrible war brings with it a veritable *Iliad* of woes, and very nearly elimi-
nates all culture from the world. . . . Here we daily experience news of a second
naval battle, unless perchance your fleet has again retired into harbor. The courage
which you hint is the subject of debate among you is of a bestial kind, not human.
For if men acted under the guidance of reason, they would not so tear one another
to pieces, as anyone can see. But why do I complain? There will be wickedness as
long as there are men: but even so, wickedness is not without pause, and is occasionally counterbalanced by better things.[42]

Spinoza shared Oldenburg's frustration with the international political
situation. He, too, found therein an opportunity for reflection on human
nature, with his thoughts on the "warriors sated with blood" perfectly at-
tuned to his own philosophical beliefs.

If that famous scoffer [i.e., the fifth-century Greek philosopher Democritus] were
alive today, he would surely be dying of laughter. For my part, these troubles move
me neither to laughter nor again to tears, but rather to philosophising, and to a
closer observation of human nature. For I do not think it right to laugh at nature,
and far less to grieve over it, reflecting that men, like all else, are only a part of nature, and that I do not know how each part of nature harmonises with the whole,
and how it coheres with other parts. And I realize that it is merely through such
lack of understanding that certain features of nature – which I thus perceive only
partly and in a fragmentary way, and which are not in keeping with our philosophical attitude of mind – once seemed to me vain, disordered and absurd. But
now I let everyone go his own way. Those who wish can by all means die for their
own good, as long as I am allowed to live for truth.[43]

Spinoza and Oldenburg talk much in their letters about Huygens, with
whom Spinoza was now well acquainted. They may have met casually in

The Hague, perhaps attending the same gathering or through an intermediary. It is also possible, however, that Spinoza sought Huygens out
soon after moving to Voorburg. When Oldenburg paid his visit to Spinoza
in Rijnsburg several years earlier, he could not have failed to talk about
Huygens to his new scientific colleague. After all, he was in the Netherlands to call on Huygens, and, after talking with Spinoza, he must have realized how much the two had in common.[44] Besides their shared interest
in various areas of natural philosophy, particularly of the Cartesian variety, both were skilled in mathematics, optics, and polishing lenses.[45] The
two men did, indeed, hit it off quite well. Often, when Spinoza came into
The Hague, he would call on Huygens, who in turn would be sure to visit
Spinoza during his frequent trips to the family's estate just outside Voorburg. Their philosophical intercourse was made even easier in the summer and fall of 1664, when the plague hit The Hague and Huygens and his
brother Constantijn made an extended stay at "Hofwijk." Spinoza and
Huygens seem to have spent a good amount of time together between 1663
and 1666 discussing astronomy and a number of problems in physics, such
as the errors in Descartes's calculations of the laws of motion.[46]

Huygens, the author of an important work on optical theory, the *Diop-
trics*, admired Spinoza's lenses and his instruments – "the [lenses] that the
Jew of Voorburg has in his microscopes have an admirable polish," he
wrote to his brother in 1667[47] – while Spinoza kept up with Huygens's
own progress in that area. He told Oldenburg that "Huygens has been, and
still is, fully occupied in polishing dioptrical glasses. For this purpose he
has devised a machine in which he can turn plates, and a very neat affair
it is. I do not yet know what success he has had with it, and, to tell the truth,
I do not particularly want to know. For experience has taught me that in
polishing spherical plates a free hand yields safer and better results than
any machine."[48] Huygens's "machine" allowed the polisher to place the
glass in a device that would then be brought to the grinding lathe; Spinoza preferred to hold the glass with his hands against the lathe, a large
wooden structure that was powered by a foot pedal.

Spinoza and Huygens made an unlikely pair. The one was a Jew from a
merchant family who preferred to live simply and earn his means by a
craft. The other was a Dutch aristocrat who also polished lenses but refused to engage in selling them, as he considered it an occupation beneath
his station. And, despite their intellectual camaraderie, there seems to have
been a lack of true warmth and intimacy in their relationship. When Huygens wrote to his brother from Paris, he referred to Spinoza not by name

but as "the Jew from Voorburg" or "the Israelite." Moreover, however much he appreciated Spinoza's practical skills with lenses, he did not think much of his knowledge of theoretical optics. And when the Abbé Gallois asked Huygens for a copy of Spinoza's *Theological-Political Treatise* and of the *Opera posthuma* in 1682, he responded by saying, "I should hope that there is something better I could do for you to give you pleasure."[49] Spinoza, for his part, did not seem to have for Huygens the feelings and trust that he had for some of his other friends. There was a certain distance between the two men, evident in a remark Spinoza made some years later to the Amsterdam physician Georg Schuller. In 1675, Walther Ehrenfried von Tschirnhaus, a mutual friend of theirs, was getting acquainted with Huygens in Paris, as Schuller and Spinoza had recommended him to do. Huygens had seen the *Theological-Political Treatise*, a copy of which Spinoza sent to him, and was now pressing Tschirnhaus – who had seen the manuscript of the *Ethics* – to tell him if Spinoza had published anything else. This was just a few months after Spinoza halted the publication of the *Ethics* out of a desire to avoid the denunciations that would inevitably follow. Tschirnhaus, knowing of Spinoza's caution and keeping to the promise of secrecy he had made when he was allowed to see the *Ethics*, replied to Huygens, according to Schuller, that "he knows of none except for the 'Proofs of the First and Second Parts of Descartes' Philosophy'. Otherwise he said nothing about you except for the above, and hopes that this will not displease you."[50] Spinoza told Schuller that he was pleased that Tschirnhaus "has, in his conversations with Mr. Huygens, conducted himself with discretion."[51] Spinoza may have had a better relationship with Christiaan's brother Constantijn, who shared his interest in lenses – and in drawing! – and with whom he seems to have continued to meet for a couple of years after Christiaan's departure for Paris in 1666.[52]

Spinoza had other reasons besides the Huygens brothers for visiting The Hague. He even had access to a pied à terre in the city: the house "Adam and Eve" on the Baggynestraat, which Daniel Tydeman owned and where his brother, Mesach, lived.[53] While no match for Amsterdam in terms of cosmopolitan culture, there was a critical mass of savants in The Hague with whom to converse and compare notes. Before he moved to Paris, Huygens probably introduced Spinoza to a fellow mathematician, optical theorist, and lense grinder (and also the author of the *Parva dioptrica*), Johannes Hudde.[54] Born in 1628 in Amsterdam to a regent family, Hudde studied medicine at Leiden in the late 1650s (where, as a fellow student of Lodewijk Meyer, it is possible he first met Spinoza). He wrote two mathematical treatises and corresponded with a number of prominent individuals on matters of science and Cartesian geometry, but eventually gave up the philosophical life for the political. In 1667, he became a member of Amsterdam's *vroedschap*, the governing council; and in 1672 he began the first of numerous stints as one of the city's burgemeesters. He and Spinoza corresponded briefly in the first half of 1666, mainly over questions of the existence and uniqueness of God (the demonstrations of which from the *Ethics* Spinoza rehearsed for him) and the geometry of refraction. A friendly acquaintance with Hudde had the potential of being of long-term practical value, as Spinoza was constantly on the lookout for some protection against the orthodox preachers from the political elite, to which Hudde surely belonged. It may have been for just this reason that he cultivated their relationship.

ૐ

In the spring of 1665, before the defeat of the Dutch fleet, Spinoza was once again in Amsterdam, this time for a couple of weeks. He probably saw all his old friends, including De Vries, Bouwmeester, and Serrarius, as well as Meyer, who was now the director of the Amsterdam Municipal Theater.[55] He may have paid a visit to Boreel, now hosting Collegiant meetings in his house on the Rokin,[56] and dropped by Rieuwertsz's bookshop to see what was new in the world of freethinking publishing. Bouwmeester seems to have been somewhat aloof, and Spinoza, upon his return to Voorburg, was somewhat hurt by his friend's odd behavior. First, the physician failed to keep a farewell appointment when Spinoza was leaving Amsterdam. He then neglected to pay Spinoza a visit when he was in The Hague.

I don't know whether you have completely forgotten me, but many things concur that raise the suspicion. First, when I was about to leave [Amsterdam], I wanted to say goodbye to you, and since you yourself had invited me, I thought that without doubt I would find you at home. But I learned that you had gone to The Hague. I returned to Voorburg, not doubting that you would at least visit us in passing. But you have returned home, God willing, without greeting your friend. Finally, I have waited three weeks, and in all that time I have no letter from you.[57]

Still, all is forgiven. He is mindful of Bouwmeester's tender feelings and encourages him to "pursue serious work energetically and with true enthusiasm, and to be willing to devote the better part of your life to the cultivation of your intellect and soul." Bouwmeester, diffident to begin with, appears to have been undergoing a prolonged crisis of confidence. Spinoza hoped, through a continued philosophical correspondence, to build up his friend's self-esteem. "You should know that I have previously suspected, and am almost certain, that you have less confidence in your ability than you should." Spinoza tells him to feel free to communicate his thoughts to him, something that Bouwmeester, feeling unworthy, apparently hesitated doing lest Spinoza show the letters to others who would then mock him. "I give you my word," Spinoza promised, "that henceforth I will keep them scrupulously and will not communicate them to any other mortal without your permission." Bouwmeester's failure to visit Spinoza when he was in the vicinity of Voorburg was probably due to these feelings of inferiority before his learned and increasingly well-known friend, and Spinoza, trying to put him at ease, was sensitive to this. He was, it seems, as solicitous of his friends as they were of him and cared greatly not just for their physical health but also for their intellectual and emotional well-being.

Spinoza's own health, however, was suffering. After his return from Amsterdam, he bled himself to help reduce a fever. "After I left I opened a vein once, but the fever did not stop (though I was somewhat more active even before the bloodletting – because of the change of air, I think)."[58] In the letter to Bouwmeester, written in June 1665, is the first indication of the respiratory problems that Spinoza probably inherited from his mother and would kill him twelve years later. He asked Bouwmeester for the "conserve of red roses" that the doctor had promised him. This is a mixture of rosebuds – a source of vitamin C – crushed with an equal amount of sugar, then cooked in water until reduced to a thick consistency. It was considered to be a remedy for respiratory ailments. Though Spinoza says that he has been fine for a while now, he probably expected more bouts in the future. He also claims to have suffered several times from tertian fever – a form of malaria that often results in febrile convulsions – but adds that "by good diet I have got rid of it and sent it I know not where."

≈

Despite the distractions of war, plague, illness, and the letters of Blijenbergh, work on the grand geometrical presentation of his metaphysical, psychological, and moral ideas – including much of the material taken up in less rigorous form in the *Short Treatise* and cautiously suggested in the "Metaphysical Thoughts" – proceeded apace throughout 1664 and early 1665. By June 1665, Spinoza appears to have regarded what he had written so far as a nearly complete draft of his *Philosophia*, later to be called the *Ethics*. He envisioned at this point a three-part work – perhaps corresponding to the tripartite *Short Treatise* ("on God, man and his well-being") – although the definitive version that he possessed around 1675, and that his friends finally published after his death, was supplemented, revised, and reorganized into five parts (on God, the human mind, the passions, human bondage to the passions, and freedom via the power of the intellect), with the original Part Three being expanded into Parts Three through Five.[59] The draft of Part One, *De Deo*, that had been circulating among his friends in 1663 now existed in both Latin and Dutch manuscripts, as did Part Two (*De natura & origine mentis*, "On the nature and origin of the mind"), all translated by Balling.[60] In March 1665, he spoke to Blijenbergh of material that, in the published version, appears at the conclusion of the penultimate Part Four,[61] but that now belonged to Part Three. By June, he was near the end of this part. He felt that, while there was still some more to be written, most of Part Three was ready to begin being translated into Dutch. The letter to Bouwmeester from that month was intended, in part, to sound him out on the possibility of his doing the translating, most likely because Balling had died.[62]

As for the third part of our philosophy, I shall soon send some of it either to you (if you wish to be its translator) or to friend De Vries. Although I had decided to send nothing until I finished it, nevertheless, because it is turning out to be longer than I thought, I don't want to hold you back too long.[63]

Part Three of 1665 must have contained much of the material from Parts Four and Five of the published version. It is hard to believe that Spinoza would have regarded the final part as ready for the commencement of translation – and thus, one would presume, as practically complete – before he had covered, if only in a preliminary manner, "the power of the intellect," human freedom, and blessedness, the most important conclusions of the work and all issues taken up in the published Part Five.[64] When Spinoza put aside the three-part *Ethics* in the autumn of 1665 to work on his *Theological-Political Treatise*, then, he most likely had at hand what he, at the time, considered a substantially complete draft, albeit one that, while broadly representative of the final version, would undergo significant reworking in subsequent years.

The *Ethics* is an ambitious and multifaceted work. It is also bold to the point of audacity, as one would expect of a systematic and unforgiving critique of the traditional philosophical conceptions of God, the human being, and the universe, and, above all, of the religions and the theological and moral beliefs grounded thereon. Despite a dearth of explicit references to past thinkers, the book exhibits enormous erudition. Spinoza's knowledge of classical, medieval, Renaissance, and modern authors – pagan, Christian, and Jewish – is evident throughout. Plato, Aristotle, the Stoics, Maimonides, Bacon, Descartes, and Hobbes (among others) all belong to the intellectual background of the work. At the same time, it is one of the most radically original treatises in the history of philosophy.

It is also one of the most difficult, not the least because of its format. At first approach, the mere appearance of the *Ethics* is daunting, even intimidating to the nonphilosopher. With its Euclidean architecture of definitions, axioms, postulates, propositions, scholia, and corollaries, it looks all but impenetrable. But the geometrical layout, to which Spinoza had been committed since late 1661, is not some superficial shell for material that could have been presented in a different, more accessible manner. Besides being methodologically essential (and perhaps rhetorically and pedagogically useful) to the certainty and persuasiveness of his conclusions – the "deductions" constitute the argument for Spinoza's theses – the geometrical method bears an intimate relationship to the content of Spinoza's metaphysics and epistemology. The structure of the universe, with its causally necessary connections, is mirrored by the structure of ideas, with their logically necessary connections. Moreover, Spinoza's conception of what constitutes knowledge in its ideal form, the intuitive perception of the essences of things, initially involves a dynamic, rationally discursive apprehension not unlike the way in which the propositions of the *Ethics* are related.[65]

Despite the difficulty of the book, Spinoza clearly believed that anyone – and we are all endowed with the same cognitive faculties – with sufficient self-mastery and intellectual attentiveness can perceive the truth to the highest degree. This is probably why he seems from the start to have wanted to make sure that a Dutch translation of the *Ethics* was available, so that "the truth" would be accessible to the many. For it is our natural *eudaimonia*, our happiness or well-being, that is at stake, and for Spinoza this consists in the knowledge embodied in the propositions of the *Ethics*.

What that knowledge consists in – and what Spinoza intends to demonstrate (in the strongest sense of that word) – is the truth about God, nature, and ourselves; about society, religion, and life. Despite the great deal of metaphysics, physics, anthropology, and psychology that take up Parts One through Three, Spinoza took the crucial message of the work to be ethical in nature. It consists in showing that our happiness and well-being lie, not in a life enslaved to the passions and to the transitory goods we ordinarily pursue, nor in the related unreflective attachment to the superstitions that pass as religion, but rather in the life of reason. To clarify and support these broadly ethical conclusions, however, Spinoza must first demystify the universe and show it for what it really is. This requires laying out some metaphysical foundations, the project of Part One.

"On God" begins with some deceptively simple definitions of terms that would be familiar to any seventeenth-century philosopher. "By substance I understand what is in itself and is conceived through itself"; "By attribute I understand what the intellect perceives of a substance, as constituting its essence"; "By God I understand a being absolutely infinite, i.e., a substance consisting of an infinity of attributes, of which each one expresses an eternal and infinite essence." The definitions of Part One are technically Spinoza's absolute starting points, although some of his critics complained that they already assumed too much. To a query by Simon de Vries, however, he replied that a definition need not be true or provable, but only "explain a thing as we conceive it or can conceive it."[66] The definitions are, in effect, simply clear concepts that ground the rest of his system. They are followed by a number of axioms that, he assumes, will be regarded as obvious and unproblematic by the philosophically informed ("Whatever is, is either in itself or in another"; "From a given determinate cause the effect follows necessarily"). From these, the first proposition necessarily follows, and every subsequent proposition can be demonstrated using only what precedes it.

In Propositions One through Fifteen, Spinoza presents the basic elements of his picture of God. God is the infinite, necessarily existing (that is, uncaused), unique substance of the universe. There is only one substance in the universe; it is God; and everything else that is, is in God.

P1: A substance is prior in nature to its affections.

P2: Two substances having different attributes have nothing in common with one another. (In other words, if two substances differ in nature, then they have nothing in common).

P3: If things have nothing in common with one another, one of them cannot be the cause of the other.

P4: Two or more distinct things are distinguished from one another, either by a difference in the attributes [i.e., the natures or essences] of the substances or by a difference in their affections [i.e., their accidental properties].

P5: In nature, there cannot be two or more substances of the same nature or attribute.

P6: One substance cannot be produced by another substance.

P7: It pertains to the nature of a substance to exist.

P8: Every substance is necessarily infinite.

P9: The more reality or being each thing has, the more attributes belong to it.

P10: Each attribute of a substance must be conceived through itself.

P11: God, or a substance consisting of infinite attributes, each of which expresses eternal and infinite essence, necessarily exists. (The proof of this proposition consists simply in the classic "ontological proof for God's existence." Spinoza writes that "if you deny this, conceive, if you can, that God does not exist. Therefore, by axiom 7 ['If a thing can be conceived as not existing, its essence does not involve existence'], his essence does not involve existence. But this, by proposition 7, is absurd. Therefore, God necessarily exists, q.e.d.")

P12: No attribute of a substance can be truly conceived, from which it follows that the substance can be divided.

P13: A substance which is absolutely infinite is indivisible.

P14: Except God, no substance can be or be conceived.

This proof that God – an infinite, necessary, and uncaused, indivisible being – is the only substance of the universe is stunning in its economy and efficiency, with the simple beauty peculiar to a well-crafted logical deduction. First, establish that no two substances can share an attribute or essence (P5). Then, prove that there is a substance with infinite attributes (i.e., God; P11). It follows, in conclusion, that the existence of that infinite substance precludes the existence of any other substance. For if there *were* to be a second substance, it would have to have *some* attribute or essence. But since God has *all* possible attributes, then the attribute to be possessed by this second substance would be one of the attributes already possessed by God. But it has already been established that no two substances can have the same attribute. Therefore, there can be, besides God, no such second substance.

If God is the only substance, and (by axiom 1) whatever is, is either a substance or *in* a substance, then everything else must be in God. "Whatever is, is in God, and nothing can be or be conceived without God" (P15).

As soon as this preliminary conclusion has been established, Spinoza immediately reveals the objective of his attack. His definition of God – condemned since his excommunication from the Jewish community as a "God existing in only a philosophical sense" – is meant to preclude any anthropomorphizing of the divine being. In the scholium to Proposition 15, he writes against "those who feign a God, like man, consisting of a body and a mind, and subject to passions. But how far they wander from the true knowledge of God, is sufficiently established by what has already been demonstrated." Besides being false, such an anthropomorphic conception of God can have only deleterious effects on human freedom and activity.

Much of the technical language of Book One is, to all appearances, right out of Descartes. But even the most devoted Cartesian would have had a hard time understanding the full import of Propositions 1–15. What does it mean to say that God is substance and everything else is "in" God? Is Spinoza saying that rocks, tables, chairs, birds, mountains, rivers, and human beings are all *properties* of God, and hence can be predicated of God (just as one would say that the table "is red")? It seems very odd to think that objects and individuals – what we ordinarily think of as independent "things" – are, in fact, merely properties of a thing. Spinoza was sensitive to the strangeness of this kind of talk, not to mention the philosophical problems to which it gives rise. When a person feels pain, does it follow that the pain is ultimately just a *property* of God, and thus that God feels pain? Conundrums such as this may explain why, as of Proposition 16, there is a subtle but important shift in Spinoza's language. God is now described not so much as the underlying substance of all things, but as the universal, immanent, and sustaining cause of all that exists: "From the necessity of the divine nature there must follow infinitely many things in infinitely many modes (i.e., everything that can fall under an infinite intellect)."

According to the traditional Judeo-Christian conception of divinity, God is a transcendent creator, a being who causes a world distinct from himself to come into being by creating it out of nothing. God creates that world by a spontaneous act of free will and could just as easily have not created

anything outside himself. By contrast, Spinoza's God is the cause of all
things because all things follow causally and necessarily from the divine
nature. Or, as he puts it, from God's infinite power or nature "all things
have necessarily flowed, or always followed, by the same necessity and in
the same way as from the nature of a triangle it follows, from eternity and
to eternity, that its three angles are equal to two right angles."[67] The existence of the world is thus mathematically necessary. It is impossible that
God should exist but not the world. This does not mean that God does not
cause the world to come into being freely, as nothing *outside* of God con-
strains him to bring it into existence. But Spinoza does deny that God created the world by some arbitrary and undetermined act of free will. God
could not have done otherwise. There are no possible alternatives to the
actual world, and absolutely no contingency or spontaneity within that
world. Everything is absolutely and necessarily determined.

P29: In nature there is nothing contingent, but all things have been determined
from the necessity of the divine nature to exist and produce an effect in a
certain way.

P33: Things could have been produced by God in no other way, and in no other
order than they have been produced.

There are, however, differences in the way things depend on God. Some
features of the universe follow necessarily from God alone – or, more precisely, from the absolute nature of one of God's attributes itself. These are
the universal, infinite, and eternal aspects of the world, and they do not
come into or go out of being. They include the most general laws of the
universe, together governing all things in all ways. From the attribute of
extension there follow the laws governing all extended objects (the truths
of geometry) and laws governing the motion and rest of bodies (the laws
of physics); from the attribute of thought, there follow laws of thought
(logic) and what Spinoza calls "God's intellect." Particular and individual
things are causally more remote from God. They are nothing but finite
"affections of God's attributes, or modes by which God's attributes are expressed in a certain and determinate way."[68]

There are two causal orders or dimensions governing the production
and actions of particular things. On the one hand, they are determined by
the general laws of the universe that follow immediately from God's natures. On the other hand, each particular thing is determined to act and to
be acted upon by other particular things. Thus, the actual behavior of a
body in motion is a function not just of the universal laws of motion, but

also of the other bodies in motion and rest surrounding it and with which it comes into contact.[69]

Spinoza's metaphysics of God is neatly summed up in a phrase that occurs in the Latin (but not the Dutch!) edition of the *Ethics:* "God, or Nature," *Deus, sive Natura:* "That eternal and infinite being we call God, or Nature, acts from the same necessity from which he exists."[70] It is an ambiguous phrase, as Spinoza could be read as trying either to divinize nature or to naturalize God. But for the careful reader there is no mistaking Spinoza's intention. The friends who, after his death, published his writings must have left out the "or Nature" clause from the more widely accessible Dutch version out of fear of the reaction this identification would predictably arouse among a vernacular audience.

There are, Spinoza insists, two sides of Nature. First, there is the active, productive aspect of the universe – God and his attributes, from which all else follows. This is what Spinoza, employing the same terms he used in the *Short Treatise,* calls *Natura naturans,* "naturing Nature." Strictly speaking, this is identical with God. The other aspect of the universe is that which is produced and sustained by the active aspect, *Natura naturata,* "natured Nature."

> By *Natura naturata* I understand whatever follows from the necessity of God's nature, or from any of God's attributes, i.e., all the modes of God's attributes insofar as they are considered as things that are in God, and can neither be nor be conceived without God.[71]

Spinoza's fundamental insight in Book One is that Nature is an indivisible, uncaused, substantial whole – in fact, it is the *only* substantial whole. Outside of Nature, there is nothing, and everything that exists is a part of Nature and is brought into being by Nature with a deterministic necessity. This unified, unique, productive, necessary being just *is* what is meant by "God." Because of the necessity inherent in Nature, there is no teleology in the universe. Nature does not act for any ends, and things do not exist for any set purposes. There are no "final causes" (to use the common Aristotelian phrase). God does not "do" things for the sake of anything else. The order of things just follows from God's essences with an inviolable determinism. All talk of God's purposes, intentions, goals, preferences, or aims is just an anthropomorphizing fiction.

> All the prejudices I here undertake to expose depend on this one: that men commonly suppose that all natural things act, as men do, on account of an end; indeed,

they maintain as certain that God himself directs all things to some certain end, for they say that God has made all things for man, and man that he might worship God.[72]

God is not some goal-oriented planner who then judges things by how well they conform to his purposes. Things happen only because of Nature and its laws. "Nature has no end set before it. . . . All things proceed by a certain eternal necessity of nature." To believe otherwise is to fall prey to the same superstitions that lie at the heart of the organized religions.

[People] find – both in themselves and outside themselves – many means that are very helpful in seeking their own advantage, e.g., eyes for seeing, teeth for chewing, plants and animals for food, the sun for light, the sea for supporting fish. . . . Hence, they consider all natural things as means to their own advantage. And knowing that they had found these means, not provided them for themselves, they had reason to believe that there was someone else who had prepared those means for their use. For after they considered things as means, they could not believe that the things had made themselves; but from the means they were accustomed to prepare for themselves, they had to infer that there was a ruler, or a number of rulers of nature, endowed with human freedom, who had taken care of all things for them, and made all things for their use.

And since they had never heard anything about the temperament of these rulers, they had to judge it from their own. Hence, they maintained that the Gods direct all things for the use of men in order to bind men to them and be held by men in the highest honor. So it has happened that each of them has thought up from his own temperament different ways of worshipping God, so that God might love them above all the rest, and direct the whole of Nature according to the needs of their blind desire and insatiable greed. Thus this prejudice was changed into superstition, and struck deep roots in their minds.[73]

A judging God who has plans and acts purposively is a God to be obeyed and placated. Opportunistic preachers are then able to play on our hopes and fears in the face of such a God. They prescribe ways of acting that are calculated to avoid being punished by that God and earn his rewards. But, Spinoza insists, to see God or Nature as acting for the sake of ends – to find purpose in Nature – is to misconstrue Nature and "turn it upside down" by putting the effect (the end result) before the true cause.

Nor does God perform miracles, because there are no departures whatsoever from the necessary course of nature. The belief in miracles is due only to ignorance of the true causes of phenomena.

If a stone has fallen from a roof onto someone's head and killed him, they will show, in the following way, that the stone fell in order to kill the man. For if it did not fall to that end, God willing it, how could so many circumstances have concurred by chance (for often many circumstances do concur at once)? Perhaps you will answer that it happened because the wind was blowing hard and the man was walking that way. But they will persist: why was the wind blowing hard at that time? why was the man walking that way at that time? If you answer again that the wind arose then because on the preceding day, while the weather was still calm, the sea began to toss, and that the man had been invited by a friend, they will press on – for there is no end to the questions which can be asked: but why was the sea tossing? why was the man invited at just that time? And so they will not stop asking for the causes of causes until you take refuge in the will of God, i.e., the sanctuary of ignorance.[74]

This is strong language, and Spinoza is clearly not unaware of the risks of his position. The same preachers who take advantage of our credulity will fulminate against anyone who tries to pull aside the curtain and reveal the truths of Nature. "One who seeks the true causes of miracles, and is eager, like an educated man, to understand natural things, not to wonder at them, like a fool, is generally considered and denounced as an impious heretic by those whom the people honor as interpreters of nature and the Gods. For they know that if ignorance is taken away, then foolish wonder, the only means they have of arguing and defending their authority, is also taken away."

In Part Two, Spinoza turns to the origin and nature of the human being. The two attributes of God of which we have cognizance are extension and thought. This, in itself, involves what would have been an astounding thesis in the eyes of his contemporaries, one that was usually misunderstood and always vilified. When Spinoza claims in Proposition 2 that "Extension is an attribute of God, or God is an extended thing," he was almost universally – but erroneously – interpreted as saying that God is literally corporeal. For just this reason "Spinozism" became, for his critics, synonymous with atheistic materialism.

What is in God is not matter itself, however, but extension as an essence. And extension and thought are two distinct essences that have absolutely nothing in common. The modes or expressions of extension are physical bodies; the modes of thought are ideas. Because extension and thought have nothing in common, the two realms of matter and mind are causally closed systems. Everything that is extended follows from the attribute of extension alone. Every bodily event is part of an infinite causal series of bodily events and is determined only by the nature of extension and its laws, in conjunction with its relations to other extended bodies. Similarly, every idea follows only from the attribute of thought. Any idea is an integral part of an infinite series of ideas and is determined by the nature of thought and its laws, along with its relations to other ideas. There is, in other words, no causal interaction between bodies and ideas, between the physical and the mental. There is, however, a thoroughgoing correlation and parallelism between the two series. For every mode in extension that is a relatively stable collection of matter, there is a corresponding mode in thought. In fact, he insists, "a mode of extension and the idea of that mode are one and the same thing, but expressed in two ways."[75] Because of the fundamental and underlying unity of Nature, or of substance, thought and extension are just two different ways of "comprehending" one and the same Nature. Every material thing thus has its own particular idea – a kind of Platonic concept – that expresses or represents it. As that idea is just a mode of one of God's attributes – thought – it is in God, and the infinite series of ideas constitutes God's mind. As he explains:

A circle existing in nature and the idea of the existing circle, which is also in God, are one and the same thing, which is explained through different attributes. Therefore, whether we conceive nature under the attribute of Extension, or under the attribute of Thought, or under any other attribute, we shall find one and the same order, or one and the same connection of causes, i.e., that the same things follow one another.

It follows from this, he argues, that the causal relations between bodies is mirrored in the logical relations between God's ideas. Or, as Spinoza notes in Proposition 7, "the order and connection of ideas is the same as the order and connection of things."

One kind of extended body, however, is significantly more complex than any other in its composition and in its dispositions to act and be acted upon. That complexity is reflected in its corresponding idea. The body in question is the human body; and its corresponding idea is the human mind or soul. The mind, then, like any other idea, is simply one particular mode of God's attribute, thought. Whatever happens in the body is reflected or expressed in the mind. In this way, the mind perceives, more or less obscurely, what is taking place in its body. And through its body's interactions with other bodies, the mind is aware of what is happening in the physical world around it. But the human mind no more interacts with its body than any mode of thought interacts with a mode of extension.

One of the pressing questions in seventeenth-century philosophy, and perhaps the most celebrated legacy of Descartes's dualism, is the problem of how two radically different substances such as mind and body enter into a union in a human being and cause effects in each other. How can the extended body causally engage the unextended mind, which is incapable of contact or motion, and "move" it, that is, cause mental effects such as pains, sensations, and perceptions. Spinoza, in effect, denies that the human being is a union of two *substances*. The human mind and the human body are two different expressions – under thought and under extension – of one and the same thing. And because there is no causal interaction between the mind and the body, the so-called mind–body problem does not, technically speaking, arise.

The human mind, like God, contains ideas. Some of these ideas – sensory images, qualitative "feels" (like pains and pleasures), perceptual data – are imprecise qualitative phenomena, being the expression in thought of states of the body as it is affected by the bodies surrounding it. Such ideas do not convey adequate and true knowledge of the world, but only a relative, partial, and subjective picture of how things presently seem to be to the perceiver. There is no systematic order to these perceptions, nor any critical oversight by reason. "As long as the human Mind perceives things from the common order of nature, it does not have an adequate, but only a confused and mutilated knowledge of itself, of its own Body, and of external bodies."[76] Under such circumstances, we are simply determined in our ideas by our fortuitous and haphazard encounter with things in the external world. This superficial acquaintance will never provide us with knowledge of the essences of those things. In fact, it is an invariable source of falsehood and error. This "knowledge from random experience" is also the origin of great delusions, as we – thinking ourselves free – are, in our ignorance, unaware of just how we *are* determined by causes.

Adequate ideas, on the other hand, are formed in a rational and orderly manner, and are necessarily true and revelatory of the essences of things. "Reason," the second kind of knowledge (after "random experience"), is the apprehension of the essence of a thing through a discursive, inferential procedure. "A true idea means nothing other than knowing a thing perfectly, or in the best way." It involves grasping a thing's causal connections not just to other objects but, more importantly, to the attributes of God and the infinite modes (the laws of nature) that follow immediately from them. The adequate idea of a thing clearly and distinctly situates its object in all of its causal nexuses and shows not just *that* it is, but *how* and *why* it is. The person who truly knows a thing sees the reasons why the thing was determined to be and could not have been otherwise. "It is of the nature of Reason to regard things as necessary, not as contingent."[77] The belief that some thing is accidental or spontaneous can be based only on an inadequate grasp of the thing's causal explanation, on a partial and "mutilated" familiarity with it. To perceive by way of adequate ideas is to perceive the necessity inherent in Nature.

Sense experience alone could never provide the information conveyed by an adequate idea. The senses present things only as they appear from a given perspective at a given moment in time. An adequate idea, on the other hand, by showing how a thing follows necessarily from one or another of God's attributes, presents it in its "eternal" aspects – *sub specie aeternitatis*, as Spinoza puts it – without any relation to time. "It is of the nature of Reason to regard things as necessary and not as contingent. And Reason perceives this necessity of things truly, i.e., as it is in itself. But this necessity of things is the very necessity of God's eternal nature. Therefore, it is of the nature of Reason to regard things under this species of eternity." The third kind of knowledge, intuition, takes what is known by reason and grasps it in a single act of the mind.

Spinoza's conception of adequate knowledge reveals an unrivaled optimism in the cognitive powers of the human being. Not even Descartes believed that we could know all of Nature and its innermost secrets with the degree of depth and certainty that Spinoza thought possible. Lodewijk Meyer himself, in his preface to *Descartes' Principles of Philosophy*, alerts the reader to this difference between the two.

We must not fail to note that what is found in some places [of this work] – viz. *that this or that surpasses the human understanding* – must be taken . . . as said only on behalf of Descartes. For it must not be thought that our Author offers this as his own opinion. He judges that all those things, and even many others more sublime and subtle, can not only be conceived clearly and distinctly, but also explained very satisfactorily – provided only that the human Intellect is guided in the search for truth and knowledge of things along a different path from that which Descartes opened up and made smooth.[78]

Most remarkably, because Spinoza thought that the adequate knowledge of any object, and of Nature as a whole, involves a thorough knowledge of

God and of how things are related to God and his attributes, he also had
no scruples about claiming that we can, at least in principle, know God
perfectly and adequately: "The knowledge of God's eternal and infinite
essence that each idea involves is adequate and perfect."[79] "The human
Mind has an adequate knowledge of God's eternal and infinite essence."[80]
No other philosopher in history has been willing to make this claim. But,
then again, no other philosopher identified God with Nature.

Spinoza engages in such a detailed analysis of the composition of the
human being because it is essential to his goal of showing how the human
being is a part of nature, existing within the same causal nexuses as other
extended and mental beings. This has serious ethical implications. First, it
implies that a human being is not endowed with freedom, at least in the ordinary sense of that term. Because our minds and the events in our minds
are simply ideas existing within the causal series of ideas that follows from
God's attribute thought, our actions and volitions are as necessarily determined as any other natural events. "In the Mind there is no absolute, or
free, will, but the Mind is determined to will this or that by a cause that is
also determined by another, and this again by another, and so to infinity."

What is true of the will (and, of course, of our bodies) is true of all the
phenomena of our psychological lives. Spinoza believes that this is something that has not been sufficiently understood by previous thinkers, who
seem to have wanted to place the human being on a pedestal outside of (or
above) nature.

Most of those who have written about the Affects, and men's way of living, seem
to treat, not of natural things, which follow the common laws of nature, but of
things that are outside nature. Indeed they seem to conceive man in nature as a
dominion within a dominion. For they believe that man disturbs, rather than follows, the order of nature, that he has absolute power over his actions, and that he
is determined only by himself.[81]

Descartes, for example, believed that if the freedom of the human being
is to be preserved, the soul must be exempt from the kind of deterministic laws that rule over the material universe.

Spinoza's aim in what, in the published version, are Parts Three and
Four is, as he says in his preface to Part Three, to restore the human be-
ing and his volitional and emotional life into their proper place in nature.
For nothing stands outside of nature, not even the human mind.

Nature is always the same, and its virtue and power of acting are everywhere one and
the same, i.e., the laws and rules of nature, according to which all things happen, and

change from one form to another, are always and everywhere the same. So the way of understanding the nature of anything, of whatever kind, must also be the same, viz. through the universal laws and rules of nature.

Our affects – our love, anger, hate, envy, pride, jealousy, and so on – "follow from the same necessity and force of nature as the other singular things." Spinoza, therefore, explains these emotions – as determined in their occurrence as are a body in motion and the properties of a mathematical figure – just as he would explain any other things in nature. "I shall treat the nature and power of the Affects, and the power of the Mind over them, by the same Method by which, in the preceding parts, I treated God and the Mind, and I shall consider human actions and appetites just as if it were a question of lines, planes, and bodies."

Our affects are divided into actions and passions. When the cause of an event lies in our own nature – more particularly, our knowledge or adequate ideas – then it is a case of the mind acting. On the other hand, when something happens in us the cause of which lies outside of our nature, then we are passive and being acted upon. Usually what takes place, both when we are acting and when we are being acted upon, is some change in our mental or physical capacities, what Spinoza calls "an increase or decrease in our power of acting" or in our "power to persevere in being." All beings are naturally endowed with such a power or striving. This *conatus,* a kind of existential inertia, constitutes the "essence" of any being. "Each thing, as far as it can by its own power, strives to persevere in its being."[82] An affect just *is* any change in this power, for better or for worse. Affects that are actions are changes in this power that have their source (or "adequate cause") in our nature alone; affects that are passions are those changes in this power that originate outside of us.

What we should strive for is to be free from the passions – or, as this is not absolutely possible, at least to learn how to moderate and restrain them – and become active, autonomous beings. If we can achieve this, then we will be "free" to the extent that whatever happens to us will result not from our relations with things outside us, but from our own nature (as that follows from, and is ultimately and necessarily determined by, the attributes of God, that is, by the substance of which our minds and bodies are modes). We will, consequently, be truly liberated from the troublesome emotional ups and downs of this life. The way to bring this about is to increase our knowledge, our store of adequate ideas, and to eliminate as far as possible our inadequate ideas, which follow not from the nature of the mind alone but from its being an expression of how our body is affected by other bodies. In other words, we need to free ourselves from a reliance on the senses and the imagination, as a life of the senses and images is a life being affected and led by the objects around us, and rely as much as we can only on our rational faculties.

Because of our innate striving to persevere – which, in the human being, is called "will" or "appetite" – we naturally pursue those things which we believe will benefit us by increasing our power of acting and shun or flee those things that we believe will harm us by decreasing our power of acting. This provides Spinoza with a foundation for cataloging the human passions. For the passions are all functions of the ways in which external things affect our powers or capacities. Joy, for example, is simply the movement or passage to a greater capacity for action. "By Joy . . . I shall understand that passion by which the Mind passes to a greater perfection."[83] Being a passion, joy is always brought about by some external object. Sadness, on the other hand, is the passage to a lesser state of perfection, also occasioned by a thing outside us. Love is simply Joy accompanied by an awareness of the external cause that brings about the passage to a greater perfection. We love that object which benefits us and causes us joy. Hate is nothing but "Sadness with the accompanying idea of an external cause." Hope is simply "an inconstant Joy which has arisen from the image of a future or past thing whose outcome we doubt." We hope for a thing whose presence, as yet uncertain, will bring about joy. We fear, however, a thing whose presence, equally uncertain, will bring about sadness. When that whose outcome was doubtful becomes certain, hope is changed into confidence, while fear is changed into despair.

All of the human emotions, insofar as they are passions, are constantly directed outward, toward things and their capacities to affect us in one way or another. Aroused by our passions and desires, we seek or flee those objects that we believe cause joy or sadness. "We strive to further the occurrence of whatever we imagine will lead to Joy, and to avert or destroy what we imagine is contrary to it, or will lead to Sadness."[84] Our hopes and fears fluctuate depending on whether we regard the objects of our desires or aversions as remote, near, necessary, possible, or unlikely. But the objects of our passions, being external to us, are completely beyond our control. Thus, the more we allow ourselves to be controlled by *them*, the more we are subject to passions and the less active and free we are. The upshot is a

fairly pathetic picture of a life mired in the passions and pursuing and fleeing the changeable and fleeting objects that occasion them: "We are driven
about in many ways by external causes, and . . . like waves on the sea, driven
by contrary winds, we toss about, not knowing our outcome and fate."[85]
The title of Part 4 of the *Ethics* reveals with perfect clarity Spinoza's eval-
uation of such a life for a human being: "On Human Bondage, or the Powers of the Affects." He explains that the human being's "lack of power to
moderate and restrain the affects I call Bondage. For the man who is subject to affects is under the control, not of himself, but of fortune, in whose
power he so greatly is that often, though he sees the better for himself, he
is still forced to follow the worse." It is, he says, a kind of "sickness of the
mind" to suffer too much love for a thing "that is liable to many variations
and that we can never fully possess."[86]

The solution to this predicament is an ancient one. Since we cannot
control the objects that we tend to value and allow to influence our well-
being, we ought instead to try to control our evaluations themselves and
thereby minimize the sway that external objects and the passions have over
us. We can never eliminate the passive affects entirely; nor would that even
be desirable in this life. We are essentially a part of nature and can never
fully remove ourselves from the causal series that link us to external things.
"It is impossible that a man should not be a part of Nature, and that he
should be able to undergo no changes except those which can be understood through his own nature alone, and of which he is the adequate
cause. . . . From this it follows that man is necessarily always subject to passions, that he follows and obeys the common order of Nature, and accom-
modates himself to it as much as the nature of things requires."[87] But we
can, ultimately, counteract the passions, control them, and achieve a certain degree of relief from their turmoil.

The path to restraining and moderating the affects is through virtue.
Spinoza is a psychological and ethical egoist. All beings naturally seek their
own advantage – to preserve their own being – and it is right for them to
do so. This is what virtue consists in. Because we are thinking beings, endowed with intelligence and reason, what is to our greatest advantage is
knowledge. Our virtue, therefore, consists in the pursuit of knowledge and
understanding, of adequate ideas. The best kind of knowledge is a purely
intellectual intuition of the essences of things. This "third kind of knowledge" – beyond both random experience and ratiocination – sees things
not in their temporal dimension, not in their duration and in relation to

other particular things, but under the aspect of eternity, that is, abstracted from all considerations of time and place and situated in their relationship to God and his attributes. They are apprehended, that is, in their conceptual and causal relationship to the universal essences (thought and extension) and the eternal laws of nature.

We conceive things as actual in two ways: either insofar as we conceive them to exist in relation to a certain time and place, or insofar as we conceive them to be contained in God and to follow from the necessity of the divine nature. But the things we conceive in this second way as true, or real, we conceive under a species of eternity, and to that extent they involve the eternal and infinite essence of God.[88]

But this is just to say that, ultimately, we strive for a knowledge of God. The concept of any body involves the concept of extension; and the concept of any idea or mind involves the concept of thought. But thought and extension are just God's attributes. So the proper and adequate conception of any body or mind necessarily involves the concept or knowledge of God. "The third kind of knowledge proceeds from an adequate idea of certain attributes of God to an adequate knowledge of the essence of things, and the more we understand things in this way, the more we understand God."[89] Knowledge of God is, thus, the mind's greatest good and its greatest virtue.

What we see when we understand things through the third kind of knowledge, under the aspect of eternity and in relation to God, is the deterministic necessity of all things. We see that all bodies and their states follow necessarily from the essence of matter and the universal laws of physics; and we see that all ideas, including all the properties of minds, follow necessarily from the essence of thought and its universal laws. This insight can only weaken the power that the passions have over us. We are no longer hopeful or fearful of what shall come to pass, and no longer anxious or despondent over our possessions. We regard all things with equanimity, and we are not inordinately and irrationally affected in different ways by past, present or future events. The results are self-control and a calmness of mind.

The more this knowledge that things are necessary is concerned with singular things, which we imagine more distinctly and vividly, the greater is this power of the Mind over the affects, as experience itself also testifies. For we see that Sadness over some good which has perished is lessened as soon as the man who has lost it realizes that this good could not, in any way, have been kept. Similarly, we see that [because we regard infancy as a natural and necessary thing] no one pities infants because of their inability to speak, to walk, or to reason, or because they live so many years, as it were, unconscious of themselves.[90]

Our affects themselves can be understood in this way, which further diminishes their power over us.

Spinoza's ethical theory is, to a certain degree, Stoic,[91] and recalling the doctrines of thinkers such as Cicero and Seneca:

We do not have an absolute power to adapt things outside us to our use. Nevertheless, we shall bear calmly those things that happen to us contrary to what the principle of our advantage demands, if we are conscious that we have done our duty, that the power we have could not have extended itself to the point where we could have avoided those things, and that we are a part of the whole of nature, whose order we follow. If we understand this clearly and distinctly, that part of us which is defined by understanding, i.e., the better part of us, will be entirely satisfied with this, and will strive to persevere in that satisfaction. For insofar as we understand, we can want nothing except what is necessary, nor absolutely be satisfied with anything except what is true.[92]

What, in the end, replaces the passionate love for ephemeral "goods" is an intellectual love for an eternal, immutable good that we can fully and stably possess, God. The third kind of knowledge generates a love for its object, and in this love consists not joy, a passion, but blessedness itself. Taking his cue from Maimonides' view of human *eudaimonia*, Spinoza argues that the mind's intellectual love of God *is* our understanding of the universe, our virtue, our happiness, our well-being, and our "salvation."[93] It is also our freedom and autonomy, as we approach the condition wherein what happens to us follows from our nature (as a determinate and determined mode of one of God's attributes) alone and not as a result of the ways in which external things affect us. Spinoza's "free person" is one who bears the gifts and losses of fortune with equanimity, does only those things which he believes to be "the most important in life," takes care for the well-being of others (doing what he can to ensure that they, too, achieve some relief from the disturbances of the passions through understanding), and is not anxious about death.[94] The free person neither hopes for any eternal, otherworldly rewards nor fears any eternal punishments. He knows that the soul is not immortal in any personal sense, but is endowed only with a certain kind of eternity. The more the mind consists of true and adequate ideas (which are eternal), the more of it remains – within God's attribute of thought – after the death of the body and the disappearance of that part of the mind that corresponds to the body's duration.[95] This understanding of his place in the natural scheme of things brings to the free individual true peace of mind.

A number of social and political ramifications that follow from Spinoza's ethical doctrines of human action and well-being, all related to questions that came more and more to occupy his mind by the mid-1660s. Because disagreement and discord among human beings is always the result of our different and changeable passions, "free" individuals – all of whom share the same nature and act on the same principles – will naturally and effortlessly form a harmonious society. "Insofar as men are torn by affects that are passions, they can be contrary to one another. . . . [But] insofar as men live according to the guidance of reason, they must do only those things that are good for human nature, and hence, for each man, i.e., those things that agree with the nature of each man. Hence, insofar as men live according to the guidance of reason, they must always agree among themselves."[96] Free human beings will be mutually beneficial and useful, and will be tolerant of the opinions and even the errors of others. However, human beings do not generally live under the guidance of reason. The state or sovereign, therefore, is required in order to ensure – not by reason, but by the threat of force – that individuals are protected from the unrestrained pursuit of self-interest on the part of other individuals. The transition from a state of nature, where each seeks his own advantage without limits, to a civil state involves the universal renunciation of certain natural rights – such as "the right everyone has of avenging himself, and of judging good and evil" – and the investment of those prerogatives in a central authority. As long as human beings are guided by their passions, the state is necessary to bring it about that they "live harmoniously and be of assistance to one another."[97]

Explicitly political questions inhabit only a small corner of the *Ethics*. Perhaps Spinoza put that work aside in 1665 just because of what he might have regarded as the more pressing political issues that had begun once again to disturb the peace of Voorburg, and of the Dutch Republic as a whole, around that time. It would be a good number of years – and possibly not until after the assassination of Johan de Witt and the end of the period of "True Freedom" – before Spinoza returned to work seriously on his metaphysical-moral treatise.

Perhaps, too, he hoped for a time more propitious for the reception of the geometrical presentation of his radical ideas on God, nature, and the human being. Spinoza was, by nature, a very cautious individual – his signet ring was inscribed with the motto *Caute*, "Caution!" – and he was hesitant about revealing the more profound and potentially troublesome aspects of his doctrines and their theological implications to people outside of the immediate circle of friends who had been reading the manuscript drafts all along. Even Oldenburg – who had been entrusted in 1661 with only a cryptic taste of Spinoza's ideas on God and substance[98] – was now allowed nothing more than a partial explanation of the work's metaphysical theses. In a letter from around November 1665, Spinoza responded to Oldenburg's request to explain further to him and Boyle "how each part of Nature accords with its whole, and the manner of its coherence with other parts." Spinoza replied at length about how body and mind are parts of infinite extension and infinite thought, respectively, and thus "parts of Nature," but without mentioning (or even hinting) that extension and thought are attributes of God.[99] From Oldenburg's letter – which displays, at the very least, the man's persistence ("Would that you may at last bring to birth the offspring of your own mind and entrust it to the world of philosophers to cherish and foster") – it is fairly clear that he does not have a clue about Spinoza's full position:

Why do you hesitate, my friend, what do you fear? Make the attempt, go to it, bring to completion a task of such high importance, and you will see the entire company of genuine philosophers supporting you. I venture to pledge my word, which I would not do if I doubted my ability to redeem it. In no way could I believe that you have in mind to contrive something against the existence and providence of God, and with these crucial supports intact religion stands on a firm footing, and any reflections of a philosophical nature can either be readily defended or excused. So away with delays, and suffer nothing to divert you.[100]

Spinoza's caution was, no doubt, warranted. But if he thought that public reaction to a less formally composed treatise on Scripture, religion, and the limits of political and theological authority would be more measured and accommodating, and could possibly pave the way for his metaphysical and ethical doctrines, he was badly mistaken.

10

Homo Politicus

L IFE IN THE DUTCH COUNTRYSIDE, though peaceful, also has its down
sides particularly for someone who thrives on intellectual exchange
with others. When the weather is bad, Spinoza tells Oldenburg in November 1665, he is stranded in Voorburg, unable to get into The Hague to
see people or send letters. He also invariably receives his own mail late. "I
wrote this letter last week, but I could not send it because the wind prevented my going to The Hague. This is the disadvantage of living in the
country. Rarely do I receive a letter at the proper time, for unless an opportunity should chance to arise for sending it in good time, one or two
weeks go by before I receive it."[1] Still, in the house on the Kerkstraat,
Spinoza was able to work uninterrupted and without the distractions of a
major city.

The calm of Voorburg, however, was briefly but perhaps for Spinoza
permanently disturbed just as he was nearing completion of the draft of
the *Ethics*, and the incident may even have played a role in his decision to
put the treatise aside. In 1665, he was apparently drawn into the local religious dispute that, in its theological and political dimensions, reflected
the schisms characterizing Dutch society at large. Jacob van Oosterwijck,
through either death or retirement, had just vacated his post as preacher
in the local church, probably the same church for which the street Daniel
Tydeman's house sat on was named. Tydeman served on the committee
that was appointed to select a new preacher. He, the diocese's bishop, Hendrick van Gaelen, and a former bishop named Rotteveel nominated, in a
petition to the magistrates of Delft, a Zeelander named Van de Wiele. The
Collegiant Tydeman and his colleagues, with their liberal, possibly Remonstrant persuasions, were opposed in their choice by more orthodox members of the church, who sent their own petition to Delft. The conservatives
accused the nominating committee of deliberate provocation and made
known their own preference for a pastor named Westerneyn. The town's

burgemeesters sided with the conservative faction, although it is not clear that Westerneyn was appointed either.[2] It seems, from the conservatives' petition, that Spinoza was allied with Tydeman's group; and it is possible he even had a hand in drafting their original petition.[3] In the minds of many of his Reformed neighbors in Voorburg, Spinoza, that man "born of Jewish parents," now had a reputation. He was, more so than his liberal accomplices in this affair, a danger to society: "[He] is now (so it is said) an atheist, or someone who mocks all religions and thus surely is a harmful instrument in this republic, as many learned individuals and preachers . . . can attest."[4]

Spinoza was always deeply offended by the accusation that he was an atheist. Responding to Lambert van Velthuysen's attack on the *Theological-Political Treatise* and his denunciation of Spinoza as "teaching sheer atheism with furtive and disguised arguments,"[5] he accused Van Velthuysen of having "perversely misinterpreted my meaning," and protested that his critic should be ashamed of leveling such a charge against him. "If he had known [what manner of life I pursue] he would not have been so readily convinced that I teach atheism. For atheists are usually inordinately fond of honors and riches, which I have always despised, as is known to all who are acquainted with me."[6] It was, nonetheless, a label that accompanied his name for a long time after his death, abetted by receiving the imprimatur in the eighteenth century of no less an authority than the generally tolerant Pierre Bayle. Despite his admiration for Spinoza's character, Bayle begins his entry for Spinoza in his *Dictionnaire* by describing him as "a Jew by birth, and afterwards a deserter from Judaism, and lastly an atheist." He insists that Spinoza "died completely convinced of his atheism" and sowed the seeds for the corruption of others.

Whatever may be the general ambiguities in the epithet "atheist," the meaning of the term becomes expecially hazy when viewed in the volatile religious environment of seventeenth-century Holland. To the churchgoing citizens of Voorburg, at least, it meant one who showed disrespect for religion. Spinoza certainly did not have a very high opinion of organized religion, especially as it existed in his day. But he did believe in what he called the "true religion," something not unlike what his nonconfessional friends probably practiced. Thus, he was taken aback by Van Velthuysen's claim that he had "renounced all religion." "Does that man, pray, renounce all religion, who declares that God must be acknowledged as the highest good, and that he must be loved as such in a free spirit? And that in this alone does our supreme happiness and our highest freedom consist?"[7] What he does have contempt for, he admits, is the religion, based in the passions and superstition, of people like Van Velthuysen:

I think I see in what mire this man is stuck. He finds nothing to please him in virtue itself and in intellect, and would choose to live under the impulsion of his passions but for one obstacle, his fear of punishment. So he abstains from evil deeds and obeys the divine commandments like a slave, reluctantly and waveringly, and in return for this servitude he expects to reap rewards from God far sweeter to him than the divine love itself, and the more so as he dislikes the good that he does, and does it unwillingly. Consequently, he believes that all who are not restrained by this fear lead unbridled lives and renounce all religion.

Did Spinoza's system rule out a belief even in the existence of God? Over the years, Spinoza emphatically and repeatedly denied this. He certainly did discourage the belief in a God endowed with the characteristics traditionally attributed to him by theologians. But had not Spinoza demonstrated that these properties are, in fact, incompatible with the true definition of God? His contemporaries, however, seemed more interested in the scandal surrounding his name than in any close study of his arguments. This provided much work for Spinoza's friends and defenders. During his sojourn in the Netherlands, Gottlieb Stolle asked Burchard de Volder, who knew Spinoza fairly well – and certainly better than anyone still living at the time of his interview (1703) – about Spinoza's alleged lack of religion: "He is an atheist, isn't he?" To which De Volder, probably exasperated by a question he may have been asked a thousand times before, replied that he could not agree.[8]

Spinoza's sensitivity to the charge of atheism was one of the motivating factors behind his decision to put aside the *Ethics* for a while in order to compose a treatise on theological and political matters. In September 1665, Oldenburg good-naturedly teased Spinoza about his decision to turn to such questions. "I see that you are not so much philosophising as theologising, if one may use that term, for you are recording your thoughts about angels, prophecy and miracles."[9] In his reply, Spinoza explained the reason for his change of plans.

I am now writing a treatise on my views regarding Scripture. The reasons that move me to do so are: 1. The prejudices of theologians. For I know that these are the main obstacles that prevent men from giving their minds to philosophy. So I apply myself to exposing such prejudices and removing them from the minds of sensible people. 2. The opinion of me held by the common people, who constantly accuse me of atheism. I am driven to avert this accusation, too, as far as I can. 3. The freedom to philosophise and to say what we think. This I want to vindicate completely, for here it is in every way suppressed by the excessive authority and egotism of preachers.[10]

There is an edge on Spinoza's voice here. He was probably resentful about the outcome of the Voorburg affair, and particularly about the way he and his landlord may have been talked about and treated by a number of important people in town. He was undoubtedly indignant about the way Reformed ministers, for whom he never had much respect, tried to dominate civic affairs there and elsewhere. By the time he published the work – and, despite his distaste for "brawling" with theologians, publish it he would – a number of events had transformed his resentment into outright anger.

It seems, in fact, to have been not so much a new project that Spinoza undertook in the fall of 1665 as a return to an old one. Among the many theological and political issues that he addresses in the *Theological-Political Treatise* – the status and interpretation of Scripture; the election of the Jewish people; the origins of the state; the nature, legitimacy, and bounds of political and religious authority, and the imperative for toleration – are ones that we have reasons for thinking were of concern to Spinoza as far back as the period of his excommunication from the Jewish community. The testimonies about his religious beliefs from around 1655–6 all mention views on Scripture that are – if the generally hostile witnesses are to be trusted – essentially those of the book published in 1670. And the reports about the *Apology* that he is alleged to have written soon after the *cherem*, as well as the mention of a *tractatus theologico-politicus* from late 1659 or early 1660 in Adriaen Paets's letter to Poelenberg,[11] suggest that Spinoza had been contemplating, and perhaps actually working on, a composition at least partly like the *Theological-Political Treatise* for some time.

It is not clear whether, in the initial letter – long since lost – that provoked Oldenburg's comment, Spinoza was any more forthcoming about the details of his views on the Bible and religion than he was regarding the theological implications of his metaphysics. One suspects he was not, for Oldenburg, who took his Christianity seriously, responded to Spinoza's explanation with his usual enthusiasm. "The reasons that you mention as having induced you to compose a treatise on Scripture have my entire approval, and I am desperately eager to see with my own eyes your thoughts on that subject."[12] He is expecting Serrarius soon to be sending him a parcel from Amsterdam and hopes Spinoza will be able to include in it what he has already written.

This would have been perfectly convenient for Spinoza, for he was still making the occasional journey to Amsterdam. Besides his visits with his older circle of friends, he seems also to have been meeting around this time with Hudde and De Volder, apparently to discuss natural philosophy and mathematics.[13] These trips would also have given him the opportunity to keep abreast of some recent events that must have been of great interest to him and would have served only to confirm in his mind his view of the superstitious nature of "popular" religion.

The year 1666, as one might expect, was invested by many people with great significance. Christian millenarians, taking their numerical clue from the Book of Revelations, believed it to be the year of the Second Coming and the establishment of the "rule of the saints." Many philo-Semites who still felt the disappointment of 1656, the previous date expected for the conversion of the Jews (an important sign that Christ's return was near), were on the lookout for any indications that this time their faith would be rewarded. Jewish messianists, for their part, had been anxious for the coming of the Messiah and the gathering of all of Israel in the Holy Land under his dominion ever since Menasseh ben Israel's report sixteen years earlier on Montezino's discovery of some of the "Lost Tribes" in the New World. It looked, for a time, as if the hopes of both groups were finally to be fulfilled in the person of Sabbatai Zevi, the Messiah from Smyrna.

Zevi was born in 1626, in Smyrna, Turkey, to an Ashkenazic family from Greece.[14] The date on which he was born on the Jewish calender, the ninth of Av (Tisha b'Av), a day devoted to mourning for the destruction of the First and Second Temples, was traditionally regarded by rabbis as the birthday of the Messiah, and Zevi eventually came to take this coincidence very seriously. As a boy, he was a precocious and talented, if rather melancholic, scholar. Having undergone a traditional religious training in Talmud and rabbinical law, Zevi turned at an early age to a close study of the *Zohar,* a work of Jewish mysticism from thirteenth-century Castile, and other kabbalistic texts. He received the title *chacham* while still in his teens, although he never formally functioned as the rabbi for a congregation. Zevi was, however, a charismatic individual and attracted a good number of followers over a relatively short period of time. They studied Talmud under him, and the more devoted ones followed him in his strict, ascetic practices to prepare themselves for mystical insight into the hidden secrets of the Torah. (Among these practices was sexual abstinence; Zevi is reported not to have consummated any of his several marriages.) Zevi was also, apparently, a manic-depressive, subject to great mood swings and bouts of paranoia. As Gershom Scholem, the great scholar of Jewish mysticism, puts it, "there is no doubt that Sabbatai Zevi was a sick man."[15]

Zevi's beliefs about the meaning of Torah, the nature and presence of God, and the path to enlightenment focused on the traditional distinction in kabbalah between the hidden "core" of God's being, *En Sof,* and the various manifestations of God in the world, the so-called *sefirot.* According to the *Zohar,* the Tetragrammaton – the four Hebrew letters that stand in for God's name in the Torah (YHWH, יהוה) – denotes, not the hidden and inaccessible core from which the *sefirot* emanate, but rather that one of the seven manifest *sefirot* in which are comprehended the others that are the active and passive forces constituting the visible universe. It is this dominant *sefirah* to which the divine attributes pertain, and thus it is the divine essence that is the God of Israel who is creator and lawgiver. It is that which the people of Israel worship in prayer and from which the divine commandments issue. Zevi, though inspired by this classic kabbalistic scheme, reportedly modified it in a significant way. He is said to have asserted that the God of Israel (and the object named by the Tetragrammaton) is, in fact, found not among the *sefirot,* the emanation, but rather in something superior to them but still distinct from *En Sof* – a kind of "divine self" that derives from the hidden core and governs the *sefirot* (and, thus, the world) from above.[16]

In 1648, a year marked for the redemption of the Jews according to some rabbis, Zevi began frequently pronouncing the Tetragrammaton, a practice forbidden by rabbinical Judaism and taken as a sign of his psychological instability by the religious authorities. After his expulsion from Smyrna around 1651 – a punishment for both his deeds and his opinions – he wandered around the Mediterranean, reaching Palestine in the early 1660s. In Jerusalem, he briefly came into contact with a yeshiva student named Abraham Nathan ben Elisha Chaim Ashkenazi. Shortly thereafter, this young man, while studying kabbalah in Gaza – and inspired perhaps by Zevi's alternately saintly and bizarre behavior, as well as by his unorthodox and mystical opinions and the rumors that Zevi thought himself the Messiah – underwent a mystical "vision" and was awakened to Sabbatai's messianic mission.[17] In early 1665, "Nathan of Gaza" publicly announced that Zevi was the Messiah. He soon convinced Sabbatai himself, and by May 1665 Zevi proclaimed himself to be the Messiah. Acting as the Messiah's prophet – in effect, taking on the role of Elijah – Nathan succeeded in generating an enormous amount of enthusiasm for his master. Not everyone was persuaded, however. Zevi was quickly excommunicated by the Jerusalem rabbinate and banished from Palestine in the summer of 1665, at which point he made his way back to Smyrna. After taking over the city's synagogue, suspending the force of Jewish law, and proclaiming himself "the Lord's Anointed," he announced that the Redemption would take place on June 18, 1666. Word began to spread about the coming of the Messiah (but not, apparently, about his having been put under a ban by Jerusalem's rabbis). Over a relatively short period of time, Jews in various parts of the Middle East and Europe were taken by a messianistic frenzy. They began selling their goods, violating the commandments (particularly regarding fasts and festivals), and preparing for their joint return to the Holy Land. Their opponents, fearful for their lives and property, kept silent.

Sephardim were particularly, but not exclusively, susceptible to the Sabbatean madness. Jewish communities in Salonika, Constantinople, Leghorn, Venice, London, Hamburg, and even the West Indies were affected, but so were Ashkenazim in Poland and Germany. Perhaps the most important center of messianistic activity around Zevi's appearance, though, was Amsterdam. By the second half of the seventeenth century, many Portuguese Jews throughout Europe were looking to the Dutch community as an intellectual and spiritual bellwether, as is evident from the scolding that the members of the Talmud Torah congregation received from Rabbi Jacob Sasportas of Hamburg, the most vocal and vehement of the anti-Sabbateans: "The eyes of all Israel were upon you when this error began, and if you had rejected the reports, or [at least] not accepted them as certainties, the other communities would not have fallen into error, for they followed your example."[18]

Having witnessed the effects on their country of the ongoing war with England and of the plague of 1664–5 – with a death rate exacerbated, in the minds of many, by the comet of 1664 – the more messianistic spirits among Amsterdam's Jews (who seem not to have been hit as hard by the latest pestilence as other groups) were looking for an indication that all this suffering had some purpose. When the reports about Zevi – one of whose wives, fleeing the Cossack massacres in 1648, had found refuge among the

Amsterdam Ashkenazim – began arriving in November 1665, there was much rejoicing. Rabbi Sasportas wrote:

there was a great commotion in the city of Amsterdam, so that it was a very great trembling. They rejoiced exceedingly, with timbrels and with dances, in all the streets. The scrolls of the Law were taken out of the Ark [for ceremonial processional] with their beautiful ornaments, without considering the possible danger from the jealousy and hatred of the gentiles. On the contrary, they publicly proclaimed [the news] and informed the gentiles of all the reports.[19]

The members of the community, led by the kabbalist Rabbi Aboab (the chief rabbi since Mortera's death in 1660), threw all caution to the winds as they abandoned themselves to their joy in the anticipated return of the exiles. Merchants neglected their businesses, and ordinary life (not to mention religious life) was disrupted in the extended celebration. Many, dropping all practical affairs and exercising no foresight, made immediate arrangements to travel to the Holy Land. Before leaving for Jerusalem, Abraham Pereira, one of the wealthiest members of the community and a fervent Sabbatean, offered to sell his country house at a substantial loss, but refused to take any money from the buyer "until he be convinced in his own conscience that the Jews have a King."[20] The Amsterdam Jews named their children Sabbatai and Nathan, added new prayers to their liturgy, introduced weekly recitations of the priestly blessing (which formerly was pronounced only on major festivals), and planned on exhuming their dead from the cemetery in Ouderkerk to take them to Palestine. Amsterdam's Jewish publishers also began producing Hebrew, Spanish, and Portuguese editions of the prayer book composed by Nathan of Gaza. In a letter to his friend Sasportas, Rabbi Aaron Sapharti, a colleague of Aboab's and a fellow Sabbatean, reported on the general delirium of

the Holy Congregation whose fervor is beyond description. If you beheld it with your eyes you would agree that this is the Lord's doing. For they spend all day and all night in the synagogue as on the Day of Atonement, and on the Sabbath they offered more than ten thousand silver florins. More benches had to be added to our yeshiva [for the many penitents and worshipers] and [if you were here] you would behold the world upside down. For [at] all the houses where they used to play at dice and lotteries, they have of themselves stopped it, without [waiting for] an order from the heads of the congregation, and all day and night they put the Law of the Lord to their hearts.[21]

Not everyone was so taken by the false Messiah and his prophet, although few were brave enough to make their views known in public. Leyb ben

Ozer, an Ashkenazic notary in Amsterdam at the turn of the eighteenth century, describes the boldness of one unbeliever:

A Sephardic merchant called Alatino denied all the reports and letters, and said in public, "You are mad! Where are the signs? Where are the tidings that the prophet Elijah is himself to bring? Where is the celestial Temple [that is to descend on Jerusalem]? Where are the [eschatological] wars that are foretold? Why have we not heard of the Messiah b. Joseph who is to fall in battle?" But everyone cursed him and said, "Surely he shall not behold the face of the messiah."[22]

Leyb notes that Alatino's end was seen as prophetic: "One day as he had returned from the Bourse in order to have his meal, between the washing of the hands and the breaking of the bread he fell down and died suddenly. When this became known to the Jews, and to the gentiles too, a great fear and trembling fell upon them." Rabbi Aboab told Sasportas of the "quarrel and contention" that had divided the members of the congregation into camps, with the Sabbateans far outnumbering their opponents and "set on mischief against whoever opposes their faith."[23]

In 1666, the world of the Sabbatean enthusiasts came rudely crashing down upon them. In February of that year, Zevi was arrested in Constantinople by the sultan and imprisoned at the fortress at Gallipoli. The charges by the Turkish authorities, who had been watching the messianic movement in their midst with increasing concern, included fomenting sedition and immorality. Zevi was given a choice between death and conversion to Islam. He chose the latter and in September became a Muslim, adopting the name Aziz Mehemed Effendi, although he continued to practice some form of Judaism in secret. His followers were crestfallen. Most simply cursed the false Messiah and returned to their ordinary lives, or whatever was left of them. A good number, however, continued to believe Zevi to be the Messiah. They simply saw his apostasy as part of the grand plan, and tried to rationalize it in various ways.

Millenarian Christians took a strong interest in the events of 1665–6. Serrarius, in fact, played an active role in spreading the word of Sabbatai's anointment among Protestants. Believing that Jews and Christians were awaiting the same Messiah,[24] he saw the activity among the Jews as a sure sign of their imminent conversion, which he had been anticipating would occur in 1666, and as the prelude for the Second Coming and the inauguration of Christ's thousand-year reign. He worked on a translation of Nathan's book of prayers in early 1666, and (faithful to the end) died at the age of eighty-nine in 1669 en route to Turkey to meet Zevi face to face.

Because there is only one extant letter from Spinoza for the years 1668–70, we are not able to learn directly about what must have been Spinoza's great sorrow over this loss of a longtime friend. Serrarius had done much for Spinoza, particularly immediately after the excommunication, when he probably introduced the banished (and possibly homeless) Spinoza around Amsterdam's millenarian circles, including its Quaker community.

Oldenburg, too, closely monitored the rumors about a Messiah arising among the Jews and inquired of a number of his correspondents to see what they knew of the recent events. He was moved by more than just idle curiosity. The restoration of a Jewish kingdom in the Holy Land would, he believed, be an event of great political significance. He probably heard much about the Sabbatean movement in Amsterdam from Serrarius himself. In December 1665, he wrote to their mutual friend in Voorburg to see what he thought of the whole affair.

Here there is a wide-spread rumor that the Israelites, who have been dispersed for more than two thousand years, are to return to their homeland. Few hereabouts believe it, but many wish it. Do let your friend know what you hear about this matter, and what you think. For my part, I cannot put any faith in this news as long as it is not reported by trustworthy men from the city of Constantinople, which is most of all concerned in this matter. I am anxious to know what the Jews of Amsterdam have heard about it, and how they are affected by so momentous an announcement, which, if true, is likely to bring about a world crisis.[25]

There is no extant reply by Spinoza to this query. But he could not have been unaware of, much less indifferent to, the mania overwhelming Europe's Jewish population. He, too, would have known about the state of affairs in Amsterdam by way of reports from Serrarius, although he would have also learned much firsthand when he was in town on one of his visits. Spinoza must have regarded the activities of his former teachers, neighbors, and business associates at best with amusement, and possibly with scorn for their superstitious and ridiculous behavior. The whole escapade, no doubt, confirmed for him everything he had been thinking and writing about the ways in which the credulity and passions of ordinary people can be manipulated by self-proclaimed religious authorities.

೬

Although by mid-1667 the war with England was winding down, the domestic peace of the Netherlands was once again veering toward one of its periodic disasters. Debates over the conduct of the war (and over the terms of peace) reopened the fissures in Dutch politics and society that had been only cosmetically sealed ever since De Witt succeeded, by force of personality and legislation, in excluding any Stadholder from taking office in Holland.

Johan de Witt was arguably the greatest statesman of the Dutch Republic in the seventeenth century, and perhaps even in all of Dutch history. His accomplishments appear all the more impressive when seen in light not just of the difficulties that he faced on the international scene – with the republic constantly being menaced on one side or another, by England, France, Spain, and various German princes – but particularly of the opposition he faced at home. De Witt was born into a wealthy Dordrecht family on September 25, 1625.[26] Both he and his older brother Cornelis, another important actor on the Dutch political stage, studied law at the University of Leiden, although Johan also developed a strong interest in mathematics under the tutelage of the Cartesian Frans van Schooten the elder. They were sworn in as lawyers at the Court of Holland in 1647, and Johan did his legal apprenticeship in The Hague with a lawyer known for his Remonstrant sympathies. De Witt showed no real interest in politics at this time, however, and mathematics continued to be his real passion for a number of years. He composed a treatise on conic sections and had a fairly wide reputation for his geometric skills. Both Huygens and Newton later admired his work in this area.

In the summer of 1650, when the conflict between the stadholder William II and the States of Holland came to a head, Johan's father, Jacob, a deputy to the states from Dordrecht and a staunch republican, was arrested along with five other deputies. Johan worked hard on his father's behalf, and Jacob was released by August. After the stadholder's sudden death in November of that year, the De Witts saw their political fortunes rise again when Johan was appointed to be one of the two town pensionaries of Dordrecht. This also made him Dordrecht's permanent deputy to the States of Holland. The position was an important one, as Dordrecht's pensionary had the role of standing in for the Grand Pensionary of the States of Holland – at this time, Jacob Cats – when necessary. De Witt took a leading role in the debate over the abolition of the stadholdership that dominated the Great Assembly, called to determine the political future of the republic, in 1651. He forcefully presented Holland's case against continuing to fill an office that, in the view of many, was a medieval relic from the time when the Low Countries were governed in absentia by the dukes of Burgundy. When Cats resigned as Grand Pensionary at the age of seventy-four in 1652, his predecessor, Adriaan Pauw, reluctantly stepped back in. But Pauw was soon off to England on diplomatic business, and De Witt performed most of his domestic work. When Pauw died in early 1653, Johan de Witt found himself occupying the most powerful political post of the land.

De Witt was a true republican. He was devoted to the Netherlands as a constitutional state without any quasi-monarchical offices such as Stadholder and captain-general (although he was willing to let each province decide for itself whether or not to appoint a Stadholder). In his view, the governing bodies of the republic's towns and provinces – the city councils and the provincial states – had the right to choose anyone they wished for local and provincial office and to represent them at the federal level in the States General. With his conception of the "True Freedom," he pressed for the devolution of Dutch politics. Sovereignty, he insisted, resided in the provinces. The States General should exercise only those powers granted to it by the Union of Utrecht, namely, waging war and making peace. All other powers belonged properly to the provincial states, each of which in turn derived its powers and prerogatives from the towns that sent it their deputies. De Witt was not, however, a democrat. He was as wedded to the oligarchic system from which he benefited as any other member of the regent class. His marriage was well suited, in fact, to admitting him to Amsterdam's regent society: his wife, Wendela Bicker, came from one of that city's most powerful clans. Although Spinoza and other radical democrats were natural political allies of De Witt and his faction representing the interests of the states against their Orangist opponents, there was a substantial political and ideological divide between them.[27] There is a report that, after reading the *Theological-Political Treatise* when it was published in 1670, De Witt so disapproved of its democratic sentiments that he refused to meet with Spinoza: "When Spinoza was told that his Excellency had disapproved of his book, he sent somebody to his Excellency in order to speak with him on the subject. But he was answered that his excellency did not want to see him pass his threshold."[28]

De Witt was also an advocate of toleration, although not of the absolute variety. He defended the freedom to philosophize, within limits, when he intervened in the university debates over Cartesianism in 1656.[29] He also favored freedom of religious belief, while insisting on respect for the preeminence of the Reformed faith over all others. Here, again, he parted company with Spinoza, Koerbagh, and their fellow travelers. Even the most liberal of regents was not willing to do away with all censorship and practical restraints on intellectual and religious dissent; and the Grand Pensionary had a very clear vision of the limits beyond which authors were expected not to trespass. De Witt's commitment was, above all, to the well-being and stability of the Dutch Republic. A recent biographer calls him "Machiavellian," but in service to the state, not his own power.[30]

Much of De Witt's attitude toward toleration and other pressing issues can be explained by the fact that he was in a very tight situation. The Orangists, perpetually resentful over De Witt's power (and especially his work on behalf of the Exclusion Act that kept William III from the stadholdership of Holland), had been eager to conclude peace with England and establish good relations with Charles II, William's uncle, who (they believed, perhaps naively) would then help them press for their own "Restoration." De Witt and his faction, on the other hand, insisted on a military defeat that would be a humiliation for the English and a triumph for the States of Holland, with strong conditions set for any peace treaty. When Admiral de Ruyter and his ships sailed up the Thames on June 17, 1667, and inflicted great damage on the English fleet, Charles had no choice but to come to terms. It was not just a victory for the Dutch navy and an economic blessing for Dutch trade, effectively ending English control of the shipping lanes, but also a clear political triumph for De Witt himself. Still, the Orangists and their allies among the orthodox Reformed clergy kept up the pressure. Soon after the Peace of Breda – called by one contemporary wit the "snarling peace" – the States of Holland issued the "Eternal Edict . . . for the Preservation of Freedom" in an attempt to pacify De Witt's opponents and supplement the "True Freedom" with the "Great Harmony." While the resolution permanently abolished the post of Stadholder in Holland and gave all the political functions of that office to the States, it nonetheless expressed the province's support for appointing the Prince of Orange to the Council of State – in effect, an attempt to coopt him – and held out the possibility of his eventually assuming the position of captain-general. The Orangists saw this as an attempt to undercut William's rightful claims, while the states-party faction saw it as a brilliant defense of republican principles. De Witt himself regarded it simply as a pragmatic compromise.[31] His enemies were not satisfied by this half-measure, and they bided their time until the right opportunity arose for their revenge.

The great defender of De Witt and his republican principles in the 1660s was Pierre de la Court (Pieter van den Hove), a textile manufacturer from Leiden who would achieve an international reputation for his political writings. In his book *The Interest of Holland,* published in 1662, he argued for the abolition of the stadholdership, insisting that such an office was contrary to Holland's best interests. He blamed the war with England on the militaristic monarchism of the Orangists and maintained that the republican form of government was the most conducive to peace and economic prosperity. De Witt had a hand in composing the treatise, and he endorsed most of its recommendations. In his *Political Discourses,* published the same year, De la Court went further and presented a strong case against monarchical and quasi-monarchical systems of government. He also insisted that the well-being of society required that the church – in this case, the Reformed preachers – keep to its proper sphere, the spiritual condition of its flock, and not be allowed any influence in the political arena.[32]

Spinoza read De la Court's writings – he owned a copy of the *Political Discourses,* as well as a book by his brother, Jan – and was influenced by his ideas.[33] These two outstanding political theorists of the seventeenth century may also have been acquainted with each other. It is not clear, however, whether Spinoza had a personal relationship with De Witt himself. Although Spinoza the principled democrat and De Witt the pragmatic liberal did not hold the same political views, historical circumstances nonetheless seem to have united their fates. They did share the privilege of being despised and slandered by the same religious authorities of the Dutch Reformed Church, and they were held in equal disdain by De Witt's political enemies. Equally strong in his commitment to the Dutch Republic, Spinoza was sympathetic to De Witt's predicament in his confrontation with the *predikanten;* and, as a practical matter, he supported the Grand Pensionary in his limited political goals of defending a secular and relatively tolerant state. (Spinoza, of course, had no romantic notions about the Stadholder's place in Dutch history; and he commented disparagingly to Oldenburg, in November 1665, on the movement in Overijsel to bring in the Prince of Orange to serve as mediator with the English.)[34] The tendency of their hostile contemporaries, who had no need for fine distinctions, was to lump the two men together. One Calvinist critic of De Witt even believed that "Mr. Jan and his accomplices" had had a hand in editing and publishing the *Theological-Political Treatise.*[35] It has often been taken for granted that the two men, with their common penchants for republicanism and mathematics, were active political allies and even close friends, with De Witt visiting Spinoza at his lodgings after he moved from Voorburg to The Hague.[36] Here is how Lucas initiated the myth:

[Spinoza] had the advantage of knowing the Grand Pensionary De Wit [*sic*], who wanted to learn mathematics from him, and who often did him the honor of consulting with him on important matters. But he [Spinoza] had so little craving for the goods of fortune that, after the death of M. de Wit, who gave him a pension of two hundred florins, when the signature of Spinoza's Maecenas was shown to his heirs, who raised some difficulties over continuing it, [Spinoza] left it in their hands with so much tranquility as if he had the resources elsewhere. This disinterested manner making them reconsider, they granted him with joy what they had just refused him. It was on this that he depended for the greater part of his subsistence, having inherited from his father nothing but some complicated business affairs.[37]

It is hard to believe that De Witt had much to learn from Spinoza in the way of mathematics. And neither Spinoza nor De Witt mentions the other man even once in their extant correspondence.[38] Moreover, there is no evidence, other than Lucas's report, that De Witt left Spinoza an annuity. While it is possible that Lucas heard about the pension from Spinoza himself, it is doubtful that Spinoza, who was reluctant to accept a stipend even from his close friends, would have taken any money from the leader of a political faction, even one he favored.[39] And yet the idea of an at least casual, if not particularly warm, relationship between two of the great personalities of the Dutch Golden Age is a seductive one. During the years 1664–6, De Witt, Huygens, and Hudde working together on the calculation of probabilities, a set of mathematical problems in which Spinoza had an interest at exactly the same time.[40] Given his close relationship with both Huygens and Hudde, who could not have been unaware of his interest and skill in the material, it hardly seems likely that his two friends would not have tried to include him in their project. Still, the nature of Spinoza's personal relationship with De Witt remains purely a matter of speculation.

꒰ꔷ

One of the casualities of the war with England had been Spinoza's relationship with Oldenburg. Although communication between Voorburg and London was difficult during the hostilities, the two managed, with

Serrarius's help in Amsterdam, to correspond through December 1665.
But the real blow came when Oldenburg was arrested at the beginning of
the summer of 1667. On June 20, he was escorted to the Tower of London, accused, he tells one correspondent, of "dangerous desseins and
practises." He was not entirely sure what exactly he had done to warrant
such a charge, but he suspected – and this seems to have been confirmed
to him by someone – that it was because he had criticized the conduct of
the war in some letters and conversations. His situation was certainly not
helped by the fact that he was known to have favored the cause of Cromwell over that of Charles II. Oldenburg denied the accusations against him,
while admitting to his correspondent that he had indeed expressed some
reservations about the way the war was being run, but only out of concern
for the safety and well-being of England.

That those expressions of mine, whatever they were, proceeded from a reall trouble of mine, to see things goe no better for England, than they did; and yt I
thought, there were oversights and omissions some where, wch might prove very
prejudiciall to ye honor of ye King and ye prosperity of ye nation; being heartily
afflicted to see such insolence acted against England by a people [i.e., the Dutch],
that but 80. years agoe, wth folded hands implored ye compassion and assistance
of England, and are in great part obliged to England for their present prosperity.
Thus, this expressed from me some words of complaint of neglect and security on
our side; wch having given offence, I am ready to beg his Majies pardon for, upon
my knees. But as to ill desseins, I shall say wth all chearfulness; I am not guilty of
any, and all yt know me well, can attest my love, concern and zeale for the kings
and the kindgoms interest and prosperity.[41]

Oldenburg seems, in particular, to have been critical of the policies and
strategies that had allowed the "insolent" Dutch to proceed so far up the
Thames that month. He now regrets the "rashnes and folly of my expressions."[42] He also believed that the fact that he, foreign-born, had many
overseas contacts, especially in Holland and France, contributed to the
suspicions about his loyalty. But he had always allowed his letters from
those parts to be inspected ever since the war began. Once he was granted
pen and paper in his prison cell, he wrote directly to the king to protest
his innocence. Although, he tells Charles, "yr Majies Petitioner finds to
his extreme grief, yt he has incurred yr Majies displeasure, by writing sev-
erall rash and censorious expressions, for wch he now stands committed
to yr Majies Tower," he swears that he is, as many will attest, "a true and
loyall Englishman."[43]

Oldenburg was released from the Tower on August 26, when the war was over. He was in poor financial and physical condition, and worried about how people would now think of him. He was especially anxious to resume his role as correspondent to Europe's great and far-flung scientific community, but feared that many of his friends would be hesitant to recommence writing to him lest they place him, once again, under suspicion. He told Boyle that he was concerned "that forrainers, especially in the neighboring parts, may be grown shy to reassume that commerce, they were wont to entertain with me, out of some tenderness and concern for my safety, wch they may judge may be endangered as well by their freenes of writing to me, as by mine of writing to ym."[44] It was some time before he and Spinoza resumed their exchange of letters.

One month after Oldenburg was set free, Spinoza's circle of friends suffered an irreplacable loss. On September 26, 1667, Simon Joosten de Vries was buried in Amsterdam. Because almost all of Spinoza's letters that were mainly of personal, not philosophical, import were destroyed by his posthumous editors, we cannot see Spinoza in what must have been a deeply felt grief for the death of a dear friend. De Vries had been immensely devoted to Spinoza. Both Lucas and Colerus report that De Vries offered to support Spinoza with an annual stipend but that Spinoza refused to accept it. As Lucas tells it, "when one of his intimate friends, a well-off man, wanted to make him a present of two thousand florins, so as to enable him to live more comfortably, he declined them with his usual politeness, saying that he had no need of them."[45] Colerus adds that Spinoza replied that accepting so much money "might distract him from his occupations and contemplations."[46] Some time later, De Vries raised the subject again – and this indicates that his death came as no surprise to Spinoza – when discussing with his friend the terms of the will he was drafting. As De Vries never married, he wanted to make Spinoza his sole heir. Spinoza protested that it would be unfair to De Vries's brother "if he disposed of his estate in favor of a stranger, however much friendship he bore him."[47] De Vries acceded to Spinoza's wishes but in the end had his way, at least in part: he left Spinoza an annuity of five hundred guilders to be paid out of his estate. Spinoza thought this still excessive, particularly given his modest needs, and he had the amount decreased to three hundred guilders.[48] Colerus claims that after Simon's death the money was paid by Simon's brother, "living at Schiedam." But all of the De Vries brothers were dead by 1667, and none of them had ever lived in Schiedam. Simon did have a

sister in that village, however: Trijntje Joosten de Vries. It was in the house
that she shared with her husband, Alewijn Gijsen, that Spinoza had spent
those few months during the plague in the winter of 1664–5. In all likelihood, Trijntje inherited her brother's estate, and Alewijn – who would
have had full fiduciary control over his wife's money – respected his late
brother-in-law's wishes and continued to support Spinoza, with whom he
was well acquainted.[49]

While this extra income must have been useful, Spinoza never did have
great financial concerns. Whatever he earned from polishing lenses had always been supplemented by the generosity of his friends.[50] And all the evidence suggests that he led a very frugal existence. "He cared little for the
goods of fortune," Lucas writes:

> Not only did riches not tempt him, but he even did not at all fear the odious con-
> sequences of poverty. Virtue raised him above all these things, and although he was
> not strong in the good graces of Fortune, he never cajoled her nor murmered
> against her. If his fortune was mediocre, his soul, in recompense, was among the
> most well-endowed with that which makes men great. Even when in extreme need,
> he was liberal, lending what little he had from the largesse of his friends with as
> much generosity as if he were living in wealth. Having heard that someone who
> owed him two hundred florins had gone bankrupt, far from being upset by it, he
> said, while smiling, "I must reduce my daily needs to make up for this small loss.
> That is the price," he added, "of fortitude."[51]

Spinoza's daily needs were modest and his clothes and furnishings "sober
and humble." He dressed plainly and without much fuss (at least according to Colerus, who notes that "in his clothing he was simple and common").[52] He did not have a great many expenses, and although he did not
oppose "honest pleasures," those of the body "touched him little."[53]
Spinoza himself insisted that whoever would devote himself to the search
for truth should "enjoy pleasures just so far for safeguarding one's health."
"As far as sensual pleasure is concerned," he argued, "the mind gets so
caught up in it . . . that it is quite prevented from thinking of anything else.
But after the enjoyment of sensual pleasure is past, the greatest sadness
follows. . . . And there are innumerable examples of people who have hastened their death through too much sensual pleasure."[54] Bayle relays a report from Spinoza's neighbors that he was moderate in his food and drink,
and did not worry much about money.[55] He was content, we are told, "to
live from hand to mouth"; and what went into that mouth was, apparently,
not of great concern to him:

It appears [from some papers I (Colerus) found at his death] that he lived a whole day upon a milk soup made with butter, which cost three stuivers, and drank a pot of beer, which cost one and a half stuivers. Another day he ate nothing but gruel made with raisins and butter, which cost four stuivers and eight pennies. In a whole month I found only two half pints of wine among his reckonings; and although he was often invited to the table of another, he preferred however to eat his own bread.[56]

Like many Dutchmen of his time, he also enjoyed smoking tobacco in a pipe,[57] no doubt a long-stem clay one such as appears in many still lifes of the period. This was probably one of very few vices he allowed to intrude upon a generally austere regimen. To all appearances, Spinoza abided by the provisional "rules for living" that he recommended to anyone who desired to achieve "the highest human perfection" and lead the philosophical life: "seek money, or anything else, just so far as suffices for sustaining life and health."[58]

᠔

Because there are only three extant letters between March 1667 and the beginning of 1671, all of them to Jarig Jellesz, the details of Spinoza's activities during this period and his thoughts on current events – some of which touched him quite directly – are obscure. He probably moved his lodgings to another part of Voorburg in May 1668, just before the arrests of his friends Adriaan and Johannes Koerbagh, when his landlord Tydeman bought a new house on the Herenstraat. Spinoza also seems to have been helping Jellesz in his study of Descartes's philosophy. The letters to Jellesz show a continuing interest in scientific matters, particularly optics and hydrodynamics, as well as a more than passing curiosity about some alchemical experiments recently performed by Johannes Helvetius, the Prince of Orange's personal physician and a resident of The Hague. Helvetius had stolen a tiny piece off a "Philosopher's Stone" from a visiting alchemist. He put the fragment in a pot and melted some lead with it. The lead was allegedly transmuted into gold. There was much excitement in town over this event, which had been "confirmed" by some local "experts," including a silversmith named Brechtelt. When Spinoza heard about it, he asked Isaac Vossius – once a friend of Menasseh ben Israel's, and now a colleague of Huygens's who shared his and Spinoza's interest in light and optics – for his opinion. Vossius "laughed heartily at it, and even expressed surprise that I should question him about such a silly thing."[59] Undeterred by his friend's mockery, Spinoza pursued his inquiries into the matter. He took the time in early 1667 to pay a visit to Brechtelt in The Hague, who offered his account. He even went to see Helvetius himself, of whom Huygens had a fairly low opinion.[60]

Around this time, Spinoza may also have been working on a short treatise on the geometrical optics underlying the phenomenon of the rainbow. Jellesz, Lucas, Colerus, and others mention that Spinoza wrote such a work. He was probably reading Boyle's *Experiments and Considerations concerning Colours* soon after Oldenburg alerted him in 1665 to the existence of a Latin translation. His letters to Hudde in mid-1666 and to Jellesz in March 1667 all testify to a particular preoccupation in the second half of the decade with practical and theoretical optical questions, material virtually absent from all prior correspondence. His earliest biographers, however, are also in almost unanimous agreement that whatever Spinoza wrote about the rainbow was "consigned to the flames" a little while before his death.[61] In 1687, however, an anonymous pamphlet entitled "The Algebraic Calculation of the Rainbow" was published in The Hague by Levyn van Dyck, the official printer for the city's municipal authorities, and some have insisted it is the piece that Spinoza is alleged to have written.[62] There is no evidence to support this claim, and it seems fairly certain that Spinoza is not the author of the work.[63] Its calculations are based on a thorough acceptance of Descartes's account of the nature of the rainbow, the important elements of which, by the late 1660s, had been refuted by Huygens – a fact of which Spinoza could not possibly have been unaware. Descartes had used Snel's law of refraction to calculate geometrically how the rays of light falling on a droplet of water would be affected in their motion. He was particularly interested in the angle at which those rays would, after reflection and refraction (but not diffraction) from various points on the droplet, strike the eye of an observer.[64] The author of the pamphlet, whoever it may have been, used Descartes's analytic (or algebraic) geometry and the rules of refraction to calculate the height of the arc of both the primary and secondary rainbows. The mathematical work in the treatise is perfectly competent, but the scientific content is a bit dated for its time, given the latest developments in optical theory and doctrines of the nature of light.

ॐ

With the exception of the loss of De Vries and Balling, nothing in the 1660s could have affected Spinoza more – both emotionally and intellectually – than the sequence of events leading up to the death in prison, in 1669, of

Adriaan Koerbagh. The Koerbagh affair held great significance not just for his immediate associates but for the future of toleration and secularism in the Netherlands as a whole. The influence exercised by the Reformed Church in the proceedings against Adriaan and his brother Jan signaled, to some, the waning of the "True Freedom." It also made it clearer than ever to Spinoza that a strong stand needed to be taken in defense of the basic principles of De Witt's republic, principles for which De Witt himself now seemed, to Spinoza, unwilling to fight.

As early as 1666, Jan Koerbagh, himself a Reformed preacher, was under suspicion by his ecclesiastical superiors for harboring unorthodox opinions, while Adriaan, who had had a child out of wedlock, was considered to be leading a life of debauchery. In that year, they were interrogated by the Amsterdam consistory. Adriaan was warned about his immoral behavior and Jan was queried about his thoughts on God and other matters. He replied with a remarkably Spinozistic explanation: "Since God is an infinite being outside of which nothing exists, all creatures are not beings but only modifications or ways of being determined or extended by their rest and movement."[65] Two years later, in February 1668, Adriaan published his *Een Bloemhof van allerley lieflijkheyd* (A flower garden composed of all kinds of loveliness). In this book, the elder brother – who had always had an interest in the history and usage of the Dutch language – undertook to set forth his philosophical and theological views under the guise of simply clarifying those foreign words which have crept into the legal, medical, devotional, and colloquial vocabularies of Dutch. His intention was clearly to criticize, even mock, nearly all organized religions, and his tone often alternates between sarcasm and contempt. He took particular delight in deriding what he took to be the superstitions of Catholicism.

Altar: a place where one slaughters. Among those of the Roman Catholic faith, they are even holy places, where priests daily celebrate the divine service. But it no longer consists in the slaughter of animals, as among the Jews or pagans, but in a more marvelous affair, that is, in the creation of a human being. For they can do what even God cannot do, at any hour of the day: make a human creature from a small piece of wheatcake. This piece of cake remains what it was beforehand, and they give it to someone to eat while saying it is a man – not simply a man, but the God-Man. What an absurdity![66]

Throughout Koerbagh's works, there is, underneath the ridicule, a serious metaphysical theology and a philosophy of religion that Koerbagh shared, in important respects, with his friends Spinoza, Van den Enden, and Lodewijk Meyer. Among other things, Koerbagh denied the divine authorship of the Bible. It is, he insisted, a human work, compiled from a variety of other writings by "Esdras" (a reference to Ezra, who, according to Spinoza – from whom Koerbagh probably learned many of his skills in biblical exegesis – performed the role of redactor of the Pentateuch). And the proper method for interpreting the meaning of Scripture is, as for any book, a naturalistic one, relying mainly on the language and the historical context of its authors and texts. For grasping the *truth* in Scripture, on the other hand, nothing is needed but human reason.

> Bible: . . . In general, a book, of any sort, including the story of Renard or Eulen-spiegel. . . . One cannot know who the authors of the Jewish writings were. Among the most famous theologians, some think that a certain Esdras compiled them from other Jewish writings. . . . Meanwhile, there is, in Scripture, something that is certain and that agrees with reason, the sole thing that I hold as scripture, and that must have served for the composition of other writings. But the rest is, for us, useless and vain, and can be rejected without difficulty.[67]

Both in the *Bloemhof* and in a book he composed later that same year, *Een Ligt schijnende in duystere plaatsen* (A light shining in dark places), Koerbagh attacked the irrationality of most religions, with their superstitious rites and ceremonies. The real teaching of God, the "true religion," is simply a knowledge of and obedience to God and a love of one's neighbor. Fearlessly inviting the charge of Socinianism, he denied that Jesus was divine and rejected all trinitarian doctrines. God is one, being nothing but the substance of the universe. This being is composed of an infinite number of infinite attributes, of which two alone are known to us: thought and extension. As such, God is identical with nature as a necessary and deterministic system. Miracles, understood as divinely caused departures from the laws of nature, are thus impossible.[68] On the political side, Koerbagh was a radical democrat. He believed strongly in the virtues of a secular republic and warned of the dangers of the usurpation of political power by the church. In a pamphlet published in 1664, he presented the case for De Witt's conception of the republic as a federation of sovereign and autonomous provinces and argued for the subordination of religious to civil authority.[69]

Although Koerbagh was a learned scholar who was clearly influenced by his reading of the classics, as well as by contemporary thinkers such as

Hobbes,[70] there is no denying the Spinozist tenor of his doctrines. He must have closely studied the manuscripts of the *Ethics* and the *Theological-Political Treatise*, still a work in progress. Tragically, he did not share Spinoza's caution. He published the *Bloemhof* under his own name and in Dutch, thus exacerbating the fear of the authorities that many more people would read and be corrupted by it than would be possible had it been it written in academic Latin. He tried to do the same with *A Light Shining in Dark Places*, but the publisher, Everardus van Eede of Utrecht, suspended the printing when he realized what a potentially scandalous (and thus, for him, dangerous) work he was producing.[71] Jan tried to convince the printer that the book had the approval of De Witt, but this was surely a ruse. The patrician De Witt would have had no intention of publicly endorsing the blasphemies of Koerbagh, or even the democratic republicanism of men like Spinoza and Meyer. If Koerbagh and his allies saw the Grand Pensionary and other regents as sympathetic to their political and religious cause – and it is safe to assume that Spinoza, at least, did not harbor any such illusions – they were hopelessly mistaken. De Witt had too fine a line to walk. He resented any attempts by the *predikanten* to meddle in affairs of state, but he could not afford to ignore or antagonize them. He certainly was not about to attach his political fortunes – and perhaps even his life – to the more extreme views held by these radicals. Even Pierre de la Court, more of a democrat than De Witt, would have found Koerbagh's views too immoderate for his taste.[72]

Van Eede was not persuaded by Jan's assurances, and he notified the authorities. The sheriff of Utrecht immediately confiscated the chapters already printed and forwarded them to his colleagues in Amsterdam. Jan, whom the investigators suspected of being one of the authors of the book, was arrested on May 10. Adriaan fled, but was eventually arrested in Leiden on July 18 – after his whereabouts were revealed by "an excellent friend" in exchange for fifteen hundred guilders – and returned to Amsterdam, chained in an open cart. The brothers were interrogated at length by a committee of municipal officers, with the encouragement and full cooperation of the Reformed consistory. Among their interrogators was Johan Hudde, Spinoza's erstwhile colleague in optical research and now one of Amsterdam's magistrates.

The questions put to Adriaan during his examination reveal that, although Spinoza had as yet published only the *Descartes' Principles of Philosophy*, along with its metaphysical appendix, his views on Scripture and his political opinions were sufficiently well known that he had, by mid-1668, come to the attention of the regents in Amsterdam.

Adriaan Koerbagh, lawyer and medical doctor, of Amsterdam, thirty-five years old. Question: Had he composed a work entitled *Een Bloemhof*? Response: yes. Question: Did he do it by himself? Response: yes, he was aided by no one. Question: Did the doctor [Abraham] van Berckel [another friend of Spinoza's, and the first to translate Hobbes's *Leviathan* into Dutch, in 1667] help? Response: no, although it is not impossible that he talked about it with someone. But his brother [Jan] had not read the book until after it was completely printed. The latter had, with his consent, corrected a chapter, but not one of the provocative ones. Question: Who shared his opinions? Response: no one, to his knowledge. He added that he had not spoken about them with Van Berckel nor with anyone else, not even with Spinoza or with his brother. . . . He admitted to having spent some time with Spinoza, to having gone to his home on different occasions, but he had never spoken of this affair with him. He had composed the *Bloemhof* with the sole intention of teaching people to speak correct Dutch. Question: Did he understand Hebrew? Response: only with the help of a dictionary. Question: What did the Hebrew word *shabunot* mean? Response: I do not know and would have to look it up in Buxtorf's lexicon. The accused admitted to having had relations with Van Berckel and others, but affirms that he never spoke of this doctrine with Spinoza.[73]

We do not know when, or even how often, Koerbagh visited Spinoza in Voorburg. Any evidence of their relationship that may have been contained in Spinoza's correspondence, and particularly whatever letters might have been written between Spinoza and either one of the brothers, was most likely destroyed by Spinoza's friends after his death, for understandable reasons. Koerbagh had also been in contact with Van den Enden in 1662–3, as he confessed in the course of his response to a line of questioning that also revealed that Koerbagh denied the divinity of Jesus and the virginity of Mary. "We do not really know who was, in truth, the father of this Savior (Jesus). That is why some ignorant people have affirmed that it was God, the God of eternity, and a son of the God of eternity, and that he was born of a virgin without the intervention of a man. But these theses, too, are foreign to Scripture and contrary to the truth." Koerbagh was asked if he spoke about this with Spinoza. "Response: no . . . nor with his brother. But he confessed to having visited one or two times the home of Van den Enden five or six years earlier."[74]

The inquest took several weeks. Jan, who had already spent more than six weeks in jail, got off with a warning. His judges agreed that he was not the author of either blasphemous treatise. One of the magistrates remarked that, "in our country, in the absence of public gatherings or writings, we are not so particular about the opinions that people hold regarding the Church."[75] Adriaan, on the other hand, was sentenced on July 29 to ten years in prison, followed by ten years in exile, and charged a fine of four thousand guilders. This was severe but (thanks to the influence of Hudde and others) better than the punishment recommended by one member of the commission: that his right thumb be cut off, that his tongue have a hole bored through it with a red-hot iron, and that he be imprisoned for thirty years, with all of his possessions confiscated and all of his books burned.[76] He was conveyed to the harsh confines of the Amsterdam prison, usually reserved for violent offenders condemned to hard labor. Seven weeks later, and ill from his incarceration, he was moved to Het Willige Rasphuis, another prison in the city that had more tolerable conditions and an infirmary. Koerbagh's health took a serious and rapid turn in his confinement, and on October 15, 1669 – just over a year after being sentenced – he was dead.

Adriaan Koerbagh's treatment at the hands of the magistrates and the church authorities – in Spinoza's eyes, a dangerous collusion between the secular and the sectarian – gave him the impetus to put the final touches on his *Theological-Political Treatise* and begin preparing it for publication. He had been working continuously on the book for at least three and a half years. During that time, he saw two acquaintances arrested by political authorities, one of whom died in a prison cell. By the end of 1668, almost all of Spinoza's energy must have been devoted to completing his treatise on religion and the state – now, to his mind, a matter of pressing importance, both public and personal.

By this point, Spinoza can have been under no illusions about the reception his ideas would receive, and he took the necessary precautions to protect both himself and his publisher. The first edition of the *Theological-Political Treatise,* though it was published in Amsterdam by Jan Rieuwertsz sometime in late 1669 or early 1670, bore on its title page a false publisher and place of publication: "at Hamburg, by Heinrich [Henricum] Künraht." The author's name did not appear at all. These measures were not unreasonable, particularly because the Reformed consistory, having been alerted to certain blasphemous and heretical works that were being published in Amsterdam, was keeping an especially close watch on Rieuwertsz's shop in 1669.[77] Spinoza may have traveled to Amsterdam for an extended stay to oversee the production of the work, although he would have had complete confidence in the skills and judgment of his printer friend, who was well seasoned in and sympathetic to his ideas.

The subtitle of the book makes clear the nature of its author's project and its relevance to the contemporary political context: "Wherein it is shown that freedom to philosophize cannot only be granted without injury to piety and the peace of the Commonwealth, but that the peace of the Commonwealth and Piety are endangered by the suppression of this freedom." Spinoza's ultimate intention is to undercut the political power exercised in the Republic by religious authorities. For it is the "excessive authority and egotism of preachers," as he told Oldenburg, which most threatens that freedom "to say what we think."[78] If he cannot transform the Netherlands into the kind of democratic republic that, he believes, is the best and most natural form of government, he can at least help ensure that it stays true to the tradition of toleration and secular constitutional principles which have sustained it ever since independence. The key to diminishing the influence of the clergy, who justify their abuses by appealing to the holiness of a certain book as the word of God, is to demonstrate the true nature of Scripture and its message, eliminate the "superstitious adornments" of popular religion, and argue for ideal principles of political government on the basis of the original conditions under which civil society arises in the first place.

It was a project for which Spinoza was particularly suited – certainly more so than any other philosopher of the period, given his familiarity with the worlds of Jewish and Gentile learning. The task required both skills in biblical exegesis and a sophisticated grasp of political theory. Spinoza was well endowed with the former, prepared not just by his long-standing knowledge of Hebrew, Torah, and the rabbinical tradition, but also by his familiarity with classic and contemporary Jewish philosophical texts, orthodox and heterodox, ranging from Maimonides' *Guide of the Perplexed* to Menasseh's *Conciliador*. And since his days in Amsterdam under the tutelage of Van den Enden, he had never stopped studying the important political thinkers of the sixteenth and early seventeenth centuries, such as Machiavelli and Hugo Grotius. In the 1660s, he supplemented this historical political education with the just published works of Hobbes (both the *Leviathan*, translated into Dutch in 1667 and into Latin in 1668, and the *De Cive*), De la Court, and others.

Despite the obvious differences in style and theme, there is an essential continuity between the *Theological-Political Treatise* and the *Ethics*. In fact, the metaphysics, theology, and ethics of the *Ethics* lay the groundwork – sometimes explicitly invoked – for the political, social, moral and religious theses of the *Treatise*. In discussing God's "election" of the Hebrew people in the *Treatise*, for example, Spinoza says:

> By God's direction I mean the fixed and immutable order of Nature, or the chain of natural events; for I have said above, and have already shown elsewhere, that the universal laws of Nature according to which all things happen and are determined are nothing but God's eternal decrees, which always involve eternal truth and necessity. So it is the same thing whether we say that all things happen according to Nature's laws or that they are regulated by God's decree and direction.[79]

The *Treatise* is also informed by the "merely philosophical" and anti-anthropomorphic picture of God found in the *Ethics:* "[Moses] imagined God as a ruler, lawgiver, king, merciful, just, and so forth; whereas these are all merely attributes of human nature, and not at all applicable to the divine nature";[80] and by the *Ethics*'s conception of human happiness and blessedness as consisting in the knowledge of nature and, consequently, the intellectual love of God ("Everything in nature involves and expresses the conception of God in proportion to its essence and perfection; and therefore we acquire a greater and more perfect knowledge of God as we gain more knowledge of natural phenomena").[81] Moreover, the *Treatise* presents many of the ideas of the *Ethics* in a nongeometrical – and, hence, more accessible – format, sometimes filling in details that the other work omits.[82]

Spinoza begins the treatise by alerting his readers, through a kind of "natural history of religion," to just those superstitious beliefs and behaviors that clergy, by playing on ordinary human emotions, encourage in their followers. A person guided by fear and hope, the main emotions in a life devoted to the pursuit of temporal advantages, turns, in the face of the vagaries of fortune, to behaviors calculated to secure the goods he desires. Thus we pray, worship, make votive offerings, sacrifice, and engage in all the various rituals of popular religion. But the emotions are as fleeting as the objects that occasion them, and thus the superstitions grounded in those emotions are subject to fluctuations. Ambitious and self-serving clergy do their best to stabilize this situation and give some permanence to those beliefs and behaviors. "Immense efforts have been made to invest religion, true or false, with such pomp and ceremony that it can sustain any shock and constantly evoke the deepest reverence in all its worship-pers."[83] Religious leaders are generally abetted in their purposes by the civil authority, which threatens to punish all deviations from theological orthodoxy as "sedition." The result is a state religion that has no rational foundations, a mere "respect for ecclesiastics" that involves adulation and mysteries but no true worship of God.

The solution to this state of affairs, Spinoza believes, is to examine the Bible anew and find the doctrines of the "true religion." Only then will we be able to delimit exactly what we need to do to show proper respect for God and obtain blessedness. This will reduce the sway that religious au-thorities have over our emotional, intellectual, and physical lives, and re-instate a proper and healthy relationship between the state and religion. A close analysis of the Bible is particularly important for any argument that the freedom of philosophizing – essentially, freedom of thought and speech – is not prejudicial to piety. If it can be demonstrated that Scrip-ture is not a source of "natural truth," but the bearer of only a simple moral message ("Love your neighbor"), then people will see that "faith is something separate from philosophy." Spinoza intends to show that in that moral message alone – and not in Scripture's words or history – lies the sacredness of what is otherwise merely a human document. The Bible teaches only "obedience [to God]," not knowledge. Thus, philosophy and religion, reason and faith, inhabit two distinct and exclusive spheres, and neither should tread in the domain of the other. The freedom to philoso-phize and speculate can therefore be granted without any harm to true re-ligion. In fact, such freedom is essential to public peace and piety, as most civil disturbances arise from sectarian disputes. The real danger to the re-public comes from those who would worship, not God, but some words on a page: "It will be said that, although God's law is inscribed in our hearts, Scripture is nevertheless the Word of God, and it is no more permissible to say of Scripture that it is mutilated and contaminated than to say this of God's Word. In reply, I have to say that such objectors are carrying their piety too far, and are turning religion into superstition; indeed, instead of God's Word they are beginning to worship likenesses and images, that is, paper and ink."[84]

From a proper and informed reading of Scripture, a number of things become clear. First, the prophets were not men of exceptional intellectual talents – they were not, that is, naturally gifted philosophers – but simply very pious, even morally superior, individuals endowed with vivid imaginations. They were able to perceive God's revelation through their imaginative faculties via words or real or imaginary figures. This is what allowed them to apprehend that which lies beyond the boundary of the intellect. Moreover, the content of a prophecy varied according to the physical temperament, imaginative powers, and particular opinions or prejudices of the prophet. It follows that prophecy, while it has its origins in the power of God – and in this respect it is, in Spinoza's metaphysical scheme, no different from any other natural event – does not provide privileged knowledge of natural or spiritual phenomena. The prophets are not necessarily to be trusted when it comes to matters of the intellect, on questions of philosophy, history, or science; and their pronouncements set no parameters on what should or should not be believed about the natural world on the basis of our rational faculties.

Nothing in Scripture could be clearer than that Joshua, and perhaps the writer who composed his history, thought that the sun goes round the earth and the earth does not move, and that the sun stood still for a time. Yet there are many who, refusing to admit that there can be any mutability in the heavens, explain this passage so that it means something quite different. Others, who have adopted a more scientific attitude and understand that the earth moves and the sun is motionless or does not revolve around the earth, make every effort to extort this meaning in the teeth of the Scriptural text. Indeed, I wonder at them. Do we have to believe that the soldier Joshua was a skilled astronomer, that a miracle could not be revealed to him, or that the sun's light could not remain above the horizon for longer than usual without Joshua's understanding the cause? Both alternatives seem to me ridiculous. I prefer the simple view that Joshua did not know the cause of that extension of daylight, and that he and all the host along with him believed that the sun revolves around the earth with a diurnal motion and on that day it stood still for a while, this being the cause of the prolonged daylight.[85]

Spinoza provides an equally deflationary account of God's election, or the "vocation," of the Hebrews. It is "childish," he insists, for anyone to base their happiness on the uniqueness of their gifts; in the case of the Jews, it would be the uniqueness of their being chosen among all people. The ancient Hebrews, in fact, did not surpass other nations in their wisdom or in their proximity to God. They were neither intellectually nor morally superior to other peoples. They were "chosen" only with respect to their social organization and political good fortune. God (or Nature) gave them a set of laws and they obeyed those laws, with the natural result that their society was well-ordered and their autonomous government persisted for a long time. Their election was thus a temporal and conditional one, and their kingdom is now long gone. Thus, "at the present time there is nothing whatsoever that the Jews can arrogate to themselves above other nations."[86] Spinoza thereby rejects the particularism that many – including Amsterdam's Sephardic rabbis – insisted was essential to Judaism. True piety and blessedness are universal in their scope and accessible to anyone, regardless of their confessional creed.

Central to Spinoza's analysis of the Jewish religion – although it is applicable to any religion whatsoever – is the distinction between divine law and ceremonial law. The law of God commands only the knowledge and love of God and the actions required for attaining that condition. Such love must arise, not from fear of possible penalties or hope for any rewards, but solely from the goodness of its object. The divine law does *not* demand any particular rites or ceremonies such as sacrifices or dietary restrictions or festival observances. The six hundred and thirteen precepts of the Torah have nothing to do with blessedness or virtue. They were directed only at the Hebrews so that they might govern themselves in an autonomous state. The ceremonial laws helped to preserve their kingdom and ensure its prosperity, but were valid only as long as that political entity lasted. They are not binding on all Jews under all circumstances. They were, in fact, instituted by Moses for a purely practical reason: so that people might do their duty and not go their own way.

Moses, by his divine power and authority, introduced a state religion . . . to make people do their duty from devotion rather than fear. Furthermore, he bound them by consideration of benefits received, while promising many more benefits from God in the future. . . . This, then, was the object of ceremonial observance, that men should never act of their own volition but always at another's behest, and that in their actions and inward thoughts they should at all times acknowledge that they were not their own masters but completely subordinate to another.[87]

This is true not just of the rites and practices of Judaism, but of the outer ceremonies of all religions. None of these activities have anything to do with true happiness or piety. They serve only to control people's behavior and preserve a particular society.

A similar practical function is served by stories of miracles. Scripture speaks in a language adapted to affect the imagination of ordinary people and compel their obedience. Rather than appealing to the natural and real causes of all events, its authors sometimes narrate things in a way calculated to move people – particularly uneducated people – to devotion. "If Scripture were to describe the downfall of an empire in the style adopted by political historians, the common people would not be stirred. . . ." Strictly speaking, however, miracles – understood as divinely caused departures from the ordinary course of nature – are impossible. Every event, no matter how extraordinary, has a natural cause and explanation. "Nothing happens in nature that does not follow from her laws." This is simply a consequence of Spinoza's metaphysical doctrines. Miracles as traditionally conceived require that there be a distinction between God and nature, something that Spinoza's philosophy rules out in principle. Moreover, nature's order is inviolable insofar as the sequence of events in nature is a necessary consequence of God's attributes.

The universal laws of nature are merely God's decrees, following from the necessity and perfection of the divine nature. So if anything were to happen in nature contrary to her universal laws, it would also be necessarily contrary to the decree, intellect and nature of God. Or if anyone were to maintain that God performs some act contrary to the laws of Nature, he would at the same time have to maintain that God acts contrary to his own nature – than which nothing could be more absurd.[88]

There certainly are "miracles" in the sense of events whose natural causes are unknown to us, and which we therefore attribute to the powers of a supernatural God. But this is, once again, to retreat to superstition, "the bitter enemy of all true knowledge and true morality."

By analyzing prophecy in terms of vividness of imagination, Jewish election as political fortune, the ceremonial law as a kind of social and political expediency, and the belief in miracles as an ignorance of nature's necessary causal operations, Spinoza naturalizes (and, consequently, demystifies) some of the fundamental elements of Judaism and other religions and undermines the foundations of their external, superstitious rites. At the same time, he thereby reduces the fundamental doctrine of piety to a simple and universal formula, naturalistic in itself, involving love and knowledge. This process of naturalization achieves its stunning climax when Spinoza turns to consider the authorship and interpretation of the Bible itself. Spinoza's views on Scripture constitute, without question, the most radical theses of the *Treatise* and explain why he was attacked with such vitriol by his contemporaries. Others before him had suggested that Moses was not the author of the entire Pentateuch. But no one had taken that claim to the extreme limit that Spinoza did, arguing for it with such boldness and at such length. Nor had anyone before Spinoza been willing to draw from it the conclusions about the status, meaning, and interpretation of Scripture that he drew.[89]

Spinoza denies that Moses wrote all or even most of the Torah. The references in the Pentateuch to Moses in the third person; the narration of his death and, particularly, of events following his death; and the fact that some places are called by names they did not bear in the time of Moses all "make it clear beyond a shadow of a doubt" that the writings commonly referred to as "the Five Books of Moses" were, in fact, written by someone who lived many generations after him. Moses did, to be sure, compose some books of history and law; and remnants of those long-lost books can be found in the Pentateuch. But the Torah as we have it, as well as other books of the Hebrew Bible (such as Joshua, Judges, Samuel, and Kings) were written neither by the individuals whose names they bear nor by any person appearing in them. Spinoza argues that these were, in fact, all composed by a single historian living many generations after the events narrated, and that this was most likely Ezra. It was the postexilic leader who took the many writings that had come down to him and began weaving them into a single (but not seamless) narrative. Ezra's work was later completed and supplemented by the editorial labors of others. What we now possess, then, is nothing but a compilation – and a rather mismanaged, haphazard, and "mutilated" one at that.

If one merely observes that all the contents of these five books, histories and precepts, are set forth with no distinction or order and with no regard to chronology, and that frequently the same story is repeated, with variations, it will readily be recognised that all these materials were collected indiscriminately and stored together with view to examining them and arranging them more conveniently at some later time. And not only the contents of these five books but the other histories in the remaining seven books right down to the destruction of the city were compiled in the same way.[90]

As for the books of the Prophets, they are of even later provenance, compiled (or "heaped together," in Spinoza's view) by a chronicler or scribe perhaps as late as the Second Temple period. Canonization into Scripture occurred only in the second century B.C.E., when the Pharisees selected a number of texts from a multitude of others. Because the process of transmission was a historical one, involving the conveyance of writings of human origin over a long period of time through numerous scribes, and because the decision to include some books but not others was made by ordinary, fallible human beings, there are good reasons for believing that a significant portion of the text of the "Old Testament" is corrupt.

Spinoza was working within a well-known tradition. The claim that Moses was not the author of the entire Pentateuch had already been made in the twelfth century by Ibn Ezra, in his commentary on Deuteronomy. He argued, for example, that Moses could not have written the account of his own death. Spinoza knew and admired Ibn Ezra's writings, and there is no question that his views on the authorship of the Torah were influenced by them. But he was also familiar with Isaac La Peyrère's more recent *Pre-Adamitae*, in which the French Calvinist millenarian questioned not only the Mosaic authorship of the Bible but also the reliability of the transmission process and, hence, the accuracy of the biblical texts. In 1660, Samuel Fisher, the Quaker leader in Amsterdam, published *The Rustic's Alarm to the Rabbies*. Scripture, Fisher insisted, is a historical document, a text written by human beings, and therefore should not be confused with the Word of God, which is ahistorical and eternal. Moses' contribution was simply to begin the process of writing down God's message. Fisher cast doubt on the authenticity of what now passes for Holy Scripture. The books that we have are, in fact, copies of copies of copies, and so on, all of which passed through numerous hands. During the transmission process, alterations and omissions must have crept into the texts, which now are fairly corrupt. Spinoza could not read English, but his possible personal connection with Fisher in the late 1650s in Amsterdam could explain any influence that Fisher's views might have had on him. Finally, there is the English philosopher Thomas Hobbes who, in his *Leviathan* – which Spinoza clearly studied very closely – insists that most of the five books attributed to Moses were actually written long after his time, though Moses did indeed compose some of what appears in them.[91]

To be sure, denying the Mosaic authorship of the Bible was still an exceedingly unorthodox view. Spinoza noted that "the author [of the Pentateuch] is almost universally believed to be Moses," and he knew that rejecting that dogma would earn an author the condemnation of religious authorities. But there was nothing novel, by 1670, in claiming that Moses did not write all of the Torah, nor in suggesting that Scripture was composed by human beings and transmitted through a fallible historical process. Spinoza's radical and innovative claim was to argue that this holds great significance for how Scripture is to be read and interpreted. He was dismayed by the way in which Scripture itself was worshiped, by the reverence accorded to the words on the page rather than to the message they sought to convey. If the Bible is a historical and thus natural document, then it should be treated like any other work of nature. The study of Scripture, or biblical hermeneutics, should therefore proceed as the study of nature or natural science proceeds: by gathering and evaluating empirical data, that is, by examining the "book" itself for its general principles:

> I hold that the method of interpreting Scripture is no different from the method of interpreting Nature, and is in fact in complete accord with it. For the method of interpreting Nature consists essentially in composing a detailed study of Nature from which, as being the source of our assured data, we can deduce the definitions of the things of Nature. Now in exactly the same way the task of Scriptural interpretation requires us to make a straightforward study of Scripture, and from this, as the source of our fixed data and principles, to deduce by logical inference the meaning of the authors of Scripture. In this way – that is, by allowing no other principles or data for the interpretation of Scripture and study of its contents except those that can be gathered only from Scripture itself and from a historical study of Scripture – steady progress can be made without any danger of error, and one can deal with matters that surpass our understanding with no less confidence than those matters that are known to us by the natural light of reason.[92]

Just as the knowledge of nature must be sought from nature alone, so must the knowledge of Scripture – an apprehension of its intended meaning – be sought from Scripture alone. Spinoza explicitly took issue with Maimonides' view in the *Guide of the Perplexed*.[93] The great twelfth-century rabbi, as much of a rationalist as Spinoza, had argued that deciphering the meaning of Scripture is a matter of seeing what is consistent with reason. Because Scripture is the Word of God, its intended meaning must be identical with the truth. Therefore, if some passage, when read literally, cannot possibly be accepted as true, then the literal meaning must be rejected in favor of a figurative one. The Bible speaks, on occasion, of divine bodily parts. But reason tells us that an eternal, immaterial God does not have a body. Therefore, any references in Scripture to God's feet or hands must be read metaphorically.[94] For Spinoza, this type of exegesis is illegitimate insofar as it goes beyond Scripture itself – to some external standard of rationality or truth – in order to interpret Scripture. "The question as to whether Moses did or did not believe that God is fire must in no wise be decided by the rationality or irrationality of the belief, but solely from other pronouncements of Moses."[95] A distinction must be made between the meaning of Scripture, which is what one is after when interpreting it, and what is philosophically or historically true. Much of what Scripture relates is not, in fact, true. Scripture is not a source of knowledge, least of all knowledge about God, the heavens, or even human nature. It is not, in other words, philosophy, and therefore the principles of reason must not serve as our sole guide in interpreting Scripture. The moral message of Scripture does, indeed, agree with reason in the sense that our rational faculties approve of it. But *that* Scripture teaches such a message can be discovered only through the "historical" method.

The implementation of that method to discover what the authors of Scripture intended to teach requires a number of linguistic, historical, and textual skills. One should know the language in which Scripture was written, Hebrew, as well as the life, times, and even the "prejudices" of its authors and the nature of their audiences. Only by placing a book in its personal and historical context can one hope to decipher what the writer was trying to communicate.

Our historical study should set forth the circumstances relevant to all the extant books of the prophets, giving the life, character and pursuits of the author of every book, detailing who he was, on what occasion, at what time, for whom, and in what language he wrote. Again, it should be related what happened to each book, how it was first received, into whose hands it fell, how many variant versions there were, by whose decision it was received into the canon, and, finally, how all the books, now universally regarded as sacred, were united into a single whole. All these details . . . should be available from an historical study of Scripture; for in order to know which pronouncements were set forth as laws and which as moral teaching, it is important to be acquainted with the life, character and interests of the author. Furthermore, as we have a better understanding of a person's character and temperament, so we can more easily explain his words.[96]

One consequence of Spinoza's views is that the interpretation of Scripture is open and accessible to any person endowed with intelligence who is able and willing to acquire the necessary skills. There are, of course, various obstacles standing in the way of even the most well-trained of scholars – the fragmentary knowledge of the Hebrew language as it existed in the seventeenth century; the inherent ambiguities in its alphabet, vocabulary, and grammar; and the difficulty of accurately reconstructing the history surrounding such ancient writings. Nonetheless, Spinoza insists

that his method of interpreting Scripture "requires only the aid of natural reason." There is no need for lengthy and complex commentaries or
ordained intermediaries such as priests, rabbis, or pastors. "Since the
supreme authority for the interpretation of Scripture is vested in each individual, the rule that governs interpretation must be nothing other than
the natural light that is common to all, and not any supernatural right, nor
any external authority."[97]

When properly interpreted, the universal message conveyed by Scripture is a simple moral one: "To know and love God, and to love one's
neighbor as oneself." This is the *real* word of God and the foundation of
true piety, and it lies uncorrupted in a faulty, tampered, and corrupt text.
The lesson involves no metaphysical doctrines about God or nature and
requires no sophisticated training in philosophy. The object of Scripture
is not to impart knowledge, but to compel obedience and regulate our
conduct. "Scriptural doctrine contains not abstruse speculation or philosophic reasoning, but very simple matters able to be understood by the
most sluggish mind."[98] Spinoza claims, in fact, that a familiarity with Scripture is not even necessary for piety and blessedness, because its message
can be known by our rational faculties alone, although with great difficulty
for most people. "He who, while unacquainted with these writings, nevertheless knows by the natural light that there is a God having the attributes we have recounted, and who also pursues a true way of life, is altogether blessed."[99]

It follows that the only practical commandments that properly belong
to religion are those which are necessary to carry out the moral precept
and "confirm in our hearts the love of our neighbor." All the rest is, as
Rabbi Hillel said, mere commentary. "A catholic faith should therefore
contain only those dogmas which obedience to God absolutely demands,
and without which such obedience is absolutely impossible . . . these must
all be directed to this one end: that there is a Supreme Being who loves
justice and charity, whom all must obey in order to be saved, and must worship by practicing justice and charity to their neighbor." As for other dogmas, "every person should embrace those that he, being the best judge of
himself, feels will do most to strengthen in him love of justice."[100]

This is the heart of Spinoza's case for toleration, for freedom of philosophizing, and for freedom of religious expression. By reducing the central message of Scripture – and the essential content of piety – to a simple
moral maxim, one that is free of any superfluous speculative doctrines or

ceremonial practices; and by freeing Scripture of the burden of having to communicate specific philosophical truths or of prescribing (or proscribing) a multitude of required behaviors, he has demonstrated both that philosophy is independent of religion and that the liberty of each individual to interpret religion as he wishes can be upheld without any detriment to piety.

> As to the question of what God, the exemplar of true life, really is, whether he is fire, or spirit, or light, or thought, or something else, this is irrelevant to faith. And so likewise is the question as to why he is the exemplar of true life, whether this is because he has a just and merciful disposition, or because all things exist and act through him and consequently we, too, understand through him, and through him we see what is true, just and good. On these questions it matters not what beliefs a man holds. Nor, again, does it matter for faith whether one believes that God is omnipresent in essence or in potency, whether he directs everything from free will or from the necessity of his nature, whether he lays down laws as a rule or teaches them as being eternal truths, whether man obeys God from free will or from the necessity of the divine decree, whether the rewarding of the good and the punishing of the wicked is natural or supernatural. The view one takes on these and similar questions has no bearing on faith, provided that such a belief does not lead to the assumption of greater license to sin, or hinders submission to God. Indeed . . . every person is in duty bound to adapt these religious dogmas to his own understanding and to interpret them for himself in whatever way makes him feel that he can the more readily accept them with full confidence and conviction.[101]

Faith and piety belong not to the person who has the most rational argument for the existence of God or the most thorough philosophical understanding of his attributes, but to the person "who best displays works of justice and charity."

Spinoza's account of religion has clear political ramifications. There had always been a quasi-political agenda behind his decision to write the *Treatise,* as his attack was directed at political meddling by religious authorities. But he also took the opportunity to give a more detailed and thorough presentation of a general theory of the state that might, at that time, have been only sketchily present in the manuscript of the *Ethics.*[102] Such an examination of the true nature of political society is particularly important to his argument for intellectual and religious freedom, for he must show that such freedom is not only compatible with political well-being but essential to it.

The individual egoism of the *Ethics* plays itself out in a prepolitical context – the so-called state of nature, a universal condition where there is no law or religion or moral right and wrong – as the right of every individual to do whatever he can to preserve himself. "Whatever every person, whenever he is considered as solely under the dominion of Nature, believes to be to his advantage, whether under the guidance of sound reason or under passion's sway, he may by sovereign natural right seek and get for himself by any means, by force, deceit, entreaty, or in any other way he best can, and he may consequently regard as his enemy anyone who tries to hinder him from getting what he wants."[103] Naturally, this is a rather insecure and dangerous condition under which to live. In Hobbes's celebrated phrase, life in the state of nature is "solitary, poor, nasty, brutish and short."[104] As rational creatures, we soon realize that we would be better off, still from a thoroughly egoistic perspective, to come to an agreement among ourselves to restrain our opposing desires and the unbounded pursuit of self-interest – in sum, that it would be in our greater self-interest to live under the law of reason rather than the law of nature. We thus agree to hand over to a sovereign our natural right and power to do whatever we can to satisfy our interests. That sovereign – whether it be an individual (in which case the resulting state is a monarchy), a small group of individuals (an oligarchy), or the body politic as a whole (a democracy) – will be absolute and unrestrained in the scope of its powers. It will be charged with holding all the members of society to the agreement, mostly by playing on their fear of the consequences of breaking the "social contract."

Obedience to the sovereign does not infringe upon our autonomy because in following the commands of the sovereign we are following an authority whom we have freely authorized and whose commands have no other object than our own rational self-interest.

Perhaps it will be thought that . . . we are turning subjects into slaves, the slave being one who acts under orders and the free man who does as he pleases. But this is not completely true, for the real slave is one who lives under pleasure's sway and can neither see nor do what is for his own good, and only he is free who lives wholeheartedly under the sole guidance of reason. Action under orders – that is, obedience – is indeed to some extent an infringement of freedom, but it does not automatically make a man a slave; the reason for the action must enter into account. If the purpose of the action is not to the advantage of the doer but of him who commands, then the doer is a slave, and does not serve his own interest. But in a sovereign state where the welfare of the whole people, not the ruler, is the supreme law, he who obeys the sovereign power in all things should be called a subject, not a slave who does not serve his own interest.[105]

The type of government most likely to issue laws based on sound reason and to serve the ends for which government is instituted is democracy. It is the "most natural" form of governing arising out of a social contract – because in a democracy the people obey only laws that issue from the general will of the body politic – and the least subject to various abuses of power. In a democracy, the rationality of the sovereign's commands is practically secured, as it is unlikely that a majority of a large number of people will agree to an irrational design. Monarchy, on the other hand, is the least stable form of government and the one most likely to degenerate into tyranny.

Lest his readers miss the relevance of his theoretical claims to the present political scene, Spinoza gets right to the point:

As for the States of Holland, as far as we know they never had kings, but counts, to whom the right of sovereignty was never transferred. As the High States of Holland make plain in the document published by them at the time of Count Leicester,[106] they have always reserved to themselves the authority to remind the said counts of their duty, and have retained the power to uphold this authority of theirs and the freedom of the citizens, to assert their rights against the counts if the latter proved tyrannical, and to keep them on such a tight rein that they could do nothing without the permission and approval of the States. From this it follows that sovereign right was always vested in the States, and it was this sovereignty that the last count [Philip II of Spain] attempted to usurp. . . . These examples fully confirm our assertion that every state must necessarily preserve its own form, and cannot be changed without incurring the danger of utter ruin.[107]

There can be no doubt that the Orangist camp, clamoring for the return of the Stadholder in the person of William III, recognized the object of Spinoza's attack here.

Although he relies strongly on the example of the ancient Hebrew state, Spinoza was again thinking of the current situation in the Dutch Republic when he argued that the security, stability, and persistence of any state whatsoever depends on keeping all authority on all public matters in the hands of the sovereign alone. The second Jewish commonwealth was destroyed from within when the priestly caste started usurping political power, while the first commonwealth was weakened by the division of power between the kings and the Levites, who administered all religious affairs. There is a clear lesson here for the Calvinist preachers in the Dutch Republic:

How disastrous it is for both religion and state to grant to religious functionaries any right to issue decrees or to concern themselves with state business. Stability

is far better assured if these officials are restricted to giving answers only when requested, and at other times to teaching and practicing only what is acknowledged
as customary and traditional.[108]

As the outward practices of religion impinge upon the comportment and
relations of citizens, they fall under "state business" and thus within the
sphere of the sovereign's power. It would have taken a particularly dim wit
for a contemporary *predikant* not to recognize himself in Spinoza's depic-
tion of the Jewish high priests, who "usurped the rights of secular rulers
and at last wished to be styled kings."

The sovereign, then, should have complete dominion in all public matters, secular and spiritual. There should be no church separate from the
religion instituted and regulated by the state. This will prevent sectarianism and the multiplication of religious disputes. All questions concerning
external religious rites and ceremonies are in the hands of the sovereign.
This is in the best interest of everyone, as the sovereign will, ideally and
in conformity with his "contractual" duty, ensure that such practices are
in accord with public peace and safety and social well-being.

Since it is the duty of the sovereign alone to decide what is necessary for the welfare of the entire people and the security of the state, and to command what it
judges to be thus necessary, it follows that it is also the duty of the sovereign alone
to decide what form piety towards one's neighbor should take, that is, in what way
every man is required to obey God. From this we clearly understand in what way the
sovereign is the interpreter of religion; and, furthermore, we see that no one can
rightly obey God unless his practice of piety – which is the duty of every person –
conforms with the public good, and consequently, unless he obeys all the decrees
of the sovereign.[109]

The sovereign should rule in such a way that his commands enforce God's
law. Justice and charity thereby acquire the force of civil law, backed by the
power of the sovereign.

On the other hand, dominion over the "inward worship of God" and
the beliefs accompanying it – in other words, inner piety – belongs exclusively to the individual. This is a matter of inalienable, private right, and
it cannot be legislated, not even by the sovereign. No one can limit or control another person's thoughts anyway, and it would be foolhardy and destructive to the polity for a sovereign to attempt to do so. Nor can speech
ever truly and effectively be controlled, as people will always say want they
want, at least in private. "Everyone is by absolute natural right the master

of his own thoughts, and thus utter failure will attend any attempt in a commonwealth to force men to speak only as prescribed by the sovereign despite their different and opposing opinions."[110] There must, Spinoza grants, be *some* limits to speech and teaching. Seditious discourse that encourages individuals to nullify the social contract should not be tolerated. But the best government will err on the side of leniency and allow the freedom of philosophical speculation and the freedom of religious belief. Certain "inconveniences" will, no doubt, sometimes result from such an extensive liberty. But the attempt to regulate everything by law is "more likely to arouse vices than to reform them." In a passage that foreshadows John Stuart Mill's utilitarian defense of liberty nearly two centuries later, Spinoza adds that "this freedom is of the first importance in fostering the sciences and the arts, for only those whose judgment is free and unbiased can attain success in these fields."[111]

At the end of the *Treatise,* Spinoza allows himself one final and bitter swipe at those who were responsible for the death of Adriaan Koerbagh: the Reformed consistory and its allies.

It is clearer than the noonday sun that the real schismatics are those who condemn the writings of others and seditiously incite the quarrelsome mob against the writers, rather than the writers themselves, who usually write only for scholars and appeal to reason alone . . . the real disturbers of the peace are those who, in a free commonwealth, vainly seek to abolish freedom of judgment, which cannot be suppressed.[112]

The state, he concludes, can pursue "no safer course than to regard piety and religion as consisting solely in the exercise of charity and justice." The right of the sovereign should extend only to people's actions, "with everyone being allowed to think what he will and to say what he thinks."

The *Theological-Political Treatise* is one of the most eloquent arguments for a secular, democratic state in the history of political thought. Spinoza felt deeply about the issues he addressed, and – in contrast to the generally dispassionate *Ethics* – his sentiments in the *Treatise* are strong and unmistakable. Nonetheless, he recognized the political realities of the time and exercised some caution. He must have known how the book would be received by the clergy and certainly pulled no punches in his assault on their authority. But he wisely played to the urban regent class, his natural allies in his campaign against "theocracy" and, for the most part, no less committed than he to keeping William III from assuming the stadholdership.

Thus, the *Treatise* is sprinkled with statements likely to flatter the oligarchs of Amsterdam (and, perhaps, those of The Hague).

To confirm that any disadvantages consequent on this freedom [of judgment] can be avoided simply by the sovereign's authority, and by this authority alone people can be restrained from harming one another even when their opinions are in open conflict, examples are ready to hand, and I need go no distance to find them. Take the city of Amsterdam, which enjoys the fruits of this freedom, to its own considerable prosperity and the admiration of the world. In this flourishing state, a city of the highest renown, men of every race and sect live in complete harmony; and before entrusting their property to some person they will want to know no more than this, whether he is rich or poor and whether he has been honest or dishonest in his dealings. As for religion or sect, that is of no account, because such considerations are regarded as irrelevant in a court of law; and no sect whatsoever is so hated that its adherents – provided that they injure no one, render to each what is his own, and live upright lives – are denied the protection of the civil authorities.[113]

This is either a brilliant example of cutting irony, particularly when read in light of the city's treatment of Koerbagh, or an attempt to coopt the regents, to persuade them to look kindly upon his work and even see him as an articulate defender of their cause – a cause which they themselves may temporarily have forgotten. The regents would also have recognized that, in his call for state control over religion, Spinoza was simply renewing a proposal advocated sixty years earlier by Oldenbarneveldt in his ultimately fatal confrontation with the Counter-Remonstrants.[114] Given Oldenbarneveldt's near-mythical stature among arch-republicans, this could have held a very potent appeal for them. Regents of a Remonstrant persuasion in particular, being no less resistant than Spinoza to the confessional conformity that the orthodox Reformed hoped to impose, would have felt great sympathy for Spinoza's abstraction of religion from all external rites, its reduction to an essentially *moral* creed, and his antidogmatism.

Spinoza seems, in fact, to have actively courted protection from some powerful members of the regent class. This could explain why Adriaan Paets, a fairly liberal Amsterdam regent, possessed a copy of a work entitled *tractatus theologico-politicus* in the early 1660s. Spinoza is alleged – albeit by one of De Witt's enemies, hoping no doubt to lump together De Witt and the notorious atheist – also to have sent a copy of the finished manuscript of the *Treatise* to De Witt.[115] Spinoza may have hoped for some support from the Grand Pensionary. Lucas and others say that De Witt did provide cover for the philosopher and even helped ensure that the book was not banned as long as he was alive, but there is no independent evidence for this.[116] Spinoza probably hoped, above all, that his humble submission to "the scrutiny and judgment of my country's government" (meaning, most likely, the provincial States of Holland) would deflect any attacks that might come from the ruling class. He insists, both at the beginning and at the end of the work, that, "if they consider any part of my writing to be contrary to the laws of my country or to be prejudicial to the general good, I retract it." That hope was quickly dashed.

11

Calm and Turmoil
in The Hague

NOW THAT THE WORK on the *Theological-Political Treatise* was behind him and the book in press, Spinoza decided it was time to move to The Hague. He may have begun to tire of life in the country, with its various drawbacks. He probably also sought easier access to the intellectual life of the city. With his many friends and acquaintances in town, he would have found it much more convenient to live there rather than to commute from Voorburg. They reportedly encouraged him in this design. "He had many friends in The Hague," Colerus says, "some in the military, others of high position and eminence, who often visited and discoursed with him. It was at their request that he finally went to live in The Hague."[1] Spinoza left Voorburg sometime at the end of 1669 or early in 1670 and initially took some rooms in the rear of the third floor – essentially an attic – of a house on a back wharf called De Stille Veerkade (The Quiet Ferry Quay). The house was owned by a widow named Van der Werve, and she would be Colerus's own landlady when he lodged in the same rooms twenty years later. Her husband, a lawyer named Willem, had recently died, and she was apparently renting rooms to make up for the lost income. She told Colerus that Spinoza generally kept to himself, often having his meals in his rooms. He sometimes did not come out for several days.

The Hague was an expensive city, and the rent at Van der Werve's too steep for Spinoza's limited means. After a little over a year, at the beginning of May 1671, he made the final relocation of his life to a nearby house owned by Hendrik van der Spyck. The house was on the Paviljoensgracht, on the periphery of the city. He took a large single room on the first floor of this house, paying eighty guilders a year. Like Spinoza's landlord in Voorburg, the Lutheran Van der Spyck was a master painter. He concentrated mainly on interior decorations, although he was known to take a turn at portraiture as well.[2] The house had originally been owned by the landscape painter Jan van Goyen, and Van der Spyck may have acquired it

through his connections in the Guild of St. Luke. He supplemented the
income from his craft not only with rent from his tenants but also with
earnings from his services as a registered military solicitor.[3] Members of
the military were generally paid their salary a year in arrears, and often
turned to well-off citizens for loans (usually at an interest rate of 6 percent)
to carry them through until payday.

Van der Spyck's house could not have been a very quiet one. By the time
Spinoza moved in, the painter and his wife, Ida Margareta Ketteringh, had
three children; four more were born between 1671 and 1677. Still, it must
have been sufficiently tranquil for Spinoza's purposes, for he stayed there
until the day he died, five and a half years after he moved in. He furnished
his room plainly and functionally, and his possessions were few. The room
contained a bed; a small oak table, a three-legged corner table, and two
smaller tables; his lense-grinding equipment, and about a hundred and
fifty books in a bookcase. One painting, a portrait in a black frame, hung
on the wall. There was also a chessboard.[4] He was careful with his expenses
and proud of the simplicity of his living. Spinoza often told his house-
mates, whom Colerus interviewed, "I am just like a serpent who has his
tail in his mouth; I seek to have nothing left over at the end of the year, beyond what is necessary for a decent burial. My relatives shall inherit nothing from me, just as they have left me nothing."[5]

Spinoza seems to have had a friendly, even intimate, relationship with Van
der Spyck's family. They had many good things to say about their lodger
to Colerus. As Colerus was the Lutheran preacher in The Hague, they were
members of his congregation. He would have had frequent opportunities
to speak with them and so was able to draw what must be a fairly reliable
picture of Spinoza's personality and habits; and because Colerus was no
admirer of Spinoza, his account also avoids the usual pitfalls of hagiogra-
phy. Spinoza apparently spent a good deal of time in his room, working on
either his lenses or his writing, or perhaps just reading. "When he was at
home, he was troublesome to no one. . . . When he tired of his investigations, he came down and spoke with his house companions on whatever
was going on, even about trivial matters." For diversion, he liked to collect spiders and have them fight each other, or throw flies into their webs,
creating "battles," which so entertained him "that he would break out
laughing." Far from being the morose, even antisocial recluse of legend,
Spinoza was, when he did put down his work, gregarious, self-controlled,
and possessed of a pleasing and even-tempered disposition – much as one

would expect from the author of the *Ethics*. He was kind and considerate, and enjoyed the company of others, who seem in turn to have enjoyed his.

His conversation and way of life were calm and retiring. He knew how to control his passions in an admirable way. No one ever saw him sad or merry. He could control or hold in his anger and his discontent, making it known only by a sign or a single short word, or standing up and leaving out of a fear that his passion might get the better of him. He was, moreover, friendly and sociable in his daily intercourse. If the housewife or other members of the household were sick, he never failed to comfort them and to console them and to encourage them to endure that which, he told them, was the lot assigned to them by God. He exorted the children of the house to be polite and to be respectful of their elders and to go to public worship often.[6]

Spinoza showed an interest in the family's religious observance. "When the members of the household returned from church, he often asked them what they had learned from the sermon." He held Colerus's predecessor as Lutheran preacher, a man named Cordes, in high esteem, going to hear him preach on occasion, and advised Van der Spyck and his family and lodgers "not to miss any sermon of so excellent a preacher." Spinoza even praised the Lutheran faith of his hosts, although (one suspects) more out of politeness than anything else. One day, when Van der Spyck's wife asked Spinoza whether he thought she could be saved in the religion that she professed, he replied: "Your religion is good, and you need not search for another one in order to be saved, as long as you apply yourself to a peaceful and pious life."[7]

Colerus's narrative, along with the reports of others,[8] have given rise to the belief that Spinoza actually became a practicing Christian. While this is very hard to believe, what makes resolving the issue particularly difficult are the numerous references to Jesus as "Christ" in his writings, along with his evident admiration for Jesus' teachings. He believed that Jesus, as a recipient of the revelation of God's Word, equaled and perhaps even surpassed Moses. In the *Theological-Political Treatise*, he wrote that "the Voice of Christ can thus be called the Voice of God in the same way as that which Moses heard. In that sense it can also be said that the Wisdom of God – that is, wisdom that is more than human – took on human nature in Christ, and that Christ was the way of salvation."[9] He also insists that "he who is totally unacquainted with the Biblical narratives, but nevertheless holds salutary beliefs and pursues the true way of life, is absolutely blessed and has within him the spirit of Christ."[10] Most of Spinoza's explanations of Jesus' prophecy, however, can either be read as proposed interpretations of Scripture – in which case he is simply elaborating what Scripture appears to relate about Jesus – or be construed in a thoroughly naturalistic and moralistic manner, without implying any essentially Christian supernatural dogma. The claim that "God revealed himself to Christ, or to Christ's mind, directly" should, for example, be read merely as a claim about Jesus' clear and distinct apprehension of the truth.[11] Spinoza certainly did not believe that Jesus was the son of God in the literal sense Christianity demands; nor did he believe either that Jesus' birth involved something miraculous or that anything like a resurrection took place.

Oldenburg, after reading the *Theological-Political Treatise*, started to have some doubts about Spinoza's conformity to Christian piety and pressed him on just these issues: "[Some] say that you are concealing your opinion with regard to Jesus Christ, Redeemer of the World, sole Mediator for mankind, and of his Incarnation and Atonement, and they request you to disclose your attitude clearly on these three heads. If you do so, and in this matter satisfy reasonable and intelligent Christians, I think your position will be secure."[12] Spinoza's response must have disappointed him. "The passion, death and burial of Christ I accept literally, but his resurrection I understand in an allegorical sense."[13] He insists that to speak of "Christ's resurrection from the dead" is really to speak only of his spiritual influence, to indicate that "by his life and death he provided an example of surpassing holiness."[14] As for the Incarnation, it, too, should be understood only in the sense that God's wisdom was present in the highest degree in Jesus. But "as to the additional teaching of certain Churches, that God took upon himself human nature, I have expressly indicated that I do not understand what they say. Indeed, to tell the truth, they seem to me to speak no less absurdly than one who might tell me that a circle has taken on the nature of a square."[15] Spinoza *did* believe that Jesus was a supremely gifted moral teacher, and that much of what he had to say about blessedness and piety was true. But, then, those same principles are accessible to any sufficiently rational being; and "salvation" in no way requires recognition of Jesus as God's anointed. None of Spinoza's words in the *Treatise* or elsewhere should be taken as expressions of adherence to Christianity as an organized religion or to its central theological doctrines.

Spinoza's refusal to embrace Christianity in a formal way, as opposed to accepting what he saw as its original moral message, certainly did not, however, stem from any vestigial feelings of Jewishness. Spinoza, as an adult, did not see himself as a Jew; in no way was his self-identity bound up with his Jewish birth and upbringing. The clearest indication of this can be found in the *Treatise* itself, where the Jews are always referred to in the third person: it is "they" who have nothing to boast about in terms of God's election over and above other peoples. Spinoza belonged to no confessional religion and had no intention of joining any "sect." To judge by his philosophy, this must have been a matter of principle and not merely of historical accident. To become a practicing Christian would have been just as hypocritical, for him, as to have taken the bribe allegedly offered by the rabbis and remained a member of the Talmud Torah congregation.

ા

Spinoza received many visitors in his room on the Paviljoensgracht, and the Van der Spycks must have gotten used to the traffic in their house. He now had a reputation – a somewhat notorious one in the minds of many – in The Hague and elsewhere. Although the *Theological-Political Treatise* had been published anonymously, who the author was was no deep secret. One of his acquaintances reports that Spinoza was visited by "all types of curious minds, and even by upper-class girls [*filles de qualité*], who prided themselves on having a superior mind for their sex."[16] Colerus mentions that some of Spinoza's friends were in the military. This might explain why, in February 1673, Spinoza's name appeared as a witness on a notary document involving some members of the army. A Lieutenant-Colonel Don Nicolas de Oliver Fullana, a Spanish-speaking mercenary from Majorca, was helping the Dutch in their new fight against the French, who had invaded the Netherlands the year before. Because of his connections with another officer who had been arrested and executed in January 1673 for abandoning his post, it was important to Fullana – perhaps for the purpose of securing loans from a solicitor like Van der Spyck, either for himself or for the officers under his command – that it be publicly known that he was not under arrest as well, or even under suspicion. Thus, in the company of the sergeant-major of his regiment, Ferdinand Le Fevre, and Werner Matthijssen, a captain in the marines, as well as Gabriel Milan, a man of some international standing, Fullana went to the notary Johannes Beeckman in The Hague and had his witnesses declare that

it is truly the case that they were very well acquainted with Lieutenant-Colonel Fullana, that the same lieutenant-Colonel was at present here in The Hague, free, unmolested, at liberty, coming and going as he will, and I, the notary, declare like-wise that I too am very well acquainted with the said Lieutenant-colonel Fullana, and that the said Lieutenant-colonel is at present resident here, free from arrest or molestation of any kind; certifying that the above-mentioned parties have, this very day, seen Lieutenant-Colonel Fullana walking at liberty, and have spoken with him. Thus executed at The Hague, in the presence of Mr. Benedictus Spin-osa and Davidt Simonsen, solicited witnesses hereto.[17]

Fullana was, it seems, a Jew of converso heritage. He lived for a while in Brussels's marrano community, and later settled among the Portuguese Jews in Amsterdam. Fullana could not have known very much Dutch at the time of the document, and perhaps Spinoza – a "solicited witness," presumably paid for his service – was brought in to help translate for him. It may have been Van der Spyck who facilitated this arrangement, since as a solicitor to the military he could have had connections with any one of the officers involved. Or maybe Fullana was one of Spinoza's "military friends." As he lived in The Hague but spoke only Spanish, he and Spin-oza – who, no doubt, spoke that language – could have fallen in together under some circumstance or another. They might have been introduced by Milan, a well-connected agent representing the interests of the King of Denmark at The Hague. Like Spinoza, Milan was from a Portuguese-Jewish merchant family, in Hamburg. He lived in Amsterdam in the 1660s, but moved in 1670 to The Hague, where all court business took place, to serve his Danish employers. With so much in common, it would not be surprising if Spinoza and Milan, both local celebrities of a sort, were ac-quainted with each other in a relatively small place like The Hague.

The Hague is no farther from Amsterdam than Voorburg is, and Spin-oza continued to travel occasionally to the city of his birth in the 1670s. He may have been invited by his old Latin teacher, or even by the groom himself, to help celebrate the wedding of Maria van den Enden and Dirk Kerckrinck on February 27, 1671, in Amsterdam. Spinoza owned a cou-ple of books published by Kerckrinck in 1670 and 1671, which suggests that the two were still in touch during those years. Kerckrinck had to convert to Catholicism to marry Van den Enden's daughter, a move per-haps made necessary by the fact that his ex-Jesuit father-in-law was, re-portedly, about to begin service as medical adviser to the French monarch, Louis XIV, a man as much an enemy of Protestantism as he was of the Dutch Republic. We do not know if Spinoza was one of the guests in the French chapel of the Carmelites. The story about his own love for Maria and his failed ambition to marry her is highly implausible. But if it is true, it means that his friends' marriage would have been a bittersweet experience for him.

Spinoza may also have made the trip to Amsterdam to attend some of the meetings of the intellectual and cultural society to which his friends Lodewijk Meyer and Johannes Bouwmeester belonged. A new "academy" originated in November 1669, when a dozen people met at the Stil Malta on the Singel, a canal at the heart of the city surrounded by affluent homes.[18] Besides the physicians Meyer and Bouwmeester, they included Antonides van der Goes, who had been a student at Van den Enden's along with Spinoza, and a couple of prominent lawyers, at least one of whom came from a regent family. What brought them all together was a common interest in the theater, particularly of the French variety. The society, which they called Nil Volentibus Arduum (Nothing Is Difficult to Those Who Are Willing), met every Tuesday evening from five to eight to discuss tragedy, comedy, poetry, dramatic theory, the translation of Latin and French classicist plays, and various other cultural matters. The preceding year had been a difficult one for both Meyer and Bouwmeester, and Meyer, at least, was probably looking for new creative outlets for his considerable energies. He had been ousted as director of the Municipal Theater in 1669 over differences of opinion with the theater's regents – which may explain his desire to begin his *own* theater society. Bouwmeester, on the other hand, had just barely escaped being implicated in the blasphemy charges against Adriaan Koerbagh, on whose book the *Bloemhof* he had collaborated.

At the meetings of the association, one member would present some ideas on a set theme, either in writing or orally, which they would then discuss as a group. They also collaborated on translations of French plays, which they published at Rieuwertsz's shop. By 1671, their discussions had broadened to include distinctly philosophical issues. On May 19, "each member was asked to reflect on the nature and properties of our language," and in December someone led a roundtable on the question of whether a person alone on an island could, solely by way of his rational faculties, arrive at a proper conception of God and nature. Meyer was even introducing Spinozistic themes into their conversations. Nil Volentibus Arduum seems, in fact, to have functioned at times much as the Amsterdam circle of Spinoza's friends did in the early 1660s.[19] Meyer spoke on the nature of good and evil – inspired, no doubt, by Spinoza's account of these moral qualities in the manuscript of the *Ethics* – while Bouwmeester presented something on "truth." Surprisingly, neither Jellesz nor Rieuwertsz seems to have attended these meetings. It is tempting to assume that Spinoza, however, may have been present at least once or twice.

೩ം

If Spinoza sincerely thought that his "treatise on Scripture" would, as he said to Oldenburg in 1665, allow him to silence those "who constantly accuse me of atheism" and dispel the impression that he denied all religion, then he was in for a rude awakening. The book reached the Dutch reading public in early 1670. The reaction, far and wide, was immediate, harsh, and unforgiving. Spinoza quickly became identified as an enemy – perhaps *the* enemy – of piety and religion. Some of his more extreme critics accused him of being an agent of Satan, perhaps even the Antichrist himself.

The first attack came from Jacob Thomasius, a professor of theology in Leipzig, in May 1670. He wrote a long diatribe against "an anonymous treatise on the freedom of philosophizing," a "godless" document, he insisted. Regnier Mansveld, a professor at Utrecht, wrote, "in my opinion, that Treatise ought to be buried forever in an eternal oblivion."[20] They were soon joined, not surprisingly, by Willem van Blijenbergh, who had earlier so earnestly entreated Spinoza to explain the principles of his philosophy to him. He wrote, in a commentary on the *Treatise* in 1674, that "it is a book full of studious abominations and an accumulation of opinions which have been forged in hell, which every reasonable person, indeed every Christian should find abhorrent." Spinoza, he proclaimed, had tried to overthrow the Christian religion, along with "all our hopes that are grounded in it," and to replace it either with atheism or with some "natural religion formed according to the interests and humors of the sovereign."[21] The book was attacked by Remonstrants, Cartesians, and even Collegiants such as Johannes Bredenburg, a businessman from Rotterdam. Bredenburg objected most vehemently to Spinoza's conception of God and to the determinism at the heart of the system. In his *Enervatio Tractatus Theologico-Politici* (Refutation of the *Theological-Political Treatise*), written in 1675, Bredenburg argued that Spinoza's "fatalism" was harmful to all true religion and the worship of God. Nearly all of Spinoza's critics saw the *Treatise* as a dangerous and subversive work that, under the cover of a nominal belief in God, was intended to spread atheism and libertinism.[22] Even Thomas Hobbes, not one to be squeamish when it came to political and theological controversy, was taken aback by Spinoza's audacity. According to his biographer, the English philosopher claimed that the

Treatise "cut through him a bar's length, for he durst not write so boldly."[23]

Official condemnation by the religious authorities did not lag far behind these individual efforts. On June 30, 1670, the ecclesiastic court of the Reformed Church in Amsterdam, ever on guard against "Socinianism and licentiousness," decided that the matter was serious enough to warrant a general synod of the city, which in turn denounced the *Treatise* as "blasphemous and dangerous." In July, the district synod of The Hague followed suit and warned the provincial synod to be on guard against the "idolatrous and superstitious treatise." The consistories of Leiden, Utrecht, and Haarlem had already taken up the threat posed by this "vicious and harmful book" and concluded that something had to be done.[24] By late summer, the matter reached the synods of North and South Holland, both of which strongly condemned the work. The delegates to the Synod of South Holland concluded that the *Theological-Political Treatise* was "as vile and blasphemous a book as the world has ever seen," and they issued a call to all preachers to be on guard against its pernicious influence. They also told them to press their local magistrates to take action to stop the printing and circulation of the work.

The secular authorities varied in their willingness to comply with these petitions. Although the Leiden burgemeesters did order the sheriff to seize all remaining copies of the *Treatise* from local booksellers, the councils of many towns – including Amsterdam – and the provincial governors of Holland dragged their feet. In April 1671, the Hof van Holland, Court of Holland – the highest legal tribunal in the province, although, by the latter half of the seventeenth century, of questionable practical authority over the lower courts of the towns – acting on the provincial synods' requests, examined "various blasphemous books," including the Dutch translation of Hobbes's *Leviathan*, Meyer's *Philosophy, Interpreter of Holy Scripture*, and Spinoza's *Theological-Political Treatise*. The court agreed that the works in question contained many "scandalous opinions" and "Godless thoughts" and basically concluded that the magistrates in those towns which had banned and confiscated copies of Meyer's and Spinoza's books had, in the light of past legislation, acted properly. The strategy employed by the consistories in appealing to the "Socinianism" of the *Treatise* paid off. The court proclaimed that the publication and dissemination of the book explicitly contravened the order issued by the States of Holland on September 17, 1653, authorizing the suppression of "Socinian" and similarly offensive works.[25] The judges in The Hague decreed, further, that the publication, distribution, and sale of such works should be forbidden by a specific ordinance. They authorized the magistrates of the province's towns to order inquiries into the identity of the books' authors, publishers, printers, and sellers, and enjoined them to prosecute the responsible parties "without any pity," as required by the 1653 law.

A week later, the States of Holland took due notice of the court's judgment and set up a commission to look into the matter of the offending books. But, significantly, the States did not issue an independent edict forbidding the distribution of the *Treatise* and other "repugnant" works, as the synods and the court had requested. The regents who dominated the provincial assembly were, in all likelihood, simply reluctant to start banning books that were not written in the vernacular. Moreover, De Witt was still Grand Pensionary and in firm control of the States. With his own, albeit limited, commitment to the freedom of philosophizing, he may have exercised some influence over this decision. The synods nonetheless kept up the pressure, constantly reminding the municipal and provincial authorities of their duty. The Reformed Church was unanimous in its condemnation of the *Treatise*, and within a few years the *predikanten* of Amsterdam, Leiden, The Hague, Dordrecht, Utrecht, Gelderland, and Friesland had all passed numerous resolutions against "that corrupting and detestable book."[26] The practical efficacy of such resolutions was, of course, in the hands of the local magistrates. For the most part, it remained possible, throughout the early 1670s, to buy the *Treatise* in bookstores in the major towns. Still, the bookseller had to be discreet. And Leiden was probably not the only town actually to impound copies of the book right off the shelves.

Spinoza was aware that it was because his book was written in Latin that he did not suffer the same fate as Koerbagh. There was, indeed, an early and impressive demand for a Dutch edition of the *Treatise*. Rieuwertsz[27] – without first checking with Spinoza – decided to commission one right away from Jan Hendrik Glazemaker, who had translated Descartes's works into Dutch for Rieuwertsz's press some years before. But Spinoza had never given his permission for a translation, and appears not to have wanted one. When, in early 1671, he heard, that Glazemaker's was already in the process of being printed, he immediately tried put an end to it. Fearful of the consequences of the appearance of a Dutch edition, he wrote to Jellesz in February to ask for his friend's help in stopping the work's production:

When Professor – [possibly Theodore Craanen, a Cartesian professor from Leiden] recently paid me a visit, he told me, among other things, that he had heard that my *Tractatus Theologico-Politicus* had been translated into Dutch, and that somebody, he did not know who, proposed to get it printed. I therefore beg you most earnestly please to look into this, and, if possible, to stop the printing. This is not only my request but that of many of my good friends who would not wish to see the book banned, as will undoubtedly happen if it is published in Dutch. I have every confidence that you will do me and our cause this service.[28]

His appeal was successful, and Glazemaker's translation did not appear until 1693. With the memory of the events of 1668–9 still vivid, Spinoza was no doubt thinking of his personal safety as well.

He was not surprised by the attacks from the ecclesiastical authorities, nor, perhaps, even by those from academic circles. He was ever conscious, as he had told Oldenburg several years before, of how easily "the theologians of our time . . . with their customary spleen" take offense at unorthodox opinions.[29] In most cases, he maintained his equanimity and dismissed the objections as having their origin in ignorance and a refusal to give his ideas an honest and unprejudiced reading. Writing to Jellesz in 1674 about Mansveld's critique, he notes that

I have seen [the book which the Utrecht professor wrote against mine] in a bookseller's window. From the little that I then read of it, I judged it not worth reading through, and far less answering. So I left the book lying there, and its author to remain such as he was. I smiled as I reflected that the ignorant are usually the most venturesome and most ready to write. It seemed to me that they . . . set out their wares for sale in the same way as do shopkeepers, who always display the worse first. They say the devil is a crafty fellow, but in my opinion these people's resourcefulness far surpasses him in cunning.[30]

Spinoza's boast that he did not read, or even buy, Mansveld's work may be a lie. For among the books in his library – and perhaps, indeed, it was a gift left unread – was a copy of the professor's *Adversus anonymum Theologo-politicum*.[31] Nonetheless, Spinoza was generally unmoved – both intellectually and, to all appearances, emotionally – by the violence of the onslaught. The experience did, however, make him even more cautious about publishing the *Ethics*, to which he returned soon after moving to The Hague.

In October 1671, Spinoza received a letter from Gottfried Wilhelm Leibniz, a young German recently graduated with a law degree from the University of Altdorf and now serving the Elector of Mainz as a cultural and diplomatic councillor. Leibniz, of course, became one of the great philosophers and mathematicians of the modern period, independently developing the calculus at around the same time Newton did. But when he initiated his correspondence with Spinoza he was still an unknown. Leibniz had a great interest in scientific questions – he served for a while as the secretary of an alchemical society in Nuremberg – and had already published a treatise on matter and motion. Writing from Frankfurt, Leibniz introduced himself to Spinoza by way of their common interest in optics, having heard reports about "your remarkable skills" in that area. He asked Spinoza to comment on a paper he enclosed, "A Note on Advanced Optics," in which he discusses some principles concerning the gathering of light rays that have been refracted by a glass lense and their implication for the aperture sizes of polished glasses.[32] It is clear, however, that Leibniz was after more than a conversation about technical optical questions. Although he does not mention this to Spinoza, he had already read the *Theological-Political Treatise*[33] – a copy of which may have been given to him by Thomasius who was, in addition to being among Spinoza's earliest critics, Leibniz's former professor at Leipzig – and perhaps also *Descartes' Principles of Philosophy*. He was undoubtedly now interested in entering into a dialogue with their author on philosophical issues. Spinoza, unprompted by anything in Leibniz's letter, gave him just the opening he was looking for: "I have no doubt that you know somebody here at The Hague who would be willing to take charge of our correspondence. I should like to know who it is, so that our letters can be dispatched more conveniently and safely. If the *Tractatus Theologico-Politicus* has not yet reached you, I shall send you a copy if you care to have it."[34] Regrettably, no other letters of the correspondence between Spinoza and Leibniz survive. The two men must have discussed many of the metaphysical and theological issues raised in the *Treatise,* and given Leibniz's natural brilliance and wide-ranging interests in practically all intellectual disciplines, it was probably the most useful philosophical exchange in which Spinoza ever engaged.[35]

Spinoza, however, did not have full confidence in the sincerity of his new colleague. Leibniz's letters contained all the politeness and deference one would expect from a man well versed in the protocols of diplomacy and the niceties of court life, but Spinoza remained unsure of his motives for some time. In 1672, the Elector of Mainz sent Leibniz to Paris, where he remained until 1676, to try to persuade Louis XIV to stop troubling the peace of Europe and redirect his military ambitions toward Egypt. While in Paris, Leibniz fell in with that city's large circle of savants, including Huygens and another acquaintance of Spinoza's, Ehrenfried Walther von Tschirnhaus. A learned member of a noble German family, Tschirnhaus, who was born in 1651, had spent some time in the Netherlands for his education. He studied law at the University of Leiden, where he may have first been exposed to Spinoza's ideas, in the early 1670s. While at Leiden, he met a medical student named Georg Hermann Schuller, who lived in the same house as he and seemed to share his philosophical interests. After his studies, Tschirnhaus decided to remain in the Dutch Republic, initially spending some time as a volunteer soldier. By 1674, he was living in Amsterdam where, meeting up again with Schuller – who, by this point, had somehow gotten to know Spinoza – he came into contact with Rieuwertsz, Meyer, and Bouwmeester. He did not stay in that city for long, however, soon moving to London (where he met Oldenburg, Boyle, and Newton) and Paris. On his departure from Amsterdam, Tschirnhaus carried with him a copy of the manuscript of the *Ethics* (or, at least, a substantial portion of it), which he must have picked up from one of Spinoza's Amsterdam friends – or perhaps even from Spinoza himself[36] – on the condition that he keep it to himself and not show it around. In the fall of 1675, Schuller, who served as an intermediary between the peripatetic Tschirnhaus and Spinoza, wrote to The Hague to tell Spinoza that Tschirnhaus had met Leibniz in Paris and that their friend – almost certainly implored by Leibniz – would like to show him his copy of the *Ethics*.

He has met [in Paris] a man named Leibniz of remarkable learning, most skilled in the various sciences and free from the common theological prejudices. He has established a close friendship with him, based on the fact that like him he is working at the problem of the perfecting of the intellect, and indeed he considers there is nothing better or more important than this. In ethics, he says, Leibniz is most practiced, and speaks solely from the dictates of reason uninfluenced by emotion. He adds that in physics and especially in metaphysical studies of God and the Soul he is most skilled, and he finally concludes that he is a person most worthy of having your writings communicated to him, if [your] consent is first given; for he thinks that the Author will derive considerable advantage therefrom, as he undertakes to show at some length, if this should please you. If not, have no doubt that he will honorably keep them secret in accordance with his promise, just as in fact he has made not the slightest mention of them.[37]

As if Tschirnhaus, through Schuller, has not already said enough to try to make Spinoza favorably disposed toward Leibniz and allow him to show the manuscript to his fellow German, he adds that "this same Leibniz thinks highly of the *Tractatus Theologico-Politicus*, on which subject he once wrote you a letter, if you remember." Schuller ends the letter by adding his own endorsement to Tschirnhaus's request: "I would therefore ask you out of your gracious kindliness, unless there is strong reason against it, not to refuse your permission, but if you can, to let me know your decision as soon as possible."

Tschirnhaus's description of Leibniz's opinion of the *Treatise* is thoroughly misleading, although Tschirnhaus himself (given Leibniz's tactfulness, or perhaps duplicitousness) may not have been aware of the fact. Leibniz did, indeed, have great respect for Spinoza's learning and profundity. But in the autumn of 1670, well before his initial letter to Spinoza, Leibniz wrote to Thomasius lauding his "refutation" of the *Treatise:* "You have treated this intolerably impudent book on the liberty of philosophising as it deserves."[38] Leibniz may not have known the identity of the work's author at the time, but he certainly did know it when he wrote his letter in May 1671 to Johan Georg Graevius, Professor of Rhetoric at the University of Utrecht:

I have read the book by Spinoza. I am saddened by the fact that such a learned man has, as it seems, sunk so low. The critique that he launches against the holy books has its foundations in the *Leviathan* of Hobbes, but it is not difficult to show that it is often defective. Writings of this sort tend to undermine the Christian religion, consolidated by the precious blood, sweat and vigilance of martyrs. If only they can stimulate someone equal to Spinoza in erudition but exceeding him in his respect for Christianity to refute his numerous paralogisms and his abuse of eastern letters.[39]

Leibniz was responding to Graevius's report of "a most pestilential book [*liber pestilentissimus*] entitled *Discursus Theologico-Politicus*," whose author "is said to be a Jew named Spinoza, but who was cast out of the synagogue [ἀποσυνάγωγος] because of his monstrous opinions."[40]

Spinoza, aware of the treatment his book was receiving in both Germany and France, may have had his suspicions about Leibniz's views, although it is more likely that he was moved simply by his naturally cautious nature. Either way, he refused to give his consent to Tschirnhaus's request.

I believe I know Leibniz, of whom he writes, through correspondence, but I do not understand why he, a councillor of Frankfurt, has gone to France. As far as I can judge from his letter, he seemed to me a person of liberal mind and well versed in every science. Still, I think it imprudent to entrust my writings to him so hastily. I should first like to know what he is doing in France, and to hear our friend Tschirnhaus's opinion of him after a longer acquaintance and a closer knowledge of his character.[41]

Spinoza's reluctance here could, in part, have had something to do with the political context as well. The republic was still at war with France in 1675, and Spinoza's desire to know what exactly a diplomat from Mainz was doing in Paris might have been grounded in a fear that Leibniz, on behalf of his employer, was somehow working with the French, who had also recently executed his former Latin tutor. On the other hand, Spinoza may have just wanted to minimize the number of people who had access to a work that he knew would only compound the public outcry against him. He believed that the *Ethics* was, in many respects, a more radical book than the *Theological-Political Treatise*, which, with its argument for freedom of thought and expression, he had hoped would open the public way for it. Having never met Leibniz in person, he did not know him well enough to trust him not to pass along what he had learned from reading the *Ethics* to hostile critics, or perhaps even to undertake his own attack on the work.

Tschirnhaus, acceding to his friend's wishes, did not show the manuscript to Leibniz. But, observing the letter but perhaps not the spirit of Spinoza's request, he *did* describe its contents to him. "Tschirnhaus has told me many things about the book manuscript of Spinoza," Leibniz wrote in 1676. "Spinoza's book will be about God, the mind, happiness or the idea of the perfect human being, the improvement of the mind, the improvement of the body, etc."[42] In the end, Leibniz, as is clear from his later writings, agreed with some things he found in Spinoza's posthumously published works (they contain, he wrote, "a lot of good thoughts"); but, more often than not, he found them full of "wild and absurd," even dangerous, opinions.[43] He did not, however, allow this to cloud his judgment of Spinoza, whom he sometimes referred to as "that discerning Jew," as a person:

Piety commands that when people's dogmas are harmful their bad effects should be pointed out, where it is appropriate to do so: for example, beliefs that go against the providence of a perfectly good, wise and just God, or against that immortality of souls that lays them open to the operations of his justice; not to mention other opinions that are dangerous to morality and public order. I know that some excellent and well-meaning people maintain that these theoretical opinions have less practical effect than is generally thought. I know too that there are people with fine characters who would never be induced by doctrines to do anything unworthy of themselves; moreover, those who reach these erroneous opinions through speculation are not only inclined by nature to be aloof from the vices to which ordinary men are prone, but also are concerned for the good name of the sect of which they are, as it were, the leaders. One can acknowledge that Epicurus and Spinoza, for instance, led exemplary lives.[44]

ॐ

In the spring of 1672, disaster struck the republic when the army of Louis XIV invaded Dutch territory.[45] France and the Netherlands had participated in an uneasy alliance ever since the Franco-Dutch treaty of 1662. Louis was initially useful to the Dutch in their second war against England and had even helped to restrain threats to the republic from the east from the prince-bishop of Münster. But always lurking in the background behind the professed amity were tensions over French ambitions toward the Spanish Netherlands. Louis sought to expand his dominion into the southern Low Countries, which, two centuries earlier, had belonged to the Duke of Burgundy. When, in the mid-1660s, a substantially weakened Spain began withdrawing its forces from its Flemish and Wallonian possessions, the king of France saw that the opportunity was ripe to make his move. This caused no small amount of concern among De Witt and his colleagues. The Netherlands needed some parity between the powers of Spain and France so that they would keep each other in check, lest one of the greedy monarchs turn his sights on Dutch territory. Now, an unopposed France could mean only trouble for the republic. At one point, as a kind of appeasement, De Witt offered to renew the Franco-Dutch partition treaty of 1635, which would have allowed France to appropriate a large part of the Spanish Netherlands while leaving some of the Flemish lands to the Dutch.

Relations between France and the Netherlands were deteriorating on the economic front as well. When Dutch exports – such as cloth, herring, tobacco, and sugar – began assuming a large share of the French market, Louis's finance minister, Jean-Baptiste Colbert, imposed, in April 1667, a harsh tariff on all foreign imports. This measure hit the Dutch particularly hard, given the importance of the French trade to their domestic economy. Combined with the recent establishment by France of East and

West Indies Companies to compete with their Dutch counterparts, Colbert's move served only to increase the anger and resentment – not to mention the anxiety – of the Dutch public. The citizens of the republic were reaching the end of their patience.

The French army entered the Spanish Netherlands late in the spring of 1667. After inconclusive negotiations with Spain over how best to counter the French threat, the republic formed the Triple Alliance with England and Sweden in 1668. This armed coalition sought to defuse the growing conflict between France and Spain over the southern Netherlands, recommending a settlement that was, for the most part, in France's favor and threatening military intervention if France refused to halt its offensive moves. There was a great deal of disagreement even within the States-party faction in the Netherlands over how to deal with France. De Witt believed that nothing would be gained by war, and that an at least outwardly amicable relationship with France was essential to Dutch security. Consequently, he tried to avoid intervention at all costs. Others, however, were less sanguine about the possibility of a negotiated settlement. By 1671, with Louis fuming over the Triple Alliance and plotting his revenge, a significant number of Dutch policymakers were pressing for at least economic retaliation, arguing for bans on French imports such as wine, paper, and vinegar. The States General passed one such measure in November 1671.

In January 1672, all hope for a peaceful resolution seemed lost as France entered into an alliance with Cologne and Münster against the republic. The Dutch were now surrounded by hostile states. Louis XIV seemed intent not just on taking over the Spanish Netherlands but also in defeating the Republic of the Netherlands itself and transforming it into a monarchy, with William III as its sovereign. If he thought that this would at least earn him the support of the Orangist faction in the republic, he was a poor judge of Dutch character. His threats to both the republic's honor and its sovereignty incited De Witt's Orangist opponents to press for a strong response. Even the regents of Amsterdam were willing to put aside their differences with the Orangists to find some role for William, now reaching his majority, in running the republic's affairs. As war with France seemed ever more likely, there was increasing support on all sides for the appointment of William as Stadholder in Holland and other provinces, and as captain-general and admiral-general of the republic's forces. Finally, in February 1672, the States General gave him the supervised command of the army and navy.

Two months later, Louis declared war on the Dutch; he was soon followed by the king of England, the prince-bishop of Münster, and the Elector of Cologne. The Dutch were overwhelmed, and initially lost quite a bit of territory. On June 23, when the French entered Utrecht, a contingent of French and Münsterite troops captured several other cities. Most of the blame for the debacle fell on De Witt and his regent allies. De Witt had always executed a magnificent diplomatic game, playing the great international powers of Spain, France, England, Sweden, Denmark, and the imperial states off against each other. He was a pragmatist, above all else, and was willing to make an alliance with whomever he believed would best serve Dutch interests at the moment. But in 1672, with the memory of the second Anglo-Dutch war still fresh in their minds, the people of the Netherlands were no longer willing to settle for pragmatic solutions. The Grand Pensionary's position was weaker than it had ever been. He was being accused in anonymous pamphlets of military incompetence, of siphoning public funds into his private accounts, and even of plotting to hand the republic over to its enemies so that he could rule it on their behalf.

On the night of June 21, as De Witt was walking home from the Binnenhof, where the States of Holland met in The Hague, he was attacked with a knife and wounded by four young men from good families. Only one of the assailants was caught, and he was beheaded six days later. Though De Witt's wounds were not very serious, he fell ill while recovering from the attack. His incapacitation only increased the cry for stronger leadership, and at the beginning of July, William III was proclaimed Stadholder by the provinces of Holland and Zeeland. De Witt, although recovered by the end of the month and asked to continue in his post by a gracious William, bowed to political necessity and resigned the office of Grand Pensionary of the States of Holland on August 4. Meanwhile, De Witt's brother, Cornelis, had been arrested on July 23 for allegedly plotting against the Stadholder's life, certainly a trumped-up charge. After a lengthy interrogation, he was formally acquitted of the accusations against him on August 20. However, a hostile mob assembled outside the prison in which Cornelis was being held. The crowd had been stirred up by Orangists incensed over the verdict, and Johan de Witt was led to believe that his brother had asked him to come and help escort him away. De Witt arrived at the prison to take Cornelis to a relative's house nearby; but when he reached his brother's cell, the two realized the difficult situation in which they found themselves. As they walked out of the gate, there was a cry that the "traitors" were coming and they were forced back into the building. The States of Holland, meeting nearby, tried to prevent any harm from coming to the men. But the mob by now was out of hand. Although there were armed soldiers stationed outside the prison, rumors of an approaching crowd of peasants intent on wreaking havoc in The Hague necessitated their moving to the town bridges. Upon leaving their position the commander of the cavalry is said to have commented, "I shall obey, but now the De Witts are dead men."[46]

Now facing only a small band of civic guardsmen, the crowd rallied against the men trapped inside and broke into the prison. They reportedly found Cornelis reading a book of French plays in bed, while Johan sat at the foot of the bed with a Bible in hand. The two men were forced downstairs and pushed into the waiting mob. The intention was to hang them, but they were so viciously attacked that they died before reaching the scaffold. The bodies were then hung up by the feet, stripped bare, and literally torn to pieces.

Spinoza was stunned by these acts of barbarity, perpetrated not by some roving band of thieves but by a crowd of citizens that included respectable, middle-class burghers. Leibniz spoke with Spinoza about the events surrounding the deaths of the De Witt brothers when he was passing through The Hague in 1676: "I have spent several hours with Spinoza, after dinner. He said to me that, on the day of the massacres of the De Witts, he wanted to go out at night and post a placard near the site of the massacre, reading *ultimi barbarorum* [roughly translated, "You are the greatest of barbarians"]. But his host locked the house to keep him from going out, for he would be exposed to being torn to pieces."[47] Van der Spyck was no doubt also thinking about his own safety and the condition of his house. He had good reason to be concerned, for Spinoza's name, both among the learned and in the popular imagination, was intimately linked with that of De Witt. The Grand Pensionary's enemies, in fact, used his purported connections with "the evil Spinoza" to cast aspersions on both him and his brother. A pamphlet from 1672 proclaims that De Witt basically gave Spinoza the protection he needed to publish the *Theological-Political Treatise*. The author of the pamphlet alleges that among De Witt's books and manuscripts was found a copy of the *Treatise*, "brought forth from hell by the fallen Jew Spinoza, in which it is proven, in an unprecedented, atheistic fashion, that the word of God must be explained and understood through Philosophy, and which was published with the knowledge of Mr. Jan."[48]

One of the immediate effects of the downfall of De Witt and his regime was the end of the "True Freedom," with its policy of provincial (and even municipal) autonomy and a generally tolerant intellectual atmosphere. A widespread purge of the town councils was begun. Regents seen as sympathetic to the De Witts were replaced by individuals who were unequivocally Orangist and favorably disposed to the aims of the orthodox Calvinists. Political power became more centralized as it moved back from the towns and the provincial states to the Stadholder and the States General, over which William had great influence. Consequently, it became easier for the authorities to exercise a broader and more consistent control over what was said and done in the republic. This 1672 *wetsverzetting* both in the distribution of power and in the policies to be pursued almost certainly explains why Spinoza henceforth had to contend, not just with condemnations from ecclesiastical authorities, but also with proscriptions from the secular side of officialdom as well.

The changes in the political winds may also account for the fact that, after 1672, Spinoza found himself the object of attack by Cartesian academic philosophers and theologians as well. It might, at first glance, seem surprising that people such as Regnier Mansveld at the University of Utrecht, Johannes de Raey, Christopher Wittich, and Theodore Craanen at the University of Leiden, and Lambert van Velthuysen were all united in their opposition to Spinoza. After all, these were men committed, to one degree or another, to the propagation of the new philosophy and science. But given the political realities of the 1670s, they really had no choice but to come down hard on "radical Cartesians" and their Spinozist allies. Although they certainly had serious disagreements with many of the methodological and metaphysical doctrines of Spinoza, Meyer, Van den Enden, and others, their hostility was also, at least in part, a strategic defensive maneuver made necessary by their own difficult circumstances.

Since 1650, the polarization between liberals and conservatives within the Reformed Church had taken the form of a contest between two doctrinal camps, each united behind a charismatic personality. On the one hand, there was the formidable Gisbertus Voetius, Dean of the University of Utrecht and one of Descartes's most implacable foes. Strongly orthodox in theology and conservative in social and political policy, Voetius refused to tolerate any deviations from his narrow view of the Reformed faith and his broad view of its role in society and academia. His opponent, Johannes Cocceius, was a professor of theology at the University of Leiden.

Cocceius was fairly liberal in his interpretation of the demands of Calvinism. He also took a nonfundamentalist view of the Bible. The words of
Scripture should not always be read literally, he argued, but rather interpreted in the light of their linguistic, literary, and historical context.

The dispute between the "Voetians" and the "Cocceians" began in the
Leiden theological faculty in 1655 as a disagreement over social mores,
stemming mainly from a difference of opinion regarding the observance
of the Sabbath. The Voetians had been pushing for more "godliness" in
the lifestyles of ordinary people. They generally discouraged many of the
recreations that the Dutch of the seventeenth century enjoyed so much,
such as dancing and gaming. They took particular exception to any kind
of work or play on the Sabbath. The Lord's Day was a day for rest and
prayer, not ice-skating parties along the canals. The Cocceians responded
that a strict observance of the Fourth Commandment was not really necessary in their day and age. Piety no longer required one to stop working
or to abandon all amusements. By 1659, the debate had become so heated
that the Synod of South Holland, urged by the States of Holland (who
rightly saw that any theological dispute in the republic threatened inevitably to turn into a political one), tried to quell the Sabbath argument
by forbidding any further discussion of the issue.

Of course, like the Remonstrant/Counter-Remonstrant battle of the
1610s, the schism between the Voetians and the Cocceians in the late 1650s
did become politically and culturally charged. The Cocceian side tended
to be supported by members of the States-party faction, that is, De Witt
and his allies, since they were all trying to check the political and social influence of the orthodox Reformed preachers. Voetians were joined, on the
other hand, by Orangists, as both groups opposed the power of the States
of Holland: the Voetians because that body was in the hands of the more
tolerant (and therefore theologically "lax") regents; the Orangists because
the deputies to the States of Holland stood in the way of the appointment
of their beloved William III. The Cocceians also came to be seen – to an
important extent, correctly – as allied with the Cartesians. De Witt, Cocceians, and Cartesians all insisted on the separation of philosophy from
theology. Descartes and his followers claimed, in unequivocal terms, that
philosophy must not presume to pronounce on theological matters, and
that theologians should, when it is not a question of an article of faith, leave
philosophers free to pursue their inquiries through reason alone. This was
a convenient distinction for academic Cartesians, because it meant for

them a certain degree of independence in their teaching from the oversight of the theologians. For De Witt, the separation of the two disciplines – and, in the universities, the two faculties – was especially important as a move for reducing the power of the theologians. To limit their sphere of control it was necessary to support (and even expand) the freedom to philosophize. If philosophy and theology were kept separate, then there were clear and well-defined boundaries beyond which theologians must not tread. The Voetians not only resented the attempt to limit the scope of their authority, but also argued that if theology were not placed above philosophy and allowed to control it, then eventually philosophy would subordinate theology.

The Cocceians, with their nonliteral approach to Scripture, were also regarded as lending support to the Cartesian project in natural philosophy and the new science. If it was no longer necessary to read all of the Bible literally, then its reports of miracles – that is, purported violations of the mathematical laws of a mechanistic universe – were open to a figurative interpretation. Cocceian exegetical methods also cleared the way for a Copernican rereading of those passages that, traditionally, were seen as sustaining the view that a stationary earth was the center of the universe.[49] Over time, the Cartesian-Cocceians became bolder, and much of what they said went well beyond anything explicitly endorsed by Cocceius himself. Theologians such as Frans Burman and humanist scholars such as Graevius were not shy about advertising their sympathy for Cartesian method, metaphysics, and physics. One historian notes that the Cocceian project was nothing less than the "assimilation of Calvinist theology with Cartesian science and philosophy."[50]

In most places, things quieted down for a while in the 1660s. Cocceius himself died in 1669, and the Cartesians controlled the major universities of Leiden and Utrecht. But when De Witt was overthrown in 1672 and the Voetians and their political supporters gained the upper hand, a new reaction against the Cocceians and the Cartesians set in. There was a general purge of Cartesian professors of philosophy and Cocceian professors of theology at the universities. But this time the net was cast even wider and was aimed not just at moderate Cartesians with university appointments but also at independent radicals such as Meyer and Spinoza. In fact, Meyer's hyperrationalistic treatise, *Philosophy, Interpreter of Holy Scripture* – wherein he argued that the proper guide for apprehending the meaning of the Bible is reason itself, and which had been the object of orthodox (and even Cartesian) ire ever since its publication in 1666 – served only to confirm the Voetians' worst fears. To the Voetians in the late 1660s and early 1670s, Cocceianism looked very much like Meyer's extreme brand of Cartesianism.[51] The secular authorities, taking their lead from the theologians, were practically incapable of distinguishing between the different varieties of Cartesians and Cocceians. Among the twenty "Cocceian-Cartesian" propositions condemned by the States of Holland in 1676 is one claiming that philosophy should be the interpreter of Scripture. It did not help the cause of the moderate Cartesians that the first published work by the author of the *Theological-Political Treatise* was a summary of Descartes's philosophy.

The Cartesian (and Cocceian) backlash against Spinoza, then, needs to be seen in the light of this Voetian attack on the Cartesians and Cocceians. By turning their own forces on Spinoza and on radical Cartesians, the more moderate Cartesians hoped to distinguish themselves in the minds of their critics from the more "dangerous" strains of freethinking infecting the republic. They strongly and loudly criticized anyone who dared to push the principles of rationalist philosophy so far as to start denying the immortality of the soul, the divine origin of Scripture, the doctrine of the Trinity, and the possibility of divine miracles. It was not *only* a tactical maneuver. There were, indeed, substantive philosophical differences between Spinoza and the Cartesians, and only a naive reader of the *Descartes' Principles of Philosophy* and the *Theological-Political Treatise* would think that Spinoza should be identified as a "Cartesian" in any meaningful sense. But there can be no question that, if the Cartesians themselves were going to mount an effective defense, they had to distance themselves publicly from Spinoza, even if this meant exaggerating their real philosophical differences with him. Spinoza himself saw through their strategy. Writing to Oldenburg in September 1675, he complained that "the stupid Cartesians, in order to remove this suspicion from themselves because they are thought to be on my side, ceased not to denounce everywhere my opinions and my writings, and still continue to do so."[52]

The Cocceians, too, had good cause for concern. Many of their fundamental doctrines resembled the kinds of things Spinoza argued for in the *Treatise*. They, like Spinoza, distinguished between God's moral law and the ceremonial law, a distinction that allowed them to claim that the commandment to observe the Sabbath strictly is a ritual law intended only for the Jews, to whom it was directly given. They also argued that religious authorities should play no role in secular political affairs. And they believed that Scripture should be understood on its own terms, that is (to use Spinoza's words), "from Scripture itself."[53] These similarities gave the Cocceians sufficient motivation for trying to make it clear that they, too, were no Spinozists.

&

In the midst of the campaign against him that began after De Witt's murder, Spinoza must have been pleased to learn that *some* people, at least, appreciated his philosophical talents, although it is not clear that those people were working from a very solid basis. In February 1673, Spinoza received the following letter from Johann Ludwig Fabricius, acting on behalf of Karl Ludwig, Elector of Palatine, one of the German imperial states.

Renowned Sir,
His Serene Highness the Elector Palatine, my most gracious lord, has commanded me to write to you who, while as yet unknown to me, are strongly recommended to his Serene Highness, and to ask you whether you would be willing to accept a regular Professorship of Philosophy in his illustrious university. The annual salary will be that currently paid to regular professors. You will not find elsewhere a Prince more favorably disposed to men of exceptional genius, among whom he ranks you. You will have the most extensive freedom in philosophizing, which he believes you will not misuse to disturb the publicly established religion. I have pleasure in complying with the request of the most wise Prince. . . . I will add only this, that if you come here, you will have the pleasure of living a life worthy of a philosopher, unless everything turns out contrary to our hope and expectation.
    And so farewell, with my greetings, most honored sir,
                                                    From your most devoted,
                                                    J. Ludwig Fabritius
Professor at the University of Heidelberg and Councillor to the Elector Palatine.[54]

This offer of a chair in philosophy at the University of Heidelberg must have been flattering to Spinoza. Before the Thirty Years' War, Heidelberg – the capital city of the Elector's domain – had one of the great universities of Europe, and Karl Ludwig was trying to restore to it its former luster. Since the death of Johannes Freinsheim in 1660, there had been no regular philosophy professor occupying a chair in the lower faculties. An offer first went out to Tannequil Lefevre, a professor at the Protestant academy in Saumur, France. He accepted the post but died in February 1672, just before leaving for Heidelberg. Freinsheim had been a Cartesian, and the Elector was probably seeking to replace him with a like-minded teacher. He had been encouraged in his plan to make an offer to Spinoza by Urbain Chevreau, an expatriate French Catholic serving the Elector as an adviser in intellectual affairs, a kind of resident *homme de lettres*. "Being at the court of the Elector," Chevreau wrote some years later, "I was speaking very advantageously of Spinoza, although I knew this Jewish Protestant only through the first and second parts of the Philosophy of Mr. Descartes, printed in Amsterdam by Jan Rieuwertsz in 1663. The Elector had this book, and after having read to him a few chapters of it, he resolved to appoint him in the Academy of Heidelberg to teach philosophy there, on the condition that he not dogmatize."[55] This would not be the first time that a Jew held a teaching post at the university. Jacob Israel, in fact, was not only professor of physiology but rector of the entire institution.

Both Chevreau and Karl Ludwig were apparently unfamiliar with the *Theological-Political Treatise*. This was not the case with the man commissioned by the Elector to write the invitation to Spinoza. Johann Fabricius, a stern Calvinist, occupied a chair in the theology faculty at Heidelberg and was a good friend and adviser to Karl Ludwig. *He*, at least, had read the *Treatise*, and his opinion of it was no different from the opinion of almost all other theologians. In 1671, Fabricius, after going through the work, told his friend and biographer, Johann Heidegger, that "I shudder when I see such unbridled licentiousness being presented in a public display, and the Christian religion itself and Holy Scripture being so openly blasphemed."[56] Now the poor man, under order of his sovereign, had to invite the author of such a "horrible book" to become his colleague. Fabricius put his animosity – and his pride – aside and wrote the letter.

Spinoza took the offer seriously, even going so far as to obtain a copy of an old book by Fabricius's brother that he had dedicated to Karl Ludwig.[57] But, after thinking about it for a month, he decided graciously to decline.

If I had ever had any desire to undertake a professorship in any faculty, I could have wished for none other than that which is offered me through you by His Serene Highness the Elector Palatine, especially on account of the freedom to philosophize that this most gracious Prince is pleased to grant, not to mention my long-felt wish to live under the rule of a Prince whose wisdom is universally admired. But since I have never intended to engage in public teaching, I cannot induce myself to embrace this excellent opportunity, although I have given long consideration to the matter.

The offer may have been particularly tempting in light of recent events in The Hague and the dark outlook for philosophical freedom in the republic in the near future. But besides the facts that Spinoza had never left the Netherlands for even a short stay elsewhere – and this would remain true for his entire life – and that he had many good friends in The Hague and in Amsterdam, there were two main considerations that led him to refuse the offer. First, he was reluctant to lose precious time to teaching. "I reflect that if I am to find time to instruct young students, I must give up my further progress in philosophy." Second, and this may have been an even more important factor, he was worried by the portentous stipulation in Fabricius's letter that he not "misuse" his philosophical freedom "to disturb the publicly established religion." He was troubled by the ambiguity in the phrase.

I do not know within what limits the freedom to philosophize must be confined if I am to avoid appearing to disturb the publicly established religion. For divisions arise not so much from an ardent devotion to religion as from the different dispositions of men, or through their love of contradiction that leads them to distort or to condemn all things, even those that are stated aright. Now since I have already experienced this while leading a private and solitary life, it would be much more to be feared after I have risen to this position of eminence. So you see, most Honorable Sir, that my reluctance is not due to the hope of some better fortune, but to my love of peace, which I believe I can enjoy in some measure if I refrain from lecturing in public.

Spinoza concludes by asking the Elector "to grant me more time to deliberate on this matter," but it is clear that he has no intention of accepting.[58]

We do not know if the Elector, in giving his instructions to Fabricius, told him explicitly to mention in his letter to Spinoza that his "freedom in philosophizing" would be conditional. Chevreau claims that all Karl Ludwig insisted upon was "that he not dogmatize." And this might have meant merely that Spinoza's lecturing duties would be confined to philosophy and that he should not make any pronouncements on church doctrine. In other words, it could have been an expression of a commitment to a separation of philosophy and theology. In his letter, Fabricius gives it a more ominous twist, as if even purely philosophical lectures could get Spinoza into trouble if religious authorities found the content of his lectures disturbing. Perhaps the hostile Fabricius, while complying with the letter of the Elector's order, was trying to sabotage the appointment by scaring off Spinoza.[59] If that was his strategy, then, at least in Chevreau's mind, it worked: "We searched for reasons for his refusal, and after several letters which I received from The Hague and Amsterdam [it is not clear if these are letters from Spinoza himself], I conjectured that these words, 'On the condition that you not dogmatize', made him afraid." All to the good, Chevreau concluded, for "he was better off in Holland, where he could carry on a great commerce with Oldenburg and other Englishmen, and where he had complete liberty to entertain with his opinions and maxims those who were curious enough to visit him, and to turn them all into his disciples, either deists or atheists."[60] Karl Ludwig must have been disappointed, however. He was a highly educated, cultured, and tolerant ruler. He had grown up in the Netherlands, where his father – Frederick V, the so-called Winter King – was forced to take refuge during the Thirty Years' War. A Calvinist, Karl Ludwig was, in his religion and politics, relatively liberal and would certainly not have found Spinoza's philosophy – not even the *Theological-Political Treatise* – as abhorrent as did those around him.

As for Spinoza, it was a good thing for him that he did not accept the offer. He would have had no patience for the protocols of court life – and he would surely have been expected to attend, from time to time, to the intellectual and pedagogical needs of the Elector and his family – or for the politics and intrigue of Heidelberg's academic circles. It was also a prudent move, for the following year the French army moved into Heidelberg and closed down the university. All of its professors were banished. Spinoza's predicament would have been particularly difficult, as he might have encountered some difficulty in trying to return to his peaceful existence in The Hague. For by taking up Karl Ludwig's offer and abandoning the republic, he probably would have exacerbated the hostility against him among those who, still associating him with the De Witt brothers, suspected him of traitorous inclinations.

Suspicions about Spinoza's loyalty to the Dutch cause, in fact, reached a high point that summer of 1672 when he made a potentially dangerous (and possibly ill-advised) but fruitful trip behind enemy lines. Things had not gone well for the Dutch forces, now under the command of William III, in the early stages of the war. Throughout 1672, the republic suffered a series of significant military defeats. By late summer, the greater part of the Netherlands was in either French or Münsterite hands. Town after town was falling to the enemy, sometimes without a fight. The city of Utrecht, in no mood for an extended siege, capitulated to the prince of Condé on June 13. For the next year and a half, until November 1673, it remained under French control. A lieutenant-colonel in Condé's retinue, Jean-Baptiste Stouppe, was made commandant of the city.

Stouppe – or Stoppa, as his name was probably pronounced in his northern Italian hometown – was from a French Protestant family.[61] He served as a minister to Huguenots in London in the late 1640s and 1650s, doing some intelligence work on the side for Cromwell, including trying to foment Protestant rebellion in France. At one point, he reportedly offered, on the Lord Protector's behalf, the French crown to the prince of Condé, Louis II of Bourbon, if he would take charge of the revolt. Condé, who a short time later would be one of the leaders of the Fronde rebellion, prudently declined, replying – no doubt, sarcastically – that he would be happy to oblige as soon as Cromwell's army was in France. Stouppe fled England when Charles II was restored to the throne and joined Condé's army, in which his brother was an officer. He was, however, personally criticized by a Swiss Protestant professor of theology for participating in the assault on a Protestant nation, the Netherlands, in the service of a Catholic sovereign.

Stouppe responded to the theologian by composing his *La Religion des Hollandois*, an indictment of purported Dutch religiosity. He argued that the Dutch were not the upstanding and devout Protestants the good professor believed them to be. In fact, their religious observance and theological orthodoxy left much to be desired. They tolerated all kinds of deviant and bizarre religious sects, and even allowed freethinkers and atheists to publish their views without making any effort to refute them. Stouppe used the example of Spinoza, of whose piety he had a fairly low opinion, to make his point:

[There is] an illustrious and learned man, who has, I am told, a large number of followers who are completely attached to his views. I am talking of a man who was born Jewish, whose name is Spinosa, and who has not abjured the religion of the Jews nor embraced the Christian religion; thus, he is a very bad Jew and no better a Christian. A few years ago he wrote a book in Latin, whose title is *Theological-Political Treatise*, in which his principal goal seems to be to destroy all religions, particularly the Jewish and Christian ones, and to introduce atheism, libertinage and the freedom of all religions. . . . His followers do not dare disclose themselves, because his book absolutely undermines the foundations of all religion.[62]

Stouppe is particularly impressed by Spinoza's erudition, which, to his mind, makes it especially important to refute his "pernicious" book. The Dutch must be leaving him alone either because they lack the courage or the resources to criticize him, or – which is more worrisome – because they share his sentiments. Stouppe has his suspicions that the latter is the case. He notes laxity among the Dutch in their observance of the exterior rites of the Christian religion, particularly those who are abroad on business. Dutch sailors and merchants in the Far East, for example, are known to neglect their observance of Christian rites, and even (on occasion) to forbid it. Here Stouppe is relying on Spinoza's own account of Dutch behavior in Japan when, in the *Treatise,* he claims that the Dutch East Indies Company has ordered its employees there not to engage in outwardly Christian practices because the Japanese have forbidden them.[63] Spinoza was using the example to argue that religious ceremonies are inessential to true piety. To Stouppe, it was a sign that the Dutch put their business interests ahead of their religious duties. More important, it showed that they were, at heart, Spinozists.[64]

Stouppe's attack on Spinoza and on the Dutch who so scandalously allowed Spinoza's book to circulate was written in May 1673. This makes it all the more surprising that less than two months later this same man was escorting Spinoza from The Hague to visit his commanding officer, the prince of Condé, at his headquarters in Utrecht. Indeed, Stouppe himself had encouraged the general to invite Spinoza in the first place. This apparent hypocrisy did not escape the notice of Jean Brun (Johannes Braun), a Cocceian theologian at Groningen who wrote a defense of Dutch Protestantism in response to Stouppe's book: "I must note how surprised I am to see Stouppe rant so forcefully against Spinoza and go on so over the fact that so many people in this country [the Netherlands] visit him, seeing as how he himself cultivated a direct friendship with the man while he was in Utrecht. For I have been assured that it was he who solicited the Prince of Condé to bring [Spinoza] from The Hague to Utrecht expressly to confer with him, and that Stouppe praised him highly and was greatly familiar in his company."[65]

Stouppe was obviously not so doctrinaire and prejudiced against Spinoza that he was without any interest in getting to know one of the republic's greatest – if most notorious – intellectual celebrities. He seems to have become personally acquainted with Spinoza even while writing his book against him, perhaps at one point paying him a visit in The Hague.[66]

Stouppe was also conscious of his commanding officer's interest in matters philosophical, his taste for freethinking, and his habit of surrounding himself with learned (and libertine) company.[67] When Condé was living in Chantilly, his patronage supported a number of important writers, including Molière, Racine, and La Fontaine.[68] He now tried to recreate in Utrecht, as far as possible under the circumstances, the kind of cultural environment on which he depended, this time supplementing his imported French courtiers with a Dutch cast. "The Prince of Condé," Colerus reports, "wanted very much to speak with Spinoza," and even offered to win for him a pension from Louis XIV if only Spinoza would dedicate one of his books to the French monarch.[69] Spinoza eventually, and "with all the civility he was capable of," declined the offer of a pension, adding that "he had no desire to dedicate any book to the King of France." But, with some reluctance at having to interrupt his work, he did accept the invitation to come to Utrecht.

It could not have been an easy trip in the summer of 1673. Not only was there the problem of evading Dutch troops in order to enter French-occupied territory. As a defensive maneuver, the Dutch had opened the dikes and flooded much of the land lying between The Hague and Utrecht, making it impossible to cross directly eastward from the one city to the other. Both Lucas and Colerus claim that Spinoza was welcomed into the French camp with great courtesy, although the prince himself had been called away on royal business some days before. "M. de Luxembourg, who received Spinoza in the Prince's absence, showed him a thousand devotions and assured him of the good will of His Highness."[70] Spinoza found himself in good company. Among the local savants who risked the enmity of their fellow Dutch citizens – who felt nothing but hatred for the French occupiers and, one would suspect, for their friends as well – and paid their respects to Condé by joining him on occasion for intellectual discourse were Professors Graevius and Van Velthuysen from the University of Utrecht. During his stay in Utrecht, Spinoza got to know both of these men, who were among his severest critics. Despite Van Velthuysen's rather harsh judgment of the *Theological-Political Treatise* two and a half years earlier, he (at heart, a liberal) and Spinoza apparently ironed out their differences – or, better, agreed to disagree. The tone of their correspondence a few years later is significantly more cordial than it had been in 1671, with Spinoza acknowledging the Cartesian professor's "devotion to the pursuit of truth and . . . exceptional sincerity of mind."[71]

It seems pretty clear, however, that Spinoza never got to meet the prince of Condé himself. Condé left the city on July 15, and it is practically certain that Spinoza did not arrive before July 18.[72] Condé had left word that Spinoza should wait for his return. Bayle – alone among Spinoza's early biographers – claims that the two did eventually meet and converse a number of times, with Condé even trying (with the help of an offer of a hefty pension) to persuade Spinoza to return with him to France and join his court. Spinoza, of course, declined, saying that "all of His Highness's power would not be able to protect him against the bigotry of the Court, in so far as his name is already hated on account of the *Theological-Political Treatise*."[73] Bayle relies on the testimony of Henriquez Morales ("Henri Morelli"), an Egyptian Jewish doctor who knew Spinoza well and who claimed to have talked with Spinoza about the trip,[74] and that of a Monsieur Boussière, Condé's surgeon who was present with the army at Utrecht and insisted that he saw Spinoza enter the prince's rooms.[75] Colerus, on the other hand, says that Van der Spyck and his wife assured him that Spinoza never got to see Condé at all.[76] Lucas agrees, noting that some weeks after Spinoza's arrival the prince sent a message that he would not be returning to Utrecht for quite a while. Soon thereafter, and at the end of what must have been a relatively pleasant stay – probably longer than anticipated but no doubt laced with intellectual and other entertainment and interesting new acquaintances – Spinoza took his leave, to the great disappointment of his hosts.

Not surprisingly, when Spinoza got back to The Hague he received something less than a hero's welcome. Once again, his landlord had to take care both for his lodger's safety and for the protection of his house. "Having come back from Utrecht, he had the rabble incensed against him," Van der Spyck told Colerus.

They considered him a spy, and mumbled that he corresponded with the French over state affairs. Because his landlord became worried about this, and was afraid that they would break into his house to look for Spinoza, Spinoza calmed him with these words: "Do not be afraid! I am not guilty, and there are many people at the highest office who know well why I have gone to Utrecht. As soon as they make any noise at your door, I will go out to the people, even if they should deal with me as they did with the good De Witt brothers. I am an upright Republican, and the welfare of the state is my goal."[77]

Spinoza's claim that there were individuals in high places who knew why he had made the trip to the enemy's camp has given rise to the speculation that perhaps he was on an official diplomatic mission, possibly carrying some overture to peace negotiations from the government at The Hague to the head of the French army. There can be no question that Spinoza and Stouppe – and, if they met, Condé – talked a great deal about the war between their nations, and may even have come up with various suggestions about how to end it expeditiously. But the suggestion that Spinoza would have been employed by those in power at The Hague seems highly improbable. These were the days of the Orangists, not the De Witts. Even if the Stadholder or the States were inclined to communicate with the French, they would not have entrusted so sensitive a task to someone they perceived as an enemy of the republic.

Spinoza was not, of course, an enemy of the republic. All of his writing is directed toward the "happiness" and well-being, not just of his fellow human beings, but also of the political society they composed and upon which they depended. There is, thus, a bit of pathos in his short speech to his landlord. What he probably felt most of all when thinking about an unreasonable crowd gathering in front of the house on the Paviljoensgracht was not fear of suffering the same violent end as De Witt, but fear for the future of the republic and, more important, for the principles for which it once stood.

12

"A free man thinks
least of all of death"

W ITH PETER BALLING, Simon de Vries, and Adriaan Koerbagh gone,
Spinoza's circle of friends in Amsterdam had, by the early 1670s,
lost a significant core of its membership – even, for a time, its critical mass.
Van den Enden had departed, too – off to Paris, where he was executed in
1674 for his role in the plot against Louis XIV. But there were still Bouwmeester and Meyer, who probably made the trip to The Hague to see Spinoza from time to time. Rieuwertsz was still around as well, although he
was probably fairly busy with new publishing projects and with trying to
keep his bookshop functioning under the vigilant eyes of the city authorities. And by 1674, these older acquaintances were joined by a second generation of eager Spinozists and fellow travelers, including Schuller, Pieter
van Gent – a friend of Schuller's from their days of medical studies at Leiden – and, for a few months, Tschirnhaus. Thus, there probably continued
to be an active group of Spinoza's "disciples" in Amsterdam throughout
the 1670s, most likely meeting at Rieuwertsz's shop and carrying on the
work of the circle from the late 1650s.

And then there was Jarig Jellesz. Ever faithful, he was, in the years
1673–4, slowly moving from his study of Descartes and of the *Ethics* to the
Theological-Political Treatise, which he must have been reading in Glazemaker's unpublished Dutch translation. In a letter now lost, he asked Spinoza how his own theory of natural right and his account of the state differed from those of Hobbes. He probably also expressed his concern over
the recent attacks against his friend's book.[1] Jellesz does not seem to have
been an active participant in Meyer's literary club, if he ever attended at all,
and in his philosophical studies he appears to have been working mainly
on his own. Jellesz may, anyway, have always fit in only awkwardly with Spinoza's other acquaintances. He was probably the least formally educated
member of the group. He never went to a university, and did not even
know Latin. He might also have been slightly put off by the freethinking

tendencies of Meyer and others. Jellesz was a person of a deep and simple faith. In the spring of 1673, he sent Spinoza a copy of his "Confession of the Universal and Christian Faith," in which he attempted to lay out only the most basic tenets required for "a universal confession acceptable to all Christians." The work is the expression of a rationalist, nonconfessional, unitarian faith. It takes its inspiration from Luther and Erasmus as well as from Descartes and Spinoza. Beatitude and grace are identified with "a purely rational knowledge" of eternal truths. Jellesz dismisses all particular ceremonial rites as unecessary for – in fact, as possible hindrances to – piety and true religion. Understanding and moral behavior alone are essential for salvation. This is the real teaching of Jesus, a human being who, more than anyone else, was informed by the Holy Spirit, that is, by divine wisdom and reason.[2] Spinoza, though he reportedly "gave [Jellesz] no praise nor many indications of approval," wrote to him that "it is with pleasure that I have read through the writings that you sent me, and found them such that I can suggest no alterations in them."[3]

Spinoza's relationship with Jellesz, harking back to their days as merchants on the Amsterdam Exchange, was older than any other current ties in his life. Jellesz's continuing friendship, and perhaps his financial support, must have been of great importance to Spinoza during these difficult days. For despite his even temper and the dispassion with which he received the vitriolic attacks on the *Theological-Political Treatise*, Spinoza cannot have been totally unmoved by the news in December 1673 that the representatives to the States of Holland and West Friesland were calling for strong measures to be taken against "profane" books published under false titles. What the deputies had immediately in mind, and that occasioned their new crusade, was not so much the *Treatise* per se – which, though its cover page carried a false publisher and place of publication nevertheless gave the correct title – as the appearance earlier that year of an edition of the *Treatise* bound together with Meyer's *Philosophy, Interpreter of Holy Scripture* in a single volume and printed in three versions under different false titles: the *Totius medicinae idea nova*, by Franciscus de le Boe Sylvius, a deceased professor of medicine at the University of Leiden; the *Operum historicorum collectio*, by Daniel Heinsius, a humanist who had died eighteen years earlier; and the *Opera chiurgica omnia*, a collection of medical treatises by Francisco Henriquez de Villacorta. The states were particularly incensed by the "fraudulence" involved in such undertakings. They asked the Court of Holland to put an end to such pestilential writings once and for all and to issue an order to the effect that Spinoza's and Meyer's books should be suppressed and confiscated throughout the entire province.

The court found sufficient cause for action. Consequently, on July 19, 1674, the *Tractatus Theologico-Politicus* – along with other "Socinian and blasphemous books" such as Hobbes's *Leviathan* and Meyer's *Philosophia Sacrae Scripturae Interpres* – was officially banned by the secular authorities of the province of Holland.[4] All of these books were found "not only to reverse the teaching of the true, Christian Reformed religion, but also to overflow with blasphemies against God, his attributes and his admirable Trinity, against the divinity of Jesus Christ and his true blessedness." It was judged that the works undermined both the fundamental principles of Christianity and the authority of Holy Scripture. Therefore, the court decreed, it would henceforth be forbidden to print, sell, or disseminate the books in question, and violators would be punished accordingly.[5]

The spirit of De Witt, it was clear, was dead. Both the States of Holland and the Hof, not to mention the town councils, were now in the hands of noticeably unsympathetic regents. Spinoza could no longer count on either lax enforcement of provincial decrees or protection by local officials. At the same time, the leaders of the Reformed Church and the philosophers and theologians of the universities, particularly the Cartesians, kept up their pressure. Between the summer of 1673 and the fall of 1674 alone – from just before the provincial States made their finding to just after the court issued its writ – the *Treatise* was condemned by three provincial synods (of North Holland, South Holland, and Utrecht) and the consistory of one major city (Leiden; the consistory of Amsterdam had already registered its denunciation, and The Hague would soon follow in 1675).

Spinoza must have felt embattled on all sides. Still, he never wavered from his policy of not engaging in direct responses to these attacks. He had no taste whatsoever for disputation and public feuding. As he told Oldenburg years before, in explaining why, in anticipation of the response of theologians, he was not publishing the *Short Treatise*, "I absolutely dread quarrels."[6] By 1675, his attitude toward his critics had become even more contemptuous: "I have never had in mind to rebut any of my adversaries, so undeserving of reply did they all seem to me."[7]

Besides, he was too busy with his own work to engage in time-consuming written polemics with his numerous critics. At some point in the early 1670s, Spinoza returned to the *Ethics*. He concentrated especially on reworking material from what had once been an extensive Part Three but that he was now organizing into Parts Four and Five. This included much of his moral psychology, his account of human bondage to the passions, and the picture of the "free human being." It is likely that much of what Spinoza has to say in the *Ethics* of a political and social nature and on religion and true freedom underwent significant revision after 1670. The latter parts of the manuscript that he picked up after a hiatus of at least six years now had to be recast in the light, not just of his reading in the intervening period – especially Hobbes's *Leviathan* – but, more importantly, of the theory of the state and civil society that he himself set forth in the *Theological-Political Treatise*. We do not know exactly how far Spinoza got before he put the *Ethics* aside in 1665, although it was clearly a pretty substantial draft; consequently, we do not know how much of the completed work stems only from the 1670s. Given what appears to be a general continuity in his metaphysical, moral, and political thinking between the early 1660s and early 1670s, however, it is unlikely that the additions or changes made to the *Ethics* after his move to The Hague represented any significant revision of his basic doctrines. The political implications of his theory of the human being and human motivation may have become clearer and more elaborate after his completion of the *Treatise*, but they could never have been very far from his mind even when he began the geometrical presentation of his system around 1661.

Spinoza continued to work on other projects as well. There is a possibility that, as late as the winter of 1674–5, he was still thinking of finishing the *Treatise on the Emendation of the Intellect*. He may also have been considering composing a short work on physics. Both of these plans are cryptically suggested in an exchange with Tschirnhaus in January 1675. Dr. Schuller had given Tschirnhaus a copy of the manuscript of the methodological treatise while Tschirnhaus was still in Amsterdam,[8] and Tschirnhaus later asked Spinoza when he was planning on publishing the work. Spinoza noted tersely in reply that "as for your questions concerning motion, and those which concern method, since my views on these are not yet written out in due order, I reserve them for another occasion."[9] He also envisioned a series of notes to be added to the text of the *Theological-Political Treatise* in a subsequent edition that would, "if possible, remove prejudices that have been conceived against it." He thus asked Oldenburg, in the fall of 1675, to point out those passages which, in his opinion, "have proved a stumbling block to learned men."[10] He hoped to include, in addition, the critical remarks of Van Velthuysen and his response to them. Now that he had met the professor from Utrecht, he thought more highly of him. He wrote to Van Velthuysen to ask for his permission, adding the stipulation that if he found any of Spinoza's remarks in his reply too harsh, he should be free to correct or delete them.[11]

It was probably around this time, if not a few years earlier, that Spinoza undertook to compose a Hebrew grammar.[12] In the *Theological-Political Treatise*, he insists on the necessity of a knowledge of Hebrew for interpreting Scripture properly. "Since all the writers of both the Old and New Testaments were Hebrews, a study of the Hebrew language must undoubtedly be a prime requisite not only for an understanding of the books of the Old Testament, which were written in that language, but also for the New Testament. For although the latter books were published in other languages, their idiom is Hebraic."[13] But the people who actually *used* Hebrew on an everyday basis, he complains, have left us no information concerning the basic principles of their language. There were, of course, numerous Hebrew grammars, old and new, available in the seventeenth century, including those written by Rabbi Mortera (1642) and Rabbi Menasseh ben Israel (1647). Spinoza himself owned several books on the Hebrew language, including Buxtorf's 1629 *Thesaurus grammaticus linguae Sanctae Hebraeae*. But in addition to the irremediable problems that will necessarily plague any latter-day account of Hebrew – "Nearly all the words for fruits, birds, fishes have perished with the passage of time, together with numerous other words. . . . And the idiom and modes of speech peculiar to the Hebrew nation have almost all been consigned to oblivion by the ravages of time" – there is a further problem in all previous grammars from which, Spinoza claims, his will not suffer. As the title to Buxtorf's work indicates, it is a grammar of Hebrew as a "sacred" language, as the language of Holy Scripture. Spinoza proposes, on the other hand, to write a grammar of Hebrew as a *natural* language, which, he argues, it surely is. "There are many who have written a grammar of Scripture, but no one has written a grammar of the Hebrew language."[14] Oddly, the only texts from which he works and draws examples are, in fact, the books of the Hebrew Bible. But his method is perfectly consistent with his account of Scripture. If the Bible is a work of human hands, composed over time in the natural way in which all books are produced, as he argues in the *Theological-Political Treatise*, then its language should be understood not as the supernatural language of some transcendent being but as the lived language of a specific people. As Scripture is just another human text, so is Hebrew just another human tongue.

Thus, Spinoza's goal in the work published posthumously as the *Compendium of Hebrew Grammar*, and which was left uncompleted at the time of his death, is to provide a kind of secularization of Hebrew by recreating its rules and practices as a natural language and not as a "holy tongue." It is, he suggests, a work "for those who desire to speak Hebrew, and not just chant it."[15] He intended it primarily for the private use of his friends, at whose request he began writing it in the first place. Answering Spinoza's own call to interpret Scripture "from Scripture alone," as well as the demand of their Protestant upbringing to turn to "the Book" itself, they wanted him to provide them some kind of initiation into the rudiments of the language to help them in their study. Jellesz reveals that there were several manuscript copies of the work circulating among the Amsterdam group.[16] It may be that Spinoza was perfectly satisfied with this kind of distribution, never intending it to be published formally.

The *Compendium*, which Jellesz also claims was to have been presented in the "geometric manner" of the *Ethics*, was supposed to contain two parts. Part One, of which thirty-three chapters were completed, would present basic etymology, laying out the Hebrew alphabet and the principles governing Hebrew nouns, verbs, and other parts of speech. Here Spinoza could begin clearing up some of the more tractable problems confronting those who wish to study the Torah that he had pointed out in the *Theological-Political Treatise*, such as possible confusions arising from the similarities of some Hebrew letters and the difficulties attending vocalization, punctuation, and accentuation. Part Two, which he never began, was to present the rules of Hebrew syntax.[17]

In organizing his grammar, Spinoza relied, to some extent, on the works of other Hebraists, Jewish and Gentile. In addition to Buxtorf's text, he owned a sixteenth-century edition of the grammar written by Moses Kimchi, the great twelfth-century Bible commentator, as well as one by Eliyahu Levita. Still, the resulting treatise is a highly idiosyncratic work. Among its most striking peculiarities is Spinoza's compression of Hebrew grammar into the categories and structures of Latin. For example, Hebrew nouns are said to decline into six cases: nominative, genitive, dative, accusative, vocative, and ablative. Thus, the noun דָּבָר ("word," or "thing") appears, in Spinoza's account, in the dative case as לְדָבָר, which is really just the noun compounded with the preposition signifying "to."[18] Hebrew verbs are given various "conjugations" conforming to the standard Latin paradigms. Moreover, although the material is not presented *in more geometrico*,

Spinoza nevertheless offers a hyperrationalistic account of Hebrew as distilled from Scripture. He is concerned, above all, with showing how it is a thoroughly law-governed language. His penchant for reducing all constructions and variations to rules and for eliminating, as far as possible, all irregular forms leads him to hypothesize an eighth "conjugation" (one more than the usual seven verb forms), a passive form of the reflexive *hitpael*.[19] Perhaps Spinoza's most original, although untenable, contribution to the history of Semitic languages is his theory of the primacy of the noun. "All Hebrew words," he asserts, "have the force and properties of nouns."[20] On his account, all verbs, adjectives, and other elements derive from the substantive. This may, as some scholars have suggested, be simply the expression in linguistic theory of his basic metaphysical doctrines, in which "substance" is the foundational category.[21]

We have no indication of how helpful Spinoza's friends found his Hebrew grammar. It is not a work suitable for beginners. There are also noticeable errors in his lessons – the result, perhaps, of the fact that it had been nearly twenty-five years since Spinoza had worked regularly on Hebrew texts. And yet, by writing the *Compendium* for his Christian companions, Spinoza was unwittingly fulfilling the aims of Grotius when he argued in 1618 that Jews should be allowed to settle in the Netherlands: "Plainly God has desired them to live somewhere. Why, then, not here rather than elsewhere? . . . Besides, the scholars among them may be of some service to us by teaching us the Hebrew language."

ċ⁊

In the midst of these various projects, and with his health already causing him some concern, time and energy became more and more precious to Spinoza. As his fame increased, a greater part of his day was taken up with receiving visitors and responding to letters. For example, there are the inquiries made in the fall of 1674 by Hugo Boxel, onetime Pensionary of Gorinchem, as to whether Spinoza believed in ghosts. Boxel certainly did, on the basis of credible stories (ancient and modern) and on reasonable principles – although, he insisted, they are never female, as ghosts do not give birth.[22] Spinoza, out of respect for his correspondent, whom he may have met during his stay in Utrecht the year before, does not deny the existence of ghosts outright, but in the end claims that there is no evidence in its favor. The belief in such things, he suspects, is a product of imagination, not reason. When Boxel replies that Spinoza's prejudices may be preventing him from searching for the truth in this matter, Spinoza, now that he is pushed, comes right out and admits that ghost stories are all nonsense. "I confess that I was not a little amazed, not at the stories that are narrated, but at those who write them. I am surprised that men of ability and judgement [such as Pliny and Suetonius] should squander their gift of eloquence and misuse it to persuade us of such rubbish."[23] As for the claim that all ghosts are male, "those who have seen naked spirits have not cast their eyes on the genital parts; perhaps they were too afraid, or ignorant of the difference."

Boxel is nothing if not persistent. He takes issue with Spinoza's conception of God and of the necessity inherent in the universe, to which Spinoza had appealed in replying to Boxel's claim that a belief in the existence of ghosts and spirits does greater honor to God's glory, because such creatures would express God's image more than would corporeal beings. Spinoza, losing his patience, suggests that their exchange is not getting anywhere, and that perhaps it would be best to end the conversation. "When two people follow different first principles, the difficulty they experience in coming together and reaching agreement in a matter involving many other questions might be shown simply from this discussion of ours."[24] He believes that they disagree so much on fundamentals – such as God, necessity, and human nature – that they will never be able to resolve their differences on this issue of secondary importance. What is particularly bothersome to Spinoza is Boxel's adherence to the anthropomorphic conception of the God of popular imagination.

When you say that you do not see what sort of God I have if I deny in him the actions of seeing, hearing, attending, willing, etc. and that he possesses those faculties in an eminent degree, I suspect that you believe there is no greater perfection than can be explicated by the aforementioned attributes. I am not surprised, for I believe that a triangle, if it could speak, would likewise say that God is eminently triangular, and a circle that God's nature is eminently circular. In this way each would ascribe to God its own attributes, assuming itself to be like God and regarding all else as ill-formed.

So far as we know, Boxel never wrote to Spinoza again.

Spinoza engaged in a philosophically more fruitful discussion later that year when Tschirnhaus began his correspondence with him, with Schuller acting as go-between. While he was in Amsterdam in the fall of 1674, Tschirnhaus began a close study of the *Ethics*, most likely in the company of Schuller and others. He seems to have been concerned, above all, with the problem of freedom of the will. Writing to Spinoza in October, he observes that human freedom does not require the absence of all determination. We can, he claims, consider ourselves free just as long as, while determined in our actions by definite causes, we are not constrained or compelled by external circumstances in such a way that it would have been impossible to do otherwise than as we have done. Tschirnhaus suggests to Spinoza that everything that he says in the *Ethics* about the deterministic nature of the universe can be true without that implying that human beings are not free. Spinoza replied to Tschirnhaus – to whom he is still referring as "your" friend in his first letter to Schuller – that in a universe where "every single thing is necessarily determined by a determinate cause to exist and to act in a fixed and determinate way" freedom is, for human beings, nothing but an illusion. We are no different from any other created thing, such as a stone flung through the air.

Conceive, if you please, that while continuing in motion the stone thinks, and knows that it is endeavoring, as far as in it lies, to continue in motion. Now this stone, since it is conscious only of its endeavor and is not at all indifferent, will surely think it is completely free, and that it continues in motion for no other reason than that it so wishes. This, then, is that human freedom which all men boast of possessing, and which consists solely in this, that men are conscious of their desire and unaware of the causes by which they are determined. In the same way a baby thinks that it freely desires milk, an angry child revenge and a coward flight. Similarly, a drunken man believes that it is from his free decision that he says what he later, when sober, would wish to be left unsaid.[25]

Spinoza and Tschirnhaus seem to be genuinely impressed with each other. The philosophical nobleman is intrigued by Spinoza's system, even favorably inclined toward it, particularly "the method for seeking out truth," which he finds to be of "surpassing excellence." Their exchange led to a face-to-face meeting in late 1674, probably in Amsterdam. Even after his move first to London and later to Paris – where he secured an appointment as tutor to the son of Colbert, Louis XIV's finance minister – Tschirnhaus continued to work hard at understanding the finer details of the metaphysics of God and nature in the *Ethics* and presented Spinoza with a number of probing and intelligent questions. This was no doubt a pleasant change of pace for Spinoza from either the bothersome queries of a Blijenbergh or the prejudiced condemnation of a Van Velthuysen.

Years later, and despite a body of incriminating evidence, Tschirnhaus would never admit publicly to having been influenced by Spinoza, even going so far at one point as to deny that he had known him personally. In private lettters and conversations, however, he vigorously defended his friend against the charges of his critics. But the most he would openly concede, in an unguarded moment, was that "even if I were a follower of a philosopher who is Jewish, that is of no importance, since almost all the Scholastics were committed to Aristotle, who certainly was not a Christian."[26]

The following spring, Spinoza was also able to renew his correspondence with Oldenburg. By the 1670s, after a number of very difficult years, the secretary of the Royal Society was a changed man. As a result of the loss of his wife to the plague, his brief but damaging imprisonment, and burdensome financial difficulties while raising two children by himself, Oldenburg was now a humbler, quieter, perhaps more introspective and conservative man. During his travails he probably derived great comfort from his religious faith, a fairly conventional faith that had always run deep. It must have been with great alarm, then, that he read his friend's "treatise on Scripture," most likely just after its publication. Spinoza had sent him a copy of the *Theological-Political Treatise*,[27] and Oldenburg's initial response – expressed in a letter no longer extant but probably from 1670 – was decidedly negative. This may be the reason there are no letters between the two men until Oldenburg, regretting the harshness of his earlier dispatch, wrote again in June 1675: "At the time [of my first letter] some things seemed to me to tend to the endangerment of religion," he tells Spinoza. He admits, however, that his first judgment was "far too premature" and was based only on "the standard set by the common run of theologians and the accepted formulae of the Creeds (which seem to me far too influenced by partisan bias)." He assures Spinoza that he has now given the book "more proper attention" and is persuaded that, "so far from intending any harm to true religion and sound philosophy, on the contrary you are endeavoring to commend and establish the true purpose of the Christian religion, together with the divine sublimity and excellence of a fruitful philosophy."[28]

It is hard to assess Oldenburg's honesty here. He was certainly capable of great duplicity, a useful talent for the corresponding secretary of a scientific society whose job is to collect information. And he did not want to scare the ever-cautious Spinoza off from any future exchanges, particularly as he was desirous of obtaining a copy of the *Ethics*, which he and Tschirnhaus apparently discussed in London and the publication of which he believed to be imminent. In fact, his motives in his June letter are fairly transparent. Just after reassuring Spinoza of his confidence that the philosopher's aim was to "commend and establish" true Christianity and "fruitful" philosophy, he adds that

since I now believe this to be your set intention, I most earnestly beg you to be good enough to explain what you are now preparing and have in mind to this end, writing regularly to your old and sincere friend who wholeheartedly longs for a most successful outcome for such a divine undertaking. I promise on my sacred oath that I will divulge nothing of this to any mortal, if you enjoin silence on me, and that I will strive only for this, gradually to prepare the minds of good and wise men to embrace those truths which you will one day bring forth into the broader light of day, and to dispel the prejudices that have been conceived against your thoughts.

In a letter the following month, the careful Oldenburg – still smarting, perhaps, from his time in the Tower of London – quickly adds that if Spinoza *is* willing to send him some copies of the *Ethics* to distribute "among my various friends," he would appreciate a little discretion. "I would only ask this of you, that in due course they should be addressed to a certain Dutch merchant staying in London, who will then have them sent to me. There would be no need to mention the fact that the particular books have been forwarded to me. . . . "[29]

It is, of course, possible that there was nothing calculated or devious about Oldenburg's expression of regret for the 1670 letter. To the almost obsessively cordial Oldenburg, his first response to the *Theological-Political Treatise* must have seemed, in retrospect, a rather brusque way to reestablish contact after an extended hiatus in their correspondence, which had broken off before his imprisonment. Although five years is a long time to wait before making amends, he may have been thinking, in 1675, only of what was due to the feelings of someone whom he still considered a friend. Or he may have truly changed his mind about the *Treatise*, perhaps with a little coaxing from Tschirnhaus. Tschirnhaus reports, through Schuller, about what seemed to him to have been a productive rendezvous with Oldenburg in the spring of 1675, just before Oldenburg's letter to Spinoza: "[Tschirnhaus] relates that Mr. Boyle and Oldenburg had formed a very strange idea of your character. He has not only dispelled this, but has furthermore given them reasons that have induced them to return to a most worthy and favorable opinion of you, and also to hold in high esteem the *Tractatus Theologico-Politicus*."[30]

In light of his subsequent letters to Spinoza, however, Oldenburg's profession of approval in June 1675 cannot but seem less than sincere. For until the end of his life Oldenburg, despite what appears to be an unfeigned affection for Spinoza, clearly had misgivings about his friend's philosophical and theological views (as well as his piety). The likely explanation for Tschirnhaus's confidence in a real change of opinion in Oldenburg is that when Boyle and Oldenburg saw that Tschirnhaus was not only a friend of Spinoza's but also more favorably inclined toward his views than they were, they must have realized the need for tact.

Part of the problem is that Oldenburg just did not understand the essence of Spinoza's views.

I cannot but approve your purpose in signifying your willingness to elucidate and moderate those passages in the *Tractatus Theologico-Politicus* which have proved a stumbling-block to readers. I refer in particular to those which appear to treat in an ambiguous way of God and Nature, which many people consider you have confused with each other. In addition, many are of the opinion that you take away the authority and validity of miracles, which almost all Christians are convinced form the sole basis on which the certainty of Divine Revelation can rest. Furthermore, they say that you are concealing your opinion with regard to Jesus Christ, Redeemer of the World, sole Mediator for mankind, and of his Incarnation and Atonement, and they request you to disclose your attitude clearly on these three heads. If you do so, and in this matter satisfy reasonable and intelligent Christians, I think your position will be secure.[31]

Spinoza must have wondered, indeed, how closely Oldenburg had read the *Treatise*. In his reply in December 1675, he sets Oldenburg straight. Although he insists that those who think that he *identifies* God with the whole of nature ("by which they understand a kind of mass or corporeal matter") are mistaken, he concedes that "I entertain an opinion on God and Nature far different from that which modern Christians are wont to uphold." As for miracles, "I am on the contrary convinced that the certainty of divine revelation can be based solely on the wisdom of doctrine, and not on miracles, that is, on ignorance." Finally, he dispels any illusions that Oldenburg might be harboring about Spinoza's adherence to Christian dogmas, particularly regarding Jesus as the literal incarnation of God.[32] Oldenburg found the clarifications even more unsettling than his original uncertainty about the orthodoxy of Spinoza's opinions.

From his conversations with Tschirnhaus, Oldenburg also had some idea of the content of the "five-part Treatise." On this basis, he advised Spinoza, "out of your genuine affection for me, not to include in it anything that may seem in any way to undermine the practice of religious virtue. This I strongly urge because there is nothing our degenerate and wicked age looks for more eagerly than the kind of doctrines whose conclusions may appear to give encouragement to prevalent vices."[33] Although throughout this second phase of their correspondence Oldenburg refers to what "your readers" will find troublesome in the work, there can be no doubt that he was, for the most part, giving expression to his own objections. Spinoza was most anxious to know what he could possibly have said that not only would prove unacceptable to contentious theologians but also would threaten "the practice of religious virtue." Oldenburg revealed that he was concerned, above all, with Spinoza's necessitarianism and what he refers to as the "fatalism" inherent in his views.

> You appear to postulate a fatalistic necessity in all things and actions. If this is conceded and affirmed, they say, the sinews of all law, all virtue and religion are severed, and all rewards and punishments are pointless. They consider that whatever compels or brings necessity to bear, excuses; and they hold that no one will thus be without excuse in the sight of God. If we are driven by fate, and if all things, unrolled by its unrelenting hand, follow a fixed and inevitable course, they do not see what place there is for blame and punishment.[34]

Spinoza denied, in an immediate return letter, that his views absolved people of responsibility for their actions. Moral precepts are still "salutary" and binding upon us. For just because good necessarily and inevitably follows from virtue (and evil from vice), the practice of virtue "will not on that account be more or less desirable." He adds, further, that "men are without excuse before God for no other reason than that they are in God's hands as clay in the hands of the potter, who from the same lump makes vessels, some to honor and some to dishonor."[35] No one, he argues, can complain against God – that is, against the necessity of Nature – for having given him the character and nature he has received.

> Just as it would be absurd for a circle to complain that God has not given it the properties of a sphere, or a child suffering from kidney-stone that God has not given it a healthy body, it would be equally absurd for a person of feeble character to complain that God has denied him strength of spirit and true knowledge and love of God, and has given him so weak a nature that he cannot contain or

control his desires. In the case of each thing, it is only that which follows necessarily from its given cause that is within its competence. That it is not within the competence of every person that he should be of strong character, and that it is no more within our power to have a healthy body than to have a healthy mind, nobody can deny without flying in the face of both experience and reason.

Yes, Spinoza grants, all people who sin from the necessity of their nature are therefore excusable. And if one wishes to conclude from this that God cannot be angry with them, Spinoza agrees, but only because God is not a being subject to anger in the first place. But he is not willing to concede that it follows that all people are worthy of blessedness. "For people may be excusable, but nevertheless be without blessedness and afflicted in many ways. A horse is excusable for being a horse, and not a human; nevertheless, he needs must be a horse and not a human. He who goes mad from the bite of a dog is indeed to be excused; still, it is right that he should die of suffocation. Finally, he who cannot control his desires and keep them in check through fear of the law, although he also is to be excused for his weakness, nevertheless cannot enjoy tranquility of mind and the knowledge and love of God, but of necessity he is lost."[36] Oldenburg remained unconvinced by Spinoza's defense of views that he found rather harsh. "It seems very cruel that God should deliver people up to eternal, or at least dreadful temporary torments because of sins that they could in no way have avoided."[37]

Oldenburg's reading of the *Theological-Political Treatise* and the ensuing correspondence seem to have had a significant effect on his regard for Spinoza. He does not appear to have wavered in his warm personal feelings for him. But the truth is, Oldenburg never really did know Spinoza very well. They had met only once, fifteen years earlier, and it was for a very brief time. As the true nature of Spinoza's views slowly but finally emerged late in their correspondence, and as it dawned on him that they subscribed to radically different conceptions of "true piety and religion," Oldenburg probably did, as Tschirnhaus relayed to Spinoza, entertain "a very strange idea" of his character.

༉

By early July 1675, Spinoza was sufficiently satisfied with his progress on the *Ethics* to decide it was finally time to publish it. The manuscript of which he had been so protective as to allow only a select few to see it – and even then only on the condition that they not talk about it to others – was, it seemed, about to be made public. He made the trip to Amsterdam toward the end of the month and handed over his manuscript – or, more likely, a newly made fair copy – to Rieuwertsz. It is unclear whether Spinoza was planning to withold his name from the title page, as he had done with the *Theological-Political Treatise*. It is unlikely, however, that he any longer felt the need to take such precautions. Much had happened in the fifteen years since he began the work, particularly the five since the appearance of the *Treatise*, and there would be very little mystery about who its author was.

Also, there was very little to be gained by anonymous publication. Ever since France's forced withdrawal from Utrecht and other towns in the fall of 1674, the Stadholder had held a high place in the minds of the Dutch people. A member of the House of Orange was seen, once again, as having saved the Netherlands from disaster. William and his supporters came down hard on those republicans who resisted his consolidation of powers. Wheras liberal regents and much of the merchant class wanted to end the war quickly and get back to the political – and economic – status quo ante, the Orangists insisted on continuing the war until France was finally defeated and taught a lesson. Given their control of the States General, the States of Holland, and some important town councils, the Orangists inevitably had their way in most matters political and military. Their Voetian allies had a similar monopoly in the theological domain. Thus, the rules of the game had changed considerably since 1670, and there was no reason to think that simply by publishing a treatise anonymously one would be saved from a fate like that of the more brazen Koerbagh. Still, the game had to be played. Perhaps a sympathetic magistrate, when pressed by the *predikanten*, could use the opportunity to drag his feet and reply that everything was being done to find out who the author of such a pernicious work was.

While he was in town on business, Spinoza may have been drawn by curiosity to pay a visit to his old neighborhood. He could not have failed to have heard about the huge new synagogue that his former congregation was building at the end of the Breestraat. Construction had begun in 1671 under the direction of a Dutch architect, Elias Bouwman, and carpenter, Gillis van der Veen. (The use of Dutch builders was necessitated by the fact the Jews were still not allowed to join any of the city's guilds.) Although work was suspended for over two years after the first calamities of 1672, the structure was finished by the time Spinoza came to Amsterdam in the summer of 1675. He may have even had a mind to be present at the new building's consecration, which took place on August 5. It was a magnificent affair for a complex that had cost almost one hundred and sixty five thousand guilders. There were eight days of ceremonies and celebrations, and *le tout Amsterdam* was in attendance, including members of prominent regent families. One astonished spectator remarked that he could not believe he was witnessing the inauguration of a synagogue by a people technically still in exile.[38]

Spinoza stayed in Amsterdam for two weeks. But no sooner had he begun overseeing the production of his book than he abruptly stopped the printing. Back in The Hague by early September, he explained to Oldenburg the reasons for his decision:

While I was engaged in this business, a rumor became widespread that a certain book of mine about God was in the press, and that in it I endeavor to show that there is no God. This rumor found credence with many. So certain theologians, who may have started this rumor, seized the opportunity to complain of me before the Prince and the Magistrates. Moreover, the stupid Cartesians, to remove this suspicion from themselves because they are thought to be on my side, ceased not to denounce everywhere my opinions and my writings, and still continue to do so. Having gathered this from certain trustworthy men who also declared that the theologians were everywhere plotting against me, I decided to postpone the publication I had in hand until I should see how matters would turn out, intending to let you know what course I would then pursue. But the situation seems to worsen day by day, and I am not sure what to do about it.[39]

Part of what must have troubled Spinoza was the resolution against him issued by the consistory in his city of residence in June of that year. The Reformed leaders in The Hague had already condemned the *Theological-Political Treatise* five years earlier. But this time their attack seemed more personal and ominous. At an ordinary gathering of the assembly, the members of the consistory, whose discussion was entered into the record of their proceedings under the simple label "Spinoza," noted that, "as the consistory understands that the most blasphemous opinions of Spinoza are beginning to spread more and more, as much in this town as elsewhere, each of the members of this body is earnestly asked to see what they can learn about this, whether there is any other book by him that might happen to be in press, and what danger further lies here, in order to report back about it to this gathering and then, after a finding, to do something about it."[40] However, this did not deter Spinoza from leaving for Amsterdam a month later, with his plans to publish the *Ethics* intact.

More worrisome than the occasional broadside from the preachers, which he had come to expect, were, as his letter to Oldenburg indicates, the intimations that the secular authorities might, at the instigation of the theologians, be preparing to act once again. Spinoza was well served by his informants regarding the less-than-friendly murmurings about the content of his forthcoming book. From The Hague, Theodore Rijckius wrote to an influential friend on August 14 that "there is talk among us that the author of the *Tractatus Theologico-Politicus* is about to issue a book on God and the mind, one even more dangerous than the first. It will be the responsibility of you and those who, with you, are occupied with governing the Republic, to make sure that this book is not published. For it is incredible how much that man, who has striven to overthrow the principles of our most holy faith, has already harmed the Republic."[41] If the point of publishing the *Treatise* before the *Ethics* had been to prepare the way for his extreme metaphysical and moral views by first setting out the arguments for freedom of philosophizing, Spinoza badly miscalculated. In fact, given Spinoza's distaste for controversy, the *Treatise* may have made the publication of the *Ethics* impossible in his lifetime.

ஐ

September 1675 brought, among other correspondence, a long letter from Albert Burgh, the scion of a wealthy regent family and a friend (and perhaps a pupil) of Spinoza's from his days at Van den Enden's. Albert, now twenty-four years old and writing from Florence, began his letter innocently enough.

On leaving my country, I promised to write to you, should anything worthy of note occur during my journey. Since such an occasion has now arisen, and one of the greatest importance, I am discharging my debt. I have to tell you that, through God's infinite mercy, I have been brought back to the Catholic Church and have been made a member thereof.[42]

This in itself, though disheartening, was no news to Spinoza. He had heard the talk in Amsterdam and elsewhere about the conversion of the son of Conraad Burgh, Treasurer of the Republic of the Netherlands. And, indeed, there was much to talk about. It was, by all accounts, a spectacular and – in the eyes of one admirer – "edifying" conversion.[43] Burgh had been, according to this same witness, on the verge of moving "from heresy to atheism, on account of the friendship he had entered into with Spinoza, the most impious and most dangerous man of the century," had it not been for the fact that "God took pity on him" and led him abroad.[44] He came to realize his true vocation through a religious experience he had while sojourning in Padua and Venice. In Rome, under the tutelage of a Dominican friar from Amsterdam, he took a vow of poverty and adopted the dress and demeanor of a mendicant. Burgh was extreme in his austerity. He reportedly traveled long distances in an old habit and bare feet, no matter what the weather. His family, of course, was greatly distressed over this turn of events. They made every effort to bring him home and back into the Calvinist fold; they even cut off his allowance. It was all in vain, however, for Albert only scoffed at their lack of understanding and mocked their anguish.

Spinoza may at first have been pleased that an old acquaintance, however wayward, was making an effort to renew their friendship. His pleasure, however, would have quickly dissipated as he read further into the letter. For in it all of Albert's considerable energies are devoted to trying to persuade Spinoza to mend the errors of his ways, save his soul, and turn to Christ and "be born again."

The more I have admired you in the past for the penetration and acuity of your mind, the more do I now moan and lament for you. For although you are a man of outstanding talent, with a mind on which God has bestowed splendid gifts, a lover of truth and indeed a most eager one, yet you allow yourself to be entrapped and deceived by that most wretched and arrogant Prince of evil spirits. For what does all your philosophy amount to, except sheer illusion and chimera? Yet you entrust to it not only your peace of mind in this life, but the eternal salvation of your soul.

Burgh goes on to attack Spinoza's views in the *Theological-Political Treatise,* that "impious" and "diabolical" book, and warns him to "acknowledge your evil heresy, regain your senses after this distortion of your true nature, and be reconciled with the Church. . . . For if you do not believe in Christ, you are more wretched than I can say." Why, he asks Spinoza, "will you keep on raving, with your idle and futile chatter on the subject of the countless miracles and signs which, after Christ, his apostles and disciples and thereafter many thousands of saints have performed through the omnipotent power of God in witness to and confirmation of the truth of the Catholic faith?" There is still a way for Spinoza to save himself: "turn away from your sins, try to realize the deadly arrogance of your wretched insane way of reasoning." But he fears that pride will stand in the way of

Spinoza's seeing the light. "Think how little reason you have to scoff at the whole world except your wretched adorers, how foolishly proud and puffed up you have become by the thought of the superiority of your talent and by men's admiration of your vain – indeed utterly false and impious – doctrine."

The poor man seems truly to have lost his mind, and Spinoza tells him as much. He did not write back right away, perhaps being unsure about how best to deal with such a diatribe. But in December, at the personal request of Burgh's father, who asked Spinoza for help in bringing his son back to his senses, he finally wrote a reply.

I had intended to make no answer to your letter, being convinced that time rather than argument was what you needed so as to be restored to yourself and your family. . . . But some of my friends, who with me had formed great hopes for you from your excellent natural abilities, have strenuously urged me not to fail in the duties of a friend, and to reflect on what you lately were rather than what you now are.[45]

Spinoza was, as so many observed, a man of calm demeanor, gentle and slow to anger. But when pushed, especially in such a direct and personal manner, he was perfectly capable of responding in kind. Stung by the harsh words of an erstwhile friend, he holds back nothing in his response to Burgh's vitriol. He tries, of course, to appeal to what is left of Albert's reason and asks him to remember that tolerance which is due to differences in religious observance: "Unless perchance you have lost your memory together with your reason, you will not be able to deny that in every Church there are very many honorable men who worship God with justice and charity." The principles of the *Theological-Political Treatise* are evident in his plea to Albert to consider a more universalist and less sectarian conception of piety.

Whatever distinguishes the Roman Church from others is of no real significance, and consequently is constructed merely from superstition. For, as I have said with John, justice and charity are the one sure sign of the true catholic faith, the true fruits of the Holy Spirit, and wherever these are found, there Christ really is, and where they are not, Christ is not. For only by the Spirit of Christ can we be led to the love of justice and charity. Had you been willing to meditate aright on these things, you would not have ruined yourself nor would you have brought bitter grief on your kinsfolk who now sorrowfully bewail your plight.

But rather than sticking with gentle persuasion, as Albert's father might have preferred, Spinoza decides to play at the young man's game and returns fire for fire. "Do you bewail me, wretched man? And do you call my philosophy, which you have never beheld, a chimera? O youth deprived of understanding, who has bewitched you into believing that you eat, and hold in your intestines, that which is supreme and eternal." To Albert's question as to how he can be so sure that he has found the best philosophy of all, Spinoza replies:

I have far better right to put that question to you. For I do not presume that I have found the best philosophy, but I know that what I understand is the true one. If you ask me how I know this, I reply that I know it in the same way that you know that the three angles of a triangle are equal to two right angles. That this suffices no one will deny who has a sound brain and does not dream of unclean spirits who inspire us with false ideas as if they were true. . . . But you, who presume that you have at last found the best religion, or rather, the best men to whom you have pledged your credulity, how do you know that they are the best out of all those who have taught other religions, are teaching them now, or will teach them in the future? Have you examined all those religions, both ancient and modern, that are taught here and in India and throughout the whole world?

All such religions are, anyway, nothing but institutionalized superstition. This is especially true, Spinoza insists, of the Roman Catholic Church. "I would not believe that there is any better [church] arranged for deceiving the people and controlling people's minds if it were not for the organization of the Mahomedan Church, which far surpasses it. For ever since this superstition originated, no schisms have arisen in their Church." In the end, Burgh's letter only confirmed for Spinoza the account of the irrational psychological motives behind confessional religious beliefs that he sketched in both the *Treatise* and the *Ethics:* "You have become the slave of this Church not so much through love of God as fear of Hell, which is the single cause of superstition. . . . Do you take it for arrogance and pride that I resort to reason, and that I give my acceptance to this, the true word of God, which is in the mind and can never be distorted or corrupted?"

Spinoza closes with a final, unforgiving exhortation:

Away with this destructive superstition and acknowledge the faculty of reason that God gave you, and cultivate it, unless you would be counted among the beasts. . . . If you will pay attention to these things [the principles in the *Treatise*] and also examine the histories of the Church (of which I see that you are quite ignorant) so as to realize how false are many Papal traditions, and through what turn of events and with what craft the Pope of Rome finally gained supremacy over the Church six hundred years after the birth of Christ, I have no doubt that you will at last recover your senses. That this may come about is my sincere wish for you.

Albert was back in Amsterdam sometime late that year, and Spinoza may have addressed his letter to him at his parents' house (Burgh *père* may have asked for Spinoza's help only after his son's return). Burgh made the trip from Italy, of course, barefoot and in a torn smock, begging for alms along the way. He scandalized his family with his behavior, and before long his father and mother were at their wits' end. To their great dismay, Spinoza's counteroffensive had no visible effect. After a short stay, and no doubt unable to bear the luxurious surroundings of the family home, Albert Burgh joined the Franciscans and went off to live the monastic life in Rome.[46]

&

Throughout 1676, Spinoza carried on his philosophical exchanges with Tschirnhaus and Oldenburg and continued to work on notes for an amended edition of the *Theological-Political Treatise*. His health must have been slowly but noticeably deteriorating, however, his congenital respiratory problems having been exacerbated by years of inhaling the glass dust produced by his lense grinding. He probably did not travel very much during this year, although he continued to take time out from his work to entertain numerous visitors. Among the guests who dropped by the house on the Paviljoensgracht was Leibniz, the German philosopher-diplomat who had written to him five years earlier and with whom Tschirnhaus had become friendly in Paris. Leibniz was on his way back to Hanover to take up his duties as court librarian to Johan Frederick, duke of Brunswick. He left Paris in October and made a week-long stopover in London, where he spent some time with Oldenburg. He and Oldenburg must have had a lengthy and sympathetic discussion concerning Spinoza's *Theological-Political Treatise*. They shared some serious objections to Spinoza's views on God, miracles, and the necessity of things and probably compared notes on their respective readings of the work. They also mulled over Spinoza's recent letters to Oldenburg, which Leibniz copied out for his own use and later annotated with copious critical and interpretive remarks.[47]

On the boat to Holland, which was delayed on the Thames because of winds, Leibniz wrote some brief papers on language, physics, and mathematics. He also readied himself for his anticipated meetings with Spinoza, probably preparing a series of notes and questions for discussion. He certainly was planning to learn more about Spinoza's views on God, nature, and the human mind, topics that were of great interest to Leibniz at this period in his life. Tschirnhaus had given him a fairly good idea of the contents of the *Ethics*. It is even possible that, despite Spinoza's refusal to grant him permission to allow Leibniz to read his manuscript copy of the work, Tschirnhaus had let him see it anyway.[48]

When Leibniz arrived in the Netherlands, he went first to Amsterdam, where he stayed for about a month. He saw Hudde (now a burgemeester of the city), with whom he discussed various mathematical and political questions, and got to know some of Spinoza's friends, particularly Schuller, to whom Tschirnhaus would have provided an introduction. He also made a trip to Delft, where he met with Anton van Leeuwenhoek.

Spinoza had been favorably prepared for Leibniz's visit by approving reports from both Tschirnhaus and Schuller. According to Leibniz, he and Spinoza met a number of times, probably over the course of several weeks. Despite their differences in outlook and style – the worldly Leibniz was the court intellectual par excellence – the two had much in common and much to talk about. Their interests intersected in many areas. Their long discussions covered a variety of important philosophical, political, and scientific topics, including the problems inherent in Descartes's laws of motion and recent events in the Dutch Republic.[49] Leibniz took the opportunity to question Spinoza about his metaphysical views, and Spinoza – now more reassured about his guest's motives and intentions than he had been a year earlier – showed him the *Ethics*, or at least some parts of it.

I saw [Spinoza] while passing through Holland, and I spoke with him several times and at great length. He has a strange metaphysics, full of paradoxes. Among other things, he believes that the world and God are but a single substantial thing, that God is the substance of all things, and that creatures are only modes or accidents. But I noticed that some of his purported demonstrations, that he showed me, are not exactly right. It is not as easy as one thinks to provide true demonstrations in metaphysics.[50]

Before one of their interviews, Leibniz had written up some of his thoughts on the ontological proof of God's existence (that is, the proof according to which God – that is, a being containing all perfections – necessarily exists because "existence" is among the number of perfections). Spinoza had employed the ontological proof in Part One of the *Ethics*, and Leibniz sought to clarify the way in which all perfections can be compatible in one and the same subject. This, according to Leibniz, was at least one area where the two men were able to reach some level of agreement.[51]

The meetings with Leibniz, stimulating and pleasant as they were, distracted Spinoza from his work on what would be the last, albeit unfinished, project of his life. Jellesz says that the *Political Treatise* was composed "shortly before his death."[52] Spinoza must have begun it no later than mid-1676. Sometime in that year, he wrote to an unknown correspondent that he was "engaged in a certain matter which I believe to be more important, and which I think will be more to your liking, namely, in composing a Political Treatise, which I began some time ago at your suggestion." Spinoza further notes that, by the time of this letter, whose exact date is also unknown, he had already finished six chapters of the work.

The *Political Treatise* is, in some respects, a sequel to the *Theological-Political Treatise*. If the 1670 treatise establishes the basic foundations and most general principles of civil society, regardless of the form which sovereignty takes in the state (whether it be a monarchy, an aristocracy, or a democracy), the new work concerns more particularly how states of different constitutions can be made to function well. Spinoza also intended – an intention that remained unfulfilled – to show that, of all constitutions, the democratic one is to be preferred. No less than the *Theological-Political Treatise*, the composition of the *Political Treatise* is intimately related to the contemporary political scene in the Dutch Republic. Spinoza treats a number of universal political-philosophical themes with an immediate historical relevance, even urgency.

The *Political Treatise* is a very concrete work. Spinoza begins, in fact, by dismissing utopian schemes and idealistic hopes for a society of individuals leading the life of reason. "Those who persuade themselves that the multitude or people distracted by politics can ever be induced to live according to the bare dictate of reason must be dreaming of the golden age of the Poets, or some fable."[53] Any useful political science must start, instead, from a realistic assessment of human nature and its passions considered as natural, necessary phenomena – in other words, from the egoistic psychology of the *Ethics*. Only then can one deduce political principles that, in accordance with experience, will best serve as the foundation of a polity.

On applying my mind to politics, I have resolved to demonstrate by a certain and undoubted course of argument, to deduce from the very condition of human nature, not what is new and unheard of, but only such things as agree best with practice. And that I might investigate the subject matter of this science with the same freedom of spirit as we generally use in mathematics, I have labored carefully not to mock, lament or execrate, but to understand human actions; and to this end I have looked upon passions, such as love, hatred, anger, envy, ambition, pity, and the other disturbances of the mind, not as vices of human nature, but as properties, which belong to it just as heat, cold, storm, thunder and the like belong to the nature of the atmosphere, which phenomena, though inconvenient, are yet necessary, and have fixed causes, by means of which we endeavor to understand their nature.[54]

Sound political theory also requires a familiarity with history and with the variety of constitutions, successful and otherwise, that have actually been instituted in different times and places. Spinoza himself, in preparing this work, made a careful study of the constitutions of Genoa and Venice, two famous republics, and read up on different forms of government and their leaders – real and legendary – as related by ancient and modern writers.

In addition to a realistic understanding of human nature, particularly of human action and motivation, political philosophy requires an account of rights. For Spinoza, natural right is, once again, determined by the basic law of nature that proclaims that every thing essentially pursues its own preservation. In the case of beings endowed with appetite, this law means that every individual is led by desire to seek and obtain that which he perceives to be in his self-interest. Any person, therefore, has the *right* to do that which, by nature, he necessarily does, and his right extends as far as his power will allow him to go.

But human beings in a state of nature are quick to recognize that their natural rights are best secured by combining together and agreeing to live according to the general judgment of all as embodied in laws. Led by the passions of hope and fear, and desirous of defending their lives and properties from the violent assaults of others, "a multitude comes together and wishes to be guided, as it were, by one mind." Therefore, by common consent, they entrust the affairs of state to a sovereign power, which henceforth wields "dominion" over them as subjects. This sovereign is authorized to do what it can to preserve peace and establish the conditions for well-being, to "remove general fear and prevent general sufferings," and basically to express and enforce the will of the multitude by issuing laws that serve the interests of its subjects. Ideally, the sovereign will be guided by reason, not passion, to pursue effectively "that very end that sound reason teaches is to the interest of all people." The multitude will then recognize the identity of purpose between themselves and their sovereign. This will lead to a stable and prosperous commonwealth, one in which peace and security are grounded, not in fear alone, but also in a sense of civic virtue among its citizens.

Democracy is the best form of commonwealth. In a democracy, the citizens who make up the multitude reserve the sovereignty for themselves. Every member of the commonwealth has the right to vote in the body that makes the laws and to hold public office. Dominion is thus directly in the hands of all the people who are governed. This guarantees, to the highest practical degree, that the laws enacted by the sovereign will reflect the will of the people and serve their interests. Democracy, Spinoza noted in the *Theological-Political Treatise*, is "the most natural form of state." He died before he got very far into the chapters on democracy in the *Political Treatise*, but there is no reason to think that the mob's behavior in 1672 changed his mind. However, he also recognized that not every state will, in fact, be a democratic one, and that many states – because of their historical or political traditions or some other factors – would not be fit to make a transition to a democratic constitution. He believed, moreover, that a state should not consider lightly effecting a radical change in the basic structure of its established government, whatever it might be. For these reasons, the main question of the *Political Treatise* concerns, not how to actualize an ideal state per se, but rather how best in practice, and under realistic conditions, to institute a monarchical, an aristocratic, or a democratic constitution so that it comes as close as possible to serving the purposes for which government exists. Spinoza's aim is to show how each form of government can be perfected relative to its kind and optimized in terms of how well it functions as an effective sovereign.

The ideal monarchy, where political authority is conferred on one person, will not be an absolute one. The laws of the land must not be subject to the inconstant and potentially irrational will of one individual. "For kings are not gods, but human beings, who are often led captive by the Siren's song."[55] The monarch must be limited in his powers by a strong and independent council. This council, which needs to be a representative assembly embodying a cross-section of the entire population ("from every sort or class of citizens"), will be responsible for offering the king advice on what laws to issue and what courses of action to take. The king must always choose one of the options recommended by the council and, ideally, will select the one that received the support of the majority of the council, as that will be what is in the interest of the greater part of his subjects.

The duty of he who holds dominion is always to know its state and condition, to watch over the common welfare of all, and to execute whatever is to the interest of the majority of the subjects. . . . [But] a king cannot by himself know what will be in the interest of the dominion. . . . Therefore, the king's utmost right is but to choose one of the opinions offered by the council, not to decree anything or offer any opinion contrary to the mind of all the council at once.[56]

The ideal monarchy, in other words, is a constitutional monarchy; and the king must answer to the will of the people as expressed by their deputies. In this way, "every law will be an explicit will of the king, but not every will of the king will be a law."[57]

Spinoza's concern with perfecting the monarchical form of government was no idle speculation geared only for the likes of Spain, England, and France. There was, in fact, significant support within the Netherlands for making the Stadholder – technically, only a servant and officer of the States of the province(s) where he held office, although in some provinces he was also designated the "First Noble" – into a royal figure. After his victories in 1674, William III's stadholdership in the province of Holland was made perpetual and hereditary, while the States of Gelderland, in January 1675, wanted to grant the prince of Orange true sovereignty over the province, offering, in effect, to make him "duke of Gelderland." Dutch republicans were appalled. In the face of strong opposition by Amsterdam and other major cities, William declined the honor. This affair, in fact, signaled the beginning of the decline of the Stadholder's popularity; and by the time Spinoza wrote the *Political Treatise* the immediate threat of monarchy was greatly diminished.[58] But the passions that led to Gelderland's move remained. Spinoza was intent on ensuring that any steps away from a purely republican form of government and toward a monarchist one would be as benign as possible.

The aristocratic constitution sketched by Spinoza resembles, in many important respects, the type of system then in place throughout most of the Netherlands. And here, too, Spinoza was suggesting ways to ameliorate some of the weaknesses to which this kind of government is naturally prone – weaknesses that, to his mind, had been responsible for many of the republic's problems during the last decade. The aristocracy that Spinoza prescribes is a city run by three bodies: a legislative assembly, an executive board of "syndics," and a judicial court. All of the members of these are drawn from a patrician class. There is oversight between the organs of state and clear delineation among their respective prerogatives, but together they wield absolute authority in the commonwealth. "The multitude" has no

political power whatsoever. Thus commoners must rely on the wisdom
and virtue of the ruling class.

The largest and most important of the political bodies is the "supreme
council," which is responsible for making the laws and whose membership
consists in the patrician population at large. Spinoza argues that the key to
a successful aristocracy is a regent class large enough to ensure that there
will be a sufficient number of men (and he is clear that it is to be a patri-
archy) who "excel in knowledge and counsel," "first-rate men" who surpass all others in character, honesty, and wisdom. He recommends a ratio
of multitude to patricians of fifty to one. In a city with a population of two
hundred and fifty thousand, that would mean a regent class of five thousand, which in turn would guarantee an elite group of at least a hundred
lawmakers (with the assumption that only two or three out of every hundred men will be truly suited for the task of wise government), the minimum number necessary to enact wise laws for a city of that size. Members
are to be elected (or "coopted") into the ruling class by the sitting members themselves, with no requirements as to property, wealth, or family.

Spinoza believed that an ideal aristocratic state of the kind he sketched
would not suffer the problems the Dutch Republic did in the late 1660s
and early 1670s. Had the regent class in Amsterdam and Holland been
larger and entry less restricted, it could easily have acted more decisively
and opposed the pressure of the Orangists. De Witt, serving as the regent's
agent, would then have been able to persevere through his difficulties and
pursue the policies that he believed were in the republic's best interests.
There would not have been the wide distribution of power that stymied
the town councils and the provincial States. As things stood, however,
"those who actually held dominion were far too few to govern the multitude and suppress their powerful adversaries. Whence it has come to pass
that the latter have often been able to plot against them with impunity, and
at last to overthrow them." Spinoza firmly believed that one of the contributing causes to what he calls "the overthrow of the Dutch Republic"
in 1672 was "the fewness of its rulers."

Spinoza had another lesson in mind for his contemporaries when he
moved from considering the aristocratic government of an individual city-
state to that of a multicity polity. When there are several municipalities involved in a federation, each with its own patrician class – which was essentially the case in the Dutch Republic – political power must remain
decentralized, with each city governing itself. "The patricians of every

city, who, according to its size, should be more or fewer, have supreme right over their own city, and in that city's supreme council, they have supreme authority to fortify the city and enlarge its walls, to impose taxes, to pass and repeal laws, and, in general, to do everything which they judge necessary to their city's preservation and increase."[59] This kind of local autonomy was one of the central principles of De Witt's "True Freedom." Only affairs that are of common concern should be dealt with by a general senate, to which each city is to send representatives. The number of representatives allowed a city, moreover, is to be proportionate to its size and power. This will prevent the smaller cities from interfering with the policies that a majority have decided are in their common interest, something that Spinoza felt was a weakness in the provincial States and in the States General of the Netherlands. Every town that sent representatives to the States of Holland, whether it was a large city like Amsterdam or a small town like Purmerend, had one vote; and every province in the republic, no matter what its size or financial contribution to the generality budget, had one vote in the States General. This allowed the Orangists to counterbalance the power of States-party cities and De Witt's allies in the States of Holland.

If decentralization is consistently respected, and the regent class is sufficiently large and strong, with no ambiguities as to who has political power at what level, there will be no need for any dominant, quasi-monarchical position in the multicity aristocracy. Unfortunately, the Dutch never took these precautions when they formally excluded the Stadholder in the 1650s.

If anyone retorts that the dominion of the Dutch has not long endured without a count or someone to fill his place, let him have this reply: that the Dutch thought that to maintain their liberty it was enough to abandon their count, and to behead the body of their dominion, but never thought of remodeling it, and left its limbs just as they had been first constituted, so that the province of Holland has remained without a count, like a headless body, and the actual dominion has persisted without the name. And so it is no wonder that most of its subjects have not known with whom the authority of the dominion lay.[60]

There will, of course, always be the danger that people, moved by their irrational passions, will, in times of trouble, try to put themselves in the hands of a single individual. "When a dominion is in extreme difficulties, when all, as sometimes happens, are seized by a sort of panicky terror, they will, without regard to the future or the laws, approve only that which their actual fear suggests and turn towards the man who is renowned for his victories and set him free from the laws, and (establishing thereby the worst of precedents) they will allow him to continue in command, and entrust to his fidelity all affairs of state."[61] This is the first step in the degeneration from aristocracy to monarchy, and the reference to the Prince of Orange is unmistakable. But, Spinoza insisted, in the best of aristocratic or democratic commonwealths, with all ordered as it should be, this simply would not happen, for "no one could so distinguish himself by the report of his virtue as to turn towards himself the attention of all, but he must have many rivals favored by others."

Throughout Spinoza's discussion of the ideal monarchical and aristocratic constitutions, where his own utopian vision of a democratic state of free and rational human beings is compelled to give way to political, historical, and psychological realities, his most basic political and humanitarian principles still serve as the fundamental limitations upon the sovereign in any kind of state whatsoever. Whether the commonwealth is a constitutional monarchy or an aristocracy or even a democracy, liberty (understood as freedom of thought, speech, and religion) and toleration are absolutely non-negotiable. Any ideal commonwealth of any kind will preserve and maximize those liberties which are consistent with the security and well-being of the state. Moreover, the deliberations and mechanisms of power will be open. All Spinoza's ideal constitutions have provisions against secrecy in government, which he sees as the sure route to the ruin of a state.

Spinoza was among the most enlightened and liberal thinkers of his age; he was not, however, free from all its prejudices. It is unfortunate that the very last words we have by him, at the end of the extant chapters of the *Political Treatise*, are a short digression, in the opening sections on democracy, on the natural unsuitability of women to hold political power. To the question of whether "women are under men's authority by nature or institution?" Spinoza answers with an unequivocal "by nature." Women are to be excluded from government, he argues, because of their natural weakness. "One may," he concludes, "assert with perfect propriety that women have not by nature equal right with men, and that thus it cannot be that both sexes should rule alike, much less that men should be ruled by women."[62] It is odd that he did not see, not only that nothing in his philosophy necessarily leads to these conclusions, but also that, in fact, all of his principles – particularly those which imply that all human beings are equally endowed with intellect and equally capable of rational autonomy – argue against it.[63]

꒔

Spinoza was obviously not well in the winter of 1676–7. He probably allowed himself to be bled a couple of times, as this had seemed to provide some relief in the past. Given the nature of his illness, he would have been coughing frequently, and must have been paler, thinner, and weaker than usual. Still, Van der Spyck and his family told Colerus that they had "no idea that he was so near his end, even a little while before he died, and they had not the least thought of it."[64] Spinoza, stoic by nature, probably suffered his infirmity with much reserve and little fuss. Always trying to be as faithful as possible to his philosophical principles in his own life, he was not given to pondering his mortality. This was an activity, rather, for the superstitious multitude who, moved by hope and fear, worry about what is to come in some alleged hereafter. As he proclaims in the *Ethics,* "a free man thinks least of all of death, and his wisdom is a meditation on life, not on death."[65]

In fact, Spinoza himself may have been unprepared for the quickness of his decline, as Schuller suggested on the day after his burial: "It seems that death's unexpected debilitation took him by surprise, since he passed away from us without a testament indicating his last will."[66] This is not entirely true. There was no written will, but Spinoza did at least tell Van der Spyck that, immediately after his death, his writing desk, which contained his letters and papers (including the *Ethics*), should be sent to Rieuwertsz in Amsterdam.[67] But if Colerus's report about the final day is to be trusted – and presumably he heard it all directly from the landlord and his family, although he was writing nearly thirty years later – Spinoza, although aware of the gravity of his illness, had no idea that he would not last the afternoon.

When the landlord came home [from church] at around four o'clock [on the day before], Spinoza came downstairs from his room, smoked a pipe of tobacco and spoke with him for a long time, particularly about the sermon that was preached that afternoon. He went to bed soon afterwards in the forechamber, which was his to use and in which he slept. On Sunday morning, before church, he came downstairs again, speaking with his landlord and his wife. He had sent for a certain doctor L.M. from Amsterdam, who ordered them to buy an old cock and to cook it up that morning, so that Spinoza might, that afternoon, have some broth, which he did. And when the landlord returned with his wife, he ate it with a good appetite. In the afternoon, the landlord's family went back to church, and Dr. L.M. stayed with him alone. But when they came back from church, they heard that Spinoza had died at around three o'clock, in the presence of the physician, who just that evening returned to Amsterdam by nightboat, not even seeing to the care of the deceased. But he made off with some money that Spinoza had left lying on the table, along with some ducats and a few gold pieces, and a knife with a silver handle.[68]

Spinoza died quietly on Sunday, February 21. The doctor who was by his side when he passed away was, to all appearances, his old friend Lodewijk Meyer, although it is possible that the "doctor from Amsterdam" was, in fact, Schuller. Schuller later told Tschirnhaus that he was present on the day Spinoza died and claimed to Leibniz that he had searched through Spinoza's things "thoroughly, one by one, before and after his death."[69] Whichever physician it was, the disappearance of the money and the silverware is more likely explained as a case of memento collecting rather than theft.[70]

Van der Spyck made the arrangements for Spinoza's burial, which took place four days later. According to Colerus, "many illustrious people" followed the body to the cemetery at the New Church. Several of the mourners must have come from Amsterdam, and there were enough altogether to fill up six coaches following behind the wagon carrying the coffin. Afterward, Van der Spyck entertained them and his neighbors with some wine in his home.

Colerus does not provide any names of those who were present, and one wonders whether Spinoza's sole surviving relatives in the Netherlands, Rebecca and their nephew, Daniel de Casseres (who was also Rebecca's stepson), were among the mourners at the cemetery on February 25. What is certain is that Rebecca had not completely lost interest in her apostate brother, or at least in his possessions. On March 2, having declared herself and Daniel as Spinoza's sole legitimate heirs, she authorized Van der Spyck to draw up an inventory of her brother's goods.[71] There was, however, the problem of a number of outstanding debts owed by Spinoza. First, Johan Schröder the apothecary was due sixteen guilders for some medicine he had provided during Spinoza's illness; then there was the barber, Abraham Kervel, who wanted one guilder and eighteen stuivers for having shaved him several times over the last three months. Others came forward with unpaid bills, while Van der Spyck was owed some money for Spinoza's room, board, and burial. Confronted with such an encumbered estate, Rebecca quickly had second thoughts about pursuing her claim too vigorously. She suspected that the proceeds from the sale of her brother's meager goods might not be enough to cover all these debts. She did not want to start paying the creditors out of her own pocket, at least not without some assurance that she would be able to recoup her losses from the money brought in by the estate. Consequently, on May 30, the same day Van der Spyck authorized an agent in Amsterdam to collect what was owed him from Rebecca and Daniel as Spinoza's heirs,[72] they submitted a petition to the high court in The Hague for a conditional suspension of their rights and obligations as Spinoza's heirs.

Rebecca Espinosa and Daniel Carceris [*sic*], son of Miriam Espinosa, begotten by Samuel de Carceris, living in Amsterdam, respectfully bring to your notice that the goods left by Baruch Espinosa, brother and uncle of the supplicants who died in February of the year 1677, have fallen to the supplicants. Fearing that the estate of the said Baruch Espinosa may be encumbered by many debts, to such an extent that the simple acceptance of it may be detrimental and harmful to the supplicants, the supplicants do not think it wise to accept the said estate unless under benefit of inventory; therefore they, the supplicants, are compelled to turn to Your Lordships; requesting Your Lordships respectfully for letters of benefit of inventory with instructions to the court of The Hague, with the clause of indemnity insofar as necessary.[73]

Van der Spyck, meanwhile, had been authorized to auction off Spinoza's clothes, furniture, and books to pay some of the creditors and to recover his own expenses. The landlord held the auction in November. It was well attended and generated enough income to take care of the debts.[74] Van der Spyck himself was reimbursed for the funeral costs and Spinoza's rent by "that friend in Schiedam,"[75] almost certainly Simon de Vries's brother-in-law, Alewijn Gijsen. Colerus reports that Rebecca, seeing that nothing was left over, finally renounced her claims on Spinoza's estate.[76]

Even before the inventory, Van der Spyck had sent the writing desk and its contents to Amsterdam. Soon after receiving the manuscripts of the *Ethics*, the *Treatise on the Emendation of the Intellect*, the *Political Treatise*, the *Hebrew Grammar*, and a pile of letters, Spinoza's friends went to work preparing them for publication.[77] By the end of the year, there were Latin and Dutch editions of Spinoza's "posthumous works."[78] For Rieuwertsz's safety, the title pages contained neither the publisher's name nor the place of publication. The author, however, was now well beyond the reach of the authorities.

A Note on Sources

Spinoza's Works

Spinoza's *Opera Postuma* and the *Nagelate Schriften* were published in 1677.
They contain the *Ethica*, the *Tractatus Politicus*, the *Tractatus de intellectus
emendatione*, the *Compendium Grammatices Linguae Hebreae* (in the Latin
edition only), and seventy-five letters; the *Renati Des Cartes Principiorum
Philosophiae* and the *Tractatus Theologico-Politicus* had already been published, while the *Korte Verhandeling van God, de Mensch en deszelvs welstand*
was not recovered until the nineteenth century. In 1925, Carl Gebhardt
published the *Spinoza Opera* in four volumes (a fifth volume was added in
1987). To date, this is the standard critical edition of Spinoza's works, although in the near future it will be superseded by the edition currently
under production by the Groupe de Recherches Spinozistes. All references to Spinoza's writings in their original language are to the Gebhardt
edition, by volume number and page number (e.g., III/23). References to
the *Ethics* incorporate the relevant indications of Book, Proposition, Scholium, and Corollary; so IP15s1 is Book I, Proposition 15, scholium 1. References to English versions of the *Ethics*, the *Treatise on the Emendation of
the Intellect* (cited in the notes as *TIE*), *Descartes's Principles of Philosophy*
(cited in the notes as *PPC*), the *Short Treatise* (cited in the notes as *KV*)
and letters 1–28 refer to the translations by Edwin Curley, *The Collected
Works of Spinoza*, vol. 1 (Princeton, NJ: Princeton University Press, 1985;
cited in the endnotes as C), the now standard English edition of these writings. Volume 2 has not appeared yet. Consequently, all references to the
English version of the *Theological-Political Treatise* are to the translation
by Samuel Shirley (Leiden: Brill, 1989; cited as S), while all references to
the English version of the *Political Treatise* are to the translation by R. H. M.
Elwes (New York: Dover, 1951; cited as E). For letters 29–84, I use the translations by Samuel Shirley, *Spinoza: The Letters* (Indianapolis: Hackett

Publishing, 1995; cited as SL). Because most of Spinoza's letters are short and referencing them is relatively easy, I generally provide only the letter number (Ep.); for the longer letters, I also provide references both to the Gebhardt edition and the translations by Curley or Shirley.

Spinoza's Life

Besides Spinoza's correspondence, there are three absolutely indispensable sources for the documents concerning and surrounding his life. J. Freudenthal's *Die Lebensgeschichte Spinoza's* (Leipzig, 1899) contains the early biographical sketches by Lucas, Colerus, Bayle, Kortholt, and Monnikhoff, along with the reports and interviews by Stolle, Hallman, and others. It also contains a good many of the extant documents related to Spinoza's life: burial and marriage records, resolutions of the church and secular authorities, and a wealth of excerpts from letters and treatises. No biographer of Spinoza could function without it. Equally important, especially for Spinoza's family and early life, are the documents collected by A. M. Vaz Dias and W. G. Van der Tak in *Spinoza, mercator et autodidactus* (1932), published in an English version in *Studia Rosenthaliana* in 1982–3. Finally, there is K. O. Meinsma's *Spinoza et son cercle.* Meinsma's magisterial work (originally published in Dutch in 1896, then reissued in French with updated notes contributed by various scholars in 1983) is an extended biographical study of Spinoza and his milieu, but it is also a valuable compendium of excerpts from important documents. In trying to make sense of all of the information (and misinformation) contained in these various sources, I have found Hubbeling's collation, "Spinoza's Life: A Synopsis of the Sources and Some Documents," very helpful.

Notes

Preface

1. There is also K. O. Meinsma's *Spinoza en zijn kring*, first published in 1896, which was translated into French (as *Spinoza et son cercle*) and updated in 1983. And for a quick and illustrated overview, a reader with a knowledge of Dutch may want to look at books such as Theun de Vries's casual *Spinoza: Beeldenstormer en Wereldbouwer* (Spinoza: Iconoclast and worldbuilder).

1. Settlement

1. In his *The Origins of the Inquisition in Fifteenth Century Spain*, B. Netanyahu argues that in fact almost all conversos were full-fledged Christians and that Judaizers were few and far between.

2. Some of the best general accounts of the history of the Jews in medieval Spain and of the events leading up to the Expulsion are found in Yitzhak Baer, *A History of the Jews in Christian Spain;* Cecil Roth, *A History of the Marranos;* Jane Gerber, *The Jews of Spain;* and Béatrice Leroy, *Les Juifs dans l'Espagne chrétienne.*

3. Some reliable accounts (although not mutually consistent) are in J. S. da Silva Rosa, *Geschiedenis der Portugeesche Joden te Amsterdam;* J. d'Ancona, "Komst der Marranen in Noord-Nederland: De Portugese Gemeenten te Amsterdam tot de Vereniging," in H. Brugmans and A. Frank, eds., *Geschiedenis der Joden in Nederland;* S. W. Baron, *A Social and Religious History of the Jews*, vol. 15 (chap. 63: "Dutch Jerusalem"); Jozeph Michman, Hartog Beem, and Dan Michman, *PINKAS: Geschiedenis van de joodse gemeenschap in Nederland;* R. G. Fuks-Mansfield, *De Sefardim in Amsterdam tot 1795*; and Odette Vlessing, "Portugese Joden in de Gouden Eeuw."

4. The Nuñes story is first told by Daniel Levi de Barrios (1635–1701), poet-historian of the Portuguese Jewish community of the Netherlands, in his *Triumpho del govierno popular* (Amsterdam, ca. 1683–4). For an attempt to separate fact from fiction in de Barrios's history, see Wilhelmina Christina Pieterse, *Daniel Levi de Barrios als Geschiedschrijver van de Portugees-Israelietische Gemeente te Amsterdam in zijn "Triumpho del Govierno Popular."* The banns of the Nuñes wedding were published on November 28, 1598; see Amsterdam Municipal Archives, "Baptism, Marriage, and Burial Registers," no. 665, fol. 54. Recent scholars have discovered, however, that neither Maria nor her husband ever openly reverted to Judaism, and that in fact they eventually returned to Spain; see H. P. Salomon, "Myth or Anti-Myth: The

Oldest Account Concerning the Origin of Portuguese Judaism at Amsterdam";
and Robert Cohen, "*Memoria para os siglos futuros:* Myth and Memory on the Beginnings of the Amsterdam Sephardi Community."

5. This story was first told by Moses Halevi's grandson, Aaron's son, Uri ben Aaron Halevi, in his *Narraçao da vinda dos Judeos espanhoes a Amsterdam*, available in print as early as 1674. According to de Barrios, these events took place around 1595–7; according to Halevi, around 1603–4.

6. See H. P. Salomon, "Myth or Anti-Myth"; and Robert Cohen, "Memoria para os siglos futuros."

7. Amsterdam Municipal Archives, no. 5059, sub. 24–40 (H. Bontemantel collection), i.c. 34. See Arend H. Huussen, Jr., "The Legal Position of Sephardi Jews in Holland, circa 1600."

8. See Jonathan Israel, "Sephardic Immigration into the Dutch Republic": "The rise of Dutch Sephardic Jewry was based on its functions in international commerce. ... Sephardic immigrants were allowed to settle in those Dutch cities that accepted them, above all Amsterdam, Rotterdam, and Middelburg, essentially because they were regarded as economically useful" (45).

9. It has been suggested that most, in fact, were practicing Catholics; see Salomon, "Myth or Anti-Myth?" 302–3.

10. See Amsterdam Municipal Archives, Notarial Archives no. 76, fol. 3–4.

11. It is usually assumed that Moses Halevi played the role of spiritual leader to this early group (and later to the Beth Jacob congregation) and that he served as their first rabbi. But Odette Vlessing argues that there is no evidence to support this assumption, and in fact some evidence to the contrary; see her "New Light on the Earliest History of the Amsterdam Portuguese Jews."

12. See Huussen, "The Legal Position of Sephardi Jews in Holland, circa 1600."

13. Vlessing observes that the first real evidence that a group of Amsterdam Jews were observing Jewish law does not appear until 1610, in a notarial deed in which a number of Portuguese contract with some Dutch butchers to deliver animals for kosher slaughtering; see "New Light on the Earliest History of the Amsterdam Portuguese Jews," 47.

14. From 1607 until 1614, when the land in Ouderkerk was purchased, the Amsterdam Jews used as a burial ground a plot they acquired in Groet, outside Alkmaar.

15. The dates given for the founding of Beth Jacob vary between as early as 1600 and as late as 1608. Vlessing argues that there is reason to believe that Neve Shalom was earlier than Beth Jacob; see "New Light on the Earliest History of the Amsterdam Portuguese Jews."

16. Vlessing demonstrates that the first concrete evidence for the existence of Neve Shalom does not appear until 1612, while the first evidence of Beth Jacob's existence appears in 1614; see "Earliest History," 48–50.

17. See E. M. Koen, "Waar en voor wie werd de synagoge van 1612 gebouwed?" Koen suggests that the house was the same building that Neve Shalom erected in 1612 but was forbidden to use.

18. See Fuks-Mansfield, *De Sefardim in Amsterdam,* 53–55.

19. Quoted in Ruth E. Levine and Susan W. Morgenstein, *Jews in the Age of Rembrandt,* 5.

20. See his *Remonstratie nopend de ordre dije in de landen van Hollandt ende Westvries-land dijent gestelt op de Joden* .

21. See Huussen, "The Legal Position of Sephardi Jews in Holland, circa 1600," for a good general discussion of the steps toward recognition. See also Gérard Nahon, "Amsterdam, métropole occidentale des *Sefarades* au XVIIe siècle."

22. "Upon the request of the elders of the Jewish nation, residing within the United Provinces, as well as those in the Province of Holland, also of those in the city of Amsterdam presented to Their High Mightinesses [the Estates General] containing complaints about unjust and severe procedures applied to them for some time, by the King of Spain and his subjects with regard to their traffic and navigation as well as in other respects; the officials after deliberation do understand and declare that it should be understood and declared herewith that those of the aforementioned Jewish nation are truly subjects and residents of the United Netherlands, and that they also therefore must enjoy, possess, and profit by the conditions, rights, and advantages, provided by the Treaties of Peace and Navigation concluded with the aforementioned King of Spain. . . ." See H. J. Koenen, *Geschiedenis der Joden in Nederland*. Full emancipation, however, would not come until the next century.

23. Jonathan Israel has shown that Jewish–Dutch relations were also greatly affected by the attitude and behavior of the Spanish Crown, with whom the republic was at war until 1648; see "Spain and the Dutch Sephardim, 1609–1660."

24. See Leszek Kolakowski, *Chrétiens sans église*, chap. 2.

25. A leading Remonstrant polemicist, Uytenbogaert, claimed that the Gomarists wanted, like the pope, to place the church in charge of secular society.

26. For a good discussion of the Remonstrant crisis, see Pieter Geyl, *The Netherlands in the Seventeenth Century*, 1:38–63. Gary Schwartz demonstrates the importance of this crisis, and especially of Amsterdam's evolution into a pro-Remonstrant town, for understanding the career of Rembrandt; see *Rembrandt: His Life, His Paintings*.

27. Jozeph Michman suggests that in fact the Counter-Remonstrants were less hostile to the Jews than the Remonstrants; and that, from the perspective of the Jews, it was a good thing that the Remonstrants lost; see "Historiography of the Jews in the Netherlands."

28. Perhaps Amsterdam's warning to the Jews that they should abide closely by the Law of Moses was also an attempt to make sure that they resembled, as much as possible, the people of the "Old Testament."

29. See J. d'Ancona, "Komst der Marranen in Noord-Nederland," 261–2.

30. See Daniel M. Swetschinski, *The Portuguese-Jewish Merchants of Seventeenth Century Amsterdam*, 22–9.

31. I. S. Revah, "La Religion d'Uriel da Costa," 62.

32. See Yirmiyahu Yovel, *Spinoza and Other Heretics*, 1:19–28.

33. The Venetian Pardo was central in establishing the ritual norms of the early community; see Miriam Bodian, "Amsterdam, Venice, and the Marrano Diaspora in the Seventeenth Century," 48.

34. See d'Ancona, "Komst der Marranen," 228–39; Fuks-Mansfield, *De Sefardim in Amsterdam*, 61; M. Kayserling, "Un Conflit dans la communauté hispano-portugaise d'Amsterdam – Ses consequences."

35. Bodian, "Amsterdam, Venice, and the Marrano Diaspora," 53–7.
36. See A. M. Vaz Dias, "De scheiding in de oudste Amsterdamsche Portugeesche Gemeente Beth Jacob," 387–8.
37. A Portuguese version of the Venetian ruling is in the Amsterdam Municipal Archives, no. 334, fol. 2.
38. See I. S. Révah, "Le Premier Règlement imprimé de la 'Santa Companhia de dotar orfans e donzelas pobres.'"
39. See d'Ancona, "Komst der Marranen," 244ff.; Vlessing, "New Light on the Earliest History of the Amsterdam Portuguese Jews," 53–61.
40. There is a record of some German Jews buried in the Ouderkerk cemetery as early as 1616.
41. See Yosef Kaplan, "The Portuguese Community in Seventeenth Century Amsterdam and the Ashkenazi World"; A. M. Vaz Dias, "Nieuwe Bijdragen tot de Geschiedenis der Amsterdamsche Hoogduitsch-Joodsche Gemeente"; J Michman, Beem, and Michman, *PINCHAS: Geschiedenis van de joodse gemeenschap in Nederland*, chap. 3.
42. See Levine and Morgenstein, *Jews in the Age of Rembrandt*, 7.
43. J. G. van Dillen, "La Banque d'Amsterdam."
44. See Swetschinski, *Portuguese-Jewish Merchants*, 128.
45. See Vlessing, "Earliest History," 62–3.
46. Ibid.
47. See ibid., 54–6.
48. See Swetschinski, *Portuguese-Jewish Merchants*, 184–5; Vaz Dias and van der Tak, "The Firm of Bento y Gabriel de Spinoza," 180.
49. The most up-to-date studies of the economic status and activities of the Dutch Sephardim are Jonathan Israel, "The Economic Contribution of Dutch Sephardic Jewry to Holland's Golden Age, 1595–1713"; Daniel M. Swetschinski, "Kinship and Commerce: The Foundations of Portuguese Jewish Life in Seventeenth Century Holland"; and Odette Vlessing, "The Earliest History." See also Henry Méchoulan, *Amsterdam au temps de Spinoza: Argent et liberté;* and Herbert Bloom, *The Economic Activities of the Jews of Amsterdam in the Seventeenth and Eighteenth Centuries.*
50. The best studies of the residential demographics of Amsterdam's Jewish quarter in the seventeenth century are Vaz Dias, "Een verzoek om de Joden in Amsterdam een bepaalde woonplaats aan te wijzen," and Tirtsah Levie and Henk Zantkuyl, *Wonen in Amsterdamin de 17de en 17de eeuw*, chap. 7.
51. This raises the question of just how observant these Portuguese Jews were. For example, did they keep kosher all the time? Just in the home? At all? We do not really have an answer to this question, as Swetschinski notes (see *Portuguese-Jewish Merchants*, 437–8).

2. Abraham and Michael

1. Amsterdam Municipal Archives, notary registers for Jan Fransz. Bruyningh, register 76, fol. 3. This and the other relevant notarial records for the life of Abraham

de Spinoza can be found in Vaz Dias and Van der Tak, *Spinoza, Merchant and Autodidact*, chap. 2.

2. We know that the Isaac Espinoza who died in Rotterdam in 1627 lived, like Abraham, for a time in Nantes, because in the record book of Beth Chaim he is identified as "Isaac Espinoza, who came from Nantes to Rotterdam"; see Vaz Dias and Van der Tak, *Spinoza, Merchant and Autodidact*, 114.

3. See ibid., 126. The most prosperous members of the community were paying a 200th Penny Tax of fl. 100 or more.

4. Ibid., 119.

5. Ibid., 124.

6. Ibid., 120.

7. J. d'Ancona, "Komst der Marranen in Nord-Nederland," 233.

8. Vaz Dias and Van der Tak, *Spinoza, Merchant and Autodidact*, 114.

9. Ibid.

10. Isaac was obviously still in Portugal when Michael was born there in 1588 or 1589. Abraham was in Nantes by 1596. If Isaac and Abraham left at the same time, as seems likely, Michael would have been eight years old at the most.

11. There may have been a third child who died young. The Beth Chaim record book shows that "a grandchild of Abrah. de Espinoza" died on the twenty-ninth of December 1622. We do not know, however, if this is Abraham de Spinoza de Nantes or Abraham de Spinoza de Villa Lobos.

12. Vaz Dias and Van der Tak, *Spinoza, Merchant and Autodidact*, 131–2.

13. Ibid., 134.

14. Ibid., 135–6.

15. See Jonathan Israel, "The Changing Role of the Dutch Sephardim in International Trade, 1595–1715," for a comparison of Dutch Jewish economic fortunes before and after the Twelve Years' Truce. For the figures on the Amsterdam Exchange Bank, see p. 35.

16. Ibid., and "The Economic Contribution of Dutch Sephardic Jewry to Holland's Golden Age, 1595–1713."

17. Vaz Dias and Van der Tak, *Spinoza, Merchant and Autodidact*, 145.

18. Ibid., 139.

19. He is so identified in a notary deed of October 8, 1627: "Today, the eighth of October sixteen twenty-seven, appeared &c in the presence of &c Mendo Lopes, about 50 years old, Michiel Despinosa, about 38 years old and Jorge Fernandes Canero, about 31 years old, all of the Portuguese nation, living within the said city . . ." (Vaz Dias and Van der Tak, *Spinoza, Merchant and Autodidact*, 127). It is only from documents such as this that we have any evidence as to when Michael may have been born.

20. This is on the assumption that Isaac is Hanna's son – and hence Baruch's full brother – and not Rachel's, and that he was born *before* Baruch. It is not absolutely certain that he *was* Hanna's son. That he was older than Baruch is suggested by the fact that when their father enrolled them in the Ets Chaim society in 1637, he nonalphabetically put Isaac's name first, probably indicating that Isaac was the elder; see Vaz Dias and Van der Tak, *Spinoza, Merchant and Autodidact*, 157. Also,

the elder son would be named after the paternal grandfather, the younger son after the maternal grandfather.

21. See Swetschinski, *The Portuguese-Jewish Merchants of Amsterdam*, 694.
22. Or so argues one historian; see Levin, *Spinoza*, 39.
23. See Vaz Dias and Van der Tak, *Spinoza, Merchant and Autodidact*, 130–1.
24. All of this information on the ordinances enacted by the *deputados* and the Senhores Quinze from 1630 to 1639 is in d'Ancona, "Komst der Marranen in Noord-Nederland," 262–9.
25. Vaz Dias and Van der Tak, *Spinoza, Merchant and Autodidact*, 145.
26. Ibid.
27. Ibid., 132.

3. Bento/Baruch

1. Freudenthal, *Die Lebensgeschichte Spinoza's*, 3.
2. *Korte, dog waarachtige Levens-Beschryving van Benedictus de Spinosa, Uit Autentique Stukken en mondeling getuigenis van nog levende Personen, opgestelt,* in Freudenthal, *Die Lebensgeschichte Spinoza's,* 35. In the Dutch edition (probably a translation from a German original), Colerus gets the date of Spinoza's birth wrong, claiming he was born in December 1633. In the French edition this is corrected to November 1632. Colerus actually lived in the same house in The Hague where Spinoza briefly lived and claims to have had conversations about Spinoza with his landlord.
3. For a list of the paintings that Rembrandt made for the court of Frederik Hendrik, see Schwartz, *Rembrandt: His Life and Works*, 69.
4. Freudenthal, *Die Lebensgeschichte Spinoza's*, 3.
5. Bayle, *Dictionnaire historique et critique*, entry on "Spinoza," in Freudenthal, *Die Lebensgeschichte Spinoza's*, 29.
6. Freudenthal, 35–6.
7. See Levin, *Spinoza*.
8. See Vaz Dias and Van der Tak, *Spinoza, Merchant and Autodidact*, 139, 172–5.
9. Ibid., 171.
10. Freudenthal, *Die Lebensgeschichte Spinoza's*, 36.
11. See Vaz Dias and Van der Tak, *Spinoza, Merchant and Autodidact*, 179–83.
12. Emmanuel, *Precious Stones of the Jews of Curaçao*, 194.
13. Ibid., 193.
14. Jaap Meijer, on the other hand, claims that Gabriel was older than Baruch; see his *Encyclopedia Sephardica Neerlandica*, 2:51.
15. Vaz Dias and Van der Tak, *Spinoza, Merchant and Autodidact*, 188.
16. Ibid., 194.
17. See, for example, Sigmund Seeligmann's article in the *Maadblad Amstelodamum* of 1933, no. 2.
18. See Israel, *The Dutch Republic*, 516–31.
19. Ibid., 625.
20. Cited in Schama, *The Embarrassment of Riches*, 358.

21. In addition to Schama's illuminating discussion of the episode, see also N. W. Posthumus, "The Tulip Mania in Holland in the Years 1636 and 1637."

22. The documents in this dispute, along with an extensive and invaluable history of the events, are reprinted in Alexander Altmann, "Eternality of Punishment."

23. Ibid., 15.

24. Ibid., 19.

25. See Wiznitzer, "The Merger Agreement and the Regulations of Congregation 'Talmud Torah' of Amsterdam (1638–39)."

26. M. Fokkens, *Beschrijvinghe der Wijdtvermaarde koopstadt Amsterdam* (1622), quoted in Gans, *Memorboek*, 46.

27. The new regulations imposed by the *ma'amad* are reprinted in Gérard Nahon, "Amsterdam, Métropole occidentale des Sefarades au XVIIe siècle," 39–46.

28. Swetschinski, *The Portuguese-Jewish Merchants of Amsterdam*, 377.

29. Price, *Holland and the Dutch Republic in the Seventeenth Century*, 51–2.

30. Ibid., 38.

31. Freudenthal, *Die Lebensgeschichte Spinoza's*, 3.

32. In Sebastian Kortholt's preface to the book that his father, Christian Kortholt, wrote, *De tribus impostoribus magnis* (Hamburg, 1700); see Freudenthal, *Die Lebensgeschichte Spinoza's*, 26.

33. Vaz Dias and Van der Tak, *Spinoza, Merchant and Autodidact*, 157.

4. Talmud Torah

1. Vaz Dias and Van der Tak, *Spinoza, Merchant and Autodidact*, 150.

2. Marcus, *The Jew in the Medieval World*, 378.

3. See M. C. Paraira and J. S. da Silva Rosa, *Gedenkschrift*, for a history of the educational system of the Portuguese Jews in the seventeenth century.

4. Marcus, *The Jew in the Medieval World*, 379.

5. Ibid.

6. Roth "The Role of Spanish in the Marrano Diaspora," 115.

7. According to Bass's report, again somewhat later than Spinoza's attendance, in Marcus, *The Jew in the Medieval World*, 379.

8. Offenberg et al., *Spinoza*, 74.

9. Popkin, "Spinoza and Bible Scholarship," 384–5

10. Freudenthal, *Die Lebensgeschichte Spinoza's*, 4.

11. Ibid., 36.

12. Ibid., 20.

13. I. S. Revah, "Aux origines de la rupture spinozienne," 382. The family trees in Salomon's translation of Da Costa's *Examination of Pharisaic Traditions* show that Spinoza's mother was indeed related distantly to Da Costa's family.

14. Uriel da Costa, *Exemplar*, in Osier, *D'Uriel da Costa à Spinoza*, 139.

15. Ibid., 140.

16. Albiac, *La Synagogue vide*, pt. 2, chap. 1.

17. I. S. Revah, "La Religion d'Uriel da Costa." See also Yirmiyahu Yovel, *Spinoza and Other Heretics*, vol. 1, chap. 3.

18. Gebhardt, *Die Schriften des Uriel da Costa*, 59–62.

19. Ibid., 154–5.

20. Modena's text is found in Osier, *D'Uriel da Costa à Spinoza*, 253–92.

21. Albiac, *La Synagogue vide*, 282–3.

22. Da Costa, *Examination of the Pharisaic Traditions*, 316.

23. Osier, *D'Uriel da Costa à Spinoza*, 181–3.

24. *Exemplar*, in Osier, *D'Uriel da Costa à Spinoza*, 141.

25. H. P. Salomon, on the basis of the unique copy existing in the Royal Library in Copenhagen, has put together an edition of the *Examination*.

26. Albiac, *La Synagogue vide*, 288–9.

27. *Exemplar*, in Osier, *D'Uriel da Costa à Spinoza*, 143.

28. Ibid.

29. We do not have the text of this *cherem*.

30. *Exemplar*, in Osier, *D'Uriel da Costa à Spinoza*, 291.

31. See, for example, Revah, "La Religion d'Uriel da Costa," 48; and Vaz Dias and Van der Tak, *Uriel da Costa*.

32. The *Exemplar* was published by Philippe de Limborch, a defender of "the truth of the Christian religion."

33. See Albiac, *La Synagogue vide*, 243ff.

34. Kaplan, "The Social Functions of the *Herem* in the Portuguese Jewish Community of Amsterdam in the Seventeenth Century," 142.

35. Vaz Dias and Van der Tak, *Spinoza, Merchant and Autodidact*, 136.

36. Ibid.

37. See Chapter 1, note 22. The Jews were not fully emancipated and given all the rights of full citizenship until 1796, after the Dutch Republic had been replaced by the revolutionary Batavian Republic.

38. Gans, *Memorboek*, 47. See also Méchoulan, "A propos da la visite de Frédéric-Henri"; and David Franco Mendes's account of the visit in his *Memorias*.

39. Gans, *Memorboek*, 64.

40. For an account of this incident, see Vaz Dias and Van der Tak, "Rembrandt en zijn Portugeesche-Joodsche Buren."

41. See Schwartz, *Rembrandt*, 175.

42. See Vaz Dias and Van der Tak, "Rembrandt en zijn Portugueesche-Joodsche Buren."

43. Levine and Morgenstein, *Jews in the Age of Rembrandt*, ix.

44. Vaz Dias and Van der Tak are aware of the limited concrete evidence but is nonetheless willing to speak of "friendly mutual relations" between Rembrandt and his Jewish neighbors.

45. Schwartz, *Rembrandt*, 175.

46. See, for example, W. R. Valentiner, *Rembrandt and Spinoza: A Study of the Spiritual Conflicts in Seventeenth Century Holland*.

47. Leao took over from Menasseh in 1649.

48. This hypothesis is set forth by Valentiner.

49. Schwartz, *Rembrandt*, 371, note on p. 284. Schwartz in fact suggests that "whatever indications there are point in another direction. Spinoza's great friend in the

art world was Lodewijk Meyer, one of the founders of Nil Volentibus Arduum and
ally of Andries Pels. Their antagonism towards Rembrandt will certainly have
communicated itself to Spinoza, if they ever talked about him."

50. Vaz Dias and Van der Tak, *Spinoza, Merchant and Autodidact*, 146.

5. A Merchant of Amsterdam

1. Vaz Dias and Van der Tak, *Spinoza, Merchant and Autodidact*, 148–9, 154.
2. Portuguese Jewish Archives, Municipal Archives of Amsterdam, no. 334/1052, folio 41 recto to 47 recto.
3. Vaz Dias and Van der Tak, *Spinoza, Merchant and Autodidact*, 147.
4. See Israel, "Dutch Sephardi Jewry, Millenarian Politics, and the Struggle for Brazil (1640–1654)."
5. Ibid., 88.
6. Israel, "The Changing Role of the Dutch Sephardim in International Trade (1595–1715)," 42.
7. Ibid., 43.
8. Israel, *The Dutch Republic*, 608; Price, *Holland and the Dutch Republic*, 117–18, 163–4.
9. Israel, *The Dutch Republic*, 708–9.
10. Aitzema, *Herstelde Leeuw*, 151.
11. Vaz Dias and Van der Tak, *Spinoza, Merchant and Autodidact*, 137.
12. See Emmanuel, *Precious Stones of the Jews of Curaçao*, 193.
13. Vaz Dias and Van der Tak, *Spinoza, Merchant and Autodidact*, 180.
14. Ibid., 184.
15. Ibid., 163.
16. Ibid., 169.
17. Ibid., 189.
18. Ibid., 185–7.
19. This is Vaz Dias's conjecture; see ibid., 167.
20. All of the documents related to the Alvares episode are reprinted in ibid., 158–61.
21. Roth, *A Life of Menasseh ben Israel*, 63.
22. Vaz Dias and Van der Tak, *Spinoza, Merchant and Autodidact*, 155–6. For an analysis of De Barrios's account of *Keter Torah*, see Pieterse, *Daniel Levi de Barrios als Geschiedschrijver*, 106–8.
23. Pieterse, *Daniel Levi de Barrios als Geschiedschrijver*, 107.
24. The account of Mortera's life is from Salomon, *Saul Levi Mortera en zijn "Traktaat Betreffende de Waarheid van de Wet van Mozes."*
25. See Salomon, *Saul Levi Mortera*, lxxvii.
26. Ibid., xliv–xlvii.
27. Meijer, *Encyclopedia Sephardica Neerlandica*, 47–8.
28. Freudenthal, *Das Lebensgeschichte Spinoza's*, 4.
29. It could be that, just as many modern orthodox Jews do, Spinoza found plenty of time to study the Talmud when not engaged in business. But, as becomes clear below, by 1654 or 1655 he was devoting his spare time to studies of an entirely different and secular nature.

30. See Gebhardt, in *Spinoza Opera*, 5:231–3.

31. Menasseh ben Israel, *Conciliador*, preface to part 2.

32. Roth, *A Life of Menasseh ben Israel*, 55–6.

33. Meijer, *Beeldevorming om Baruch: "Eigentijdse" Aspecten van de Vroege Spinoza-Biografie*, 34.

34. Salomon, *Saul Levi Mortera*, xlvii.

35. Menasseh ben Israel, *The Hope of Israel*, 40.

36. *De termino vitae*, 236; quoted in Roth, *A Life of Menasseh ben Israel*, 53.

37. Albiac, *La Synagogue vide*, 301–2.

38. Menasseh ben Israel, *The Hope of Israel*, 108.

39. Jacob S. Minkin, *The Teachings of Maimonides*, 398–401.

40. *Quarta parte de la Introducción de la Fe*, 6:266.

41. Menassah ben Israel, *The Hope of Israel*, 148.

42. On this, see David Katz, *Philosemitism and the Readmission of the Jews to England: 1603–1655*, and James Shapiro, *Shakespeare and the Jews*.

43. "To His Highnesse the Lord Protector of the Commonwealth of England, Scotland, and Ireland," 81–2.

44. Roth, *A Life of Menasseh ben Israel*, chaps. 10 and 11.

45. Thus, it is perhaps going too far to say, as Roth does, that "it can hardly be doubted" that Spinoza was Menasseh's pupil (ibid., 130–1), or even that he "very probably" taught Spinoza ("Introduction," *The Hope of Israel*, 22).

46. Popkin, "Menasseh ben Israel and Isaac La Peyrère," 63.

47. This is not to say that Spinoza followed Menasseh in many of his opinions. He may, for example, have had the rabbi in mind when, in the TTP, he criticized those authors who try to reconcile the inconsistencies in Scripture (chap. 9).

48. Offenberg makes a good case for Menasseh's influence on Spinoza; see *Spinoza*, 30.

49. Freudenthal, *Die Lebensgeschichte Spinoza's*, 4.

50. II/5; C/7.

51. Freudenthal, *Die Lebensgeschichte Spinoza's*, 9.

52. Ibid., 36. According to Meinsma, it could have been the German antitrinitarian Jeremiah Felbinger, who was residing among the Collegiants in Amsterdam at this time; see *Spinoza et son cercle*, 271–2.

53. Sebastian Kortholt, in Freudenthal, *Die Lebensgeschichte Spinoza's*, 26. Kortholt may be referring to Van den Enden's daughter.

54. For Van den Enden's biography, see Meinsma, *Spinoza et son cercle*, chap. 5; and Meininger and van Suchtelen, *Liever met Wercken als met Woorden*.

55. Du Cause de Nazelle, *Memoire du temps de Louis XIV*, 98–100.

56. Freudenthal, *Die Lebensgeschichte Spinoza's*, 37.

57. Marc Bedjai is to be credited with discovering that these works were written by Van den Enden, while W. N. A. Klever has done a good deal of work on bringing out the possible (but, it seems to me, unlikely) connections with Spinoza's thought; see his edition of the *Vrye Politijke Stellingen*, as well as his summary of the works' contents in "A New Source of Spinozism."

58. Klever, "A New Source of Spinozism," 620.

59. Meininger and Suchtelen, *Liever met Wercken als met Woorden*, 68.

60. This is something on which all his earliest biographers – Lucas, Colerus, Bayle, and Jellesz – agree.

61. Van den Enden, *Vrye Politijke Stellingen*, 28.

62. Lucas relates that Van den Enden "offered to look after him and put him up in his own house without asking anything in return except his occasional help in teaching the schoolboys when he was able"; Freudenthal, *Die Lebensgeschichte Spinoza's*, 9.

63. No one has done more to help us understand Spinoza's intellectual relationship with Van den Enden than Wim Klever; see his "A New Source of Spinozism" and his introduction to Van den Enden's *Vrye Politijke Stellingen*. Klever calls Van den Enden "a kind of 'Proto-Spinoza' . . . the hidden agent behind Spinoza's genius." In an interview with the Dutch newspaper *NRC Handelsblad Dinsdag* (May 8, 1990), Klever suggests that Van den Enden bore the same relationship to Spinoza that Socrates had borne to Plato. I do not agree with this assessment, basically because it seems to give to Van den Enden more responsibility for Spinoza's intellectual development than he may be due. For an even more extreme view than Klever's, see Bedjai, "Metaphysique, éthique et politique dans l'oeuvre du docteur Franciscus van den Enden." For a critique of Klever's interpretation of the relationship between Spinoza and Van den Enden, see F. Mertens, "Franciscus van den Enden: Tijd voor een Herziening van Diens Rol in Het Ontstaan van Het Spinozisme?"; and Herman de Dijn, "Was Van den Enden Het Meesterbrein Achter Spinoza?"

64. *Observationes anatomicae*, 199.

65. Freudenthal, *Die Lebensgeschichte Spinoza's*, 37.

66. For an account of Kerckrinck's life, see Meinsma, *Spinoza et son cercle*, 189, 207–9.

67. T. Worp, *Geschiedenis van het drama en van het toneel in Nederland*, 1:30.

68. Ibid., 193ff.

69. See Meinsma, *Spinoza et son cercle*, 186–8; Meininger and Suchtelen, *Liever met Wercken als met Woorden*, 24–43.

70. Meininger and Suchtelen, *Liever met Wercken als met Woorden*, 29–30.

71. See, above all, Fokke Akkerman's "Spinoza's Tekort aan Woorden."

72. Freudenthal, *Die Lebensgeschichte Spinoza's*, 29–30. Colerus, too, declares that an attempt was made on Spinoza's life before July 1656, but claims that, according to Spinoza's landlord in The Hague, the assault was made as he was coming out of the synagogue, and the knife only tore his coat (ibid., 40–1).

73. Meinsma, *Spinoza et son cercle*, 188.

74. Ibid.

75. Freudenthal, *Die Lebensgeschichte Spinoza's*, 10.

76. Ibid., 39.

77. Letter to Balzac, May 5, 1631, *Oeuvres de Descartes*, 1:203–4

78. See Lucas, in Freudenthal, *Die Lebensgeschichte Spinoza's*, 12.

79. See Klever, "Spinoza and Van den Enden in Borch's Diary in 1661 and 1662," 318–19. These references to Van den Enden's Cartesianism come rather later than is useful, as the real question is whether Van den Enden was a devotee of Descartes's philosophy around 1654–5, when (I believe) Spinoza was studying with him.

80. However, De la Court's aristocratic sentiments may not have been to Van den En-
    den's taste, as Mertens argues; see "Franciscus van den Enden," 720–1.
81. See the fragment from Stolle's travel journal, Freudenthal, *Die Lebensgeshichte
    Spinoza's*, 229.
82. Both of these claims are made by Klever; see "A New Source of Spinozism," 631,
    and the interview with *NRC Handelsblad* cited in note 63.
83. See the *Catalogus van de Bibliotheek der Verniging Het Spinozahuis te Rijnsburg*,
    no. 57.

6. *Cherem*

1. Arnold Wiznitzer, *The Jews of Colonial Brazil*, 120ff., and Jonathan Israel, "Dutch
   Sephardi Jewry, Millenarian Politics, and the Struggle for Brazil (1640–1654)."
2. Israel, *European Jewry in the Age of Mercantilism, 1550–1750*, 154.
3. For plague statistics, see Israel, *The Dutch Republic*, 625.
4. Van der Tak, "Spinoza's Payments to the Portuguese-Israelitic Community,"
   190–2.
5. See ibid., 191.
6. Freudenthal, *Die Lebensgeschichte Spinoza's*, 114.
7. This is suggested, for example, by Revah, "Aux origines de la rupture Spinozienne," 369; and Levin, *Spinoza*, 180–2.
8. This is the interpretation favored by Van der Tak, "Spinoza's Payments," 192. He
   insists that "even if during the final months preceding his banishment his visits to
   the synagogue became less frequent, there is no question of his being estranged
   from his fellow Jews; but that on the contrary the ban must have come quite un-
   expectedly." The drop in contributions, then, "can only be explained as a result of
   decline in prosperity."
9. The document is reprinted in Vaz Dias and Van der Tak, *Spinoza, Merchant and
   Autodidact*, 163–4.
10. Ibid., 169.
11. Ibid., 191.
12. The document is in the Jewish Archives of the Municipal Archives of the City of
    Amsterdam. A copy of the Portuguese text is in Vaz Dias and Van der Tak, 164,
    with a translation on 170. The translation I have used is by Asa Kasher and Shlomo
    Biderman, "Why Was Spinoza Excommunicated?" 98–9.
13. See the entry for *cherem* in the *Encyclopedia Judaica*, as well as the discussion in
    Jacob Katz, *Tradition and Crisis*, 84–6.
14. The Talmud tells of three scholars who were expelled from the order of Pharisees
    for their opinions or behavior; see *Mishnah 'Eduyyot*, 5.6 and *Bava Metzia*, 59b.
15. *Mishneh Torah*, Hilchot Talmud Torah, chap. 7.
16. *Talmudic Encyclopedia*, "Cherem"; Méchoulan, "Le *Herem* à Amsterdam," 118.
17. *Mishneh Torah*, Talmud Torah, chap. 7, sec. 2.
18. Ibid., chap. 6.
19. See *Encyclopedia Judaica*, 352.
20. Katz, *Tradition and Crisis*, 85.

21. *Encyclopedia Judaica*, 355.

22. Freudenthal, *Die Lebensgeschichte Spinoza's*, 9–10.

23. Ibid., 42. Meijer claims that, as in Venice, the person who got the job of reading the ban was chosen by lot, and that it may have fallen to Mortera in this case; see Meijer, *Beeldvorming om Baruch*, 54.

24. Wiznitzer, "The Merger Agreement and Regulations of Congregation 'Talmud Torah' of Amsterdam (1638–39)," 131–2.

25. Kaplan, "The Social Functions of the *Herem*," 126–7.

26. Ibid., 138–40; Méchoulan, "Le *Herem* à Amsterdam," 118–19.

27. Wiznitzer, "The Merger Agreement," 132.

28. In my discussion here I rely greatly on Kaplan's analysis of excommunication in the Amsterdam community in his "The Social Functions of the *Herem*."

29. Ibid., 122–4.

30. Archives of the Portuguese Jewish Community, 334, no. 19, fol. 72 (Municipal Archives of Amsterdam).

31. All of these cases are mentioned by Kaplan, "The Social Functions of the *Herem*," 135–8.

32. Ibid., 124.

33. Archives of the Portuguese Jewish Community, 334, no. 19, fol. 16 (Municipal Archives of Amsterdam).

34. Archives of the Portuguese Jewish Community, 334, no. 19, fol. 562. On Curiel's case, see Kaplan, "The Social Functions of the *Herem*," 133–4.

35. For the text of Prado's *cherem*, see Revah, *Spinoza et Juan de Prado*, 29–30, 58–59.

36. Salomon, "La Vraie Excommunication de Spinoza." See Offenberg, "The Dating of the *Kol Bo*."

37. See Kaplan, "Karaites' in Early Eighteenth-Century Amsterdam."

38. "The Social Functions of the *Herem*," 118–19.

39. Alexander Marx, *Studies in Jewish History and Booklore*, 210–1.

40. Vlessing argues, however, that in fact the reasons behind Spinoza's excommunication were "mainly financial"; see "The Jewish Community in Transition: From Acceptance to Emancipation," 205–10. Although Vlessing puts Spinoza's bleak financial situation in perspective, her argument is unconvincing.

41. Revah, *Spinoza et Juan de Prado*, 32–3.

42. KV, 23:1–2, I/103; C/140–1; *Ethics* VP23.

43. *Ethics* I, Appendix.

44. *KV*, 2:12, I/22; C/68. *Ethics*, IP11.

45. *KV*, 18:1, I/86–7; C/127.

46. *TTP*, chap. 3.

47. *TTP*, chap. 3, III/57.

48. See Colerus in Freudenthal, *Die Lebensgeschichte Spinoza's*, 68; Bayle, ibid., 30; and Salomon Van Til's report, ibid., 237.

49. Van der Tak has done a good job of deflating the fantasies surrounding Spinoza's "apology"; see "Spinoza's Apologie." See also Revah, *Spinoza et Juan de Prado*, 40–1.

50. Freudenthal, *Die Lebensgeschichte Spinoza's*, 237. See also Stanislaus von Dunin-

Borkowski's analysis and conclusions on the relationship between the *Apologia* and the *Theological-Political Treatise* in his *Spinoza*, pt. 4, p. 125.

51. H. W. Blom and J. M. Kerkhoven, "A Letter concerning an Early Draft of Spinoza's Treatise on Religion and Politics?" 372–3.

52. Ibid., 375.

53. Wim Klever, on the other hand, has told me that he thinks it is doubtful that the work to which Paets is referring is something by Spinoza.

54. *TTP*, chap. 9, III/13.

55. Freudenthal, *Die Lebensgeschichte Spinoza's*, 221–2.

56. Ibid., 5.

57. Ibid., 7.

58. Ibid., 32.

59. *Commentary on the Mishnah, Sanhedrin*, chap. 10.

60. Hilchot Teshuvah, chap. 3.

61. On this, see Kasher and Biderman, "Why Was Spinoza Excommunicated?" 105.

62. This treatise has been lost. But Marc Saperstein attempts to reconstruct some of its contents from Mortera's sermons; see his "Saul Levi Morteira's Treatise on the Immortality of the Soul."

63. See Introduction to this work. The best and most thorough examination of the views of the rabbis of the community on just those issues on which Spinoza is said to have held heretical views is by Kasher and Biderman, "Why Was Spinoza Excommunicated?" 104–10.

64. Many of Mortera's sermons were published in 1645 in the collection *Giv'at Sha'ul*.

65. Freudenthal, *Die Lebensgeschichte Spinoza's*, 8.

66. According to Gebhardt, it was Abrabanel's book that inspired Spinoza to leave the synagogue. See also Ze'ev Levy, "Sur quelques influences juives dans le développment philosophique du jeune Spinoza," 69–71.

67. On the importance of Delmedigo to Spinoza, see d'Ancona, *Delmedigo, Menasseh ben Israel en Spinoza*.

68. There is a direct connection, however, between Spinoza's relationship with the Collegiants and his acquaintance with Van den Enden. It was probably his Mennonite/Collegiant friends who directed him to the ex-Jesuit for Latin (and philosophical) instruction.

69. For a good summary of Collegiant opinions, see Kolakowski, *Chrétiens sans église*, 166–77.

70. See Popkin, "Spinoza's Earliest Philosophical Years."

71. On Boreel, see Israel, *The Dutch Republic*, 587–8; and Meinsma, *Spinoza et son cercle*, chap. 4.

72. On the anti-Socinian campaign, see Israel, *The Dutch Republic*, 909ff.

73. Meinsma suggests that "it is likely that Spinoza aligned himself with these [Collegiants] during 1654 or the beginning of 1655" (*Spinoza et son cercle*, 152).

74. Madeleine Frances, however, argues against any Collegiant "connection" or influence on Spinoza; see *Spinoza dans les pays néerlandais*.

75. The essential work on Prado's life and thought and his relations with Spinoza was first done by Gebhardt, "Juan de Prado." See also Revah's "Aux origines de la rup-

ture spinozienne" and *Spinoza et Juan de Prado*. Kaplan's book on Orobio de Castro, *From Christianity to Judaism*, is indispensable.

76. Kaplan, *From Christianity to Judaism*, 129.
77. Ibid., 126.
78. Revah, *Spinoza et Juan de Prado*, 25–6.
79. Ibid., 28.
80. "Aux origines de la rupture spinozienne, Nouvel examen . . . ," 563.
81. Revah, *Spinoza et Juan de Prado*, 59–60.
82. Ibid., 64.
83. The text of this letter is found in Revah, "Aux origines de la rupture spinozienne," 397–8.
84. Ibid., 398–401.
85. Revah, *Spinoza et Juan de Prado*, 60–8.
86. For a reconstruction of Prado's views from Orobio's text, which is all that survives from their correspondence, see Kaplan, *From Christianity to Judaism*, 163–78; and Revah, "Aux origines de la rupture spinozienne," 375–83.
87. Revah, *Spinoza et Juan de Prado*, 22.
88. *La Certeza del Camino*, 29.
89. Albiac, *La Synagogue vide*, 329.
90. This is the thesis of Albiac, Revah, Gebhardt, Frances, and, most recently, Yovel (*Spinoza and Other Heretics*), among others.
91. In Revah's eyes, this clinches the case against the Collegiant thesis. "The Spinoza–Prado connection explains everything," he insists ("Aux origines de la rupture spinozienne," 382). The documents found in the Inquisition's files issue the coup de grace against any attempt to explain Spinoza's apostasy by appealing to Collegiant contacts (*Spinoza et Juan de Prado*, 33).
92. For Revah, "Prado's unbelief represented an essential stage in Spinoza's spiritual evolution" ("Aux origines de la rupture spinozienne," 382).
93. On the other hand, Lewis Samuel Feuer's thesis – that Spinoza's political views were diametrically opposed to the essentially monarchistic persuasions of the community's leaders, who tied their fortunes to those of the Calvinist party and the Stadholder – is hard to believe (*Spinoza and the Rise of Liberalism*, chap. 1). First, the Jewish merchants (including the rabbis) had more in common with the republican regents of the mercantile and professional classes who governed Amsterdam than with the Calvinist preachers who so often opposed them. Feuer claims that the *parnassim* would have found common cause with the Orangists in their shared hostility to Catholic Spain (and, after the Brazil debacle, Portugal). But war with Iberia was bad for business, as the Jews knew from experience. Amsterdam's Jews did appreciate the protection that Frederik Hendrik had given them while he was Stadholder; but I think it is going too far to suggest that they preferred on principle a quasi-monarchical state to a republican one. I believe that what they valued, above all else and independently of how it was achieved, was the peace and stability that allowed them to go about their affairs, along with protection from persecution.
94. Wiznitzer, "The Merger Agreement," 123–4.

95. Meijer, *Beeldvorming om Baruch*, 57.
96. Ibid., 57–8.
97. The Dutch were quite interested in what was going on in the Jewish community, as evidenced by their visits to the synagogue to watch the Jews at worship. This fact, along with the ordinary and frequent business and social contacts between the Jews and the Dutch, reveals that the Dutch would have had easy and ample opportunity to learn about such a major event in the Jewish community as Spinoza's excommunication, about which the entire congregation must have been talking.
98. For an account of the Utrecht and Leiden crises, see Theo Verbeek, *Descartes and the Dutch*, chaps. 2 and 3.
99. Pieter Geyl, *The Netherlands in the Seventeenth Century*, 2:107–9.
100. Freudenthal, *Die Lebensgeschichte Spinoza's*, 39.
101. Ibid., 8.
102. Kasher and Biderman ("When Was Spinoza Banned?") argue that this was the formal process followed in Spinoza's case. But, as Kaplan notes, there is no documentary evidence to support this; see "The Social Functions of the *cherem*," 139 n78.
103. Freudenthal, *Die Lebensgeschichte Spinoza's*, 29.
104. Ibid., 40.
105. Ibid., 29, 40.
106. They did so, for example, in the case of the Del Sotto family; see Swetschinski, "Kinship and Commerce," 70–2.
107. Revah, *Spinoza et Juan de Prado*, 32.
108. Freudenthal, *Die Lebensgeschichte Spinoza's*, 8.

7. Benedictus

1. Revah, *Spinoza et Juan de Prado*, 65, 68.
2. Freudenthal, *Die Lebensgeschichte Spinoza's*, 220.
3. Not one of these portraits, however, has been authenticated as a representation of Spinoza.
4. See Akkerman, "Spinoza's Tekort aan Woorden."
5. Many scholars do not even begin Spinoza's studies with Van den Enden until this time, usually early 1657. But this, I believe, is too late. By late 1658 or early 1659, Spinoza was back in Amsterdam, after having studied a bit in Leiden (according to Brother Tomas). That means that he was probably attending the university in Leiden by no later than early 1658, most likely even earlier. Assuming, with all probability, that he went to Leiden to study Cartesianism, then he must have known beforehand that he would need Latin. If he did not begin studying Latin with Van den Enden until 1657, that would hardly give him time to master enough Latin to be able to follow a course in philosophy.
6. Freudenthal, *Die Lebensgeschichte Spinoza's*, 10–11.
7. See Méchoulan, "Le *Herem* à Amsterdam," 132.
8. Brugmans and Frank, *Geschiedenis der Joden in Nederland*, 626–8; Frances, *Spinoza dans les pays néerlandais*, 130.

9. Meinsma, *Spinoza et son cercle*, 246.

10. Ibid., 369.

11. Freudenthal, *Die Lebensgeschichte Spinoza's*, 56; see also the report by Johannes Monikhoff in ibid., 106.

12. Meinsma, *Spinoza et son cercle*, 205, n. 26.

13. Klever, "Spinoza and Van den Enden in Borch's Diary," 314.

14. Popkin, *Spinoza's Earliest Publication?* 1. Popkin argues that this could be none other than Spinoza, and not Prado or Ribera. Klever, however, on the basis of some remarks in Borch's diary, has taken issue with Popkin's thesis of a Quaker connection; see "Spinoza and Van den Enden in Borch's Diary," 322–4.

15. Kasher and Biderman ("Why Was Spinoza Excommunicated?") consider the plausibility of Spinoza's alleged Quaker connections predating (and perhaps occasioning) the *cherem* (134–7).

16. Popkin, "Spinoza, the Quakers and the Millenarians," 113.

17. Van den Berg, "Quaker and Chiliast," 183.

18. Popkin, "Spinoza, the Quakers and the Millenarians," 123.

19. Ibid., 116–17.

20. Ibid., 117.

21. Popkin, *Spinoza's Earliest Publication?* 88–90.

22. Ibid., 105–6.

23. Popkin, "Spinoza, The Quakers and the Millenarians," 117–18.

24. Sebastian Korthalt, in Freudenthal, *Die Lebensgeschichte Spinoza's*, 27; and Bayle, in ibid., 31–2.

25. Popkin, "Spinoza, The Quakers and the Millenarians," 123–4.

26. Popkin, "Samuel Fisher and Spinoza."

27. Popkin deserves the most credit for bringing this hypothesis to our attention.

28. The letters of Ames and Caton detailing Spinoza's services are from April 1657, March 1658, and October 1658.

29. Letter to Pollot, January 8, 1644, *Oeuvres de Descartes*, 4:76–8.

30. For Heereboord's role in the various disputes at Leiden over Cartesianism, see Verbeek, *Descartes and the Dutch*, chap. 3.

31. Ibid., 87.

32. Bouillier, *Histoire de la philosophie cartésienne*, 1:270.

33. Verbeek, *Descartes and the Dutch*, 129, n. 116.

34. Among his books at his death, there were only three in French, including Antoine Arnauld's and Pierre Nicole's *La Logique, ou l'art de penser* (1665), a treatise in Cartesian logic and method. Spinoza may have had some familiarity with the language, but probably not enough to conduct his own philosophical education in it.

35. Although Spinoza never owned a copy of this work, he was familiar enough with its contents. By the late 1660s, any reader could learn about Descartes's "rules" by reading Arnauld's and Nicole's *La Logique*, the so-called Port-Royal Logic.

36. I am obliged to Theo Verbeek for this suggestion.

37. Spinoza owned both Schooten's *Principia Matheseos universalis* (1651) and his *Exercitationum Mathematicarum* (1657).

38. In the biographical sketch of the preface to Spinoza's *Opera Postuma;* see Akkerman and Hubbeling, "The Preface to Spinoza's Posthumous Works and Its Author, Jarig Jellesz" (in *Studies in the Posthumous Works of Spinoza*), 217.

39. Klever, "Spinoza and Van den Enden in Borch's Diary," 315.

40. Stolle's diary, in Freudenthal, *Die Lebensgeschichte Spinoza's,* 222.

41. Ibid., 12.

42. Van der Tak, "Jarig Jellesz' Origins." For biographical material on Jellesz, see also Akkerman and Hubbeling, "The Preface to Spinoza's Posthumous Works and Its Author, Jarig Jellesz." The author of the biographical note was probably Rieuwertsz.

43. Kolakowski, *Chrétiens sans Eglise,* 217–25.

44. For a study of Glazemaker's translating activities, as well as some family background, see Thijssen-Schoute, "Jan Hendrik Glazemaker: De Zeventiende Eeuwse Aartsvertaler."

45. Kolakowski, *Chrétiens sans église,* 210–17.

46. Freudenthal, *Die Lebensgeschichte Spinoza's,* 62.

47. According to Borch's report; see Klever, "Spinoza and Van den Enden in Borch's Diary," 314.

48. See Vandenbossche, *Adriaan Koerbagh en Spinoza.*

49. Meyer, *Philosophia S. Scripturae Interpres,* chap. 4.

50. Ibid., chap. 6, para. 3. There is no indication of whether or not Meyer recognizes that this is the same view held by Maimonides in the *Guide for the Perplexed* (I.1–70).

51. For a comparison of Meyer with Spinoza and Descartes, see Lagrée, "Louis Meyer et la *Philosophia S. Scripturae Interpres*"; and Thijssen-Schoute, "Lodewijk Meiyer en Diens Verhouding tot Descartes en Spinoza." See also Bordoli, *Ragione e scrittura tra Descartes e Spinoza.*

52. Israel, *The Dutch Republic,* 919.

53. He did not graduate from Leiden until 1660.

54. Meinsma, *Spinoza et son cercle,* 197.

55. Freudenthal, *Die Lebensgeschichte Spinoza's,* 41–2.

56. Revah, *Spinoza et Juan de Prado,* 67–8.

57. Kaplan, *From Christianity to Judaism,* 135, n. 77.

58. Ibid., 88.

59. Ibid., 204.

60. Blom and Kerkhoven, "A Letter concerning an Early Draft of Spinoza's Treatise on Religion and Politics?" Mignini's hypothesis is that the *tractatus* of 1660 consisted mainly in political material – the basic arguments of the last seven chapters of the *TTP,* and that it was only after 1665 that Spinoza started to work seriously on the chapters of the *TTP* devoted to biblical interpretation, perhaps reviving the material from the long-lost *Apologia;* see Mignini, "Données et problèmes de la chronologie spinozienne," 14.

61. Filippo Mignini first argued for the anteriority of the *TIE* to the *Short Treatise* in "Per la datazione e l'interpretazione del *Tractatus de intellectus emendatione*" and "Données et problèmes de la chronologie spinozienne entre 1656 et 1665." Mignini's hypothesis has been received with various degrees of acceptance by

Curley ("Une Nouvelle Traduction anglaise des oeuvres de Spinoza"), and Proietti ("Adulescens luxu perditus: Classici latini nell'opera di Spinoza").

62. Mignini has argued – plausibly, I think – against the view that the *TIE* was written as an introduction for the *KV* itself. He also claims – perhaps less plausibly –
that when Spinoza wrote to Oldenburg (probably around late 1661 or early 1662)
"I have written a complete short work on this subject [how things began to be and
by what bond they depend on the first cause] and also on the emendation of the
intellect" (Ep. 6: I/36; C/I, 188), he is referring simply to the *KV* and its methodological part, not to the *KV* and the *TIE* together. Following Joachim (*Spinoza's
Tractatus de Intellectus Emendatione*, 7), he rests his case partly on the fact that, at
the time of the letter, the *TIE* itself was neither a "completed" work nor part of
some "completed" work; see his "Données et problèmes de la chronologie spinozienne," as well as Curley's note on the matter, C 188, n. 53. What the *TIE* probably represents is an early version, or even a draft, of the methodological parts of
the *KV*.

63. II/7; C/9.

64. II/ 8; C/11.

65. II/30; C/35.

66. II/34, C/38; II/36, C/41. In keeping with seventeenth-century philosophical usage, the term *objectively* at the end of this passage means "cognitively" or "intel-
ligibly."

67. II/17; C/20.

68. This assumes that Mignini's theory about the dating and composition of the *TIE*
is correct, and that the work is not, as Gebhardt argued, the only part of the *KV*
to survive in both a Latin and a Dutch version.

69. Klever, "Spinoza and Van den Enden in Borch's Diary," 314. Spinoza may, of
course, simply have been visiting Amsterdam at the time, as he was wont to do after moving to Rijnsburg; but from the way in which Borch refers to him, it seems
more likely that he was still living there.

70. Akkerman and Hubbeling, "The Preface to Spinoza's Posthumous Works," 216.

71. Freudenthal, *Die Lebensgeschichte Spinoza's*, 12.

72. Offenberg, *Spinoza*, 43.

73. Freudenthal, *Die Lebensgeschichte Spinoza's*, 229.

8. A Philosopher in Rijnsburg

1. Klever, "Spinoza and Van den Enden in Borch's Diary," 314.

2. I/6; C/8–9.

3. Ep. 26, IV/159; C/394.

4. Ep. 36.

5. Freudenthal, *Die Lebensgeschichte Spinoza's*, 14.

6. Christiaan Huygens, *Oeuvres complètes*, 6:155.

7. Ibid., 158.

8. Freudenthal, *Die Lebensgeschichte Spinoza's*, 193. See also Leibniz's letter to Spinoza, Ep. 45. See Klever, "Insignis Opticus."

9. *Observationes Anatomicae,* quoted in Klever, "Spinoza's Life and Works," 33.

10. Ep. 14 reveals that Serrarius was an acquaintance of Oldenburg as well as of Spinoza.

11. This, at least, is Meinsma's suggestion; see *Spinoza et son cercle,* 223.

12. See Barbone, Rice, and Adler, "Introduction," *Spinoza: The Letters,* 8.

13. Ep. 1, IV/5; C/163.

14. Ep. 2, IV/7; C/164–5.

15. Until the discovery of two Dutch manuscripts in the middle of the nineteenth century, it was also very much a work in absentia. Neither of the two manuscripts is Spinoza's own. Most likely, they are a translation from a Latin original, which has been lost. It is highly implausible that Spinoza would have composed a complex philosophical work in Dutch, given his confessed discomfort in expressing himself on philosophical matters in that language.

16. This, at least, is the theory of Mignini, who prepared the critical edition of the *KV* for the latest Dutch edition of Spinoza's shorter writings; see Akkerman et al., Spinoza: *Korte Geschriften,* 230–40. Gebhardt had suggested that Spinoza originally dictated the work to his friends in Dutch, and only after settling in Rijnsburg revised portions of his manuscript into two separate Latin treatises: one on method, the *TIE,* and one on metaphysics, the *KV.* These were then sent back to Amsterdam to be translated into Dutch by Pieter Balling; see I/424–31.

17. See Ep. 6 and Ep. 13 (in which the reference to publishing "certain other things" seems to be to the *KV*).

18. I/112; C/149–50.

19. Strictly speaking, for Spinoza mind and body are, in fact, one and the same mode considered from two different perspectives (i.e., under two different attributes).

20. I/61; C/104.

21. I/78; C/119.

22. I/86–7; C/127.

23. See chaps. 18 and 19.

24. I/88; C/129.

25. Ep. 1, IV/6; C/164.

26. Ep. 6, IV/36; C 188.

27. Ibid.

28. Ep. 13, IV/64; C/207. A substantial part of the *Ethics* was written by this date, and it is unclear whether, in this letter, Spinoza is referring to the *KV* or to the geometrical presentation of his ideas in the *Ethics;* see Mignini ("Données et problèmes," 12–13) and Curley (C/350).

29. Ep. 12, IV/51; C/200.

30. Ep. 7, IV/37; C/189.

31. Ep. 16, IV/75; C/218.

32. Ep. 11, IV/50; C/198–9.

33. Ep. 13, IV/66–7; C/210.

34. Ep. 6.

35. Klever, "Spinoza and Van den Enden in Borch's Diary," 316–17.

36. Ep. 8, IV/40; C/192.

37. Klever, "Spinoza and Van den Enden in Borch's Diary," 315.
38. For these claims by Steno, see Ep. 67a, and Klever, "Steno's Statements on Spinoza and Spinozism."
39. Meinsma, *Spinoza et son cercle*, 230.
40. Freudenthal, *Die Lebensgeschichte Spinoza's*, 231–2.
41. Klever believes that De Volder, in fact, was a "crypto-Spinozist"; see "Burchard de Volder (1643–1709), A Crypto-Spinozist on a Leiden Cathedra."
42. Freudenthal, *Die Lebensgeschichte Spinoza's*, 22–3.
43. Meinsma, *Spinoza et son cercle*, 230–4.
44. Ep. 13, IV/63; C/207.
45. See Meyer's preface to *Descartes's Principles of Philosophy*, IV/129–30; C/227.
46. Ep. 8, IV/39; C/190.
47. Ep. 9, IV/42; C/193–4.
48. Ep. 2, IV/8; C/166. Spinoza enclosed the demonstrations in his letter, but the enclosure has since been lost. For a reconstruction of their content, see Battisti, "La dimostrazione dell'esistenza di Dio."
49. Descartes probably did not share Spinoza's optimism about the possibility of achieving mathematical certainty in the human and social sciences, although there is a great deal of debate about this.
50. In his replies to the Second Set of Objections to the *Meditations*, he does, responding to his objector's request, put some of the main arguments of the work *in more geometrico*. But he also admits that he is not persuaded that metaphysics is best served by a literally geometrical format (*Oeuvres de Descartes*, 7:156–7).
51. *Discourse on Method*, Part 2.
52. *Principles of Philosophy*, IV.206.
53. Ep. 8, IV/39; C/190.
54. Ibid.

9. "The Jew of Voorburg"

1. Freudenthal, *Die Lebensgeschichte Spinoza's*, 118–19.
2. Meinsma, *Spinoza et son cercle*, 283.
3. Lucas says that Spinoza moved to Voorburg because "he believed that it would be more peaceful there"; Freudenthal, *Die Lebensgeschichte Spinoza's*, 13.
4. Ibid., 57.
5. Ibid., 283.
6. While Colerus tells us that Spinoza taught himself how to draw, Johannes Monnikhoff, who wrote a short biography of Spinoza in the middle of the eighteenth century as an introduction to the *Short Treatise*, claims that Spinoza honed his drawing skills with Tydeman; Freudenthal, *Die Lebensgeschichte Spinoza's*, 106.
7. Ibid., 56.
8. Ep. 11, IV/63; C/207.
9. I/129; C/227. See Thijssen-Schoute, "Lodewijk Meyer en Diens Verhouding tot Descartes en Spinoza," 179.
10. Preface, *PPC*, I/127–8; C/224–5.

11. *PPC*, Preface, I/130; C/227.
12. Ep. 12a.
13. Ep. 11, IV/64; C/207.
14. See Mignini, "Chronologie Spinozienne," 11–12.
15. Ep. 15, IV/72; C/215.
16. Ep. 15, IV/73; C/216.
17. Ep. 15; Meyer repeats Spinoza's caveat almost verbatim in the preface to *PPC*, I/131; C/228–9.
18. *PPC*, I/152; C/241.
19. *PPC*, I/201; C/277.
20. I/265. This is, in fact, Maimonides' view, against which Spinoza will argue in the *TTP*.
21. See Klever, "Spinoza's Fame in 1667."
22. This, at least, is Gebhardt's opinion; see I/611. Other scholars disagree.
23. Ep. 22, IV/133; C/382.
24. Ep. 29, IV/164.
25. Ep. 14, IV/72; C/215.
26. Israel, *The Dutch Republic*, 625.
27. Ep. 17, IV/76; C/353.
28. Van der Tang, "Spinoza en Schiedam."
29. Ep. 18, IV/80–1; C/355.
30. Ep. 20, IV/122; C/373–4.
31. Ep. 21, IV/126; C/375.
32. Ep. 21, IV/126–7; C/376.
33. Ep. 23, IV/148; C/388.
34. Ep. 22, IV/134–5; C/382.
35. Ep. 24, IV/153; C/390–1.
36. Ep. 27, IV/161; C/395.
37. This is the plausible hypothesis of Curley; see C/350.
38. Israel, *The Dutch Republic*, 766.
39. Ep. 28, IV/163; C/397.
40. Ep. 25, IV/158; C/393.
41. September 28, 1665, *The Correspondence of Henry Oldenburg*, 2:553.
42. Ep. 29, IV/165; SL/182–3.
43. Ep. 30, IV/166; SL/185.
44. It is odd, however, that in a letter to Oldenburg in May 1665, Spinoza mentions how Huygens had recently "told me that he knows you" (Ep. 26). This suggests that Spinoza was *not* aware beforehand, from Oldenburg, that the two were friends.
45. Meinsma is certainly wrong when he claims that Huygens's interest in Spinoza "did not extend beyond the lenses he polished" (*Spinoza et son cercle*, 323).
46. See Ep. 26 and Ep. 30.
47. Huygens, *Oeuvres complètes*, 6:181.
48. Ep. 32, IV/174–5; SL/195–6.
49. Huygens, *Oeuvres complètes*, 8:400–2.

50. Ep. 70.

51. Ep. 72.

52. This is clear from Christiaan's letters to Constantijn from Paris between September 1667 and May 1668; see *Oeuvres complètes*, 6:148–215.

53. See Ep. 29; and Meinsma, *Spinoza et son cercle*, 300. I am assuming that Daniel Tydeman owned the house mainly because it is referred to in Spinoza's correspondence as the house of "Mr. Daniel the painter."

54. Wim Klever has suggested to me that Spinoza's acquaintance with Hudde may stem from his time in Rijnsburg, when Hudde was in the Cartesian mathematical circle at Leiden.

55. That he saw, at least, Serrarius, Rieuwertsz, and Bouwmeester can be inferred from letters 25 to 28.

56. See Meinsma, *Spinoza et son cercle*, 295.

57. Ep. 28, IV/162; C/395.

58. Ep. 28, IV/163; C/396.

59. Between 1665 and 1675, Spinoza could have done quite a bit of editing, rewriting, and adding to the text, particularly in light of the work he had meanwhile done on the *Theological-Political Treatise*. Most, if not all, of the work on the *Ethics* was most likely on Part III, and not on Parts I and II.

60. Akkerman is unsure whether Balling did all the work himself or was helped by other friends of Spinoza; see "Studies in the Posthumous Works of Spinoza," 160–1.

61. In a letter to Blijenbergh from March 1665, for example, Spinoza refers to material that, in revised form, constitutes Proposition 72 of Part Four of the published version; see Ep. 23, IV/150–1; C/389.

62. See Akkerman, *Studies in the Posthumous Works of Spinoza*, 152–3.

63. Ep. 28, IV/163; C/396.

64. It is also possible that much of what we know as Part Five (*Potentia Intellectus, seu de Libertate Humana*) was added later, perhaps around 1675. But this would imply that the draft of 1665 did not include what Spinoza must have considered perhaps the most important "ethical" dimension of the work. For discussions of the development and composition of the *Ethics*, see Steenbakkers, *Spinoza's Ethica from Manuscript to Print;* Akkerman, *Studies in the Posthumous Works of Spinoza;* and Rousset, "La Première 'Ethique.'"

65. For a fine discussion of the relationship between the form and content of the *Ethics*, see Steenbakkers, *Spinoza's Ethica from Manuscript to Print*, chap. 5. He effectively refutes Wolfson's thesis that the philosophical material is only accidentally related to its dispensable geometric form (*The Philosophy of Spinoza*, chap. 2).

66. Ep. 9, IV/43–4; C/194–5.

67. IP17s1.

68. IP25c.

69. A good analysis and interpretation of the causal orders of nature, and particularly how the eternal and infinite modes relate to the particular ones, is in Curley, *Spinoza's Metaphysics* and *Behind the Geometrical Method*.

70. The preface to Part Four.
71. IP29s.
72. Book I, Appendix.
73. Ibid., II/78–9; C/440–1.
74. Ibid., II/80–1; C/443.
75. IIP7s.
76. IIP29c.
77. IIP44.
78. I/132; C/230.
79. IIP46.
80. IIP47.
81. III, Preface.
82. IIIP6.
83. IIIP11s.
84. IIIP28.
85. IIIP59s.
86. VP20s.
87. IVP4.
88. VP39s.
89. IIP40s2.
90. VP6s.
91. Although Spinoza certainly is critical of the Stoics in important respects; see *Ethics* V, Preface.
92. IV, Appendix, II/276; C/594.
93. See Maimonides, *The Guide of the Perplexed*, III.51.
94. IVP66, 67.
95. VP38.
96. IVP34–35.
97. IVP37s2.
98. In a lost enclosure to Ep. 2. Still, in this letter, Spinoza refrains from "speaking more openly about these things," meaning the implications of his conception of substance for the nature of God.
99. Ep. 32.
100. Ep. 31.

10. *Homo Politicus*

1. Ep. 32, IV/175; SL/196.
2. Meinsma thinks that, in fact, it was Johannes Muntendam who got the post; see *Spinoza et son cercle*, 306, n. 6.
3. This, at least, is Meinsma's suggestion; ibid., 284.
4. The document is in Freudenthal, *Die Lebensgeschichte Spinoza's*, 116–18.
5. See Ep. 42.
6. Ep. 43, IV/219; SL/237.
7. Ep. 43, IV/220; SL/238.

8. See Freudenthal, *Die Lebensgeschichte Spinoza's*, 228. The text of Stolle's journal says that "Ob er [Spinoza] ein Atheus sey, könne er nicht sagen." But Klever insists that this is, in fact, a weakened version of De Volder's more strongly negative original reply; see "Burchard de Volder," 195.

9. Ep. 29, IV/165; SL/183.

10. Ep. 30.

11. Mignini finds the claim that Spinoza is the author of the treatise mentioned by Paets quite plausible; see "Données et problèmes," 13–14.

12. Ep. 31.

13. Freudenthal, *Die Lebensgeschichte Spinoza's*, 200–1.

14. The story of Zevi's life and the movement of which he was the center has been exhaustively and fascinatingly told by Gershom Scholem, *Sabbatai Sevi: The Mystical Messiah*.

15. Ibid., 125.

16. Ibid., 119–22.

17. Ibid., 199ff.

18. Ibid., 519.

19. Ibid., 521.

20. Ibid., 529–30.

21. Ibid., 523.

22. Ibid., 520.

23. Ibid.

24. Méchoulan, *Etre juif à Amsterdam au temps de Spinoza*, 122.

25. Ep. 33.

26. The standard biography of De Witt is Herbert Rowen's *John de Witt, Grand Pensionary of Holland, 1625–1672;* see also his *John de Witt: Statesman of the "True Freedom."*

27. Israel, *The Dutch Republic*, 788; Feuer, *Spinoza and the Rise of Liberalism*, 76–80.

28. This is an entry from the diary of Gronovius, a classical scholar at the University of Leiden; see Klever, "A New Document."

29. Rowen, *John de Witt: Statesman of the "True Freedom*," 58–9.

30. Ibid., 97.

31. Ibid., 131.

32. Israel, *The Dutch Republic*, 759–60.

33. See Blom's "Spinoza en De La Court."

34. Ep. 32.

35. See entry 142 in Offenberg's catalogue, *Spinoza*, 60.

36. Freudenthal and Gebhardt believe there was a close relationship between the two. Japikse, on the other hand, suggests caution in light of the lack of any concrete evidence; see "Spinoza en de Witt."

37. Freudenthal, *Die Lebensgeschichte Spinoza's*, 15–16.

38. It may be that Spinoza's friends, when editing his letters in 1677, destroyed all of his correspondence in which the disgraced and discredited (to his contemporaries) Grand Pensionary is mentioned.

39. Study of the manuscript has shown that the passage in which the pension is discussed

is probably not by Lucas; see Offenberg, *Spinoza*, 60. On the other hand, it is one thing to accept money as a handout from a friend; it is, especially in the seventeenth century, before the full development of the author's royalty, an entirely different thing to accept money as a pension for a book one has written. Perhaps Spinoza's reluctance to take charity from his friends should not be seen as evidence of a similar reluctance to accept an author's deserved pension.

40. See Hudde's letter to Huygens of April 5, 1665, in Huygens, *Oeuvres complètes*, 5:305–11; for Spinoza's interest in the calculation of probabilities, see his letter to Van der Meer, in October 1666, Ep. 38. It has been argued by some that the treatise *Reeckening van Kanssen* (On the calculation of probabilities), published together with a work called "The Algebraic Calculation of the Rainbow" in 1687, was written by Spinoza. The claim has been disputed; see, for example, De Vet, "Was Spinoza de Auteur van Stelkonstige Reeckening van den Regenboog en Reeckening van Kanssen?" There is absolutely no evidence for the attribution, and the treatise is not even mentioned by any of his earliest biographers, all of whom *do* at least take note of a treatise on the rainbow.

41. Oldenburg to Seth Ward, July 15, 1667, *The Correspondence of Henry Oldenburg*, 3:448.

42. Oldenburg to Lord Arlington, July 20, 1667, in ibid., 450.

43. Oldenburg's Petition to Charles II, in ibid., 452–3. The petition was never presented to Charles by his secretary of state.

44. September 12, 1667, in ibid., 473–4.

45. Freudenthal, *Die Lebensgeschichte Spinoza's*, 18.

46. Ibid., 62.

47. Lucas, in ibid., 18.

48. According to Stolle, the final amount was 250 guilders; see Freudenthal, 225.

49. See Van der Tang, "Spinoza en Schiedam."

50. See, for example, Leibniz's report that Spinoza was maintained by Jellesz.; Freudenthal, *Die Lebensgeschichte Spinoza's*, 201.

51. Ibid., 16.

52. Ibid., 59: "In zyn kleeding was hy slegt en borgerlijk. . . ." Lucas, on the other hand, insists that Spinoza was a tidy dresser.

53. This according to Lucas; ibid., 20.

54. *TIE*, II/6–7; C/8–9.

55. Freudenthal, *Die Lebensgeschichte Spinoza's*, 31, n. 1.

56. Colerus, in ibid., 58.

57. Ibid., 61.

58. *TIE*, II/9; C/12.

59. Ep. 40.

60. See Klever, "The Helvetius Affair, or Spinoza and the Philosopher's Stone."

61. Colerus, in Freudenthal, *Die Lebensgeschichte Spinoza's, 83*; Lucas, ibid., 25; Jellesz., preface to the *Nagelate Schriften*, in Akkerman, "The Preface to Spinoza's Posthumous Works," 219; Kortholt, in Freudenthal, 83.

62. The treatise is reprinted, in a French translation, in *Cahiers Spinoza* 5 (1984–5): 40–51.

63. See, for example, Gabbey, "Spinoza's Natural Science and Methodology," 152–4; and De Vet, "Was Spinoza de Auteur van Stelkonstige Reeckening van den Regenborg en Reeckening van Kanssen?"
64. *Meteorology*, Discourse 8.
65. Meinsma, *Spinoza et son cercle*, 340.
66. Jongeneelen, "La Philosophie politique d'Adrien Koerbagh," 248.
67. Ibid., 249–50.
68. Vandenbossche, *Adriaan Koerbagh en Spinoza*, 9–10.
69. Jongeneelen, "An Unknown Pamphlet of Adriaan Koerbagh."
70. Jongeneelen demonstrates the importance of Koerbagh's reading of Hobbes's *Leviathan*.
71. For the views of the Koerbagh brothers and a history of the events leading to their trial and to Adriaan's incarceration, see Jongeneelen, "La Philosophie politique d' Adriaen Koerbagh"; Vandenbossche, *Adriaan Koerbagh en Spinoza*, and especially Meinsma, *Spinoza et son cercle*, chaps. 9 and 10.
72. Israel, *The Dutch Republic*, 787–9.
73. An extensive quotation from the proceedings of Koerbagh's interrogation is reprinted in Meinsma, *Spinoza et son cercle*, 365–6.
74. Ibid., 366.
75. Ibid., 369.
76. Ibid., 368.
77. Ibid., 376.
78. Ep. 30.
79. *TTP* III, III/45–6; S/89.
80. *TTP* IV, III/64; S/107.
81. *TTP* IV, III/60; S/103.
82. See Curley, "Notes on a Neglected Masterpiece (II): The *Theological-Political Treatise* as a Prolegomenon to the *Ethics*."
83. *TTP*, Preface, III/6–7; S/51.
84. *TTP* XII, III/159; S/206.
85. *TTP* II, III/35–6; S/79.
86. *TTP* III, III/56; S/99.
87. *TTP* V, III/75–6; S/119.
88. *TTP* VI, III/82–3; S/126.
89. Although it should be noted that Lodewijk Meyer's views on Scripture were practically as radical as Spinoza's and that his work was attacked with equal vehemence by both ecclesiastical and secular authorities, often in the same proclamation.
90. *TTP* IX, III/131; S/175.
91. See *Leviathan*, Book III, chapter 33. For the historical and philosophical background to Spinoza's Bible scholarship, see the three articles by Richard Popkin: "Spinoza and Samuel Fisher," "Some New Light on Spinoza's Science of Bible Study," and "Spinoza and Bible Scholarship."
92. *TTP* VII, III/98; S/141.
93. Spinoza also took issue with the Cartesian methodology outlined by Lodewijk Meyer, in Meyer's *Philosophy, Interpreter of Holy Scripture*.

94. See Maimonides, *The Guide of the Perplexed*, II.25.
95. *TTP* VII, III/100–1; S/143.
96. *TTP* VII, III/101–2; S/144–5.
97. *TTP* VII, III/117; S/160.
98. *TTP* XIII, III/167; S/214.
99. *TTP* V, III/78; S/121.
100. *TTP* XIV, III/177; S/224.
101. *TTP* XIV, III/178–9; S/225.
102. It is possible – although this is sheer speculation – that much of the political material in the *Ethics* was added only after the completion of the *TTP*, although the Paets letter in 1661 regarding a "theological-political treatise" suggests that these ideas were already in Spinoza's mind.
103. *TTP* XVI, III/190; S/238.
104. *Leviathan*, I.13.ix.
105. *TTP* XVI, III/194–5; S/242–3.
106. In 1585, after the death of William I and seeking some leadership in the revolt against Spain, the United Provinces turned to England. They put themselves into the hands of the earl of Leicester, who served as "governor-general" for two years.
107. *TTP* XVIII, III/227–8; S/278–9.
108. *TTP* XVIII, III/225; S/275–6.
109. *TTP* XIX, III/232–3; S/284.
110. *TTP* XX, III/240; S/292.
111. *TTP* XX, III/243; S/295.
112. *TTP* XX, III/246; S/298.
113. *TTP* XX, III/245–6; S/298.
114. Oldenbarneveldt was simply supporting the platform of the "Remonstrance" drawn up by the Arminians in 1610; see Israel, *The Dutch Republic*, 424–5.
115. See Freudenthal, *Die Lebensgeschichte Spinoza's*, 194.
116. Meinsma is more cautious than Lucas but still finds it quite likely that the two had a personal relationship; see *Spinoza et son cercle*, 406–7.

11. Calm and Turmoil in The Hague

1. Freudenthal, *Die Lebensgeschichte Spinoza's*, 57.
2. Meinsma, *Spinoza et son cercle*, 400.
3. See Monnikhoff, in Freudenthal, 107.
4. See the inventory taken at his death in Freudenthal, 164.
5. Ibid., 58–9.
6. Ibid., 60–1.
7. Ibid., 61.
8. Including Bayle; see ibid., 31–2.
9. *TTP* I, III/20–21; S/64.
10. *TTP* V, III/79; S/122.
11. *TTP* IV, III/64–5; S/107–8.

12. Ep. 71.

13. Ep. 78.

14. Ep. 75.

15. Ep. 73.

16. This is from Stouppe's account; see Freudenthal, *Die Lebensgeschichte Spinoza's*, 195.

17. For the document, and information about the individuals connected with it, see Petry and Van Suchtelen, "Spinoza and the Military: A Newly Discovered Document."

18. For a history of the society and a survey of the topics of its discussion, see Van Suchtelen, "Nil Volentibus Arduum: Les Amis de Spinoza au travail."

19. Ibid., 397–8.

20. Freudenthal, *Die Lebensgeschichte Spinoza's*, 74.

21. Ibid., 75.

22. For Spinoza's earliest Dutch critics, see Van Bunge, "On the Early Reception of the *Tractatus Theologico-Politicus*." On Bredenburg, see Kolakowski, *Chrétiens san église*, chap. 4. See also Siebrand, *Spinoza and the Netherlanders*.

23. Aubrey, *Brief Lives*, 1:357.

24. The Utrecht consistory met on April 8; Leiden, on May 9; and Haarlem, on May 27.

25. For a study of the difficulties posed by the secular authorities for the publication and distribution of the *Treatise* before 1674, in which the traditional view that the work circulated freely and unhindered by any official action by the nonreligious municipal and provincial powers is corrected, see Israel, "The Banning of Spinoza's Works in the Dutch Republic (1670–1678)."

26. The documents, or parts thereof, of all these actions against Spinoza are in Freudenthal, *Die Lebensgeschichte Spinoza's*, 121–89.

27. It is not certain that it was Rieuwertsz who initiated the translation, but this seems the most likely hypothesis.

28. Ep. 44.

29. Ep. 6, IV/36; SL/83.

30. Ep. 50.

31. See item 67/41 in the catalogue of Spinoza's books, Freudenthal, *Die Lebensgeschichte Spinoza's*, 161.

32. Ep. 45.

33. See Leibniz's letter of May 5, 1671 to Graevius; Leibniz, *Sämtliche Schriften und Briefe* I.1, 148.

34. Ep. 46.

35. Although none of the letters of their correspondence remain, Schuller's letter (Ep. 70) indicates clearly that there was such a philosophical exchange.

36. Tschirnhaus gained at least an epistolary introduction to Spinoza through Schuller, to whom Spinoza writes about "your friend" in October 1674 (Ep. 58). By January 1675, however, Tschirnhaus and Spinoza have had at least one face-to-face conversation about philosophical matters (see Ep. 59), and Spinoza may have been sufficiently impressed by the young man to allow him to have a copy of the *Ethics*.

37. Ep. 70.
38. Leibniz, *Die Philosophischen Schriften*, 1:64.
39. Leibniz, *Sämtliche Schriften und Briefe* I.1, 148.
40. Ibid., 142.
41. Ep. 72.
42. Freudenthal, *Die Lebensgeschichte Spinoza's*, 201.
43. *Essais de Théodicée, Philosophische Schriften*, 6:217. For studies of Leibniz and Spinoza, see Friedmann, *Leibniz et Spinoza*, and the special issue of *Studia Spinozana* devoted to that theme (vol. 6, 1990).
44. *New Essays on Human Understanding*, Book IV, chap. 16, sec. 4.
45. My account of the beginning of the war with France and of the events leading up to the demise of the De Witt brothers is heavily indebted to Jonathan Israel's narrative in *The Dutch Republic*, 776–806; and Rowen, *John de Witt*, chap. 12.
46. Rowen, *John de Witt: Statesman of the True Freedom*, 216.
47. Freudenthal, *Die Lebensgeschichte Spinoza's*, 201.
48. Ibid., 194.
49. For a masterful account of the Voetian/Cocceian controversies, see Israel, *The Dutch Republic*, 660–9; 889–99. See also the material in Thijssen-Schoute, *Nederlands Cartesianisme*.
50. Kolakowski, *Chrétiens sans église*, 313.
51. See Israel, *The Dutch Republic*, 916–19.
52. Ep. 68.
53. See Kolakowski, *Chrétiens sans église*, 293–309.
54. Ep. 47.
55. Freudenthal, *Die Lebensgeschichte Spinoza's*, 219.
56. See Mayer, "Spinoza's Berufung an die Hochschule zu Heidelberg," 30.
57. See item 71/45 in the catalogue of Spinoza's books, Freudenthal, *Die Lebensgeschichte Spinoza's*, 162.
58. Ep. 48.
59. This, at least, is Mayer's conjecture; see "Spinoza's Berufung an die Hochschule zu Heidelberg," 38. He suspects, in fact, that the Elector never even gave instructions that Spinoza should not "dogmatize," and that this might be Chevreau simply summarizing the content of Fabricius's letter rather than the Elector's instructions to Fabricius.
60. Freudenthal, *Die Lebensgeschichte Spinoza's*, 219.
61. Biographical information on Stouppe can be found in Meinsma, *Spinoza et son cercle*, 420–2; and Popkin, "The First Published Reaction to Spinoza's *Tractatus*," 6–7.
62. Stouppe, *La religion des hollandais*, 66.
63. *TTP* V, III/76; S/119.
64. Stouppe, *La Religion des hollandais*, 106.
65. Freudenthal, *Die Lebensgeschichte Spinoza's*, 200.
66. This is Popkin's suggestion; see "The First Published Discussion of a Central Theme in Spinoza's Tractatus," 103. Colerus reports that Stouppe and Spinoza exchanged letters at some point (although these are, if they ever existed, now lost); see Freudenthal, *Die Lebensgeschichte Spinoza's*, 64.

67. Meinsma, *Spinoza et son cercle*, 420.
68. Among the members of Condé's circle in France was Balthazar Orobio de Castro, later Isaac Orobio de Castro and Spinoza's leading critic from the Amsterdam Portuguese community; see Kaplan, *From Christianity to Judaism*, 103–4.
69. Freudenthal, *Die Lebensgeschichte Spinoza's*, 64.
70. Lucas, in ibid., 16.
71. Ep. 69.
72. See Gustave Cohen, "Le Sèjour de Saint-Evremond en Hollande (1665–1670)," 70–1.
73. Freudenthal, *Die Lebensgeschichte Spinoza's*, 34–5.
74. See Popkin, "The First Published Reaction to Spinoza's Tractatus," 11.
75. Among recent scholars, Popkin has made the strongest case for Spinoza having actually met Condé; see "Serendipity at the Clark: Spinoza and the Prince of Condé."
76. Freudenthal, *Die Lebensgeschichte Spinoza's*, 64–5.
77. Ibid., 65.

12. "A free man thinks least of all of death"

1. See Spinoza's response to this letter on June 2, 1674, Ep. 50.
2. See Kolakowski, *Chrétiens sans église*, 217–25.
3. Ep. 48b.
4. This was not the first provincial decree in Holland taken against the work, as we saw in Chapter 11. In fact, the province of Utrecht may have already banned the book as well; see Israel, "The Banning of Spinoza's Works in the Dutch Republic (1670–1978)," 9.
5. Freudenthal, *Die Lebensgeschichte Spinoza's*, 139–40.
6. Ep. 6.
7. Ep. 69. The remark is made to Van Velthuysen, one of his critics, but with whom he is now on cordial terms.
8. Freudenthal, *Die Lebensgeschichte Spinoza's*, 207.
9. Ep. 60. Tschirnhaus had asked Spinoza, "when shall we have your Method of rightly directing the reason in acquiring knowledge of unknown truths, and also your General Treatise on Physics? I know that you have but recently made great advances in these subjects. I have already been made aware of the former, and the latter is known to me from the lemmata attached to the second part of your *Ethics*, which provide a ready solution to many problems in physics" (Ep. 59). In the published version of the *Ethics*, there is further reason to believe that Spinoza was still thinking of working on the *TIE*, or at least a later version thereof. Although it is not clear from what period of the composition of the *Ethics* this part of the text derives, in the discussion of adequate ideas and common notions in *Ethics* IIP40s, he claims that he is reserving discussion of these matters for "another Treatise"; Curley, in his note, suggests that this would be a later draft of the *TIE*.
10. Ep. 68.
11. Ep. 69.
12. Proietti argues persuasively that the composition of the Hebrew grammar should

be placed somewhere between 1670 and 1675; see "Il 'Satyricon' di Petronio e la datazione della 'Grammatica Ebraica' Spinoziana."

13. *TTP* VII, III/100; S/143.

14. I/310.

15. I/300.

16. See Akkerman, "The Preface to Spinoza's Posthumous Works," 252.

17. Ibid., 253.

18. I/324.

19. For a discussion of this aspect of the *Compendium*, see Levy, "The Problem of Normativity in Spinoza's *Hebrew Grammar.*"

20. See *Compendium*, chap. 5.

21. See Levy, "The Problem of Normativity," 372.

22. Boxel began their correspondence in September 1674, Ep. 51.

23. Ep. 54.

24. Ep. 56.

25. Ep. 58.

26. Thomasius, *Freymüthige Lustige und Ernsthafte iedoch Vernunft- und Gesetz-Mässige Gedancken*, 1:780. For a study of Tschirnhaus and Spinoza, see, Wurtz, "Un disciple hérétique de Spinoza: Ehrenfried Walther von Tschirnhaus"; and Vermij, "Le Spinozisme en Hollande: Le Cercle de Tschirnhaus."

27. Oldenburg seems not to have received the copy Spinoza sent him but got his hands on one anyway; see Ep. 61.

28. Ep. 61.

29. Ep. 62.

30. Ep. 63.

31. Ep. 71.

32. Ep. 73.

33. Ep. 62.

34. Ep. 74.

35. Ep. 75.

36. Ep. 78.

37. Ep. 79.

38. See Belinfante et al., *The Esnoga: A Monument to Portuguese-Jewish Culture*, 47.

39. Ep. 68.

40. Freudenthal, *Die Lebensgeschichte Spinoza's*, 147–8.

41. Ibid., 200.

42. Ep. 67.

43. For the details, see Arnauld, *Apologie pour les Catholiques*, II.25, in *Oeuvres*, 25:861–4.

44. Ibid., 862.

45. Ep. 76.

46. In the same month Albert Burgh wrote his letter to Spinoza, the older and more accomplished Danish scientist, Nicholas Steno, a friend of Spinoza's from his time in Leiden, wrote to Spinoza from Florence with a similar goal in mind. Steno had converted to Catholicism in 1667. He and Burgh, in fact, may have been work-

ing together in trying to get their philosopher friend to convert, although there is no hard evidence to confirm this. Steno's tone is much more gentle, reasonable, and solicitous; there is none of the harshness of Burgh's letter. He emphasizes the sterility of Spinoza's philosophy – of which he seems to have a good understanding – and the eternal rewards promised by adherence to the church. It is possible, however, that Spinoza never received the letter (Ep. 67a in his correspondence). Klever argues, moreover, that the correct dating of the letter is 1671, not 1675; see "Steno's Statements on Spinoza and Spinozism."

47. For Leibniz's comments on Spinoza's letters to Oldenburg, see Leibniz, *Philosophische Schriften*, 1:123–30. Leibniz also read and commented on Spinoza's letter to Meyer of April 1663, which Schuller showed him while he was in Amsterdam; *Philosophische Schriften*, 1:130–8.

48. Friedmann, however, does not think that Leibniz was familiar with the text of the *Ethics* by the time he was in Holland; see *Leibniz et Spinoza*, 83.

49. See Leibniz's remarks in his *Theodicy*, III.376; and the "Réfutation inédit de Spinoza."

50. Freudenthal, *Die Lebensgeschichte Spinoza's*, 206. Exactly which propositions Leibniz thought stood in need of demonstration is indicated by a paper of November 1676 in *Philosophische Schriften*, VII.262.

51. Leibniz, *Philosophische Schriften*, VII.261–2.

52. Akkerman, "The Preface to Spinoza's Posthumous Works," 249.

53. III/275; E/289.

54. III/274; E/288–9.

55. III/308; E/327.

56. III/308–10; E/328–30.

57. III/308; E/328.

58. See Israel, *The Dutch Republic*, 814–18.

59. III/348; E/371.

60. III/352; E/376.

61. III/357; E/383.

62. III/359–60; E/386–7.

63. For a rationalization and defense of Spinoza's position on the exclusion of women from full citizenship, see Matheron, "Femmes et serviteurs dans la démocratie spinoziste."

64. Freudenthal, *Die Lebensgeschichte Spinoza's*, 94.

65. IVP67.

66. Freudenthal, *Die Lebensgeschichte Spinoza's*, 202.

67. Ibid., 76.

68. Ibid., 95–6.

69. On Schuller's presence at Spinoza's death, and on his role in preparing his papers for publication, see Steenbakkers, *Spinoza's Ethica from Manuscript to Print*, 50–63.

70. The less dishonorable explanation for the disappearance of the goods was first offered by Monnikhoff; see Freudenthal, *Die Lebensgeschichte Spinoza's*, 108.

71. There had been an inventory of Spinoza's goods taken on the day of his death; for the details of the two inventories, see ibid., 154–6 and 158–65.

72. Ibid. 165–7.
73. Vaz Dias and Van der Tak, *Spinoza Merchant and Autodidact*, 171.
74. So says Kortholt; see Freudenthal, *Die Lebensgeschichte Spinoza's*, 27.
75. According to Colerus; Freudenthal, 98.
76. Freudenthal, 103.
77. Rieuwertsz, Jellesz, Meyer, Bouwmeester, Schuller, Pieter van Gent, and Glaze-maker were all involved in the project.
78. The Hebrew grammar appeared only in the Latin edition, and his friends selected only those letters they deemed to be of philosophical interest.

Bibliography

Aitzema, Lieuwe van. *Herstelde Leeuw, of Discours over 't gepasseerde in de Vereenigde Nederlanden in't jaer 1650 ende 1651.* The Hague, 1652.

Akkerman, Fokke. "Spinoza's Tekort aan Woorden." In *Mededelingen vanwege het Spinozahuis* 36 (1977).

———. "Studies in the Posthumous Works of Spinoza." Ph.D. thesis, University of Groningen, 1980.

Akkerman, Fokke, and H. G. Hubbeling. "The Preface to Spinoza's Posthumous Works (1677) and Its Author Jarig Jellesz (c. 1619/20–1683)." *LIAS* 6 (1979): 103–73.

Akkerman, Fokke, et al. *Spinoza: Korte Geschriften.* Amsterdam: Wereldbibliotheek, 1982.

Albiac, Gabriel. *La Synagogue vide.* Paris: Presses Universitaires de France, 1994.

Allison, Henry E. *Benedict de Spinoza: An Introduction.* New Haven, CT: Yale University Press, 1987.

Alquié, Ferdinand. *Le Rationalisme de Spinoza.* Paris: Presses Universitaires de France, 1981.

Altmann, Alexander. "Eternality of Punishment: A Theological Controversy within the Amsterdam Rabbinate in the Thirties of the Seventeenth Century." *Proceedings of the American Academy for Jewish Research* 40 (1972): 1–88.

d'Ancona, J. *Delmedigo, Menasseh ben Israel en Spinoza.* Amsterdam, 1940.

———. "Komst der Marranen in Noord-Nederland: De Portugese Gemeenten te Amsterdam tot de Vereniging." In Brugmans and Frank, eds., *Geschiedenis der Joden in Nederland.* Amsterdam, 1940.

Arnauld, Antoine. *Oeuvres de Messire Antoine Arnauld.* 43 vols. Brussels: Sigismond d'Arnay, 1775–83.

Aubrey, John. *Brief Lives.* Ed. Andrew Clark. Oxford: Clarendon Press, 1898.

Auffret-Ferzli. "L'Hypothèse d'une rédaction echelonné du Tractatus de Intellectus Emendatione de Spinoza." *Studia Spinozana* 8 (1992): 281–94.

Baer, Yitzhak. *A History of the Jews in Christian Spain.* Philadelphia: Jewish Publication Society, 1966.

Barbone, Steven, Lee Rice, and Jacob Adler. "Introduction." In *Spinoza: The Letters.* Trans. Samuel Shirley. Indianapolis: Hackett Publishing, 1995.

Baron, S. W. *A Social and Religious History of the Jews.* Vol. 15. New York: Columbia University Press, 1952.

Battisti, G. Saccara del Buffa. "La dimostrazione dell'esistenza di Dio.," In F. Mignini, ed., *Dio, l'uomo, la libertà: Studi sul Breve trattato di Spinoza*. L'Aquila: Japadre, 1990.

Bedjai, Marc. "Métaphysique, éthique et politique dans l'oeuvre du docteur Franciscus van den Enden (1602–1674): Contribution à l'étude des sources des écrits de B. de Spinoza." Ph.D. thesis: University of Leiden, 1990.

Belinfante, Judith C. E., et al. *The Esnoga: A Monument to Portuguese-Jewish Culture*. Amsterdam: D'Arts, 1991.

Blom, H. W. "Spinoza en De La Court." *Mededelingen vanwege het Spinozahuis* 42 (1981).

Blom, H. W., and J. M. Kerkhoven. "A Letter concerning an Early Draft of Spinoza's Treatise on Religion and Politics?" *Studia Spinozana* 1 (1985): 371–7.

Bloom, Herbert. *The Economic Activities of the Jews of Amsterdam in the Seventeenth and Eighteenth Centuries*. Williamsport, PA, 1937.

Bodian, Miriam. "Amsterdam, Venice, and the Marrano Diaspora in the Seventeenth Century." *Dutch Jewish History* 2 (1989): 47–66.

Bonger, H. *Spinoza en Coornhert. Mededelingen vanwege het Spinozahuis*. 57(1989).

Bordoli, Roberto. *Ragione e scrittura tra Descartes e Spinoza. Saggio sulla 'Philosophia s. Scripturae Interpres' di Lodewijk Meyer e sulla sua recezione*. Milan: Franco Angeli, 1997.

Bouillier, Francisque, *Histoire de la philosophie Cartésienne*. 2 vols. Paris, 1868.

Browne, Lewis. *Blessed Spinoza*. New York: Macmillan, 1932.

Brugmans, H., and A. Frank. *Geschiedenis der Joden in Nederland*. Amsterdam, 1940.

Brykman, Geneviève. *La Judéité de Spinoza*. Paris: J. Vrin, 1972.

Cohen, Gustave. "Le Séjour de Saint-Evremond en Hollande (1665–1670)." *Revue de littérature comparée* 6 (1926): 28–78.

Cohen, Robert. "*Memoria para os siglos futuros:* Myth and Memory on the Beginnings of the Amsterdam Sephardi Community." *Jewish History* 2 (1987): 67–72.

Coppier, André-Charles. "Rembrandt et Spinoza." *Revue des deux mondes* 31(1916): 160–91.

Behind the Geometrical Method: A Reading of Spinoza's Ethics. Princeton, NJ: Princeton University Press, 1988.

"Notes on a Neglected Masterpiece II: The *Theological-Political Treatise* as a Prolegomenon to the *Ethics*." in J. A. Cover and M. Kulstad, *Central Themes in Early Modern Philosophy*. Indianapolis: Hackett, 1990.

Spinoza's Metaphysics: An Essay in Interpretation. Cambridge, MA: Harvard University Press, 1969.

Curley, E. M. "Une Nouvelle Traduction anglaise des oeuvres de Spinoza." In *Spinoza entre lumières et romantisme*, Pairs: Les Cahiers de Fontenay-aux-Roses, 1985.

Da Costa, Uriel. *Examination of the Pharisaic Traditions*. Trans. H. P. Salomon and I. S. D. Sassoon, Leiden: E. J. Brill, 1993.

De Barrios, Miguel [Daniel Levi]. *Triumpho del govierno popular*. Amsterdam, ca. 1683–4.

De Deugd, Cornelius, ed., *Spinoza's Political and Theological Thought*. Amsterdam: North Holland Publishing Co., 1984.

De Dijn, Herman. "Was Van Den Enden Het Meesterbrein Achter Spinoza?" *Algemeen Nederlands Tijdschrift voor Wijsbegeerte* 1 (1994): 71–9.

Descartes, René. *Oeuvres de Descartes.* Ed. Charles Adam and Paul Tannery. 11 vol. Paris: J. Vrin, 1964–75.

De Vet, J. J. V. M. "Spinoza's Authorship of 'Stelkonstige Reeckening Van Den Regenboog' and of 'Reeckening Van Kanssen' Once More Doubtful." *Studia Spinozana* 2 (1986): 267–309.

"Was Spinoza de Auteur van Stelkonstige Reeckening van den Regenborg en Reeckening van Kanssen?" *Tijdschrift voor Filosofie* 45 (1983): 602–39.

Dunin-Borkowski, Stanislaus von. *Der Junge de Spinoza.* Münster: Aschendorffsche Verlagsbuchhandlung, 1910.

Spinoza. 4 vols. Münster: Aschendorff, 1933.

Emmanuel, Isaac S. *Precious Stones of the Jews of Curaçao. Curaçaon Jewry 1656–1957.* New York: Bock, 1957.

Feuer, Lewis Samuel. *Spinoza and the Rise of Liberalism.* Boston: Beacon Press, 1958.

Francès, Madeleine. *Spinoza dans les pays Néerlandais da la seconde moitié du XVIle siècle.* Paris, 1937.

Freudenthal, J. *Die Lebensgeschichte Spinoza's in Quellenschriften, Urkunden und Nichtamtlichen Nachrichten.* Leipzig: Verlag Von Veit, 1899.

Spinoza: Sein Leben und Seine Lehre. Stuttgart: Fr. Frommanns Verlag, 1904.

Friedmann, Georges. *Leibniz et Spinoza.* Paris: Gallimard, 1962.

Fuks-Mansfield, R. G. *De Sefardim in Amsterdam tot 1795.* Hilversum: Historische Vereniging Holland, 1989.

Gabbey, Alan. "Spinoza's Natural Science and Methodology." In *The Cambridge Companion to Spinoza.* Ed. Don Garrett. Cambridge: Cambridge University Press, 1996.

Gans, Mozes H. *Memorboek: History of Dutch Jewry from the Renaissance to 1940.* Trans. Arnold J. Pomerans. Baarn: Bosch & Keuning, 1971.

Gebhardt, Carl. "Juan de Prado." *Chronicon Spinozanum* 3 (1923): 219–91.

"Rembrandt und Spinoza." *Chronicon Spinozanum* 4 (1924–6): 160–83.

ed., *Die Schriften des Uriel da Costa.* Amsterdam: Curis Societatis Spinozanae, 1922.

Gerber, Jane. *The Jews of Spain.* New York: Free Press, 1992.

Geyl, Pieter. *The Netherlands in the Seventeenth Century.* 2 vols. London: Williams and Norgate, 1961.

Halevi, Uri ben Aaron. *Narraçao da vinda dos Judeos espanhoes a Amsterdam.* Amsterdam, 1715.

Hessing, Siegfried. *Speculum Spinozanum 1677–1977.* London: Routledge and Kegan Paul, 1977.

Hobbes, Thomas. *Leviathan.* Ed. E.M. Curley. Indianapolis: Hackett Publishing, 1994.

Hubbeling, H. G. *Spinoza.* Baarn: het Wereldvenster, 1978.

"Spinoza's Life: A Synopsis of the Sources and Some Documents." *Giornale critico della filosofia italiana* 8 (1977): 390–409.

Hunter, Graeme, ed. *Spinoza: The Enduring Questions.* Toronto: University of Toronto Press, 1994.

Huussen, Arend H. Jr. "The Legal Position of Sephardi Jews in Holland, circa 1600."
    In *Dutch Jewish History*. Vol. 3. Assen: Van Gorcum, 1993.
Huygens, Christiaan. *Oeuvres complètes*. 22 vols. The Hague: Martinus Nijhoff, 1893.
Israel, Jonathan. "The Banning of Spinoza's Works in the Dutch Republic (1670–
    1678)." In W. van Bunge and W. Klever, eds., *Disguised and Overt Spinozism around
    1670*. Leiden: Brill, 1996.
    "The Changing Role of the Dutch Sephardim in International Trade, 1595–1715."
    Dutch Jewish History 1 (1984): 31–51.
    The Dutch Republic: Its Rise, Greatness, and Fall, 1477–1806. Oxford: Oxford Uni-
    versity Press, 1995.
    "Dutch Sephardi Jewry, Millenarian Politics, and the Struggle for Brazil (1640–
    1654)." In David Katz and Jonathan Israel, eds., *Sceptics, Millenarians, and Jews*,
    76–97. Leiden: E. J. Brill, 1990.
    "The Economic Contribution of Dutch Sephardic Jewry to Holland's Golden Age,
    1595–1713." *Tijdschrift Voor Geschiedenis* 96 (1983): 505–35.
    European Jewry in the Age of Mercantilism, 1550–1750. Oxford: Oxford University
    Press, 1985.
    "Sephardic Immigration into the Dutch Republic." *Studia Rosenthaliana* 23 (1989):
    45–53.
    "Spain and the Dutch Sephardim, 1609–1660." *Studia Rosenthaliana* 12 (1978): 1–61.
Japiske, N. "Spinoza en de Witt." *Bijdragen Vaderlandse Geschiedenis* 6 (1927).
Joachim, H. H. *Spinoza's Tractatus de Intellectus Emendatione*. Oxford: Clarendon
    Press, 1901.
Jongeneelen, Gerrit. "An Unknown Pamphlet of Adriaan Koerbagh." *Studia Spin-
    ozana* 3 (1987): 405–15.
    "La Philosophie politique d'Adriaen Koerbagh." *Cahiers Spinoza* 6 (1991): 247–67.
Kaplan, Yosef. *From Christianity to Judaism: The Story of Isaac Orobio de Castro*. Ox-
    ford: Oxford University Press, 1989.
    "'Karaites' in Early Eighteenth-Century Amsterdam." In David S. Katz and Jon-
    athan Israel, eds., *Sceptics, Millenarians, and Jews*, 196–236. Leiden: E. J. Brill,
    1990.
    "The Portuguese Community in Seventeenth Century Amsterdam and the Ashke-
    nazi World." *Dutch Jewish History* 2 (1989): 23–45.
    The Portuguese Community of Amsterdam in the Seventeenth Century. Catalogue for
    the Exhibition Marking the 300th Anniversary of the Inauguration of the Por-
    tuguese Synagogue in Amsterdam. Jerusalem: Jewish National and University
    Library, 1975.
    "The Portuguese Jews in Amsterdam: From Forced Conversion to a Return to Ju-
    daism." *Studia Rosenthaliana* 15 (1981): 37–51.
    "The Social Functions of the *Herem* in the Portuguese Jewish Community of Am-
    sterdam in the Seventeenth Century." *Dutch Jewish History* 1 (1984): 111–55.
Kasher, Asa, and Shlomo Biderman. "When Was Spinoza Banned?" *Studia Rosen-
    thaliana* 12 (1978): 108–10.
    "Why Was Spinoza Excommunicated?" In David S. Katz and Jonathan Israel, eds.,
    Sceptics, Millenarians, and Jews, 98–141. Leiden: Brill, 1990.

Katz, David. *Philosemitism and the Readmission of the Jews to England: 1603–1655.* Oxford: Oxford University Press, 1982.

Katz, David S. and Jonathan Israel, ed. *Sceptics, Millenarians, and Jews.* Leiden: E. J. Brill, 1990.

Katz, Jacob. *Tradition and Crisis.* New York: New York University Press, 1993.

Kayser, Rudolf. *Spinoza: Portrait of a Spiritual Hero.* New York: The Philosophical Library, 1946.

Kayserling, M. "Un Conflit dans la communauté hispano-portugaise d'Amsterdam – Ses consequences." *Revue des Études juives* 43 (1901): 275 – 6.

Keesing, Elisabeth. "Les Frères Huygens et Spinoza." *Cahiers Spinoza* 5 (1984–5): 109–28.

Kerckrinck, Theodore. *Opera Anatomica Continentia Spicilegium Anatomicum.* Leiden: Boutesteyn, 1670.

Kistemaker, Renée, and Tirtsah Levie, eds. *Exodo: Portugezen in Amsterdam, 1600–1680.* Amsterdam: Amsterdams Historisch Museum, 1987.

Klever, W. N. A. "Burchard de Volder (1643–1709), A Crypto-Spinozist on a Leiden Cathedra." *LIAS* 15 (1988): 191–241.

"The Helvetius Affair, or Spinoza and the Philosopher's Stone: A Document on the Background of Letter 40." *Studia Spinozana* 3 (1987): 439–50.

"Insignis Opticus: Spinoza in de Geschiedenis van de Optica." *De Zeventiende Eeuw* 6 (1990): 47–63.

"A New Document on De Witt's Attitude to Spinoza." *Studia Spinozana* 9 (1993): 379–88.

"A New Source of Spinozism: Franciscus Van den Enden." *Journal of the History of Philosophy* 29 (1991): 613–31.

"Omtrent Spinoza." Address at Erasmus Universiteit, Rotterdam. November 15, 1995.

"Spinoza and Van Den Enden in Borch's Diary in 1661 and 1662." *Studia Spinozana* 5 (1989): 311–25.

"Spinoza's Fame in 1667." *Studia Spinozana* 5 (1989): 359–63.

"Spinoza's Life and Works." *The Cambridge Companion to Spinoza.* Ed. Don Garrett. Cambridge: Cambridge University Press, 1996.

"Steno's Statements on Spinoza and Spinozism." *Studia Spinozana* 6 (1990): 303–13.

Koen, E. M. "Waar en voor wie werd de synagoge van 1612 gebouwd?" *Amstelodamum* (1970): 209–12.

Koenen, H. J. *Geschiedenis der Joden in Nederland.* Utrecht, 1843.

Kolakowski, Leszek. *Chrétiens sans église.* Paris: NRF/Editions Gallimard, 1969.

Lagrée, Jacqueline. "Louis Meyer et la *Philosophia S. Scripturae Interpres.*" *Revue des Sciences Philosophiques et Théologiques* 71 (1987): 31–43.

Leibniz, Gottfried Wilhelm. *Die Philosophischen Schriften von Gottfried Wilhelm Leibniz.* Ed. C. I. Gerhardt, 7 vols. Berlin: Weidmann, 1895–90. Reprint Hildesheim: Georg Olms, 1978.

Sämtliche Schriften und Briefe. Deutsche Akademie der Wissenschaften. Multiple vols. in 7 series. Darmstadt/Leipzig/Berlin: Akademie Verlag, 1923.

Leroy, Béatrice. *Les Juifs dans L'Espagne chrétienne avant 1492.* Paris: Albin Michel,
    1993.
Levie, Tirtsah, and Henk Zantkuyl. *Wonen in Amsterdam in de 17de en 18de eeuw.* Am-
    sterdam: Amsterdam Historisch Museum, 1980.
Levin, Dan. *Spinoza: The Young Thinker Who Destroyed the Past.* New York: Weybright
    and Talley, 1970.
Levine, Ruth E., and Susan W. Morgenstein, eds. *The Jews in the Age of Rembrandt.*
    Rockville, MD: The Judaic Museum of the Jewish Community Center of Greater
    Washington, 1981–2.
Levy, Ze'ev. "The Problem of Normativity in Spinoza's *Hebrew Grammar.*" *Studia
    Spinozana* 3 (1987): 351–90.
    "Sur quelques influences juives dans le développement philosophique du jeune
    Spinoza." *Revue des Sciences Philosophiques et Théologiques* 71 (1987): 67–75.
Maimonides. *The Guide of the Perplexed.* Trans. Shlomo Pines 2 vols. Chicago: Uni-
    versity of Chicago Press, 1963.
Marcus, Jacob. *The Jew in the Medieval World.* Cincinnati: The Union of American He-
    brew Congregations, 1938.
Marx, Alexander. *Studies in Jewish Learning and Booklore.* Philadelphia: Jewish Publi-
    cation Society, 1944.
Matheron, Alexandre. "Femmes et serviteurs dans la démocratie spinoziste." *Revue
    philosophique de la France et de l'étranger* 2 (1977): 181–200.
Mayer, M. "Spinoza's Berufung an die Hochschule zu Heidelberg." *Chronicon Spin-
    ozanum* 3 (1923): 20–44.
Méchoulan, Henri. *Amsterdam au temps de Spinoza: Argent et liberté.* Paris: Presses
    Universitaires de France, 1990.
    Etre juif à Amsterdam au temps de Spinoza. Paris: Albin Michel, 1991.
    "Le *Herem* à Amsterdam et l'excommunication de Spinoza." *Cahiers Spinoza* 3
    (1980): 117–34.
    "Morteira et Spinoza au carrefour du socinianisme." *Revue des études juives* 135
    (1976): 51–65.
    "A propos de la visite de Frédéric-Henri, prince d'Orange, a la synagogue d'Ams-
    terdam." *LIAS* 5 (1978): 81–6.
    "Quelques Remarques sur le marranisme et la rupture spinoziste." *Studia Rosen-
    thaliana* 11 (1977): 113–25.
    "Spinoza face à quelques textes d'origine marrane." *Raison présente* 13 (1977):
    13–24.
Meijer, Jaap. *Beeldvorming Om Baruch: "Eigentijdse" Aspecten Van de Vroege Spinoza-
    Biografie.* Heemstede, 1986.
    Encyclopedia Sephardica Neerlandica. Amsterdam: Portugees-Israelietsche Gemeente,
    1949.
    Supplementum Sefardicum Historicum. Heemstede, 1989.
Meininger, Jan V., and Guido van Suchtelen. *Liever Met Wercken als met Woorden: De
    Levensreis Van Doctor Franciscus Van Den Enden.* Weesp: Heureka, 1980.
Meinsma, K. O. *Spinoza et son cercle.* Trans. S. Roosenberg and J.-P. Osier. Paris: J. Vrin,
    1983.

Melnick, Ralph. *From Polemics to Apologetics. Jewish-Christian Rapprochement in 17th Century Amsterdam.* Assen: Van Gorcum, 1981.

Menasseh ben Israel. *The Hope of Israel.* Ed. Henri Méchoulan and Gérard Nahon. Oxford: Oxford University Press, 1987.

Mendes, David Franco. *Memorias do estabelecimento e progresso dos Judeos Portuguezes e Espanhoes nesta famosa citade de Amsterdam. Studia Rosenthaliana* 9 (1975).

Mertens, F. "Franciscus van den Enden: Tijd voor een Herziening van Diens Rol in Het Ontstaan van Het Spinozisme?" *Tijdschrift Voor Filosofie* 56 (1994): 717–38.

Meyer, Lodewijk. *Philosophia S. Scripturae Interpres: La philosophie interprète de l'E-criture Sainte.* Trans. Jacqueline Lagree and P. F. Moreau. Paris: Intertextes, 1988.

Michman, Jozeph. "Historiography of the Jews in the Netherlands." *Dutch Jewish History* 1 (1984): 16–22.

Michman, Jozeph, Hartog Beem, and Dan Michman. *PINKAS: Geschiedenis van de joodse gemeenschap in Nederland.* Antwerp: Kluwer, 1989.

Mignini, Filippo. "Données et problèmes de la chronologie spinozienne entre 1656 et 1665." *Revue des sciences philosophiques et théologiques* 71 (1987): 9–21.

"La cronologia e l'interpretazione delle opere di Spinoza." *La cultura* 26 (1988): 339–60.

"Per la datazione e l'interpretazione del *Tractatus de intellectus emendatione* di B. Spinoza." *La cultura* 17 (1979): 87–160.

Minkin, Jacob S., ed. *The Teachings of Maimonides.* Northvale, NJ: Jason Aronson, 1987.

Moreau, Pierre-François. *Spinoza: L'expérience et l'éternité.* Paris: Presses Universitaires de France, 1994.

Mortera, Saul Levi. *Traktaat Betreffende de Waarheid van de Wet van Mozes (Tratado da verdade da lei de Moisés).* Ed. H. P. Salomon, Braga: Barbosa and Xavier, 1988. *Tratado da Verdade da Lei de Moises.* Coimbra, 1988.

Nahon, Gérard. "Amsterdam, Métropole occidentale des *Sefarades* au XVIIe siècle." *Cahiers Spinoza* 3 (1980): 15–50.

Nazelle, Du Cause de. *Mémoire du temps de Louis XIV.* Ed. Ernest Daudet. Paris: Librairie Plon, 1899.

Netanyahu, Benzion. *The Origins of the Inquisition in Fifteenth-Century Spain.* New York: Random House, 1995.

Offenberg, A. "The Dating of the *Kol Bo.*" *Studia Rosenthaliana* 6 (1972): 86–106.

"A Letter from Spinoza to Lodewijk Meyer, 26 July 1663." Ed. Siegfried Hessing. In *Speculum Spinozanum,* 426–35. London: Routledge and Kegan Paul, 1977.

"Spinoza in Amsterdam: Dichtung und Wahrheit." In *Amsterdam 1585–1672: Morgenröte des Bürgerlichen Kapitalismus.* Ed. Bernd Wilczek. Hamburg: Elster Verlag, 1986.

Offenberg, A. et al., eds. *Spinoza: Troisième centenaire de la mort du philosophe.* Catalogue of exhibition held at the Institut Néerlandais, May–June 1977. Paris, 1977.

Oldenburg, Henry. *The Correspondence of Henry Oldenburg.* Ed. A. Rupert Hall and Marie Boas Hall. 13 vols. Madison: University of Wisconsin Press, 1965–86.

Osier, Jean-Pierre. *D'Uriel da Costa à Spinoza.* Paris: Berg International, 1983.

Paraira, M. C., and J. S. da Silva Rosa. *Gedenkschrift uitgegeven ter gelegenheid van het 300-jarig bestaan der onderwijsinrichtingen Talmud Torah en Ets Haim bij de Portugueesche Israelitische Gemeente te Amsterdam.* Amsterdam, 1916.

Parker, Geoffrey. *The Dutch Revolt.* London: Allen Lane, 1977.

Petry, Michael and Guido van Suchtelen. "Spinoza and the Military: A Newly Discovered Document." *Studia Spinozana* 1 (1985): 359–63.

Peyrera, Abraham. *La Certeza del Camino.* Amsterdam, 1666.

Pieterse, Wilhelmina Christina. *Daniel Levi de Barrios als Geschiedschrijver van de Portugees-Israelietische Gemeente te Amsterdam in zijn "Triumpho del Govierno Popular.* Amsterdam, Scheltema and Holkema, 1968.

Pollock, Frederick. *Spinoza: His Life and Philosophy.* London: Duckworth & Co., 1899.

Popkin, Richard. "Christian Jews and Jewish Christians in the 17th Century." In R. Popkin and C.M. Weiner, eds. *Jewish Christians and Christian Jews.* Dordrecht: Kluwer, 1994.

"The First Published Discussion of a Central Theme in Spinoza's Tractatus." *Philosophia* 17 (1986): 101–9.

"The First Published Reaction to Spinoza's *Tractatus:* Col. J. B. Stouppe, the Condé Circle, and the Rev. Jean LeBrun." In Paolo Cristofolini, ed., *The Spinozist Heresy.* Amsterdam: APA-Holland University Press, 1995.

"Menasseh Ben Israel and Isaac La Peyrère." *Studia Rosenthaliana* 8 (1974): 59–63.

"Spinoza and La Peyrère." In Shahan and Biro, eds., *Spinoza: New Perspectives,* 177–96.

"Rabbi Nathan Shapira's Visit to Amsterdam in 1657." *Dutch Jewish History* 1 (1984): 185–205.

"Samuel Fisher and Spinoza." *Philosophia* 15 (1985): 219–36.

"Serendipity at the Clark: Spinoza and the Prince of Condé." *The Clark Newsletter* 10 (1986): 4–7.

"Some New Light on Spinoza's Science of Bible Study." In M. Grene and D. Nails, eds., *Spinoza and the Sciences.* Dordrecht: Reidel, 1980.

"Spinoza and Bible Scholarship." *The Cambridge Companion to Spinoza.* Ed. D. Garrett. Cambridge: Cambridge University Press, 1996.

"Spinoza's Earliest Philosophical Years." *Studia Spinozana* 4 (1988): 37–55.

Spinoza's Earliest Publication? The Hebrew Translation of Margaret Fell's "A Loving Salutation to the Seed of Abraham among the Jews, Wherever They Are Scattered Up and Down upon the Face of the Earth." Assen: Van Gorcum, 1987.

"Spinoza's Relations with the Quakers in Amsterdam." *Quaker History* 73 (1984): 14–28.

"Spinoza, the Quakers and the Millenarians, 1656–1658." *Manuscrito* 6 (1982): 113–33.

The Third Force in Seventeenth Century Thought. Leiden: Brill, 1992.

Porges, N. "Spinozas Compendium der Hebraïschen Grammatik." *Chronicon Spinozanum* 4 (1924–6): 123–59.

Posthumus, N. W. "The Tulip Mania in Holland in the Years 1636 and 1637." *Journal of Economic and Business History* 1 (1929): 435–65.

Price, J. L. *Holland and the Dutch Republic in the Seventeenth Century: The Politics of Particularism.* Oxford: Clarendon Press, 1994.

Proietti, O. "Adulescens luxu perditus: Classici latini nell'opera di Spinoza." *Revista di filosofia neoscolastica* 2 (1985): 210–57.

"Il 'Satyricon' di Petronio e la datazione della 'Grammatica Ebraica' Spinoziana." *Studia Spinozana* 5 (1989): 253–72.

Reijnders, Carolus. *Van "Joodsche Natien" Tot Joodse Nederlanders.* Amsterdam: [n.p.], 1970.

Rekers, Ben. "Les Points obscurs dans la biographie de Spinoza." *Tijdschrift Voor de Studie Van de Verlichting* 5–6 (1977–8): 151–66.

Revah, I. S. "Aux Origines de la rupture spinozienne: Nouveaux documents sur l'incroyance dans la Communauté judéo-portugaise D'Amsterdam à l'époque de l'excommunication de Spinoza." *Revue des Études juives* 123 (1964): 359–430.

"Aux origines de la rupture spinozienne: Nouvel examen des origines, du déroulement et des conséquences de l'affaire Spinoza-Prado-Ribera." *Annuaire du Collège de France* 70 (1970): 562 – 8.

"Le Premier Règlement imprimé de la 'Santa Companhia de Dotar Orfens e Donzalas Pobres.'" *Boletin Internacional de Bibliografia Luso-brasileira* 4 (1963).

"La Religion d'Uriel da Costa, marrane de Porto." *Revue de l'histoire des religions* 161 (1962): 44–76.

Spinoza et Juan de Prado. Paris: Mouton & Co., 1959.

Roth, Cecil. *A History of the Marranos.* New York: Harper and Row, 1966.

A Life of Menasseh ben Israel. Philadelphia: Jewish Publication Society, 1934.

"The Role of Spanish in the Marrano Diaspora." In *Studies in Books and Booklore,* 111–20. London: Gregg International Publishers, 1972.

Rousset, Bernard. "Elements et hypothèses pour une analyse des rédactions successives de *Ethique* IV." *Cahiers Spinoza* 5 (1984–5): 129–46.

"La Première *Ethique:* Méthode et perspectives." *Archives de philosophie* 51 (1988): 75–98.

Rowen, Herbert H. *John De Witt, Grand Pensionary of Holland, 1625–1672.* Princeton, NJ: Princeton University Press, 1978.

John De Witt: Statesman of the "True Freedom." Cambridge: Cambridge University Press, 1986.

Sacksteder, William. "How Much of Hobbes Might Spinoza Have Read?" *Southwestern Journal of Philosophy* 7 (1969): 25–39.

Salomon, H. P. "Myth or Anti-Myth: The Oldest Account Concerning the Origin of Portuguese Judaism at Amsterdam." *LIAS* 16 (1989): 275–309.

Saul Levi Mortera en zijn Traktaat Betreffende de Waarheid van de Wet van Mozes. Braga: Barbosa and Xavier, 1988.

"La Vraie Excommunication de Spinoza." *Forum Litterarum* 28 (1994): 181–99.

Saperstein, Marc. "Saul Levi Morteira's Treatise on the Immortality of the Soul." *Studia Rosenthaliana* 25 (1991): 131–48.

Schama, Simon. *The Embarrassment of Riches.* Berkeley and Los Angeles: University of California Press, 1988.

Scholem, Gershom. *Sabbatai Sevi: The Mystical Messiah.*, Princeton, NJ: Princeton University Press, 1973.

Schwartz, Gary. *Rembrandt: His Life, His Paintings.* Harmondsworth: Viking, 1985.

Shahan, Robert, and J. I. Biro, eds. *Spinoza: New Perspectives.* Norman: University of Oklahoma Press, 1978.

Shapiro, James. *Shakespeare and the Jews.* New York: Columbia University Press, 1996.

Siebrand, H. J. *Spinoza and the Netherlanders.* Assen: Van Gorcum, 1988.

Silva Rosa, J. S. da. *Geschiedenis der Portugeesche Joden te Amsterdam.* Amsterdam: Menno Hertzberger, 1925.

Spinoza, Baruch. *Spinoza Opera.* Ed. Carl Gebhardt. 5 vols. Heidelberg: Carl Winters Universitätsverlag, 1972 (1925).

Steenbakkers, Piet. *Spinoza's Ethica from Manuscript to Print.* Assen: Van Gorcum, 1994.

Stouppe, Jean-Baptiste. *La Religion des hollandais.* Cologne, 1673.

Swetschinski, Daniel M. "Kinship and Commerce: The Foundations of Portuguese Jewish Life in Seventeenth Century Holland." *Studia Rosenthaliana* 15 (1981): 52–74.

——— *The Portuguese-Jewish Merchants of Seventeenth Century Amsterdam: A Social Profile.* Ph.D. diss., Brandeis University. Ann Arbor: University of Michigan Microfilms, 1977.

Teicher, J. L. "Why Was Spinoza Banned?" *The Menorah Journal* 45 (1957): 41–60.

Thijssen-Schoute, C. L. "Jan Hendrik Glazemaker: De Zeventiende Eeuwse Aartsvertaler." In *Uit de Republiek Der Letteren.* The Hague: Martinus Nijhoff, 1967.

——— "Lodewijk Meyer en Diens Verhouding tot Descartes en Spinoza." In *Uit De Republiek Der Letteren* (collected essays by Thijssen-Schoute). The Hague: Martinus Nijhoff, 1967.

——— *Nederlands Cartesianisme.* Utrecht: Hess, 1954.

Thomasius, Christian. *Freymüthige Lustige und Ernsthafte iedoch Vernunft- und Gesetz-Mässige zwölff Monate des 1688. und 1689. Jahrs.* Halle: Salfeld, 1690.

Valentiner, W. R. *Rembrandt and Spinoza: A Study of the Spiritual Conflicts in Seventeenth Century Holland.* London: Phaidon, 1957.

Van Bunge, Wiep. "On the Early Reception of the *Tractatus Theologico-Politicus.*" *Studia Spinozana* 5 (1989): 225–51.

Van den Berg, Jan. "Quaker and Chiliast: The 'Contrary Thoughts' of William Ames and Petrus Serrarius." In R. Buick Know, ed., *Reformation Conformity and Dissent.* London: Epworth Press, 1977.

Vandenbossche, Hubert. *Adriaan Koerbagh en Spinoza. Mededelingen vanwege het Spinozahuis.* 39 (1978).

Van den Enden, Franciscus. *Vrije Politijke Stellingen.* Ed. W. Klever. Amsterdam: Wereldbibliotheek,1992.

Van der Tak, W. G. *Jarich Jellesz' Origins; Jellesz' Life and Business. Mededelingen vanwege het Spinozahuis* 59 (1989).

——— "Spinoza's Apologie." *De Nieuwe Gids* (1933): 499–508.

——— "Spinoza's Payments to the Portuguese-Israelitic Community; and the Language in Which He Was Raised." *Studia Rosenthaliana* 16 (1982): 190–5.

——— "Van Den Enden and Kerckrinck." *Studia Rosenthaliana* 16 (1982): 176 – 7.

Van der Tang, Aad. "Spinoza en Schiedam." *Scyedam* 10 (1984): 159–184.

Van Dillen, J. G. "La Banque d'Amsterdam." *Revue d'histoire moderne* 15 (1928).

Van Suchtelen, Guido. "Nil Volentibus Arduum: Les Amis de Spinoza au travail." *Studia Spinozana* 3 (1987): 391–404.

"The Spinoza Houses at Rijnsberg and the Hague." In Siegfried Hessing, ed., *Speculum Spinozanum*, 475–8. London: Routledge and Kegan Paul, 1977.

Vaz Dias, A. M. "De scheiding in de oudste Amsterdamsche Portugeesche Gemeente Beth Jacob." *De Vrijdagavond* 7 (1939): 387–8.

"Did Spinoza Live in 'T Opregte Tappeythuis'?" *Studia Rosenthaliana* 16 (1982): 172 – 5.

"Nieuwe Bijdragen tot de Geschiedenis der Amsterdamsche Hoogduitsch-Joodsche Gemeente." *Bijdragen en Mededelingen Van Het Genootschap Voor Joodse Wetenschap in Nederland* 6 (1940).

"Een verzoek om de Joden in Amsterdam een bepaalde woonplaats aan te wijzen." *Jaarboek Amstelodamum* 35 (1938): 180–202.

"Rembrandt en zijn Portugueesch-Joodsche Buren." *Amstelodamum* 19 (1932): 10.

Spinoza and Simon Joosten de Vries. Mededelingen Vanwege Het Spinozahuis 59 (1989).

Uriel da Costa. Nieuwe Bijdrage tot diens Levensgeschiedenis. Leiden, 1936.

"Wie Waren Rembrandt's Joodsche Buren?" *De Vrijdagavond*, Oct. 10, 1930, 22–6; Oct. 17, 1930, 40–45.

Vaz Dias, A. M., and W. G. van der Tak. "The Firm of Bento y Gabriel de Spinoza." *Studia Rosenthaliana* 16 (1982): 178–89.

Spinoza, Merchant and Autodidact, in *Studia Rosenthaliana* 16 (1982): 105–71.

Verbeek, Theo. *Descartes and the Dutch.* Carbondale: Southern Illinois University Press, 1992.

Vermij, Rienk. "Le Spinozisme en Hollande: Le Cercle de Tschirnhaus." *Cahiers Spinoza* 6 (1991): 145–68.

Vlessing, Odette. "The Jewish Community in Transition: From Acceptance to Emancipation." *Studia Rosenthaliana* 30 (1996): 195–211.

"New Light on the Earliest History of the Amsterdam Portuguese Jews." In *Dutch Jewish History.* Vol. 3. Assen: Van Gorcum, 1993.

"Portugese Joden in de Gouden Eeuw." *Opbouw* 42 (1989): 3–14.

Vloemans, A. *Spinoza. De Mensch, Het Leven en Het Werk.* The Hague, 1931.

Vries, Theun de. *Spinoza: Beeldenstormer en Wereldbouwer.* Amsterdam: H. J. W. Becht's Uitgeversmaatschappij, n.d.

Wiznitzer, Arnold. *The Jews of Colonial Brazil.* New York, 1960.

"The Merger Agreement and the Regulations of Congregation 'Talmud Torah' of Amsterdam (1638–39)." *Historia Judaica* 20–1 (1958–9): 109–32.

Wolf, A., ed. and trans. *The Oldest Biography of Spinoza.* Port Washington, NY: Kennikat Press, 1970 (1927).

Wolfson, Harry. *The Philosophy of Spinoza.* 2 vols. Cambridge, MA: Harvard University Press, 1934.

Worp, T. *Geschiedenis van het drama en van het toneel in Nederland.* 2 vols. Groningen: J. B. Wolters, 1904–8.

Wurtz, Jean-Paul. "Un disciple 'hérétique' de Spinoza: Ehrenfried Walther Von Tschirnhaus." *Cahiers Spinoza* 6 (1991): 111–43.

Yovel, Yirmiyahu. *Spinoza and Other Heretics*. Vol. 1, "The Marrano of Reason." Princeton, NJ: Princeton University Press, 1989.

"Why Was Spinoza Excommunicated?" *Commentary*, November 1977, 46–52.

Index

Aboab (da Fonseca), Isaac, 16, 18, 56,
    64, 78, 89, 91, 92, 94, 116, 124,
    130, 137, 143, 149, 157, 252
  dispute with Mortera, 52–4
Abrabanel, Jonas, 75
Abrabanel, Judah, 138
Alkmaar, 9, 356 n.14
Alvares, Anthony, 87–9
Alvares, Gabriel, 87–9
Alvares, Isaac, 87–9
Ames, William, 158, 169
Amsterdam
  and Dutch politics, 48, 83, 150, 286
  economic growth, 8, 35
  and Jews, 5–9, 10–12, 14–15, 24–6,
    148–50
  plague, 49, 212
  political organization of, 57–9
  and Remonstrant controversy, 13
  toleration in, 147
Antwerp, 5, 7–8, 103, 144
Aristotelian philosophy, 109, 112, 151,
    152, 167, 191, 197, 211
Arminius, Jacobus, 12

Bacon, Francis, 111, 193, 226
Balling, Pieter, 107, 112, 141, 169, 194,
    201, 202, 211, 212–13, 225
Barrios, Daniel Levi de, 90, 145–6
Baruch, Abraham, 56, 62, 124
Bass, Shabbethai, 61–4
Bayle, Pierre, 110, 132–3, 246
Berckel, Abraham van, 195, 268
Beth Israel (congregation), 17, 18, 31,
    39, 44, 52, 55, 128
Beth Jacob (congregation), 9, 16, 17–18,
    28, 29, 30, 31, 37–8, 43, 44, 51–2,

    55, 61, 66, 90, 91, 94, 128, 356
    n.15, n.16
Beyeren, Leendert van, 78
Bible, 53, 65, 67, 172, 131, 134, 137, 163,
    172, 216, 272–3, 275–80
Bicker, Andries, 76, 82, 84
Blijenburgh, Willem van, 47, 211,
    214–18, 295
Borch, Olaus, 158, 180
Boreel, Adam, 140–141, 159, 160, 162
Bouwmeester, Johannes, 173, 202,
    223–4, 225, 294, 300, 320
Boxel, Hugo, 326–7
Boyle, Robert, 191–3, 300, 330–1
Brazil, 45, 64, 96, 116
  Jewish community (Recife), 54, 82,
    116
  and Jewish trade, 22–3, 81–2
Bredenburg, Johannes, 295
Brun, Jean, 316
Bruno, Giordano, 111
Bueno, Ephraim, 76, 89
Bueno, Joseph, 40
Burgh, Albert, 158, 336–40
Burgh, Conraad, 158, 336, 338, 340
Burman, Frans, 309

Calvinists (Dutch Reformed Church), 6,
    12–14, 49, 83, 110, 112, 140, 147,
    148, 150, 152, 283–4, 297; see also
    Remonstrants
  and Jews, 10–12, 14, 74
  Voetian/Cocceian controversy, 307–8
Caro, Joseph, 64, 122
Cartesianism, 150–3, 163–7, 168,
    169–70, 196–8, 207–12, 307–10
Carvejal, Antonio Fernandes, 79

Casear, Johannes, 196–9, 207
Casseres, Benjamin de, 45, 86
Casseres, Daniel de, 85, 350–1
Casseres, Hana de, 86
Casseres, Michael de, 45, 86
Casseres, Samuel de, 81, 85–6, 90
Castro, Isaac Orbio de, 142, 145, 146,
    174
Castro, Mordechai de, 62
Catholics, 6, 14, 48, 49, 83, 85, 147
Caton, William, 160–2
Cats, Jacob, 49, 51, 84
Charles I (King of England), 86, 218,
    257
Charles V (Holy Roman Emperor), 5, 7
cherem, 56, 57, 94–5, 120–9, 147
    of Juan de Prado, 143–4
    of Uriel da Costa, 68–9, 71
Chevreau, Urbain, 312–14
Clauberg, Johannes, 166
Cocceianism, 308–11
Coccejus, Johannes, 185, 307–8
Cocq, Frans Banning, 76
Codde, Jacob, 39
Codde, Pieter, 25
Cohen, Samuel, 18
Colerus, Johan, 42, 43–4, 45, 65, 103,
    104, 288, 289, 349, 360 n.2.
Collegiants, 107, 112, 113, 139–41, 146,
    157, 159, 162, 167–70, 181, 194,
    295
conversos, see New Christians
Costa, Abraham da, 38, 66, 67
Costa, Bento da, 66
Costa, Branca (Sarah) da, 66, 67, 70
Costa, Uriel da, 38, 66–74, 101, 128,
    136
Craanen, Theodore, 298, 307
Crayer, Louis, 119
Cromwell, Oliver, 75, 98, 218
Curaçao, 45, 86

De la Court, Pierre, 114, 258, 267
Delmedigo, Joseph, 18, 99–100, 138
Descartes, René, 101, 111–13, 150–3,
    163–7, 193, 196–8, 200–1, 207–12,
    221, 226, 236, 307
Duarte, Manuel, 87–8

Dutch East and West Indies Companies,
    22, 23, 35, 83, 218

Elizabeth I (Queen of England), 5–6
Emden, 6, 7
England, 75, 79, 86–7, 98–9, 159,
    219–19, 257, 303, 305
Erasmus, 111

Fabricius, Johann Ludwig, 311–13
Farar, Abraham, 17, 38, 73, 79
Farar, David, 17–18, 31
Faro, Joseph de, 62
Felgenhauer, Paul, 193
Fell, Margaret, 159–62
Ferdinand of Aragon, 2–3
Fisher, Samuel, 161–3, 277
Flinck, Govert, 76
Fox, George, 161
France, 48–9, 52, 106, 255
    invasion of the Netherlands, 106, 292,
        302, 303–5, 314–15, 317, 334
    Nantes, 27, 29, 31, 32, 35
Frederick Hendrik (Stadholder), 21, 43,
    47–9, 74–5, 82
Fullana, Nicolas de Oliver, 292–3

Galilei, Galileo, 99, 111, 152
Gent, Pieter van, 320, 396 n.77
Geulincx, Arnold, 165, 194
Gijsen, Alewijn, 213, 262, 351
Gijsen, Jacob Simon, 213–14
Glauber, Johannes, 193
Glazemaker, Jan Hendrik, 168, 297
Golius, Jacob, 164
Gomes, Jacob, 62
Goyen, Jan van, 288
Graevius, Johan George, 301, 309, 317
Grotius, Hugo, 11, 111
Guerra, Joseph, 173–4

Hague, The, 42, 47, 203–4, 222, 288–9
Halevi, Aaron, 6, 9, 16, 38
Halevi, Jacob, 70
Halevi, Moses Uri, 6–7, 9, 16, 18
Hamburg, 7, 68, 69, 127, 142, 144, 251
Heereboord, Adriaan, 164, 211
Heidanus, Abraham, 164, 165, 173

Heidelberg, 311–14
Helvetius, Johannes, 263–4
Henrietta Maria (of England), 75
Henriques, Pedro, 40–1, 119
Hobbes, Thomas, 111, 130, 184, 226,
     267, 270, 277, 295–6, 322, 323
Holland (province), 48, 59, 74, 82, 83–5,
     151, 255, 257, 296–7, 322
  and Jews, 10–11
Honthorst, Gerard van, 43
Hooghe, Romeyn de, 76
Hoogstraten, Samuel van, 155
Hudde, Johannes, 183, 222–3, 249, 259,
     267, 341
Huet, Pierre Daniel, 96, 196
Hurwitz, Sabatti Scheftel, 61
Huygens, Christiaan, 183, 185, 196,
     203–4, 221–2, 255, 259, 264, 300
Huygens, Constantijn (père), 203–4
Huygens, Constantijn (fils), 221–2

ibn Ezra, Abraham, 93, 134, 277
Inquisition, 8, 23, 89, 94, 116, 130, 142,
     174; see also Portugal; Spain
Isabella of Austria (royal regent in the
     Spanish Netherlands), 47
Isabella of Castile, 2–3

Jellesz, Jarig, 107, 112, 141, 168, 169,
     194, 202, 211, 263, 294, 297,
     320–1
Jews, see also Sephardim
  Ashkenazim in Amsterdam, 19–21,
     25, 38, 49, 66, 117
  in England, 75
  relations with Dutch, 10–15, 26,
     74–6, 86, 148
  and tulip mania, 51

kabbalah, 52, 54, 89, 99, 249–50
Karl Ludwig (Elector of Palatine),
     311–14
Kerckrinck, Dirk, 108–9, 184, 195, 293
Koerbagh, Adriaan, 113, 157, 170–1,
     172, 173, 202, 257, 263, 265–70,
     285, 294
Koerbagh, Johannes (Jan), 113, 157, 195,
     202, 263, 265, 267–8

La Peyrère, Isaac, 99, 134, 277
Latréaumont, Gilles du Hamel de, 106
Leao, Judah Jacob, 78, 80
Leeuwenhoek, Anton van, 43, 341
Leibniz, Gottfried Wilhelm, 106, 155,
     184, 196, 299–302, 306, 340–2
Leiden, 45, 49, 117, 139, 163, 181, 185,
     194–5, 296, 297
  university, 12, 108, 113, 151, 158,
     163–5, 170–3, 195, 196, 255, 300,
     308, 309, 370 n.5
Levi ben Gershom (Gersonides), 93
Lievens, Jan, 76
London, 7, 8, 79, 98, 116, 212, 251
Louis II of Bourbon (Prince of Condé),
     315–19
Louis XIV (King of France), 105, 106,
     293, 303–5
Lucas, Jean-Maximilian, 42, 43, 59, 64,
     90, 100, 102, 134, 156

Machiavelli, Nicolo, 111, 130, 270
Maimonides, 53, 64, 93, 97, 121–2, 125,
     136, 138, 153, 167, 226, 242, 278
Maltranilla, Miguel Perez de, 131, 135,
     144, 146, 155, 163, 173
Manoel I (King of Portugal), 3–4
Mansveld, Regnier, 295, 298, 307
marranos, see New Christians
Maurits of Nassau, 13
Menasseh ben Israel, 16, 18, 45, 54, 64,
     75, 76, 77–8, 80, 81, 89, 91, 92,
     102, 114, 124, 130, 134, 136–7, 138,
     14, 159–60
  biographical sketch, 93–100
Mendez, Abraham, 72
Mennonites, 101, 107, 113, 139, 159,
     168–9
messianism, 96–8, 159–60, 249, 251
Meyer, Lodewijk, 171–3, 194, 202,
     205–6, 207, 266, 294, 296, 300,
     309–10, 320, 321–2, 350
Milan, Gabriel, 292–3
millenarianism, 97–8, 159–60, 249, 253
Modena, Leon, 68, 91, 128
Montaigne, Michel de, 111, 130
Montalto, Elias Rodriguez, 91
Morales, Henrique, 318

Morocco, 10, 16, 24
Mortera, Saul Levi, 16, 17, 18, 20, 23,
    30–31, 43, 45, 56, 64–5, 78, 80, 81,
    85, 94, 95, 102, 136–8, 143, 144,
    153, 156, 157
  biographical sketch, 91–3
  congregational duties, 56, 64
  dispute with Aboab, 52–4
  and Spinoza's *cherem,* 124, 128–9
  yeshivot, 89–91, 142, 145

Nathan of Gaza, 250–1
Nazelle, Du Cause de, 104, 106
Nieulant, Adriaen van, 25
Netherlands, The
  alliance with Portugal, 81–2
  arrival of Jews, 5–10'
  arrival of New Christians, 5–10
  and Brazil, 82, 116
  economy and trade, 22, 35, 47, 49, 81
  and England, 86–7, 218–19, 254–5,
    257, 303
  and France, 106, 292, 302, 303, 305,
    314–15, 317
  politics, 48–9, 74, 83–5, 112, 148,
    254–7, 283–4, 307–11, 334
  regent class, 58–9
  status of Jews, 9–15, 85, 149–50
  war with Spain, 7–8, 22–3, 28, 35, 43,
    47–9, 74, 81–2
Neve Shalom (congregation), 10, 16,
    17, 18, 39, 44, 51, 52 61, 94, 100,
    356 n.15, n.16, n.17
New Christians, 52–3, 67, 96, 116, 141
  in the Netherlands, 5–9, 15–16
  in Portugal, 3–5, 15, 52
  in Spain, 2–5, 15, 52
  trade with Amsterdam Jews, 23, 28,
    35
Newton, Isaac, 255, 299, 300
Nil Volentibus Arduum, 294–5
Nuñes, Maria, 5–6, 7, 355 n.4

Oldenbarneveldt, Johan, 12–13, 286
Oldenburg, Henry, 180, 184–6, 190–3,
    212, 219–20, 244, 247, 248, 254,
    259–61, 291–300, 329–33, 340
Oli, Jan Volkaertsz, 33, 40, 73
Osorio, Bento, 21

Ouderkerke, 10, 20, 26, 31, 38, 56, 158,
    356 n.14, 358 n.40

Paets, Adriaen, 133, 175, 286
Palache, David, 39
Palache, Samuel, 10
Palestine, 9, 90, 250, 252
Pardo, David, 10, 18, 54, 56
Pardo, Joseph, 9–10, 16, 17–18, 31, 128
Pauw, Adriaan, 11, 43, 48, 82, 84, 256
Pereira, Abraham, 89, 90, 95, 146, 252
Pereira, Isaac, 89, 95
Philip II (King of Spain), 7, 47
Philip IV (King of Spain), 47, 82
plague, 47, 49, 117, 212–13
Poelenberg, Arnold, 133
Portugal
  alliance with the Netherlands, 81–2
  dispute with the Netherlands over
    Brazil, 82
  Inquisition in, 4–5
  and Jewish trade, 22–4, 81–3
  Jews in, 3–5, 15, 52, 67
  union with Spain, 4, 81
Potter, Paulus, 25
Prado, Juan de, 90, 130, 135–6, 138,
    142–6, 154, 173–5

Quakers, 107, 138, 157, 158–63, 254

Raey, Johannes de, 165, 166, 170, 194–5,
    307
Rashi, 62, 63, 63, 93, 122
Regius, Henricus, 164, 165
Reinoso, Miguel, 173–5
Rembrandt (Rembrandt van Rijn), 25,
    43, 45, 76–9, 109, 119
Remonstrants, 48–9, 83, 84, 85, 107,
    139, 159, 286, 295
  controversy in Dutch Reformed
    Church, 12–14, 139, 148
Ribera, Daniel, 143–5
Rieuwertsz, Jan, 107, 139, 141, 168, 169,
    185, 202, 207, 269, 294, 297, 300,
    320, 334, 349
Rijnsburg, 139, 158, 180–1, 194
Robles, Tomas Solano y, 130–1, 135,
    144, 145, 146, 155, 163
Rohan, Louis de, 106

Rotterdam, 28, 31–2, 48, 117, 139
Royal Society, 185, 212

Saadya ben Joseph (Saadya Gaon), 93
Salom ben Joseph, 62–3
Salonika, 16, 55, 251
Sasportas, Jacob, 251–2
Schiedam, 213–14
Schooten, Frans van (the younger), 164
Schooten, Frans van (the elder), 166, 255
Schuller, Georg Hermann, 222, 300–1, 320, 323, 327–8, 341, 349–50
Senior, Hanna Deborah, *see* Spinoza, Hanna Deborah de
Sephardim, *see also* Jews
  and aliases, 23
  in Amsterdam: arrival and status in Amsterdam, 5–9, 10–12, 14–15, 148–50; and art, 76–7, 91–2; and Brazil, *see* Brazil; and Carribean, 87, 117; communal organizaiton, 16–19, 37, 56–9, 124; dispute in 1630s, 51–4; and Dutch politics, 369 n.93; economy and trade, 22–4, 34–5, 81–3, 86, 116; education, 18, 61–4, 89–90; neighborhood, 24–6, 27; and punishment, see *cherem;* and Sabbateanism, 251–2; synagogues, 10, 25, 27, 44, 55, 76, 149, 334–5; union agreement of, 1639, 54–5; wealth, 21
  arrival in the Netherlands, 5–10, 117
  legal status in the Netherlands, 9–12, 14–15, 47, 85
  in Portugal, 3–5
  in Spain, 1–5
Serrarius, Peter, 160, 162, 173, 185, 193, 212, 248, 253–4, 260
Silva, Samuel da, 68–9
Sixtus IV (Pope), 2
socinianism, 92, 140–1, 157, 266, 296
Soliz, Margrieta de, 73
Solms, Amalia van, 43
soul, *see also* Spinoza, on soul
  eternal punishment of, 52–4
  immorality of, 69
Spain, 303–4
  Inquisition in, 2–5

and Jewish trade, 22–4, 81–3
Jews in, 1–5, 15, 52
union with Portugal, 4, 81
war with the Netherlands, 22–3, 47–9, 81–2
Spinoza, Abraham Jesurum de, 9, 17, 27–36, 90
  arrival in Amsterdam, 27–9
  business dealings, 28–9, 35–6
  role in community, 29, 37
Spinoza, Bento (Baruch) de
  "Apologia," 132
  on Bible, 131, 134, 137, 163, 216, 272–3, 275–80, 324
  birth, 36, 42
  in business, 81, 86–89, 118–119
  and Cartesianism, 152–3, 164, 167, 170
  cherem, 120–1, 123–4, 127–9, 155
  childhood, 43–7
  and Chrisitianity, 290–2
  Compendium of Hebrew Grammar, 324–6
  condemnation (in Netherlands), 173, 295–8, 321–2, 335–6
  education, 59–65, 78, 80, 81, 89–91, 93, 99–103, 106–115
  Ethics, 131, 199, 201, 206, 225–44, 247, 298, 271, 281, 300–2, 322–3, 333–5
  family finances, 43–4, 118–20
  on freedom, 131, 189, 237, 242, 328
  on God, 131, 187, 190, 216–17, 227–33
  on happiness, 101–2, 170, 176–7, 186, 190, 241–3
  and Juan de Prado, 130, 142, 145–6, 173–5
  and Judaism, 273–4, 292
  on knowledge, 178–9, 235–7
  language, 46–7
  lense grinding, 108, 182–4, 221
  "Metaphysical Thoughts," 206, 210
  on miracles, 232–3, 274–5
  on passions, 189, 237–43
  personal habits, 193–4, 196, 262–3, 289–90
  Political Treatise, 342–9
  and Quakers, 158–163

Spinoza, Bento (Baruch) de (*cont.*)
  relationship with Talmud Torah con-
    gregation, 102, 118, 156, 173–5
  on religion, 271–2, 274–5, 280
  and Rembrandt, 78–9
  *René Descartes's Principles of Philoso-
    phy*, 107, 191, 204–12
  *Short Treatise on God, Man and His
    Well-Being*, 13, 180, 186–91, 199,
    201, 206
  on soul, 131, 137, 190, 234, 242–3
  on the state, 243, 281–5, 342–9
  Theological-Political Treatise, 131,
    132–3, 170, 175, 248, 256, 268,
    269–87, 288, 290, 292, 295–98,
    299, 301, 312, 321–2, 336, 342
  *Treatise on the Emendation of the Intel-
    lect*, 101, 175–80, 186, 323
  and University of Heidelberg, 311–314
  on virtue, 240–1
Spinoza, Esther de (Esther de Soliz), 45,
  73, 79, 85, 86
Spinoza, Gabriel (Abraham) de, 45–6,
  87, 119–20, 155, 181
Spinoza, Hanna Deborah de (Hanna
  Deborah Senior), 36, 45–6, 66, 73,
  119
Spinoza, Isaac de (Michael's father),
  27–8, 31, 359 n.10
Spinoza, Isaac de (Michael's son), 31,
  36, 45, 79, 80, 81, 359 n.20
Spinoza, Jacob de, 28–9, 32–4
Spinoza, Michael de (Miguel
  d'Espinoza), 30, 31–41, 45–6,
  59–60, 65, 66, 73, 79, 80, 81, 90,
  99, 100, 119
  arrival in Amsterdam, 31–2
  business, 32–6, 39–41, 79, 81, 83, 86
  role in community, 36–9, 43, 59–60,
    79, 81, 85
Spinoza, Miriam de, 36, 45–6, 73, 85–6
Spinoza, Rachel de, 28–9, 32
Spinoza, Rebecca de, 45, 73, 86, 181,
  350–1
Spinoza, Sara de, 27–8
Stenson, Niels, 195, 386 n.46
Stoic philosophy, 109, 226, 242
Stolle, Gottlieb, 134, 181, 247
Stouppe, Jean-Baptiste, 315–19

Talmud, 52, 54, 56, 63, 64, 68, 80, 91,
  93, 97, 114, 121
Talmud Torah (congregation), 31, 54–9,
  61, 74–5, 81, 117–18, 124–7, 141,
  147, 149, 252, 292, 334–5; *see also*
  Sephardim, in Amsterdam
Terence, 109–10, 155
Thomasius, Jacob, 295, 299, 301
Til, Salomon van, 133
Tirado, Jacob, 6–10
Torah, 62, 67, 68, 69, 72, 121, 131, 134,
  276–7
Tschirnhaus, Walther Ehrenfried von,
  222, 300–3, 320, 323, 327–9,
  330–3, 340–1
tulip mania, 50–1
Tydeman, Daniel, 203–4, 222, 245–6,
  263

Union of Utrecht, 7, 8
Utrecht, 267, 305, 315–19
  university, 151, 165, 309
Uylenburgh, Hendrik, 25, 45
Uziel, Isaac, 11, 16, 17, 18, 52, 94

Van den Enden, Clara Maria, 104,
  108–9, 293
Van den Enden, Franciscus, 78,
  103–114, 129, 139, 152, 155–6,
  158, 168, 170, 172, 193, 195, 266,
  268
Van der Spyck, Hendrik, 204, 288–90,
  292, 293, 318, 349–51
Vega, Emanuel Rodriguez, 8–9, 28
Vega, Judah, 10, 16
Velthuysen, Lambert van, 246–7, 307,
  317, 323–4
Venice, 9–10, 16, 17–18, 24, 52, 53–4,
  55, 57, 68, 69, 70, 91, 128–9,
  251
Vermeer, Johannes, 43
Voetians, 307–10, 334
Voetius, Gibertus, 151–2, 307
Volder, Burchard de, 195–6, 247, 249
Voorburg, 203–4, 243, 245–6
Vossius, Isaac, 263
Vries, Simon Joosten de, 107, 141, 169,
  194, 198, 202, 204, 261–2
Vries, Trijntje Joosten de, 213, 262

William I (William the Silent), 43, 74

William II (Stadholder), 75, 82, 83–4, 86, 218

William III (Stadholder, later King of England), 218, 257, 304–5, 314, 345

Witt, Cornelis de, 255, 305–6

Witt, Johan de, 105, 150, 151, 218, 255–9, 265, 267, 286, 297, 304–7, 308–9

Wittich, Christoph, 307

Zevi, Sabbatai, 249–53